The Asian in North America

THE ASIAN IN NORTH AMERICA

Stanford M. Lyman

ABC-Clio, Inc.

Santa Barbara, California
Oxford, England

Library of Congress Cataloging in Publication Date
Main entry under title:

The Asian in North America.

   Includes index.
   1. Chinese Americans—Addresses, essays, lectures.
2. Japanese Americans—Addresses, essays, lectures.
3. United States . . . Race relations—Addresses, essays,
lectures.   I.   Lyman, Stanford M.
E184. C5A84   301. 45′19′5073   77-9095
ISBN 0-87436-254-7

American Bibliographical Center—Clio Press
Riviera Campus, 2040 A. P. S., Box 4397
Santa Barbara, California 93103

Clio Press, Ltd.
Woodside House, Hinksey Hill
Oxford OX1 5BE, England

Composed, printed, and bound in the United States of America

To
Hideo Bernard Hata
the best of friends from the beginning

Contents

Acknowledgments

THIS BOOK, LIKE its predecessors *The Asian in the West* and the more recent *Chinese Americans,* has its origins in my adolescent and young adult years spent in San Francisco's Chinatown and in the area of that city now known as *Nihonmachi.* Friendships and intimate experiences during those years added a personal knowledge to my academic observations that cannot be duplicated. I am deeply thankful to the many Chinese Americans and Japanese Americans who opened their homes and their hearts to me. Although they remain anonymous in these pages, they are gratefully remembered.

My academic interest in the study of Asians was first kindled by the late Jacobus ten Broek, whose own analysis of the unconstitutionality of the wartime exclusion of the Japanese is a model of social scientific and legal analysis. His collaborators in that endeavor, Edward N. Barnhart and Floyd Matson, have been encouraging colleagues and thoughtful critics of my own research.

My doctoral dissertation, "The Structure of Chinese Society in Nineteenth Century America," laid the basis for my subsequent research. That work was carried on under the supervision of Kingsley Davis and H. Franz Schurmann. Professor Davis has served as both model and inspiration in sociological theory and even my own disagreements and departures from his theoretical persuasion are nevertheless colored by his influence. The Sinological studies of Franz Schurmann are challenges for any scholar to meet. His kindly interest in my studies of overseas Chinese and his constant encouragement are gratefully acknowledged although they can never be repaid.

Each of the papers in this book has been appraised and criticized by colleagues.

"The Race Relations Cycle of Robert E. Park" was first presented as the invitational paper at the annual meeting of the Pacific Sociological Association held in Long Beach, California on March 30–31, 1967. It represents research and investigation inspired by the teachings of Kenneth E. Bock at the University of California, Berkeley, and has been followed up in my book, *The Black American in Sociological Thought: A Failure of Perspective,* and in my forthcoming discussion of the neopositivist school in historical sociology in *Structure, Consciousness, and History,* coedited by Richard Harvey Brown and myself. I am indebted to two sorely-missed colleagues, Donald W. Ball and Horace R. Cayton, and to Nathan Glazer, William Petersen, and Marvin B. Scott for advice and criticism at various stages of the paper's development.

"The Chinese Diaspora" was written for and presented as the main address at the National Conference of the Chinese Historical Society of America on "The Life, Influence and Role of the Chinese in the United States, 1776–1960," held in San Francisco on July 10–12, 1975. I am indebted to Thomas W. Chinn and H. Mark Lai for giving me the opportunity to present this address and to Richard Harvey Brown, Dennis Lum, and Arthur J. Vidich for their commentary and advice.

I am indebted to David Harvey, Herbert Hill, Tetsuden Kashima, and Marvin B. Scott for critical advice on "The Significance of Asians in American Society."

"Strangers in the Cities: The Chinese on the Urban Frontier" was first presented as part of a lecture series, "Ethnic Conflict in California History," sponsored by the University of California Extension Division under the coordination of Professor Charles Wollenberg.

I am especially grateful to Professor William Willmott and Mr. Berching Ho for their collaboration on the paper "Rules of a Chinese Secret Society in British Columbia," and for their kind permission that this essay be reprinted here. I should like to acknowledge their assistance, as well as that of Eileen Beeby, Tung-Tsu Chu, Catherine Liu, Joseph Lowe, and William S. Tong, in the preparation of both papers on Chinese secret societies. For the research on Chinese secret societies I am indebted to the Committee on Social and Economic Research and the President's Committee on Research of the University of British Columbia. I would also like to thank Mr. Les Cooke of the British Columbia Parks Service for his assistance in obtaining the board upon which the rules of the Chinese secret society were written, and the Iowa Masonic Library for valuable manuscripts.

"Conflict and the Web of Group Affiliation in San Francisco's Chinatown, 1850–1910," was presented at a meeting of the Eastern Sociological Society in Boston in April, 1975. Norris Hundley, of the *Pacific Historical Review,* invited me to submit it for publication in a special edition of that journal and in the volume that emerged therefrom published by Clio Books. I am grateful to Ying-jen Chang and Steven Seidman for gathering and organizing materials related to the preparation of this essay and to Tetsuden Kashima for encouraging its publication.

"Contrasts in the Community Organization of Chinese and Japanese in North America" was first presented at the University of California, Berkeley, under the sponsorship of the Committee for Arts and Lectures, on August 23, 1966. I am grateful to Herbert Blumer, Jean Burnet, and Marvin B. Scott for criticisms of earlier drafts of this paper.

"Social Demography of the Chinese and Japanese in the United States" was first presented to the seminar in demography conducted by Kingsley Davis at the University of California in 1958–1959. I am grateful to Professor Davis for his criticism and for his encouragement in this project.

"Generation and Character: The Case of the Japanese Americans" is an outgrowth of research on character and personality in the Japanese community in San Francisco. An earlier version was presented to the medical sociology section of the University of California Medical School in 1966. I am indebted to Fred Davis and Egon Bittner for advice and criticism. Professor T. Scott Miyakawa encouraged me to revise the paper into its present form. The paper summarizes almost two decades of association with Japanese Americans in San Francisco, Berkeley, and Vancouver, British Columbia. I am especially indebted to the entire Fukuda family of San Francisco, Mr. Ted Amino, Rev. and Mrs. Taro Goto, Mr. and Mrs. Leo T. Goto, Mr. and Mrs. Howard Imazeki, Dr. Tetsuden Kashima, Mr. and Mrs. Hideo Bernard Hata, Mr. and Mrs. Harry S. Suzuki, the late Mr. Donald K. Sakuma, Mr. Kaien Shimizu, Mr. Tom Shimizu, Dr. Paul Takagi, Mr. George Yano, and the San Francisco *Nisei* group known as "The Barons."

"Red Guard on Grant Avenue" was written with the encouragement and critical advice of Howard Becker and Irving Louis Horowitz. I am also grateful for the assistance and advice of David Harvey and Tetsuden Kashima.

"Ethnicity: Strategies of Collective and Individual Impression Management," grew out of discussions I had with my coauthor, Dr. William A. Douglass, at the University of Nevada during the years 1968–1970. It was first presented at a seminar directed by Professor Benjamin Nelson at The New School for Social Research in 1972. A sequel, also coauthored with William A. Douglass, entitled "L'Ethnie: Structure, Processus Et Saillance," has been published in French in *Cahiers Internationaux de Sociologie, LXI,* 1976.

"Overseas Chinese in America and Indonesia" and "Up From the 'Hatchet Man' " are early essays inspired by my brief but happy association with the Department of Anthropology and Sociology and the reconstituted Institute of Pacific Relations at the University of British Columbia, 1960–1963. Cyril Belshaw, Harry Hawthorn, Ping-ti Ho, William Holland, Shuichi Kato, the late Kaspar Naegele, Bernard Blishen, Anthony Richmond, Yunshik Chang, Kunio Ogata, William S. Tong, Kaien Shimizu, and George Yano made my professorship and research in Canada productive and pleasant.

The eleven books discussed in separate essays and reviews represent my continuing and critical interest in the literature of Asian American studies. When I introduced a lecture series on "The Oriental in North America" at the University of California Extension Program in 1957—perhaps the first term-length course in Asian American studies taught at a major university—there were very few published works on the subject. In the next two decades there has developed a nearly defined field of study, a body of historical, anthropological, sociological, and psychological literature, and a modest increase in fiction, poetry, and drama. Hopefully the efforts so recently begun will neither falter nor fail.

When I began my formal work in the 1950s there was one recognized specialist: Professor Rose Hum Lee. Although we never met, we carried on a lively and forthright conversation through the mails, and, although our respective theoretical outlooks differed markedly, Professor Lee was gracious enough to offer me a collaborative role in her final work, *The Chinese in the United States of America.* I demurred at

the time, but never forgot her kindness to a fledgling social investigator. My obituary is a small tribute to her social scientific effort and her courage in pioneering the modern study of Chinese communities in America.

In 1971, while working in La Jolla, California, on my book *Chinese Americans,* I was interviewed by Staten Webster, a specialist in intergroup education. In the course of this very convivial discussion I discussed my own background, how I got started in Asian American Studies, and what aspects of the sociological, psychological, historical and jurisprudential perspectives are relevant to ethnic studies. Personal yet pedagogic, the interview is a fitting close to this collection of two decades of my efforts to establish a sound foundation for Asian American studies.

My lecture tours in Singapore, Hong Kong, Taiwan, and Japan have been facilitated by the United States Information Service, but in the last three countries were warmed by the hospitality of my inestimable friends, Harry and Constance Suzuki.

At various stages in the development of my studies on Asian Americans I have been aided by discussions with the late Horace R. Cayton, Wolfram Eberhard, Herbert Hill, Shuichi Kato, Ivan Light, Marvin B. Scott, Benjamin T'sou, and Arthur J. Vidich. During the years that intervened between *The Asian in the West* and the present work I have benefited from the knowledge and commentary of my friends and students, some of whom have become colleagues. Dr. Tetsuden Kashima has been invaluable as friend, critic, resource and guide. Dennis and Cynthia Lum have taught me by their example the range, depth, humanity, and good humor that can inform Asian American studies. Kaien and Suzanne Shimizu have been unfailing in keeping me informed of the Asian American situation in Canada. Charles Choy Wong has allowed me to see and comment on his excellent researches into the socio-economic conditions that prevail among Chinese and Korean businessmen in Southern California. The Chow family—Galen, Anita, and their three delightful daughters—have opened their home and—most wonderfully—their kitchen to me, introduced me to the suburban way of life among certain classes of Chinese Americans, and presented me with Galen Chow's informed memoir of his childhood days in San Francisco's Chinatown. Charles R. Freeman has served as a friendly but tough-minded critic of all that I write. Ying-jen Chang introduced me to the world of Chinese martial arts, took me through the by-ways of New York's Chinatown, and accompanied me on my quest for the vicarious thrills to be experienced in watching Kung-Fu films from Taiwan and Hong Kong.

I have dedicated this book to Hideo Bernard Hata. For more than twenty-five years "Barney" has been my chum, and, involuntarily, the custodian of my thoughts and feelings. Living with and patiently listening to my commentaries and concerns on matters affecting Chinese and Japanese Americans, his counsel and suggestions, as well as his silences, have always proved fruitful. His friendship is beyond value.

This anthology contains some materials that overlap from one paper to another. The repetitions are not merely redundancies, for they point up different angles of vision on the same material. Nonetheless for all excesses and errors I take sole and exclusive responsibility.

New York City/June, 1977   Stanford M. Lyman

Editor's Note

NINE OF THE essays appearing in this book were originally published together as *The Asian in the West* by the Desert Research Institute, University of Nevada, Reno.

Because of the continuing relevance of the material, the generally high critical reception, and the limited distribution of *The Asian in the West,* Clio Books elected to reissue the work, adding a number of related essays and reviews subsequently published by Professor Lyman.

The new matter has appeared in several scholarly journals. No attempt has been made by Clio Books or by the author to standardize editorial style (format of citations, footnotes, abbreviations, etc.).

Grateful acknowledgment is here made to the following editors and publishers who permitted the reprinting of articles originally published in their journals and books:

To Dr. Don D. Fowler and the Desert Research Institute. University of Nevada System, for permission to reprint those articles that appeared originally in *The Asian in the West,* "The Significance of Asians in American Society" and "Red Guard on Grant Avenue."

To the Publisher, Sage Publications, Inc. for "The Race Relations Cycle of Robert E. Park," originally published in *The Pacific Sociological Review,* Vol. 11, No. 2 (Spring, 1968).

To *Phylon Quarterly* for "Marriage and Family Among Chinese Immigrants to America, 1850–1960," originally published in Vol. XXIX, No. 4 (Winter, 1968).

To *Canadian Review of Sociology and Anthropology* for "Chinese Secret Societies in the Occident: Notes and Suggestions for Research in the Sociology of Secrecy," originally published in Vol. 1:2 (May, 1964); for "Contrasts in the Community Organization of Chinese and Japanese in North America" originally published in Vol. V, No. 2 (May, 1968).

To the Editorial Board, *Bulletin of the School of Oriental and African Studies* for "Rules of a Chinese Secret Society in British Columbia" originally published in Vol. 27, Pt. 3, 1964.

To *Pacific Historical Review* for "Conflict and the Web of Group Affiliation in San Francisco's Chinatown, 1850–1910" originally published in Vol. 43, No. 4 (November, 1974).

To the Chinese Historical Society of America for

"The Chinese Diaspora," originally published in *The Life, Influence and Role of the Chinese in the United States, 1776–1960,* Proceedings/Papers of the National Conference of the Chinese Historical Society of America (San Francisco: Chinese Historical Society of America, 1976).

To American Bibliographical Center, Clio Press for "Generation and Character: The Case of the Japanese Americans" which originally appeared in T. Scott Miyakawa and Hilary Conroy, *East Across the Pacific, 1972.*

To *Social Research* for "Ethnicity: Strategies of Collective and Individual Impression Management" originally published in Vol. 40, No. 2, (Summer, 1973).

To *Pacific Affairs* for "Overseas Chinese in America and Indonesia," originally published in Vol. XXXIV, No. 4 (Winter, 1961–1962); for "Up From the 'Hatchet Man'", originally published in Vol. XXXVI, No. 2 (Summer, 1963); for "Review of Roger Daniels, *The Politics of Prejudice: The Anti-Japanese Movement in California and the Struggle for Japanese Exclusion,*" originally published in Vol. XXXVII, No. 3 (Fall, 1964); for "Review of Ping Chiu, *Chinese Labor in California, 1850–1880,*" originally published in Vol. XXXVIII, No. 3–4 (Fall–Winter, 1965–1966).

To the *Journal of San Diego History* for "Review of Alexander Saxton, *The Indispensable Enemy: Labor and the Anti-Chinese Movement in California,*" originally published in Vol. XVIII, No. 2 (Spring, 1972).

To *The California Historical Society Quarterly* for "Review of Gunther Barth, *Bitter Strength: A History of the Chinese in the United States, 1850–1870,*" originally published in the December, 1966 issue.

To *Bridge: The Asian–American Magazine* for "Anti-Chinese Prejudice—A Documentation," originally published in Vol. 2, No. 3 (February, 1973).

To The American Sociological Association for "Review of Richard W. Wilson, *Learning to Be Chinese,*" originally published in *Contemporary Sociology,* (March, 1972); for "Review of Richard H. Dillon's *The Hatchet Man,*" originally published in *American Sociological Review,* Vol. 29 (June, 1964); for "In Memoriam: Rose Hum Lee," originally published in *American Sociological Review,* Vol. 30 (February, 1965).

To *Midstream: a Monthly Jewish Review* for "Chinatown in American History," originally published in Vol. XX, No. 8 (October, 1974); for "Nihonism and Judaism: A Dissent," originally published in Vol. XIX, No. 6 (June–July, 1973).

To *The Journal of Ethnic Studies* for "Review of Betty Lee Sung, *The Story of the Chinese in America,*" originally published in Vol. I, No. 1 (Spring, 1973).

To *The International Migration Review* for "Review of Integrated Education Associates, eds., *Chinese Americans: School and Community Problems,*" originally published in Vol. 7, No. 4 (Winter, 1973).

The author acknowledges that letters are on file requesting the right to reprint materials from the following journals and publications:

To Tinnon-Brown, Inc. for permission to reprint "Strangers in the Cities: The Chinese on the Urban Frontier," originally published in *Ethnic Conflict in California History,* edited by Charles Wollenberg and published in 1970.

To *Social History—A Canadian Review* for "Social Demography of the Chinese and Japanese in the United States," originally published in Vol. III, No. 3 (April, 1969).

To Intext Publishers of Scranton, Pennsylvania for "An Interview with Stanford M. Lyman," originally published in Staten W. Webster, ed., *Knowing and Understanding the Socially Disadvantaged Ethnic Minority Groups (1972).*

Articles

The Race Relations Cycle of Robert E. Park

ROBERT E. PARK'S well known race relations cycle[1] constitutes a major contribution to sociological thought, but, despite widespread discussion and criticism, its full potentiality for theory has yet to be tapped. Our concern in this paper is to arouse renewed interest in the cycle and to expose the as yet unexamined possibilities it possesses as a model through a critical examination of its uses as a descriptive theory. Not only sociological theory in race relations will benefit by a revival of interest in Park's cycle, but also a pressing problem of scientific sociology might be brought closer to solution.

The ambiguous generality in which Park couched his cycle of contact, competition, accommodation, and assimilation[2] has been a cause of major concern to those who sought to use it as a generalized law of human relations. It was at once a law of all of mankind's race relations as a whole[3] and a description of California's Oriental "problem" from 1850 to 1930.[4] It was ideology too; for Park supposed that the end of the race relations cycle cleared the social arena in which an inevitable class struggle would take place. Clouded by ideological obfuscations and befogged by its never clarified particularist-universalist ambiguity, Park's cycle appeared less useful for sociology than for politics and social reform.

More serious for its sociological potential was the cycle's apparent commitment to an evolutionist bias which, once the "functionalist" and other anti-evolutionist schools of thought had disposed of the theoretical errors of social evolutionism, made it even more hidebound. In particular Park's use of the doctrine of obstacles seemingly to explain away the empirical contradictions to the cycle's operation and direction made the race cycle, like other cycles of civilization and man's emergence, only a museum piece for students of the history of sociology. To restore the cycle's usage to sociological thought as a model, we must first carefully examine the use Park made of the doctrine of obstacles and the criticism of those who followed after him.

The Doctrine of Obstacles

Park did not carry out any full-scale study of ethnic groups to see whether his cycle approximated reality. But he did supervise the ethnic studies of his students, write numerous essays about race relations in general and various ethnic groups in particular, and he proposed a large-scale race relations survey along the Pacific Coast of the United States, especially designed to study the Chinese and Japanese in America. In 1926 a team of researchers, led by Park, made an attempt to carry out this race relations survey. Over and over their reports provided evidence contradicting the direction, and indeed, the operation of the proffered cycle. The two most famous Japanese rural communities were found to be living in a precariously balanced peace with their white neighbors, and one was torn asunder by internal ethnic rivalries.[5] The Chinatown ghetto was complexly differentiated and conflict ridden but showed no signs of political or economic disintegration.[6] The American-born Chinese and Japanese had adopted much of the culture, language, dress, habits, and opinions of conventional American society, and were less frequently the victims of assaults or race riots, but considerable discrimination and social distance still separated them from white America.[7] The evidence Park and his associates collected also suggested that a racial minority's adoption of the larger society's culture did not necessarily guarantee its acceptance into that society.

When evidence suggested that the cycle was not in fact in operation Park and his colleagues disposed of it by introducing, in effect, the age-old Aristotelian doctrine of "obstacles"—the doctrine which held that progress along an hypothesized line was inevitable, except when something interfered with it. For Park physical traits and the failure to establish interracial friendships were the chief but not the only obstacles to the working out of the cycle. Indeed, accidents of settlement, minority group size and composition, and other interferences were often cited. Thus, the orderly transition from competition to accommodation to assimilation by the Japanese living in Florin, California, in 1926 was impeded, according to Winifred Raushenbush,[8] Park's associate, in part because Florin is located near Sacramento, the seat of anti-Orientalism. But, failure to assimilate was also "due in part to an ignorant tactlessness." "It should be the first rule in the book of etiquette on race relations," continued Miss Raushenbush, "that the foreigner should never be-

come the major element in the population unless he is a slave; in fact unless the foreigner remains a very small element in the population there is inevitable friction and alarm."[9] On the other hand, Miss Raushenbush considered Livingston, California, to be "really a laboratory experiment in race relations" because the Japanese there, unlike those in Florin, did not constitute a majority of the population, did not monopolize the business interests on Main Street, had not divided into quarreling Christian and Buddhist sects, and had acquiesced quietly to business and residential segregation within a racial ghetto.[10] Characteristically, the analysis did not explain how acceptance of this "accommodated" status by Livingston's Japanese would lead to assimilation, but much evidence was introduced which suggested that it would not. Park, however, in opening the discussion of these findings, was quite sure that deepening interpersonal relations between the races would break down stereotyped thinking and thus insure assimilation. "Personal relations and personal friendships are the great moral solvents. Under their influence all distinctions of class, of caste, and even of race, are dissolved into the general flux which we sometimes call democracy."[11]

Of all the obstacles that Park enumerates—and throughout his writings many appear as *ad hoc* soldiers fighting a losing war against ultimately victorious assimilation—the one to which he always returns is the failure to establish interracial primary relations. "Peoples we know intimately we respect and esteem. In our casual contacts with aliens, however, it is the offensive rather than the pleasing traits that impress us. These impressions accumulate and reinforce natural prejudices."[12] Thus Park's prediction of the inevitable transition from accommodation to assimilation requires the "great moral solvent" of interpersonal intimacy to flow across racial lines. But Park did not worry over the fact that interracial intimacy is a consequence of the nature and frequency of contact. Indeed, he asserted that "we [students of race relations] have not reckoned with the effects of personal intercourse and the friendships that inevitably grow up out of them." These interracial friendships "cut across and eventually undermine all the barriers of racial segregation and caste by which races seek to maintain their integrity."[13] Except for his assertion that slavery assimilated African Negroes "rapidly and as a matter of course"[14] by providing for extensive intimate contacts between white masters and Negro slaves, Park eschewed analysis of the relationship between social organization and intimacy. Thus he cut off his observations at precisely the point where sociological investigation should have begun.

The doctrine of obstacles implicit in Park's thought permits him to draw a radical distinction between events and process. Nowhere does he present the history of a single racial group showing that it in fact passed through the hypothesized stages. Instead particular conditions of a variety of racial groups are used to illustrate the several stages, and the cycle is asserted to be true in all stages for each group. Although often regarded as a *theory,* Park's cycle is most fruitful if regarded as a *model.* It fails as a theory because of its built-in unfalsifiability.[15] Park did not regard contradictory data as an indication of the cycle's fruitlessness. Indeed he used disconfirming data to support the cycle's utility. Thus Park wrote, "It does not follow that because the tendencies to the assimilation and eventual amalgamation of races exist, they should not be resisted and, if possible, altogether inhibited. On the other hand, it is vain to underestimate the character and force of the tendencies that are drawing the races and peoples about the Pacific into the ever-narrowing circle of a common life. Rising tides of color and oriental exclusion laws are merely incidental evidences of these diminishing distances." [16] As Lipset has observed concerning the *theoretical* aspects of Park's cycle, "by their very nature, hypotheses about the inevitability of cycles, whether they be cycles of race relations or the rise and fall of civilization, are not testable at all."[17] It has been the fate of Park's cycle to be treated as a theory and, as such, to be regarded as empirically invalidated and theoretically unsound.

Criticism of the Race Cycle

Since Park's formulation of the cycle, unacknowledged confusion over its nature as a theory or a model has resulted in vitriolic debate over it and bitter disappointment with it. Those who have insisted that it is a universally applicable empirical generalization, a law of human behavior, have been puzzled by widespread disobedience to that law. The works of Louis Wirth[18] and Rose Hum Lee[19] illustrate the problems that arise when one adheres to Park's cycle as an unalterable description and prescription for all ethnic groups in America. Both find in their empirical studies of the Jews and Chinese in America, respectively, that complete assimilation has not in fact occurred. Wirth attributes this in part to the rise of anti-Semitism but more significantly to the presence of congregative sentiments and institutions. However, he appears to regard these as "obstacles" to the working out of the Jews' historical destiny in America. As late as 1945 Wirth seems not to have abandoned his faith in the eventual assimilation of minorities if only they are allowed to fulfill their sociological destiny, for he wrote in that year that although a race relations cycle properly includes a stage in which a minority group seeks "toleration for its cultural differences," assimilation would follow "if sufficient toleration and autonomy is attained" in the "pluralist" stage. Only if frustrated in its drive toward assimilation would a minority resort to "secessionist tendencies" or "the drive to be incorporated into another state."[20]

Rose Hum Lee is disconcerted to find that after more than a century of settlement the Chinese have not completely assimilated into American Society. Despite acculturation Chinese ghettos are still to be found in America's larger cities, and, although the absolute number of Chinatowns has declined, the population and size of the urban Chinese quarters have increased. Lee contrasts this state of affairs among the Chinese with that of the more rapidly assimilating Japanese, and noting that both groups have been victims of prejudice and discrimination, is disappointed with the character of America's Chinese. Since in recent years Sinophobia has nearly disappeared as an active force in Chinese-American relations, she can only conclude that the failure to assimilate is due in part to Chinatown's elites and their vested interests in maintaining an exclusive community, but more significantly to a lack of nerve and will on the part of the mass of Chinese. In the final pages of her study Professor Lee exhorts the Chinese to assimilate as rapidly and completely as possible, thus converting Park's prophecy into a plea.

Other adherents of the cycle as a theory were disappointed when they discovered that assimilation had not yet occurred. Bogardus[21] developed three cycles to describe the several situations which his research had uncovered. Brown asserted that either isolation, subordination, or fusion were final outcomes; assimilation and fusion are "perhaps ultimately inevitable but immediately improbable," he concluded.[22] Masuoka believes three generations are required for the fulfillment of the cycle, but that in the third "A genuine race problem arises in the history of race relations." [23] Both Glick[24] and Lieberson[25] believe that the final outcome of racial cycles is problematical, resulting in integration, nationalist movements, or permanent minority status. Etzioni has gone further than most critics in urging abandonment of Park's racial cycle as theory: "While groups are often forced into contact by the progress of technological, economic, and social change, and perhaps this is an unavoidable process, the remaining stages [of Park's race relations cycle] should be seen as alternative situations rather than links in an evolutionary process culminating in assimilation. Groups are either in conflict or accommodation or assimilation."[26]

Among the critics Brewton Berry stands out for his criticism of Park's and later sociologists' cycles and his resulting pessimism about the possibilities of theory construction in racial relations. "Some scholars," he writes, "therefore question the existence of any universal pattern and incline rather to the belief that so numerous and so various are the components that enter into race relations that each situation is unique and the making of generalizations is a hazardous procedure."[27] He then proceeds to describe race relations in Brazil, Hawaii, and between American Indians and whites and concludes that, although the course of race relations is not identical in any two situations, certain phenomena—conflict, biological mixture, cultural exchange, and domination—are widespread, if not universal and inevitable.

Other analysts have come closer to perceiving the heuristic assets of Park's cycle despite its failure as a theory. Shibutani and Kwan point out there are "so many exceptions" to Park's cycle conceived as a "natural history," but they conclude that "Park's race relations cycle is a useful way of ordering data on the manner in which immigrants become incorporated into an already-established society."[28] Frazier, after years of research, gave up the attempt to empirically verify the sequential order of Park's stages and conceded that "the different stages in the race relations cycle may exist simultaneously," but he insisted on retaining the cycle as "logical steps in a systematic sociological analysis of the subject."[29]

Seeking a path out of the profusion of research and confusion of thought arising out of Park's race relations cycle is not easy. Before dismissing what has gone before, sociologists should recognize that Park's race relations essays in general and his race cycle formulation in particular have focused critical attention on a significant aspect of human relations, provided research topics for a generation of scholars, and aided in the amelioration of social conditions. Park's stature as a theorist, empiricist, and meliorist is secure and rightfully so.[30]

Park's Cycle as a Model

The future of Park's cycle is to be realized in its value as a model. Much debate over the meaning of model and theory still goes on in sociology and this debate cannot be resolved in this paper. [31] Following Weber,[32] however, Park's cycle may be conceived as a developmental model containing four ideal types. The test of its utility lies in its ability to organize a vast body of otherwise discrete data, sensitize sociologists to specific forms of human organization, and generate hypotheses for research. There can be no doubt that Park's cycle has lived up to these desiderata. Moreover, once the cycle is regarded as a model, the questions of verification or falsification no longer are relevant. Rather, the issue is to establish the conditions under which the descriptive conditions of the model are true. In this light then, the speculations of Park and Raushenbush discussed earlier take on a new significance as notes toward hypotheses (rather unrefined, to be sure) designating the conditions under which the postulates are not true. They provide the grounds for conducting case studies testing the validity of the alleged postulate-preventing factor.

However, each of Park's stages is much in need of examination along the lines originally suggested by Weber to see whether it meets the requirements of an ideal-type. The concentration on "assimilation"[33] has been fruitful for this purpose alone—although even that ideal-type is not unambiguously represented in the contemporary sociological literature—but little more than illustration has yet been done on "contact," "competition," or "accommodation." The specific logico-empirical content of each of these is a worthy enterprise of future sociological research.

Much ambiguity continues to exist in sociological discussions of assimilation. Park himself succumbed to the doubts his colleagues had expressed about the final outcome of race relations and, at the age of 73, reformulated the racial cycle asserting that it "continues until it terminates in some predestined racial configuration, and one consistent with an established social order of which it is a part."[34] In the spirit of Park's cautious reappraisal, sociologists ought to consider just what the cultural and behavioral content of assimilation is in various societies, and in America in particular. One specific error, committed by friends and foes of Park alike,[35] is to equate assimilation with fusion, or a "melting pot" and to regard the continuing existence of identifiable ethnic groups in America as a sign of nonassimilation. The equation of fusion with assimilation is proper if and only if fusion is a core value of American society.[36] If, however, pluralism, and one of its most specific forms, racial and ethnic endogamy, are elements of the core culture, or if maintenance of ethnic group identity is a culturally permissible alternative, then a people who persist in endogamy and who maintain or establish those ancillary institutions necessary to insure endogamy are not necessarily unassimilated by those practices. Thus, if Jews or Negroes, for example, come to share in the dominant values of American society—e.g., achievement, work, moral orientations, humanitarian

mores, efficiency and practicality, progress, material comfort, equality, freedom, conformity, science and secular rationality, national patriotism, democracy, individualism, and ambivalence about the relevance of race and ethnicity[37]—but practice inmarriage and so structure the institutions of intimate contact between marriageable members of their group so that mating is likely to occur within the confines of the group, shall we not say they are indeed assimilated? It would appear that both reason and evidence would support this view of assimilation, and thus we may clear away the obfuscation that endogamy has caused for students of assimilation.

Park's Cycle as Theory: Unsolved Problems

Finally, if Park's cycle is to be treated as a theory, then all the dilemmas arising out of this kind of theory in general are applicable to it in particular. These dilemmas have not yet been resolved, but Park's cycle provides a crucial case upon which analytic thought and empirical research might be focused to help in this effort. Briefly stated these dilemmas are:

1. The debate over whether the forms of theory construction in natural science are to be adopted strictly and uncritically in social science.[38] This debate is too well known to be commented on further here, but resolution of it is vital for usage of Park's cycle as theory.

2. The debate over falsification and verification of an hypothesized developmental sequence.[39] Park's cycle takes the form: If P, then Q; if Q, then R; if R then S. Should empirical research reveal a result contrary to the prediction of the hypothesis, the hypothesis could be abandoned as incorrect, or the principle of *ceteris paribus* introduced to account for the discrepancy. However no introduction of an unlimited universe of interferences can be allowed unless we wish to be left in the unscientific position of unfalsifiability described earlier. The way out of this dilemma is to verify and construct a definite and finite set of ideal-typical interferences, the

presence of any of which would constitute an adequate explanation of the failure of the predictive hypothesis. Park's discussions of what I term "obstacles" provide a suggested beginning to this needed next step, and his work should be carefully studied for clues to and examples of the relevant interferences.

3. The debate over causal explanations in relation to developmental theories.[40] To present Park's cycle as a theory is not to account for the sequence coming to pass. Park himself, and other sociologists who subscribe to evolutionary theories, have not explicitly designated the causal nexus by which one

stage of development succeeds another. Often enough causal explanations are implicit in the descriptive statements about the stages. Future research must make explicit and empirically validate the independent variables whose form and presence are necessary and sufficient to bring on the successor stage.

Park's racial cycle, thus, is still most fruitful for the sociological enterprise. Not only does it serve as a model useful in the study of race relations in general and assimilation in particular, but it also provides an opportunity for research into the basic problems of sociological theory itself.

Notes

* Revised version of the invitational paper presented at the annual meeting of the Pacific Sociological Association, Long Beach, California, March 30–31, 1967. The author is indebted to Donald Ball, Horace R. Cayton, Nathan Glazer, William Petersen, and Marvin Scott for their criticism and advice at various stages of the paper's development.

1. The bulk of Park's work on race relations is to be found in Robert Ezra Park, *Race and Culture*, Glencoe: The Free Press, 1950. This book of essays written over the long span of Park's life was published posthumously. The date of each essay will be noted in the footnotes to follow. *Race and Culture* will be designated *RC*.

2. "Our Racial Frontier on the Pacific," *RC* p. 150. (May, 1926).

3. "The Nature of Race Relations," *RC*, p. 116, (1939).

4. "Our Racial Frontier on the Pacific," *RC*, pp. 150–151; "Behind Our Masks," *RC*, pp. 250–251. (May, 1926).

5. Winifred Raushenbush. "Their Place in the Sun." *Survey Graphic*, LVI (May, 1926), pp. 141–145.

6. Winifred Raushenbush, "The Great Wall of Chinatown," *Survey Graphic*, LVI (May, 1926), pp. 154–159 .

7. Elliot Grinnel Mears, "The Land, the Crops, and the Oriental," *Survey Graphic*, LVI (May, 1926), pp. 146–150; R. D. McKenzie, "The Oriental Finds a Job," *Ibid.*, pp. 151–153; Kazuo Kawai, "Three Roads, and None Easy," *Ibid.*, pp. 164–166; William C. Smith, "Born American, But—," *Ibid.*, pp. 167–168.

8. "Their Place in the Sun," *op. cit.*, p. 144.

9. *loc. cit.*

10. *loc. cit.*

11. "Behind Our Masks," *RC*, p. 254.

12. "Racial Assimilation in Secondary Groups with Particular Reference to the Negro," *RC*, p. 209. See also "The Bases of Race Prejudice," *Ibid.*, pp. 230–243.

13. "Our Racial Frontier on the Pacific," *RC*, p. 150.

14. "Racial Assimilation in Secondary Groups with Particular Reference to the Negro," *RC*, p. 209.

15. For a discussion of unfalsifiability in developmental theories see Kenneth E. Bock, *The Acceptance of Histories: Toward a Perspective for Social Science*, Berkeley: University of California Publications in Sociology and Social Institutions, Vol. III, 1956.

16. "Our Racial Frontier on the Pacific," *RC*, p. 151.

17. Seymour Martin Lipset, "Changing Social Status and Prejudice: The Race Theories of a Pioneering American Sociologist," *Commentary*, 9 (May, 1950), p. 479.

18. Louis Wirth, *The Ghetto*, Chicago: University of Chicago Press Phoenix Books, 1956.

19. Rose Hum Lee, *The Chinese in the United States of America*, Hong Kong: Hong Kong University Press, 1960. For further discussion of this work see Stanford M. Lyman, "Overseas Chinese in America and Indonesia," *Pacific Affairs*, XXXIV (Winter, 1961–1962), pp. 380–389.

20. Louis Wirth, "The Problem of Minority Groups," in Ralph Linton, (Ed.), *The Science of Man in the World Crisis*, New York: Columbia University Press, 1945, pp. 347–372, esp. p. 364.

21. E. S. Bogardus, "A Race Relations Cycle," *American Journal of Sociology,* 35 (January, 1930), pp. 612–617; Robert H. Ross and E. S. Bogardus, "The Second Generation Race Relations Cycle: A Study in Issei-Nisei Relationships," *Sociology and Social Research,* 24 (March, 1940), pp. 357–363. See also E. S. Bogardus, "Current Problems of Japanese Americans," *Sociology and Social Research,* 25 (July, 1941), pp. 562–571, and Robert H. Ross and Emory S. Bogardus, "Four Types of Nisei Marriage Patterns," *Sociology and Social Research,* 25 (September, 1940), pp. 63–66.

22. W. O. Brown, "Culture Contact and Race Conflict," in E. B. Reuter, (Ed.), *Race and Culture Contacts,* New York: McGraw-Hill, 1934, pp. 34–37.

23. Jitsuichi Masuoka,"Race Relations and Nisei Problems," *Sociology and Social Research,* 30 (July, 1946), pp. 452–459, at p. 459.

24. Clarence E. Glick, "Social Roles and Types in Race Relations," in A. W. Lind, (Ed.), *Race Relations in World Perspective,* Honolulu: University of Hawaii Press, 1955, pp. 239ff.

25. Stanley Lieberson, "A Societal Theory of Race and Ethnic Relations," *American Sociological Review,* 26 (December, 1961), pp. 902–910.

26. Amitai Etzioni, "The Ghetto—a Re-Evaluation," *Social Forces,* 37 (March, 1959), pp. 255–262.

27. Brewton Berry, *Race and Ethnic Relations,* Boston: Houghton-Mifflin Co., 1965 (Third Edition), p. 135. In his later work on certain groups of racial hybrids in America, *Almost White,* New York: Macmillan, 1963, Berry avoids theoretical issues entirely and, instead, concentrates on pleading for understanding and compassion. See Stanford M. Lyman, "The Spectrum of Color," *Social Research,* 31 (Autumn 1964), pp. 364–373.

28. Tamotsu Shibutani and Kian Moon Kwan, *Ethnic Stratification, a Comparative Approach,* New York: Macmillan, 1965, pp. 116–135 at p. 135.

29. E. Franklin Frazier, "Racial Problems in World Society," in Jitsuichi Masuoki and Preston Valien, (Eds.), *Race Relations, Problems and Theory: Essays in Honor of Robert E. Park,* Chapel Hill: University of North Carolina Press, 1961, p. 40. See also Frazier, *Race and Culture Contacts in the Modern World,* New York: Alfred A. Knopf, 1957, pp. 31–38.

30. See Jean Burnet, "Robert E. Park and the Chicago School of Sociology: A Centennial Tribute," *Canadian Review of Sociology and Anthropology,* 1 (August, 1964), pp. 156–169. See also the interesting exchange on Park between Ralph Ellison and Morris Janowitz in Ralph Ellison, "An American Dilemma: A Review," *Shadow and Act,* New York: Random House, 1964, pp. 304–308 and Morris Janowitz, "Review of Shadow and Act," *American Journal of Sociology,* LXX (May, 1965), pp. 732–734.

31. See Carl G. Hempel, "Typological Methods in the Social Sciences," in Maurice Natanson, (Ed.), *Philosophy of the Social Sciences,* New York: Random House, 1963, pp. 210–230; Don Martindale, "Sociological Theory and the Ideal Type," in Llewellyn Gross, (Ed.), *Symposium on Sociological Theory,* Evanston: Row, Peterson, & Co., 1959, pp. 57–91; May Brodbeck, "Models, Meaning, and Theories," *Ibid.,* pp. 373–406; Howard Becker and Harry Elmer Barnes, *Social Thought from Lore to Science,* New York: Dover Publications, 1961, II, pp. 777–787.

32. Max Weber, *The Methodology of the Social Sciences,* Glencoe: The Free Press, 1949, pp. 89–112. (Translated and Edited by Edward A. Shils and Henry A. Finch).

33. See Milton M. Gordon, *Assimilation in American Life: The Role of Race, Religion, and National Origins,* New York: Oxford University Press, 1964.

34. "The Race Relations Cycle in Hawaii," *RC,* p. 194 (1937).

35. Thus both Louis Wirth and Amitai Etzioni who strongly disagree with one another on the applicability of Park's cycle to the study of Jews in America equate assimilation with intermarriage. See Wirth, *The Ghetto, op. cit.,* pp. 68, 112–113, 125–126, 145; and Etzioni, *op. cit.,* pp. 259–261.

36. See Robin Williams, *American Society: A Sociological Interpretation,* New York: Alfred A. Knopf, 1960, pp. 80–82, 397–470.

37. *Ibid.,* pp. 415–468.

38. In addition to the articles cited in footnote 31 *supra,* see Robert O. Brown, *Explanation in Social Science,* Chicago: Aldine Press, 1963; Richard S. Rudner, *Philosophy of Social Science,* Englewood Cliffs: Prentice-Hall, 1966; and the articles by Lundberg, Natanson, Schutz, and Nagel in Natanson, *op. cit.*

39. Hempel, *op. cit.,* pp. 223–226.

40. See George A. Theodorson, "The Uses of Causation in Sociology," in Llewellyn Gross, (Ed.), *Sociological Theory: Inquiries and Paradigms,* New York: Harper & Row, 1967, pp. 131–152 and Leon J. Goldstein, "Theory in Anthropology: Developmental or Causal?" *Ibid.,* pp. 153–180.

"The Race Relations Cycle of Robert E. Park," by Stanford M. Lyman is reprinted from *Pacific Sociological Review,* Vol. II, No. 2 (Spring 1968) pp. 16–22 by permission of the Publisher, Sage Publications, Inc.

The Chinese Diaspora in America, 1850–1943

SOCIOLOGICAL STUDIES OF immigration and its effects on the social organization of the United States have taken a new turn. No longer is "assimilation" assumed to be the ineluctable final outcome of a peoples' settlement abroad. The much vaunted "melting pot" is now being increasingly recognized by sociologists and journalists as an efficacious illusion: part dream, as in the wonderful wish of J. Hector St. John de Crèvecoeur, the 18th century "American farmer," that America would dissolve in herself the divisive national identities that had made Europe such a cockpit; part tactic, as in the case of those Jews who supported and celebrated Israel Zangwill's play, *The Melting Pot* (1909), because they thought its homely message would allay widespread fears that Jews in America would remain an alien and subversive people; part ideology, as in the insistence, ritualized in the salutation to the flag, that the American people are "one nation, under God, indivisible, with liberty and justice for all." The general domestic unsettlement of the 1960s, and more especially, the renewal of racial and ethnic consciousness, the revival of nativistic movements, and the retreat of white Anglo Saxon Protes-

tant hegemony have occasioned a reinvigorated search for the basic social values that underpin social organization in the United States. There is a vague uneasiness surrounding the recent claims that Americans are living in an era of "the decline of the WASP," and "the rise of the unmeltable ethnics." Whereas Gunnar Myrdal sought a solution to the "American dilemma" by appealing to the ultimate capacity of the core values—equality and progress— to end political, social, and economic inequalities, concerned sociologists today are beginning to wonder whether any core values even prevail.

One *intellectual* problem arising out of the current disenchantment with old formulas is the absence of compelling concepts. Concepts can organize the raw reality into a new intelligibility; more important, they can sensitize sociologists to aspects of their subject that have gone hitherto unnoticed. Yet in the sociological analysis of immigration, race and ethnic relations, and minorities concept development has lagged. The very terms of reference are unsettled. In the 1920s, undoubtedly impressed by the condition of stateless but nationalistic people in Europe, American sociologists began to perceive social issues

11

in American society in terms of *majorities* and *minorities*. In this same era, impressed by the birth and maturation of the immigrants' children in America, Robert E. Park and Everett Stonequist, borrowing from the insights of Georg Simmel and Werner Sombart, coined the phrase *marginal man* to describe one who was a product of two cultures and a member of neither. For four decades sociologists have debated the efficacy, dimensions, and correlates of that concept. As different collective experiences were described the sociological vocabulary appeared always to be inadequate. Race prejudice, racism, institutionalized racism, pluralism, ghetto colonialism, congregation, segregation, and integration are all terms that have bidden for conceptual legitimacy. The rapidity of social change in this arena of American life suggests that the cultural and linguistic lag that has already been noticed will continue.

Immigrants in general, and Asian immigrants in particular, have been among the beneficiaries and victims of this sociological struggle for conceptual dominion and consensus. As new issues and problems have arisen, each people has been subjected or threatened with a re-analysis and re-evaluation of its history and present social position. Rarely have the members been consulted about their own categories of identity or experience. Rather, the social scientists, impelled by a belief in their own intellectual superiority and by a distrust of the reason that might prevail among their subjects, unilaterally defined the scope and meaning of these histories and lives.

Perhaps no other people has been subjected to more investigation in reference to an unanalyzed but much vaunted assimilation and the failure to achieve it than the Chinese in America. In 1869 Henry George opened the discussion by insisting that the Chinese were unassimilable; in 1928 Emory Bogardus suggested that the social distance between the Chinese and white Americans might decrease as the former ended their ghetto isolation and entered the middle class; but in 1960 Rose Hum Lee lamented the tardiness of the Chinese in assimilating, accused them of preserving unwarrantable special interests in Chinatown, and urged them to

develop the will and strength of character to enter fully into the mainstream of American life. The failure, however, was not that of the Chinese. Rather, there has been a failure of sociological imagination; a faltering of perspective. Assimilation, and its attendant theories and ideologies—e.g., the race relations cycle and the melting pot ideology, respectively—suffer from what Robert Blauner has called a "managerial bias," gauging the histories and attitudes of an immigrant people in accordance with the social wishes and group interests of the dominant race.

An alternative approach would seek concepts that translate the actual lived experience of people into a sociology that clarifies it. Such a sociology has not yet been developed, but several steps along the road have already been taken. The philosophical sociology of Alfred Schutz with its emphasis on the common sense understandings of the everyday world, the division of life into routine and crisis, and the significance of temporal and personal perspectives provides a groundwork for conceptual development and new empirical investigations. The ethnomethodology of Harold Garfinkel, Aaron Cicourel and their followers introduces both a healthy skepticism about absolutism in social scientific explanation and an innovative approach to the rational and social foundations of human accomplishments. Finally, a sociology of the absurd, first presented by Stanford M. Lyman and Marvin B. Scott, promises an existential and phenomenological social science that should avoid the pitfalls of ethnocentrism, managerial bias, and hidden ideological bias.

In the orientation of these new schools of thought, borrowing from them indiscriminately and yet not necessarily taking over any one of them wholly, this essay hopes to explore the Chinese experience in America. The analysis is at once historical, sociological, and, in the phenomenological sense of that term, psychological. It is also tentative, suggestive, and in the limiting sense of the term when employed in the historical sciences, experimental. My aim is to sensitize the reader to certain dimensions of the social and psychological condition of a people that arise out of their own experience.

The Chinese Diaspora

Looked at from the perspective of the immigrants, Chinese migrations have created a *diaspora,* a scattering of a portion of the Chinese people over the face of the earth. A diaspora may be said to exist where group migration has occurred, where acculturation has not taken place, where a people maintain themselves in accordance with the culture of their original homeland, and where there is at least an ideology or strong sentiment calling for an end to exile. In the case of the Chinese it is clear that their migrations were not motivated by plans for colonization, settlement, or permanent residence abroad. Rather they sought the overseas areas as places where, because of accidents of opportunity, a chance was offered to enhance their status when they returned to China. A trip abroad, a few years of work in a foreign land, and a stoic acceptance of the alien land's prejudices and discrimination could, with luck, earn a Chinese sufficient wealth to return to his village in splendor.

From Annam to Zanzibar, Chinese toiled in the hope that they would one day have enough money to retire in the land of their birth. Theirs, then, was not to be an irremediable exile, not to be the diaspora of absurdity described by Camus: permanent exile in a strange land and a life devoid of memories of a homeland left behind (Camus, 1942:18). Although they were neither involuntary migrants nor slaves in America, Chinese were excluded as much from the larger society as Negroes. But unlike the blacks, Chinese were not deprived of knowledge about and sentiment for the country of their origin. Nor did they lack hope of a return to the promised land of their past. They did not experience a divorce between themselves and their familiar lives, only a separation. They had only temporarily departed from their natural setting. A return would restore them to the fullness of their existence. They could suffer the exploitation because their hope for return to China served as a source of strength.

But the dream of an honorable return did not usually match the reality of their overseas existence. In alien lands Chinese watched helplessly as the years of toil stretched out over nearly the whole of their lives. The Chinese came as strangers, desired to be homegoers, and all too often lived, and died, as permanent sojourners. Their children became marginal men, products of two cultures, members of neither.

To speak of the Chinese as strangers is to see them in terms of the perceptive conceptualization first employed by Georg Simmel. "The stranger," he wrote in his essay of that title, "is . . . not . . . the wanderer who comes today and goes tomorrow, but rather is the person who comes today and stays tomorrow." The Chinese who journeyed to Southeast Asia, America, Europe, Africa, and Oceania were not wanderers in the strict sense of that term; they had fixed places to go, a definite purpose in mind, and a keen desire to return home to wife and kinsmen in China. Their several courses took them where opportunity beckoned. To the lonely Chinese immigrant the place where he stayed in the diaspora was his *residence;* where he happened to be was his *abode;* but only the place from which he had started out and to which he intended to return was *home.*

The Chinese as a stranger in America was *in* the society but not *of* it. He imported things into that society that were not native nor original to it.

In the most primordial sense we must necessarily recognize that the Chinese brought his body, his physiognomy, his anatomy, and his external appearance with him. In the very act he created a powerful element of his strangeness, for a part of the hierarchy of relevances, the system of priorities—the basic values—of America included the social construction and evaluation of persons as bodies categorizable into "races." It was in America that the man from Canton discovered that he belonged to a "race," that his physical features were an irreducible part of his social identity, and that he would forever exist to his hosts as an undifferentiated member of his racial category. To most Americans Chinese were impenetrable as persons, knowable only as men of "slanted" eyes and "yellow" skin. To be sure his subjective qualities could and did become at least partially known, but, as Robert E. Park's perceptive essay on the Oriental face indicated, his personal and human qualities seemed forever to be hidden "behind the mask," encapsulated within an objective physical frame from which they could not emerge.

Second, the Chinese as a stranger brought with him his language, or rather to be more exact, his languages. The peoples of Kwangtung who made up the bulk of Chinese immigrants in America spoke several dialects of the tongue Occidentals call "Chinese." Although all spoken dialects had a common written script, their verbal forms were frequently unintelligible to those who came from but a few miles away. Linguistically many of the Cantonese were strangers to each other, a phenomenon which found organizational expression in *hui kuan* (speech and territorial associations) which they established soon after their arrival in San Francisco.

However, it must be remembered that the Chinese language appeared to be but one language to Americans. To them Chinese speech seemed exotic and incomprehensible, a tongue incomparable to the more familiar languages of Europe from which their own stock had sprung. To the American the Chinese speech melody seemed a cacophony; the accent it imposed on learned English was a cause for mirth and mimicry; and its characters, formed so carefully with a brush, seemed bizarre and utterly remote from the forms of European or American writing. Finally, and most important, it seemed fundamentally to be the case that Americans did not care to learn about the language or to learn to speak it. It was the immigrants' duty to learn English or suffer the consequences of restricted communication.

Third, and derivative from his language and culture, the Chinese stranger brought with him his ways of life, familiar and taken for granted to him, unfamiliar, peculiar, and sometimes frightening to Americans. Even in his absence from hearth and home, the overseas Chinese derived strength and purpose from his family. The Chinese ideal of family loyalty found painful expression in long term bachelorhood abroad, in the association of men of common surname in clans, and in the single-minded purposefulness of returning to wife and village to retire or die. The Chinese ideal of congregation

beyond the family revealed itself in the *hui kuan* which united people of common dialect but divided persons who, though racially homogeneous, hailed from different speech communities of the same land. And the subterranean Chinese ideals of resistance, rebellion, and fraternal outlawry transplanted themselves in the form of the secret societies that sprang up wherever large numbers of Chinese settled, forming a parallel system of immigrant institutions inside the ghetto colony. Above all, the central characteristic of early Chinese community life that impressed itself on Americans was the immigrants' adherence to a system of *kadi* justice, traditional law, and patrimonial power. Clans, *hui kuan,* and secret societies governed the lives of the immigrants, dispensed justice, adjudicated quarrels, settled disputes, levied fines, punished wrongdoers, and on occasion, meted out capital punishment. To the Americans, Chinese seemed to have established an *imperium in imperio,* a parallel state, and to owe to its institutions and leaders a depth of fealty and allegiance out of proportion to its worth and out of character with what Americans expected of its immigrants. To the Chinese the social system that they established in Chinatown was a familiar form of political and economic organization. It was not universally loved or even uniformly favored, but it was respected and for some revered.

However, it was not only their institutions that puzzled and angered Americans. The personal life and style of the Chinese excited curiosity and, on all too many occasions contempt. The plaited queue in which Chinese men wore their hair was a constant source of amusement and derision. The queue originated as a symbol of subjugation imposed on the Chinese people by the Manchu conquerors in 1645. Gradually it had evolved into the badge of citizenship in the imperial state. In the first half century of their immigration to America, Chinese were taunted about their "pigtails," shaved to the scalp by mobs and miscreants, and, in 1876, ordered by law to have their queues cut off if they served a sentence in prison or were jailed while awaiting trial. To Californians the blue overalls, loose-fitting shirts, and wide-brimmed black hat favored by the Chinese seemed less a costume than a uniform, and tended to encourage the belief that they were serfs and bondmen unfit for settlement in a free society. Further, the practice of binding the feet of women, common among Chinese gentry, but by no means uniform among peasantry and laborers, aroused shock and indignation.[1] Finally, the seemingly loose and dissolute life of Chinese bachelors evoked a chorus of moral imprecations against the immigrants from the Middle Kingdom. Condemned first by Chinese custom then by American law to an almost complete celibacy in the overseas country, the Chinese lived as homeless men, turning to prostitution for sexual outlet, gambling for recreational release, and on occasion opium smoking for surcease from the cares of their lonely sojourn.

As immigrants from a traditional society who had taken up temporary residences in a frontier land to make their fortunes, the Chinese exhibited special characteristics. They were in America not to colonize nor to spread the culture of China. Neither were they there to be absorbed into America's melting pot of races and nations. Rather the special and unique character of their immigration required them to *adapt* America and its ways to their own purposes rather than *adopt* it to the exclusion and surrender of their own values. The experiences to be had in America were bracketed within the all-encompassing goal of the trip itself: to acquire wealth which in the homeland could be used to recoup status lost by flood, poverty, or war, to demand greater esteem, and to enjoy a generally better life. In this sense the familiar context in which contemporary American scholars examine immigration history—in terms of "assimilation," "contributions," and "mobility patterns"—does not describe the Chinese immigrants' own perspective. He was there to earn enough money to leave; he was there in body alone, while his spirit remained in the homeland; he was there because it offered him an opportunity to pursue his aim, not because he desired to stamp its future history with his presence.

The Chinese approached American society with the outlook characteristic of sojourner strangers in general. The most prominent features of this outlook are an enterprising spirit, a willingness to move wherever opportunity beckons, an orientation to-

ward the future which overrides both engrained tradition and current condition, and a freedom from convention. In spite of the hostile prejudices against them, the Chinese persevered and endured. Their efforts are testimony to the unsung genius and enormous capacity of an oppressed immigrant people.

The Chinese Immigrant As Sojourner

Those Chinese who stayed on in the overseas area, postponing their trip home year after year became the sojourner stock of America's pioneer Chinese (Siu, 1952: 34–44). The special psychological characteristic of the sojourner is manifested in his clinging to the culture and style of the country from which he has come. Despite having been transplanted, he retains the outlook of a Chinese villager, loyal to his family, nostalgic for the Cantonese countryside, friendly to the members of his *hui kuan*, and distant, aloof, and "objective" toward the peoples in the host society. Typically he is neither hostile nor despairing; rather he regards the conditions of his long lonely existence as a challenge to wit and patience. The overseas society exists for him as a job and an opportunity, neither as something to reject, rebuke, or revolt against. To the sojourner his own primary group—kin and friends in China—are the center of things. It is *for* them that he labors so long abroad. It is *to* them that he owes whatever his work may bring. It is *by* them that he will be honored and remembered. The sojourner is a man who remains in an alien country for a very long period of time without being assimilated by it.

As a Chinese wishing to remain Chinese the sojourner characteristically encloses himself in a Chinese world while abroad. "Chinatown," that quarter of the city reserved to Chinese businesses and residences, becomes his basic abode. To be sure his choice in this matter is not entirely voluntary; racial hostility, housing segregation, occupational exclusion, and the general pattern of discrimination in America combine to force ghettoization even on those who have more cosmopolitan outlooks. Nevertheless, in the ghetto, surrounded by compatriots who hail from his native land, the sojourner is in touch with his community and culture. The larger society is physically near but socially remote. Enclosed within the narrow confines of Chinatown, he eats, sleeps, works, and plays under the tutelage of his native values. So long as the outside society does not intrude on his solitude, he remains a Cantonese while abroad.

Even when he is bereft of a Chinese community, the sojourner may be able or be forced to retain his outlook. The lone Chinese laundryman in a white neighborhood, the solitary Chinese restauranteur in a small town, the Chinese cook on a remote ranch in the territory, [2] and the isolated Chinese student in a metropolitan university may keep their minds on their single purpose, their contacts secondary, and their associations brief. Cultural distance from the larger world may be enhanced by the language barrier, while a self-enforced isolation may reduce the possibility that major life adjustments will have to be made. Finally, the ready manner in which race contacts become institutionalized in a formal and rigid way may perforce assist the sojourner, whatever his real desire, to remain a stranger in the society.

For the sojourner life abroad is defined along the narrow lines of a job. It is something that must be done in order that something else shall follow it. Thus the overseas Chinese student studied so that he might assume a post as scientist, engineer, or diplomat in China; the overseas Chinese restauranteur cooked chop suey because that would hopefully make enough money to return home where chop suey was unknown; and the Chinese laundryman washed, ironed, and sewed because that was one of the few occupations open to Chinese men in a frontier society lacking large numbers of women. The job is not a career. It is a preparatory state of existence. But that preparatory state could and often did last the lifetime of the sojourner.

The Chinese laundryman is the sojourner *par excellence.* His job did not come to him by choice; rather it was gleaned from among the occupational leavings of the American frontier.[3] To be a laundryman in America did not entail a career commit-

ment. Instead it involved the location in a job niche, an acquisition of the skill related to it, and the willingness to continue until fortune had at last smiled. All too often the millennial dream of good fortune receded into an ever-long future. But still the laundryman toiled on. Eventually his condition became ritualized, a thing in itself, rewarded by the small satisfactions of aiding wife and children in China, continued because nothing else seemed to suggest itself. The novelist L. C. Tsung has captured this condition in a passage from his novel, *The Marginal Man:*

> The neon sign of a Chinese hand laundry reminded Charles of the several shirts he had not yet picked up. The sign said Wen Lee, but Charles had never been able to ascertain whether the proprietor's family name was Wen or Lee. He entered the shop and saw the old man still hard at work behind the counter, ironing under a naked electric bulb, although it was already ten o'clock at night . . . "How many years have you been in the States?" Charles asked out of curiosity as he paid the man.
> "Forty years," the old man answered in Cantonese, and raised his four fingers again. No expression showed on his face.
> "Do you have a family?"
> "Big family. A woman, many sons and grandsons. All back home in Tangshan."
> "Have you ever gone back since you came out here?"
> "No, I only send money," replied the old man. From underneath the counter he brought out a photograph and showed it to Charles. In the center sat a white-haired old woman, surrounded by some fifteen or twenty men, women and children, of various ages . . . The whole clan, with contented expressions on their faces, were the offspring of this emaciated old man, who supported not only himself but all of them by his two shaking, bony hands. They seemed to represent the flow of a great river of life, originating from a tiny stream. The stream may dry up some day, but the river flows on. The old man put on his glasses again and identified each person in the picture to Charles Lin. A toothless smile came to his expressionless face.
> Charles Lin realized that this picture was the old man's only comfort and relaxation. He had toiled like a beast of burden for forty years to support a large family which was his aim of existence, the sole meaning of his life. The picture to him was like a diploma, a *summa cum laude* to an honor student. Behind the facade of sadness and resignation there was the inner satisfaction which made this old man's life bearable and meaningful (Tsung, 1963: 158–159).

The Chinese Immigrant as Homegoer

Should he fulfill his dream in the overseas country, the Chinese immigrant returned home. To do so was to retranspose memory back into experience. The customs, ways, and institutions of China that he carried away with him into the diaspora were discovered again, life was recreated in its original form, and the joys of the familiar were again a source of everyday happiness. Such at any rate was the ideal. However, two sets of changes marred this wish-fulfilling picture and rendered the dream less of a possibility than the dreamer supposed.

To the Chinese the picture of returning home was clear enough. Pardee Lowe, the son of a Chinese immigrant to America, describes his father's image of what it would mean to return to China:

> Father was deeply sensible of the great honors which would be bestowed upon him if he returned to Sahn Kay Sawk. All kinsmen who returned, he remembered, were held in very high esteem. Because of their fortunes they were not treated as ordinary villagers who had never gone abroad. Instead, they were hailed as *Kum Sahn Hock* (Guests from the Golden Mountains). Nothing the village could offer was too good for him. They feasted off the fat of the land, and were treated as mandarins (Lowe, 1943:5).

This image of the return to China presumes that the historical and cultural clock will stand still, that the society that was left behind will remain as it was, that its traditions will not erode, its customs not expire, its fundamental ways not change. So long as the time between departure and the return was short and so long as no major change cracked the cake of custom in traditional China this presumption remained valid. However, for many Chinese what began as a brief and profitable sojourn abroad turned into years of exile. Thus after decades of waiting for his return a Chinese wife wrote to her husband, "You promised me to go abroad for only three years, but you have stayed there nearly thirty years now" (Siu, 1952: 35–36). As the decades abroad passed China changed. In 1911 the Manchu Empire fell before the onslaught of Sun Yat Sen and his revolutionaries. The warring factions eventually

united under Chiang Kai-Shek or joined the growing Communist Movement. A few independent warlords played politics with the scene. In 1949 the Communists succeeded in capturing the state and driving Chiang and his minions to Formosa. Throughout all this period many overseas Chinese held fast to their dream. Those who returned found a different China than the one they had left.

After 1949 the Chinese in America were cut off from remigration. In fact, although few overseas Chinese realize it, the diaspora had ended. For the aged Chinese the sojourn had become a permanent exile. In 1962 William Willmott and I interviewed an aged Chinese in Welles, British Columbia. He told us he had a wife in China he had not seen in forty-five years and a son he had never seen. He said that he received letters from them regularly. When we asked when he planned to rejoin his wife and son, he sighed and said "Maybe, next year." Then he asked if the present regime in China treated old people well; he was afraid, he said, and wondered what would happen to him if he returned.

However, even if the traditional home had not changed during his absence, the immigrant had. The years abroad in the new society could not help but leave their mark. Perhaps he had learned another language and back in his home country found himself thinking—and even occasionally, speaking—in that tongue. More likely he had acquired new skills, interests, and habits which estranged him from his fellow men at home. Some Chinese severed their queues while in America and had so come to favor the tonsorial styles of the Occident that they were embarrassed at the requirement in force until 1911 that they rebraid their hair when they remigrated to China. Abroad the Chinese immigrant had—perhaps unconsciously—come to incorporate and appreciate some of the fundamental ideas and everyday practices of America as his own. Back home in China he found himself alienated from his own people—not Chinese anymore, but certainly not an acculturated American either.

However, many of those who dreamed of going home one day from the overseas adventure could not make enough money to do so. To assuage their loneliness and, often enough, to marry and sire children, they became birds-of-passage, returning to China every few years to marry, visit with their wife, enjoy the comforts of hearth and home, and then going back to the immigrant colony where they labored in lonely solitude. Pardee Lowe recalls that his father had at one time returned to China to acquire a wife, repay the debts of his family, and retire in luxury. However, "Marriage and redemption of the family homestead soon exhausted Father's meager fortune. He returned to America, not gladly from all I heard, but reconciled. Thousands of Chinese were doing the same thing every year; spending in their native villages a fortune gained abroad, and coming back to this country to toil laboriously to acquire the necessary money to repeat their trip" (Lowe, 1945: 7).

Even some of those who returned for good did not resume an ordinary life. All too often the "fortune" that they had earned abroad was eaten up by family debts, by bribes to the ubiquitous corrupt magistrates, and by the inevitable feasts, gifts, and ostentatious splendor required of one who had made a success of himself. After funds had been exhausted some new means for making a living had to be found. Sometimes the skills acquired abroad could be turned to use nearer to home. A nice example is found in the recollections of Hosea Ballou Morse, a scholar and administrator who was quite familiar with old China:

> An incident which occurred to the author in 1893 throws some light on the usual result to a returned Chinese emigrant. At a railroad station in Formosa he was addressed in fluent and correct English by the proprietor-cook of the station restaurant; and in answer to a question of astonishment, the Chinese explained why he was there. He had returned from California with a fortune of $2,000.00. He had first to disburse heavily to remain unmolested by the magistrate and his underlings; then he had to relieve the necessities of his aged father; then an uncle, who had fallen into business difficulties, must be rescued from impending bankruptcy; and then he found he had only enough left to procure himself a wife, with a few dollars margin wherewith to establish himself in his present business, which at most would require $100.00 capital. (Morse, 1910: 166n).

Marginal Men

If the immigrant who stayed became a permanent sojourner, his children found themselves one step removed from that condition yet not fully a part of the society in which they had been born. They were, in Robert Park's memorable words, marginal men:

> The marginal man is a personality type that arises at a time and a place where, out of the conflict of races and cultures, new societies, new peoples and cultures are coming into existence. The fate which condemns him to live, at the same time, in two worlds is the same which compels him to assume, in relation to the worlds in which he lives, the role of a cosmopolitan and a stranger (Park, 1961: xvii).

As marginal men American born Chinese experienced the variety of senses in which they were cultural hybrids. The Chinese Americans were products of two cultures, partial members of two societies. They shared in the cultural traditions and social life of America and of Chinatown intimately at some times, formally at others, on occasion casually, but in some instances with excruciating if silent anguish. Not quite able to break with the manners and customs of their parents, they were still unable to completely join in the ways of America. Racial prejudice kept them at a distance from white America, while Americanization reduced their commitment to Chinatown. The Chinese American, like the second generation of other ethnic groups, "was a man on the margin of two cultures and two societies, which never completely interpenetrated and fused" (Park, 1950: 354).

One aspect of their condition that differentiated American born Chinese from children of European immigrants was race. So long as America retained its racial prejudice and racist practices, acculturation would not result in acceptance. As late as 1939 William Carlson Smith observed that "Many years will pass before American-born Chinese and Japanese in California will be accepted by the white group, no matter how thoroughly Americanized they become. Skin color and the slant (sic!) of eyes categorically classify them with their alien parents" (Smith, 1939: 369). In their relations with other

Americans, the offspring of immigrants from China discovered the ubiquitous intrusiveness of race.

Even when Chinese Americans believed that they had overcome racial prejudices and unfavorable stereotypes they unexpectedly encountered hostilities and antagonisms. A student in a midwestern college reported on an ugly inter-racial incident that later gave way to friendship:

> In college I was taken into a fraternity. In my second year I took part in the initiation of the new men. We had them lined up and were paddling them with some boards and staves. Several of the fellows had paddled them and then my turn came. After I had given one of the fellows a swat he turned around and said, 'You damned Chink! What business do you have to hit me?' That was a big shock to me. Why should he pick on me? I said nothing and when it came to the election I voted that he be received. After some time we became the best of friends (Smith, 1937: 193).

But the racial distinction often combined with cultural tradition to stigmatize a Chinese American not only in the country of his birth but also in that of his parents. Such experiences served to drive home the unique position of the second generation Chinese, impressing upon him the fact that he was caught in the middle of a conflict over which he had little control. For example, an Hawaiian-born Chinese girl who had been treated as an American in Honolulu discovered quite a different response in California:

> I gradually learned that I was a foreigner—a Chinese— that I would be wiser to admit it and to disclaim my American citizenship, particularly when I was in a Chinese group. I accepted my title as a *foreign* student more graciously. I became more accustomed to the stares of the American people, to their remarks, and to their sneers. I did not feel inferior to them. I did not feel antagonistic toward them; but I was disappointed and deeply hurt (Smith, 1939: 372).

But when this girl despaired of America, schooled herself in the Chinese language and culture, and journeyed to the land of her parents' birth, she found that she was still a foreigner, an *Americanized* Chinese and thus an alien to China's ways:

> I gave up trying to be a Chinese; for as soon as the people in China learned that I was an oversea (sic) Chinese, they remarked, 'Oh, you are a foreigner,' Some asked, 'Where did you learn to speak Chinese?' Some thought it remark-

able that I spoke Chinese at all. So you see I was quite foreign to China. I wore Chinese clothes and tried to pass as a Chinese, but I could not so I gave up and admitted my foreign birth and education (Smith, 1937: 245).

As she lived and reflected on her experiences in China and California, the girl was torn between the questions of identity. To be neither Chinese to people of her lineage nor American to people of her birthplace left her in limbo. But limbo is a land where few care to live and most journey out of it—to compromise and anguish and, perhaps, resignation. The girl concludes:

> I lack very much a Chinese background, Chinese culture, and Chinese manners and customs; I have neither their viewpoint nor their patience. Sometimes I was homesick for America. Where I had friends, I felt better. I got more or less adjusted to some things—one of them was the rickshaw. But most of the time, I had very mixed feelings. I find that unconsciously now I try to avoid the subject of China; I try to put it out of my mind and attention; I don't want to think or feel about China . . . America is really my country and my home (Smith, 1937: 243–244).

Marginality is a problem not only vis a vis the dominant racial group but also in relation to the self. It produces one of the cardinal elements of *anomie— self estrangement*. Alienation from one's own self is a probability when psychosocial acculturation is accompanied by racial stigma. In such a situation individuals find that their very bodies are problematic to them—are issues worthy of both philosophical reflection and worrisome anxiety. To an American-born Chinese the very face he presents, masking behind its Oriental visage a half-American mind, may evoke a painful, even excruciating, contradiction. Frank Chin captures this moment of self-estrangement in his haunting novel about Dirigible, a young man of San Francisco's Chinatown:

> The clean shaven face, washed and dried, cleanly drily opaque, pinkish, brownish, yellow and vaguely luminescent in the light was grand. Seeing his skin in the mirror, touching his face with his fingers, he sensed color and essence stimulated to movement through his face like petals and leaves stiffening in the sunlight. Pockmarked, lined, shadowed, full of character, like the face of a mudflat dried into a desert of potato chips. Dirigible's real face . . . The face was forced still, to be looked at in the mirror by him (Chin, 1970: 31–31).

Beneath the sense of dual and unresolved identity, and beyond the *angst* of self-estrangement, the Chinese American senses his own non-membership in the two cultures. Product of both, member of neither, he lives between them, participating in the activities appropriate to both but feeling his alien identity even as he acts. Victor Wong, a Chinese American who grew up in San Francisco's Chinatown in the 1930's, vividly recalls the pain and misunderstanding that arose from his marginal status:

> So we *were* all immigrants in those days, no matter where we were born. Between the Chinese and the English education, we had no idea where we belonged. Even to this day, if I wanted to say I'm going to China I would never say it that way; I would say *go back* to China. Because I was taught from the time I was born that this was not my country, that I would have to go to China to make my living as an adult. And I think that if it hadn't been for the Japanese War—that is with the Americans; December 7, 1941—many of us *would* probably have had to go back to China, with our parents (Wong, 1970: 70).

Until the outbreak of World War II Chinese immigrants retained a sojourner attitude not only for themselves but for their children as well. The sacred duty to be buried in the village of one's father's birth meant little to Chinese born in the United States, but prejudice and discrimination served as a constant reminder of their unequal status and limited opportunities in America. Parents would counsel their children to pay little heed to the daily slights and the legal, occupational, and social restrictions they encountered—except to let those acts of injustice remind them that their ultimate future was in China and, in the interim, in Chinatown. Therefore, parents would advise their children, both a Chinese and an American education was very important. The English schools would provide one with the training, skills, and techniques which would prove useful in China; the Chinese language school would provide one with the language, customs, and traditions which would make it possible to assume a new life in the homeland of their parents. Chinese American youths were encouraged to adopt a diligent but instrumental orientation toward America and what it had to offer. They were to acquire its methods and technics—but

they were not to be seduced by its culture, style, and way of life. Though born and reared in America, they were to remain Chinese.

At the same time the schools were interested in Americanizing the offspring of all immigrants, though not necessarily in encouraging all of them to aspire after social equality. Chinese children were required to speak, read, and write English. They were taught to revere American Revolutionary War leaders as the Founding Fathers of *their* country. Chinese Americans absorbed many of the ways of America readily and as a matter of course in school, in the mass media, and in extra-curricular activities. As Chinese Americans they found that they could not step into the white American mainstream because of severe racial prejudice and discrimination. But neither could they acquiesce to a sojourner existence; their own acculturation had progressed too far. Caught between the poles of absorption and remigration, they managed an existence, carving a way of life out of the half-a-loaf provided to them by Chinatown and the larger society, respectively.

The ambiguity of this existence produced a painful and awkward adjustment for the Chinese Americans. Many found themselves thinking more and more like their white peers but denied the opportunity to practice an American way of life. Respectful of their parents, they nevertheless could not conform to their wishes.

The remarkable difference in discipline and self-control in the American public and Chinese language schools is a reflection of the dual existence that characterized life in general for Chinese Americans. Galen Chow, who studied in San Francisco's afternoon Chinatown schools in the early 1940's, recalls the experience in a vivid description of children's life among second generation Chinese in America. Chow's parents had carefully advised him on proper behavior in public school.

> In contrast no pressure was exerted by my parents to do anything but attend Chinese school. This double standard led to a Jekyll-Hyde existence for me on school days. In public school I was a model of deportment, studious and courteous. In Chinese school I was a little terror—baiting the teacher constantly, fighting and getting into all kinds of mischief. The reason for my parents' attitudes was not lost on me. In public school, where all the teachers

were white, I had to present my best posture in order not to shame the Chinese in general and my family in particular. In Chinese school where all the students and teachers were Chinese we could revert to normal. However, probably due to the strain of my role playing in public school, I would react to an extreme when turned loose in Chinese school. Generally, I think these actions and reactions were true to some extent, more or less, in all the Chinese children.

Helen Lowe summed up this cultural generation gap when she said, "Father's American ways are not American enough, and as for his Chinese habits and ideas, they are queer, unreasonable, and humiliating!" (Lowe, 1945: 175). Her brother, Pardee, has recorded in minute detail the increasing tide of his own Americanization—the move to larger quarters for the family, the purchase and installation of a ᵇᵗub to replace the wooden bucket used through- ᵗᵈhood, the long struggle to obtain his ⁱⁿ Stanford University, ᵃ ᵘᵃˡ ⁿᵃ ᵗᵒ ᵉ ' (Lowe, 1945: ⁻ ⁻. However, the Horatio ᵘᶜᶜess story did not describe the life of all ᵤₙᵢnese Americans. Elmer Wok Wai, born at the turn of the century into the slum of San Francisco's Chinatown, saw his brother and sister sold to meet expenses, was educated in an asylum for wayward youth, and then turned out into the streets. He became a thug and strong-arm man for a Chinese secret society, killed a man, and spent seventeen years in San Quentin prison. After being parolled he ended his days as an overworked and underpaid domestic in the employ of white people (Griggs, 1969).

Even when their lives overseas were eventually crowned with success, Chinese Americans suffered because of their marginal status. Pardee Lowe became estranged from his father for two years and spoke to him only when necessary after they had quarreled bitterly over the proper way to live in America (Lowe, 1945: 176–178). Jade Snow Wong, whose ceramics became internationally renowned in the 1940's, entered into her life's work under a double burden. As a Chinese American she suffered from the prejudices and stereotypes commonly inflicted on members of her race; as a woman she had to overcome the traditional Chinese view that op-

posed the presence of women in independent professions (J. Wong, 1945: 211–246). Rose Hum Lee, born into a Montana family of Chinese descent, endured both local and family ostracism and generalized racial discrimination in her efforts to become a leading sociologist specializing in the study of Chinese Americans (Lee, 1960). Victor Wong a Chinese American born and reared in San Francisco benefitted from the greater opportunities for Chinese Americans during World War II and became an engineer. But he anguished so much over his ambiguous status in America that he first repudiated his Chinese background and sought a complete American identity, then, unhappy in that situation, he returned to an all-Chinese setting and resumed a more ethnically exclusive existence (V. Wong, 1970: 71–72).

Before World War II the likelihood that many Chinese Americans would realize a secure and productive life in America seemed remote.[4] Up until the 1940's the number of Chinese born in America had been low because of the shortage of women in the immigrant group. The few Chinese Americans who reached maturity in the first thirty years of the twentieth century entered into the business established by their kinsmen in Chinatown—restaurants, laundries, curio shops—or went to China to make a living.

The idea of a career in China excited much interest among young American-born Chinese in the 1920's and '30's. However, among those Chinese Americans who went to China were many who found themselves even more estranged than they had felt in the United States. Moreover, the social unrest that characterized China's internal condition in the first half of the century did not recommend itself to too many overseas Chinese. In some Chinatown families brothers divided over how to proceed, one choosing China, while the other chose Chinatown. In 1926 Winifred Raushenbush, a research associate of Robert E. Park, reported on what she regarded as a Chinese American success story (Raushenbush, 1926: 221). An old Chinatown family had two sons. One had become an engineer, gone to China, and was, at the time of her research, helping "Sun Yat Sen to work out his ideas about the harbors of Canton." The other had graduated from Stanford University where he had been a football player, and become a businessman and politician conciliating the warring factions in San Francisco's Chinatown. The latter "is a man who, because of his popularity as an athlete, and because of the wide diverse human curiosities which have made him a politician, finds himself at home both in America and in Chinatown, free to go back and forth from one to the other . . . He has solved in his own person a problem vastly more important to Chinatown than that of the fighting tongs; he has gotten out of the ghetto."

However, most Chinese could not get out of the ghetto. As late as the 1930's Chinese parents urged their children to prepare themselves for a life in China. Jade Snow Wong's father "encouraged her to make the mastery of Chinese her main objective; for he wanted her to go to China to study after high school graduation. He thought that a Chinese could realize his optimum achievement only in China." Her brother was also urged to think of China as his future home. "Father and son agreed that the study of medicine in China would prepare Older Brother for his career. Knowing the Chinese language, he could establish himself where medical personnel was greatly needed, and he could strengthen his ancestral ties by visits to Daddy's native village and relatives" (J. Snow Wong, 1945: 95). Victor Wong bitterly recalls that in the 1930's "it was always China that we were taught was home. In those days we were all *immigrants*. Whether we were born in America, or not, we were all immigrants . . ." (V. Wong, 1970: 24).

If China seemed uninviting and white America too formidable, then Chinatown beckoned feebly to some young Chinese Americans. In 1926 a young American-born Chinese told Winifred Raushenbush, "Just wait until the native-born ride into power here among the Chinese in San Francisco— which will happen sometime within the next ten or twelve years—and you will see a different Chinatown." (Raushenbush, 1926: 221). More Chinese Americans turned to work in restaurants, laundries, curio shops, and the Chinatown lottery in this period than went to China. But beginning in the 1930's more Chinese were being born in America

and the pressure on Chinatowns to absorb this growing population portended difficulty. In the same period the Rocky Mountain Chinatowns began to decline, and Chinese from Montana to Arizona began migrating to San Francisco, Chicago, and New York, centers of Chinese settlement in America. Chinatown's capacity to house and employ America's Chinese became taxed just as the great depression set in.

However successful it was as an arena of employment, the ghetto contained its American-born Chinese so well that they had little contact with those white outsiders with whom they might have shared a common outlook. Galen Chow recalls that during his childhood in San Francisco's Chinatown all his chums were fellow Chinese of the second generation, and with the exception of his white public school teachers, he had almost no contact with white America.

> We all played in and around the streets and buildings of Chinatown with an air of proprietorship. We knew every street, alley, unusual building, and every nook and cranny of Chinatown. We were less sure of ourselves when we ventured out of Chinatown either by ourselves or with our parents and at these times would present our stereotypical personalities of the subdued, unscrutable Oriental to the white world.

The era of Chinese diaspora in America began to erode in the decade that began with the admission of Chinese to quota status as immigrants and the right of naturalization (1943) and concluded with the triumph of the communist revolution in China. Since then Chinese have become more and more a national minority in polyglot America. With the sex ratio coming ever more into balance, the marriage of American born Chinese to one another increasing, and the birth and maturation of second and third generations in the United States, we may speak of the shift from a diasporic people to an ethnic group. Characteristic of this change is the beginnings of filiopietistic history, the interest in discovering Chinese "contributions" to America, the search for ethnic origins, and the rise of Asian American studies. There is also the noticeable difference between the attitudes of the American-born and the newly arrived immigrants. The new gangs of American Chinatowns give violent expression to this fact as they organize along lines that separate the native American from the youths recently arrived from Hong Kong. And the old institutions of Chinatown—the clans, *hui kuan,* and secret societies—struggle to maintain themselves in the face of the acculturation and suburbanization of the growing Chinese American middle class and diffidence, hostility, and intractability of the new immigrants.

Paradoxically perhaps, the best evidence of the decline of diaspora is the rise of historical and national consciousness. Membership in the people-hood of Chinese was a taken-for-granted feature of the immigrant group and the first small cohorts of American-born Chinese. It is among the Americanized generations, the college-bound, and uni-

versity educated that the gnawing sense of ambivalence and anguish over identity finds anxious expression. Seeking a break away from the brass of America that once seemed like gold to their grandfathers, this generation turns to ethnicity, rediscovers history, defines culture, and attempts to reenter the community. The new Chinese represent America as it is—neither a melting pot nor a mosaic, rather a plurality of interests, values, institutions, and sentiments in less than equal or peaceful coexistence. But that is the story for another paper. For the moment we might dwell on the realities and sentiments of the last era—diaspora and its consequences. It shall not be with us again:

Notes

1. A Chinese woman in traditional dress and with bound feet had been exhibited as a freak attraction on Broadway in 1834. Missionaries exhorted the Chinese to halt this practice and cited it frequently as evidence of the horrors and immorality that characterized pagan peoples.

2. A poignant example is provided by Frederick Remington's description of a ranch cook at the hacienda of San Jose de Bavicora in a remote part of Mexico:

> Charlie Jim, the Chinese cook, has a big room with a stove in it, and he and the stove are a never-ending wonder to all the folks, and the fame of both has gone across the mountains to Sonora and to the south. Charlie is an autocrat in his curious Chinese way, and by the dignity of his position as Mr. Jack's private cook and his unknown antecedents, he conjures the Mexicans and d———s the Texans, which latter refuse to take him seriously and kill him, as they would a "proper" man. Charlie Jim, in return, entertains ideas of Texans which he secretes, except when they dine with Jack, when he may be heard to mutter, "Cake and pie no good for puncher, make him fat and lazy"; and when he cross the patio and they fling a rope over his foot, he becomes livid; and breaks out, "Da—— puncher; da—— rope; rope man all same horse; da—— puncher; no good that way."

"An Outpost of Civilization," *Frederick Remington's Own West,* ed.

by Harold McCracken (New York: Dial Press, 1960), p. 139.

3. Lin Yutang has presented this idea in fiction in a sensitive speech by a laundryman in Chinatown:

> I did not choose, son. And it is not bad as you can see. I have made a living, and we are now all here. There was no other way. All you have is a pair of hands, and you do what the Americans do not want to do and allow you to do. When they built the railroads in the West, there were no women there. Those American men. They could not cook, and they could not wash. We Chinese cooked and washed better, so they allowed us to cook and wash. Now we wash America and cook America because we wash better and cook better. I would have opened a restaurant if I had the money (Lin Yutang, 1948: 27).

4. As the number of Chinese Americans began to grow and their education improved, Chinese community leaders expressed concern for their future. In 1929 Chinatown newspaper editor Ng Poon Chew observed:

> Perhaps the future of our American born Chinese will have to look to China for their life work. In this there is much hope China will open thousands of lines for ambitious modernized young men to utilize their learnings to help develop the country's resources (Chew, 1970: 8).

References

Blauner, Robert. 1972. *Racial Oppression in America.* New York: Harper and Row.

Bogardus, Emory. 1928. *Immigration and Race Attitudes.* Boston: D.C. Heath.

Camus, Albert. 1955. *The Myth of Sisyphus and other Essays,* translated by Justin O'Brien. New York: Vintage.

Chin, Frank. 1970. "Goong Hai Fot Choy", from *A Chinese Lady Dies,* in Ishmael Reed, ed., *19 Necromancers From Now.* Garden City: Doubleday.

Chow, Galen. 1972. "Reflections of a Yellow Boy in a White Society *circa* 1938-1950". Unpublished MS.

Cicourel, Aaron. 1974. *Cognitive Sociology: Language and Meaning in Social Interaction.* New York: The Free Press.

de Crevecoeur, J. Hector St. John. 1957. *Letters from an American Farmer.* New York: E.P. Dutton.

Garfinkel, Harold. 1967. *Studies in Ethnomethodology.* Englewood Cliffs: Prentice-Hall.

George, Henry. 1869. "The Chinese on the Pacific Coast". *New York Tribune,* May 1.

Griggs, Veta. 1969. *Chinaman's Chance: The Life Story of Elmer Wok Wai.* New York: Exposition Press.

Lee, Rose Hum. 1960. *The Chinese in the United States of America.* Hong Kong: Hong Kong University Press.

Lin Yutang. 1948. *Chinatown Family.* New York: John Day and Co.

Lowe, Pardee. 1943. *Father and Glorious Descendant.* Boston: Little, Brown and Co.

Lyman, Stanford and Scott, Marvin. 1970. *A Sociology of the Absurd,* New York: Appleton-Century-Crofts; Pacific Palisades: Goodyear Publishing Co.

McCracken, Harold, ed. 1960. *Frederick Remington's Own West.* New York: Dial Press.

Morse, Hosea Ballou. n.d. *The International Relations of the Chinese Empire. Vol. II: The Period of Submission, 1861–1893.* Taipei: No publisher listed.

Myrdal, Gunnar with the assistance of Richard Sterner and Arnold Rose. 1944. *An American Dilemma: The Negro Problem and Modern Democracy.* New York: Harper and Brothers.

Ng Poon Chew. 1970. "Letter to Samuel H. Cohn, July 4, 1929", in Edward K. Strong, *The Second Generation Japanese Problem.* New York: Arno Press and the New York Times.

Novak, Michael. 1971. *The Rise of the Unmeltable Ethnics: The New Political Force of the Seventies.* New York: Macmillan.

Park, Robert E. 1950. *Race and Culture.* The Collected Papers of Robert Ezra Park, Vol. I. Edited by Everett Cherrington Hughes, et al. Glencoe: The Free Press.

——. 1961. "Introduction" to Everett V. Stonequist, *The Marginal Man: A Study in Personality and Culture Conflict.* New York: Russell and Russell.

Raushenbush, Winifred. 1926. "The Great Wall of Chinatown: How the Chinese Mind Their Own Business Behind It". *The Survey Graphic,* LVI:3, May 1.

Schrag, Peter. 1970. *The Decline of the Wasp.* New York: Simon and Schuster.

Schutz, Alfred. 1967. *The Phenomenology of the Social World,* translated by George Walsh and Frederick Lehnert. Evanston: Northwestern University Press.

Simmel, Georg. 1950. "The Stranger", in *The Sociology of Georg Simmel,* translated and edited by Kurt Wolff. Glencoe: The Free Press.

Siu, Paul C.P. 1952. "The Sojourner". *American Journal of Sociology,* VIII, July.

Smith, William Carlson. 1937. *Americans in Process: A Study of Our Citizens of Oriental Ancestry.* Ann Arbor: Edwards Brothers.

——. 1939. *American in the Making: The Natural History of the Assimilation of Immigrants.* New York: D. Appleton-Century Co.

Sombart, Werner. 1962. *The Jews and Modern Capitalism,* translated by M. Epstein. New York: Collier Books.

Stonequist, Everett. 1961. *The Marginal Man: A Study in Personality and Culture Conflict.* New York: Russell and Russell.

Tsung, L.C. 1963. *The Marginal Man.* New York: The Pageant Press.

Wong, Jade Snow. 1945. *Fifth Chinese Daughter.* New York: Harper and Brothers.

Wong, Victor. 1970. "Childhood 1930s" and "Childhood II", in *Ting: The Cauldron: Chinese Art and Identity in San Francisco.* San Francisco: Glide Urban Center.

The Significance of Asians in American Society

TRADITIONALLY STUDIES OF race relations in America have focused on the regional character of racist practices. Thus, it is a commonplace report that Negroes in the South have been victims of a caste order;[1] that Indian troubles are a feature of westward expansion;[2] that Mexican-Americans are the principal object of ethnic intolerance in the southwest;[3] that anti-Semitism is a creature of midwestern populism;[4] and that Sinophobia and anti-Japanese sentiment are peculiar products of conditions on the Pacific Coast.[5] The image of the segmented and geographical character of American racism has facilitated a local view of the phenomenon, concentrating primarily on the origins of prejudice and discrimination in the immediate area and eschewing any analysis of racism as a central value of American society.[6] However, the 1968 report of the National Advisory Commission on Civil Disorders challenged this view when it asserted that

> Race prejudice has shaped our history decisively in the past; it now threatens to do so again. White racism is essentially responsible for the explosive mixture which has been accumulating in our cities since the end of World War II.[7]

The Kerner Report suggested that racism was endemic to America. Recent research has delved even more deeply and discovered that racism arose as a central value in the post-medieval Occident. Winthrop Jordan has shown that racist ideas were intellectual, political and social products of the encounter between Europeans on the one hand and Africans and Indians on the other in the sixteenth century and thereafter.[8] Africans were reputed to be living representatives of the once mythical savage, descendants of the Biblically accursed Ham, and an inferior species of man, while a more refined intellectual tradition failed to resolve the question of Indian origins and laid the basis for the anti-Indian sentiment of a later age.[9] The vicissitudinal moral and political character of European images of dark-skinned peoples has been documented in the works of Henri Baudet,[10] Kathleen George,[11] and Thomas Gossett.[12] Once the idea of white superiority became both accepted and diffuse, it generated a wide variety of racist practices with respect not only to the Africans and Indians, but also to the "colored" inhabitants of Oceania,[13] and the Asian Mainland.[14] The mindless genocide of the native Hawaiian population which literally decimated it in the century between Captain Cook's "discovery" of the Sandwich Islands and the American annexation of the once proud Hawaiian Kingdom,[15] the murderous destruction of the Tasmanian people by Australian and British colonists,[16] the notorious practices of "blackbirding" carried on throughout the South Pacific,[17] and the imperialist incursions into Indo-China[18] and the Chinese Empire [19] all testify to the merger of a general Occidental racism with political domination and economic advantage.[20]

Despite a new intellectual recognition of racism as part of the central value system of the western world, little research has been done to ascertain the forms in which it asserted itself and the causes for changes in those forms. It is the intent of this essay to present a hypothesis on the characteristic features and etiology of racist institutions in America and to show the pivotal role in the creation of these institutions played by Asians in the west.

American Racism in Total Institutions

America emerged in modern world history as a republic organized to promote the general welfare and provide for the continental domination and collective security of its white Anglo-Saxon denizens. At the outset of its political and social establishment, this new society was faced by three ethnic types which challenged its originating idea: settlers and immigrants from continental Europe who did not bear the Anglo-Saxon stamp of moral and social approval in their character or culture; Africans and their descendants in America, whose dark skins and cultural practices were anathema to a white racial and Anglo-Saxon cultural order; and indigenous Indians whose copper-colored bodies and social and political codes challenged the racial and territorial plans for continental domination by the white, European Occidentals. In responding to the challenges posed by these three orders of mankind, America forged both the character and institutions of a racist yet still pluralistic society. The central characteristics of this racist pluralism were its rules of inclusion and exclusion with respect to racial

types and the mechanisms adduced to enforce these rules.

Essentially the decision was made—but only gradually worked out in piecemeal fashion—that America was to be a white man's country. Eligible for inclusion within the folds of full citizenship were all those Europeans who would renounce their continental cultures in favor of at least outward conformity to the dictates of Anglo-Saxon ways.[21] "Colored" peoples, on the other hand, would be excluded from full citizenship rights, but neither expelled from the American domain nor absorbed into its mainstream by interbreeding. Color castes, created by institutionalizing the ubiquitous relevance of skin pigmentation, establishing barriers against intermarriage, and experimenting with modes of racial isolation and concentration, would control the dark-skinned peoples. Theories of cultural assimilation and doctrines of a racial hierarchy—supported at various times by state, church and science—would, supposedly, justify the arrangements to all concerned.

The Europeans were coopted slowly and steadily, with only occasional eruptions and isolated rebellions, into the Anglo-Saxon core group. The fact that English became the *lingua franca* and official dialect of discourse perhaps did more than any other single process to promote Anglo-conformity as a "natural" and "taken-for-granted" process of Americanization.[22] For Europeans acculturation proceeded naturally and as a matter of course—or so it seemed.[23] In fact, religio-ethnic enclaves managed to preserve themselves—sometimes by a self-enforced cultural and geographical isolation, as among the Amish and the Hutterians;[24] sometimes by securing linguistic, national or cultural values within the confines of church, private school or some other secluded institution[25]—and thus to create a dual national existence for themselves.

In the one hundred and thirty-seven years that separated the writing of the Constitution from the xenophobic immigration act of 1924—the final and most important victory of American nativism[26]— the Anglo-conformity doctrine triumphed over its pluralistic competitors.[27] The "melting pot" dream of the "American farmer," J. Hector St. John de Crevecoeur, was for Europeans only.[28] It was realized in the almost unnoticed erosion of Germanic culture,[29] the steady diminution and sometimes forcible eradication of Gaelic nationalism,[30] the decline of Greek-American institutions,[31] and the social isolation of steadily diminishing enclaves of other non-Anglo Europeans, including Italians,[32] Russians,[33] Poles,[34] and Jews.[35] Not a few immigrants became disenchanted and returned to their homelands.[36] More ominous was the vicissitudinal occurrence of nativist movements in America,[37] espousing a xenophobic bigotry, promoting the fear that Catholic immigrants were the advance legions of a papal conspiracy,[38] and that Jewish intelligence would subvert both Christianity and capitalism.[39] Liberty Leagues, Know-Nothing parties and the Ku Klux Klan took care to fan the flames of hatred for foreigners and to instill terror in the hearts of all those restive Negroes and as yet unacculturated Europeans.[40] Finally, ordinary newly-arrived Europeans soon learned that there were three ready testaments by which the newcomer could assure his American hosts that he was willing to assume the obligations of citizenship and fully incorporate himself into the body politic. He could share with the dominant white Americanized natives his profound pride in the fact that he too was white; he could voice his equally profound assurance that he too abhorred the "colored" peoples; he could join together with his fellow *Landsmänner* and with immigrants from other lands in associations which, whatever their social, political and economic aims, took care to exclude non-whites.[41]

The cooptation of continental Europeans was conducted concomitant with the enclosure of non-whites in total institutions. Africans were enslaved within the first half of the seventeenth century and Negro identity became coterminous with slave status.[42] Plantation slavery not only permanently excluded Negroes from the societal mainstream, but also imposed coercive controls which destroyed all but the vestiges of Old World culture.[43] The plantation dominated Negro life from the cradle to the grave. Denied the right to vote, sue, own property, make contracts, choose his place of abode, marry according to his choice and rear his own children, the slave was reduced to a pitiful existence combin-

ing the "benevolent" despotism of permanent childhood with the desperate terror of the concentration camp.[44] Despite over two hundred slave insurrections,[45] countless runaways,[46] occasional manumissions,[47] and a small but increasingly vocal free Negro population,[48] the blacks remained in nearly total subjugation until after the Civil War. Denied essential citizenship privileges and basic human rights, they were effectively excluded from the body politic and from the society.

Early attempts at enslavement of the Indians proved to be counterproductive, but the "solution" to the Indian "problem" nevertheless assumed total institutional proportions. Disease introduced by European contact took its toll in countless lives among the Red Men.[49] As the Americans pushed westward against the frontier horizons, massacre and conquest continued their decimation of the Indian nations.[50] The system of relocation, ultimately to be followed by incarceration of the Indians on wastelands unwanted by the mineral- and land-hungry "pioneers," emerged as the most efficacious "final" solution.[51] Although Indian tribes resisted unconditional surrender to white America until well past the opening of the twentieth century, and although a few escaped to Canada, the survivors of the military campaigns were eventually removed from their homelands and imprisoned on reservations.[52] There they fell under the domination of missionaries and bureaucrats who permitted them but the most modest preservation of their own way of life at the same time that they denied them knowledge about and access to the dominant society. Eating, sleeping, working, playing and mating under the ever-watchful surveillance of the Bureau of Indian Affairs, the Red Man, like the Negro, could not exercise any meaningful influence on or enter into any productive relationship with white society.[53]

Through the first half of the nineteenth century the Anglo-conformists were largely successful in their drive to insure white racial and Anglo-Saxon cultural domination of the American continent. European immigrants learned to publicly profess their desire to "Americanize" themselves, even as they stepped off the ships;[54] Negro leaders were divided over whether their people's liberation could be achieved in America or whether an exodus to Africa or to some other new land must precede jubilee day.[55] Indians retreated before the advance of white armies, many dying in proud defiance; others were degraded in the demoralizing confines of white America's fenced and guarded enclosures that were especially created to isolate them and break their spirit.[56] Freed from the aristocratic controls of Europe and almost untouched by its doctrine of *noblesse oblige,* white America subjugated its "colored" peoples. The United States appeared to have found the solution to establishing an economically thriving overseas homeland for English-speaking Caucasians of European extraction.

Then the Asian appeared on the American frontier. In light of America's treatment of "colored" peoples, the single most important fact about the first Chinese in America is that they were neither enslaved nor corralled. Arriving in California at the time of the earliest rumblings of incipient industrialism and the final onslaught on chattel slavery in America, the Chinese challenged the evil genius of this Anglo-Saxon society to wreak its racist havoc on them in some new manner, consistent with its exclusionist doctrines yet attuned to the condition of their peculiar mode of existence.[57]

Asians and the Beginnings of Modern Institutional Racism

The arrival of Asians in America preceded by but a few years the rise of industrialization and extensive urban settlement. So long as the United States depended on primary extractive and agricultural pursuits for its economic development, an excluded people—such as Negroes or Indians—might be exploited through enclosure in total institutions,[58] plantations or reservations. But with the advent of large-scale industrial production and extensive settlement in cities, the total institutional approach was not only inefficient but counterproductive.[59] A docile labor force was needed to work uncomplainingly in the new urban factories. But if such a work force was to be drawn from a people otherwise ineligible to civic, economic and social equality, methods would have to be found which would simultaneously permit the exploitation of them in a wide variety of settings and yet keep them apart from white society.[60] The Chinese arrived just in time to become what Alexander Saxton has called an "indispensable enemy."[61] In working out its response to the Asian challenge to white Anglo-Saxon dominance, America perfected the institutions of modern racism, institutions which had seen only their unorganized beginnings in the treatment of free Negroes in the slave era.

Unlike the total institutions of plantation slavery and rural reservation, modern racism is characterized by a diffuse, subtle—indeed, sometimes unconscious and invisible—prejudice found in a vast congeries of organizations, associations and social practices, none of which encompass the totality of the phenomenon, and each of which operates to degrade, demote, demoralize or defame non-white peoples.[62] Instead of finding its principal locus of operation at reservations or plantations, modern racism affects nearly all the institutions of modern industrial America—those in the political, economic, religious, educational, social and interpersonal spheres of life. Modern racism encompasses America with its rules, roles and relationships.[63]

When it became clear that Chinese and, later, Japanese might, if left to their own inclinations, ultimately participate at every level of American society and thus sully the white racial and Anglo-Saxon cultural domination which prevailed, each institutional sphere adopted restrictive or exclusionist practices to halt the potential Asian "invasion." Although some of these institutions were so situated that they operated only at a local level (during the first two decades of their American venture the Chinese were largely employed in rural mines, railroad construction, wineries, swamp drainage and agricultural labor, work in which their total supervision and segregation were assured), two important decisions at the national level gave impetus and legitimacy to even more extensive local and state institutional developments. The first of these was the limitation on family formation imposed by the Immigration Act of 1882; the second was the exclusion from naturalization imposed on Asians by legislation and judicial interpretation.

Like most immigrants to a frontier area, Chinese men had not been accompanied to America by their wives. Chinese custom and the self-acknowledged sojourner status of the first immigrants dictated this more as "natural."[64] However, when Chinese settlements appeared and the likelihood of long-term habitation in America seemed obvious, the federal government excluded the coming of the wives of immigrant Chinese laborers.[65] Not only did this legislative action insure domestic hardship and personal loneliness for the hapless Chinese working-man, it also guaranteed that no significant second generation of Chinese would be produced in America. The immigrant generation, excluded from replenishing itself by further migration after 1882, would eventually die out with no effective trace left in America.[66] The Chinese ghetto would be composed of homeless, aging bachelors whose recreational pursuits, domestic arrangements and social formations would stamp them as morally reprehensible in white American eyes.[67]

A few Chinese had been naturalized in the local communities and several states to which they had migrated before 1882.[68] However, in that year the same statute that barred the further coming of Chinese laborers and their wives also expressly excluded the Chinese from naturalization.[69] Forty years later the Supreme Court interpreted the naturalization laws then in effect to bar Japanese aliens from citizenship as well.[70] To gauge their full effect, the prohibition of the entrance of Chinese wives and the exclusion from citizenship must be read together. Even if aliens are declared to be ineligible to citizenship, their children *born on American soil* are citizens. By barring wives and declaring Chinese alienage to be permanent, the federal statutes effectively denied citizenship to almost all Chinese. Immigrants could no longer apply for naturalization and, without wives, no very significant number of natural-born citizens would arise.[71] The prohibi-

tion on acquiring citizenship had one other advantage for exclusionary procedures in a wide variety of situations. It introduced the category, "alien ineligible to citizenship" which would be used as a further bar to other rights, privileges and sanctuaries of white Anglo-Saxon domination. Laws and statutes, regulating hunting, fishing,[72] land ownership and corporate formations[73] introduced restrictions on ineligible aliens in the years that followed. Moreover, jobs, scholarships and other opportunities were foreclosed to Asians by the bar of citizenship prerequisites.

The federal legislation and judicial interpretations provided greater impetus and legislative justification for further racist practices against Asians, and for the establishment of generalized restrictions which might later be used against emancipated Negroes and detribalized Indians. Thus, in education, California's Superintendent of Education successfully complained against the presence of "Africans, Chinese, and Diggers" in 1859 and the offending races were excluded from the public schools in the following year.[74] In the years thereafter separate public schools were established for Chinese children. Even this did not contain the Asian population enough. Japanese students were ordered removed to the "Chinese school" in 1905 in what was to escalate into an international incident of bellicose proportions.[75] Nativists and patriotic organizations aroused deep-seated anxieties about intermarriage in a prolonged demagogic campaign of more than two decades to further segregate schools in the west.[76] Attempts by Chinese to desegregate San Francisco's schools in 1902[77] and those of Mississippi in 1927[78] were unsuccessful. Despite the overturn of *de jure* segregation in public schools in 1954,[79] many school systems, including those with predominant Chinese American minorities, remain segregated on a *de facto* basis. Moreover, the long history of exclusionist and separatist practice has taken its toll not only in inferior and unequal education, but also in the rise of a form of anti-racist ethnic nationalism among some Chinese. Strong feelings thus exist today among Chinese Americans attending San Francisco's almost all-Chinese Jean Parker Elementary School, Francisco Junior High

School and Galileo High School. A movement to implement not desegregation, but some form of pedagogic cultural nationalism expressible in the schools is now afoot. In public education, as elsewhere, the triumph of white racism and Anglo-conformity has produced a restive and nationalistic counter-active drive for ethnic pluralism.

State legislation controlling freedom of choice in marriage also closed the one loophole in family formation available to the homeless bachelor Chinese after 1882. Rendered ineligible for domesticity by the prohibition on immigrant wives, threatened with denial of readmission to the United States if they made home visits to their long-suffering wives in China,[80] Chinese men might have resolved their personal difficulties through intermarriage with white women as, for example, the homeless Chinese in Indonesia did when they married into the native population there.[81] However, a series of anti-miscegenation laws ultimately passed in thirty of the United States barred most Chinese from this possibility for family life.[82] Thus, the very same kind of provisions which kept black slaves from legitimately amalgamating with white masters and Indians from mingling their blood with that of all but the hated "Squaw Man," kept the Chinese from becoming a part of white America. Permitted neither to procreate nor to intermarry, the Chinese immigrant was told, in effect, to remigrate or die out—white America would not be touched by his presence.

Jobs and occupations have provided the ladder of success by which European immigrants climbed out of their original poverty and enculturation and on to the plateau of mainstream America. Entering America at a time of great industrial growth and expansion, European laborers charted the course of their own journey into America's cultural heartland by the map laid out by Anglo-Conformist leaders. Significant here is the fact that American labor's right to organize, bargain collectively and sit at the table reserved for legitimate associations were won at the price of excluding non-whites from the movement.[83] The first to be *systematically* excluded were the Chinese, although free Negroes, as Frederick Douglass's autobiography makes poignantly clear,[84] were often excluded from the workmen's associa-

tions that preceded national labor organization. The Sinophobia of Denis Kearney's Irish workers[85] and the vitriotic anti-Chinese sentiments of the Knights of Labor[86] set the stage for the wholesale exclusion of Chinese workers from the American Federation of Labor by Samuel Gompers.[87] And this exclusion of a whole race—a practice that violated Gompers' own strictures against dividing the labor force and establishing the conditions for rival racial unions to organize—in turn created the climate by which other racial and ethnic groups, notably Negroes, Indians and Mexican-Americans, might later be restricted in their labor union association or excluded altogether from the ranks and protection of organized labor.[88] Thus, the Chinese who could not vote or study beside the white man could not work beside him either. And the Chinese example, once begun, would be applied to the other colored peoples insuring a division between white and colored workers that has lasted to the present day.

Modern racism is symbolized by the presence of the urban ghetto. Typically, the scene is that of a black enclave in the recesses of a northern metropolis, surrounded by the invisible barrier of real estate restrictions and burdened with its own peculiar brands of poverty and subculture.[89] But again the ghetto arose most starkly among the Chinese and was greeted with pleasure and pressure for maintenance by the minions of modern white racist America. Chinatowns are racial ghettos whose origins are to be found in the congregative sentiments and peculiar institutions of a non-Occidental people who, in order to preserve life itself, banded together to control a piece of territory as their own.[90] They are a colonialized people's response to their condition urging, on the constructive side, that the separate culture and special identity of their own kind be preserved in dignity.[91]

But Chinatown is also and at the same time a slum. It is a gilded ghetto whose tinseled streets and brightly lit shops barely camouflage a pocket of poverty in the metropolis.[92] With the closing off of immigration, the refusal to permit amalgamation, the restriction in the public schools, and the denial of membership in the organized labor force of white America, Chinatown's survival as a ghetto was assured. With its establishment by all these institutional forces working separately but in tandem to insure the security and virginity of white Anglo America, the stage was set for similar ghettos to be established when freed Negroes tired of the caste restrictions of the Redemptionist South and moved north to find a new freedom, and when detribalized Indians moved or were thrown out of their reservations and also sought the city. The ghetto with its congregational inner spirit and its surrounding segregationist pressure, with its nationalistic fervor and its economic debilitation, with its powerful concentration and its political impotence, is a creature of modern racism whose perfection was first worked out with respect to the Asian challenge to a modern industrial racist society.

Conclusion

Until recently the Asian has occupied an insignificant place in the annals of American history and the analyses of American society. His was, he was told, but a regional and local story, perhaps of interest to the historical buffs of Pacific Coast lore, but of no importance to understanding America. Recent research suggests, however, a very different interpretation.[93] If American racism may be defined as the attempt to impose white Anglo-Saxon culture on the inhabitants of a continent, then two epochs

may be distinguished. The first, that of total exclusion for non-whites and imposed acculturation on continental Europeans, may be said to have begun in 1607 and ended in the twentieth century. Characteristic of the exclusionist mechanisms of this first period were total institutionalization of the non-white population on plantations and reservations. The second epoch continues the cultural imposition of Anglo-Saxon norms on Europeans, but substitutes segmented, partial, institutionalized racism in a wide variety of arenas of action for the abandoned and moribund method of total incarceration. The pivotal group for the study of this transition from total to partial institutionalized racism is the Asian and especially the Chinese. Neither an indigenous people to be conquered and incarcerated nor a people forcibly removed from their homeland to build the economy of a racist society, the Asian could not justifiably be enslaved or put away on reservations. In responding to the challenge of his presence, the many and varied institutions of white America segregated the schools on a racial basis, restricted citizenship to include only free whites and native-born free blacks, attempted the slow genocide possible by prohibiting family formation, and enclosed the white working class from contact with its Asian peers. In doing so it insured the survival of a Chinese ghetto and established it—the ghetto—as the urban successor to the plantation and the reservation. In treating with the Asian, white America perfected its plans for a modern, institutional, racist society.

Notes

1. The classic statements of this position are found in John Dollard, *Caste and Class in a Southern Town,* Third Edition (Garden City: Doubleday Anchor, 1957); Allison Davis, Burleigh B. Gardner, and Mary R. Gardner, *Deep South: A Social Anthropological Study of Caste and Class,* (Chicago: University of Chicago Press-Phoenix Books, 1965); Hortense Powdermaker, *After Freedom: A Cultural Study in the Deep South,* (New York: Atheneum, 1968).

2. "First of all the historic peoples to acquire California were the Indians. It is therefore pertinent to ask why it is that California is no longer an Indian country in any sense of the term. The answer . . . [is] that the Indian could not hope to compete with civilized races, though he might have rendered their occupation of California more difficult than in fact he did." Charles E. Chapman, *A History of California: The Spanish Period,* (New York: The Macmillan Co., 1921), p. 9. For a contrasting and non-ethnocentric view, see Jack D. Forbes, *Native Americans of California and Nevada* (Healdsburg, Calif: Naturegraph Publishers, 1969).

3. See Leonard Pitt, *The Decline of the Californios: A Social History of the Spanish-Speaking Californians,* 1846–1890 (Berkeley: University of California Press: 1966); Nancie L. Gonzalez, *The Spanish-Americans of New Mexico: A Heritage of Pride* (Albuquerque: University of New Mexico Press, 1969); John H. Burma, *Spanish-*

Speaking Groups in the United States (Durham: Duke University Press, 1954), pp. 3–155; William Madsen, *The Mexican-Americans of South Texas,* (New York: Holt, Rinehart, and Winston, 1964); Celia S. Heller, *Mexican American Youth: Forgotten Youth at the Crossroads,* (New York: Random House, 1966); Julian Samora, *La Raza: Forgotten Americans,* (Notre Dame: University of Notre Dame Press, 1966).

4. The populist roots of anti-Semitism were debated by major social scientists during the 1950s. For a discussion and bibliography, see John Higham, "American Anti-Semitism Historically Reconsidered," in Charles Herbert Stembler, et al. (Editors), *Jews in the Mind of America,* (New York: Basic Books, 1966), pp. 237–258. See also John Higham, "Social Discrimination Against Jews in America, 1830–1930," *Publications of the American Jewish Historical Society* XLVII (September, 1957), pp. 1–31. Of course, anti-Semitism has its original roots in Christian-Jewish divisions. In this respect, see Jules Isaac, *The Teaching of Contempt: Christian Roots of Anti-Semitism,* trans. by Helen Weaver (New York: Holt, Rinehart, and Winston, 1964). For a sociological view, see J. Milton Yinger, *Anti-Semitism: A Case Study in Prejudice and Discrimination,* (New York: Freedom Books, 1964).

5. This is the position taken in the two definitive works on the anti-Chinese movement. See Mary Coolidge, *Chinese Immigration,* (New York: Henry Holt, 1909) and Elmer C. Sandmeyer, *The Anti-Chinese Movement in California* (Urbana: University of Illinois Press, 1939). For the view that anti-Chinese sentiment existed in the East prior to the coming of the Chinese, see Stuart Creighton Miller, *The Unwelcome Immigrant: The American Image of the Chinese, 1785–1882* (Berkeley: University of California Press, 1969).

6. For a critique of this and related positions with special reference to the Negro, see Stanford M. Lyman, *The Black American in Sociological Thought: a Failure of Perspective,* (New York: G. P. Putnam's Sons, 1972).

7. *Report of the National Advisory Commission on Civil Disorders,* Otto Kerner, Chairman. (New York: Bantam Books, 1968), p. 203.

8. Winthrop Jordan, *White Over Black: American Attitudes Toward the Negro, 1550–1812,* (Chapel Hill: University of North Carolina Press, 1968), pp. 3–269. The Greco-Roman attitude toward blacks was for the most part not marred by racial prejudice. See Frank M. Snowden, Jr., *Blacks in Antiquity: Ethiopians in the Greco-Roman Experience.* (Cambridge: The Belknap Press of Harvard University Press, 1970).

9. See Lee Eldridge Huddleston, *Origins of the American Indians: European Concepts, 1492–1792.* (Austin: University of Texas Press, 1967).

10. Henri Baudet, *Paradise on Earth: Some Thoughts on European Images of Non-European Man.* Translated by Elizabeth Wentholt (New Haven: Yale University Press, 1965).

11. Kathleen George, "The Civilized West Looks at Primitive Africa: 1400–1800: A Study in Ethnocentrism," *Isis, XLIX:* Part I (March, 1958), pp. 62–72.

12. Thomas Gossett, *Race: The History of an Idea in America* (Dallas: Southern Methodist University Press, 1963).

13. See D. G. Cochrane, "Racialism in the Pacific: A Descriptive Analysis," *Oceania XL:* 1 (September, 1969), pp. 1–12.

14. See G. F. Hudson, *Europe and China: A Survey of Their Relations, from the Earliest Times to 1800* (Boston: Beacon Press, 1961) and Harold R. Isaacs, *Images of Asia: American Views of China and India,* (New York: Capricorn Books, 1962) and Harold R. Isaacs, *No Peace for Asia* (Cambridge: The M. I. T. Press, 1967), pp. 7–36, 213–242.

15. The most thorough history of this period is R. S. Kuykendall, *The Hawaiian Kingdom* (Honolulu: University of Hawaii Press, 1953, 1957, 1967). Three volumes. See also Lawrence H. Fuchs, *Hawaii Pono: A Social History* (New York: Harcourt, Brace, and World, 1961), pp. 3–39 and Andrew W. Lind, *Hawaii's People* (Honolulu: University of Hawaii Press, 1967), pp. 15–19.

16. See James Bonwick, *The Last of the Tasmanians; or, The Black War of Van Diemen's Land* (London: Sampson, Low, Son, and Marston, 1870. Australasia Facsimili Editions No. 87. Adelaide: Libraries Board of South Australia, 1969) and Clive Turnbull, *Black War: The Extermination of the Tasmanian Aborigines* (Melbourne: Cheshire-Lansdowne, 1966).

17. Douglas Oliver, *The Pacific Islands,* revised edition (Garden City: Doubleday Anchor, 1961), pp. 83–154.

18. See Marvin E. Gettleman (Editor), *Viet Nam: History, Documents, and Opinions on a Major World Crisis* (New York: Fawcett Publications, 1965), pp. 9–32; C. P. Fitzgerald, *A Concise History of East Asia* (New York: Frederick A. Praeger, 1966), pp. 218–293; Norton Ginsburg, "Indochina: The Two Viet, Cambodia, and Laos," in *The Pattern of Asia,* Norton Ginsburg, editor (Englewood Cliffs: Prentice-Hall, 1958), pp. 410–439.

19. The infamous imposition of opium on the Chinese is placed in perspective by Wen-Tsao Wu, *The Chinese Opium Question in British Opinion and Action* (New York: The Academy Press, 1928); and Arthur Waley, *The Opium War Through Chinese Eyes,* (Stanford: Stanford University Press, 1968). For the American involvement in the Pacific and China, see Foster Rhea Dulles, *America in the Pacific: A Century of Expansion* (Boston: Houghton Mifflin Co., 1932); Tyler Dennett, *Americans in Eastern Asia: a Critical Study of United States' Policy in the Far East in the Nineteenth Century* (New York: Barnes and Noble, 1963); Paul Hibbert Clyde, *United States Policy Toward China: Diplomatic and Public Documents, 1839–1939* (New York: Russell and Russell, 1964); Thomas J. McCormick, *China Market: America's Quest for Informal Empire, 1893–1901* (Chicago: Quadrangle, 1967). Perhaps still the best general account of the early period of European encroachments in China is John King Fairbanks, *Trade and Diplomacy on the China Coast: The Opening of the Treaty Ports, 1842–1854,* (Cambridge: Harvard University Press, 1964). See also W. C. Hunter, *The 'Fan Kwae' at Canton Before Treaty Days, 1825–1844* (Taipei: Ch'eng-wen Publishing Co., 1965). For the Chinese response, see Earl Swisher, *China's Management of the American Barbarians: A Study of Sino-American Relations,*

1841–1861 (New Haven: Far Eastern Publications, 1951) and Franz Schurmann and Orville Schell (Editors), *Imperial China: The Decline of the Last Dynasty and the Origins of Modern China: The 18th and 19th Centuries.* The China Reader, Volume I (New York: Random House, 1967).

20. For the Portuguese colonial empire which in many ways provided an early model of European racism in Asia and the tropics, see three works by Charles R. Boxer, *Race Relations in the Portuguese Colonial Empire, 1415–1825* (Oxford: Clarendon Press, 1963); *Portuguese Society in the Tropics: The Municipal Councils of Goa, Macao, Bahia, and Luanda, 1510–1800* (Madison, The University of Milwaukee Press, 1965); *The Dutch Seaborne Empire: 1600–1800* (New York: Alfred A. Knopf, 1965), pp. 215–241.

21. This, it seems to me, is the inescapable conclusion to be drawn from Oscar Handlin, *The Americans: A New History of the People of the United States* (Boston: Little, Brown and Co., 1963), pp. 148–162.

22. Joshua A. Fishman, *Language Loyalty in the United States: The Maintenance and Perpetuation of Non-English Mother Tongues by American Religious and Ethnic Groups* (The Hague: Mouton and Co., 1966), pp. 29–31.

23. Perhaps the best illustration of this point is the fact that groups with ambiguous racial ancestry in America strive to become "white" and to stave off the label "Negro." See Brewton Berry, *Almost White* (New York: Macmillan, 1963). For a comment, see Stanford M. Lyman, "The Spectrum of Color," *Social Research* 31 (Autumn, 1964), pp. 364–373.

24. See John A. Hostettler, *Amish Society,* revised edition. (Baltimore: Johns Hopkins Press, 1968) and John W. Bennett, *Hutterian Brethren: The Agricultural Economy and Social Organization of a Communal People* (Stanford: Stanford University Press, 1967).

25. See Nathan Glazer, "Ethnic Groups in America: From National Culture to Ideology," in Morroe Berger, et al. (Editors) *Freedom and Control in Modern Society* (New York: D. Van Nostrand Co., 1954), pp. 158–176. For the political consequences of this development, see Louis L. Gerson, *The Hyphenate in Recent American Politics and Diplomacy* (Lawrence: The University of Kansas Press, 1964).

26. See John Higham, *Strangers in the Land: Patterns of American Nativism, 1860–1925* (New York: Atheneum, 1963), pp. 300–330. For the xenophobic sources of the Immigrant Act of 1924, see William Petersen, *Population* (New York: The Macmillan Co., 1961), pp. 86–113.

27. See Barbara Miller Solomon, *Ancestors and Immigrants: A Changing New England Tradition* (New York: Science Editions, John Wiley and Sons, 1956).

28. "What then is the American, this new man? He is either an European, or the descendant of an European, hence that strange mixture of blood, which you will find in no other country. I could point out to you a family whose grandfather was an Englishman, whose wife was Dutch, whose son married a French woman, and whose present four sons now have four wives of different nations. *He* is an American, who, leaving behind him all his ancient prejudices and manners, receives new ones from the new mode of life he has embraced, the new government he obeys, and the new rank he holds. He becomes an American by being received in the broad lap of our great *Alma Mater.* Here individuals of all nations are melted into a new race of men, whose labours and posterity will one day cause great changes in the world. Americans are the western pilgrims, who are carrying along with them that great mass of arts, sciences, vigour, and industry which began long since in the east. They will finish the great circle. The Americans were once scattered all over Europe; here they are incorporated into one of the finest systems of population which has ever appeared, and which will hereafter become distinct by the power of the different climates they inhabit. The American ought therefore to love this country much better than that wherein either he or his forefathers were born." J. Hector St. John de Crevecoeur, *Letters from an American Farmer* (New York: E. P. Dutton & Co., 1957. First published in 1782), pp. 39–40.

29. Thus, Carl Schurz admonished his fellow Germans in America:

> ". . . we as Germans are not called upon here to form a separate nationality, but rather to contribute to the American nationality the strongest there is in us, and in place of our weakness to substitute the strength wherein our fellow-Americans excel us, and blend it with our wisdom. We should never forget that in the political life of this republic, we as Germans have no peculiar interests, but that the universal well-being is ours also."

Quoted in Carl Wittke, *We Who Built America: The Saga of the Immigrant* (Cleveland: The Press of Case Western Reserve University, 1967), p. 245.

30. See Oscar Handlin, *Boston's Immigrants, 1790–1800: A Study in Acculturation,* Revised Edition (New York: Atheneum, 1968); Thomas N. Brown, *Irish-American Nationalism 1870–1890* (Philadelphia: J. B. Lippincott Co., 1966); William V. Shannon, *The American Irish: A Political and Social Portrait* (New York: The Macmillan Co. 1963).

31. Theodore Saloutos, *The Greeks in the United States* (Cambridge: Harvard University Press, 1964), pp. 138–159, 232–257.

32. See Herbert J. Gans, *The Urban Villagers: Group and Class in the Life of Italian-Americans* (New York: The Free Press, 1965) and Leonard Covello, *The Social Background of the Italo-American School Child: A Study of the Southern Italian Family Mores and Their Effect on the School Situation in Italy and America* (Leiden: E. J. Brill, 1967).

33. Alex Simirenko, *Pilgrims, Colonists, and Frontiersmen: Generation-to-Generation Changes in a Russian Ethnic Community in America* (London: The Free Press of Glencoe, 1964).

34. W. I. Thomas and Florian Znaniecki, *The Polish Peasant in Europe and America* (New York: Dover Publications, 1968), II, pp. 1511–1646.

35. See Louis Wirth, *The Ghetto* (Chicago: University of Chicago

Press-Phoenix Books, 1956); Nathan Glazer, *American Judaism* (Chicago: University of Chicago Press, 1957); Albert I. Gordon, *Jews in Suburbia* (Boston: Beacon Press, 1959); Judith R. Kramer and Seymour Leventman, *Children of the Gilded Ghetto: Conflict Resolution of Three Generations of American Jews,* (New Haven: Yale University Press, 1961); Marshall Sklare and Joseph Greenblum, *Jewish Identity on the Suburban Frontier: A Study of Group Survival in the Open Society,* The Lakeville Studies, Vol. I (New York: Basic Books, 1967); Benjamin B. Ringer, *The Edge of Friendliness: A Study of Jewish-Gentile Relations,* The Lakeville Studies, Vol. II (New York: Basic Books, 1967).

36. See Theodore Saloutos, *They Remember America: The Story of the Repatriated Greek-Americans* (Berkeley: University of California Press, 1956); and Wilbur S. Shepperson, *Emigration and Disenchantment: Portraits of Englishmen Repatriated from the United States* (Norman: University of Oklahoma Press, 1965).

37. Higham, *Strangers in the Land, op. cit.*

38. Gustavus Myers, *History of Bigotry in the United States,* edited and revised by Henry M. Christman (New York: Capricorn Books, 1960), pp. 3–276.

39. Myers, *op. cit.,* pp. 277–447; Richard Hofstadter, *The Age of Reform: From Bryan to F. D. R.* (New York: Vintage Books, 1960), pp. 77–93; Higham, *Strangers in the Land, op. cit.,* pp. 13, 26–27, 66–67, 92–94, 160–161, *et passim.*

40. Solomon, *op. cit.,* pp. 82–175; Myers, *op. cit.,* pp. 92–191, 211–257; Higham, *op. cit.,* pp. 186–299. On the Ku Klux Klan and nativism, see David M. Chalmers, *Hooded Americanism: The First Century of the Ku Klux Klan, 1865 to the Present* (Garden City: Doubleday and Co. 1965); John Moffatt Mecklin, *The Ku Klux Klan: A Study of the American Mind* (New York: Russell and Russell, 1963); William Peirce Randel, *The Ku Klux Klan: A Century of Infamy* (New York: Chilton Books, 1965); Charles C. Alexander, *The Ku Klux Klan in the Southwest* (Lexington: University of Kentucky Press, 1965); Kenneth J. Jackson, *The Ku Klux Klan in the City, 1915–1930* (New York: Oxford University Press, 1967).

41. Cf. Oscar Handlin, *Boston's Immigrants, op. cit.,* pp. 133, 215–216.

42. The relation of slavery to racism has recently been debated by major students of the subject. See Oscar and Mary Handlin, "The Origins of the Southern Labor System," *William and Mary Quarterly* VII (April, 1950), pp. 199–222; Carl N. Degler, "Slavery and the Genesis of American Race Prejudice," *Comparative Studies in Society and History,* II (October, 1959), pp. 49–66; Arnold A. Sio, "Interpretations of Slavery: The Slave Status in the Americas," *Comparative Studies in Society and History,* VII (April, 1965), pp. 289–308; Herbert S. Klein, "Anglicanism, Catholicism, and the Negro Slave," *Comparative Studies in Society and History,* VIII (April, 1966), pp. 295–327; Winthrop D. Jordan, "Modern Tensions and the Origins of American Slavery," *Journal of Southern History,* XXVIII (February, 1962), pp. 18–30; David Brion Davis, *The Problem of Slavery in Western Culture* (Ithaca: Cornell University Press, 1966), pp. 3–61, 125–164, 223–290; Joseph Boskin, "Race Relations in Seventeenth Century America: The Problem of the Origins of Negro Slavery," *Sociology and Social Research,* 49 (July, 1965), pp. 446–455; Eugene Genovese, *The Political Economy of Slavery: Studies in the Economy and Society of the Slave South,* (New York: Pantheon, 1965) and Eugene Genovese, *The World the Slaveholders Made: Two Essays in Interpretation* (New York: Pantheon, 1969). See also Edgar T. Thompson, "The Natural History of Agricultural Labor in the South," *American Studies in Honor of W. K. Boyd,* edited by David K. Jackson (Durham: Duke University Press, 1940), pp. 127–145.

43. The terms for the debates over African survivals among American Negroes have been set by Melville Herskovitz, *The Myth of the Negro Past* (Boston: Beacon Press, 1958) and *The New World Negro: Selected Papers in Afroamerican Studies,* edited by Frances S. Herskovitz (Bloomington: Indiana University Press, 1966), pp. 1–12, 43–61, 83–101, 122–134, 168–173 and E. Franklin Frazier, *The Negro Family in the United States,* revised and abridged edition (Chicago: University of Chicago Press-Phoenix Books, 1966), pp. 3–208 and *The Negro in the United States,* revised edition (New York: Macmillan, 1957), pp. 3–22. See also Charles Keil, *Urban Blues* (Chicago: University of Chicago Press, 1966), pp. 1–68.

44. See Stanley M. Elkins, *Slavery: A Problem in American Institutional and Intellectual Life* (Chicago: University of Chicago Press, 1959), pp. 81–139.

45. Herbert Aptheker, *American Negro Slave Revolts* (New York: International Publishers, 1963).

46. See Henrietta Buckmaster, *Let My People Go: The Story of the Underground Railroad and the Growth of the Abolition Movement* (Boston: Beacon Press, 1959); Horatio J. Strother, *The Underground Railroad in Connecticut* (Middletown: Wesleyan University Press, 1962); Kenneth M. Stampp, *The Peculiar Institution: Slavery in the Ante-Bellum South* (New York: Alfred A. Knopf, 1963), pp. 109–132.

47. Ulrich Bonnell Phillips, *American Negro Slavery: A Survey of the Supply, Employment and Control of Negro Labor as Determined by the Plantation Regime.* (Gloucester: Peter Smith, 1959), pp. 425–431.

48. Leon Litwack, *North of Slavery: The Negro in the Free States, 1790–1860,* (Chicago: University of Chicago Press-Phoenix Books, 1965). Benjamin Quarles, *Black Abolitionists* (New York: Oxford University Press, 1969).

49. See e.g., Ralph K. Andrist, *The Long Death: The Last Days of the Plains Indians* (New York: Macmillan, 1964), pp. 14–15; Wendell H. Oswalt, *This Land Was Theirs: A Study of the North American Indian* (New York: John Wiley, 1966), pp. 245–247; Dale Van Every, *Disinherited: The Lost Birthright of the American Indian,* (New York: William Morsow, 1966), pp. 70, 251; Clark Wissler, *Indians of the United States,* revised edition, prepared by Lucy Wales Kluckhohn (Garden City: Doubleday and Co. 1966), pp. 85–86, 107–109, 148, 169, 186; William T. Hagan, *American Indians* (Chicago: University of Chicago Press, 1961), pp. 7, 12, 25, 94.

50. Roy Harvey Pearce, *Savagism and Civilization: A Study of the Indian and the American Mind.* (Baltimore: The Johns Hopkins

Press, 1967), pp. 1–238; Helen Hunt Jackson, *A Century of Dishonor: The Early Crusade for Indian Reform,* edited by Andrew F. Rolle (New York: Harper Torchbooks, 1965. Originally published in 1881), pp. 298–335.

51. Hagan, *op. cit.,* pp. 53–91.

52. Hagan, *op. cit.,* pp. 92–120; Pearce, *op. cit.,* p. 239.

53. "The Indian is never alone. The life he leads is not his to control. That is not permitted. Every aspect of his being is affected and defined by his relationship to the Federal Government—and primarily to one agency of the Federal Government: the Bureau of Indian Affairs."

"From birth to death his home, his land, his reservation, his schools, his jobs, the stores where he shops, the tribal council that governs him, the opportunities available to him, the way in which he spends his money, disposes of his property, and even the way in which he provides for his heirs after death—are all determined by the Bureau of Indian Affairs acting as the agent of the United States Government." Edgar S. Cahn, editor, *Our Brother's Keeper: The Indian in White America,* (New York: Community Press Book, World Publishing Co., 1969), p. 5.

54. See Marcus Lee Hansen, *The Immigrant in American History,* edited by Arthur M. Schlesinger, (New York: Harper Torchbooks, 1964), pp. 77–80.

55. At midcentury the champion of integration in America was Frederick Douglass. See *The Life and Writings of Frederick Douglass,* edited by Philip S. Foner (New York: International Publishers, 1950, II, pp. 168–169, 172–173, 251–254, 387–388, 441–446. Among the leading figures in favor of exodus was Martin R. Delaney who explored portions of West Africa in the hope of finding a hospitable area for Negroes to settle. See Martin R. Delany, "Official Report of the Niger Valley Exploring Party," in M. R. Delany and Robert Campbell, *Search for a Place: Black Separatism and Africa, 1860,* (Ann Arbor: The University of Michigan Press, 1969), pp. 23–148.

56. For a balanced appraisal of the role of reservations in California, whose conclusions might well apply to other areas of Indian incarceration, see Sherburne F. Cook, "The California Indian and Anglo-American Culture," in *Ethnic Conflict in California,* edited by Charles Wollenberg (Los Angeles: Tinnon-Brown, 1970), pp. 25–42.

57. See Stanford M. Lyman, "Strangers in the Cities: The Chinese on the Urban Frontier," in Wollenberg, *op. cit.,* pp. 61–100. Reprinted in this volume.

58. The term total institution is adapted from Erving Goffman, "On the Characteristics of Total Institutions," *Asylums: Essays on the Social Situation of Mental Patients and Other Inmates,* (Garden City: Doubleday Anchor, 1961), pp. 1–124. Goffman observes (p. 4): "When we review the different institutions in our Western society, we find some that are encompassing to a degree discontinuously greater than the ones next in line. Their encompassing or total character is symbolized by the barrier to social intercourse that is often built right into the physical plant, such as locked doors, high walls, barbed wire, cliffs, water, forests, or moors. These establishments I am calling *total institutions."*

59. Thus, as Richard Wade has pointed out, slavery in the cities was a halfway house to freedom. See his *Slavery in the Cities: The South, 1820–1860* (New York: Oxford University Press, 1964).

60. In a recent study of a poverty-stricken white community, David Harvey has suggested that industrialism requires surplus populations of degraded and exploitable people. He writes, "The industrial system like the school operates with a peculiar and contradictory irony. If it is to survive and maintain its career objectives intact, it must help perpetuate a 'careerless' segment of the work force. If the consumer-oriented economy is to survive, it can only do so by generating a group whose consumption ability is severely restricted . . . But why are these people stigmatized and degraded? Is this really necessary? I believe so! It is one thing to create an industrial reserve army. It is another thing to control them. How does one handle a group of people who *must* remain marginal to society if that society's institutions require them for continued existence. The answer is to render them *passive.* The most efficient way to do this is to attribute to them traits which place them outside of the category of 'reputable human.' In this way they lie beyond the concern of moral men. At the same time if the stigmatized accept the legitimacy of their own label, they can be taught that they have little right to expect more than they are presently receiving. Finally, those most stigmatized in our society are the least powerful. This includes the lower class." "Neighborhood Learning Centers as an Agent of Change in Lower Class Communities," Paper presented at the 1970 annual convention of the Council on Exceptional Children. Chicago, April 25, 1970.

61. Alexander Saxton, *The Indispensable Enemy: A Study of the Anti-Chinese Movement in California,* unpublished Ph.D. dissertation, University of California, Berkeley, 1967. (Ann Arbor: University Microfilms, 1970).

62. Cf. Louis L. Knowles and Kenneth Prewitt, editors, *Institutional Racism in America* (Englewood Cliffs: Prentice-Hall, 1969), pp. 4–14.

63. See Roger Daniels and Harry H. L. Kitano, *American Racism: Exploration of the Nature of Prejudice* (Englewood Cliffs: Prentice-Hall, 1970), pp. 5–28.

64. See Stanford M. Lyman, "Marriage and the Family Among Chinese Immigrants to America, 1850–1960," *Phylon Quarterly* 29 (Winter, 1968), pp. 321–330. Reprinted in this volume.

65. The point was litigated in the federal courts. See *Case of the Chinese Wife* 21 Fed. 785 (1884).

66. Thus Robert E. Park, writing in 1926, was moved to observe, "The Chinese population is slowly declining in the United States, but San Francisco, at any rate, will miss its Chinese quarter when it goes." "Our Racial Frontier on the Pacific," *Survey Graphic* LVI (May, 1926), p. 196.

67. See the sympathetic account of Jacob A. Riis, *How the Other Half Lives: Studies Among the Tenements of New York* (New York: Sagamore Press, Inc., 1957. First published in 1890), pp. 67–76.

68. Maurice R. Davie, *World Immigration: With Special Reference to the United States* (New York: Macmillan, 1949), p. 328.

69. Milton R. Konvitz, *The Alien and Asiatic in American Law,* (Ithaca: Cornell University Press, 1946), p. 10, 7Ϛ–96.

70. *Ozawa vs United States* 260 U.S. 178 (1922). For the full particulars of the case, see *Documented History of Law Cases Affecting Japanese in the United States, Vol I: Naturalization Cases and Cases Affecting Constitutional and Treaty Rights,* (San Francisco: Consulate-General of Japan, 1925), pp. 1–121.

71. See Roderick D. McKenzie, *Oriental Exclusion: The Effect of American Immigration Laws, Regulations and Judicial Decisions Upon the Chinese and Japanese on the American Pacific Coast,* (Chicago: University of Chicago Press, 1928), pp. 79–97.

72. Milton R. Knovitz, *op. cit.,* pp. 161–169, 185–186.

73. Thus California stripped Chinese aliens of their fishing licenses in 1864, Japanese and other ineligible aliens of their fishing licenses in 1943, and all aliens ineligible to citizenship of the right to own land or form corporations in 1913.

74. William Warren Ferrier, *Ninety Years of Education in California, 1846–1936* (Berkeley: Sather Gate Book Shop, 1937), p. 98.

75. T. A. Bailey, *Theodore Roosevelt and the Japanese-American Crises: An Account of the International Complications Arising from the Race Problem on the Pacific Coast* (Gloucester: Peter Smith, 1964).

76. Yamato Ichihashi, *Japanese in the United States: A Critical Study of the Problems of the Japanese Immigrants and Their Children,* (New York: Arno Press and the New York Times, 1969), pp. 228–282; and Jacobus ten Broek, Edward N. Barnhart, and Floyd Matson, *Prejudice, War, and the Constitution.* Japanese American Evacuation and Resettlement, Vol. III, (Berkeley: University of California Press, 1954), pp. 11–67.

77. *Wong Hin vs Callahan,* 119 Fed. 381 (1902).

78. *Gong Lum vs Rice* 275 U.S. 78 (1927).

79. *Brown vs. Board of Education* 348 U.S. 483 (1954).

80. Cf. *Chew Heong vs United States* 112 U.S. 536 (1884); *United States vs Jung Ah Lung* 124 U.S. 621 (1887); *The Chinese Exclusion Case* 130 U.S. 581 (1889).

81. See Donald Earl Willmott, *The Chinese of Semarang: A Changing Minority Community in Indonesia,* (Ithaca: Cornell University Press, 1960), pp. 103–116.

82. In fourteen of these laws there was a specific prohibition on marriage between Chinese, or "Mongolians," and whites. California's anti-miscegenation statute was originally enacted in 1872 to bar marriages between Negroes and whites. In 1906 it was amended to prohibit marriages between whites and "Mongolians." In 1948 it was declared unconstitutional. See Huang Tsen-ming, *The Legal Status of the Chinese Abroad,* (Taipei: China Cultural Service, 1954), pp. 260–262. See also Fowler V. Harper and Jerome Skolnick, *Problems of the Family* (Indianapolis:

Bobbs-Merrill, 1962), pp. 96–99. For the California case invalidating the miscegenation statute, see *Perez vs Sharp,* 32 Cal. 711, 2nd Ser. (1948).

83. See Herbert Hill, "The Racial Practices of Organized Labor—the Age of Gompers and After," in *Employment, Race, and Poverty: A Critical Study of the Disadvantaged Status of Negro Workers from 1865 to 1965,* edited by Arthur M. Ross and Herbert Hill (New York: Harcourt, Brace, and World, 1967), pp. 365–402.

84. See Frederick Douglass, *Narrative of the Life of Frederick Douglass, an American Slave* (Garden City: Doubleday Dolphin, 1963, originally published in 1845), pp. 113–114.

85. See James Bryce, "Kearneyism in California," *The American Commonwealth* (New York: Macmillan, 1901), II, pp. 425–488. See also Doyce B. Nunis, Jr., "The Demagogue and the Demographer: Correspondence of Denis Kearney and Lord Bryce," *Pacific Historical Review,* 36 (August, 1967), pp. 269–288.

86. See W. W. Stone, "The Knights of Labor on the Chinese Question," *Overland Monthly,* 2nd Ser., VII (March, 1886), pp. 225–230.

87. See Samuel Gompers, *Seventy Years of Life and Labor: An Autobiography* (New York: E. P. Dutton, 1925), I, pp. 216–217, 304–305; II, pp. 162–169.

88. The definitive studies of occupational discrimination against Negroes have been done by Herbert Hill. A partial bibliography of his works on the subject would include: *No Harvest for the Reaper: The Story of the Migratory Agricultural Worker in the United States* (New York: N.A.A.C.P., n.d.); "A Record of Negro Disfranchisement," *Midstream* (Autumn, 1957), pp. 3–12; "Labor Unions and the Negro," *Commentary* (December, 1959), n.p.; "Racial Inequality in Employment: The Patterns of Discrimination," *Annals of the American Academy of Political and Social Science, CCCLVII* (January, 1965), pp. 30–47; "Planning the End of the American Ghetto: A Program of Economic Development for Equal Rights," *Poverty and Human Resources Abstracts* II (March–April, 1967), pp. 23–36; "No End of Pledges: Continuing Discrimination in the Construction Unions," *Commonweal LXXXVII* (March 15, 1968), pp. 709–712; "Sewing Machines and Union Machines," *The Nation* (July 3, 1967), n.p.; "The Racial Practices of Organized Labor: The Contemporary Record," in *The Negro and the American Labor Movement,* edited by Julius Jacobson (Garden City: Doubleday Anchor, 1968), pp. 286–357; "Employment, Manpower Training and the Black Worker," *Journal of Negro Education* (Summer, 1969), pp. 204–217; "Black Protest and the Struggle for Union Democracy," *Issues in Industrial Society* I (1969), pp. 19–29, 48; "Black Labor in The American Economy," *In Black America, 1968: The Year of Awakening,* edited by Pat Romero (Washington, D. C.: United Publishing Corp., 1969), pp. 179–216.

For discrimination against Mexican-Americans, see Ernesto Galarza, *Merchants of Labor: The Mexican Bracero Story* (San Jose: The Rosicrucian Press, 1964); Truman E. Moore, *The Slaves We Rent* (New York: Random House, 1965); Eugene Nelson, *Huelga: The First Hundred Days of the Great Delano Grape Strike* (Delano,

Calif.: Farm Worker Press, 1966); Peter Matthiessen, *Sal Si Puedes: Cesar Chavez and the New American Revolution* (New York: Random House, 1969); Stan Steiner, *La Raza: The Mexican Americans* (New York: Harper and Row, 1969); Charles Wollenberg, "Conflict in the Fields: Mexican Workers in California Agri-business," in Wollenberg, *op. cit.,* pp. 135–152.

For discrimination against and response among Indians, see Edmund Wilson, *Apologies to the Iroquois* (New York: Vintage Books, 1966); Cahn, *op. cit.;* Alan L. Sorkin, "American Indians Industrialize to Combat Poverty," *Monthly Labor Review* (March, 1969), pp. 19–25; Stan Steiner, *The New Indians* (New York: Harper and Row, 1968; Vine Deloria, Jr., *Custer Died for Your Sins: an Indian Manifesto* (New York: Macmillan, 1969).

89. See among many studies, Kenneth B. Clark, *Dark Ghetto: Dilemmas of Social Power* (New York: Harper and Row, 1965). For a recent penetrating analysis of black subculture in America, see Ulf Hannerz, *Soulside: Inquiries into Ghetto Community and Culture,* (New York: Columbia University Press, 1969).

90. See D. Y. Yuan, "Voluntary Segregation: a Study of New York Chinatown," *Phylon Quarterly* (Fall, 1963), pp. 255–265. For the concept of territoriality and its applications to Chinatown, see Stanford M. Lyman and Marvin B. Scott, "Territoriality: A Neglected Sociological Dimension," *Social Problems* 15 (Fall, 1967), pp. 236–249.

91. Cf. Robert Blauner, "Internal Colonialism and Ghetto Revolt," *Social Problems* XVI (Spring, 1969), pp. 393–408.

92. See, e.g., Stuart H. Cattell, *Health, Welfare, and Social Organization in Chinatown* (New York: Community Service Society, 1962), and Stanford M. Lyman, "Red Guard on Grant Avenue," *Trans-action* 7 (April, 1970), pp. 21–34. Extended and reprinted in this volume.

93. The closing of mainland China to Occidental study since 1949 has, understandably, increased the academic attention paid to overseas Chinese communities. Until recently this new interest was largely confined to Southeast Asia. See Maurice Freedman, "A Chinese Phase in Social Anthropology," *British Journal of Sociology* XIV (March, 1963), pp. 1–19. In the last few years, however, an interest in Chinese communities within Occidental settings has arisen. Although none of the works has developed the thesis presented in this paper, they are of substantial interest for just such possibilities. For reviews of the early phase of this renewed interest, see Maurice Freedman and William Willmott, "Southeast Asia, with Special Reference to the Chinese," *International Social Science Journal,* 13:2 (1961), pp. 245–270. Stanford M. Lyman, "Overseas Chinese in Indonesia and America," *Pacific Affairs* XXXIV (Winter, 1961–1962); and Stanford M. Lyman, "Up From the 'Hatchet Man'," *Pacific Affairs,* XXXVI (Summer, 1963), pp. 160–171.

————————

Reports and monographs are now appearing on the Chinese in Canada and Mexico. For the former, see three essays by William Willmott, "Chinese Clan Associations in Vancouver," *Man* LXIV (March–April, 1965), pp. 33–37; "Some Aspects of Chinese Communities in British Columbia Towns," *B. C. Studies* I (Winter, 1968–1969), pp. 27–36; "Approaches to the Study of the Chinese in British Columbia," *B. C. Studies* 4 (Spring, 1970), pp. 38–52. See also Stanford M. Lyman, W. E. Willmott, and Berching Ho, "Rules of a Chinese Secret Society in British Columbia," *Bulletin of the School of Oriental and African Studies* 27:3 (1964), pp. 530–539. Reprinted in this volume.

For Mexico, see Charles C. Cumberland, "The Sonora Chinese and the Mexican Revolution," *Hispanic American Historical Review,* XL (May, 1960) pp. 191–211.

Strangers in the City:
The Chinese on the Urban Frontier

TO SPEAK OF the Chinese in San Francisco and, for that matter, in Seattle, Vancouver, New York City and other large cities, as *strangers*, is to describe them in terms first projected by the great sociologist, Georg Simmel. "The stranger," he wrote in his essay of that title, "is . . . not . . . the wanderer who comes today and goes tomorrow, but rather is the person who comes today and stays tomorrow."[1] Chinese immigrants who journeyed to America and other foreign shores in the last century were wanderers to be sure, but they were not without fixed places to go. Their course took them where opportunity beckoned, but never without the hope of one day returning to the homeland which would call them back from their diaspora and invite them once more to the warmth of hearth and domesticity.[2]

While abroad they were *in* the host society, but never were they *of* it. The culture, ideas and ideals they brought were foreign to native Americans and would never have seen birth among the host society's people had it not been for the influx of these strangers.

As strangers, the Chinese aroused much interest and curiosity, but not without hostility. Ideas about the newcomers were not based on actual knowledge; they were, rather, stereotypes, categorical images built upon flimsy shreds of information about China and supplemented by cursory observations devoid of any profound cultural, social or historical intelligence.[3] As time passed, the original pejorative impressions were reinforced by reiteration and legitimized by the proclamations of social and political elites. At last the stereotypes became the basis for both legislative restrictions and popular uprisings against the Chinese. Only after the newcomers had declined somewhat in numbers and accommodated themselves to a ghetto existence within the urban structure—only when it appeared that other racial and ethnic groups posed a greater threat—did hostilities toward the Chinese begin to subside. The stereotypes did not vanish, but they took on more benign forms. These, unfortunately, were couched in patronizing and indulgent terms. As both symbol and artifice they facilitate the social distance that persists even to today.

Chinese Immigration to America

American interest in China antedates immigration from that nation by more than a half century. The *Chinoiserie* movement[4] which swept over Europe from the sixteenth century had by the end of the eighteenth left its mark on America where Chinese bric-a-brac was to be found in colonial homes and by the nineteenth century in frontier cabins as well.[5] Chinese art collections were the early prized possessions of both private individuals and museums.[6] Several magnificent houses were built in the "Chinese style" in Colonial America, and Chinese tapestries adorned many a wall of American gentlemen and traders.[7] Indeed, one of the compelling economic reasons for the American Revolution was the desire of American merchants and traders to wrest control of the China trade from British domination. China's importance to the new republic was symbolized by the early appointment of Major Samuel Shaw as Consul at Canton in 1786, the first American Consulate beyond the Cape of Good Hope.[8]

Interest in China's art, architecture and government was not however accompanied by much knowledge of or deep compassion for the Chinese people. To be sure, the Jesuits in sixteenth century Peking had exaggerated an image of efficient public administration and lack of military aggression in China which had impressed Europeans and some Americans.[9] But these ideas were not spread far and wide in America; rather, there was a general indifference about the Chinese people and only occasional approval of China's policy of isolation from foreign influence.[10]

From 1787 until 1848 few Chinese visited the United States. A Chinese colony, settled in Nootka Sound in 1788 only lasted until 1789, and other Chinese brought to the Northwest coast of America travelled on ships along the Pacific coast until around 1791, a few deserting in Mexico.[11] An earlier Chinese settlement in Mexico City in 1635 had also come to naught.[12] A few Chinese seamen had been temporarily abandoned in Pennsylvania in 1785–1786, while others worked occasionally as sailors on the New England ships that engaged in the China trade, even though an American law of 1817 limited

foreign sailors on American ships to no more than one-third of the crew. One Chinese cook shipped as "George Harrison of Charlestown, Mass."[13] By representing one of his Chinese crew members as an important mandarin who had to be returned to his native land, in 1809, John Jacob Astor persuaded President Jefferson to exempt his ship from the embargo on China then in force.[14] Four years later the American ship *Sally* docked in Plymouth with a Chinese passenger who attended the Sabbath meeting the following Sunday in full mandarin regalia.[15] In 1830 John P. Cushing, one of the most influential merchants in the China trade, retired with a retinue of Chinese servants.[16]

The education of Chinese in America had interested some Americans, such as James Magee who brought a Chinese over to learn English in 1800.[17] In 1818 the first of five Chinese youths was admitted to the school for foreign students at Cornwall, Connecticut. This institution was begun for the "education in our own country of Heathen youth, in such manner, as with subsequent professional instruction, will qualify them to become useful Missionaries, Physicians, Surgeons, School Masters or interpreters, and to communicate to the Heathen Nations such knowledge in agriculture and the arts as may prove the means of promoting Christianity and civilization."[18] The students' history at the school, as well as the denouement of the school itself, has been reported by a descendant of the school's founders: "Wong Arce came in 1818 from Canton. He was brought by a New York merchant who had employed him in Canton and was soon dismissed for disobedience and immorality. In 1823 Ah Lan and Ah Lum came from Philadelphia, stayed two years and were also dismissed for misconduct. In 1825 Chop Ah See was in the school for a while. From 1822–25 Lieaou Ah See, known also as William Botelho, came from Boston and is regarded as the first Protestant convert. Lieaou who was reported as faithful but far from brilliant, is supposed to have died a Christian in China. The boys were supported partly by charity but mainly by manual labor. The school was closed in 1827 because two Cherokee Indians married two prominent white girls in Cornwall. There was no correspondence recorded with the Chinese after their departure from the school and the experiment seems, as far as the Chinese were concerned, to have been a failure."[19]

Forty-five years were to pass before the Chinese Government, urged by Yung Wing, who had become America's first Chinese college graduate when he matriculated from Yale University in 1854,[20] would send over one hundred Chinese young men to study in America as part of the ill-fated Chinese Educational Mission. In 1881, concerned over the growing Americanization of these Chinese youth— their popularity with white girls, their neglect and even deprecation of Chinese studies, ethics, and practices (including the wearing of the queue which they had petitioned their tutor for permission to sever[21])—the Chinese government recalled the entire mission and required that the students return to China.[22]

That Americans regarded Chinese persons with a mixture of curiosity and amazement is indicated in the reactions to some of the early visitors. In 1808 a Chinese equestrian was employed as a stage performer in New York City. A Chinese juggler performed in the same city in 1842.[23] Chinese sailors and their dog, aboard the junk *Ke Ying* docked at Providence in 1847, were nearly as great a curiosity to the Rhode Island visitors as was the ship itself.[24] One year after the junk left, P. T. Barnum opened his Chinese museum in New York City.

Two traits of the Chinese continued to puzzle and astonish Americans throughout the nineteenth century. One was the plaited queue worn by Chinese men, a mark of subjection imposed on them by the Manchu conquerors in 1645. The queue was a constant source of amusement and derision to Californians who plagued Chinese immigrants by cutting off or pulling on their "pigtails,"[25] and who in the 1870's attempted to punish Chinese by prohibiting the wearing of this badge of citizenship.[26] The other was the practice among Chinese of binding the feet of their women, a custom so remarkable to Occidentals that as late as 1834 a Chinese woman in traditional dress and with bound feet was exhibited as a freak attraction on Broadway.[27] Although "pigtails" and footbinding were the most commented upon features of Chinese life—not only by American

but other peoples, such as the Japanese, who tried to extirpate the practices when they assumed rule in Taiwan[28]—other traits and customs aroused curiosity, astonishment or indignation. The fact that they had "yellow" complexions and "slanted" eyes, that Chinese men all wore the same style of clothing,—a loose blue blouse, with matching trousers and a broad brimmed hat,—that they regularly remitted money and the corpses of their dead to China, that they spoke an "unintelligible" cacophanous language, that they seemed to adopt only a crude "pidgin" English, that they appeared to gamble incessantly and be addicted to opium smoking, that they carried peculiar diseases, and that they came without their wives or sweethearts— each and every one of these real and imagined, alleged and exaggerated traits contributed to the belief that the Chinese were a strange, exotic and even a dangerous people.

Chinese immigration to America effectively began in 1847. A coincidence of catastrophe in China and opportunity in California supplied the expulsive and attractive elements that linked the Middle Kingdom to the United States. Political unrest had been a constant feature of life in Kwangtung and Fukien Provinces since the Manchu conquest of 1644.[29] Overpopulation, once considered no problem at all, presented ever-increasing pressures on agricultural production and distribution after 1800.[30] In addition, foreign intrigues by several of the European nations and the United States had seriously encroached upon Chinese sovereignty, arousing an incipient nationalism directed against both the foreigners and the Manchu regime.[31] Then, in 1849, a terrible flood wreaked havoc on the already wretched lives of southeastern China's peasants. "The rains have been falling for forty days," said a memorial to the emperor, "until the rivers, and the sea, and the lakes, and the streams, have joined in one sheet over the land for several hundred *li* [three *li* are equal to one English mile] and there is no outlet by which the waters may retire."[32] The observer who wrote for *Blackwood's Magazine* noted that on the basis of missionary reports, "ten thousand people were destroyed, and domestic animals drowned in untold numbers;

crowds even of first families were begging bread, and (horror of horrors to the pious Celestials!) coffins were floating about everywhere on the face of the waters. . . . Such an inundation is too stupendous for the European mind adequately to comprehend its extent, and is said to have exceeded any similar disaster within the memory of the present generation."[33]

Natural disaster was followed by rebellion and revolution. In 1851 the Taiping revolutionaries raised their standard against the empire in a civil insurrection that lasted for fourteen years and resulted in casualties estimated to be greater than 30,000,000. [34] In the same period the Cantonese unsuccessfully fought against invasions from British, French and American mercenary forces and also against Hakkas invading from the northwest.[35] The stage was set for continuous anti-Manchu rebellions and anti-foreign uprisings.[36] As a result of all these catastrophic and dislocating events, hundreds of thousands of Chinese were uprooted from their villages. Many fled to the coastal seaports of Canton, Hong Kong and Macao where they hoped to find work, to secure aid from kinsmen, or to go abroad temporarily until they could recoup their losses and return to loved ones as wealthy men.

Then gold was discovered in California.[37] A few Chinese merchants had already arrived in California, and they sent word back to kinsmen and friends of the remarkable discovery.[38] Meanwhile shipping lines and independent sea captains, realizing the profits to be made in adding passenger traffic to the brisk commercial trade with China, sailed into southeastern Chinese ports with circulars advertising the gold discovery and offering cheap passage to California.[39] The excitement created by the news, coupled with the fabulous accounts brought back by the first Chinese returnees, started a brisk passenger trade which, while its vicissitudes were many during the period of "free" immigration, did not subside markedly until American law placed restrictive limits on it in 1882.[40]

The method by which most Chinese came to California was a variant of the indenture system which two centuries earlier had brought Englishmen to the colonies[41] and which a few decades hence would bring southern and eastern Europeans to work in the burgeoning industries of the Northeast.[42] The "credit-ticket" system, as it has been called,[43] enabled an impoverished Chinese to come across the ocean without putting up any cash, find food and lodging in San Francisco, and assistance in going to work in the mines, on the railroads, or in the midwest or east as a strikebreaker. Money for his passage was obtained from kinsmen or fellow-villagers who assigned the collection of the debt to kinsmen or *Landsmänner* in San Francisco. The latter, organized into caravansaries, met the immigrant at the point of debarkation, accompanied him to the hostel in which his compatriots dwelt, provided him with food, a place to sleep, and a certain amount of protection from anti-Chinese elements. Most important, the merchant leaders of the *hui kuan* (*Landsmannschaften*) acted as contractors or subcontractors and sent gangs of men out to work. The debts incurred by the Chinese immigrants were deducted from their wages by Chinese headmen, and defalcating debtors were prevented from escaping back to China by special arrangements between the Chinese creditor associations and the merchant fleet. The entire system was fraught with corruption and undoubtedly not a few Chinese found themselves poorer off in the end than they had been when they began their American adventure, and many were forced to stay overseas much longer than they had anticipated.[44]

Although an American law of 1862 forbade the immigration of involuntary contract labor, the ignorance and corruptibility of American consuls at Canton and the nefarious methods of Chinese "crimps" combined to effect the illegal traffic in human flesh.[45] One incident is of particular importance because it introduced Chinese laborers into the South and indicates the limited interest held by Americans in the Chinese. Following the Civil War there was a severe labor shortage on plantations in Louisiana, Arkansas and other states of the defunct Confederacy. This vexing situation resulted in a bizarre scheme to import Chinese. Originated at the Memphis convention of 1869, subsidized by two major railroads, supported by newspapers in the North as well as the South, and effected by the "crimping" activities of the notorious labor contractor Tye Kim Orr and the mysterious shipmaster Cornelius Koopmanschap, the "Chinese experiment" resulted in the inveiglement of 200 Chinese aboard the ship *Ville de St. Lo* in 1870. Some jumped overboard when they learned their fate; others bided their time and ran away when the ship deposited its human cargo in New Orleans.[46] Some of them may have made up the early Chinese settlements in the south; others probably migrated into the midwest, journeyed to California, or moved into the industrial northeast.[47]

The appearance of Chinese in the midwest and south took place after the anti-Chinese movement had begun in California. Riots against the Chinese seem not to have occurred in the former Confederate states, largely because the Chinese there were not perceived as a competitive but rather as an exploitable element in the labor force, often to be used as a club against recalcitrant Negro laborers. In Colorado, however, where Chinese began to settle in 1870, one of the worst riots ever against the immigrants from the Middle Kingdom took place in Denver on October 31, 1880.[49] It was one of the signals that the Sinophobic virus, once but a localized malady, had become a nearly national epidemic.

The Beginnings of the Anti-Chinese Movement

At first there were but a few Chinese in America. Most of them were located in San Francisco where they acted as purveyors of art goods, foods and prefabricated houses which they floated across the Pacific and reassembled in the city crowded with gold-seekers.[50] During the first few months of their stay in California, Chinese merchants were regarded as a curious but welcome addition to the already heterogeneous population composed of Mexicans, Indians, Americans, Chileans, Australians and various Europeans. They participated in civic festivals, thrived in their mercantile establishments and were expected, as one San Francisco newspaper prophesied, soon to serve in the legislature.[51] "We shall undoubtedly have a very large addition to our population," wrote an editor of the *Daily Alta Californian* on May 12, 1851, "and it may not be many years before the halls of Congress are graced by the presence of a long-queued Mandarin sitting, voting, and speaking beside a don from Santa Fe and a Kanaker from Hawaii . . . The 'China boys' will yet vote at the same polls, study at the same schools, and bow at the same altar as our own countrymen."

However, this period of welcome, this sense of social toleration and sympathetic response, this recognition of California as a culturally plural society, disappeared quickly when Chinese began to appear in the gold mines.[52] The gold mines of California and other states where the precious ore was discovered were never dominated by the Chinese. Indeed, it would appear that they often worked mines already abandoned by white men.[53] Nevertheless, they were attacked vigorously and viciously by both public laws and popular uprisings. California's infamous Foreign Miners' Tax, first enacted in 1850, and then repealed, reenacted and reset irregularly until it was declared void in 1870, was from the beginning enforced almost exclusively against the Chinese who paid 50 percent of the total revenues obtained from it during its first four years and 98 percent during its final sixteen years of enforcement.[54] Moreover, beginning in 1852, the California legislature began what would be more than a quarter of a century of vain experimentation with laws designed to restrict or exclude altogether the coming of Chinese to the state.[55]

In addition to harassing and restrictive legislation, the Chinese were subjected to popular tribunals and mob violence in the mines. In the town of Chinese Camp as early as 1849 an uprising took place against 60 Chinese miners. At Marysville white miners drew up a resolution in 1852 asserting that "no Chinaman was to be thenceforth allowed to hold any mining claim in the neighborhood."[56] There followed a general uprising in the area against the Chinese and, accompanied by a marching band, white miners expelled the Chinese from North Forks, Horseshoe Bar and other neighboring mining camps.[57] By 1856 the following laws were in operation in California's Columbia mining district: "Neither Asiatics nor South-Sea Islanders shall be allowed to mine in this district, either for themselves or for others." "Any person who shall sell a claim to an Asiatic or a South-Sea Islander shall not be allowed to hold another claim in this district for the space of six months."[58] In New Kanaka Camp, Tuolomne Colony, the Chinese were excluded entirely, "not allowed to own either by purchase or pre-emption."[59] As late as 1882 the laws of Churn Creek District forbade any miner to sell a claim to the Chinese,[60] and Chinese were rarely to be seen in that county. In 1858 and 1859 there were again attempts to expel the Chinese from the placers, and Chinese were routed out of Vallecito, Douglas Flat, Sacramento Bar, Coyote Flat, Sand Flat, Rock Creek, Spring Creek and Buckeye.[61]

By the end of the decade gold mining was coming to an end for Chinese and other pioneers alike. Gold strikes in British Columbia in 1858, and gold, silver and copper mining in the Rocky Mountain area attracted some Chinese for the next thirty years, extending the miners' anti-Chinese movement eastward and northward into Canada. However, by the mid-1860s many Chinese were beginning to move into other occupations: railroad building and food, laundry, manufacturing, mercantile and domestic services, occupations which located them in cities. As the 1850s closed, the Chinese accounted for twenty-five percent of California's miners, yet this fact alone, as Rodman W. Paul has pointed out, suggests the decline of the mines.[62] Descriptions of Chinese miners in the 1860s indicate the reduced state of the industry. Writing in the 1860s an anomymous erstwhile miner described the area around Sonora: "Whole acres of land have been upturned and the earth and sand passed through a second and third washing, and apparently every particle of gold extracted; yet the less ambitious Chinese and Mexicans find enough in these deserted places to reward them for their tedious labors."[63] In Tuolomne County Chinese worked mines so far

below the streams that the ore had to be "packed" up to the water: "Here we see troops of sturdy Chinamen groaning along under the weight of huge sacks of earth brought to the surface from a depth of eighteen feet and deposited in heaps after a weary tramp along the banks of a muddy pool."[64] William H. Brewer who traveled throughout California between 1860 and 1864 described the town of Weaver as "a *purely* mining town . . . so it is like California in bygone times." There he found a church "sluiced around until only enough land remains for it to stand upon . . . and multitudes of Chinese—the men miners, the women 'frail,' very frail, industrious in their calling." At Eureka: "Ten white men and two Chinamen slept in the little garret of the 'hotel.' Our horses fared but little better, and our bill was the modest little sum of fifteen dollars." Along the Klamath River: "Here and there a poor Chinaman plies his rocker, gleaning gold from sand, once worked over with more profit, but there are few white inhabitants left until we reach Happy Camp."[65]

Despite the decline of the mining industry, or perhaps because of it, Chinese were still expelled from areas in which they had settled to work or were forcibly driven out of their jobs. A few Chinese were employed in and around some quicksilver mines near Calistoga until 1900; they were indulged as servants so long as they appeared docile and obsequious, but they were as often suspected of thievery and kept under surveillance.[66] The Chinese who had been employed in quartz mining, often "for certain inferior purposes, such as dumping cars, surface excavations, etc.,"[67] were driven out of that occupation in Sutter Creek as a concession to striking white miners in 1871.[68] In 1885, the leading citizens of Eureka ordered the entire Chinese population to leave Humboldt County on one day's notice or suffer the injuries of an outraged mob. When a few Chinese were brought to the area in 1906 the town again forcibly removed them. As late as 1937 Humboldt County boasted of its riddance of the hated Chinese.[69] The 1880s witnessed the beginning of over two decades of public threats, popular agitation and prejudicial reporting about the Chinese in Napa County which ended with their decline or departure around the turn of the century.[70] By the end of the nineteenth century the California Chinese had, for the most part, died off, returned to China, moved eastward or settled into those ghettoes of American cities referred to as "Chinatowns." There they would remain to the present day.

The mining frontier of the west moved eastward and with it went some of the Chinese—and after them came nativist movements to remove their tiny colonies or restrict their meager opportunities.[71] Oregon, Idaho, Montana, Nevada and Wyoming felt a Chinese presence in the last three decades of the nineteenth century. British Columbia and Alaska also employed Chinese at first and then attempted to exclude them during this period. Chinese entered Oregon in the late 1860s, apparently following after the whites who worked the newly discovered gold fields in the eastern part of that state. By 1870 mining had declined considerably in Oregon as was evidenced by the fact that of the 3,965 miners there the Chinese numbered 2,428.[72] A similar decline in Idaho mining caused many whites to sell out to Chinese so that by 1870 more than one-half the state's miners were Chinese; by 1880 the ratio of Chinese to whites in Idaho was higher than in any state or territory in the Union.[73] Chinese settlement in Montana began at least as early as 1869 and continued to increase irregularly until 1910, after which it declined until in 1940 only 258 were left in Butte, a city which had once complained of over 2,500 Chinese.[74] Nevada had a small Chinese population by the mid-1850s, a fact testified by the renaming of the settlement first known as Hall's Station to Chinatown;[75] by the 1870s a thriving Chinese community had been established at Virginia City as a result of the Comstock mining boom, and it was soon the object of curiosity and suspicion.[76] The Chinese community at Rock Springs, Wyoming was the scene in 1885 of one of the worst riots ever spawned by the anti-Oriental feeling in America.[77] Chinese settlement in British Columbia began with the Fraser River gold strike in 1858 which brought several thousand Chinese from California's sluiced out

fields,[78] and it was increased by the importation of Chinese to build the Canadian Pacific Railroad.[79] In Alaska the Chinese stay was as brutish as it was short. Imported to work the picked-over gold mines of John Treadwell in 1885, they were confronted by the angry, demoralized, unemployed white and Indian mine laborers and attacked with dynamite. One year later they were incarcerated and expelled from the Territory; after 1886 no more Chinese were employed in Alaskan mines.[80]

The Sinophobia which gripped California spread to the Rocky Mountain area in the wake of the Chinese miners. An editorial in an Arizona newspaper is typical of its genre and reveals both the nature and depth of the hatred against the Chinese:

> The Chinese are the least desired immigrants who have ever sought the United States . . . the Almond-eyed Mongolian with his pig-tail, his heathenism, his filthy habits, his thrift and careful accumulation of savings to be sent back to the flowery kingdom.
> The most we can do is to insist that he is a heathen, a devourer of soup made from the fragrant juice of the rat, filthy, disagreeable, and undesirable generally, an incumbrance that we do not know how to get rid of, but whose tribe we have determined shall not increase in this part of the world.[81]

Similar views inflamed the people of other states in the Rockies, occasionally modified by a recognition of the benefits obtained from the Chinese. Thus, in Silver City, Idaho, the *Owyhee Avalanche* asserted, "They are in many respects a disgusting element of the population but not wholly unprofitable."[82] However, more people seemed to agree with the Montana journalist who wrote, "We don't mind hearing of a Chinaman being killed now and then, but it has been coming too thick of late . . . soon there will be a scarcity of Chinese cheap labor in the country . . . Don't kill them unless they deserve it, but when they do—why kill 'em lots."[83] Opposition to the Chinese was not merely a pastime of journalists; Montana Governor James M. Ashley expressed the views of much of the citizenry and many of his fellow governors in the west when he said that his state needed "Norwegian, Swedes, and Germans," not Chinese:

> It will be conceded by all practical men who have given this subject any thought, that Montana is better adopted

[sic] to the hardy races of men and women from Great Britain and Northern Europe . . . I am . . . opposed to the importation of laborers from any of the barbarous or semi-civilized races of men, and do not propose to co-operate in any scheme organized to bring such laborers into Montana, or into any part of the country.[84]

By 1880 the drive to exclude Chinese, which started in California and moved eastward to the Rockies, had spread throughout the nation and laid the basis for America's first bill to restrict immigration on the basis of race. In 1870 Chinese laborers had been shipped from California to North Adams, Massachusetts, to break a strike of shoemakers. Hailed at first by those opposed to the striking union, the Knights of St. Crispin, the Chinese were subsequently the objects of anti-coolie meetings held in Boston to protest the reduction of American labor to the standards of "rice and rats."[85] In 1877 another gang of Chinese were imported from California to break a cutlery manufacturing strike in Beaver Falls, Pennsylvania.[86] The *Cincinnati Enquirer* and other Ohio papers protested against the use of Chinese labor in the cigar-making industry,[87] the industry whose union leader, Samuel Gompers, was to become a lifelong foe of the Chinese and one of the most potent forces in denying them equal opportunity in craft work.[88] America's labor unions fulminated against the Chinese and demanded their exclusion from the nation and their expulsion from the labor force. "The political issue after 1877 was racial, not financial, and the weapon was not merely the ballot, but also 'direct action'—violence. The anti-Chinese agitation in California, culminating as it did in the Exclusion Law passed by Congress in 1882, was doubtless the most important single factor in the history of American labor, for without it the entire country might have been overrun by Mongolian labor and the labor movement might have become a conflict of races instead of one of classes."[89] That a historian of labor, writing in the twentieth century, could make this statement is indicative of the depth to which Sinophobia had worked itself into at least one sector of the American population.

Settlement in Cities

One of the outstanding characteristics of the Chinese in America is their settlement in cities. Unlike the Japanese, for example, the Chinese have not had a long habitation on agricultural hinterlands followed by the migration of second and third generation offspring to urban areas.[90] A few Chinese agricultural settlements existed briefly in the California interior,[91] and some Chinese farmers are to be found in the rural environs of Vancouver, British Columbia, but the bulk of Chinese have always dwelt in cities or small towns.[92] Even when Chinese were employed on railroads—such as the Central Pacific in the late 1860s—or in digging the tunnels of California's vineyards,[93] their places of work were but temporary abodes; when the work was done they returned to the city. "San Francisco," testified Frank M. Pixley, politician, publisher and opponent of Chinese immigration, "is the heart and hive and home of all the Chinese upon this coast. Our Chinese quarter, as it is called, is their place really of residence. If they go to a wash house in the vicinity, to a suburban manufactory, to gardening near the town, or if to build railroads in San Bernardino or on the Colorado, or to reclaim tule lands in the interior, their departure there is temporary, and their return here is certain; therefore the number in San Francisco depends upon seasons and the contract labor market."[94]

The Chinese population of San Francisco grew both in an absolute and a proportional sense in the decades after 1860. In 1860 the Chinese in San Francisco numbered 2,719 persons and were only 7.8% of the state's total Asian population. By 1870 it had jumped to 12,030 and 24.4%; ten years later it had risen to 21,745 and 28.9%; in 1890 the Chinese in San Francisco had grown to 25,833 and 35.7%. Only in 1900 did the Chinese in San Francisco show a decline. The enforcement of the exclusion laws, the return of numerous successful or discouraged Chinese to China, and the departure of others for the midwest and beyond left the number at 13,954, still 30.5% of the state's Chinese population.[95]

The city always meant the Chinese quarter, a ghetto called "Chinatown." It was in Chinatown that the lonely Chinese laborer could find fellowship, companions, social familiarity and solace. Chinatown acted as a partial buffer against the prejudices, hatreds and depredations of hostile whites. Chinatown included the offices and hostelries of the various Chinese benevolent and protective associations, places where one could get a bunk for the night, some food, a stake, and a knowledge of the number, kinds and conditions of available jobs. Chinatown also housed the Chinese elite, the merchants of the ghetto who acted as spokesmen for and protectors of the laborers and who held the latter in a state of political dependence and debt bondage. The Chinatowns of America and elsewhere[96] cannot be said to be either products of white racism on the one hand or congregative sentiments among the Chinese on the other. Rather, they must be seen as complex emergents produced by these two elements acting simultaneously. A powerful sense of group feelings and social needs found institutionalized expression in Chinatown at the same time that white aversion and hostility gave added reasons for those Chinese institutions to continue to flourish.

Chinese Social Organization

The Chinese quarter of San Francisco and other cities where Chinatowns have been established are characterized by a high degree and complex mesh of organization. To the present day most Americans are unaware of the actual nature and functions of Chinese associations and tend to regard them in unilluminating stereotypy. There are three basic types of association established in Chinatown as well as subsidiary and ancillary groupings. At the apex of the organizational pyramid is a confederation of associations which tends to govern the community. First there are clans. Clans have their origin in the Chinese lineage communities so prevalent in southeastern China, communities which united their male inhabitants with bonds of blood loyalty based on descent from a common ancestor.[97] In the New World the lineage unit was replaced by a net sprung wider than the original geographically compact village of origin to include all those bearing the same surname. The clan provided the boundaries of the incest taboo by prohibiting marriage within the same surname group.[98] Clan officials established hostelries for their kinsmen, and the clan association became a kind of immigrant aid society providing food, shelter, employment, protection and advice. The clans further served to remind the sojourner of his ties to village and family in China, and in the absence of the original lineal authorities, assumed a role *in loco parentis.*[99] In some instances clans obtained a monopoly over some trades or professions in Chinatown and effectively resisted encroachments on these monopolies by ambitious Chinese from other clans.[100] More recently clan authority has been undermined by the acculturation of Chinese born in America and by a resentment against both its traditional despotism and the clans' failure to ameliorate social conditions.[101]

In addition to clans, however, there developed among immigrant Chinese a functionally similar but structurally different type of association. The *hui kuan* united all those who spoke a common dialect, hailed from the same district of origin in China or belonged to the same tribal or ethnic group. The *hui kuan*, like the clan, originated in China, and by the mid-nineteenth century there were associations of this type throughout the Celestial Empire. In many ways these Chinese associations were similar to those immigrant aid and benevolent societies formed by Europeans in America, and the German term which has been applied to the latter, *Landsmannschaften*, is applicable to the Chinese *hui kuan* as well.[102]

The several *Landsmannschaften* established in San Francisco and other cities where Chinese dwelt served as caravansaries, hostelries, credit associations and employment agencies for their members. They also represented their constituency in dealings with other *Landsmannschaften* and with white officials. Finally, they conducted arbitration and mediation hearings between individuals and groups and adjudicated disputes. In San Francisco, Vancouver and New York City the several *hui kuan* confederated together with other associations, often including clans and secret societies, to form a supra-community association. The Chinese Benevolent Association, as it is usually called, provides Chinatown-wide governance on the one hand and a united front in relations with white America on the other.[103] During the first half century of Chinese settlement in America the consolidated association of *hui kuan* commanded at the least the grudging allegiance and obedience of the toiling Chinese laborers and the respect of many well-meaning whites; however, in more recent times the association's alleged involvement in illegal immigration, its failure to meet the needs of San Francisco's new Chinese immigrant youth, its conservative and traditional orientation toward welfare, and its anachronistic appearance to acculturated American-born Chinese have led to a certain decline in its community power and a slight dampening of its popularity with white America.[104] Nevertheless, it retains considerable authority and can still exert sanctions against recalcitrant and defalcating Chinese in the ghetto.[105]

The third major type of organization in Chinatown is the secret society. Like the clan and the *hui kuan*, the secret society originated in China where for centuries it served as the principal agency for protest, rebellion and banditry. It also provided a haven for those who blamed officialdom for their agricultural or professional failures, for those who had been expelled from their village, expunged from their lineage or who had run afoul of the law.[106] After 1644 in Kwangtung and Fukien secret societies were the most notorious opponents of Manchu rule, and for more than 250 years they pursued sporadic guerrilla warfare against Ch'ing officials, seaport towns and wealthy merchants. The overseas branches contributed to Sun Yat-sen's revolution in 1911, but in China secret societies continued to plague both revolutionary forces and republican power holders—both of which tried to crush or co-opt them—well into the middle of the twentieth century. After the advent of the Communist regime, attempts were again made to "coordinate" them or stamp them out, although it is by no means clear how successful these efforts have been.[107]

Nineteenth century migrants from Kwangtung and Fukien included not a few of the members of the Triad Society, the most famous of China's clandestine associations. In nearly every overseas Chinese community of size secret societies sprang up as chapters of or models based on that order. In Malaya, an area in which much information on these societies has been gathered, the several secret fraternal brotherhoods not only organized much of the social, economic, political, criminal and recreational life of the Chinese community, but also played a significant role in the industrial and political development and the foreign relations of the British colony.[108]

In the United States and Canada early immigrants established Chinese secret societies in the cities and in the outlying areas where Chinese miners gathered to organize their meager elements of livelihood and daily life. In the mining country of British Columbia, for example, a Chinese secret society provided a carefully run hostelry, adjudicated disputes and regulated the boundaries of the claims.[109] In the cities the secret societies soon took over control of gambling and prostitution in the American Chinatowns, and it is with these activities rather than with their political or eleemosynary work that they are most often associated in the minds of non-Chinese in America.

The different associations often fell out with one another; their so-called "tong wars"—in actual fact, violent altercations that involved clans, *hui kuan* and secret societies—are a frequent source of apocryphal history and stereotypy of the Chinese in America. The charitable works of secret societies were confined for the most part to mutual aid to their constituents, the establishment of buildings and club-houses where fraternity might be found, and, in recent years, some care and solicitation for their aged and infirm members. Political activities of the secret societies in North America were limited to occasional interest in the fortunes of China's regimes, and they did not interfere with or participate in the national politics of the United States or Canada.

At the turn of the century and in the decade thereafter Sun Yat-sen obtained considerable financial support from chapters of the *Chih-kung T'ang* in North America.[110] In San Francisco over 2,000,000 dollars in revolutionary currency were printed, while in rural California a few hundred inspired Chinese young men drilled in preparation to join the fighting forces of Sun's revolution.[111] When Dr. Sun was stranded without funds in New York City at a critical moment in the revolution, Seto May-tong, a Triad Society official who was to continue to exercise influence on the international relations of China and secret societies for more than thirty years, raised the necessary funds to finance his fateful return to China. In 1912 Seto mortgaged the society's buildings in Victoria, Vancouver and Toronto, raising $150,000 for the revolution.[112]

In more recent years Chinese secret societies may have lost some of their erstwhile functions and declined in influence and power. Their unity in support of Sun Yat-sen collapsed with the failure of the Republic to establish consensus and legitimacy. Although the Triad Society reorganized as a political party in 1947, it was ineffectual in arranging a peace between the Communist and Kuomintang forces, and since has been devoid of political influence.[113] Meanwhile, in the Chinatowns of America prostitution and gambling—the traditional sources of secret society revenue—have declined with the infirmity and death of the bachelor immigrants, the establishment of families in America, and the acculturation of the American-born Chinese.[114] Finally, the general rejection of traditional Chinese societies by the present generation of immigrants and Chinese-Americans has added to secret society desuetude.[115] At the present time it would appear that, barring some unforeseen source for their rejuvenation, Chinese secret societies will soon disappear from the American scene.

The Shortage of Women

The principal social problem affecting the Chinese in America was the shortage of women. So few Chinese women came to America that it was not until the middle of the twentieth century that there occurred even a proximity in balancing the sex ratio. During the entire period of unrestricted immigration (1850–1882) a total of only 8,848 Chinese women journeyed to American shores. In that same period over 100,000 men arrived in the United States. Many of the women could not stand the rigors of life in America and died or returned to China. By 1890 only 3,868 Chinese women were reported to be in the country. The number of Chinese males continued to grow during the latter three decades of the nineteenth century. In 1860 the census reported 33,149 male Chinese; in 1870, 58,633; in 1880, 100,686; and in 1890 there were 102,620 Chinese men in America. Only in 1900 did the census of Chinese males reveal a halt in the growth of this portion of the Chinese population in America. In that year 85,341 Chinese males were reported. Between 1860 and 1890 the ratio of Chinese males per 100 Chinese females was alarmingly high: 1,858 in 1860; 1,284 in 1870; 2,106 in 1880; 2,678 in 1890; and 1,887 in 1900.[116]

The imbalance in the sex ratio was slowly reduced during the first half of the twentieth century. By 1920, despite the birth of a few females among the Chinese in America, the males still far outnumbered the females: for every 100 women there were more than 695 men. By 1960 the situation had been only partially mitigated. The number of males had grown to 135,430, but the number of females was only 100,654.[117] The low number of females among the Chinese in America and elsewhere[118] has been one of the most salient features shaping their personal, social and community life.[119]

Ideally, Chinese custom held that a wife should remain in the household of her husband's parents, even in the event that her husband went abroad. Should his parents die during his absence, the wife was expected to perform the burial and mourning rites.[120] Village headmen often secured a prospective emigrant's loyalty to his village by requiring that he marry before departing and that he promise to remit money for the support of his wife and family and the village community.[121] Overseas the clan or *hui kuan* often assumed the obligation of collecting the remittances from the laboring immigrants and sending them to the appropriate villages in China.[122] The lonely laborer toiled in the hope that one day he would return to his wife and family as a wealthy and respected man. In fact, however, this rarely occurred; instead, the sojourner was usually forced to put off his remigration to China year after year. The promise of America's gold turned to dross, but still he labored. For some there was a temporary respite in a visit to China, the siring of a son there, and the hope, sometimes realized, that the son would join the father in the American adventure when he came of age.[123]

If Chinese custom, often misunderstood in America,[124] prevented Chinese women from joining their husbands overseas in the first three decades of unrestricted immigration, American law continued the bar against them after 1882. According to the Chinese Exclusion Act of that year, as interpreted by the courts two years later,[125] a Chinese woman acquired the legal status of her husband upon marriage. Thus, the wives of Chinese laborers were excluded by the same law which excluded Chinese laborers from coming to the United States. In the many changes made in the immigration laws before they were all repealed and a quota system imposed in 1943, the few liberalizations that were granted were applied almost exclusively to the Chinese wives of American citizens and the wives and offspring of Chinese merchants and other classes exempted in the original exclusion act.[126]

The consequences of the barring of Chinese women were many and tragic. In the rural mining areas the few Chinese women who had come abroad often became unwilling prostitutes servicing the sexual needs of homeless, lonely Chinese laborers.[127] "The Chinese are hardly used here," wrote Horace Greeley from a California mining camp in 1859. He went on to say that "he has no family here (the few Chinese women brought to this country being utterly shameless and abandoned), so that he forms no domestic ties, and enjoys no social standing."[128] "Very few bring wives with them," wrote Henryk Sienkiwicz in 1880 in one of his letters from America, "and for that reason it so happens that when among ten Chinese occupying a dwelling place there is but one woman, they all live together with her. I encountered such examples of polyandry quite frequently, particularly in the country."[129]

In the cities in which the Chinese congregated, prostitution was organized under the direct or tributary control of the secret societies. Young girls were brought to America from China after being kidnapped, sold into indentured servitude by their parents, captured by pirates or raiding bands, or lured abroad by a meretricious promise of proxy marriage. Once having arrived in America they were placed under contract to individual Chinese, or more often, to brothels in the Chinese quarter. They might be sold and resold again and again. The brothel keepers guarded their interest in "slave girls" by bribing court interpreters and offering perjured testimony in numerous litigations, and by invoking the assistance of secret society thugs to put off Chinese men who wished to marry a girl under contract.[130]

Organized prostitution and secret society vice domination continued well into the twentieth century.[131] A close observer of Chicago's Chinatown wrote in 1934: "Women are another temptation. Be it remembered that out of a total of some 5,000 Chinese in Chicago there are only about 40 women, and one can imagine the social problem involved. The Chinese Exclusion Act has prevented the Chinese from importing their women. Taking advantage of this situation, the tong men smuggle young girls from China for this purpose. The owner of the prostitution house owns the victims and pays tax to the tong which delivered the girls, and gives to the owner protection. Prostitution houses in the town are in the guise of hotels, and gambling houses, as stores."[132] Rather than recognize that the source of the problem was America's restrictive immigration laws, most journalists and politicians were content to rail against the Chinese on the grounds of immorality. Only Jacob A. Riis, himself an immigrant, having toured New York's Chinatown in 1890, seemed to grasp the enormity of the problem. He offered a solution: "This is a time for plain speaking on the subject. Rather than banish the Chinaman, I would have the door opened wider—for his wife; make it a condition of his coming or staying that he bring his wife with him. Then, at least, he might not be what he now is and remains, a homeless stranger among us. Upon this hinges the real Chinese question, in our city at all events, as I see it."[133]

The Anti-Chinese Movement in the Cities

The presence of Chinese in large numbers in San Francisco should not have seemed so strange in view of the polyglot population already in that city. The heterogeneous denizens of San Francisco were described in an observant report in 1852:

> The population of both the State and city was largely increased in 1852. The departures by sea from San Francisco were only 23,196 while there were 66,988 arrivals. This immigration was about double the amount that had taken place in 1851. The immigrants from the Atlantic States generally crossed the Isthmus, while the greater number of European foreigners came round Cape Horn. The Germans, a most valuable and industrious class of men, and the French, perhaps by nature not quite so steady and hard-working a race, though still a useful body of citizens, were year by year arriving in large numbers, and were readily remarked among the motley population. The most untutored eye could distinguish and contrast the natural phlegm and common-sense philosophy of the fat Teuton, and the "lean and hungry look" and restless gestures of the Celt . . . The English, Scotch and Irish immigrants, were also numerous, but their characteristics, although something different, were less distinguishable from those of native Americans than were the manners and customs of other foreigners. Besides there were always arriving numerous specimens of most other European nations,—Spaniards, Portuguese, Italians, Swiss, Greeks, Hungarians, Poles, Russians, Prussians, Dutch, Swedes, Danes, Turks, too—all visited California.

> Many of them went to the mines, although a considerable proportion never left San Francisco. The country and city were wide enough to hold them all, and rich enough to give them all a moderate independence in the course of a few years . . .

> Upwards of twenty thousand Chinese are included in the general number of arrivals above given. Such people were becoming very numerous in San Francisco . . . at one period of 1852 there were supposed to be about 27,000 Chinese in the state. A considerable number of people of "color" (*par excellence*) also arrived. These were probably afraid to proceed to the mines to labor beside the domineering white races, and therefore they remained to drudge, and to make much money and spend it in San Francisco, like almost every body else. Mexicans from Sonora and other provinces of Mexico, and many Chileans, and a few Peruvians from South America, were likewise continually coming and going between San Francisco and the ports of their own countries. The Chinese immigrants had their mandarins, their merchants, rich, educated, and respectable men, in San Francisco; but all the Mexicans and Chileans, like the people of negro descent, were only of the commonest description. The women of all these various races were nearly all of the vilest character, and openly practiced the most shameful commerce. The lewdness of fallen white females is shocking enough to witness, but it is far exceeded by the disgusting practices of these tawny visaged creatures.[134]

As late as 1875, San Francisco still attracted comment because of its many peoples, cosmopolitan atmosphere and colorful character. Samuel Wells Williams, the noted missionary to China, wrote of it in tones of genuine rapture:

> San Francisco is probably the most cosmopolitan city of its size in the world. Nowhere else are witnessed the fusing of so many races, the juxtaposition of so many nationalities, the Babel of so many tongues. Every country on the globe, every state and principality, almost every island of the sea, finds here its representative. Your next door neighbor may be a native of Central Asia; your vis-a-vis at the restaurant table may have been born under the shadow of the great wall of China; the man who waits on you at table may be a lascar from the East Indies. If you go to the theater, you may find sitting next to you a lady from the Sandwich Islands; if you go to the Opera, you may hear, in the pauses of the music, French, German, Italian, Spanish, Russian, Swedish, Modern Greek, spoken by people dressed in the most scrupulous evening costume. If you take a ride in the horse-cars, you may find yourself wedged in between a parson from Massachusetts and a parsee from Hindostan; if you go to the bank, you may be jostled by a gentleman from Damascus, or a prince of the Society Islands. In three minutes' walk from your place of

business, you enter an Oriental city—surrounded by the symbols of a civilization older than that of the Pharaohs."[135]

Yet, the strange customs, peculiar habits and frugal life of the Chinese seemed to astonish, alarm, or disgust the San Franciscans within a short time after the arrival of Chinese laborers. Chinese merchants, with their indispensable supply of hot cooked foods, objects d'art and household necessities, were a small but favored group. Chinese laborers on the other hand, were, "unfair" competition in the mines and elsewhere, and morally degenerate, socially undesirable and politically irrelevant. The derision of the Chinese, the hatred directed against them, and the vicious half-truths and distortions that were to make up the anti-Chinese stereotype were already visible in 1852. Although, according to San Francisco's annalists of that year, the Chinese were described as "generally quiet and industrious members of society, charitable among themselves, not given to intemperance and the rude vices which drink induces, and . . . reputed to be remarkably attached to their parents," they were despised in California:

> The manners and habits of the Chinese are very repugnant to Americans in California. Of different language, blood, religion, and character, inferior in most mental and bodily qualities, the Chinaman is looked upon by some as only a little superior to the Negro, and by others as somewhat inferior. It is needless to reason upon such a matter. Those who have mingled with "celestials" have commonly felt before long an uncontrollable sort of loathing against them. "John's" person does not smell very sweetly; his color and the features of his face are unusual; his penuriousness; his lying, knavery, and natural cowardice are proverbial; he dwells apart from white persons, herding only with country-men, unable to communicate his ideas to such as are not of his nation, or to show the better part of his nature. He is poor and mean, somewhat slavish and crouching, and is despised by the whites, who would only laugh in derision if even a divine were to pretend to place the two races on an equality. In short there is a strong feeling,—prejudice it may be,— existing in California against all Chinamen, and they are nicknamed, cuffed about and treated very unceremoniously by every other class.[136]

That the racial hostility toward the Chinese stemmed in great measure from their alleged competition with urban white labor was indicated in 1852 when the California State Senate turned down Senator Tingley's infamous Bill number 63, "An Act to Enforce Contracts and Obligations to Perform Work and Labor," commonly known as the "Coolie Bill."[137] In the committee's minority report, eventually adopted by the Senate, Senator Philip Roach, who was to be a leader in the fight for Chinese exclusion for the next thirty years, wrote that he did not oppose the importation of Oriental contract labor for agriculture: "There is ample room for its employment in draining the swamplands, in cultivating rice, raising silk, or planting tea. Our State is supposed to have great natural advantages for those objects; but if these present not field enough for their labor, then sugar, cotton, and tobacco invite their attention. For these special objects I have no objection to the introduction of contract laborers, provided they are excluded from citizenship; for those staples cannot be cultivated without 'cheap labor'; but from all other branches I would recommend its exclusion." Roach's conclusion about Chinese in the skilled labor occupations was quite emphatic. "I do not want to see Chinese or Kanaka carpenters, masons, or blacksmiths, brought here in swarms under contracts, to compete with our own mechanics, whose labor is as honorable and as well entitled to social and political rights as the pursuits designated 'learned professions.' "[138] By the 1870s California labor's "social and political rights" took the form of an organized movement dedicated to the restriction of Chinese immigration and the exclusion of Chinese workers from the labor market.

After two decades of mining and railroad building, work which had kept large numbers of Chinese away from the cities, the Chinese began to settle down in the urban Chinatowns of the west and to become a principal part of the labor force in newly developing urban industries. During the 1870s and 1880s Chinese in San Francisco were employed in the woolen, textile, clothing, shoe, cigar, gunpowder and a few other industrial factories which at that time played a vital part in the city's economy.[139] When the depression of the 1870s put large numbers of white laborers out of work, Chinese workers became the objects of labor union hostility. Popular demagogues—of whom Denis Kearney was the most famous[140]— railed against their presence in industries which, they held, belonged to white labor exclusively. Mob actions against the Chinese were organized, harassing laws were passed, and eventually the Chinese were driven out of the industries and in many cases out of the cities as well.

The polemics against the Chinese were inflammatory and exaggerated allegations against their character and culture, and they served as incitements to riot and abuse. Mark Twain, one of the most acute observers of the western scene, bitterly satirized the mistreatment of Chinese, calling attention to the unequal protection of the laws, popular prejudices and injurious practices from which they suffered daily. He had hoped that the Burlingame Treaty of 1868 would put an end to these abuses, but when its protective provisions were winked at, he fulminated against the street boys and politicians, workers and legislators who perpetrated torture and terror on the inoffensive Chinese. As he so carefully observed, the popular attacks on Chinese were not simply the outrages of sick or savage individuals, but rather the product of the campaign of Sinophobic vilification which had been created by the political, labor and media leaders.[141] Similarly, Thomas Nast, the political cartoonist, turned his sharp pen to satirizing the inconsistent laws and hate-ridden ideologies that barred Chinese from citizenship and the franchise and condemned them to be the mud-sills of America. Later, however, Nast appears to have withdrawn the bite from his criticism and to have accepted the permanent place of Chinese in this country as an abused minority.[142]

Negro leaders such as Frederick Douglass carefully distinguished their opposition to the coolie trade and to the exploitation of Chinese laborers from any opposition to Chinese as laborers or citizens,[143] but occasionally a California Negro journalist would take up the anti-Chinese cry contrasting the latter's alleged inability to assimilate with the rapidly Americanizing Negro.[144] As the racist movement spread throughout the United States, the anti-Chinese diatribes became confused with those levelled against the Negro. Comparisons, sometimes favoring one, sometimes the other were made, but in the end both Negroes and Chinese were declared inimical and inferior to white society in general and to white labor in particular.[145]

The demagogic voice of Denis Kearney of California was a major factor in elevating the anti-Chinese movement to national importance. In a letter to Lord Bryce, Kearney defended himself against Bryce's criticism, stating, "My only crime seems to have been that I opposed the Mongolization of my State in the interest of our own people and their civilization."[146] The Workingmen's Party of California, led by Kearney, adopted the slogan "The Chinese Must Go," and as its numbers and influence increased, affected California politics and legislation in a remarkable manner. In 1879 it sent a large and vociferous delegation to the state constitutional convention and played an important part in bringing about the infamous Article XIX of the California Constitution. In its vitriolic volley against the Chinese the Workingmen's Party rose to new heights of rhetorical invective:

> The Chinese coolie represents the most debased order of humanity known to the civilized world. No touch of refinement can ever reach him. He comes to this country in a condition of voluntary servitude, from which by the insidious precautions of the Chinese Six Companies, under whose auspices this immigration is carried on, he is scarcely ever able to escape—brings with him all the loathsome and vicious habits of his native country.
>
> No amount of association or example can change in the least iota his repulsive filthiness, or wean him in the slightest degree from the ways of his race. His personal habits are of the most loathsome. He knows nothing of the family relation, nothing of the sanctity of an oath, regards no right of property except as controlled through absolute fear, and utterly refuses to assimilate in any measure with the people to whom his presence is a curse. As a race, the thirty years of their presence in California has not been able to influence them to a solitary change of habit. They maintain their separate dress, retain their language and religion, institute their own secret courts, levying fines and enforcing decrees, even to the applying of the death sentence, in utter defiance of the laws of the State.
>
> They establish and carry on the most thorough and complete system of gambling, protect and encourage debauchery in its worst form, and under the cover of their laws, openly provide the most polluted system of prostitution ever known. Wherever they locate as a class in a city or town, it is as if the horrid touch of leprosy had grasped it. Straightway all Caucasian civilization is driven away

from the quarter they settle upon; property values are destroyed, and as is the case in San Francisco a proscribed quarter known as "Chinatown" is made, with as exactly defined limits and as complete an isolation from the civilized portion of the community as the line by the Great Wall which divided their own country from Tartary.

Disgusting and nauseating as is the contemplation of the personal habits of the race, it is, however, to the influence which their competition with the intelligent and civilized labor of the State in all our industries will have upon the future, that the people are looking with most concern, and from which unwholesome and unnatural competition the people are anxiously seeking for relief . . .[147]

The vicious anti-Chinese stereotype was perhaps never so well combined with a fanatical religious anthropology and the racist interests of white labor organizations as in the testimony presented by Frank M. Pixley before the Senate committee investigating Chinese immigration in 1877:

> The Chinese are inferior to any race God ever made . . . I think there are none so low . . . Their people have got the perfection of crimes of 4,000 years . . . The Divine Wisdom has said that He would divide this country and the world as a heritage of five great families; that to the Blacks He would give Africa; and Asia he would give to the Yellow races. He inspired us with the determination, not only to have prepared our own inheritance, but to have stolen from the Red Man, America; and it is now settled that the Saxon, American or European groups of families, the White Race, is to have the inheritance of Europe and America and that the Yellow races are to be confined to what the Almighty originally gave them; and as they are not a favored people, they are not to be permitted to steal from us what we have robbed the American savage of . . . I believe the Chinese have no souls to save, and if they have, they are not worth the saving . . .
>
> The burden of our accusations against them is that they come in conflict with our labor interests; that they can never assimilate with us; that they are a perpetual unchanging and unchangeable alien element that can never become homogeneous; that their civilization is demoralizing and degrading to our people; that they degrade and dishonor labor; that they never become citizens, and that an alien, degraded labor class, without desire of citizenship, without education and without interest in the country it inhabits, is an element both demoralizing and dangerous to the community within which it exists.[148]

Sparked by the agitation of labor leaders and politicians, the urban anti-Chinese movement entered a violent phase. Riots against the Chinese occurred in the major cities of the west. The first significant urban uprising took place in San Francisco in 1869,[149] and another far more serious riot occurred in the midst of a tong war in Los Angeles' Chinatown on October 24, 1871. After two policemen and a bystander had been killed, a white mob descended on the Chinese quarter and in but four hours killed at least nineteen Chinese, including women and children, burned several buildings and looted shops.[150] Six years later unemployed laborers burned and looted San Francisco's Chinese ghetto for several weeks without any significant interference by public agencies of law enforcement.[151] In 1880 an anti-Chinese riot occurred in Denver.[152] Five years later uprisings against the Chinese occurred in Rock Springs, Wyoming and in Tacoma and Seattle, Washington.[153] In 1907 labor-inspired agitation caused a mob of 15,000 white persons, led by some of the city's most prominent citizens, to descend on the Chinese and Japanese quarters of Vancouver, British Columbia; in response, the Orientals called a city-wide general strike which was only settled after intervention by the king of England and his representative William Lyon Mackenzie King.[154] Riots and assaults on the Chinese also occurred in smaller cities and towns of the West: at Gold Hill and Virginia City, Nevada in 1869; at Martinez, California in 1871; at Truckee, California, in 1878, during which 1000 Chinese were driven out; and in many other towns from Napa to Eureka in California and elsewhere.[155]

Anti-Chinese legislation was of three kinds. The first consisted of state and ultimately federal laws to restrict or exclude the Chinese altogether from this country. California experimented for twenty-five years with immigration laws which were consistently declared unconstitutional. Only after the anti-Chinese movement had escalated from a sectional to a national issue did the federal government pass the first exclusion act. The second type of law sought to eliminate Chinese from those occupations in which they allegedly competed "unfairly" with white labor. Finally, a number of laws were passed which had either a punitive or harassing intent.

Among the laws passed in California perhaps the most infamous was Article XIX of the State Constitution, added in the Convention of 1879. This amendment forbade the employment of Chinese in any corporation formed in the state, on any state, municipal and county public works, and provided for legislation whereby any city or town might expel its Chinese inhabitants. Much of this amendment was rendered inoperative by judicial decisions.[156]

Additional city and state ordinances adversely affected Chinese laundrymen, fishermen and farmers. San Francisco sought to limit the activities of Chinese washmen by laws which limited the hours, arbitrarily licensed the laundry buildings, and taxed persons who used poles to deliver goods or traveled from house to house without a vehicle or horse. Some of these laws survived judicial scrutiny, but most of them fell before the unusually sharp eye of the justices of the Supreme Court.[157] In other states, including Nevada and Montana[158] laws or collective action sought the elimination of the peaceful Chinese laundrymen. Chinese fishermen were excluded from fishing by a law excluding aliens ineligible for citizenship from obtaining a license. After this ordinance ran afoul of the courts, a tax law made fishing expensive. California's second law denying fishing licenses to aliens ineligible to citizenship was passed after Chinese became eligible for naturalization and was directed against the Japanese. It too was declared unconstitutional.[159] Under the guise of protecting land and resources from aliens, California forbade nonnaturalizable citizens from obtaining land in 1913 and only after four decades of fruitless legal challenges was this anti-Oriental legislation declared void.[160] Even though much of California's anti-Chinese legislation was declared unconstitutional, its intent was realized by successful labor agitation which resulted in the firing of Chinese workers in nearly every urban industry in which they had thrived and their retreat into Chinatown.[161]

The most outrageous of the punitive and harassing legislation were the "lodging house" and "queue-cutting" ordinances passed in San Francisco and subsequently enacted as state laws. A law requiring 500 cubic feet of air space for each person inhabiting any public hostelry was enforced solely against the Chinese after 1873. When the Chinese

combined to resist the law by refusing to pay the fines and crowding the jails so that there was less than five hundred cubic feet of air space per person in them, the Board of Supervisors retaliated with a vengeance. A vehicle tax on Chinese laundrymen, a prohibition on returning the dead to China, and a public health ordinance ordering the cutting of queues were proposed and sent on to the mayor for signature. Mayor Alvord vetoed the ordinances, but in 1876 they were enacted over the signature of Mayor Bryant. A court case against these laws was started and on July 7, 1879 the Circuit Court of the United States invalidated the law that had forced Chinese to be deprived of their badge of citizenship in the Chinese Empire. The prohibition on the removal of the dead from county burial plots, unless a physician's certificate was obtained, was upheld by the Supreme Court in the same year.[162]

In addition to their abuse by outraged mobs, their victimization and deprivations by legislative enactments and the discriminatory attacks on them by organized labor, the Chinese were also denied the right to testify in California courts and were segregated in several of the states' public schools. According to a ruling by California's twenty-nine year old Chief Justice, Chinese were declared to be Indians and as such were ineligible to testify in any case involving a white man. This ruling, making Chinese vulnerable to any kind of otherwise illegal treatment by whites so long as only Chinese witnessed the evil, remained in force from 1854 to 1875.[163]

California's Superintendent of Education complained bitterly of the presence of Chinese and other minorities in the public schools in 1859: "Had it been intended by the framers of the education law that the children of the inferior races should be educated side by side with the whites, it is manifest the census would have included children of all colors. If this attempt to force Africans, Chinese, and Diggers into one school is persisted in it must result in the ruin of the schools. The great mass of our citizens will not associate on terms of equality with these inferior races; nor will they consent that their children should do so."[164] The state legislature acquiesced to Superintendent Moulder's request and in 1860 delegated to him the power to withhold public funds from any school which admitted the proscribed minorities. Provision for separate schools was made, and a Chinese school operated irregularly in San Francisco after 1860. In later years, modifications of the law permitted admission of non-whites if whites did not object, but this law of 1866 had little effect in subsequent years. Chinese brought suit to desegregate the state's public schools in 1902 but were unsuccessful.[165] Twenty-five years later Chinese in Mississippi failed in another attempt to desegregate schools and subsequently refused to send their children to the schools established for "colored" pupils.[166] Since 1954 school segregation has been illegal, but *de facto* segregation still persists in the Chinese as well as other non-white ghettos.

Conclusion

The Chinese were truly strangers in a strange land. They had come suddenly to a frontier area, bringing with them cherished values and deeply engrained customs which, together with their physical distinctiveness, caused them to stand out and apart from the general population. It would not be unfair to point out that the Chinese had very few friends or sympathizers in the American West. Neither radicals nor reactionaries, liberals nor conservatives were interested in defending—much less understanding—them. The radical intellectuals and labor leaders were with rare exception notorious for their fulminations against the hapless Chinese.[167]

Reactionaries, racists, demagogues, nativists and know-nothings seized upon "the Chinese question" to ride to power in California. Occasionally a Protestant missionary, men such as A.W. Loomis and Otis Gibson, took a sympathetic interest in and assumed a protective posture toward the Chinese. But when conversions proved to be few in number, these brave souls deserted the field and in some instances turned against their former charges. The Catholics remained almost universally opposed to the Chinese, preferring to serve their Irish flock and even to minister to its Sinophobia.[168]

A few officials and attorneys, possessed of a sense of noblesse oblige or moved to defend civil rights,— Hall McAllister, Colonel Frederick A. Bee and Benjamin S. Brooks—accepted the challenge of the Chinese presence and strove manfully to maintain their liberties and defend their lives and property. But these men were effective in the courts; they could not stop the violence of aroused mobs nor could they counter the invective and organization of the anti-Chinese unions. In the end the Chinese were forced to retreat behind the "walls" which prejudice and discrimination had erected; they returned to the ghetto and inside attempted to build a secure if not prosperous life.

By the turn of the century the Chinese were isolated, neglected and demoralized. Located inside the Chinatowns of American cities they achieved some sense of cultural freedom, a relaxation of tensions and a precarious independence. Some found a new sense of freedom in giving support to Sun Yat-sen's liberation movement for China; a few prospered as merchants and gained political and social power in the ghetto, but most remained homeless and trapped, too poor to return to China and too oppressed to enter fully into American society. Sojourners without wives, they could not procreate a second generation which, had it been born, might have succeeded like the second generation of other immigrant groups. Only after 1930 were there enough Chinese women present in America to guarantee that a new generation of significant proportions would develop in the next two decades. The much-vaunted Chinese family remained but an idea in Chinatown for eight remorseless decades.

Today, America and its Chinese are beginning to sense the legacy of the nineteenth century. The children of the immigrants, born in America, growing up in a period of relative tolerance and burgeoning civil rights, educated in public schools and emancipated from Chinese tradition, have left Chinatown for the professions, the suburbs and the rest of the American dream. To be sure, they still encounter discrimination in housing and in certain occupations, and they still must silently wince at the gauche pretensions of toleration which often accompany white "acceptance." Meanwhile, inside

Chinatown, the old elite, composed of executives of the clans, *hui kuans* and secret societies, continues to hold sway at the expense of their subjects over whom they exercise a benevolent but despotic authority.

The mass of Chinatowners may be divided into four groups for whom life holds varying degrees of promise and poverty. The aged bachelors live in tiny, cold, unkempt, rooms, suffer from tuberculosis and other diseases not prevalent in the metropolis and contribute to Chinatown's alarming suicide rate. The shopkeepers and restaurateurs thrive on a tourist trade but privately worry about the effects of America's foreign policy on their fortunes. The new immigrants find themselves doubly estranged and alienated—they cannot bow to the authority of the Chinatown elites, but they lack the language and skill with which they might enter the American mainstream. Some work in the garment sweatshops, eking out a meager living from a production system that was once the horror of every humane Occiden-

tal but has now all but disappeared except in Chinatown. The youthful immigrants are angry and militant, and in their outcry against a seemingly pitiless system, sound a call like that of the Negro and other minority groups seeking independence and identity. The American-born school dropouts, those who for one reason or another have not made it into white America, are estranged from their immigrant peers by culture and language, but enjoined from white or Chinese-American middle-class life by their academic and occupational failures. Imbued with a new spirit born of desperation and vague radicalism, they too have assumed the posture of late of an independent group seeking not assimilation but liberty. Chinatown's future lies with its people. As some sociologists are realizing, it is as problematic and unpredictable as America is as a whole. One step in understanding its present is a knowledge of its past.

Notes

1. Georg Simmel, "The Stranger," in *The Sociology of Georg Simmel*, Glencoe: The Free Press, 1950, p. 402 (Translated and edited by Kurt Wolff).

2. See Paul C.P. Siu, "The Sojourner," *American Journal of Sociology*, VIII, (July, 1952), pp. 32–44.

3. Cf. Harold Isaacs, *Images of Asia: American Views of China and India*, New York: Capricorn, 1962, pp. 63–238.

4. See Arthur O. Lovejoy, "The Chinese Origin of a Romanticism," *Essays in the History of Ideas*, New York: Capricorn, 1960, pp. 99–135.

5. Foster Rhea Dulles, *China and America: The Story of Their Relations Since 1784*, Princeton: Princeton University Press, 1946, pp. 6–7.

6. George H. Danton, *The Culture Contacts of the United States and China: The Earliest Sino-American Culture Contacts, 1784–1844*, New York: Columbia University Press, 1931, pp. 29, 33.

7. See Clay Lancaster, *The Japanese Influence in America*, New York: Walton H. Rawls, 1963, pp. 1–41.

8. Kenneth Scott Latourette, *The History of the Early Relations Between the United States and China, 1784–1844*, Transactions of the Connecticut Academy of Arts and Sciences, 22 (August, 1917)

pp. 16–17. New York: Kraus Reprint Corp., 1964. See also Robert Glass Cleland, "Asiatic Trade and American Occupation of the Pacific Coast," *Annual Report of the American Historical Association for the Year 1914*, I (Washington, 1916), pp. 283–289. For Shaw's own account of his days in China see Joseph Quincy, *The Journals of Major Samuel Shaw, the First American Consul at Canton, with a Life of the Author*, Taipei: Cheng-wen Publishing Co., 1968. (Originally published in 1848).

9. See *China in the 16th Century: The Journals of Matthew Ricci, 1583–1610*, New York: Random House, 1952, pp. 41–58. (Translated by Louis J. Gallagher, S.J.). The "American farmer," J. Hector St. John de Crevecoeur, wrote in 1782 that "The American father thus ploughing with his child, and to feed his family, is inferior only to the emperor of China ploughing as an example to his kingdom." *Letters From An American Farmer*, New York: E.P. Dutton, 1957, p. 21. The 1765 catalogue of the private Union Library of Philadelphia contained among its titles *Chinese Tales*, a book so popular the librarian had had to advertise for its return in 1764. Carl and Jessica Bridenbaugh, *Rebels and Gentlemen: Philadelphia in the Age of Franklin*, New York: Oxford Hesperides, 1962, p. 87.

10. See *Niles Register*, Feb. 23, 1822; June 18, 1835. Quoted in Danton, *op. cit.*, p. 11n. There also was a considerable respect for

China's developments in agriculture and conveniences. Thus, the first volume of the *American Philosophical Society* wished that America "could be so fortunate as to introduce the industry of the Chinese, their arts of living, and improvements in husbandry . . . [so that] America might become in time as populous as China." And as late as 1840 *Hunt's Merchants' Magazine* wrote, "The industry and ingenuity of the Chinese in all that relates to the conveniences of life are remarkable: the origin among them of several arts of comparatively recent date in Europe, is lost in the night of time." Quoted in Latourette, *op. cit.*, p. 124.

Respect for the Chinese government, originating in the 16th century Jesuit praises of the Peking administration, died down after Lord Macartney vividly contrasted the old Chinese order with that imposed after 1644 by the Manchus. He wrote, "The government as it now stands is properly the tyranny of a handful of Tartars over more than three hundred millions of Chinese . . . A series of two hundred years in the succession of eight or ten monarchs did not change the Mongol into a Hindu, nor has a century and a half made Ch'ien-lung a Chinese. He remains at this hour, in all his maxims of policy, as true a Tartar as any of his ancestors." *An Embassy to China: Being the Journal Kept by Lord Macartney During his Embassy to the Emperor Ch'ien Lung, 1793–1794,* Hamden, Conn.: Archon, 1963 (Edited by J. C. Crammer-Byng), pp. 236–237. By the mid-nineteenth century the Chinese emperor's ability to keep Anglo-American ministers from the capital and to bottle them up with local officialdom was a matter of keen consternation. See, e.g., Laurence Oliphant, *Narrative of the Earl of Elgin's Mission to China and Japan in the Years 1857, '58, '59,* New York: Harper and Brothers, 1888, pp. 276–281.

11. George I. Quimby, "Culture Contact on the Northwest Coast, 1785–1795," *American Anthropologist,* 50 (April–June, 1948), pp. 247–255. See also Margaret Ormsby, *British Columbia: A History,* Vancouver: Macmillans in Canada, 1958, pp. 16–19.

12. Homer H. Dubs and Robert S. Smith, "Chinese in Mexico City in 1635," *Far Eastern Quarterly,* I (August, 1942), pp. 387–389. See also William Lytle Schurz, *The Manila Galleon,* New York: E.P. Dutton, 1959, pp. 63–98.

13. For the Chinese in Pennsylvania see R.L. Brunhouse, "Lascars in Pennsylvania: A Sidelight on the China Trade," *Pennsylvania History,* January, 1940, pp. 20–30. For the role of the Chinese in early New England see Samuel Eliot Morison, *The Maritime History of Massachusetts, 1783–1860,* Boston: Houghton Mifflin, 1961, p. 354 et passim.

14. Dulles, *op. cit.*, p. 39.

15. Morison, *op. cit.*, p. 203.

16. Dulles, *loc. cit.*; Morison, *op. cit.*, p. 240, 273.

17. Latourette, *op. cit.*, p. 123.

18. Danton, *op. cit.*, p. 102.

19. Charles Gold to George Danton. Reported in Danton, *op. cit.*, pp. 102–103.

20. For the life of Yung Wing see Yung Wing, *My Life in China and America,* New York: Henry Holt & Co., 1909; Lo Hsiang-lin, *Hong Kong and Western Cultures,* Honolulu: East West Center Press, 1964, pp. 86–156; Edmund H. Worthy, Jr., "Yung Wing in America," *Pacific Historical Review,* XXXIV (August, 1965), pp. 265–288.

21. See Tyler Dennet, *Americans in Eastern Asia,* New York: Barnes and Noble, 1963, p. 545n. for a personal report to this effect.

22. Y.C. Wang, *Chinese Intellectuals and the West, 1872–1949,* Chapel Hill: University of North Carolina Press, 1966, pp. 42–45. For the fate of the Chinese returnees, many of whom led distinguished lives in China, see Lo Hsiang-lin, *op. cit.*, pp. 125–144.

23. Richard H. Dillon, *The Hatchet Men: The Story of the Tong Wars in San Francisco's Chinatown,* New York: Coward-McCann, 1962, p. 30.

24. Howard M. Chapin, "The Chinese Junk Ke Ying at Providence," *Rhode Island Historical Society Collections,* 27 (January, 1934), pp. 5–12.

25. For a popular account which, despite the author's lack of social criticism, reveals the hostility directed against Chinese and the cruel pranks played upon them see Lucius Beebe and Charles Clegg, "The Heathen Chinese," *The American West,* New York: E.P. Dutton, 1955, pp. 318–335. Mark Twain documented the numerous attacks on Chinese, attacks which took place nearly every day. See, e.g., "Those Blasted Children," *New York Sunday Mercury,* March 27, 1865. Reprinted in Bernard Taper, (Editor), *Mark Twain's San Francisco,* New York: McGraw Hill, 1963, pp. 27–33. Many of the songs of Gold Rush California derided the Chinese for his queue. See Richard A. Dwyer and Richard E. Lingenfelter *The Songs of the Gold Rush,* Berkeley: University of California Press, 1964, pp. 112–113, 119, 121 et passim. The Chinese queue was also a stereotypical feature of humorous drama about the Chinese in the nineteenth century. See Stewart W. Hyde, "The Chinese Stereotype in American Melodrama," *California Historical Society Quarterly,* December, 1955, pp. 357–367.

26. B.S. Brooks, "History of the Legislation of the Supervisors of the City of San Francisco Against the Chinese, Culminating in the Passage of the Present Ordinance Generally known as the 'Queue Cutting Ordinance' . . ." *Appendix. The Invalidity of the Queue Ordinance of the City and County of San Francisco,* San Francisco: J.L. Rice and Co., 1879, pp. 15–43.

27. Latourette, *op. cit.*, p. 123; Dillon, *op. cit.*, p. 30. The definitive work on the subject is Howard S. Levy, *Chinese Footbinding: The History of a Curious and Erotic Custom,* New York: Walton Rawls, 1966.

28. Levy, *op. cit.*, pp. 95–99, 276–281.

29. Thomas Taylor Meadows, *The Chinese and their Rebellions,* Stanford: Academic Reprints, n.d. [originally published in 1856], pp. 34–50, 112–122; J. Thomson, *The Straits of Malacca, Indo-*

China, and China; or Ten Years' Travels, Adventures, and Residence Abroad, New York: Harper and Brothers, 1875, pp. 46–48.

30. Ping-ti Ho, *Studies on the Population of China, 1368–1953,* Cambridge: Harvard University Press, 1959, pp. 101–280.

31. Hosea Ballou Morse, *The Trade and Administration of the Chinese Empire,* Shanghai: Kelly and Walsh, 1908, pp. 175–351; John King Fairbank, *Trade and Diplomacy on the China Coast: The Opening of the Treaty Ports, 1842–1854,* Cambridge: Harvard University Press, 1964. (One volume edition); W.C. Hunter, *The 'Fan Kwae' at Canton Before Treaty Days, 1825–1844,* Taipei: Ch'eng-wen Publishing Co., 1965; Victor Purcell, *China,* London: Ernest Bann, 1962, pp. 52–61; Edgar Holt, *The Opium Wars in China,* London: Putnam, 1964.

32. "The Celestials at Home and Abroad," *Littell's Living Age,* 430 (August 14, 1852), p. 294.

33. *loc. cit.*

34. For a careful analysis of casualties during the Taiping Rebellion see Ping-ti Ho, *op. cit.,* pp. 236–247, 275. The Taiping insurrection has been a continuous source of Sinological study. For some representative works see Meadows, *op. cit.*; Vincent C. Y. Shih, *The Taiping Ideology: Its Sources, Interpretations and Influences,* Seattle: University of Washington Press, 1967; Franz Michael in collaboration with Chung-li Chang, *The Taiping Rebellion: History and Documents; Vol. 1: History,* Seattle: University of Washington Press, 1966; Eugene Powers Boardman, *Christian Influence upon the Ideology of the Taiping Rebellion, 1851–1865,* Madison: University of Wisconsin Press, 1952; J.C. Cheng, *Chinese Sources for the Taiping Rebellion, 1850–1864,* Hong Kong: Hong Kong University Press, 1963; Lady Flavia Anderson, *The Rebel Emperor,* London: Victor Gollancz, 1958.

35. Oliphant, *op. cit.,* pp. 75–300; Meadows, *op. cit.,* pp. 74–492; Robert Fortune, *A Residence Among the Chinese: Inland, On the Coast, and at Sea. Being a Narrative of Scenes and Adventures During a Third Visit to China from 1853 to 1856 . . . With Suggestions on the Present War,* London: John Murray, 1857, pp. 1–22, 423–440; S. Wells Williams, *The Middle Kingdom: A Survey of the Geography, Government, Education, Social Life, Arts, Religion, etc., of the Chinese Empire and its Inhabitants . . .* New York: John Wiley, 1853. Third Edition, Vol. II, pp. 417–604. For the Hakka-Punti War see Leon Comber, *Chinese Secret Societies in Malaya: A Survey of the Triad Society from 1800 to 1900,* Locust Valley: J.J. Augustin, 1959, pp. 28–29. For the American participation in the Taiping hostilities see Robert S. Rantoul, *Frederick Townsend Ward: Organizer and First Commander of the 'Ever Victorious Army' in the Tai Ping Rebellion,* Salem: Essex Institute, 1908. Historical Collections of the Essex Institute, Vol. XLIV.

36. Arthur Waley, *The Opium War Through Chinese Eyes,* Stanford: Stanford University Press, 1968; Siang-Tseh Chiang, *The Nien Rebellion,* Seattle: University of Washington Press, 1954; *The Boxer Uprising: A History of the Boxer Trouble in China,* New York: Paragon, 1967; Victor Purcell, *The Boxer Uprising: A Background Study,*

Cambridge: University Press, 1963.

37. "The Discovery of Gold in California," *Hutchings' California Magazine,* II (November, 1857), pp. 194–202. Articles by John A. Sutter and James W. Marshall. Reprinted in John A. Hawgood, *America's Western Frontiers: The Exploration and Settlement of the Trans-Mississippi West,* New York: Alfred A. Knopf, 1967, pp. 189–198.

38. "Quite a large number of the Celestials have arrived among us of late, enticed hither by the golden romance which has filled the world. Scarcely a ship arrives here that does not bring an increase to this worthy integer of our population; and we hear, by China papers, and private advices from that empire, that the feeling is spreading all through the sea-board, and, as a consequence, nearly all the vessels that are up for this country are so for the prospect of passengers. A few Chinamen have returned, taking home with them some thousands of dollars in California gold, and have thus given an impetus to the spirit of emigration from their fatherland which is not likely to abate for some years to come." *Daily Alta California,* May 12, 1851.

39. For circulars used in 1862, 1868, and 1870 see Hubert Howe Bancroft, *The New Pacific,* New York: The Bancroft Co., 1915, pp. 413–414. Third Edition.

40. A full discussion of all the ramifications of Chinese immigration is beyond the scope of this paper. For good accounts see Pyau Ling, "Causes of Chinese Emigration," *Annals of the American Academy of Political and Social Science,* XXXIX (January, 1912), pp. 74–82; Ta Chen, "Chinese Migrations, with Special Reference to Labor Conditions," *Bulletin of the United States Bureau of Labor Statistics,* No. 340, Washington, D.C.: Government Printing Office, 1923; Wu Ching-ch'ao, "Chinese Immigration in the Pacific Area," *Chinese Social and Political Science Review,* XII–XIII (October, 1928, January, 1929, April, 1929), pp. 543–560, 50–76, 161–182; Tin-Yuke Char, "Legal Restrictions on Chinese in English-Speaking Countries of the Pacific," *Chinese Social and Political Science Review,* XVI (January 4, 1933), pp. 472–513.

41. See Warren B. Smith, *White Servitude in Colonial South Carolina,* Columbia: University of South Carolina Press, 1961; Carl Bridenbaugh, *Vexed and Troubled Englishmen, 1590–1642,* New York: Oxford University Press, 1968, pp. 210, 421–424; Oscar Handlin, *The Americans: A New History of the People of the United States,* Boston: Atlantic-Little, Brown, 1963, pp. 20–22.

42. See Theodore Saloutos, *They Remember America: The Story of the Repatriated Greek-Americans,* Berkeley: University of California Press, 1956, pp. 16–17; Oscar Handlin, *Boston's Immigrants, 1790–1880: A Study in Acculturation,* New York: Atheneum, 1968, pp. 70–71.

43. Persia Crawford Campbell, *Chinese Coolie Emigration to Countries within the British Empire,* London: King and Sons, 1923, pp. xvii–xix, 28–39, 150–151.

44. For a complete discussion see Stanford M. Lyman, *The*

Structure of Chinese Society in Nineteenth Century America, unpublished Ph.D. dissertation, University of California, Berkeley, 1961.

That the Chinese migrant to California was often the loser in an unprofitable venture is illustrated in this incident related by the distinguished historian Hosea Ballou Morse:

> "An incident which occurred to the author in 1893 throws some light on the usual result to a returned Chinese emigrant. At a railway station in Formosa he was addressed in fluent and correct English by the proprietor-cook of the station restaurant; and in answer to an expression of astonishment, the Chinese explained why he was there. He had returned from California with a fortune of $2000. He had first to disburse heavily to remain unmolested by the magistrate and his underlings; then he had to relieve the necessities of his aged father; then an uncle, who had fallen into business difficulties, must be rescued from impending bankruptcy; and then he found he had only enough left to procure himself a wife, with a few dollars margin wherewith to establish himself in his present business, which at most would require $100 capital."

The International Relations of the Chinese Empire, Volume II: The Period of Submission, 1861–1893, Taipei: Book World Co., n.d. (Originally published in 1910), p. 166n.

45. For the early maltreatment of Chinese by American sea captains see the account of the infamous *"Robert Brown" incident"* in Earl B. Swisher, *China's Management of the American Barbarians: A Study of Sino-American Relations, 1841–1861,* New Haven: Far Eastern, 1951, pp. 179–205. For the corruption of American officials at Canton see the Testimony of Thomas H. King in *Report of the Joint Special Committee to Investigate Chinese Immigration.* U.S. Congress. Senate. 44th Congress. 2nd Session. Report No. 689. February, 1877, p. 93; Testimony of Governor F. F. Low and Testimony of Charles Wolcott Brooks in "Chinese Immigration: Its Social, Moral, and Political Effects." *Report to the California State Senate of its Special Committee on Chinese Emigration,* Sacramento: 1878, pp. 70, 101–102. See also Charles Wolcott Brooks, "The Chinese Labor Problem," *Overland Monthly,* November, 1869, pp. 407–419.

46. The entire incident may be pieced together from documents and articles which appeared at the time. For the Memphis convention see the report of its Committee on Chinese Labor in John R. Commons et al., *A Documentary History of American Industrial Society,* Cleveland: A.H. Clark, 1910–1911, Vol. IX, pp. 80–84. The whole scheme was debated in the South's most prominent journal. See William M. Burwell, "Science and the Mechanic Arts Against Coolies," *De Bow's Review,* (July, 1869), pp. 557–571; A.P. Merrill, "Southern Labor," *Ibid,* pp. 586–592; William M. Burwell, "The Cooley-ite Controversy," *Ibid.,* (August, 1869), pp. 709–724; "Our Chamber of Commerce—The Chinese Labor Question," *Ibid.,* pp. 669–701. For the character of Tye Kim Orr see Edward Jenkins, *The Coolie—His Rights and Wrongs,* New York: Routledge and Sons, 1871, pp. 114–116. For the Chinese reaction see the Testimony of T.H. King in *Report of the Joint Special Committee . . . op. cit.,* p. 93. For Koopmanschap see Gunther Barth, *Bitter Strength: A History of the Chinese in the United States, 1850–1870,* Cambridge: Harvard University Press,

1964, pp. 60, 117, 190–196. For a contemporary favorable account of Koopmanschap's Southern plan see "The Chinese Again," *Hunt's Merchants' Magazine,* LXI (September, 1869), pp. 214–217.

47. Chinese had appeared in Kansas in 1859. During the Reconstruction Period gangs of Chinese were employed in various kinds of work in several southern states. See Barth, *op. cit.,* pp. 187–198. For the Chinese in Mississippi see Robert W. O'Brien, "Status of Chinese in the Mississippi Delta," *Social Forces* 19 (March, 1941), pp. 386–390.

48. See, e.g., Barth, *op. cit.,* p. 189.

49. Patricia K. Ourada, "The Chinese in Colorado," *The Colorado Magazine* XXIX (October, 1952), pp. 273–283.

50. James J. O'Meara, "The Chinese in Early Days," *Overland Monthly,* IV (May, 1884), p. 477.

51. Mary R. Coolidge, *Chinese Immigration,* New York: Henry Holt, 1909, pp. 22–25.

52. Signs of racism and xenophobia had appeared earlier. The hostilities to Australians, Chileans, Mexicans, Peruvians and Pacific Islanders and the early attempts to bar Negroes from the State have been attributed, by one recent careful researcher, to the "respectable" American white middle class settlers' desire for "order." See Leonard Pitt, "The Beginnings of Nativism in California," *Pacific Historical Review* 30 (February, 1961), pp. 23–38. For a recent analysis of the Negro question in the West, see Eugene H. Berwanger, *The Frontier Against Slavery: Western Anti-Negro Prejudice and the Slavery Extension Controversy,* Urbana: University of Illinois Press, 1967. For an excellent example of California gubernatorial policy directed against the Negroes see "The First Annual Message of the Governor of California," December 21, 1849. *California Senate Journal. First Session.* 1849–1850, pp. 30–41.

53. For descriptions of Chinese miners see "Mining Life in California," *Harper's Weekly,* October 3, 1857, pp. 632–634; J.D. Borthwick, *Three Years in California,* Edinburgh and London: Blackwood, 1857, chapter 17.

54. See "Report of the Committee on Mines and Mining Interests," *Assembly Journal.* California State Legislature, 4th Session. 1853. *Appendix,* pp. 7–12; see also Coolidge, *op. cit.,* pp. 26–40.

55. See *People vs. Downer* 7 Cal. 169 (1857); *Lin Sing vs. Washburn,* 20 Cal. 534 (1863); *In re Ah Fong,* 3 Sawyer 144 (1874); *Chy Lung vs Freeman* 92 U.S. 275 (1876). See also Elmer C. Sandmeyer, "California Anti-Chinese Legislation and the Federal Courts: A Study in Federal Relations," *Pacific Historical Review,* 5 (September, 1936), pp. 189–211.

56. For the attack at Chinese Camp see Thedore Hittel, *History of California,* San Francisco: N.J. Stone, 1897, Vol. IV p. 102. The resolution against Chinese miners at Marysville will be found in the Marysville *Herald,* May 4, 1852.

57. *Sacramento Union,* May 2, 1852.

58. Charles Howard Shinn, *Mining Camps: A Study in American Frontier Government*, New York: Harper "Torchbooks," 1965. Originally published in 1884. (Edited by Rodman Wilson Paul), p. 246.

59. *Ibid.*, p. 248.

60. *Ibid.*, p. 213.

61. *Sacramento Union*, December 29, 30, 1858; March 5–10; July 16, 25, 1859. Coolidge, *op. cit.*, p. 255n.

62. "By 1859 the white miners had abandoned a large part of the American River, the original home of river mining, to the Chinese, and by the close of 1863 the Asiatics had inherited the greater part of the river claims throughout the state. The fact that the whites no longer desired the claims for themselves is conclusive evidence of the declining profitableness of this once great type of mining." Rodman W. Paul, *California Gold: The Beginning of Mining in the Far West*, Lincoln: University of Nebraska Press, 1947, p. 130. See also Rodman W. Paul, *Mining Frontiers of the Far West, 1848–1880*, New York: Holt, Rinehart, and Winston, 1963, pp. 35–36.

63. "How We Get Gold in California," *Harper's New Monthly Magazine*, April, 1860. Reprinted in Milo Miltin Quaife, *Pictures of Gold Rush California*, New York: Citadel, 1967, p. 197.

64. *Ibid.*, p. 199.

65. *Up and Down California in 1860–1861: The Journal of William H. Brewer*, Berkeley: University of California Press, 1966, pp. 329–330, 455, 481. (Edited by Francis P. Farquhar).

66. Helen Rocca Goss, "The Celestials," *Life and Death of a Quicksilver Mine*, Los Angeles: Historical Society of Southern California, 1958, pp. 63–86.

67. Rossiter W. Raymond, *Statistics of Mines and Mining in the States and Territories West of the Rocky Mountains*, Washington: Government Printing Office, 1872, p. 4. Quoted in Paul, *California Gold, op. cit.*, p. 322.

68. Paul, *California Gold, op. cit.*, pp. 329–330.

69. Lynwood Carranco, "Chinese Expulsion from Humboldt County," *Pacific Historical Review*, 30 (November, 1961), pp. 329–340.

70. Charlotte T. Miller, *Grapes, Queues, and Quicksilver*, unpublished manuscript in possession of the author.

71. Larry D. Quinn, " 'Chink Chink Chinaman': the Beginnings of Nativism in Montana," *Pacific Northwest Quarterly* 58 (April, 1967), pp. 82–89.

72. A circular recruiting labor in Hong Kong for Oregon in 1862 tells part of the story:

> To the countrymen of Au Chan! There are laborers wanted in the land of Oregon, in the United States, in America. There is much inducement to go to this new country, as they have many great works there which are not in our own country. They will supply good houses and plenty of food. They will pay you $28 a month after your arrival, and treat you considerately when you arrive. There is no fear of slavery. All is nice. The ship is now going and will take all who can pay their passage. The money required is $54. Persons having property can have it sold for them by correspondents, or borrow money of me upon security. I cannot take security on your children or your wife. Come to me in Hongkong and I will take care for you until you start. The ship is substantial and convenient.—(signed) Au Chan

Quoted in Rhoda Hoff, *America's Immigrants: Adventures in Eyewitness History*, New York: Henry Z. Walck, 1967, pp. 74–75. For the rise and decline of Chinese miners in Oregon see Rodman W. Paul, *Mining Frontiers . . . op. cit.*, p. 149.

73. *Ibid.*, pp. 143–144.

74. Rose Hum Lee, *The Chinese in the United States of America*, Hong Kong: Hong Kong University Press, 1960, pp. 189–190.

75. James M. Hulse, *The Nevada Adventure: A History*, Reno: University of Nevada Press, 1966, p. 79.

76. Dan DeQuille (Pseudonym for William Wright), *History of the Big Bonanza: An Authentic Account of the Discovery, History, and Working of the World Renowned Comstock Silver Lode of Nevada*, San Francisco: Hartford Publishing Co., A. L. Bancroft & Co., 1876. The section on Chinatown is reprinted in Robert Kirsch and William S. Murphy, *West of the West: Witnesses to the California Experience, 1542–1906*, New York: E. P. Dutton, 1967, pp. 409–411.

77. *The Chinese Massacre at Rock Springs, Wyoming Territory, September 2, 1885*, Boston: Franklin Press, Rand Avery and Co., 1886. For a debate over whether the Chinese "deserved" to be the victims of a riotous lynch mob see A.A. Sargent, "The Wyoming Anti-Chinese Riot," *Overland Monthly* VI (November, 1885), pp. 507–512 and J., " 'The Wyoming Anti-Chinese Riot'—Another View," *Overland Monthly*, VI (December, 1885), pp. 573–576.

78. Pierre Lamoureux, "Les Premieres Années de L'immigration Chinoise au Canada,". *Revue Canadienne de Geographie*, 9 (January–March, 1955), pp. 9–28.

79. Ormsby, *op. cit.*, pp. 167, 281.

80. Ted C. Hinckley, "Prospectors, Profits, and Prejudice," *The American West*, II (Spring, 1965). pp. 58–65.

81. *Tombstone Epitaph*, February 13, 1882. Quoted in Duane A. Smith, *Rocky Mountain Mining Camps: The Urban Frontier*, Bloomington: Indiana University Press, 1967, p. 31.

82. *Owyhee Avalanche*, June 23, 1866. Quoted in Smith, *op. cit.*, p. 32.

83. *Mountanian*, March 27, 1873. Quoted in Larry Barsness, *Gold Camp: Alder Gulch and Virginia City, Montana*, New York: Hastings House, 1962, p. 239.

84. *Governor's Message, Delivered to the Two Houses of the Montana Legislative Assembly at Virginia City*, December 11, 1869. Helena, 1869, p. 8. Quoted in Quinn, *op. cit.*, p. 83. Cf. "Special Message from the Governor of California to the Senate and Assembly of

California in Relation to Asiatic Emigrations," *California Senate Journal, Third Session.* April 23, 1852.

85. Springfield *Republican,* June 7, 1870; Boston *Transcript,* June 13, 1870; Boston *Commonwealth,* June 25, 1870; Boston *Investigator,* July 6, 1870. See also Frederick Rudolph, "Chinamen in Yakeedom: Anti-Unionism in Massachusetts," *American Historical Review,* 53 (October, 1947), pp. 1–29.

86. Albert Rhodes, "The Chinese at Beaver Falls," *Lippincott's Magazine,* 19 (June, 1877), pp. 708–714.

87. Cincinnati *Enquirer,* January 8, April 11, June 24, 1870; Cleveland *Leader,* June 6, 1870; *Ohio State Journal,* November 3, 1873. Quoted in Carl Wittke, *We Who Built America,* New York: Prentice-Hall, 1948, pp. 460–461.

88. Samuel Gompers, *Seventy Years of Life and Labor: An Autobiography,* New York: E.P. Dutton, 1925, Vol. I, pp. 216–217, 304–305; Vol. II, pp. 162–169. For Gompers' racism see Herbert Hill, "The Racial Practices of Organized Labor—the Age of Gompers and After," in Arthur Ross and Herbert Hill, (Editors), *Employment, Race, and Poverty: A Critical Study of the Disadvantaged Status of Negro Workers, from 1865 to 1965,* New York: Harcourt, Brace, and World, 1967, pp. 365–402.

89. Selig Perlman, *The History of Trade Unionism in The United States,* New York: Augustus Kelley, 1950, p. 52.

90. See Stanford M. Lyman, "Contrasts in the Community Organization of Chinese and Japanese in North America," *Canadian Review of Sociology and Anthropology* 5 (May, 1968), pp. 51–67.

91. For the Chinese in agriculture see Carey McWilliams, *Factories in the Fields: The Story of Migratory Farm Labor in California,* Boston: Little, Brown, 1939, pp. 66–88; McWilliams, *Southern California Country: an Island on the Land,* New York: Duell, Sloan, and Pearce, 1946, pp. 84–95; Ping Chiu, *Chinese Labor in California, 1850–1880,* Madison: State Historical Society of Wisconsin, 1963, pp. 67–88.

92. See Rose Hum Lee "The Decline of Chinatowns in the United States," *American Journal of Sociology,* (March, 1949), pp. 422–432.

93. For the Chinese in railroad work see Alexander Saxton, "The Army of Canton in the High Sierra," *Pacific Historical Review* XXXV (May, 1966) pp. 141–152. Chinese were also employed in digging the tunnels for California's vineyards; many were killed in tunnel collapses. They also worked as pickers of grapes, strawberries, cotton and other crops, and at a variety of other laboring and menial tasks. See A.W. Loomis, "How Our Chinamen Are Employed," *Overland Monthly,* (March, 1869), pp. 231–240; H.C. Bennett, "The Chinese in California, Their Numbers and Significance," *Sacramento Daily Union,* November 27, 1869, p. 8; Ping Chiu, *op. cit.,* pp. 40–128.

94. Testimony of the Hon. Frank M. Pixley, *Report of the Joint Special Committee . . . op. cit.,* p. 12.

95. See the table in Coolidge, *op. cit.,* p. 503.

96. The diaspora of Chinese since the sixteenth century has made Chinatown an ubiquitous phenomenon in countries of Asia, Africa, Europe, and Latin America. For some representative descriptions see Shelland Bradley "Calcutta's Chinatown," *Cornhill Magazine,* LVII (September, 1924), pp. 277–285; Tsien Tchehao. "La vie sociale des Chinois a Madagascar," *Comparative Studies in Society and History,* III (January, 1961), pp. 170–181; A. Dupouy, "Un Camp de Chinois," *Reveue de Paris,* 25 (November, 1919), pp. 146–162; P. Le Monnyer, "Les Chinois de Paris," *L'Illustration,* 82 (November 1, 1924), pp. 406–407; Christopher Driver, "The Tiger Balm Community," *The Guardian* (January 2, 1962); Ng Kwee Choo, *The Chinese in London,* London: Oxford University Press, 1968; Leonard Broom, "The Social Differentiation of Jamaica," *American Sociological Review* XIX (April, 1954), pp. 115–124.

97. See Maurice Freedman, *Lineage Organization in Southeastern China,* London: The Athlone Press, 1958 and Freedman, *Chinese Lineage and Society: Fukien and Kwangtung,* London: The Athlone Press, 1966.

98. "Whenever any persons having the same family name intermarry, the parties and the contractor of the marriage shall each receive 60 blows, and the marriage being null and void, the man and woman shall be separated, and the marriage-presents forfeited to government." Sir George Thomas Staunton, *Tsa Tsing Leu Lee: Being the Fundamental Laws and a Selection from the Supplementary Statutes of the Penal Code of China . . .* London, 1810, p. 114. Quoted in Freedman, *Lineage Organization . . . op. cit.,* p. 4n. Overseas this rule has been relaxed as more and more Chinese-Americans refuse to recognize an incest taboo that runs counter to that of the American kinship system. However, only a decade ago, one Chinese-American college student told me that his mother would be furious if she knew he was dating a girl with his own surname. Clan exogamy has been seen as one of the principal reasons for the decline of small, i.e., four clan, Chinatowns in the United States. Marriageable men migrate to the larger urban Chinese communities to have a greater choice in mate selection. See Rose Hum Lee, "The Decline of Chinatowns . . ." *op. cit.*

99. San Francisco Chinese Chamber of Commerce, *San Francisco's Chinatown, History, Function, and Importance of Social Organization,* San Francisco, 1953, pp. 2–4. Space does not permit a complex discussion of overseas clans. See Stanford M. Lyman, *The Structure of Chinese Society . . . op. cit.,* 164–178 and William Willmott, "Chinese Clan Associations in Vancouver," *Man* LXIV (March–April, 1964), pp. 33–37.

100. See Chinese Chamber of Commerce, *op. cit.,* p. 3. See also the discussion in Rose Hum Lee, *The Chinese in the United States of America, op. cit.,* pp. 136–137, 164–165, 264.

101. See Calvin Lee, *Chinatown, U.S.A.: A History and Guide,* Garden City: Doubleday, 1965, pp. 31–34. For the nature of

intra-clan disputes and disharmony see Milton L. Barnett, "Kinship as a Factor Affecting Cantonese Economic Adjustment in the United States," *Human Organization,* 19 (Spring, 1960), pp. 40–46.

102. The definitive work on the subject is Ping-ti Ho, *Chung-kuo hui-kuan shih-leuh.* [An Historical Survey of *Landsmannschaften* in China], Taipei: Student Publishing Co., 1966. For brief accounts see Ping-ti Ho, "Salient Aspects of China's Heritage," in Ping-ti Ho and Tang Tsou, (Editors), *China in Crisis: China's Heritage and the Communist Political System,* Chicago: University of Chicago Press, 1968, Vol. I, Book 1, pp. 34–35; and Francis L. K. Hsu, "Chinese Kinship and Chinese Behavior," *Ibid.,* Vol I, Book 2, pp. 588–589. See also D. J. Macgowan, "Chinese Guilds or Chambers of Commerce and Trades Unions," *Journal of the Royal Asiatic Society, North China Branch,* August 1886, pp. 133–192; and Hosea Ballou Morse, *The Gilds of China—with an account of the Gild Merchant or Co-Hong of Canton,* Shanghai: Kelly and Walsh, 1932.

103. See A.W. Loomis, "The Six Chinese Companies," *Overland Monthly,* New Series, 2 (September, 1868), pp. 221–227; William Speer, "Democracy of the Chinese," *Harper's Monthly,* XXXVII (November, 1868), pp. 844–846; Richard Hay Drayton, "The Chinese Six Companies," *The Californian Illustrated Magazine,* IV (August, 1893), pp. 472–477; Fong Kum Ngon (Walter N. Fong), "The Chinese Six Companies," *Overland Monthly,* (May 1894), pp. 519–526; Charles Frederick Holder, "The Dragon in America: Being an Account of the Workings of the Chinese Six Companies in America and its Population of the United States with Chinese," *The Arena,* XXXII (August, 1904), pp. 113–122; William Hoy, *The Chinese Six Companies,* San Francisco: Chinese Consolidated Benevolent Association, 1942; Tin-Yuke Char, "Immigrant Chinese Societies in Hawaii," *Sixty-First Annual Report of the Hawaiian Historical Society,* Honolulu: Advertiser Publishing Co., 1953, pp. 29–32; Chu Chai, "Administration of Law Among the Chinese in Chicago," *Journal of Criminal Law,* 22 (March, 1932), pp. 806–818.

104. See Rose Hum Lee, *The Chinese in the United States of America, op. cit.,* pp. 147–161; Calvin Lee, *op. cit.,* pp. 34–35. In Canada a crackdown on illegal immigration from Hong Kong and China led to a highly misleading article attacking the Chinese in racist innuendoes and accusing the Chinese Benevolent Association of complicity in the crimes. See Alan Phillips, "The Criminal Society that Dominates the Chinese in Canada," *Maclean's: Canada's National Magazine,* 75 (April 7, 1962), pp. 11, 42–44 and the letter from Stanford Lyman and William Willmott to the Editor in *Ibid.,* 75 (May 19, 1962), p. 6. Recently in San Francisco disaffected immigrant Chinese youth and disenchanted American-born youth have formed separate associations and publicly rebuked the Chinese Six Companies for their insensitivity in Chinatown. See the San Francisco *Chronicle,* March 18, 19, 1968. News of this effort is regularly reported in *East-West,* a San Francisco Journal published in Chinatown. For the New York community's social problems, see Stuart H. Cattel, *Health, Welfare, and the Social Organization in Chinatown* New York: Community Service Society, 1962, pp. 20–90.

105. The Six Companies aroused the ire of impoverished Chinese, a few missionaries, and an occasional sea captain for its ruthless and unstinting efforts to collect debts. See Otis Gibson, *The Chinese in America,* Cincinnati: Hitchcock and Walden, 1877, pp. 339–344; A.W. Loomis, "The Six Chinese Companies," *op. cit.,* p. 223; Testimony of Thomas H. King, *Report of the Joint Special Committee . . . op. cit.,* p. 95. It still collected debts from departing Chinese as late as 1942 and also required those returning to China to pay a departure fee. See Hoy, *op. cit.,* pp. 23–24.

106. In the following there is only a brief discussion of one of the most fascinating elements of overseas Chinese life. For a more complete discussion see Stanford M. Lyman, "Chinese Secret Societies in the Occident: Notes and Suggestions for Research on the Sociology of Secrecy," *Canadian Review of Sociology and Anthropology,* I (May, 1964), pp. 79–102.

107. Thomas Taylor Meadows, *op. cit.,* pp. 112–120. Sun Yatsen's relations with secret societies is described in S.Y. Teng, "Dr. Sun Yat-sen and Chinese Secret Societies," in Robert Sakai, (Editor), *Studies on Asia, 1963,* Lincoln: University of Nebraska Press, 1963, pp. 81–99; Sun Yat Sen, *Memoirs of a Chinese Revolutionary: A Programme of National Reconstruction for China,* London: Hutchinson & Co., n.d., pp. 184–224. See also James Cantlie and C. Sheridan Jones, *Sun Yat Sen and the Awakening of China,* New York: Fleming H. Revell, 1912, pp. 86–126; Stephen Chen and Robert Payne, *Sun Yat-sen: A Portrait,* New York: John Day, 1946, pp. 1–176; Marius B. Jansen, *The Japanese and Sun Yat-sen,* Cambridge: Harvard University Press, 1954, pp. 59–130; Shao Chuan Leng and Norman D. Palmer, *Sun Yat-sen and Communism,* London: Thames and Hudson, 1962, pp. 1–34; Paul Linebarger, *Sun Yat Sen and the Chinese Republic,* New York: Century, 1925, pp. 115–282; Mariano Ponce, *Sun Yat-sen: The Founder of the Republic of China,* Manila: Filipino-Chinese Cultural Foundation, 1965; Lyon Sharman, *Sun Yat-sen: His Life and its Meeting—a Critical Biography,* Hamden, Conn.: Archon, 1965, pp. 29, 61–64, 84–86, 97, 109, 113–114; Henry Bond Restarick, *Sun Yat Sen: Liberator of China,* New Haven: Yale University Press, 1931, pp. 11–108. Two post-1949 Chinese publications also speak of Dr. Sun's relations with secret societies: *Dr. Sun Yat-sen: Commemorative Articles and Speeches by Mao Tse-tung, Soong Ching Linn, Chou En-lai, and Others,* Peking: Foreign Languages Press, 1957, pp. 14–16, 70–72; Wu Yu-chang, *The Revolution of 1911: a Great Democratic Revolution of China,* Peking: Foreign Languages Press, 1962, pp. 16–30. For the communist suppression of secret societies see A. Doak Barnett, *China on the Eve of Communist Takeover,* New York: Praeger, 1963, pp. 83, 91–92, 126–129; Theodore H.E. Chen, *Thought Reform of the Chinese Intellectuals,* Hong Kong: Hong Kong University Press, 1960, pp. 108–111.

108. In addition to Leon Comber, *op. cit.,* see J.S.M. Ward and W.G. Stirling, *The Hung Society or the Society of Heaven and Earth,* London: Baskerville Press, 1925-6, 3 vols.; Mervyn Llewelyn Wynne, *Triad and Tabut: A Survey of the Origin and Diffusion of Chinese and Mohammedan Secret Societies in the Malay Peninsula, A.D. 1800–1935,* Singapore: Government Printing Office, 1941; J.M. Gul-

lick, *The Story of Early Kuala Lumpur,* Singapore: Donald Moore, 1956; J.M. Gullick, *A History of Selangor, 1742–1957,* Singapore: Eastern Universities Press, 1960, pp. 41–90; Maurice Freedman, "Immigrants and Associations: Chinese in Nineteenth-Century Singapore," *Comparative Studies in Society and History,* III (October, 1960), pp. 25–48; Song Ong Siang, *One Hundred Years' History of the Chinese in Singapore,* Singapore: University of Malaya Press, 1967; Chen Mock Hock, *The Early Chinese Newspapers of Singapore, 1881–1912,* Singapore: University of Malaya Press, 1967, pp. 46–47, 59–60, 82, 95–97, 119, 138–139.

109. Stanford M. Lyman, W.E. Willmott, and Berching Ho, "Rules of a Chinese Secret Society in British Columbia," *Bulletin of the School of Oriental and African Studies,* XXVII, 3 (1964) pp. 530–539.

110. See the three essays by Stewart Culin, "Chinese Secret Societies in the United States," *Journal of American Folk-Lore,* III (January–March, 1890), pp. 39–43; "The I Hing or 'Patriotic Rising,' A Secret Society Among the Chinese in America," *Report of the Proceedings of the Numismatic and Antiquarian Society of Philadelphia for the Years 1887–1889,* November 3, 1887, pp. 51–58; "The Gambling Games of the Chinese in America," *Publications of the University of Pennsylvania. Series in Philology, Literature, and Archaeology,* 1:4 (1891), pp. 1–17. For Dr. Sun's skepticism about the Chinese secret societies in America see Sun Yat Sen, *op. cit.,* pp. 190–191, 215; for his skepticism about those in Malaya see Chen Mock Hock, *op. cit.,* pp. 95–97n.

111. Alexander McLeod, *Pigtails and Gold Dust: A Panorama of Chinese Life in Early California,* Caldwell, Idaho: Caxton, 1947, pp. 149–150; Carl Glick, *Double Ten: Captain O'Banion's Story of the Chinese Revolution,* New York: Whittlesey House, 1945; Henry Bond Restarick, *op. cit.,* p. 103.

112. Information on Seto May-tong is from *An Appeal for the Contribution of Essays Celebrating the Eighty-first Birthday of Mr. Seto May-tong and for Monetary Gifts Serving as the Foundation Fund of the May-tong Memorial School,* (1948), a document in Chinese presented to the author by a former member of the *Chih-kung T'ang.*

113. *Chung-Kuo Hung-Mun Ming-Tse Tang Declaration, Political Outline, and Constitution,* Shanghai, September 1947; *The Declaration of Alliance of Middle Parties,* Shanghai and Nanking, February 21, 1948. These documents are in possession of the author.

114. See Stanford M. Lyman, "Chinese Secret Societies . . ." *op. cit.,* pp. 99–100.

115. Calvin Lee, *op. cit.,* pp. 34–37.

116. Sixteenth Census of the United States, "Characteristics of the Non-white Population by Race," p. 7; "Race by Nativity and Sex for the United States, 1850–1940," p. 19; Seventeenth Census of the United States, "Non-white Population by Race," p. 3B–19. See also Coolidge, *op. cit.,* p. 502.

117. United States Population Census, 1960, "Non-white Population by Race." *Final Report,* PC (2)-1C. Washington, D.C., 1963, p. 4.

118. Two settlements of Chinese—one in Trinidad in 1806–1814, the other in Hawaii in 1852—foundered because of the failure of Chinese women to join the men in the overseas venture. See Eric Williams, *History of the People of Trinidad and Tobago,* Port-of-Spain: PNM Publishing Co., 1962, p. 77 and Ralph S. Kuykendall, *The Hawaiian Kingdom: Foundation and Transformation, 1778–1854,* Honolulu: University of Hawaii Press, 1957, p. 329.

119. See Stanford M. Lyman, "Marriage and the Family Among Chinese Immigrants to America, 1850–1960," *Phylon Quarterly,* 29 (Winter, 1968), pp. 321–330.

120. Freedman, *Lineage Organization . . . op. cit.,* pp. 19–20, 32, 101–105. There was much variation in practice. See Freedman, *Chinese Lineage and Society . . . op. cit.,* pp. 43–67. See also Wen Yen Tsao, "The Chinese Family from Customary Law to Positive Law," *Hastings Law Journal,* 17 (May, 1966), pp. 727–765.

121. For a good fictional account see James A. Michener, *Hawaii,* New York: Random House, 1959, pp. 399–401.

122. The remittances continued well into the twentieth century and were a principal element of the Republican economy. See Arthur N. Young, *China and the Helping Hand, 1937–1945,* Cambridge: Harvard University Press, 1963, pp. 79, 178, 262–263. From July, 1937 to December, 1941 the Chinese Overseas Affairs Commission reported receipt of $61,985 from the United States. Chinese Ministry of Information, (compiler), *China Handbook, 1937–1943: A Comprehensive Survey of Major Developments in China in Six Years of War,* New York: Macmillan, 1943, p. 37.

123. See Paul C.P. Siu, *op. cit.,* pp. 35–41. See also Paul C.P. Siu, "The Isolation of the Chinese Laundryman," in Ernest W. Burgess and Donald Bogue, *Contributions to Urban Sociology,* Chicago: University of Chicago Press, 1964, pp. 429–442.

124. A good example is found in a United States Government report: "The Chinese coolie seldom or never removes his wife or family from his original domicile. They are left to represent his home interest with his ancestral divinities. The women are still less inclined to travel than the men. Without any education or mental development, Chinese females cherish exaggerated terrors of the fierce 'outside barbarians,' and of the tempestuous seas. A number of high class females have arrived in this country, the wives of intelligent merchants and business men, whose belief in the popular creed is not more profound than that which the ancient philosophers cherished for the classic mythology; but of the laboring classes it is believed that not à single instance of this character has yet been reported . . . It is evident, that with the Chinese female immigration already secured, no permanent family organization can be expected, and that consequently the Chinese race will not be propagated in this country. Their continuance as part of our population is then limited to the natural life of the immigrant." "Chinese Labor in Agriculture," *U.S. Department of Agriculture Reports:* 1870, pp. 573–574.

125. *Case of the Chinese Wife,* 21 Fed. 785 (1884); Huang Tsen-ming, *op. cit.,* pp. 84–85.

126. Timothy J. Molloy, "A Century of Chinese Immigration: A Brief Review," *Monthly Review of the United States Immigration and Naturalization Service,* V (December, 1947), pp. 69–75.

127. From a silver mining camp in Nevada in 1869 comes a terrible incident: "None were treated as beastly as the Chinese women from the brothels. One prostitute tried to run away from her owner and hide in the hills, but she was finally captured and held prisoner. Living in the open, exposed to the elements during her brief period of freedom, she had frozen both feet. The flesh fell away from the bones before her master asked admission to the hospital for her and then both feet had to be amputated. Although the wounds healed rapidly, the patient courted death, refusing to take medicine or food. She was eventually returned to the home of her owner to pass into oblivion without a protest from society." W. Turrentine Jackson, *Treasure Hill: Portrait of a Silver Mining Camp,* Tucson: University of Arizona Press, 1963, p. 65.

128. Horace Greeley, "California Mines and Mining," Sacramento, August 7, 1859, in Horace Greeley, *An Overland Journey: From New York to San Francisco in the Summer of 1859,* New York: Knopf, 1964, pp. 245–246 (Edited by Charles T. Duncan).

129. Henryk Sienkiwicz, *Portrait of America,* New York: Columbia University Press, 1959, p. 255.

130. A.W. Loomis, "Chinese Women in California," *Overland Monthly,* 3 (April, 1869), pp. 344–351; Charles Frederick Holder, "Chinese Slavery in America," *North American Review,* 165 (July, 1897), pp. 288–294; Louis J. Beck, *New York's Chinatown: An Historical Presentation of its People and Places,* New York: Bohemia Publishing Co., 1898, pp. 107–121; Carol Green Wilson, *Chinatown Quest: The Life Adventures of Donaldina Cameron,* Stanford: Stanford University Press, 1950.

131. The situation might have been mitigated if Chinese had been able to intermarry into the white population. In other areas of Chinese settlement, such as Indonesia, Chinese did intermarry. (See Donald Earl Willmott, *The Chinese of Semarang: A Changing Minority Community in Indonesia,* Ithaca: Cornell University Press, 1960, pp. 103–116). However, in the United States, racial intermarriage has been illegal in thirty-nine states. In fourteen of these states the law specifically prohibited marriage between Chinese or "Mongolians" and whites. California's anti-miscegenation statute was originally enacted in 1872 to prohibit marriage between Negroes or mulattoes; in 1906 it was amended to prohibit marriages between whites and "Mongolians." See Huang Tsen-ming, *op. cit.,* pp. 260–262; Fowler V. Harper and Jerome Skolnick, *Problems of the Family,* Indianapolis: Bobbs Merrill, 1962, pp. 96–99; *Perez vs. Sharp,* 32 Cal. 711 (2nd Ser.), 1948; Andrew D. Weinberger, "A Reappraisal of the Constitutionality of 'Miscegenation' Statutes," in Ashley Montagu, *Man's Most Dangerous Myth: The Fallacy of Race,* Cleveland: Meridian Books, World Publishing Co., 1964, pp. 402–424.

132. Remigio B. Ronquillo, "The Administration of Law Among the Chinese in Chicago," *Journal of Criminal Law,* 25 (July, 1934), pp. 205–224.

133. Jacob A. Riis, *How the Other Half Lives: Studies Among the Tenements of New York,* New York: Sagamore Press, 1957, p. 76.

134. Frank Soule, John H. Gihon, and James Nisbet, *The Annals of San Francisco,* Palo Alto: Lewis Osborne, 1966, pp. 411–412. (Originally published in 1855).

135. Samuel Wells Williams, "The City of the Golden Gate," *Scribner's Monthly,* X (July, 1875), pp. 272–273.

136. Frank Soule, John H. Gihon, and James Nisbet, *op. cit.,* pp. 378–379.

137. *California Senate Journal. Third Session.* 1852. pp. 168, 192, 205, 217.

138. "Minority Report of the Select Committee on Senate Bill No. 63 . . ." *California Senate Journal. Third Session. Appendix* March 20, 1852, p. 671.

139. Ping Chiu, *op. cit.,* pp. 89–128.

140. See James Bryce, "Kearneyism in California," *The American Commonwealth,* New York: The Macmillan Co., 1901, Vol. II, pp. 425–448, and "Appendix," pp. 878–880. See also Doyce B. Nunis, Jr., "The Demagogue and the Demographer: Correspondence of Denis Kearney and Lord Bryce," *Pacific Historical Review* XXXVI (August, 1967), pp. 269–288.

141. See Philip S. Foner, *Mark Twain: Social Critic,* New York: International Publishers, 1958, pp. 182–192.

142. Morton Keller, *The Art and Politics of Thomas Nast,* New York: Oxford University Press, 1968, pp. 217–242.

143. Philip S. Foner, *The Life and Writings of Frederick Douglass, Vol. IV: Reconstruction and After,* New York: International Publishers, 1955, pp. 46, 222, 262–266, 282, 339, 349, 352, 385, 440.

144. See Leon Litwack, *North of Slavery: The Negro in the Free States, 1790–1860,* Chicago: University of Chicago Press, 1965, pp. 167–168.

145. See Forrest G. Wood, *Black Scare: The Racist Response to Emancipation and Reconstruction,* Berkeley: University of California Press, 1968, pp. 97–101.

146. Bryce, *op. cit.,* Vol. II, p. 880.

147. *The Workingmen's Party of California,* San Francisco: Bacon and Co., 1878. Quoted in N. Ray Gilmore and Gladys Gilmore, (Editors), *Readings in California History,* New York: Thomas Y. Crowell, 1966, pp. 200–203.

148. Testimony of Frank M. Pixley in *Report of the Joint Special Committee . . . op. cit.,* p. 22.

149. Coolidge, *op. cit.,* p. 259.

150. C.P. Dorland, "Chinese Massacre at Los Angeles in 1871," *Annual Publication of the Historical Society of Southern California,* Los Angeles, 1894, pp. 22–26.

151. Coolidge, *op. cit.,* p. 265–266; Oscar Lewis, *San Francisco: Mission to Metropolis,* Berkeley: Howell-North, 1966, pp. 136–139.

152. Patricia K. Ourada, *op. cit.*

153. B.P. Wilcox, "Anti-Chinese Riots in Washington," *Washington Historical Quarterly,* 20 (July, 1929), pp. 204–212; Jules Alexander Karlin, "The Anti-Chinese Outbreaks in Seattle, 1885–1886," *Pacific Northwest Quarterly,* XXXIX (April, 1948), pp. 103–130; Karlin, "The Anti-Chinese Outbreak in Tacoma, 1885," *Pacific Historical Review,* 23 (August, 1954), pp. 271–283; Murray Morgan, *Skid Road: An Informal Portrait of Seattle,* New York: Viking, 1960, pp. 84–102.

154. Alan Morley, *Vancouver: From Milltown to Metropolis,* Vancouver: Mitchell Press, 1961 pp. 121–126.

155. Eliot Lord, *Comstock Mining and Miners,* Berkeley: Howell-North, 1959, pp. 355–359 (Originally Published in 1883); Coolidge, *op. cit.,* pp. 254–277; Lewis, *op. cit.,* pp. 139–140; Vardis Fisher and Opal Laurel Holmes, *Gold Rushes and Mining Camps of the Early American West,* Caldwell, Idaho: Caxton Printers, 1968, pp. 262–265, 272–273.

156. *In re Tiburcio Parrot,* 6 Sawyer 349 (1879); *In re Ah Chong,* 6 Sawyer 451 (1880); *In re Lee Sing,* 43 Fed. 359 (1890).

157. See *Soon Hing vs. Crowley,* 113 U.S. 713 (1880); *People vs. Soon Kung,* unreported (1874); *People vs. Ex Parte Ashbury* reported in *Daily Alta Californian,* February 5, 1871; *Yick Wo vs. Hopkins* 118 U.S. 356 (1885).

158. Fisher and Holmes, *op. cit.,* pp. 263–264; Rose Hum Lee, *The Chinese in the United States of America, op. cit.,* p. 267.

159. Coolidge, *op. cit.,* pp. 72–73; *Takahashi vs. Fish and Game Commission of California,* 334 U.S. 410 (1947).

160. *Terrace vs. Thompson,* 263 U.S. 197 (1923); *Porterfield vs. Webb,* 263 U.S. 255 (1923); *Webb vs. O'Brien,* 263 U.S. 313 (1923); *Frick vs. Webb,* 263 U.S. 326 (1923); *Mott vs. Cline,* 200 Cal. 434 (1927); *Morrison vs. California,* 291 U.S. 82 (1934); *Oyama vs. California,* 322 U.S. 633 (1927); *Sei Fuji vs. State of California,* 242 P2nd 617 (1952).

161. See *Report of the Immigration Commission. Immigrants in Industry. Japanese and other Immigrant Races in the Pacific Coast and Rocky Mountain States.* United States Congress. Senate. 61st Congress, 2nd Session. Senate Document 633, Vol. III, Washington, D.C.: Government Printing Office 1911, pp. 411–413.

162. *The Invalidity of the Queue Ordinance, op. cit., Appendix,* pp. 15–43; *Ho Ah Kow vs. Matthew Nunan,* 5 Sawyer 552 (1879); Sandmeyer, *op. cit.,* pp. 54–55.

163. *People vs. Hall,* 4 California 399 (1854); *Speer vs. See Yup,* 13 California 73 (1885); *People vs. Elyea,* 14 California 144 (1855).

164. Quoted in William Warren Ferrier, *Ninety Years of Education in California, 1846–1936,* Berkeley: Sather Gate Book Shop, 1937, p. 98.

165. Ferrier, *op. cit.,* pp. 98–104. *Wong Hin vs. Callahan* 119 Fed. 381 (1902).

166. *Gong Lum vs. Rice* 275 U.S. 78 (1927).

167. See, e.g., Cameron H. King Jr., "Asiatic Exclusion," *International Socialist Review,* 8 (May, 1908), pp. 661–669. A few exceptions to the general anti-Chinese sentiment of organized labor were found among the "radicals" who organized the International Workers of the World, The United Mine Workers of British Columbia, and the American Labor Union. The division among labor unions on "The Chinese Question" is documented in Philip S. Foner, *History of the Labor Movement in the United States,* New York: International Publishers, 1957–1965, Vol. I: *From Colonial Times to the Founding of the American Republic,* pp. 425–428, 488–493; Vol II: *From the Founding of the American Federation of Labor to the Emergence of American Imperialism,* pp. 58–60, 204–205; Vol. III: *The Policies and Practices of the American Federation of Labor, 1900–1909,* pp. 274–279, 426–429; Vol IV: *The Industrial Workers of the World, 1905–1917,* pp. 81–82, 123–124.

168. Robert Seagar II, "Some Denominational Reactions to Chinese Immigration to California," *Pacific Historical Review,* February, 1959, pp. 49–66.

Marriage and the Family among Chinese Immigrants to America, 1850–1960

WHETHER OR NOT an immigrant group established families in America had a profound effect on its subsequent community organization and acculturation. The single male or the husband who had left his wife behind evaluated the host country primarily in terms of its economic opportunities and estimated the time and effort required to earn enough money to return home. The estimates often proved to be woefully incorrect,[1] but so long as the immigrant country held out promise, the immigrant remained a sojourner, or a bird-of-passage,[2] saving his hard-earned cash and remitting what he could spare to wife and loved ones at home.[3] A homeless man while overseas, the immigrant depended on his compatriots and his associational ties for help when in need of protection and friendship. To the extent of his needs the association commanded his allegiance, respect, and obedience.

The immigrant who brought a wife with him or sent for her later was in a different position. Although he might continue to regard himself as a sojourner, the longer he and his family remained abroad the stronger their roots in the immigrant country would be implanted. Should his children be born and reared in the host country, his stake there was even more firmly established.[4] The children spoke the language of the immigrant country, attended its schools, accepted its customs and mores as their own, and unless disabused by experiences of their own, regarded their father's homeland as more foreign than the country of their own birth.[5] Moreover, the establishment of conjugal and domestic life by an immigrant served to loosen his dependence on immigrant associations. Sexual gratification, companionship, and help became more of a family and less of an organizational affair for the married immigrant. To the extent of his marital commitment, he was isolated from the pressures of external organizations and relieved of his obligations to them. By the same token the associations diminished in importance and were reduced in power as their domestic and hedonistic functions were assumed by the family.

Similar in composition to most peoples migrating to a frontier society,[6] the sex ratio of the Chinese and Japanese was unbalanced. The number of males far exceeded that of females. However, the Chinese and Japanese tended to respond to the shortage of women in quite different ways. The Japanese came less and less to depend on their mutual aid societies as they founded families in America. The Chinese, living in enforced bachelorhood, required the special services of *Landsmannschaften* and secret societies to satisfy their social and sexual needs.

So few Chinese women came to the United States that not even a near numerical equality in the sexes was achieved until the middle of the twentieth century. During the entire period of unrestricted immigration (1850–1882) a total of only 8,848 Chinese women journeyed across the Pacific. Many of the women could not withstand the rigors of life in America and died or returned to China. By 1890 only 3,868 Chinese women were reported to be in the country. During the same period the number of Chinese men emigrating from China to America was much larger. The census reported 33,149 male Chinese in 1860; 58,633 in 1870; 100,686 in 1880; 102,620 in 1890; 85,341 in 1900. Between 1860 and 1900 the ratio of Chinese males per 100 Chinese females was alarmingly high: 1,858 in 1860; 1,284 in 1870; 2,106 in 1880; 2,678 in 1890; and 1,887 in 1900.[7]

As the decennial census reports indicate, the imbalance in the sex ratio among Chinese was slowly reduced during the first half of the twentieth century. By 1920, despite the birth of a few females among the Chinese immigrants, the males still far outnumbered the females: for every 100 women there were more than 695 men. By 1960 the situation had been only partially mitigated. The total number of males had climbed to 135,430, but the number of females was only 100,654.[8] The low number of females among the Chinese has been one of the most important facts shaping their personal, social, and community life. It is hardly possible to speak of a conjugal family life for most Chinese men in the United States until after the third decade of the twentieth century.

The settlement abroad by Chinese men unaccompanied by wives or sweethearts was not confined to the United States. Chinese communities in the Straits Settlements, New Zealand, and Thailand were also conspicuous by their superfluity of males.[9]

In Trinidad an early experiment in Chinese immigration foundered on the shortage of women.

> In 1806, 147 Chinese workers arrived in Trinidad, followed by a further 192 in the same year. But the following year thirty or forty applied for permission to return to China . . . One of the difficulties was that Chinese women did not accompany the workers, and the free women of colour in Trinidad, it was alleged, considered themselves superior to the Chinese who, though free in name, were performing the work of slaves. So the Governor reported in 1807 . . . By 1814 the hopes placed on China had failed. Those who remained, about thirty in number, were regarded as useful fishermen and butchers. Had they, in the Governor's opinion, brought with them wives and families and priests, they would have been a very valuable addition to the Trinidad population.[10]

Chinese custom and family law required that a wife remain in the home of her husband's parents even if her husband had to seek work elsewhere. Should his parents die in his absence the wife was expected to perform the burial and mourning rites in place of her husband. Village headmen often secured an emigrant's loyalty to his village by requiring that he marry before he depart and that he remit money regularly for support of his wife, family, and the village community.[11] Overseas, the *Landsmannschaften* often assumed the obligation of collecting the remittances from the laboring immigrants and sending them to the appropriate villages in China.[12] When, in 1884, a United States federal court ruling made it impossible for any Chinese woman except the wife of a Chinese merchant or other member of the classes exempted under the Chinese Exclusion Act to enter the country,[13] it enforced and exacerbated with American law the Chinese practice, already widespread among immigrants, of requiring wives and sweethearts to remain in China while their husbands and fiances worked abroad.

Although exact statistical evidence is unavailable to verify the fact, it appears that at least half of the Chinese men who came to America were married.[14] Many others were young single men at the time of their arrival in America, but, having acquired a small amount of money, returned to China, married, and remigrated back to America without their wives.[15]

With the exception of the small but affluent and powerful merchant class, most of the Chinese remained absentee husbands while in America, "The Chinese coolie seldom or never removes his wife or family from his original domicile," reported a federal agricultural release in 1870. "They are left to represent his home interest with his ancestral divinities. The women are still less inclined to travel than the men." The report goes on to explain that, "Without any education or mental development, Chinese females cherish exaggerated terrors of the fierce 'outside barbarians,' and of the tempestuous seas." However, "A number of higher-class Chinese females have arrived in this country, the wives of intelligent merchants and businessmen . . ."[16] In 1892, some credence was given to the allegedly "exaggerated terrors" that Chinese females supposedly felt about Americans. Mary Chapman reported, "Very few of Boston's Chinese have brought their wives and families, largely because they are unwilling to expose their families to the persecutions which they themselves have suffered. The women are not anxious to come."[17] But whether or not they were moved by traditional custom or motivated by fears for their safety, Chinese laborers could not legally bring their wives to America after 1884. In the few changes made in the laws before they were all repealed in 1943 and a quota system established, what liberalizations were granted were applied almost exclusively to wives and offsprings of merchants and other classes exempted in the exclusion law of 1882 and to the Chinese wives of certain American citizens.[18]

The few Chinese wives who did join their husbands in America were usually married to merchants or to those who could assume the legal status of merchants. They were kept in seclusion by their husbands and seldom ventured forth alone into the Chinese community and almost never beyond it into that of white America. "No virtuous and respectable Chinese woman, whether married or single, is ever permitted to show herself in public," wrote a careful observer of New York's Chinese quarter in 1898: "Especially is the wife thus carefully excluded from view, except to those of her own sex; and if she

has occasion to visit another woman every precaution must be taken to avoid observation. Usually a closed carriage is employed to convey her, even though the distance be less than a block away."[19]

The shortage of women among the Chinese immigrants to America might have been mitigated if Chinese had had the opportunity to intermarry with the native white population. In other areas of Chinese settlement intermarriage has occurred and has had a profound effect on Chinese community organization and family life. In Semarang, Indonesia, for example, Chinese immigrants took wives from the Indonesian women; their progeny are known as *Peranakans* and are usually distinguished from the ethnically and culturally Chinese *Totoks*.[20] But very few Chinese in America intermarried. The mutual peculiarities of dress, language, habits, customs, and diets, not to mention the physical distinctiveness of both racial identities kept Chinese and Americans apart. In addition, both Americans and Chinese have tended to enclose themselves in mutually exclusive associations, thus reducing the amount of personal contact to a minimum and severely restricting the possibility for romantic attachments to arise. In California and elsewhere the practice, begun in 1860 and continued long into the twentieth century, of segregating schools,[21] churches, and youth associations[22] according to race, further reduced contact between the two peoples. Moreover, anti-miscegenation laws made marriages between Chinese and Caucasians illegal in many states, the District of Columbia, and the Virgin Islands. In Maryland and North Carolina the prohibition on intermarriage extended to members of two different nonwhite races. Thirty-nine states at one time prohibited intermarriage between whites and other races, and in 1962 twenty-one states still had such laws in force. In fourteen states the laws specifically designated Chinese or "Mongolians" as ineligible to marry whites.[23]

Thus, for the bulk of Chinese immigrants, the establishment of a family in America was impossible. They lived the lives of homeless men and resorted to meeting their sex and social needs through the services of certain community organizations. The superfluity of males in the Chinese communities overseas and the inaccessibility of native women had as their inevitable sequel the establishment of prostitution. Before the turn of the century the Chinatowns of America's cities were honeycombed with brothels. Other recreations also were established in Chinatown—places where opium might be purchased and smoked, and gambling halls. Control over prostitution, opium selling, and gambling did not long remain in the hands of individual entrepreneurs, but passed quickly under the domination of several rival secret societies which had emerged in Chinatown.

In rural areas prostitution among the Chinese was a more personal and disorganized affair. "Very few bring wives with them," wrote Henryk Sienkiwicz in 1880 in one of his letters from America, "and for that reason it so happens that when among ten Chinese occupying a dwelling there is but one woman, they all live together with her. I encountered such examples of polyandry quite frequently, particularly in the country."[24] Horace Greeley, visiting the gold diggings in California in 1859, grasped the excessive burden the lonely Chinese faced: "[He] has no family here (the few Chinese women brought to this country being utterly shameless and abandoned), so that he forms no domestic ties, and enjoys no social standing."[25]

In the cities of America where thousands of Chinese men congregated in congested ghettos, prostitution and concubinage were carried on as a business under the ownership or control of secret societies. From China young girls were brought to America after they had been kidnapped from their home villages, sold by their impoverished parents, captured by pirates or raiding bands, or lured abroad by a meretricious promise of proxy marriage. Once having arrived in North America, they were placed under contract to individual Chinese or, more often, to brothels in the Chinese quarter. They might be sold and resold again and again. Younger girls might be used as domestics while older ones were used to satisfy the sex needs of homeless men of Chinatown. Some of these girls found a way to escape the dreaded life into which they had been

cast by seeking asylum among the missionaries who served Chinatown; others became concubines or second wives to already married but lonely Chinese men and hoped to enjoy the status accorded to a concubine when their man returned to China; still a few others found love among one of their patrons and married in America. Many, however, were unable to escape and lived a life that was as brutish as it was short.[26]

Control over the provision of sex and recreation to a community of womanless men provided those who had it with wealth and power. Evidence of the importance of this domination over illicit services is documented in the vigorous and unstinting opposition which the secret societies offered to those who sought to undermine vice in Chinatown or take control of it away from them. The kidnapping of a girl from a brothel by her sweetheart or a rival society was likely to bring on a violent fight. Police were bribed to look the other way with respect to brothel operations. When missionary societies actively sought to end the trade and use of "slave girls" in Chinatown, they were met by counteraction in courts. Astute attorneys, perjured testimony, and purposefully misleading translations by Chinese interpreters sometimes secured the release of a girl from the mission to which she had fled and forced her return to a brothel or to her former owner.[27]

Prostitution and its attendant opportunities for affluence and community power continued well into the twentieth century. In Chicago's Chinatown, for example, an observer noted in 1934, "there are only about 40 women . . . One can imagine the social problem involved . . . the owner of the prostitution house owns the victims and pays tax to the tong which delivered the girls, and gives to the owner, protection."[28]

The extreme imbalance in the sex ratio among the Chinese also meant that the birth and maturation of a substantial American-born generation was delayed. In 1890, forty years after Chinese had begun to migrate to the United States, the American-born Chinese constituted only 2.7 percent of the Chinese population in America. In 1920 this had risen to 30 percent, but it was not until 1950 that the American-born Chinese came to be more than half of the total Chinese population in America. The 1960 census indicated that 93,288 or more than 35 percent of the total Chinese population in the United States, was foreign-born.[29]

It was the habit of the Chinese migrant to return to China periodically, visit his wife, sire a child, hopefully a son, and then return to America alone.[30] Later, these China-born sons would be brought to America and asked to help out in and eventually take over the father's business.[31] If the immigrant father had acquired American citizenship—which was possible in a few instances before 1882 and again after 1943, but not in the intervening period— he might bestow derivative United States citizenship upon his China-born son and effect his entry to the United States legally. In other instances, entry might be effected illegally. A few have been able to claim derivative citizenship meretriciously and enter the country; others entered as "slots;" i.e., as "sons" of a "paper Chinese father" legally eligible to bring his children to the United States.[32]

The China-born sons found themselves estranged both from their fathers (real or "paper") and from the American environment in which they found themselves. However, their financial straits and—if they were illegal entries—their security from detection and deportation depended on their seclusion and protection within Chinatown. Thus, many of them were forced to become part of the heavily exploited work force of the Chinatown shops, restaurants, and factories and also to maintain obedience to their kinsmen—actual or fictitious—and to the associations that provided mutual aid and defense.[33] In 1956, a federal grand jury was presented an affidavit from a lawyer for the Retail Clerks International Union charging that fifty Chinese employees of Chinese-owned supermarkets in Yuba City, California, had been forced to work ten hours per day, six days a week and to "kick back" an estimated $265,000 from their wages to their four employers between 1951 and 1954. The affidavit went on to assert that the fifty Chinese employees "were confined to barracks-like quarters and prevented from leading a normal life."[34] A study

conducted in San Francisco and Oakland found that the newly arrived sons were disillusioned by the contrast between their fathers' ostentatious affluence and largesse when they had visited in China and their isolation and poverty in Chinatown. Moreover, the status of the sons fell sharply when they arrived in Chinatown. Their poor English and lack of specialized skills, not to mention local job discrimination, distinguished them sharply from their American-born peers and kept them inside Chinatown. The married sons were unable to effect the entry of their wives; the affianced were required to marry their fiancees before the latter could enter the United States; the single, unattached men could not find suitable mates. "As a result, a large number of idle and malcontented youth roamed the streets, sulked at home, or disturbed the community with their antics and unsocial behavior."[35]

The long womanless condition of the Chinese in America is one of the most profound and least discussed factors affecting Chinese communities and acculturation. With the vast Pacific Ocean separating him from domestic joys and companionship, the Chinese sojourner relied on the tong-controlled brothels for sex, attended the gambling and opium dens for recreation and respite from the day's toil, and paid homage and allegiance to his clansmen, *Landsmänner,* and fraternal brothers to secure mutual aid, protection and a job. Unable to procreate and rear children in America, the homeless sojourner watched helplessly as his estranged China-born sons followed in his footsteps and fell into the established Chinatown way of life. At the turn of the century, above the chorus of Sinophobic voices debating "the Chinese question," a compassionate journalist, himself an immigrant, boldly stated the heart of the matter:

This is a time for plain speaking on this subject. Rather than banish the Chinaman, I would have the door opened wider—for his wife; make it a condition of his coming or staying that he bring his wife with him. Then, at least, he might not be what he now is and remains, a homeless stranger among us. Upon this hinges the real Chinese question, in our city at all events, as I see it.[36]

Notes

1. The distinguished historian, Hosea Ballou Morse, recounts:

> An incident which occurred to the author in 1893 throws some light on the usual result of a returned Chinese emigrant. At a railway station in Formosa he was addressed in fluent and correct English by the proprietor-cook of the station restaurant; and in answer to an expression of astonishment, the Chinese explained why he was there. He had returned from California with a fortune of $2,000. He had first to disburse heavily to remain unmolested by the magistrate and his underlings; then he had to relieve the necessities of his aged father; then an uncle, who had fallen into business difficulties, must be rescued from impending bankruptcy; and then he found he had only enough to procure himself a wife, with a few dollars margin wherewith to establish himself in his present business, which at most would require $100 capital.

The International Relations of the Chinese Empire, The Period of Submission, 1861–1893 (Taipei, n.d.), p. 199n.

2. "Upwards of 800 Chinese have returned from California," wrote an emigration officer at Hong Kong in 1853. "They appeared all of them to have plenty of money and stated their intention of returning to California . . . The return of Chinese under such favorable circumstances must naturally stimulate emigration to that quarter . . ." Letter of J. T. White, Hong Kong, December 26, 1853. Cited in *ibid.*, p. 166n.

3. In British Columbia the author interviewed a Chinese hermit who had lived in the province for over sixty years and had made but one return trip to China, forty-five years before the interview, to get married. He had sired a son but left China to return to Canada before he was born. Although he had not seen his wife in over four decades and had never seen his son, he continued to remit money to them and hoped one day soon to return to China.

The total remittances of all overseas Chinese rose to $1,328,-610,000 in 1940 according to China's Overseas Affairs Commission. "A Survey of Chinese Emigration," *International Labor Review,* LX (September, 1949), 293. Between 1937 and 1940 "no less than $2,000,000,000 had been sent by the overseas Chinese to their families in China." Chinese Ministry of Information. *China Handbook, 1937–1943* (New York, 1943), p. 38.

For a sociological discussion of the overseas Chinese migrant as a social type see Paul C. P. Siu, "The Sojourner," *American Journal of Sociology,* LVIII (July, 1952), 33–34.

4. The author has been told of cases where American-born Japanese children granted the wish of their aged parents and helped finance their return to Japan to spend their last days in the land of their birth only to have the parents return to America after a short stay in Japan and acknowledge that the United States is in truth their home.

5. Among the first immigrant Japanese parents it was a practice to send the eldest or youngest son to Japan for education and then to have him return to America. The psychological and social problems of these returned Japanese, *Kibei,* as they are called, were severe. Many found that they were estranged from their parents and peers alike. Truly marginal men, they were products of two cultures and members of neither.

6. See, *e.g.,* Rodman Wilson Paul, *Mining Frontiers of the Far West, 1848–1880* (New York, 1963), pp. 164–65, "Because of the dearth of ladies, men often devised impromptu dancing matches with their male companions in the saloons." W. Turrentine Jackson, *Treasure Hill: Portrait of a Silver Mining Camp* (Tucson, 1963), p. 76.

7. Mary Coolidge, *Chinese Immigration* (New York, 1909), p. 502; U. S. Department of Commerce, Bureau of the Census, *Sixteenth Census of the United States,* "Characteristics of the Non-white Population by Race," p. 7; "Race by Nativity and Sex for the United States: 1850–1940," p. 19; *Seventeenth Census of the United States,* "Non-white Population by Race," p. 3B–19.

8. U. S. Department of Commerce, Bureau of the Census, "Non-white Population by Race," 1960. Final Report PC (2)-1C (Washington, D. C.: 1963), p. 4.

9. The following table gives some representative figures:

Chinese in Selected Areas of Southeast Asia by Year and Sex

Area	Year	Total	Males	Females
Straits Settlements[a]	1881	86,766	75,571	14,195
New Zealand[b]	1906	2,570	2,515	55
Thailand[c]	1919	260,194	205,470	54,724
	1929	445,274	313,764	131,510
	1937	524,062	335,524	188,538
	1947	476,582	319,196	157,386

Sources: a: M. Freedman "Immigrants and Associations: Chinese in Nineteenth Century Singapore," *Comparative Studies in Society and History,* III (October, 1960), 26. b: Ng Bickleen Fong, *The Chinese in New Zealand* (Hong Kong, 1959), p. 28. c: R.J. Coughlin, *Double Identity: The Chinese in Modern Thailand* (Hong Kong, 1960), p. 23.

10. Eric Williams, *History of the People of Trinidad and Tobago* (Port of Spain, Trinidad, 1962), p. 77. The British bark *Thetis* brought 200 Chinese coolies to Hawaii in 1852. The Chinese proved satisfactory, but it was suggested that their wives should be brought with them. Ralph S. Kuykendall, *The Hawaiian Kingdom: Foundation and Transformation, 1778–1854* (Honolulu, 1957), p. 329.

11. James Michener has furnished his readers with a coldly realistic scene depicting the manner in which Chinese village leaders secured loyalty from departing emigrants:

> Chun Fat . . . said slowly . . . , "I want everyone who, for the honor of his family, has volunteered to go to the Fragrant Tree Country [Hawaii] to get married before he leaves this village. . . . You young travelers, like Mun Ki, must not think that because you are required to marry here in the Low Village that you may not also take wives in the new land. Oh no, indeed! There is only one

reason why you must get married here, and establish your home here, with your legal wife waiting patiently for your return. If you do these things, then no matter where you go, you will always think of this village as permanent home. You will yearn for the day when, like me, you stride up these sacred steps," and sweeping his expensive gown about him, he marched into the ancestral hall, from which he cried with real passion, "and you will bow humbly before the tablets of your ancestors. For your home is here. . . . When the white men abused me in California, I remembered this pavilion with my family tablets, and I gained strength to endure their abuse. When the snows were unbearable in Nevada, I remembered this ancestral hall, and they became endurable. Marry a girl from this valley, as I did thirty years ago. Leave her here with your home, and no matter where you go you will come back." Then, adding a more immediately practical note, he reminded them: "And you will always send money back to this village." *Hawaii* (New York, 1959), pp. 399–401.

See also Norman S. Hayner and Charles N. Reynolds, "Chinese Family Life in America," *American Sociological Review, II* (October, 1937), 630–37. Reprinted in Arnold Rose, ed., *Race Prejudice and Discrimination: Readings in Intergroup Relations in the United States* (New York, 1953), pp. 352–61.

12. Rose Hum Lee, *The Chinese in the United States of America* (Hong Kong, 1960), pp. 84–85, 111, 258, 358.

13. *Case of the Chinese Wife,* 21 Fed. 785 (1884). *United States vs. Mrs. Gue Lim,* 176 U. S. 459(1900).

14. Coolidge, *op. cit.,* pp. 17–20.

15. Stewart Culin, "China in America: Social Life of the Chinese in Eastern Cities of the United States" (Paper read before the American Association for the Advancement of Science, Section on Anthropology [Philadelphia, 1887], p. 7).

16. "Chinese Labor in Agriculture," U. S., Department of Agriculture, *Reports,* (1870), 573.

17. Mary Chapman, "Notes on the Chinese in Boston," *Journal of American Folk-lore, V* (October-December, 1892), 321.

18. Tin-Yuke Char, "Legal Restrictions on Chinese in English-Speaking Countries of the Pacific," *Chinese Social and Political Science Review,* XVI (January, 1933), 489–90, 505: Huang-Tsen Ming, *The Legal Status of the Chinese Abroad* (Taipei, 1954), pp. 84, 179. In 1931 the Chinese wife of an American citizen who was married prior to the approval of the Immigration Act passed on May 26, 1924, was permitted to enter the United States. "An Act to Admit to the United States Chinese Wives of Certain American Citizens," *American Journal of International Law,* XXV (October, 1931), 229. Since all Chinese except those born in the United States or its possession were held to be aliens ineligible to citizenship, this provision was not of too much assistance.

19. Louis J. Beck, *New York's Chinatown: An Historical Presentation of its People and Places* (New York, 1898), pp.34–35. Cf. the description by Bancroft: "The wealthy [Chinese] merchant is content with the one small room behind the store, but it is the embodiment of neatness. . . . Married people indulge in a little more room than the bachelor of the same class, but the furniture even of the merchant's family home is of the simplest, and more limited than at the store establishment save an extra plant or so. Indeed, the wife is kept so secluded that all show may be dispensed with." Hubert Howe Bancroft, "Mongolianism in America," *Essays and Miscellany* (San Francisco, 1890), pp. 327–28.

20. Donald Earl Willmott, *The Chinese of Semarang: A Changing Minority Community in Indonesia* (Ithaca, 1960), pp. 103–16 *et passim.*

21. California at first excluded Negroes, Indians and "Mongolians" from public schools. Later, laws provided that if white parents did not object, colored children might be admitted to the "white" school, but when separate schools were established, the colored children were no longer to be admitted. California's decision to exclude an American citizen of Chinese descent from a white school was upheld by the Circuit Court, *Wong Hin vs. Callahan,* 119 Fed. 381 (1902). Segregated school systems have been held to be unconstitutional since 1954. *Brown vs. Board of Education,* 347 U. S. 483. But *de facto* segregation of schools is still an issue in California and elsewhere and has an effect on Chinese as well as Negro students. It, too, may be unconstitutional. See Richard A. Hicks, "California Suggests *De Facto* Segregation Must End," *Stanford Law Review* XVI (March, 1964), 434–42.

Segregation of Chinese children has also occurred in the South. In Mississippi, when a Chinese boy received the highest honors in the school at Ruleville, the white citzens excluded all Orientals from the school. Chinese had attended the white schools in that state until 1925 when a Chinese was expelled from the white school in Dublin. He carried his case to the Mississippi Supreme Court which ruled against him. Associate Justice McGowen said in his opinion that "the dominant purpose of the segregated school system in Mississippi was to preserve the purity and integrity of the white race, and prevent amalgamation; and further, to preserve, as far as possible, the social system of race segregation." *School and Society,* XXVIII (September 29, 1928), 389. The Chinese refused to attend the schools for Negroes and ten years later the State agreed to establish separate Chinese schools. In some communities the students were taught by tutors, Robert W. O'Brien, "Status of Chinese on the Mississippi Delta," *Social Forces,* XIX (March, 1941), 387–88.

In *Gong Lum vs. Rice,* 275 U.S. 78 (1927), the United States Supreme Court ruled that Martha Lum, along with others who were not white, was "colored," and that therefore Mississippi was not violating the Constitution in requiring her to attend the separate state-supported school for colored children. See Albert P. Blaustein and Clarence C. Ferguson, Jr., *Desegregation and the Law: The Meaning and Effect of the School Segregation Cases* (New York, 1962), pp. 102–03.

22. In San Francisco, the Young Men's Christian Association and the Presbyterian Church have always maintained separate chapters and churches, respectively, for Chinese, Japanese and

whites. See Clifford Drury, *San Francisco YMCA: 100 Years by the Golden Gate, 1853–1953* (Glendale, 1963), pp. 19, 33, 65–67, 151–54, 169–72, 223, 227.

23. Arizona, California, Georgia, Idaho, Mississippi, Missouri, Montana, Nebraska, Nevada, Oregon, South Dakota, Utah, Virginia, Wyoming. Huang-Tsen Ming, *op. cit.,* pp. 260–62. See also Fowler V. Harper and Jerome Skolnick, *Problems of the Family* (Indianapolis, 1962), pp. 96–99. The California case is *Perez vs. Sharp*, 32 Cal. 711 (2nd Ser.); see Paul Hartman, *Civil Rights and Minorities* (New York, 1962), pp. 12–13. Only recently have some of these laws been declared unconstitutional or repealed.

24. Henryk Sienkiwicz, *Portrait of America* (New York, 1959), p. 225.

25. Horace Greeley, "California Mines and Mining," dispatch to the New York *Tribune* from Sacramento, August 7, 1859, in Horace Greeley, *An Overland Journey From New York to San Francisco in the Summer of 1859*, ed. by Charles T. Duncan (New York, 1964).

26. See Bancroft, *op. cit.,* pp. 356–58; A. W. Loomis, "Chinese Women in California," *Overland Monthly*, III (April, 1869), 334–51; Charles Frederick Holder, "Chinese Slavery in America," *North American Review*, CXLV (July, 1897), 288–94; C. P. Dorland, "Chinese Massacre at Los Angeles in 1871," Annual Publication of the Historical Society of Southern California, III, Part 2 (January 7, 1894), 22–26; Beck, *op. cit.,* pp. 107–21. See also Richard H. Dillon, *The Hatchet Men: The Story of the Tong Wars in San Francisco's Chinatown* (New York, 1962), pp. 221–40, *et passim*.

27. C. P. Dorland, *loc. cit.;* San Francisco *Chronicle*, November 11, 1919; February 7, 1910; January 25, 1915; March 29, 1921. The citations from the *Chronicle* have been reprinted in William Hogan and William German (eds.), *The San Francisco Chronicle Reader*(New York, 1962), pp. 25–33; Winifred Raushenbush, "The Great Wall of Chinatown; How the Chinese Mind Their Own Business Behind It," *Survey Graphic*, IX (May 1, 1926), 156; Carol Green Wilson, *Chinatown Quest: The Life Adventures of Donaldina Cameron* (Stanford, 1950). See also Curt Gentry, *The Madams of San Francisco, A Highly Irreverent History of the City by the Golden Gate* (Garden City, 1964), pp. 50–59; Adela Rogers St. John, *Final Verdict* (New York, 1962), pp. 190–204.

28. Remigio B. Ronquillo, "The Administration of Law Among the Chinese in Chicago," *Journal of Criminal Law, XXV (July, 1934), 217.*

29. *Abstract of the Twelfth Census of the United States, 1900,* Table IV, p. 8; *Abstract of the Fifteenth Census of the United States, 1930,* Table p. 81; *Sixteenth Census of the United States, 1940,* "Population: Characteristics of the Non-white Population by Race," Table 1, p. 5; *United States Census of Population, 1950,* Special Reports: "Non-white Population by Race," Table 29, 3B–87; *United States Census of Population, 1960,* "Non-white Population by Race," Final Report PC(2)-1C, Table 4, p. 4, Table 7. p. 7 Table 8, p. 8, Table 12, p. 19, Table 30, p. 97.

30. The wife left behind in the home of her husband's parents

did not always acquiesce meekly. "You promised me to go abroad for only three years," an embittered wife of a Chinese laundryman wrote her husband, "but you have stayed there nearly thirty years now." Quoted in Siu, *op. cit.,* pp. 35–36.

A Chinese sojourner in Peru returned to China after ten years but his wife had committed suicide. He returned to Peru, obtained a visitor's visa to the United States, and until it expired he stayed with his son in California. Faced with deportation to China without relatives there to help him, he hanged himself in his son's orchard. Oakland *Tribune,* December 10, 1963; San Francisco *Examiner,* December 10, 1963.

Recently changes in American law have made it possible for wives and children to join their long-absent husbands. In Chinese communities all over the United States reunions of Chinese families separated for many years have been reported. See Stockton, California, *Record,* November 14, 1963; Keyport (New Jersey) *Weekly,* November 7, 1963; New York *Daily News,* November 13, 1963; Des Moines *Tribune,* November 7, 1963; Matawan (New Jersey) *Journal,* November 7, 1963; Jackson (Mississippi) *Clarion-Ledger,* November 17, 1963; Seattle *Post Intelligence,* December 10, 1963.

31. "A third factor aiding the growth of the Chinese community [in the Mississippi Delta region] was the fact that in many instances the stores were passed from father to son or to some other relative. During the early days the men would leave the Delta region for the trip home where they would be married, have children, and then return alone to the United States. After the boys in the family had been reared and educated in China, they migrated to the Delta to take over the stores from their fathers. Family groups did not appear, commonly, until the twentieth century. In fact, the 1930 census lists 438 males to 123 female Chinese, including the children . . ." O'Brien, *op. cit.,* p. 388.

The Chinese laundryman and restauranteur in America is a typical sojourner. The attitude of one who had been a bird-of-passage, traveling between China and America for more than thirty years, was described thus: "At the present time (1948) Mr. C. is very much interested in getting his son over to this country. He was told that he could apply for American citizenship so that he could get his wife into this country nonquota. His son, however, cannot come nonquota, for when the youth was born, his father was not naturalized—nor is he naturalized yet. It seems that Mr. C. cares mostly to have his son in this country; like most of his countrymen, his wife's coming has not been in his mind. He is not going to apply for citizenship now. At least he has not made up his mind." Siu, *op. cit.,* p. 41. See also Paul C. P. Siu, "The Isolation of the Chinese Laundrymen," in Ernest W. Burgess and Donald Bogue, *Contributions to Urban Sociology* (Chicago, 1964), pp. 429–42.

32. Timothy J. Molloy, "A Century of Chinese Immigration: A Brief Review," *Immigration and Naturalization Service Monthly Review,* December, 1947, pp. 69–75; Rhoads Murphy "Boston's Chinatown," *Economic Geography,* XXVIII (July, 1952), 254–55; for a recent case see *The Matter of Leong,* Int. Dec. 1284, File A-12653531, May 16, 1963, in *Interpreter Releases,* 40, 36 (September

27, 1963), 271–72.

Canada recently conducted a crackdown and investigation of allegedly illegal Chinese immigration. Between 1961 and 1963 stories of "slots" and the "slot racket" appear regularly in newspapers in Vancouver, Calgary, Winnipeg, Toronto and Ottawa.

33. In 1954, a prominent Chinatown leader was convicted of bringing thirty-five Chinese illegally into the United States. Although he denied it, testimony was offered that he had received between $1,000 and $3,000 for each entry. The convicted man had been president of the Chinese Chamber of Commerce and owned a famous restaurant in Chinatown. San Francisco *Examiner* November 19, 1963; San Francisco *Chronicle,* November 19, 1963; San Francisco *Call-Bulletin,* November 19, 1963.

Present law permits deportation for those who smuggle aliens into the United States "for gain." Gain is construed to mean not only direct monetary rewards, but also other services such as use of the smuggled aliens' services. *Gallegos vs. Hoy,* Fed. 665 (C. A. 9, 1958), cert. denied, 360. U. S. 935.

34. "California: Chinese in Slavery?" *Newsweek,* XLVII (March 26, 1956), 30.

35. Rose Hum Lee, "The Recent Immigrant Chinese Families of the San Francisco-Oakland Area." *Marriage and Family Living,* XVIII (February, 1956), 14–24; Rose Hum Lee, "The Established Families of the San Francisco Bay Area," *The Midwest Sociologist,* XIX (December, 1957), 19–25.

36. Jacob A. Riis, *How the Other Half Lives,* (New York, 1957), p. 76.

Chinese Secret Societies in the Occident: Notes and Suggestions for Research in the Sociology of Secrecy

DESPITE THE INCREASING documentation of nearly all aspects of life in the Occident, and the great number of studies of minorities, including the Chinese, Chinese secret societies have, with the assistance of misinformed or misguided researchers, remained secret. Information about the history and ritual of Chinese secret societies is now available for China and Southeast Asia, but the lacunae in information about these societies among Chinese in North America and other Occidental countries is remarkable. Purcell wrote in 1951, "The complex social and political life of the Chinese is often dismissed with reference to 'secret societies' or 'Tong wars';" while this is no longer valid for Chinese communities in Southeast Asia, it is still true for those in the United States, Canada, Latin America and Europe.[1] This article embodies the bibliographic and substantive information I have been able to collect. It is not comprehensive nor exhaustive, but I hope it will point up the direction, and also the misdirection, of earlier research and encourage further examination of the subject.

During the nineteenth century, except for Stewart Culin,[2] whose few but important works are largely unread today, the only persons concerned with Chinese secret societies in the United States were Sinophobes, journalists and local police. The several investigations conducted by the city of San Francisco, the State of California, and the United States Congress between 1870 and 1890 and information submitted to the United States Industrial Commission in 1901 disclosed a little about the more unsavory activities of these societies. Anti-Chinese writers seized upon the data to support their case for exclusion of Chinese labourers from the country. Around the turn of the century an enterprising San Francisco journalist who had lived in Canton as a boy and spoke Chinese fluently arranged to be initiated into the "Chee Kung Tong" and wrote a sensational article describing the ceremony.[3] Police collected a number of documents—manifestoes, instructions to paid mercenaries, and declarations beginning or ending inter-society feuds—in their numerous raids on the Chinese quarter of the city, but, unlike their counterparts in Southeast Asia, never made use of these materials for social analysis.

Sinophilic writers and certain historians and sociologists have minimized the activities of secret

77

societies, or failed to mention them at all.[4] An American writer in 1896 claimed that even though they engaged in violent altercations chapters of Chinese secret societies in America were less dangerous to the nation than Nihilists or Anarchists. Chester Holcombe argued that the importance of Chinese secret societies had been grossly exaggerated by romantic writers and that they were "not in evidence as having any serious influence upon the [Chinese] nation." The first sociologist to turn her attention to America's Chinese, Dr. Mary Coolidge, dismissed secret society activities as the work of a few bad men. Later sociologists, more interested in inter-group relations and the sources of prejudice, have treated the societies only insofar as they formed part of the psychological structure of the Sinophobic syndrome.

In 1937 an American sociologist, apparently unaware of Culin's earlier work or of the literature on the subject from China and Southeast Asia, collected newspaper clippings on "Tong wars" in California for two five-year periods and published a brief analysis. He noticed that "very little of this material, however, is free from the deep coloring of an outside, Occidental mind that fails to sense the existence of basic cultural elements accounting for the appearance of the tongs and for the subsequent evolution of their activities." Since 1940, Rose Hum Lee has done extensive research on the Chinese in America, but her treatment of secret societies is limited by her desire to see the Chinese assimilated into American society and her antipathy toward immigrant institutions and their leaders. Another recent work on the Chinese in America mentions Chinese "tongs" and the "tong wars" briefly but gives the impression that both are things of a past best forgotten. A local social historian of San Francisco has issued a well-documented account of the internecine strife between Chinese secret societies in the period before the great earthquake and fire of 1906, but, like many local histories, this work is oversimplified and makes only the briefest mention of the Sinic origins of the societies. The nature and significance of Chinese secret societies in America is yet imperfectly understood and awaits dispassionate analysis.

Despite the importance of secret societies in Chinese history since the Han period, almost nothing about them was known in the Occident before the nineteenth century.[5] An account of the activities of the Triad Society by a Protestant missionary, Dr. Milne, published in 1827, appears to be the earliest notice of any Chinese secret society in the West. With the exception of a translation of a Triad "manifesto" by Dr. Milne's colleague, Rev. R. Morrison, a few years later, no new information on the society was disclosed until the famous article by Lieutenant T. J. Newbold and Major-General F. W. Wilson in 1841, which designated nine separate secret societies in China, and pointed out that the Triad "is the one that prevails in Canton, and obtains almost exclusively in the Straits of Malacca and the vast islands of the Indian Archipelago . . ."

The first "authentic" history of the society was written by the interpreter in Chinese to the Netherlands Indies Government on the basis of material obtained from a bundle of books seized in a police raid at Padang, Sumatra, in 1863. Published in 1866 in Batavia, this work has served as a standard guide to the Triad Society ever since.[6] In 1900 William Stanton, whose "long intercourse, as a Police Detective Officer with the Chinese, and especially with the classes to which members of the Society mainly belong, and his ability to converse with them in their own tongue, have afforded him opportunities, such as few foreigners have had, of obtaining books and insignia and of gathering information," published an account of the Triad Society's activities to that date. Twenty-four years later Colonial officers Ward and Stirling produced a three-volume description of the society. Mervyn Llewelyn Wynne, whose work was cut short by his untimely death, left in the custody of the Malayan police an incomplete manuscript based on his exhaustive examination of the literature on Chinese and Mohammedan secret societies in Malaya. Published by the Government Printing Office in Singapore in 1941, with an introduction by W. L. Blythe, this invaluable work was first classified as "confidential—for authorized use only" and has only recently become available to western scholars. Recently, Leon Comber, formerly a superintendent of the Malayan Police, published an account of the secret societies which relies heavily upon earlier works and a hitherto unexamined manuscript by the Japanese political adventurer, Amane Hirayama. The most recent study is of the Chinese Triad Society in Hong Kong by the British police superintendent there. Considering the difficulties of acquiring information about clandestine associations and the nature of their activities, it is understandable that secret societies have become the preserve of police analysts. The objectivity and erudition of these officers have been remarkable in the face of their avowed interest in suppressing the societies, and students should be grateful for their prodigious efforts.

Myth and Legitimacy: Masonic and Chinese Secret Societies

One group in the Occident that has not been indifferent to Chinese secret societies is the order of Freemasons. The interest taken by Freemasonry in Chinese secret societies both provides an unusual case study in secret society legitimation and suggests the need for a more precise sociology of secrecy.

When the Occident was first learning of Chinese secret societies there was widespread anti-masonic activity in Europe and North America. Apparently Freemasons seized upon the new discovery to "prove" that their own order had originated in antiquity. Freemason intellectuals created the myth that the Chinese and Masonic orders were descendants from a common mystic ancestor. According to the Masonic "historians" their order had originated in the ancient Near East and "diffused" into Oriental and Occidental societies.[7] Thus Schlegel wrote, "Perhaps masonry divided itself into two branches: one passing to the West, . . . and the other directing itself to the East and finding fertile soil for its development in China." Dr. Milne, Newbold and Wilson, and a German Mason, Dr. Joseph Schauberg, expressed with varying degrees of certainty their belief in the masonic character of the best known Chinese secret order, the Triad Society.

Ward and Stirling continued the argument, the former beginning his Preface to their joint study with the assertion:

> Like Freemasonry in the West, the Hung or Triad Society seems justly entitled to claim that it is a lineal descendant of the Ancient Mysteries. Its signs are of primeval antiquity, but it represents the Higher Degrees in Freemasonry rather than the Craft in that the main part of the ritual deals with what is supposed to befall a man after death.

Stirling explained that he had become a Mason shortly after coming to Malaya "and on taking the ordinary three degrees, the Mark and the Royal Arch degrees, I was immediately struck by the very marked resemblance to the Chinese Triad Society." Their three-volume treatise contains the lengthiest treatment of the argument that Masonry and the Hung or Triad Society have a common origin. Wynne subscribes to the thesis that modern secret societies are the descendants of those that originated with the "ancient mysteries," and he opens his work with a long peroration in which he traces out from the "common unity of mankind" the "diffusion" which produced the Masonic, Triad and other contemporary secret orders.

However, although they chose to identify Chinese secret societies as the Asian descendants of their own order, the Freemasons did not wish to accept responsibility for or identity with the contemporary clandestine associations in China. As a result the relationship between contemporary Chinese secret societies and Occidental Freemasonry became a subject of frequent and polemical discussion in Masonic journals. Masonic writers, some of whom had distinguished careers in Sinology, agreed on the similarity between certain symbolic items and rituals found in Chinese institutions and in Masonry but were unwilling to grant recognition to the Chinese Triad Society or other societies designated as "Chinese Freemasons."[8] Thus, Herbert A. Giles argued that Freemasonry did exist in China if by that term was meant

> that higher and more ethereal scheme of morality, veiled in an allegory and illustrated by symbols drawn from operative Masonry, which was initiated in prehistoric times when the human race, emerging gradually from savagery and barbarism, first turned to contemplate the wondrous works of the Great Architect of the Universe

and began to recognize the mutual obligations of man to man.

William B. Pettus asserted that

> it would seem to be certain that the ancient Masonry of Asia was finally divided up and a part went to Europe where it remained pure and has so been handed down to subsequent ages throughout the world; whereas that branch which remained in China became orientalized and localized, finally dying out altogether or being merged into smaller tongs which have adopted other purposes than the pure one which the true Order inculcates.

One year later Pettus showed that the "Chinese Grand Lodge" of Freemasons in Shanghai had "no historic connection with the Free and Accepted Order of Masons of Europe and America." In 1916 in the face of reports of persecutions of Chinese "Freemasons" in Kirin and Heilungkiang Provinces, a Mason wrote that "there is no such body of 100,000 Freemasons, as we know Freemasonry in Manchuria." Other Occidental Masons were more emphatic and ethnocentric in their dissociation of western Freemasonry from so-called Chinese Freemasonry. E. J. Hudson wrote in 1920 that

> China teems with secret societies, and though they are similar to Freemasonry, yet, they, being of so political a nature, we (who do not understand the Chinese mind, which mind causes them to talk in symbols, so that if we cannot grasp the symbol their object in intentionally deceiving us is achieved) can scarcely expect the Chinese mind to understand or fathom our ideas of a society which teaches a 'peculiar system of morality, veiled in allegory and illustrated by symbol.'

Freemasons soon discovered that, in creating their own mythical history, they had inadvertently provided an avenue of legitimation for Chinese secret societies in the Occident. The Chinese clandestine orders, some of which were engaged in the sale of drugs, the operation of gambling dens and houses of prostitution, and the mounting of local wars and rebellions, began to call themselves "Chinese Freemasons" and to demand the rights and privileges accorded to the Occidental order. Colonial officers in Southeast Asia, some of whom were Freemasons, were careful to exempt their own order from the ban placed on all secret societies and directed specifically against those of the Chinese.

However, in other areas of Chinese settlement such as the United States and Canada the designation "Chinese Freemasons" took hold and is still commonly used for Chinese secret societies.

Whatever their beliefs about the Oriental origins of Freemasonry, Occidental Masons declared that chapters of Chinese societies in the western world which designated themselves "Masonic" were not bona fide.[9] Discussing one of these societies as it existed in China and New Zealand, J. B. Page wrote, "Such a society is sure to interest us, because although it has no direct connection with our own, yet it appears to have some similar ideals, and to make use of the same symbols." He concluded that "the Chinese Masonic Society" was the same as the Chinese Triad; that it had no connection with Freemasonry "as we understand it;" that it was not and never had been recognized by the English or any other Grand Lodge nor by the Provincial Grand Lodge in Hong Kong; that it had no connection with "operative masonry or with any branch of the Art of Building;" that its ritual and teaching contained no reference to the building of King Solomon's temple on which Masonic ritual was based; that, though some of its rituals, signs and symbols were the same as those of Masonry, its interpretation of these might be different; and that it had devoted its activities to political work and the defense of China against foreign invasions. He further pointed out that although the chapter in Auckland made use of the square, compass and the letter G, these were "a stereotyped pattern" the meaning of which was unknown to the membership. In 1891 a writer noted that the "Chinese Masonic Lodge" in New York City was a "native organization, not adhed (*sic*) directly to the Free and Accepted Masons, but said to be founded on principles very nearly akin." Another Mason complained that though he had "searched the length and breadth of China for a Chinese Masonic Lodge," he had never found one, but had finally discovered such a society in Sacramento, California, in 1911. He asserted that the adoption of the square and compass emblems by this society had been motivated by the desire "of gaining prestige and to be known as good men . . ." He came away "convinced that it was a meeting place for one of the many Tongs so prevalent in this country." Still another Mason pointed out that occasionally individual Chinese were admitted into membership in American Masonic chapters, but the Chinese chapters, although they were "accomplishing much for the betterment of their race," were not "recognized as regular by American jurisdictions, although the objectives are the same." "While Negro and Chinese Masonry is regarded as irregular by us," he concluded, "and cannot be recognized according to our constitutions, we must regard their origins as ancient and their object most honorable."

Occidental chapters of the Masonic order have, on occasion, given an unofficial recognition to Chinese societies which appeared to have Masonic characteristics.[10] The *Masonic Tribune* of Seattle, Washington, reprinted without comment articles which had appeared in the *Seattle Post-Intelligencer* describing the dedication ceremonies for the new "Bing Kong Bow Leong Tong" building and which designated the order as a "lodge of Chinese Freemasonry." The members of Spokane Lodge No. 34, attended the initiation ceremony of "the Chinese Lodge" after they had found a suitable rationale to justify their violation of the prohibition on visiting a "Lodge of clandestine Masons." "I will only add," concluded the anonymous Masonic reporter of this incident, "that the Master was killed by a hatchetman in the alleyway back of the lodge room a few days after we made our visit." In Manila a Chinese society called "Yee Yin Koong Sie" approached the American Manila Lodge No. 342 with a request for recognition which was denied. But the American Masons, among whom were an army general and a justice of the Supreme Court of the Philippine Islands, did attend a meeting of the Chinese society, and later, when several members of that society were assassinated, made representations on its behalf to the government of China.

It is not startling that secret societies seek justification in the eyes of both their own members and a curious and often suspicious and hostile outside world. Initiates must believe that they have concealed their activities from public scrutiny for good reason, and that the cause which they serve in secret would be worthy and honourable if it were fully understood by outsiders. Hence, whatever its real purposes, a secret society ususally seeks to legitimize itself before outsiders by an appeal to some general aim or some ideology sufficiently well-known and respected beyond its own clandestine arcana to be accorded public honour.

Nineteenth-century Freemason intellectuals adopted the then popular "comparative method" to demonstrate to their own members and outsiders that their worthiness and their mandate dated from honourable antiquity. However, their peculiar methodology, the "discovery" of a long-lost "sister-society" (as Schlegel called the Triad Society) in China, created a potential tie between them and the contemporary Chinese secret Societies. Further, it opened the door to reciprocal claims on the part of the Chinese. The Masons attempted, albeit only partly successfully, to restrict their commitment to "historic" identity with the rituals "common" to their own and the Chinese societies. But as the evidence presented indicates, the link between Masonry and Chinese secret societies did in fact go beyond merely a heuristic exegesis in history: local chapters visited with lodges of the Chinese societies; at least a nominal "brotherhood" has been established and continued between the two orders; and, finally, in a few recorded instances masonic chapters have extended aid to the Chinese societies.

There are very few data on the reciprocal influence of Masonic recognition on the Chinese secret societies. No investigation of this question has been carried out. However, the Chinese secret societies are known to have attempted to turn the unusual opportunity afforded them by Occidental Freemasonry to their own advantage. How successful their endeavour has been is difficult to say. In some instances, notably in North America, the facade of masonry has promoted the probity of the societies and added still another cloak of concealment over their aims and activities. But has masonry had unintended effects? Have the Chinese societies been able to retain their pristine nature since they accepted "membership" in the masonic brotherhood? If so, how have they resolved the dilemma of accepting only the nominal accoutrements of masonry and resisting the claims, if there were any, made upon them by their adoption of the formal masonic identity? What have been the nature and consequences of the cross-pressures put upon Chinese secret societies because of masonic recognition? Have the aims or activities of the Chinese societies been modified or inhibited? Hypotheses suggested in the works of Simmel, Coser, Gluckman and Arendt might fruitfully be tested utilizing data about Masonic-Chinese secret society relations.

These suggested research problems on Chinese and Masonic secret societies will be theoretically enriched and formulated more precisely if a typology of secret societies is developed. Clandestine societies may be classified first according to their *attitude* toward the prevailing norms of the society. Some societies, such as the American Freemasons, are in close accord with dominant social values. Others, the African Mau Mau, for instance, are hostile to the central values and social institutions of the society in which they are established. The former may be called *conformative;* the latter *alienative.* Secret societies may be further distinguished according to the *mode* by which they manifest their attitude toward the central values of the larger society. Here we consider the stated objectives and actual practices of the society. Some secret societies exist primarily to provide certain activities and benefits for their members and do not concern themselves directly with the larger social order. Present-day college fraternities are an obvious example. Other associations exist not primarily for the benefit of their own members but to effect some change in the larger society or to actively resist change in it. The radical Irish labour society in America known as the Molly Maguires is an historical instance. Some societies have played both roles, and indeed it would probably be impossible to find a perfectly unambiguous example of any single type. The two modes by which secret societies manifest their attitude toward the larger society may be designated *expressive* and *instrumental,* respectively.

The distinctive attitudes towards society and modes of expression may be combined into a classificatory schema. Such a schema illustrates and distinguishes the varying roles which secret societies play in relation to the larger social order. It also provides categories for use in comparing secret societies. Further, it suggests that research should be done on the causes and conditions of existence for the different types of secret societies.

A Typology of Secret Societies
with Suggested Examples

Mode of Adaptation	Attitude Toward Larger Society	
	Conformative	Alienative
Instrumental	John Birch Society	Chinese Triad Society
Expressive	Twentieth Century Freemasons	African Mani

Simmel[11] suggests that secret societies seek to conceal their rituals from outsiders because the total secrecy protects the actual purposes of the society from discovery. The typology of secret societies proposed here suggests a modification and addition to his hypothesis. Rituals and ritualistic secrecy seem to serve different functions according to the nature and purpose of the society. The naive Masonic attempt to legitimate its secret order by comparing its own ritual with that of the Chinese Triad Society illustrates the need to reformulate Simmel's sociology of secrecy.

The alleged similarities between the rites, oaths and initiation ceremonies of the Masonic and Chinese Triad orders are less a testimony to "diffusion" from a common source than evidence that similar rituals are found in almost all clandestine societies. It is not so much that Triad and Masonic rituals resemble each other, but that they both conform to what we know about secret societies in general. In their ritualistic humiliation of neophytes, awful threats of death or torture to those members who reveal the secrets of the order, oaths of eternal brotherhood sworn by actual or symbolic commingling of blood, and solemn promises of lifelong and altruistic service to the cause of the society, both the Chinese and Masonic secret society rites bear resemblance to those of the African Mau Mau, the Ku Klux Klan, and many college fraternities. At once it becomes clear how superficial such comparisons of the purely formal aspects of ritual are. For some of the societies named above—the Mau Mau, the Ku Klux Klan, the Chinese Triad—the ritual is more than a purely ceremonial rite: it is symbolic of entrance into an order proscribed by and hostile to the larger order. The vows of secrecy are taken less to protect the esoteric ritual from discovery than to protect the order from betrayal to the authorities. For alienative secret societies, then, and especially for alienative-instrumental societies, the arcana of mysticism and esoterica are not the effective secrets of the order, but are symbolic representations of or camouflage for them. But for conformative societies, such as the contemporary Freemasons and most college fraternities, the ritual is symbolic of entrance into an order which is hardly at variance with the social order at all. One need of such a society is to concoct an artificial distinction between its elect few and outsiders. Thus, the ritual and mystery may be the *only real secrets*. It is understandable why the Masons and college fraternities put so much store on preserving the secrecy of their watchwords and formal initiation rites. If the rites are revealed the only distinction between the society and outsiders may be lost.

On the other hand, for the criminal or rebellious society, and more specifically for its hard core of committed adherents, the ceremonies might be held in lighter regard. Indeed, a purely ceremonial or mystic interest in a clandestine order by outsiders might deflect attention from its more practical purposes, and concentrate it on the purely esoteric distinctions between the order and the larger society. In the Mason-Chinese secret society relationship the Masons contributed unwittingly to their own and the public's deception. Schlegel, appointed by the Dutch colonial authorities to unravel the mystery surrounding the criminal activities of the Chinese Hung-league, or Heaven-Earth League, another name for the Triad Society in the East Indies, having confirmed the parallel between its rituals and those of the Masonic order, declared:

> Freemasonry, persecuted formerly as a most dangerous institution, has proved itself, after its recognition, to be not only innocuous, but even highly beneficial. Now, that we trust that the secret of the Hung-league is sufficiently cleared up to be well understood, the similar forbearance might, perhaps, be shown to this sister-society the Heaven-Earth League.[12]

The sociology of secrecy and ritual, hence, might throw more light on the vulnerability and viability of secret societies and the roots of the "torment of secrecy." Not only should sociologists proceed to compare and contrast Masonic and other conformative societies with those at odds with the social order, but they should also focus on the similarities and differences among rebellious societies. For example, there is need for as full an exposition as possible of the sociological nature of the Mafia, apparently a loose confederation of secret criminal gangs begun in Sicily under conditions similar to those that spawned the Triad Society in China, and transported to America by immigrants. What is the career of these rustic non-ideological societies in an industrial setting? Do they, as is suggested by the works by Hobsbawm, Bell and Bendix,[13] provide an alternative to the alleged "modern" tendency of rebelliousness to become political and ideological? From what strata do they recruit their members? What is their fate in the foreseeable future?

The Chinese Triad Society: Social Banditry and Revolution in China

Of the several secret societies said to have existed in China, the one which has aroused considerable interest there and abroad and which deserves much more sociological attention is the Triad Society, or to use one of its most often-heard names among the overseas Chinese, the Chih-Kung T'ang. The name "Triad" derives from the mystical significance which the society attaches to the number three and refers specifically to the order's belief in the connection between what it asserts are the three basic elements, heaven, earth and man. The term Chih-Kung T'ang may be rendered "Patriotic Rising Society" and connotes the political character of the society. The fact that this political name is apparently not found among the chapters of the society in China but is one of its most widely used names among overseas Chinese suggests a difference in emphasis at home and abroad.

The Triad society is one of the oldest of existing Chinese secret societies. Its origins are obscured by its own semi-mythical history, but it had been established by the early eighteenth century in southeastern China. It apparently arose as an ethicopolitical cult with the avowed aim of overthrowing the Ch'ing or Manchu Dynasty (1644–1911) and restoring that of the Ming which reigned between 1368 and 1644. Its founders are said to have been the five survivors from among the Shaolin monks whose monastery was attacked and destroyed by agents of the Emperor Yung Ching in 1734. However, the society itself, or a precursor, may have existed in 1674 or even earlier, and, whenever it actually was formed, it certainly incorporated into its ritual and organization features of the earlier White Lotus Sect and the ancient Carnation Eyebrows Society. Shortly after its establishment the Triad Society broke up into many autonomous chapters in Southeastern China. It has remained in loose confederation ever since. When Chinese moved overseas, chapters of the society accompanied the immigrants into diaspora.

In traditional China the secret society was the principal instrument for the expression of popular grievances against the superior power of imperial authority. In some instances local dissatisfaction was expressed by withdrawal: the aggrieved parties would retire from society and seclude themselves within the confines of an other-worldly religious order. In other cases, anger and alienation would be translated into what E. J. Hobsbawm has characterized as "social banditry." The aggrieved parties would form a society of outlaws or join an already existing one. Proscribed by the law, the men would seek concealment in secrecy and live by their wits and off the land. They would prey upon the countryside and hide in the hills. The popularity so often enjoyed by social bandits stemmed from their actual or imputed identification with the masses, and their opposition to the imposition of imperial authority on local, more or less independent, institutions. In China as elsewhere social banditry and its attendant agency, the secret society, arose under conditions of stress, in areas where government had little popular support, and among classes not yet influenced by fully articulated ideological considerations.

Depending on the particular situation, social banditry in China took on a populist or a conservative character.[14] In the former instance, the bandits identified with or needed the protection of the local poor, and became "Robin Hoods," robbing the rich and distributing a portion of their booty to the poor. They also righted local wrongs, especially when a bandit and his followers came into control of a whole village or town and adjudicated the problems of its inhabitants. The bandits were conservative when they were employed by local landlords to make sure that peasants and other poor and exploited elements did not translate their accumulated grievances into organized armed violence. A "conservative" bandit society might thus find itself at war with a "populist" one. The activities of the Chinese Triad Society during the struggles between peasantry, landlords and officials indicate that occasionally this actually occurred. In one instance, the Yao Revolt (1832), the Triad Society fought at first for and then against the rebels, and at one time acted as mediator between the rebels and the government.[15] Ninety-five years later Mao Tse-tung commented on the conservative use of the secret societies during the early stages of the Communist-Kuomintang struggle in China: "They often degenerated into the tools of the landlords and bureaucrats and even turned into definitely reactionary bodies. In his counter-revolutionary *coup d'etat* of 1927, Chiang Kai-shek utilized them to disrupt the unity of the masses and to destroy the revolution."[16]

It is in their maintenance of a rebellious attitude on the one hand and their refusal to become revolutionary on the other that the Chinese secret societies reveal their unique sociological character. Their political activities have been limited to what Reinhard Bendix calls "populist legitimism, . . . violent protests against existing conditions for the purpose of setting to right an established order that has been wilfully abused by those who exercise immediate authority."[17] Populist legitimism, rebellion within a frame of reference that accepts the established political order, has had a long history in China.[18] Its most vivid exposition occurred when revolutionary forces actively threatened to establish an entirely new order. The revolution in China, popularly but inaccurately (in terms of our distinctions) known as the Tai P'ing Rebellion (1850–1864), provides an outstanding case in point.[19] This revolution was led by the fanatical, proto-Christian apostle of a new order for China, Hung Hsiu-Ch'uan. Hung had studied briefly with the American missionary, Issachar J. Roberts, and had adapted his revolutionary ideology from Christian eschatology. Hung organized his followers into a radical sect, the Godworshippers, and made a nearly successful attempt to overthrow the Manchu regime. During the early stages of the revolt, certain Triad Society chieftains allied themselves temporarily with Hung, but when they discovered the religious zealousness of his cause and the fundamental changes he anticipated in the social order after his victory, they withdrew their support and made war upon his armies. At the same time they expressed their continuing dissatisfaction with the government in power, but not with the *political system of empire itself,* by attacking and capturing Amoy and Shanghai and holding those two cities against imperial siege for several months. Hung's famous denunciation of the society as vulgar and anachronistic anticipated the essentially similar conclusions to be drawn later by other Chinese revolutionaries.

In the century after 1850, Chinese secret societies, despite their non-revolutionary character, continued to appeal to radicals who hoped to establish a new political and social order in China. Their mass membership, ritually enforced solidarity, and organized institutions were regarded as the base from which a full scale assault on the government might be launched. At the turn of the century a few members of the small but important anarchist movement which flourished among Chinese students in Paris and Tokyo toyed briefly with the idea of infiltrating the secret societies in order to acquire mass support for anarchistic principles.[20] Similarly, the Communist movement in China hoped to utilize the secret societies in behalf of its revolutionary cause.[19] Thus in March, 1926, Mao Tse-tung noted that China's "proletariat" was divided into a small body of industrial workers and

> In addition there is a fairly large number of *lumpen*-proletarians, that is, peasants who have lost their land and

handicraftsmen who are denied all opportunity of employment. They lead a most precarious life. They have formed, as their mutual-aid organizations in political and economic struggle, secret societies in various places, for instance, the Triune Society in Fukien and Kwang-tung, the Society of Big Swords in Anhwei, Honan and Shantung, the Society of Rational Life in Chihli and the three north-eastern provinces, and the Blue Band in Shanghai and elsewhere. To assign these people to their proper role is one of the difficult problems in China. Good fighters but apt to be destructive, they can become a revolutionary force if given proper guidance.

By 1939, however, "proper guidance" had not yet been fully effective, for Mao wrote in that year:

> China's colonial and semi-colonial status has created an enormous army of rural and urban unemployed. Denied any lawful way of making a living, many of them are forced to resort to unlawful means, hence the robbers, gangsters, beggars, prostitutes and all those who cash in on popular superstitions. This social stratum is vacillating in character: while some are easily bought over by the reactionary forces, others may join the revolution. Tending to destruction rather than construction, these people after joining the revolution are the source of ideology of the roving bands of rebels and of anarchism. Therefore, we must know how to remold them and forestall their destructiveness.

The one apparently successful employment of the secret societies on behalf of a revolutionary cause occurred during the eighteen year period in which Sun Yat-sen planned and executed the overthrow of the Manchu Dynasty (1894–1912).[22] In 1886, Sun enrolled as a medical student at the Pok Tsai Hospital in Canton, where, according to a recent official biography, he met Cheng Shih-liang, "who was much influenced by Dr. Sun's revolutionary ideas. Cheng had connections with the secret societies, and was able to give Dr. Sun much help later to stir up the secret societies against the Manchu regime." In addition to founding several revolutionary societies, Sun himself was a member of the Triad Society and a "fighter" official in overseas chapters of the society in Honolulu, San Francisco and Chicago.

Among the overseas Chinese Sun found considerable support for his anti-Manchu movement. As his widow was later to recall,

> Actually he found that the idea of nationalism was in a latent state, it had not died out among the overseas Chinese, even though the homeland had been ruled by the Manchu conquerors for more than two centuries. The

scholars of the Ming dynasty (1368–1644 A.D.) had through a secret society kept alive the idea of the Chinese nation during the whole of that period, and this secret order was still in existence among the overseas survivors of the Ming officials.[23]

Sun Yat-sen made three world tours (1895–1899, 1903–1905, 1909–1911), visiting overseas Chinese communities and government officials in Asia, North America and Europe in order to gather support and funds for the revolution. His activities in Asia and Europe have been described elsewhere, but his work within Chinese communities in North America and his relations with secret societies there are less well known and more difficult to document.

Apparently Sun was aided in North America by Seto May-tong, an official of the "Hung-men Society," another name for the Triad Society.[24] When Sun was arrested by the American officials for landing at San Francisco with a forged passport, Seto and two other anti-Manchu supporters arranged for his release and raised the necessary $5,000 bail. When, in 1911, Dr. Sun was trapped without funds in New York City at a crucial moment in the revolution, Seto and his colleagues raised the necessary $450 to start him on his journey back to China. In addition, Seto organized fund-raising campaigns among the overseas Chinese, not all of whom, by any means, were members of the secret societies. Revolutionary currency was printed in workshops in San Francisco's Chinatown. In 1912 Dr. Sun cabled Seto for more funds. Seto convoked a meeting of the Canadian chapters of the Chih-kung T'ang, and it was there resolved to mortgage the society buildings in Victoria, Vancouver, and Toronto to raise the necessary funds. The sum of $150,000 was raised and remitted to China. The importance which Sun attached to the aid given to the revolutionary cause by Seto and his associates is evidenced by Sun's offer to appoint Seto as Privy Councillor in the new government, an offer that was politely refused.

How was Sun able to obtain continued support for his revolutionary cause from the secret societies when others had failed to do so? A definite answer to this question is difficult to offer, but some suggestions may be advanced. Sun treated his revolution quite pragmatically. The goals of his movement were never stated precisely. His supporters agreed

on little else than that they wished to depose the Manchu regime and establish a new government. That there was little unity of purpose among the revolutionaries was indicated soon after the first revolutionary government took power: the erstwhile allies fell out with one another and a long factional war began. Moreover, to this day both the Kuomintang and Communist movements claim Sun as their own political forebear and ideological guide. More specifically, Sun differed sharply from earlier and later revolutionaries by never directly repudiating the age-old traditional objective of the Triad Society, the restoration of the Ming dynasty. Instead he capitalized on this aim and appealed to the overseas Chinese to support him because he would restore "ming"—which means "brightness"—to China. Sun's recognition of the strategic importance of maintaining his revolution's identification with the traditional objective of the secret societies is suggested in the elaborate ceremonies he ordered performed before the tomb of the last Ming emperor shortly after the overthrow of the Manchus. Sun himself delivered the principal invocation, a long peroration recounting the history of the revolt and identifying his republican cause with the aims of the long-dead Ming ruler:

> How could we have attained this measure of victory had not Your Majesty's soul in heaven bestowed upon us your protecting influence? . . . Your people have come here today to inform Your Majesty of the final victory. May this shrine wherein you rest gain fresh lustre from today's event and may your example inspire your descendants in the times which are to come.[25]

By never directly attacking the particular brand of populist legitimism so deeply rooted in the secret societies, and by appealing generally to their anti-Manchu sentiments, Sun was able to obtain secret society support for the establishment of the government quite out of keeping with their traditional aims.

Chinese Secret Societies in the Occident

After Chinese migrated overseas, secret societies sprang up in the immigrant settlements. In the Straits Settlements, as the area today comprising

Malaysia was called in the nineteenth century, clandestine associations which were chapters of or modelled after the Chinese Triad Society not only organized much of the social, economic and hedonistic life of the Chinese community, but also played a significant part in the political and economic development of the British colony. In nineteenth century Singapore, according to a recent study, secret societies bound together in a single unit the separate solidarities of clan, dialect, territory and occupation. However, the study of Chinese secret societies in southeast Asia is sufficiently advanced and well-known today to need no further exposition here.

There has been almost no sociological analysis of the organization and activities of Chinese secret societies in North America. Yet it appears that there has been nearly as extensive an organization of these societies on the latter continent as in southeast Asia.

In the United States of America, Chinese secret societies were organized along with Cantonese speech and prefectural associations.[26] Before there had been a decade of Chinese immigration to California Chinese immigrants from Kwangtung had established five separate associations which served to demarcate the linguistic and "ethnic" distinctions among them. In addition at least two secret societies had been established. Before the turn of the century there were nine speech and prefectural associations and over fifty secret society chapters in San Francisco. It is not clear how many of these "tongs," as they are often called, were overseas chapters of the Triad Society or some other society having its origins in China, and how many were autochthonous in America. In British Columbia, Canada, however, all the secret societies seem to have been locals of the Chih-kung T'ang. Chapters of that order appear to have been established shortly after Chinese from California joined in the Fraser River gold rush to British Columbia (1858). They may have been established as early as 1862 in Barkerville and certainly had been established in one Cariboo town in 1876 and another in 1882. The Chinese Benevolent Association in Victoria was not founded until 1884, suggesting that the secret societies in rural British Columbia bound together the solidarities of clan, language and district of origin.

The scope of operations of secret societies in the Chinese communities was by no means narrow. On the basis of available data it would appear that their activities may be classified according to their political, criminal and benevolent character. They played a significant role in the overseas Chinese community and also occasionally attempted to influence the course of political events in China.

The political interests of the societies were Janus-headed. On the one hand they continued to seek a voice in the organization of politics and society in China; on the other hand, they sought and obtained an influential position in the community power structure of Chinatowns. There is no evidence to suggest that the secret societies sought to participate in the national politics of the United States or Canada.

The role played by secret societies in the establishment of the first Chinese Republic has already been mentioned. Their interest in China's politics did not entirely abate after Sun's first victory, but it did lose some of its intensity.[27] Political activity since 1911 appears to have been sporadic and occasioned by crises. A few of the Chinese "soldiers" trained secretly in Hawaii and America to fight for the Republican cause went to China after the revolution but most of the small Chinese "army" abroad apparently disintegrated without seeing any action. The breach between the Kuomintang and the Chinese Communist Party in 1927 was echoed abroad by factionalism among the secret society chapters. Seto May-tong, representing the North American branches of the Chih-kung T'ang, sent telegrams urging unity and harmony on the warring factions in China. The failure to reconstitute the Communist-Kuomintang alliance resulted in a deterioration of relations between the Kuomintang and Triad Chapters in America, Canada and Cuba which has lasted to this day. Following the Marco Polo Bridge incident in 1937, Seto organized fund-raising campaigns on behalf of the Chinese in the eastern cities of the United States under the direction of the On Leong Association, a mercantile branch of the Triad Society which he had established in 1903. Seto served four years as chairman of the fund-raising campaign, and was awarded the position of Counselor in the Executive Yuan of

Generalissimo Chiang Kai-shek's government. In 1941 the American chapters elected Seto as their delegate and representative in the Republican government. Trapped in Hong Kong by the outbreak of hostilities, Seto arranged for tbe Hong Kong chapters of the Triad Society to support the defense against the Japanese siege and to preserve order in the British colony.

As China's political organization was modernized, its adoption of new forms was reflected in the structure of the overseas secret societies. In October, 1923, an international Congress of Triad delegates met in San Francisco and announced formation of a political party. On March 11, 1935, a convention of the North and South American chapters in New York City renamed the party, and in 1947 it was reorganized at a convention in Shanghai. It is interesting to note that the revised Constitution of 1947 specifically enjoins the members to keep the party "secrets" and provides a graded system of punishments for those who violate this as well as any other of its provisions.

The role of the overseas Chinese secret societies has not been clear since the communist takeover in China. The societies made a valiant but unsuccessful effort to effect a reunification of the Kuomintang and Communist Parties in 1947. At the Shanghai convention, still represented by the venerable Seto May-tong, the party, newly renamed the Chung-kuo Hung-Mun Ming-tsi T'ang (Chinese Hung Society Party of the People) and called the Chinese Freemason Democratic Party in press releases to English-speaking journalists, issued a call to unity, urged an immediate cease-fire in the Nationalist-Communist struggle, demanded the formation of a new coalition government representing a wide spectrum of political views, and offered a general political and economic program which it declared all parties should adopt in the interest of unifying and pacifying China.

Following the communist takeover, Chinese secret society involvement in China's politics seems to have declined and become less unified. Occasionally one hears that the Triad Society, or one of its local chapters, is engaged in support of a "third force" movement aimed at establishing a non-ideological,

broadly representative, and democratic government in China.[28] The chapter of the society on the Chinese mainland has not been destroyed but reorganized, according to a recent study, as a nominally separate political party charged with the task of appealing to overseas Chinese on behalf of the Communist cause.[29] There is no evidence that any overseas branch has identified with the aims of the mainland chapter.

The influential role of the Chinese secret societies within the overseas Chinese communities is more understandable once we appraise their criminal activities and provision of mutual aid.

The Chinese who migrated to America were, for the most part, married and single men. Chinese custom, supported by the immigrants' belief that they were sojourners only temporarily resident in America, dictated that women be left behind. Later American law converted the customary practice into a legal prohibition. As a result, prostitution, gambling and the smoking of opium became organized activities in Chinatown feeding on the needs and deprivations of the lonely, uncared-for Chinese labourers. Before the turn of the century American Chinatowns were known to both Sinophobes and the more benevolently disposed as communities in which organized vice was the order of the day. Provision of illegal goods and services was under the control of the several secret societies. The societies placed captured women under indenture-servitude in brothels, first imported and later smuggled opium into the country, and controlled gambling through a tributary collection of its profits.

The efforts of American law enforcement agencies to prevent these illegal activities and to suppress the societies were largely unsuccessful. Policemen were easily bribed, and in some cases the Chinese gambler used the police and courts to his own advantage. In one instance, Fong Ching, a notorious Chinese criminal and secret society leader in San Francisco at the turn of the century, regularly informed the police of the illegal activities of rival societies, and, after the police had arrested the malefactors, reopened their establishments under a protected status.[30] A set of instructions to a gunman employed by the Chih-kung T'ang, dated July 2,

1887, was captured in Victoria, B. C. in 1899. The society promised to provide for his family's financial security should he be captured, maimed or killed, and guaranteed perjured testimony on his behalf should he be apprehended and tried.[31] The decline in vice activities, and especially prostitution and opium-smoking, may be dated from 1930, the point at which the sex-ratio among Chinese in America reached almost reasonablè proportions and the birth of a new generation of Chinese in this country was certainly foreshadowed. As recently as 1934 an astute observer described the vice activities in Chicago's Chinatown and the control secret societies had over them.[32] Today, however, it would appear that prostitution, as an intra-community institution, has all but disappeared in Chinatown, and that gambling and opium-smoking is confined to aged residents, sojourners who never returned to China. The decline in vice probably has reduced considerably the revenue of the secret societies.

The benevolent activities of the early American chapters of the Chih-kung T'ang were little known until the recent discovery of a set of rules of a nineteenth century lodge in British Columbia.[33] The rules indicate that charity and mutual aid among the members, most of whom were miners working along the northern reaches of the Fraser River, were carefully limited to succouring the aged, indigent and disabled, and providing shelter for transient members. No funds were to be drawn from its treasury to defray cost of births, marriages or death. If a poor member should again become solvent, or a disabled man return to work, the money advanced to him was to be repaid. Today, the "Chinese Freemasons" of Vancouver claim that much of their energies and income is spent on charitable activities and care of their aged and indigent members. Spacious rooms in a new society building in the heart of Vancouver's Chinatown—a building, it should be added, emblazoned with the Masonic square, compass and letter G—appear to be given over to the aged members who congregate there to read, play games or watch television.

Chinese communities in America have enjoyed an extra-territorial status to a far greater extent than other ethnic communities. Denied the franchise for a long period, the Chinese, unlike other immigrants, were not the objects of any local ward politician's attention.[34] In place of the political machine and wardheeler, the Chinese were protected and represented by their own ethnic associations. In effect the Chinese in America have been kept in an unofficial "colonial" dependency. Indeed, the relations between the North American Chinese communities and local city government bear a close resemblance to those between the Chinese and other minorities in Southeast Asia, and British and Dutch colonial officers. The "mayor of Chinatown" tacitly acknowledged by city officials in America is, in many respects, nothing less than the American equivalent of the *Kapitan China* once officially recognized in colonial southeast Asia.

Inside Chinatown a merchant class soon became the power elite.[35] This elite controlled the immigrant associations, dispensed jobs, settled disputes and represented the Chinese immigrant before white society. Community power rested, fundamentally, on control over the traditionally powerful clans and speech and prefectural associations. In San Francisco, the separate prefectural and speech associations soon confederated into the powerful Chinese Six Companies, an association still in existence. Similar confederations, consolidating merchant control, took place in New York, Vancouver and other cities before the end of the nineteenth century. The respect according to Chinese merchants by white Americans ratified the elite's power and further secured its domination over the Chinese community.

At first the speech and prefectural associations prohibited secret society members from holding office and even sought to aid American police in suppressing the societies. By the 1870s, however, the secret societies had infiltrated the "respectable" associations and secret society moguls also became presidents of the associations. At the same time the associations appear also to have begun to engage in some criminal and vice activities, and for this era the distinctions between the activities of the speech and prefectural associations and the secret societies becomes harder to draw.[36]

Chinese communities were neither ruled by mobs

nor orderly and peaceful. Conflicts between the several associations were not uncommon. Fights arose over scarce and valuable "resources"—power, wealth and women. In these fights, erroneously called "tong wars" in America, clans, speech and prefectural associations, and secret societies were the antagonists. The recourse to violence, the mode of fighting, and the institutions for peace-making were all regulated by custom understood by the opposed parties. Indeed, early Chinese communities in America were "united" by the conflicts within them, which made no sense to non-Chinese outsiders and therefore isolated the contending parties and bound them together in "antagonistic cooperation."

Beginning in the second decade of the twentieth century Chinese community power elites became consolidated in a complex interlocking directorate of clan, speech and prefectural association, and secret society leaders. The Chinese Peace Association, created in San Francisco in 1913 to prevent Chinatown disputes from erupting in violence, contained delegates from all three types of association. The community-wide organization, in most communities called the Chinese Benevolent Association, which once excluded secret society representation, also admitted representatives from the clandestine orders. Conflict within and between associations has not disappeared, but violence has declined in the last fifty years.

The greatest gap in information about secret societies is for the years since 1910. Much more investigation of the modern period is needed. Research on Chinese secret societies is impeded by the desire of the societies to conceal their true nature and by the general suspicion and distrust with which researchers, especially white researchers, are regarded. Nevertheless, it is possible to discover a few details about the societies and their modern fate.

One leader of the "Chinese Freemasons" in Vancouver told the author that the society had lost the importance and meaning it once had for the community. There is evidence that needs once served by secret societies and other Chinese societies no longer exist or are served better by other associations. As Chinese have gained access to the political, legal, occupational and social positions once open only to Caucasians, they have drifted away from Chinatown, losing interest in its insular institutions, and shutting themselves off from its benefits and influence. The sex ratio of the Chinese is more balanced than in the past, and the womanless immigrant generation has largely died out, returned to China, or become too enfeebled to be served by prostitution. Gambling is still the habit of some aged Chinese, and is today carried on in tiny gambling dens hidden in the recesses of stores and hotels. Vancouver's Chinatown is no longer an inescapable residential ghetto: of the 2,662 names listed in the 1961 Chinese business telephone directory, 1,809 had addresses outside of Chinatown; of the 5,287 Chinese without telephones, 2,146 were residing outside of Chinatown. Moreover, 673 Chinese-owned businesses, more than half of the 1,113 listed, were also located outside of Chinatown.

The Chinese born in America or Canada since 1930 appear to have less nationalistic interest in China than the much smaller and ill-treated earlier generations of Chinese-Americans or the immigrants. Communist China is closed to them, and there is no noticeable Sinic "zionism" among them. One former leader of Vancouver's "Chinese Freemasons," who, along with Seto May-tong had represented the overseas Chinese at the ill-fated mediation meetings in Shanghai and Hong Kong in 1947, has since resigned from the society and now devotes himself to portrait-painting and to the publication of a mimeographed sheet urging world leaders to establish international peace.

Chinatown is declining, although the decline has not been accepted with equanimity. Chinese community leaders in Vancouver have carried on a campaign, largely unsuccessful, to halt or modify the city's slum clearance program in that area.[37] The city's redevelopment plan, if completed, will level the tiny "bachelor houses" where clusters of aged immigrants are living out their last days and replace them with modern single-unit apartment houses. It will also relocate many Chinese away from Chinatown. Chinatown leaders have argued that the community's culture, business and traditional associations would be severely damaged by the civic plans. They have won one important concession: the right to submit an alternate but equally "modern" proposal for the rehabilitation of Chinatown.

Chinese secret societies must not be hastily consigned to disappearance from the Occidental scene; the Chih-kung T'ang has shown a remarkable ability to survive. Undoubtedly its ostensible objective, the restoration of the Ming dynasty, has not been the most significant factor in its longevity. Secret societies, like other institutions, serve many purposes, not all of them manifest.[38] In China the secret society traditionally served for the redress of grievances, the shelter of outcasts and renegades, and the securing of dynastic change. Overseas the secret society united various traditional solidarities into an organization, gave aid and protection to its members, engaged in control over and sale of illicit goods and services, and provided an occupation and avenue to upward mobility for those unable to achieve success through legitimate means. It was also a means through which the overseas Chinese could exercise an unusual amount of influence over the course of political events in China. Viewed from a different perspective, the secret society, together with the clan, speech and prefectural associations provided the unassimilated Chinese with many of the services the local political machine gave to the enfranchised European immigrant in America. Access to and acceptance of the institutions of the host society threaten the immigrant institutions. For some of these assimilation has meant destruction, for others survival in a new form. Further research on Chinese secret societies is needed to establish their latent functions and their potential for survival in new forms or in relation to different needs. In addition, we need to know more about the nature of their appeal and to what classes of the community their appeal is directed. From such research may come more accurate generalizations about their ability to survive in different epochs and different environments.

Moreover, research on Chinese and other secret societies will increase our knowledge about the range and alternatives of expression for protesting and rebellious behaviour. The existence of secret "bandit" associations in an industrial society suggests that, contrary to the formulation and implicit argument in the work of Hobsbawm, non-ideological political rebellion *coexists with* rather than *precedes* the ideological expression of political differences.

The analysis of Chinese secret societies in the Occident presented here also suggests a modification in the recently developed theory of overseas Chinese community development. In an illuminating article rich in historical data and even richer in theoretical perspective, Maurice Freedman has written:

> If we take [contemporary] Sarawak as the model of a simple and relatively small-scale overseas settlement, we may assume that in their earliest phase the Singapore Chinese bound all their solidarities together in a similar fashion, the secret society acting as the knot. In later times increasing complexity and growth of scale forced individual principles of grouping to crystallize in different types of association. Later Singapore is presumably the model of the most developed form of immigrant Chinese settlement in Southeast Asia.[39]

Freedman has presented an intriguing model for the study of social change in the overseas Chinese community. However, his model appears to be derived from certain *a priori* evolutionist assumptions and suffers from the defects of that type of theory. The doubtful thesis that change is always in one direction, from small to large, from simple to complex, and from functionally diffuse to specific formations, apparently has been taken over without qualification by Freedman. It leads him to assume that the relatively small and simple Chinese social organization in modern Sarawak is the model for early Singapore and, perhaps, all early overseas Chinese organization. In other words, there is in Freedman's formulation the familiar evolutionist fallacy and the equally familiar methodological device used to demonstrate the evolutionist theme— the rearrangement of contemporary geographically separate societies into a temporal sequence. There is evidence in Freedman's own historical narrative to suggest that early Singapore's Chinese community was quite complex. Secret societies coexisted with dialect and clan groupings, and as Freedman has demonstrated so well, these alignments cut across one another, modifying and mitigating the structure of conflict. There is good reason to expect any large-scale overseas Chinese organization to be complex from its inception, since it was derived from the already complicated and sometimes contradictory principles of kin, village, speech and secret society organization and alignment existent in southeastern China. Introduction of evolutionistic models to describe social change distorts and oversimplifies the extremely complex state of affairs that was and still is overseas Chinese society.

The study of Chinese secret societies in America suggests that the overseas Chinese settlement in which the secret society bound together the otherwise separate solidarities of clan and speech, such as the rural nineteenth century Chinese communities in British Columbia, was a particular historical phenomenon to be accounted for in terms of the peculiar conditions that occasioned it, such as the local origins of the immigrants, the size of the community, and the tactics of organization necessitated by the situation. Where large numbers of Chinese settled in cities such as San Francisco, complex Chinese social organization and social conflict quickly emerged.

Social change has certainly occurred in Chinese communities. The study of this change will proceed more fruitfully if it does not take the change for granted, or assume *a priori* the causes or direction of change. In the study of Chinese society, as in other sociological studies, it is necessary not only to describe but also, and more important, to *account for* change.

Notes

1. Victor Purcell, *The Chinese in Southeast Asia* (London, 1951), 639. For information on Chinese secret societies in China and southeast Asia see Maurice Freedman, *Lineage Organization in Southeastern China* (London, 1958), 92–140; C. K. Yang, *Religion in Chinese Society* (Berkeley, 1961), 144–79; Donald Willmott, *The Chinese of Semarang: A Changing Minority Community in Indonesia* (Ithaca, 1960), 132–4; Lea Williams, *Overseas Chinese Nationalism: The Genesis of the Pan-Chinese Movement in Indonesia* (Glencoe, 1960), *passim;* G. William Skinner, *Chinese Society in Thailand: An Analytical History* (Ithaca, 1957), *passim;* G. William Skinner, *Leadership and Power in the Chinese Community in Thailand* (Ithaca, 1958), 5–11; William H. Newell, *Treacherous River: A Study of Rural Chinese in North Malaya* (Kuala Lumpur, 1962), 140–2.

2. Stewart Culin, *The Religious Ceremonies of the Chinese in the Eastern Cities of the United States* (Philadelphia, 1887); "The I Hing or 'Patriotic Rising,' A Secret Society Among the Chinese in America," *Report of the Proceedings of the Numismatic and Antiquarian Society of Philadelphia*, 1891, 51–8; "Social Life of the Chinese in the Eastern Cities of the United States," Philadelphia, 1887; "Chinese Games with Dice," Philadelphia, 1889, 5–21; "Chinese Secret Societies in the United States," *Journal of American Folk-Lore*, January–March, 1890, 39–43; "Customs of the Chinese in America," *Journal of American Folk-Lore*, July–September, 1890, 191–200; "The Gambling Games of the Chinese in America," *Publications of the University of Pennsylvania, Series in Philology, Literature, and Archaeology*, I, 4, 1891; "Chinese Games with Dice and Dominoes," *Report of the United States National Museum, Smithsonian Institute*, 1893, 489–537.

3. B. Church Williams in the San Francisco *Call*, January 9, 1898.

4. Sources for the material reported are Helen F. Clark, "The Chinese of New York Contrasted with their Foreign Neighbors," *The Century Magazine*, November, 1896, 104–13; Chester Holcombe, *The Real Chinese Question* (New York, 1900), 100–14; Mary Coolidge, *Chinese Immigration* (New York, 1909); C. N. Reynolds, "The Chinese Tongs," *American Journal of Sociology*, XL, March, 1935, 612–3; Rose Hum Lee, *The Chinese in the United States of America* (Hongkong, 1960), 142–84, 299–324, 405–30; S. W. Kung, *Chinese in American Life: Some Aspects of their History, Status, Problems, and Contributions* (Seattle, 1962), 202–4; Richard H. Dillon, *The Hatchet Men: The Story of the Tong Wars in San Francisco's Chinatown* (New York, 1962).

5. For comments on the underworld of Han China see Ping-ti Ho, "Records of China's Grand Historian: Some Problems of Translation," *Pacific Affairs*, Summer, 1963, 171–82. Bibliography for the materials in this paragraph includes D. Milne, "Some Account of a Secret Association in China, entitled The Triad Society," *Transactions of the Royal Asiatic Society*, I, Pt. 1, London, 1827; R. Morrison, "A Transcript in Roman Characters, with a Translation, of a Manifesto in the Chinese Language issued by the Triad Society," *Journal of the Royal Asiatic Society*, I, London, 1834, 93–5; T. J. Newbold and F. W. Wilson, "The Chinese Secret Society of the Tien-ti-huih," *Journal of the Royal Asiatic Society*, VI, London, 1841, 120–158.

6. Gustave Schlegel, *Thian Ti Hwui. The Hung-League or Heaven-*

Earth-League. A Secret Society with the Chinese in China and India (Batavia, 1866). Bibliography for materials in this paragraph includes William Stanton, *The Triad Society or Heaven and Earth Association* (Shanghai, 1900); J. S. M. Ward and G. W. Stirling, *The Hung Society, or The Society of Heaven and Earth* (London, 1925), 3 vols.; Mervyn Llewelyn Wynne, *Triad and Tabut: A Survey of the Origin and Diffusion of Chinese and Mohammedan Secret Societies in the Malay Peninsula, A. D. 1800–1935* (Singapore, 1941); Leon Comber, *Chinese Secret Societies in Malaya: A Survey of the Triad Society from 1800 to 1900* (Locust Valley, 1959); W. P. Morgan, *Triad Societies in Hongkong* (Hong Kong, 1960).

7. Information and quotations in this paragraph are from Schlegel, *op. cit.,* p. X; Joseph Schauberg, *Symbolik der Freimaurerei,* Zurich, 1861, Theil I, 178; Ward and Stirling, *The Hung Society,* p. i; Wynne, *Triad and Tabut,* XV–LVII.

8. Quotations in this paragraph are from Herbert A. Giles, "Freemasonry in China" (Shanghai, 1890), reprinted in *The Texas Grand Lodge Magazine,* July, 1936, 18; W. B. Pettus and Theodore E. Simman, "The Temple of Heaven at Peking, China," *The New Age,* September, 1927, 559; W. P. Pettus, "The So-Called Chinese Grand Lodge," *The New Age,* February, 1928, 105; W. A. De Wolf-Smith, "Chinese Freemasonry," *The New Age,* December, 1916, 572; E. J. Hudson, "Freemasonry and Native Societies," *Trestle Board,* October, 1923, 23.

9. Quotations in this paragraph are from J. B. Page, "The Chinese Masonic Society," *The Masonic Analyst,* October 1, 1929, 13, 15; "Chinese Masonry," *The Canadian Craftsman,* June, 1891, 366; E. A. Normann Tandberg, "Chinese Masonry vs. Masonry in China," *The Masonic Digest,* June, 1925, 90; E. M. Wilson, "White-Black-Yellow," *The Masonic Analyst,* April, 1927, 8.

10. Quotations in this paragraph are from "Chinese Masonry," *Masonic Tribune,* March 1, 1917; D., "Celestial Masonry." *The Trestle Board,* October, 1898, 454–455; "Chinese Masonry in 1904," *Montana Mason,* March, 1929, 7–8.

11. Georg Simmel, "The Secret and the Secret Society," in Kurt Wolff, trans. and ed., *The Sociology of Georg Simmel* (Glencoe, Ill., 1950), 307–78, esp. 358–60.

12. Schlegel, *Thian Ti Hwui,* XL.

13. See E. J. Hobsbawm, *Social Bandits and Primitive Rebels* (Glencoe, 1959); Daniel Bell, "Crime as an American Way of Life," *Antioch Review,* Summer, 1953, 131–53; Daniel Bell, "The Racket-Ridden Longshoremen," *Dissent,* Autumn, 1959, 417–29; Daniel Bell, "The Myth of the Cosa Nostra," *The New Leader,* December 23, 1963, 12–5; Reinhard Bendix, "The Lower Classes and the 'Democratic Revolution'," *Industrial Relations,* October, 1961, 91–116.

14. Bendix, "The Lower Classes and the 'Democratic Revolution,' " 97–9.

15. Comber, *Chinese Secret Societies in Malaya,* 19–31.

16. Mao Tse-tung, *Analysis of the Classes in Chinese Society* (Peking, 1960), 14, n. 2.

17. Bendix, "The Lower Classes and the 'Democratic Revolution,' " 98–9.

18. Thomas Taylor Meadows, *The Chinese and Their Rebellions* (Stanford, n.d., [1856]).

19. Meadows, *The Chinese and Their Rebellions, passim;* Comber, *Chinese Secret Societies in Malaya,* 22–8; Stanton, *The Triad Society,* 15–8; G. Hughes, "The Small-Knife Rebels (An Unpublished Chapter of Amoy History)," *The China Review,* L, 4, 1872–1873, abridged in Wynne, *Triad and Tabut,* 62–3.

20. Robert A. Scalapino and George T. Yu, *The Chinese Anarchist Movement* (Berkeley, 1961), 16–7.

21. Mao Tse-tung, *Analysis of the Classes in Chinese Society,* 13–4, and Mao Tse-tung, *The Chinese Revolution and the Chinese Communist Party* (Peking, 1960), 41–2.

22. Sun Yat-sen's relations with secret societies is described in *Dr. Sun Yat-sen: Commemorative Articles and Speeches by Mao Tse-tung, Soong Ching Ling, Chou En-lai, and Others* (Peking, 1957), James Cantlie and Sheridan Jones, *Sun Yat-sen and the Awakening of China* (New York, 1912), 86–126; Carl Glick, *Double Ten: Captain O'Banion's Story of the Chinese Revolution* (London, 1945); Henry Bond Restarick, *Sun Yat-sen: Liberator of China* (New Haven, 1931), 11–108.

23. Soong Ching Ling, "Sun Yat-sen—Great Revolutionary Son of the Chinese People," in *Dr. Sun Yat-sen: Commemorative Articles,* 14.

24. Information on Seto May-tong and his activities with the secret societies in North America is from *An Appeal for the Contribution of Essays Celebrating the Eighty-first Birthday of Mr. Seto May-Tong and for Monetary Gifts Serving as the Foundation Fund of the May-Tong Memorial School* (1948), a document in Chinese presented to the author by a former member of the Chih-kung T'ang.

25. Cantlie and Sheridan, *Sun Yat-sen and the Awakening of China,* 132–4.

26. A more complete discussion will be found in Stanford M. Lyman, *The Structure of Chinese Society in Nineteenth Century America,* unpublished Ph.D. dissertation, University of California, 1961.

27. The following is based on an analysis of certain documents of the society turned over to the author: *Chung-Kuo Hung-Mun Ming-Tse Tang Declaration, Political Outline, and Constitution,* Shanghai, September, 1947; *Chung-Kuo Hung-Mun Ming-Tse Tang Political Outline,* Shanghai, 1947; *The Declaration of Alliance of Middle Parties,* Shanghai and Nanking, February 21, 1948. See also Leong Gor Yun, *Chinatown Inside Out* (New York, 1936), 136–42; A. Doak Barnett, *China on the Eve of Communist Takeover* (New York, 1963), 83, 91–2, 126–9.

28. Burton Wolfe, "Chinatown, U.S.A.: The Unassimilated Peo-

ple," *The California Liberal,* February, 1960, 1, 3–5.

29. Theodore H. E. Chen, *Thought Reform of the Chinese Intellectuals* (Hongkong, 1960), 110.

30. Lyman, *The Structure of Chinese Society in Nineteenth Century America,* 351, and sources cited therein.

31. "Letter of Instructions to a Highbinder or Salaried Soldier," exhibits attached to statement of J. Endicott Gardner. *Reports of the United States Industrial Commission . . . Chinese and Japanese Labor in the Mountain and Pacific States.* XV, Part IV, Washington, D. C., 1901, 771.

32. Remigio B. Ronquillo, "The Administration of Law Among the Chinese in Chicago," *Journal of Criminal Law,* July, 1934, 216–7.

33. Stanford M. Lyman, William Willmott, and Berching Ho, "Rules of a Chinese Secret Society in British Columbia," *Bulletin of the School of African and Oriental Studies,* October, 1964. For a discussion of Chinese settlement in British Columbia see Pierre Lamoreux, "Les premières années de l'immigration Chinoise au Canada," *Review Canadienne de Geographie,* January–March, 1955,

9–28.

34. See Robert K. Merton, *Social Theory and Social Structure* (Glencoe, 1957), 71–82.

35. The situation was similar in Australia. See G. Oddie, "The Lower Class Chinese and the Merchant Elite in Victoria, 1870–1890," *Historical Studies: Australia and New Zealand,* November, 1961, 65–9.

36. William Hoy, *The Chinese Six Companies* (San Francisco, 1942).

37. *Submission of the Chinatown Property Owners Association to Mr. J. V. Clyne, Royal Commission, Property Expropriation, Regarding Vancouver Redevelopment in Area "A"* (undated), and *Brief of the Chinatown Property Owners Association presented to the Royal Commission on Expropriation Laws and Procedures,* July 17, 1961.

38. See Camilla H. Wedgwood, "The Nature and Function of Secret Societies," *Oceania,* July, 1930, 129–45.

39. Maurice Freedman, "Immigrants and Associations: Chinese in Nineteenth Century Singapore," *Comparative Studies in Society and History,* October, 1960, 25–48, at p. 45.

Rules of a Chinese Secret Society in British Columbia

(with W. E. WILLMOTT and BERCHING HO)

THE BODY OF rules translated below was first discovered by a Park Ranger employed to restore the erstwhile gold-mining town of Barkerville, British Columbia, as an historical monument. Searching for authentic artifacts in an abandoned 'Chinese Freemason' hall in the neighbouring town of Quesnel Forks, he came upon some tattered ceremonial robes, a Chinese book of codes and signs, and a board approximately 10 feet in length inscribed with Chinese characters. These (with some other items) were stored by the ranger at Barkerville, in a box marked 'unidentified materials', which was found by the authors in the summer of 1961, while carrying out field research on Chinese social organization in the Cariboo region of British Columbia. Mr. Ho identified the calligraphy on the board as a set of rules of the *Chih-kung T'ang*.[1]

This is the first body of rules of a Chinese secret society in North America to fall into the hands of Occidental researchers. In the nineteenth century municipal police occasionally captured code books, rules, or notices of the outbreak of inter-society feuds, but they apparently made little analytic use of them.[2] In 1899 an American missionary turned over to the United States Industrial Commission a letter of instructions to a paid mercenary of the 'Chee Kung Tong'.[3] From time to time an enterprising journalist or a few Occidental Freemasons were able to witness the initiation or building dedication ceremonies of chapters of Chinese secret societies.[4] The American ethnologist Stewart Culin gained access to a few of the chapters and utilized documents captured in police raids for his published accounts of their organization and activities.[5] The rules translated below add to the available material and throw further light on the operations and internal organization of these societies.

We have been unable to identify the town in which these rules originated or to establish the exact date on which they were promulgated. From the text it appears that they were written at some time shortly after 1882. At another point in the text we are told that the British Columbia lodge of the *Chih-kung T'ang* was first established in 1876, and that six years later the chapter for which these rules apply was founded. However, from other sources it is believed that the first chapter of this society was established at Barkerville in 1862. There may have been rival chapters of the lodge established in British Columbia, each claiming authenticity for itself. At another place in the text the writer warns of fraud and misrepresentation by persons claiming to be empowered to found new chapters. Apparently one object intended by the promulgation of these rules was to put a stop to interlopers seeking to organize 'false' chapters of the society.

Chinese from California began to migrate into British Columbia in 1858 after gold was discovered along the Fraser River. A chapter of the *Chih-kung T'ang* was founded at Barkerville in 1862 and, according to the document here translated, chapters were established in other gold-mining towns in 1876 and 1882. The order, or a rival society, had been established in Victoria by 1897, for in that year a newspaper article in Rossland reported that a Chinese merchant of that town had been threatened by 'high binders' but had written 'to the chief of the gang in Victoria who wrote out an order prohibiting hostilities against him.'[6] A letter of instructions to a 'highbinder or salaried soldier' dated 2 July 1887 and embossed with the seal of the 'Che Kung Tong' was captured at Victoria in 1899. By 1903 the order had been hierarchically organized with local, regional, and provincial divisions.[7] The establishment of the *Chih-kung T'ang* in British Columbia pre-dates by 22 years the formation of the Chinese Benevolent Association, which was founded in Victoria in 1884.[8] As the rules below indicate, the Chinese miners in the British Columbia hinterlands organized mutual aid, protection, and other matters through chapters of secret societies. Later, with the advent of a merchant élite in Victoria, the community-wide association was established.[9]

The *Chih-kung T'ang* is but one appellation for one of the oldest of existing Chinese fraternal orders. Its origins are obscured by its own semi-mythical history and by the still popular belief that it is the Oriental branch of world Freemasonry, the latter being said to have originated in the ancient Near East and to have 'diffused' into Oriental and Occidental orders.[10] It would appear, though that the society originated as an ethico-political cult in the seventeenth century with the avowed aim of overthrowing the Ch'ing and restoring the Ming dynasties.

From its inception the Triad Society, as it is commonly called, divided into many chapters in south-eastern China. Triad chapters participated in several of the insurrections against the Manchu régime between 1787 and 1911. Some of the Society's more daring exploits took place during the Taiping rebellion (1850–64), when Triad chieftains first joined with and then turned against Hung Hsiu-ch'uan, the revolutionary leader of the 'God-worshippers', and Triad sea raiders captured and held the cities of Amoy and Shanghai against the siege of imperial troops.[11] After 1850, in China and abroad, the Triad Society was heavily involved in nearly every revolutionary attempt to end Manchu rule in China.

In the nineteenth century people from Kwangtung and Fukien Provinces migrated to South East Asia and North and South America. Not a few of these immigrants were members of or knew about the Triad Society, for in nearly every overseas Chinese community secret associations sprang up which were branches of or modelled on that order. In Malaya, an area in which much information about these societies has been gathered, the several fraternal orders not only organized much of the social, economic, political, and recreational life of the Chinese community, but also played a significant role in the industrial and political development of the British colony.[12]

In the United States Chinese secret societies as well as speech-group and territorial *Landsmannschaften* were established as mutual aid societies within the confines of the Chinese quarter of the city. The secret societies soon took over control of gambling and prostitution in the American 'China-towns', and it is with these two activities rather than their political or eleemosynary work that they are most often associated in the minds of non-Chinese in America. The different associations often fell out with one another; their 'tong wars' are a frequent source of apocryphal history and stereotypy of the Chinese in America. Political activities of the secret societies in North America were cofined to sporadic interest in the fortunes of China's régimes, and they did not interfere with or participate in the national politics of the United States or Canada. At the turn of the century San Yat-sen obtained considerable financial support from chapters of the *Chih-kung T'ang* in North America. In San Francisco over 2,000,000 dollars in revolutionary currency were printed;[13] in British Columbia the chapters mortgaged their buildings to raise money for the republican cause.[14]

The rules translated below consist of a preamble and 42 regulations governing the conduct of the members of the society. The regulations are divided into three sets. The first set contains 24 items; the second, 9; the third, 9. The three sets are not only substantially different from one another but are also divided in accordance with the mystical significance in which the number three and its multiples were held by the society.[15]

The preamble is an attempt in classical style and grandiloquent language to justify the promulgation of the rules.[16] Although imperfect in syntax and vocabulary, it contains the metaphorical images and parallel constructions found in philosophical and legal treatises. Some of the phraseology might have been borrowed from famous literary or philosophical passages and adapted to the needs of the local situation.

The first 24 rules are concerned with fiscal policies and revenues, the rights, privileges, and obligations of dues-paying members, and the conditions under which novices might be instructed, arbitration carried out, and disputes settled. In a manner consistent with the attitudes towards public law in Manchu China,[17] the rules warn several times against members appealing to the legally established judiciary for aid, or conspiring with outsiders to collect debts of fellow-members or to "oppress" fellow-members.

The second set of 9 rules is of a more specific and local nature, and as the seventh item suggests, indicates that separate chapters adopted regulations suitable to the conditions at hand. Five of the regulations concern mining, setting out the areas beyond which mining might be carried out, the size

of a mine allotted to each person, and the offenses for which punishments would be imposed. The rest of the rules govern the manner in which disputes will be settled, the conditions under which the society will render financial aid to individuals, the limitations on the use of the *T'ang* hostelry, and the requirements of secrecy.

The final 9 rules are not those of the whole society but a set of house rules adopted by the lodgers in the *T'ang* hostelry. The 9 rules set out in precise and detailed instructions the domestic arrangements under which fellow-members shall live together.

Rules of the *Chih-kung T'ang*[18]

It is said that a well-organized society is ruled by reason and that the security and harmony of society depend on the cultivation of harmonious sentiments. The nation treats peace and prosperity as matters of paramount importance: the cangue is moistened by rain. In a hostel a friendly relationship among the lodgers is of paramount importance: the gentle breeze is important on a sea voyage. If everything is carefully planned at the beginning, there will be no regrettable results at the end. One must straighten out one's own life before one can straighten out the lives of others.

The purpose in forming the *Chih-kung T'ang* is to maintain a friendly relationship among our countrymen and to accumulate wealth through proper business methods for the benefit of all members. Thus, those who do mental work and those who do physical work are devoting their strength to this common goal.

Recently rumours and slander about our organization have been spread increasingly abroad. Fortunately, in the face of danger, our comrades have held on to the truth firmly and unflinchingly, have carried on the work with steadfastness of heart, and have relied on self-confidence in the face of slander. All these efforts are made for the perfection and continuing progress of our organization. Thus, once again, it is high time to clarify the constitution and regulations, which are of paramount importance for the guidance of T'ang affairs, so that our organization does not have an abortive development. Since a good thing grows slowly, we want to construct a hostel to meet the needs of our society. Among travellers there is no distinction between host and guest. When there is a common purpose we should work together; we arrive at the principle by being aware of the basic situation; we shall not be confused or shaken by slander; we act in the name of justice. In this way our organization shall enjoy a flourishing future; peace shall reign permanently within our hostel; members who are disciplined shall enjoy living together. There is a method in the making of money; one also enjoys the profit which is inherent in the rare items one has for sale. Hence why should anyone worry if a wanderer does not return to his homeland because gold has not filled his sack?

Regulations of the T'ang

The treasurer will make an annual financial report of the T'ang. The balance sheet will be posted in the T'ang hall at the end of the year. There should be no delay in producing the annual financial report.

On 1 December of each year the Head[19] of the T'ang and the other officers will audit the accounts, to see that there is no mistake or discrepancy.

In case of disagreements on matters affecting the T'ang, a meeting will be called. All ceremonial procedures must be followed. Instruments for punishment must also be displayed. The officers will be seated in order. No noise will be allowed. Justice, not personal favour, will decide who is right and who is wrong.

No member will be permitted to act for outsiders to collect bad debts from T'ang members. Anyone who uses force to collect bad debts on behalf of outsiders and is convicted through evidence will be subject to punishment without clemency.

No member will be allowed to speak in the T'ang whose membership fees are not paid.

When new businesses are opened by the T'ang and helpers are needed, only members who have paid dues and have seniority in the T'ang are qualified for these posts. Any competition or strug-

gle for these posts among members will not be permitted.

If any member makes trouble in the brothel or gambling house and if complaints have been made to the T'ang, he will be brought back to the T'ang for severe punishment without clemency.

In the events of Red and White[20] a donation may be suggested but such a donation must be voluntary. Public accounts of the T'ang will not be spent for these purposes.

Members who collaborate with outsiders and use the name of the *Chih-kung T'ang* to threaten others for financial gain may be punished. If anyone makes such a complaint and can identify such a member, that member will be brought back for punishment.

Members in good standing may ask the T'ang for assistance in cases of urgent need. Membership identification may be obtained from the T'ang and membership must be registered with the headquarters. Those who fail to register and do not pay membership dues must submit 30 dollars supplementary fees when requesting the assistance of the T'ang in disputes.

If members are suffering as a result of natural disasters, or if, after investigation, they have been found to be innocent victims of false accusations or oppression by others, the Headmen, in association with the executive members, shall arbitrate a settlement of the matter in order that brotherhood be maintained.

This T'ang was originally founded at *Mau-si*[21] in 1876, and in 1882 it was established in this town. Since then no other T'angs have been formed. Anyone who intends to form a new T'ang and create trouble will be prosecuted.

Members, no matter whether they are living in town, in mining areas, in ports, or in cities must maintain fair practices in business. Anyone who uses an advantageous position in business to oppress our countrymen will be brought back for punishment in accordance with the constitution if a complaint is made and evidence presented.

Members, no matter whether they are living in town, in mining areas, in ports, or in cities must follow a policy of first come, first served when selling or buying businesses or mines. Anyone who does not follow this regulation will be punished in accordance with the regulations if a complaint is made and evidence presented.

Members, no matter whether they are living in town, in mining areas, in ports, or in cities will not be permitted to reduce wages or to spread slander against each other in order to compete in hiring. Anyone committing these acts will be punished if a complaint is made and evidence presented.

Headmen from San Francisco intending to establish a forum for teaching disciples whether in the town or in the mining areas must hold a license from the *Chih-kung T'ang*. Anyone without such a license pretending to be a Headman in order to establish a school will be prosecuted.

The senior member and officers in other towns and mining areas who invite the Headman to open a forum must investigate to be sure the Headman holds a license from the *Chih-kung T'ang*. New recruits trained by self-styled Headmen without a license will not be considered as T'ang members.

Those persons living in other towns and mines, near or far, who need assistance from our officers for arbitration in case of trouble must pay the travelling expenses of the officer. The T'ang will not be responsible for expenses.

The officer sent by the T'ang on a mission to arbitrate in a dispute must act justly; he must make every effort to find a solution to satisfy both sides. The officer who is corrupt in any way in mediation will face severe punishment.

Any dispute or mutual suspicion among members should be settled in the T'ang in accordance with reason. Those who persist in quarrelling with one another or who appeal to the courts either create more trouble and expense or damage friendships.

Members who come to the T'ang for settlement of a dispute will be heard without prejudice. Right and wrong will be assessed by the T'ang. Any criticism of the T'ang outside the meeting will diminish the prestige of the T'ang.

The Junior or Senior Headman who is chosen by the T'ang to go to other towns and mining areas to open a forum must follow the regulations of the T'ang. A membership fee of two dollars from each new member must be remitted to the T'ang. A Headman who fails to submit such fees will not be allowed to open a forum.

Members since 1876 who fail to pay their dues and other donations for ceremonies, or who do not register their names at the headquarters will not be permitted to speak in the *Chung-i T'ang*.[22] Such members must pay a 50-dollar fine when they ask the T'ang for assistance in case of trouble. The senior member and officers will then call a meeting to decide whether or not the T'ang will give such assistance. If, after investigating the request, the T'ang decides there is sufficient evidence to show that the demand is reasonable, it will provide assistance. If the request is not reasonable and the purpose is to use the prestige of the T'ang to oppress others, the person making the request will be punished.

Criticism must only be made in the T'ang meeting. Anyone who makes criticisms behind the scenes or utters slander against other members outside the meeting will be sentenced to 21 stripes.

The above 24 items were adopted by the conference of the T'ang. All members must obey these regulations.

Mining Regulations

Hung-men[23] brothers who engage in gold-mining must mine beyond the boundary line. Anyone who mines within the boundary line will be considered as invading private property and will be prosecuted.

Members who openly collaborate with outsiders to invade other members' mines will be punished in accordance with the regulations by having both ears cut off. Intercession by senior members will not be permitted. Members who hide behind the scenes but persuade outsiders to invade other members' mines, if discovered, will be brought back and punished in accordance with the regulations by having one ear cut off. Intercession will not be permitted.

A member who bribes outsiders to plot against his opponent in a dispute, thus causing physical harm to another member, will be sentenced, upon evidence, to losing both ears. Intercession by members will not be permitted.

Any quarrel and dispute among members may be referred to the T'ang, which will call a meeting to settle the dispute. The member losing the case will be fined one dollar. If he fails to pay the fine immediately, he will be sentenced to six stripes. Sentence will be decided by the senior members, who will judge the severity of the error committed. Sentence will be carried out in the T'ang.

Any members who have found good mines are limited to 100 feet for each person. If both sides of the border-line are marked but the person mining has not yet had the time to go to the Land Office to register his claim, and another member, aware of this, secretly rushes to the Office to register the claim, the latter will be considered as having invaded the property of another member and will be prosecuted.

The important matters of the Lodge are confidential. Any member who gives information about such matters to an outsider will be sentenced, upon evidence, to 108 stripes without clemency.

Since the establishment of the chapter in this town, the regulations of the T'ang have been based mainly on the constitution of the *Chih-kung T'ang,* supplemented by regulations adapted to suit local conditions. It has been decided that the regulations should be in writing on a board and should hang in the Hall in order that they be made known to members.

All the money received by the T'ang is for conducting T'ang affairs. However, those members who are old or sick, or who have suffered disaster caused either by natural calamities or by accidents, and who have no means nor anyone to look after them, may receive care from the T'ang. When sick members are in good health and start working again, medical expenses paid by the T'ang must be refunded. If the medical expenses amount to a large sum beyond the ability of the member to repay, the treasurer should report the case to the meeting, and a collection may be taken up among the members, so that brotherhood will be maintained.

Members who are either newly arrived in this town or just back from the mining area and who

have no way of finding a place to stay may register with the chapter. Accommodation for sleeping and two meals will be provided. Beyond this, the member must take care of himself. Members should not stay longer than necessary. It would be embarrassing if a member had to be accused to his face of overstaying.

The above regulations should be made known and will apply to all members. Anyone who neglects these regulations will be punished without clemency.

Issued by the T'ang.

Hostel regulations

All those who reside in the hostel have to look after each other. Friendly relationships and kindness among lodgers are most precious.

Lodgers who go out at night must take precautions against fire; the safety measures of the hostel must not be neglected.

The daily needs of wood and water for the hostel will be supplied by all lodgers, who will take turns in performing such duties according to the schedule. No excuse will be allowed without special arrangement in advance. Those who need to launder clothes must supply their own water.

The daily needs of tea, salt, light, and fuel in the hostel will be counted each week, and assessed equally from all lodgers. For those who have not stayed a full week, the account will be reckoned by days. No person will be allowed to evade his contribution. Those who are not willing to share these expenses may look elsewhere for accommodation. Lodgers who need candles must supply their own. Candles belonging to the hostel may not be taken by individuals.

In the case of vacancy of bunks in the hostel: first come, first served. The hostel will accommodate all and strife over bunks will not be permitted. Every bunk should be kept clean, and in this matter lodgers may check on each other.

Time for using the kitchen should be by schedule. The chopping-block must be cleaned each time after use.

The hostel is primarily to serve travelling members. However, those who come here for slaughtering cattle or for selling goods may stay one week. Beyond this time-limit, rental may be charged by the hostel.

The working tools and personal belongings of the lodgers should be clearly marked with personal identification to avoid mistakes by others. Articles should be carefully examined before being removed in order to avoid the exchange of old articles for new ones.

The friend of a newly arrived merchant or guest staying in the hostel may yield his bunk to his friend to show his hospitality. All lodgers should be polite to each other.

The above regulations are adopted by the meeting of the lodgers. Actions against these regulations will be prosecuted.

Issued by the Hostel.

Notes

1. Part of the research on which this article is based was financed by grants to Messrs. Lyman and Willmott by the Institute of Social and Economic Research and the President's Committee on Research, both of the University of British Columbia. The rules were originally translated by Mr. Ho, whose draft was then edited by Mr. Willmott and later by Dr. Lyman. The authors gratefully acknowledge assistance in the final revision by Miss Catherine L. Liu and Professor T'ung-tsu Ch'ü, both of the Department of Asian Studies at the University of British Columbia, and by Mr. William S. Tong. Mr. Les Cooke, of the British Columbia Parks Service, kindly loaned the board to the University of British Columbia so that it could be photographed and studied. The book of codes, oaths, and rites of the *Chih-kung T'ang,* also found by Mr. Cooke, has been presented to the University of British Columbia Library through the courtesy of the British Columbia Parks Service.

The introductory statement has been prepared by Dr. Lyman.

2. Police sergeant John J. Manion of the San Francisco Police Department turned over a typed manuscript titled 'Tongs and tong wars' to police headquarters. A portion of this unpublished document is reprinted in C. N. Reynolds, 'The Chinese tongs', *American Journal of Sociology,* XL, 5, 1935, 612–23. There is as yet no available history of Chinese society in the United States. Useful information can be found in Louis J. Beck, *New York's Chinatown: an historical presentation of its people and places,* New York, Bohemia Publishing Co., 1898; Mary Coolidge, *Chinese immigration,* New York, Henry Holt, 1909; Elmer Sandmeyer, *The Anti-Chinese movement in California,* Urbana, University of Illinois Press, 1939; Alexander Mc Leod, *Pigtails and gold dust,* Caldwell, Idaho, Caxton Printers, 1947; Rose Hum Lee, *The Chinese in the United States of America,* Hong Kong, Hong Kong University Press, 1960; Richard H. Dillon, *The hatchet men: the story of the tong wars in San Francisco's Chinatown,* New York, Coward-McCann, 1962; S. W. Kung, *Chinese in American life: some aspects of their history, status, problems, and contributions,* Seattle, University of Washington Press, 1962. For a sociological analysis see Stanford M. Lyman, *The structure of Chinese society in nineteenth century America,* unpublished Ph.D. dissertation, University of California, Berkeley, 1961.

3. 'Letter of instructions to a highbinder or salaried soldier'. Exhibits attached to statement of J. Endicott Gardner, *Reports of the United States Industrial Commission. . . . Chinese and Japanese labor in the mountain and Pacific states,* XV, Pt. IV, Washington, D. C., Government Printing Office, 1901, 771.

4. B. Church Williams, in the *San Francisco Call,* 9 January 1898; 'Chinese Masonry', *Canadian Craftsman,* XXIV, 12, 1891, 366–7; E. A. Normann Tandberg, 'Chinese masonry vs. masonry in China,' *Masonic Digest,* IV, 12, 1925, 90; Carter Brooke Jones, 'Chinese masonry', *Masonry Tribune,* 1, 12, 1917, 1; D., 'Celestial Masonry', *Trestle Board,* XII, 10, 1898, 454–5; 'Chinese celebrate,' *Rossland Miner* (British Columbia), 13 October 1903.

5. Stewart Culin, 'The I Hing or "Patriotic Rising", a secret society among the Chinese in America', *Proceedings of the Numismatic and Antiquarian Society of Philadelphia for the years 1887–9,* 3 November 1887, 51–7; 'Chinese secret societies in the United States', *Journal of American Folk-Lore,* III, 10, 1890, 191–200; 'The gambling games of the Chinese in America', *Publications of the University of Pennsylvania, Series in Philology, Literature, and Archaeology,* 1, 4, 1891, 17 pp.; 'Chinese games with dice and dominoes', *Report of the United States National Museum, Smithsonian Institute,* 1893, 489–537.

6. *Rossland Miner,* 21 October 1897.

7. At the dedication of the 'Gee Kong Tong' building in Rossland, those present included the 'local president', the 'Kootenay master', and 'the master of the Fraternity for British Columbia', *Rossland Miner,* 27 October 1903.

8. Margaret Ormsby, *British Columbia, a history,* Vancouver, Macmillan Co. of Canada, 1958, 303.

9. For the rural-urban distribution of the Chinese in nineteenth-century British Columbia see Pierre Lamoureaux, 'Les Premières années de l'immigration chinoise au Canada', *Revue Canadienne de Geographie,* IX 1, 1955, 9–28.

10. J. S. M. Ward and W. G. Stirling, *The Hung Society or the Society of Heaven and Earth,* London, Baskerville Press, 1925–6, 3 vols.;

Mervyn Llewelyn Wynne, *Triad and Tabut: a survey of the origin and diffusion of Chinese and Mohammedan secret societies in the Malay Peninsula, A. D. 1800–1935,* Singapore, Government Printing Office, 1941, xvii–lvii; Gustave Schlegel, *Thian ti-hwui, the Hung League or Heaven-Earth League: a secret society with the Chinese in China and India,* Batavia, Lange, 1866.

11. Thomas Taylor Meadows, *The Chinese and their rebellions,* London, Smith, Elder, 1856, 150–2; William Stanton, *The Triad Society or Heaven and Earth Association,* Hong Kong, Kelly and Walsh, 1900, 8–24.

12. Leon Comber, *Chinese secret societies in Malaya: a survey of the Triad Society from 1800 to 1900,* Locust Valley, N. Y., J. J. Augustin, 1959; J. M. Gullick, *The story of early Kuala Lumpur,* Singapore, Donald Moore, 1956; J. M. Gullick, *A history of Selangor, 1742–1957,* Singapore, Eastern Universities Press, 1960, 41–90; Maurice Freedman, 'Immigrants and associations: Chinese in nineteenth-century Singapore', *Comparative Studies in Society and History,* III, 1, 1960, 25–48.

13. McLeod, op. cit., 149–50.

14. W. E. Willmott, 'Chinese communities in British Columbia towns', unpublished MS. According to a recent study Sun Yat-sen 'was a Triad official of long standing and is reported to have been a 426 "Fighter" official of the Kwok On Wui, as it was called in Cantonese, in Honolulu and Chicago; this society came under the general supervision of the Cantonese-named Chi Kung Tong, a mainly overseas section of the Triad Hung Mun' (W. P.

Morgan, *Triad societies in Hong Kong,* Hong Kong, Government Press. 1960, 25).

15. Schlegel, op. cit., xvii–xxvii.

16. The authors are indebted to Miss Liu for helpful comments on the preamble.

17. See Sybille van der Sprenkel, *Legal institutions in Manchu China* (London School of Economics. Monographs on Social Anthropology, No. 24), London, Athlone Press, 1962, 80–111.

18. The calligrapher placed no title at the head of his work, but began immediately with the preamble.

19. Literally, 'elder brother'. It is meant in this context as the executive officer of the society.

20. Red and white are the customary colours used in connexion with the *rites de passage* in China; red for marriage, birth, or birthdays; white for death and funerals.

21. We have not been able to locate any town in nineteenth-century British Columbia for which this might be the translation. It may refer to the area of Barkerville, within the district termed Moose Heights (the term is no longer current except as the name of a small settlement north of Quesnel).

22. The *Chung-i T'ang* refers to the meeting-hall within the buildings of the *Chih-kung T'ang.*

23. The *Chih-kung T'ang* considers itself a branch of the *Hung-men Society,* another name for the Triad Society.

Conflict and the Web of Group Affiliation in San Francisco's Chinatown, 1850–1910

ALTHOUGH THE EARLY history of the Chinese in America has been explored by many authorities, most attention has been focused on the anti-Chinese movement. The structure and operations of Chinese associations established in the Oriental ghettoes of the West have received scant and stereotyped treatment.[1] The net effect of these analyses has been a perfectly correct but one-sided image of victimization unrelieved by any analytical accounts of the organizational activity or associational creativity of the Asian victims.

Most of the contemporary reports on nineteenth-century Chinatowns that treat the basic types of traditional Chinese organizations—clans, *Landsmannschaften,* and secret societies—betray a Sinophobia deeply embedded in the general racism of that era. It is not surprising that scholars of a later generation, seeking to redress this racist balance, would concentrate on the popular tribunals, prejudicial reports, and painful pejorative heaped upon the hapless Chinese. Moreover, in seeking to overturn the obloquy and slander of a whole people, sympathetic American scholars have tended to engage in a selective perception reflecting their own

less venal outlook. Clans became "family associations," *Landsmannschaften* were transformed into "benevolent societies," and the activities of the once feared secret societies were said to be vastly exaggerated, if not wholly fabricated. To these liberal-minded scholars Chinese immigrants were white men with yellow skins.

In fact the first six decades of Chinese settlement in San Francisco were distinguished by the fact that Chinese immigrants, beset with a hostile racist movement opposing their very presence in America,[2] built their own special community. This community—Chinatown—was remarkable for its fierce internal conflicts, its lack of solidarity, and its intensive disharmony. Popularly known as "tong wars," the violent battles in Chinatown actually involved clans, *Landsmannschaften,* and secret societies. These fights raged intermittently but frequently for sixty years. Then, in the years closing the first decade of the twentieth century, an era seemed to come to an end. The last major reorganization of the immigrants' prefectural associations—the absorption of the Yan Hoi group into the Sue Hing Association—occurred in 1909. Three years later

103

secret society and merchant leaders—who had been at odds with one another for more than fifty years—formed the Chinese Peace Society in the hope that they could end tong wars in Chinatown. In 1911 the Republican Revolution ended dynastic rule in China and ushered in an era of class and cosmopolitan politics that also found expression in political and radical parties in the overseas Chinese colonies. By 1910 most of the immigrant Chinese laborers had been driven off the farmlands and out of most of the urban jobs in and around San Francisco and forced to work as well as live in Chinatown. An aging population that could not be replenished by immigration—forbidden since 1882—or by procreation—prevented by the enormous imbalance in the sex ratio—seemed in danger of extinction during the next half century.[3] But instead of disappearing, Chinatown in the years following 1910 became an established tourist attraction, dominated by its merchant and association leaders, exploiting the labor of its poorer elements, and hiding its fetid squalor under the show of its pagoda roofs, parades on Chinese New Year, and patriotic drives in behalf of the *Kuomintang*.[4] Yet, beneath the surface, the basic structure that had been established at such fearful cost during its first sixty years remained. It still does.

In this paper, the structure and operation of San Francisco's nineteenth-century Chinatown are presented in a schematic and sociological fashion. The argument can be stated quite succinctly: Nineteenth-century Chinatown was a complex, highly organized community whose associations were not in constant harmony with one another. Most important were the activities of the secret societies, whose competition for control of vice and whose political battles were fierce. As a result of inter-society conflicts and traditional modes of resolving them, violent altercations erupted repeatedly within the ghetto. Since these disputes were intramural, they acted as a further barrier to contacts with the larger society, placed many individuals under cross-pressures of loyalty to the several associations whose membership overlapped, and fastened on the Chinese community a pattern of antagonistic coopera-

tion. Thus intra-community conflict and cooperation acted together to help isolate the Chinese from the metropolis.

Chinese communities in the United States have enjoyed a measure of isolation and communal self-government far exceeding that of other ethnic communities.[5] One reason for the unusual separation of Chinatowns from regular public municipal controls was their long period of electoral irrelevance to American politics. Denied naturalization and the franchise for nearly a century, the Chinese, unlike European immigrants, were not the objects of any local ward politician's solicitations. Left to themselves—except during anti-Chinese campaigns—the Chinese organized their own benevolent, protective, and governmental bodies. In effect, the Chinese community in America is more like a colonial dependency than an immigrant settlement in an open society. The relationship between the ghetto community and metropolitan authorities bears a close resemblance to that which prevailed in the British, Dutch, and French colonies in Oceania and Southeast Asia.[6] The "mayor of chinatown,"[7] a person whose authority is tacitly acknowledged by civic officials in the United States, is, in most respects, nothing less than an American equivalent of the *Kapitan China,* an official who represented the Chinese inhabitants of the European colonies in Southeast Asia.[8]

Inside a Chinatown like that which developed in San Francisco, a merchant class soon became the ruling elite.[9] Because commercial success was so closely tied to social acceptance and moral probity in America, this elite enjoyed good relations with public officials. Chinatown merchants controlled immigrant associations, dispensed jobs and opportunities, settled disputes, and acted as advocates for the Chinese sojourners before white society.[10] The power of these merchants rested on a traditional foundation. They governed Chinatown through the complex interrelationships of clans and *Landsmann-schaften,* or mutual aid societies.[11] Opposition to this system of authority came primarily from members of secret societies. Eventually secret society leaders infiltrated the legitimate associations and a mercantile power structure emerged uniting the purveyors of legal and illegal goods and services.

Clans

One of the most important of the legitimate associations was the clan, an organization which traces its origins to the lineage communities of southeastern China.[12] Although descent in the lineage community was usually carefully recorded so as to exclude all except direct descendants, such meticulousness was impossible to maintain in the fast-changing social conditions of the overseas colonies. There the surname alone established identity, and clan brothers assumed their blood relationship on the basis of their common name.[13] Moreover, practical considerations often superseded loyalty to ideals of lineal purity, producing combinations of clan names and the admission of different surnames into the same association.[14] Real or assumed kinship provided the basis for clan solidarity, while "practical reasoning" resolved those questions which tended to engender disunity.[15]

Overseas clans were organized by prominent ghetto merchants who assumed many of the duties and responsibilities that lineage communities had been responsible for in China. In place of the territorially compact village, the overseas clan was organized around a leading merchant's store.[16] The merchant usually exerted leadership in his clan, established a hostelry above the store for his kinsmen, and provided aid, advice, comfort, and shelter. The clan provided the boundary of the incest taboo, and marriage was prohibited among persons bearing the same surname.[17] Clans further served to remind the sojourner of his obligations to village and family in China, and, in the absence of lineage authorities, overseas clan leaders acted *in loco parentis*.[18]

In addition to their assumption of traditional lineage authority, clans afforded an opportunity for commercial monopoly. Just as certain clans in China kept trade secrets confined to their members and restricted the entrance of upstarts,[19] so the overseas clans organized brotherhoods in trade, manufacture, and types of labor. The Dear clan, for example, operated San Francisco Chinatown's fruit and candy-stores; the Yee and Lee clans owned better-class restaurants and supplied most of the cooks in domestic service. Because they varied in location and membership, the clans could (and still can) be classified according to their economic and community dominance.[20] Thus, the Lees are most prominent in Philadelphia; the Toms in New York City; the Loys in Cleveland; the Ongs in Phoenix. In some Chinatowns more than one clan is conspicuous by its size. Thus, the Fongs and Yees both predominate in Sacramento as do the Moys and Chins in Chicago. Small Chinatowns probably sprang up on the basis of a single clan, and in the smaller towns of the Rocky Mountain areas, there have rarely been more than four clans.[21]

Hui Kuan

In addition to clans, immigrant Chinese, during the first decade of their sojourn in America (1851–1862), established five *hui kuan,* organizations which were functionally similar to but structurally different from the clan.[22] The overseas *hui kuan,* similar to its urban counterpart in China,[23] unites all those who speak a common dialect, hail from the same district of origin, or belong to the same ethnic group. In many ways it is similar to those immigrant aid societies *(Landsmannschaften)* formed by Europeans in America; however, the scope of *hui kuan* controls and the diversity of its functions far exceed those of its European counterparts. For example, wherever Chinese groups settled, their local *hui kuan* served as caravansary, credit and loan society, and employment agency.[24] It also acted in a representative capacity, speaking for its members to other *hui kuan* and to white society as well.[25] In addition, it provided arbitration and mediation services for its members, settling disputes and adjudicating issues that might otherwise erupt in open violence, or, among a people who trusted public law more than the Chinese, might have found their way into the municipal courts.[26] As a combined eleemosynary, judicial, representative, and mutual aid society, the *hui kuan* exercised a wide span of control over its members. Precisely because of its multiplicity of functions, the *hui kuan* could command allegiance. To the individual Chinese who refused it fealty, it could withhold financial aid, order social ostracism, render a punitive judgment in a suit brought before its tribunal, and arrange for false charges and incriminating testimony in public courts.[27]

The *hui kuan* confederated in 1858, i.e., during the first decade of Chinese settlement in San Francisco. At first composed of five prominent *Landsmannschaften,*[28] the confederation expanded because of the addition of new speech groups, the disintegration and reformation of already established *hui kuan,* and the admission, after much pressure, of secret societies and other associations.[29] The consolidated federation of *hui kuan* commanded at least the grudging allegiance and obedience of the Chinatown masses during the latter half of the nineteenth century, and it also earned the respect of many urban whites. Popularly called the Chinese Six Companies[30] in San Francisco, the Chinese Consolidated Benevolent Association acted as an unofficial government inside Chinatown and was the most important voice of the Chinese immigrants speaking to American officials.

As a spokesman group the Chinese Consolidated Benevolent Association has frequently protested against the legal impositions and social indignities heaped upon Chinese immigrants in America, and on occasion it has requested judicial extraterritorial rights over those Chinese likely to be accused of crimes. Among its more significant proclamations and protests were the "Letter of the Chinamen to his Excellency Governor Bigler" in 1852; the "Reply to the Message of His Excellency, Governor John Bigler" in 1855; a "Remonstrance from Chinese in California to the Congress of the United States" in 1868; a "Memorial from the Six Chinese Com-

panies: an address to the Senate and House of Representatives of the United States" in 1877; and, in 1916, a protest to the President of the United States over the onerous burden of America's exclusionist immigration practices.[31]

However, despite its growth in status, the Consolidated Benevolent Association did not have much success in preventing the passage of or revoking already existent discriminatory laws.[32] Neither did it succeed in establishing exclusive jurisdiction over Chinese criminals or in stopping the mobs that attacked Chinatowns throughout the latter decades of the nineteenth century.[33] For many years the Chinese spokesmen could not overcome the charge—levelled against them by anti-Chinese demagogues—that they held the people they claimed to represent in unlawful serfdom.[34] On the other hand, they were not always able to command complete obedience. For example, in 1893, when they ordered Chinese not to register in accordance with a newly enacted immigration act, and subsequently lost their appeal against the act in the courts, they encountered open resistance in Chinatown.[35] To most Chinese, the consequence of failure to register—deportation—was simply too grave. Eventually, however, after the worst phase of the anti-Chinese movement was over, and with the aid of white apologists who exaggerated its community services and charitable deeds, the confederated *hui kuan* achieved recognition as the sole spokesman for Chinese in America.[36] But recognition by white America was not matched by appreciation from the inhabitants of Chinatown. The latter often grumbled about the exploitative power of the combined *hui kuan* and occasionally revolted, without success, against its excesses.[37]

The community dominance of the Consolidated Benevolent Association was rooted not only in its traditional authority, but also in its control over debts, labor, commerce, and disputes.[38] The bulk of Chinese immigrants were debtors, and their obligations were owned or supervised by the *hui kuan* merchants. Moreover, the *hui kuan* acted as a general collection agency and creditor for its more affluent members. In addition, it charged its members entrance and departure fees and insisted that all debts be cleared before an immigrant returned to China. The *hui kuan* also provided the organizational base for a rotating credit system that became the principal source of capital for entrepreneurship and business development in Chinatown. Its power to give or withhold needed money served as a source of anger among those who suffered from its onerous exactions or its outright refusal to make needed loans.[39]

The *hui kuan* appear to have supervised contract labor among the immigrants and also to have provided an organizational basis for craft and commercial guilds.[40] Although apologists for the Chinese denied that the *hui kuan* had anything to do with the labor system that existed among the sojourners, there is evidence that the *hui kuan* operated the "credit-ticket" system (by which Chinese borrowed money to come to America), acted as subcontractors for white labor recruiters, and may have supplied the bosses for Chinese labor gangs deployed in various parts of the country.[41]

The pattern of both labor and business organization in Chinatown reflected the *hui kuan's* interest. Common laborers, service workers, and skilled operatives were organized according to their dialect or their district of origin in China.[42] Crafts and commercial establishments were similarly organized so that district and linguistic group monopolies over labor and business prevailed in every major Chinatown. Stores and restaurants in Chinatown were allocated space according to a traditional property right system under the control of the *hui kuan*. The property right system protected group monopolies from excessive competition and the entrance of upstarts.[43]

Perhaps the most important power of the consolidated *hui kuan* was jurisdictional in nature.[44] Mention has already been made of the mediation and arbitration service provided individual clans and *hui kuan*. When an individual felt wronged in his original suit or when disputes arose among associations, an appeal could be lodged with the tribunal of the confederated *hui kuan*. The Benevolent Association was thus the supreme organ for settlement of disputes. So long as the Chinese were either denied the right to testify in public courts or unwilling to employ the American legal system,[45] the merchant

elite of Chinatown exercised an awesome authority. Persons who were not in good standing with their clan or *hui kuan* could be refused a hearing. Those who openly revolted against the Chinatown establishment might be stripped of their property, boycotted, ostracized, or, in extreme cases, given even more violent treatment.[46]

Secret Societies

Clans and *hui kuan* were traditional and lawful societies in China and in the overseas colonies; secret societies were traditional in China, but they usually became criminal or subversive associations. Nineteenth-century migrants from Kwangtung included not a few members of the Triad Society, China's most famous clandestine association.[47] Active in rebellions and crime for centuries in China, the Triad Society provided the model for the secret societies that sprang up overseas.[48] In some settlements, such as those in rural British Columbia, where clans and *hui kuan* had failed to form, secret societies became the sole community organization.[49] The secret societies enrolled members according to interest, rather than by kin or district ties, and in one recorded instance in 1898 admitted an American journalist.[50] From the beginning of Chinese settlement in America the secret societies, popularly known as *tongs*,[51] have remained a significant part of Chinatown's organizational structure.

The scope of operations of secret societies was wide, but confined for the most part to Chinatown. On the basis of available data, their activities may be classified according to their political, protest, criminal, and benevolent character.

Political Activities

Secret societies in the Chinese community of the United States and other areas of immigrant settlement did not seek to alter, oppose, or subvert the national political structure of their host countries. They did, however, attempt to influence the course of political events in China. For the most part, their political activities failed, but in the establishment of Dr. Sun Yat Sen's republic in 1911 their efforts were significant. Sun found considerable support for his anti-Manchu movement among the overseas Chinese and especially within the secret societies.[52] A founder of two revolutionary societies himself, Sun joined or participated with many others and persuaded them to give money and, on a few occasions, men to the cause.[53] On his trip to the United States in 1904 he worked with the *Chih-kung T'ang,* an overseas branch of the Triad Society, because "there was at the time no other organization which could claim membership all over America."[54] Purposefully vague about the precise nature of his revolutionary aims, Sun did not openly challenge the secret societies' interest in restoring the Ming Dynasty.[55] Ultimately he prevailed over several rival insurrectionist groups by organizing his own revolutionary party and by gaining the support of Christian and non-Christian Chinese, a few prominent whites, and most of the secret societies.[56] So successful was Sun's movement in America—the money for the new republic was printed in San Francisco's Chinatown—that by 1910 he seriously considered transferring his headquarters from Japan to the United States.[57]

Protest

As was the case in China, secret societies provided the organizational base and the muscle for protest against individual or collective oppression. However, the secret societies in the United States did not direct their actions against white racism, Sinophobic legislation, or anti-Chinese mobs. Rather, their attention was concentrated on the power elite of Chinatown. The secret societies provided a check on clan and *hui kuan* exploitation and control over the sojourners.

There is evidence to suggest that the more notorious toughs and thugs employed by the secret societies in the United States were recruited from those who revolted against or were alienated from the merchant elite oligarchy of the *hui kuan.* Elmer Wok Wai, severely disturbed by the way of life in his broken family and bereft of clan protection, ran away from home at fifteen, became a gunman for the *Hop Sing Tong,* and served seventeen years in prison before he went to work as a domestic servant for a white family.[58] Mock Wah, certain that his inability to secure a favorable hearing before the Chinese Six Companies' tribunal stemmed from the fact that he came from a weak clan, established the *Kwong Duck Tong.*[59] Num Sing Bark, a scholar and intellectual from China, founded the *Hip Sing Tong* to take revenge on those powerful Chinatown clans that he blamed for his failure in business.[60]

Business failure because of Chinatown's clan and *hui kuan* monopolies also led Wong du King and Gaut Sing Dock to join secret societies, while an unsuccessful suit before the tribunal of the Chinese Consolidated Benevolent Association caused Yee Low Dai to form the *Suey Sing Tong* and to take by force what he could not obtain by law.[61] Hong Ah Kay, a notorious gunman for the *Suey Sing Tong,* entered the society only after losing both his father and his mistress through clan and *hui kuan* machinations.[62] Two tong leaders were apparently alienated intellectuals. Kung Ah Get of the San Jose chapter of the *Hip Sing Tong* was a self-educated and illiterate orator of considerable eloquence, while another *Hip Sing* leader, Ton Back Woo, was an erstwhile military student in China who had passed only the first of his examinations before adverse circumstances forced him to emigrate to New York City.[63] Just as the secret societies of China recruited those Chinese who had fallen or been forced out of the traditional ascriptive associations, so the clandestine lodges among the Chinese in America gathered their members from among those angered by and ostracized from Chinatown's more powerful clans and *hui kuan.*[64] However, unlike the situation in China, where bandit dynasties had occasionally been established, a tong bandit could not hope to utilize his overseas tong connections to become an emperor.[65] He might occasionally participate from afar in China's political upheavals, but usually he spent his days looking after the society's criminal operations and fighting in its many feuds.

Criminal Activities

Provision of illegal goods and services—opium, gambling, and prostitution—became the economic base for secret societies.[66] A few early efforts of the clans and *hui kuan* to subvert tong business operations were successful. However, American authorities refused the merchant leaders' requests for extraterritorial rights over Chinese criminals in America.[67] Later, after 1882—the precise date is not clear—secret society leaders were admitted to the ruling elite of Chinatown; thereafter, the strong opposition of the secret societies to traditional authorities was gradually replaced by attempts to hide and to regulate vice operations. By 1913, secret society members held positions in the Chinese Peace Society, which had been established to end internecine fights in Chinatown.[68]

The criminal activities of the secret societies were nearly impervious to American agencies of law enforcement. Policemen on the Chinatown detail were easily bribed.[69] Moreover, the widespread police practice of vice control, rather than total abolition, led them into tacit cooperation with the secret societies.[70] In some cases a Chinese tong leader used both the police and the courts to his own advantage. For example, Fong Ching, popularly known as "Little Pete," regularly informed the police about vice operations in San Francisco's Chinatown. After the arrest of the malefactors, he would reopen their establishments under police protection, the reward for being an informer.[71] The municipal courts could also be subverted by tong machinations. Tong gunmen could count on perjured testimony to be presented in their behalf and on the effective bribery of court interpreters as well.[72] Indeed, according to a set of instructions taken from a secret society thug in British Columbia in 1887, the tong promised its "salaried soldiers" protection against conviction in the courts, and, should that fail, the society further guaranteed financial aid for the convicted felon and for his family while he served his prison sentence, and burial and other death benefits should he die while working in behalf of his secret society.[73]

Benevolent Activities

The charitable and fraternal activities of the secret societies were confined to aiding their own members. As the societies prospered they erected elaborate halls in Chinatown which not only reflected their affluence, but also were used for fraternal and charitable purposes. For example, when the Chinese Society of Free Masons, a euphemism for the Triad Society,[74] opened a new building in San Francisco in 1907, a local newspaper reported that one of its floors would house destitute widows and orphans because "care will be taken of all those in any way connected with the lodge, who have been overtaken with misfortune."[75] Mutual aid was also a feature of rural lodges of the secret societies, but charity was chastened by a cautious regard for the small treasury available and by the fear that interlopers would presume upon the tong's benevolence. A set of secret society rules from a lodge in the Fraser River area illustrates the conservatism and apprehensions of the small isolated chapters. The society provided a bunkhouse, arbitration and mediation services, and sickness and death benefits, but, perhaps in keeping with the womanless condition of the miners, no funds were provided for expenses related to childbirth, marriage, or funerals.[76] A partial exception to this rule seems to have been made in the case of secret society thugs. There is evidence that at least one such thug was promised a $500 death benefit, free medical care, a subvention of $10 per month, and a flat fee of $250 plus the cost of transportation back to China in case of permanent disability.[77] The rural chapters, beset by local problems and worried about interlopers from San Francisco's Chinatown, took care to protect their jurisdiction from frauds. A British Columbia lodge rule read: "Headmen from San Francisco intending to establish a forum for teaching disciples whether in the town or in the mining areas must hold a license from the *Chih-kung-T'ang.* Anyone without such a license pretending to be a Headman will be prosecuted."[78] Penury and fear seemed to place significant limitations on mutual aid and benevolence within the secret societies.

Conflict and the Web of Group Affiliation in
Chinatown

Chinese communities were highly organized, but
organizations rested on different and in some cases
contradictory foundations. The aims of the clans,
hui kuan, and secret societies often clashed, and their
peaceful competition not infrequently gave way to
violence. Chinese immigrants frequently fell out
with one another in quarrels over women, money, or
politics. Sometimes these disputes escalated into
group conflicts. Although the term "tong war"
suggests that the violent altercations within America's Chinatowns were confined to the several secret
societies, in fact these struggles included all three of
the basic types of associations. For many decades the
internal conflicts among the Chinese sojourners
isolated them from the larger society and bound
them together in an antagonistic cooperation.

Violent conflicts in Chinatown arose for the most
part out of four major kinds of situations: rival
aspirations for control of the illegal commerce in
drugs, gambling, and prostitution; transplantation
of mainland civil wars or revolutions to the overseas
Chinatowns; revolts of the poor against the merchant oligarchy of Chinatown; and rival claims to a
woman. The first is illustrated by the unfortunate
career of Fong Ching, a secret society leader whose
daring plan to take control of vice in San Francisco's
Chinese quarter resulted in the formation of a
coalition of tongs to oppose his scheme and, finally,
in his assassination in a Chinatown barbershop.[79]
The second by the Weaverville War (1854), the
California version of China's Hakka-Punti War
(1855–1868).[80] The third by the war between the
wealthy Yee clan and the On Yick Tong, a secret
society composed largely of underpaid workers.[81]
The last has countless illustrations. The shortage of
women among the overseas Chinese led many of the
young male immigrants to resort to prostitutes, most
of whom were Chinese girls brought to America
under contract as indentured domestic servants and
put to work in the brothels that dotted San Francisco's Chinatown.[82]

At the turn of the century, several powerful secret

societies fought one another for monopoly of vice
operations in Chinatowns throughout the United
States.[83] The worst of these fights occurred in San
Francisco and New York, although branches and
chapters in smaller Chinese settlements also took
part. Since stakes in these battles were high, the
fighting was fierce. Ultimately the less powerful
secret societies were destroyed or coopted into the
larger ones. The outcome of these struggles was the
admission of secret society leaders into the councils
of the confederated *hui kuan* and a consolidation of
crime and vice in Chinatown under the control of a
restive secret society oligopoly.

Although secret societies were at first opposed by
clan and *hui kuan* leaders, the latter's efforts to stamp
them out failed. Buoyed by their success in vice, the
secret societies challenged the right of the clan-*hui
kuan* elites to dominate Chinatown. In the late 1880's
a violent struggle broke out between the Suey Sing
Tong and the Wong Clan in San Francisco;[84] a few
years later another bloody fight between the Yee
Clan and the On Yick Tong ended the armed truce
that characterized Chinatown after the Suey Sing-
Wong fight had ended.[85] In another bloody fight in
1893 the secret societies sought to end *hui kuan*
authority in Chinatown. After a financially exhaustive and abortive attempt by San Francisco's Six
Companies to test the constitutionality of the Geary
Act, several secret societies combined in a violent
and vituperative campaign to persuade the rank
and file Chinese to renounce their allegiance to the
confederation of *hui kuan.*[86] That effort failed, but
secret society leaders were soon established within
the power structure of Chinatown.[87]

Not all the fights in Chinatown were related to
local matters. Another source of violence in the
Chinese communities of San Francisco and elsewhere were the rivalries between lineage communities and ethnic groups in southeastern China that
were carried overseas by the emigrants.[88] A local
incident might spark the renewal of a feud that had
originated in the homeland. Thus, the Hakka-Punti
war was fought not only in Kwangtung between
1855 and 1868, but also in Malaya as the Larut War
of 1872–1873 and in the United States as the
Weaverville War of 1854.[89] In the American phase of

this war, the *Sam Yap Hui Kuan,* composed of Cantonese, fell out with the *Yan Wo Hui Kuan,* which represented the Hakka group, at China Camp and at Weaverville, California. In one battle at Kentucky Ranch, some 900 "soldiers" of the Yan Wo met 1200 of the Sam Yap "army" and fought until the latter were victorious.[90] Both groups secured military assistance from local white Californians.

After 1900 not a few of the so-called "tong wars" in America's Chinatowns were among rival factions seeking to overthrow the Manchu dynasty. Although Dr. Sun was able to unite the warring factions in many overseas areas, including the United States, these united fronts did not last long. Disputes among societies supporting different leaders and ideologists broke out before and after the Chinese Revolution of 1911.[91] Because the secret societies were essentially criminal and rebellious rather than political and revolutionary, these fights also coincided with local struggles for power, wealth, and women.

Some of the conflicts in San Francisco's Chinatown were primitive class conflicts. They represented the inarticulate, non-ideological revolts of poor Chinese against a system which they resented and did not control. One example of this premodern class struggle is found in the war between the Yee Clan and the On Yick Tong.[92] Ostensibly begun because of an argument over a prostitute, the bloody fight also reflected the resentment of the secret society members toward the Yee clan because of its wealth, status, and power. The clan was composed of many prosperous merchants, and its treasury allegedly contained hundreds of thousands of dollars. In sharp contrast the On Yick group consisted primarily of laborers, cooks, and restaurant workers, who lived in the Chinatowns of Stockton, San Francisco, and Portland. In this "war," as in most such fights, the merchants were eventually victorious.

Still another source of hostility in San Francisco and elsewhere was the extreme imbalance in Chinatown's sex ratio, a situation which helps explain the numerous fights that broke out over women.[93] These quarrels between suitors were often used as a pretext to reopen old feuds, or as a justification for violent seizure of power. Not only did such fights break out between rival suitors but also between love-struck men and the brothel keepers who held girls under contract.[94] Sometimes a young Chinese would offer to buy up a girl's contract, and if he was refused he would kidnap her. The brothel-keeper would call on his secret society protectors to recover the girl, and the kidnapper would enlist the aid of his clan or *hui kuan.* The resulting struggle would be short, bloody, and usually fatal for the couple.[95] So long as the shortage of females in Chinatown remained acute, and it remained so until the late 1920s, rivalries and feuds over women continued to generate wars among associations.

This analysis of the first six decades of organizational life inside Chinatown permits a concluding discussion that is both sociological and historical. In the first sixty years of their settlement in San Francisco, Chinese immigrants, hard-pressed by the anti-Chinese movement, still managed to forge a community in the strange and hostile environment of the West. It was a traditional community, transplanting to the urban overseas Chinatown many of the institutions and customs of imperial China. Thus clans, *hui kuan,* and secret societies emerged among the immigrants as the principal organizations promoting, respectively, familial solidarity, mutual aid, and organized crime and rebellion. In the new Chinatowns these traditional associations vied with one another for the allegiance of the immigrants, overall community domination, and, in the case of the *hui kuan,* the jurisdictional right to speak for all the Chinese in the city.

The organizational developments and internecine fights that took place in Chinatown from 1850 to 1910 indicate that forming an overseas Chinese community was not an easy task. Principles of clan solidarity, barriers of language and dialect, allegiance to rebellious secret societies, and their own competitive interest in making enough money to permit retirement in China divided the loyalties of the Chinese immigrants. Yet during the same period the depredations of anti-Chinese mobs, the difficulties and indignities imposed by restrictive immigration legislation, the occupational discrimination created by state and local laws prohibiting or limiting the employment of Chinese, and the active opposition of the American labor movement to the Chinese workingman all seemed to call for a community united in the face of its enemies. What emerged out of this condition of pressures from without the ghetto and divisions within was a pattern alternating between order and violence. By 1910 this pattern had assumed a complex but recognizable sociological form: that of the community whose members are bound to one another not only because of external hostility but also because of deadly internal factionalism.[96]

Both community order and inter-association conflict developed patterns and rituals in Chinatown. When order did prevail in the Chinese quarter, it was grounded in the community's institutions of law, arbitration, and conflict resolution. Most of the disputes within and among clans, *hui kuan,* and secret societies were settled by arbitration, and many appeals were amicably resolved by the tribunal of the confederation of *hui kuan.* Of course, some litigants did not accept the judgments of the tribunals. In some cases angry losers to a suit would withdraw from the association, join or found a new *hui kuan* or secret society, or rebel against the established authority in Chinatown.[97] But any system of law and order implies, if it does not generate, resistance and rebellion. Although the desire for order in Chinatown was strong during the nineteenth century, conflict was more in evidence. Even during the peaceful periods, ghetto life more nearly resembled an armed truce than a harmonious community.

If order in Chinatown was governed by traditional law, the violence in the ghetto had a definite ritual to it. In accordance with Chinese custom, no inter-association feud began without a ceremonial exchange of insults and the posting of a *chun hung,* i.e., a declaration of war.[98] Thus, the Weaverville War of 1854 began with the antagonists hurling carefully worded abusive statements at one another followed by a challenge to fight. In another case, that of the abortive attempt to overthrow the president of San Francisco's Consolidated Benevolent Association in 1893, the secret societies posted a properly worded and insulting *chun hung* on the bulletin boards and store windows of Chinatown.[99] The mode of fighting and the designation of those who would be permitted to engage in armed violence were also carefully regulated. The secret societies maintained their own bands of "salaried soldiers," and, although the evidence is not so clear, the clans and *hui kuan* probably did the same.[100] According to the instructions given to one thug by his secret society, he was forbidden to use weapons except in service to the tong.[101] In any fight the number of casualties on each side was carefully enumerated, and a crude version of the *lex talionis* seems to have governed the taking of life. A fight was brought to an end by diplomatic negotiations carried out by representatives of the belligerent parties and, often enough, presided over by a neutral mediator. The end of a "tong war" was solemnized by the signing of a treaty of peace and followed by a ceremonial banquet.[102] These rules, codes, and rituals provided a measure of stability to the wars and even curbed, but did not altogether eliminate, violence.[103]

San Francisco's Chinatown witnessed both a considerable amount of conflict and an increasingly complex web of group affiliation in the years between 1850 and 1910. On the one hand, the intramural struggles for wealth, women, and power certainly did not lend themselves to peaceful relations among the immigrants. On the other hand, the fabric of group affiliation was woven more tightly[104] as wars generated the need for allies and a system of collective security. And throughout this period of intra-community conflict, the *hui kuan* leaders presented themselves to municipal authorities, state legislators, and congressional investigators as spokesmen for the entire Chinese community.[105]

Viewed from the perspective of a sociology of conflict, Chinatown in the years between 1850 and 1910 appears to be an extremely complex example of the thesis first developed by Georg Simmel and elaborated by Edward Alsworth Ross and Lewis Coser.[106] As Coser states it: "It seems to be generally accepted by sociologists that the distinction between 'ourselves, the we-group, or in-group, and everybody else, or the other-groups, out-groups' is established in and through conflict."[107] The social organization of San Francisco's Chinatown was comprised of a number of we-groups, each one of which looked at the others as an out-group. At times these we-groups were arrayed against one another in deadly combat. Yet, at other times, for example, when the Chinese immigrants as a whole felt threatened by white American racism, these opposed groups would postpone or put aside their differences and appear to form a united front.[108] The oscillation between intramural wars and the semblance of solidarity required in the face of a common enemy must have modified the strength and character of the Chinese associations, although, one must add, the evidence for this statement is not readily available.

The intramural conflicts probably added to the already considerable isolation of the Chinese community from the larger society. Feuds among clans, tong wars, and fights to depose the headmen of the Consolidated Benevolent Association must have seemed incomprehensible to most white Americans, who were not informed about traditional Chinese modes of organization or conflict resolution. These wars did generate a widespread stereotype of Chinatown that included lurid stories about opium dens, sing-song girls, hatchet men, and tong wars.[109] The real Chinese society was difficult to discern behind this kind of romantic illusion.

However, if intramural conflicts isolated Chinatown from the metropolis, they also very probably challenged the complex structures of solidarity inside the ghetto. Although we need much more evidence than we now have, including such documents as the biographies and papers of many ordinary Chinatowners, it is not unreasonable to suppose that feuds and fights among associations were the occasions for discovering and testing group loyalty. Clan, *hui kuan,* and secret society leaders very likely made demands of allegiance, service, and money on their members during times of hostilities in the ghetto. And it seems equally reasonable to suppose that, at different times and in different situations, the ordinary clan, *hui kuan,* or secret society member was variously disposed to regard his own association with warm feelings, fierce patrio-

tism, troublesome annoyance, and even, perhaps, nagging fear. Yet in times of fighting, there was no mass exit of Chinese from Chinatown. At the very least, then, it would appear that the ordinary Chinese immigrant acquiesced in the difficulties imposed by his ghetto situation, and, at the most, some must have joined feverishly in support of their associations.

Simmel pointed to the fact that enmities and reciprocal antagonisms maintain established systems by encouraging a balance among their components.[110] The conflicts in Chinatown seem to bear out his observation in two distinct ways. First, the very fact that fights were confined to the ghetto and limited to matters affecting its Chinese denizens helped to establish and maintain the boundaries of the ghetto community. Chinese clans feuded with one another and not with white American families or Irish or any other ethnic group's clans. The *hui kuan* established its merchant oligopoly in Chinatown and not throughout the city, and the primitive class conflicts against its economic domination took place inside the Chinese quarter. The secret societies organized vice and crime in the ghetto and not elsewhere, and their gang wars were also confined to Chinatown. Moreover, the fights that broke out among the associations were aimed at issues and elements that were physically, socially, and politically located inside Chinatown (or, on occasion, in China). It is true that occasionally outsiders—police, clergy, diplomats, and the representatives of the Chinese government—became involved in the wars in Chinatown. But outsiders served only in an *ad hoc* capacity; their services were employed to balance the power of one or another of the contending factions.

The second sense in which Chinatown conflict provided for balance in the community arises from the fact that it was not directed at the absolute obliteration of opponents.[111] It must be remembered that hardly any struggle in Chinatown ever ended with unconditional surrender or total annihilation. The balance of power among contending parties prevented such an outcome. And this balance established the precarious stability in the community's structure. When peace treaties were signed, each party recognized the rights of the other to exist and to continue in the competition for women, wealth, and power. Chinatown was thus something of a Hobbesian cockpit, except that no fight ever escalated into a war of all against all or ended with a genocidal "final solution." We may speculate that the condition of long-term armed watchfulness probably generated an interest in the conservation of the existing institutions, since any party had an interest in knowing just who was representing any other body of Chinese and how many persons he represented. Thus, community conflict and group maintenance complemented one another. Conflict in Chinatown generated the need for groups to form and cohere; groups found added sources of *esprit de corps* in the conflicts that erupted. Conflict and group affiliation were the warp and woof of the first six decades of the Chinese community.

Notes

1. See, e.g., George F. Seward, *Chinese Immigration, in Its Social and Economical Aspects* (New York, 1881), 223–242, 261–291; Mary Coolidge, *Chinese Immigration* (New York, 1909), 401–422; Carl Glick, *Shake Hands with the Dragon* (New York, 1941), 34–44, 81–92, 244–245; S. W. Kung, *Chinese in American Life: Some Aspects of their History, Status, Problems, and Contributions* (Seattle, 1962), 76–78, 197–227; Calvin Lee, *Chinatown, U.S.A.* (Garden City, 1965) 28–37, 82–128; Betty Lee Sung, *Mountain of Gold: The Story of the Chinese in America* (New York, 1967), 130–186; Roger Daniels, "Westerners from the East: Oriental Immigrants Reappraised," *Pacific Historical Review,* XXXV (1966), 378–384.

2. See Seward, *Chinese Immigration,* 292–310; Coolidge, *Chinese Immigration,* 26–336; Elmer C. Sandmeyer, *The Anti-Chinese Movement in California* (Urbana, 1939), 25–111.

3. Victor G. Nee and Brett de Bary Nee, *Longtime Californ': A Documentary Study of an American Chinatown* (New York, 1972), 272–273; Richard Dillon, *The Hatchet Men: The Story of the Tong Wars in San Francisco's Chinatown* (New York, 1962), 361; H. Mark Lai, "A Historical Survey of Organizations of the Left among the Chinese in America," *Bulletin of Concerned Asian Scholars,* IV (Fall, 1972), 10–19; Samuel Gompers, *Seventy Years of Life and Labor* (New York, 1925), I, 216–217, 304–305; II, 160–169; Herbert Hill, "The Racial Practices of Organized Labor—The Age of Gompers and After," in *Employment, Race and Poverty: A Critical Study of the Disadvantaged Status of Negro Workers from 1865 to 1965,* edited by Arthur M. Ross and Herbert Hill (New York, 1967), 365–402; Hill, "Anti-Oriental Agitation and the Rise of Working-Class Racism," *Society,* X (Jan.–Feb., 1973), 43–54; Carey McWilliams, *Factories in the Fields: The Story of Migratory Farm Labor in California* (Boston, 1939), 66–88; Lyman, *The Asian in the West,* 9–26, 65–80.

4. Stanford M. Lyman, *Chinese Americans* (New York, 1974); Ivan Light, "From Vice District to Tourist Attraction: The Moral Career of American Chinatowns, 1880–1940," *Pacific Historical Review,* XLIII (1974), 367–394; Victor Nee, "The Kuomintang in Chinatown," *Bridge Magazine* I (May–June, 1972), 20–24.

5. Thus, there has never been a "mayor of Little Tokyo" in the United States, nor have European immigrant *Landsmannschaften* ever secured such a broad span of power over their communities as that of the Chinese *hui kuan.* See Stanford M. Lyman, "The Structure of Chinese Society in Nineteenth Century America" (Ph.D. dissertation, University of California, Berkeley, 1961), 272–276.

6. See C. S. Wong, *A Gallery of Chinese Kapitans* (Singapore, 1964).

7. Stewart Culin, "Customs of the Chinese in America," *Journal of American Folk-Lore,* III (July–Sept. 1890), 193.

8. According to the system of colonial administration developed in the British, Dutch, and French colonies in Southeast Asia, a *Kapitan China* was the representative of the Chinese inhabitants. He served on the various advisory councils, and usually represented the interests of the dominant clan, speech, or secret societies within the Chinese community. Usually he was elected by the Chinese societies and approved for appointment by the European colonial administration, but the method of securing this office varied. See, for example, J. M. Gullick, *The Story of Kuala Lumpur* (Singapore, 1956), 16–25, 64–79; W. E. Willmott, *The Political Structure of the Chinese Community in Cambodia* (New York, 1970), 111–126, 141–160.

9. For early evidence, see "Letter of the Chinamen to his Excellency Gov. Bigler," dated San Francisco, April 29, 1852, in *Littel's Living Age,* XXIV (July 3, 1852), 32–34.

10. See "New Rules of the Yeung Wo Ui Kun" and "Sze Yap Company," reprinted in William Speer, "Democracy of the Chinese," *Harper's Monthly,* XXXVII (Nov. 1868), 836–848; A. W. Loomis, "The Six Chinese Companies," *Overland Monthly,* I (Sept. 1868), 221–227; "Address of the Chinese Six Companies to the American Public," April 5, 1876, in "Report of the Joint Special Committee to Investigate Chinese Immigration," 44 Cong., 2 sess., *S. Rept. 689* (Feb. 27, 1877), 39; Pun Chi, "A Remonstrance from the Chinese in California to the Congress of the United States," 1855, in William Speer, *The Oldest and Newest Empire: China and the United States* (Hartford, 1870), 575–581.

11. *Landsmannschaften* is perhaps the only appropriate term to describe the several kinds of mutual aid societies established by Chinese in America. These societies originated in China as dialect groups founded by rural Chinese who had migrated to China's cities. See Ping-ti Ho, *Chung-Kuo hui kuan shih-lun* (Taipei, 1966).

12. See Maurice Freedman, *Lineage Organization in Southeastern China* (London, 1958).

13. Herbert A. Giles, "The Family Names," *Journal of the Royal Asiatic Society, North China Branch,* XXI (Aug. 1886), 255–288; Leong Gor Yun, *Chinatown Inside Out* (New York, 1936), 54–66.

14. Leong Gor Yun, *Chinatown Inside Out,* 59; W. E. Wilmott, "Chinese Clan Associations in Vancouver," *Man,* LXIV (1964), 33–37.

15. For example, in the United States and Canada there are two distinct clans using the surname "Wong." The characters forming the surname of the two clans are quite distinguishable in written script, but their Anglicization is the same, that is, the English term "Wong." There are members of both clans in each clan organization.

16. Stewart Culin, *China in America: A Study of the Social Life of the Chinese in Eastern Cities of the United States* (Philadelphia, 1887), 10.

17. Sir George Thomas Staunton, trans., *Ta Tsing Leu Lee; Being the Fundamental Laws, and a Selection from the Supplementary Statutes of the Penal Code of China; Originally Printed and Published in Pekin in Various Successive Editions . . .* (London, 1810), 114.

18. See the letters from a mother in China to her son in California and to his clan brothers, in A. W. Loomis, "The Old East in the New West," *Overland Monthly,* I (Oct. 1868), 362.

19. Max Weber, *The Religion of China: Confucianism and Taoism,* trans. Hans H. Gerth (Glencoe, 1951), 86–91.

20. Chinese Chamber of Commerce, *San Francisco's Chinatown: History, Function and Importance of Social Organization* (San Francisco, 1953), 3.

21. Leong Gor Yun, *Chinatown Inside Out,* 54–66; Chinese Chamber of Commerce, *San Francisco's Chinatown,* 3; Mary Chapman, "Notes on the Chinese in Boston," *Journal of American Folk-Lore,* V (Oct.–Dec. 1892), 324; Rose Hum Lee, "The Decline of Chinatowns in the United States," *American Journal of Sociology,* LIV (1949), 422–432.

22. Cf. Maurice Freedman, "Immigrants and Associations: Chinese in Nineteenth-Century Singapore," *Comparative Studies in Society and History,* III (1960), 25–48.

23. Ping-ti Ho, "Salient Aspects of China's Heritage," in *China in Crisis,* ed. Ping-ti Ho and Tang Tsou (Chicago, 1968), Vol. I, Book I, 32–33.

24. Otis Gibson, *The Chinese in America* (Cincinnati, 1879), 49–51; "Report of the Joint Special Committee to Investigate Chinese Immigration," 24; Lyman, "The Structure of Chinese Society," 283–308.

25. Lyman, "The Structure of Chinese Society," 314.

26. Fong Kum Ngon [Walter N. Fong], "The Chinese Six Companies," *Overland Monthly,* XXIII (May, 1894), 524–525; Speer, "The Oldest and Newest Empire," 836–848.

27. Loomis, "The Six Chinese Companies," 221–227; Gibson, *The Chinese in America,* 339–343; Leong Gor Yun, *Chinatown Inside Out,* 49–50; "Report of the Joint Special Committee to Investigate Chinese Immigration," 95.

28. *Hui kuan* formed, dissolved, and reconstituted themselves throughout the first sixty years of Chinese settlement. The Canton Association, formed in 1851, reconstituted itself as the Sam Yup Association in the same year; the Sze Yup Association, formed in 1851, dissolved over internal disputes into the Hop Wo Association (also incorporating the entire Yee clan, which had withdrawn from the Ning Yung Association) in 1862 and the Kong Chow Association in 1867; the Young Wo Association formed in 1852; the Sun On Association, formed in 1851, reconstituted itself as the Yan Wo Association in 1854; the Ning Yung Association, formed in 1853, suffered the loss of the Yee clan in 1862 but continued to represent immigrants from Toishan; the Sue Hing Association was formed during the years 1879–1882 by dissidents from the Hop Wo Association, while the Yan Hoi Association was founded in 1898, again by Hop Wo defectors; the Look Yup Association was established in 1901 by a coalition of groups from the Sam Yup Association and the Kong Chow Association; in 1909 the Yan Hoi Association was absorbed by the Sue Hing Association. The structure remained stable thereafter for forty-two years; in 1951 the Fa Yuan Association formed as a splinter from the Sam Yup Association. See the historical chart made by Him Mark Lai in Nee and Nee, *Longtime Californ',* 272–273.

29. William Hoy, *The Chinese Six Companies* (San Francisco, 1942), 5, 28, 59–62; Chinese Chamber of Commerce, *San Francisco's Chinatown,* 5; Leong Gor Yun, *Chinatown Inside Out,* 6–9; Culin, *China in America,* 28.

30. Although the number of *hui kuan* increased beyond six, that number has been stereotypically associated with the confederation in San Francisco.

31. See footnotes 9 and 10 *supra;* see also Speer, *The Oldest and Newest Empire,* 578–581; Gibson, *The Chinese in America,* 315–323; J. S. Tow, *The Real Chinese in America* (New York, 1923), 118–119.

32. The legislation is summarized in Lucille Eaves, *A History of Labor Legislation in California* (Berkeley, 1909), 105–195; Ira B. Cross, *A History of the Labor Movement in California* (Berkeley, 1935), 73–130; Coolidge, *Chinese Immigration,* 55–82; Sandmeyer, *The Anti-Chinese Movement in California,* 40–77; Lyman, "The Structure of Chinese Society," 383–386; Lyman, *The Asian in the West,* 23–24; Robert F. Heizer and Alan F. Almquist, *The Other Californians: Prejudice and Discrimination under Spain, Mexico, and the United States* (Berkeley, 1971), 154–177.

33. For Chinese merchant elites' abortive attempts to obtain extraterritorial rights over Chinese immigrant criminals, see

Speer, *The Oldest and Newest Empire,* 579–580, 600–601; Gibson, *The Chinese in America,* 315–323. For unchecked mob actions in Chinatown, see Lyman, *The Asian in the West,* 12–16, 19–23.

34. See, for example, Richard Hay Drayton, "The Chinese Six Companies," *The Californian Illustrated Magazine,* IV (Aug. 1893), 472–479.

35. *Fong Yue Ting v. U.S.,* 149 U.S. 698 (1893). It was this decision, sustaining the Geary Act and requiring all Chinese in the United States to register with the collector of internal revenue, that sparked a rebellion against Chun Ti Chu, the Six Companies' president. Chun had provoked the case by ordering Chinese to refuse to register. Thousands of Chinese might have been deported had not Congress, under pressure from the employers of Chinese, hastily enacted the McCreary Amendment, extending the deadline for registration another six months. See Drayton, "The Chinese Six Companies," 472–493; Fong, "The Chinese Six Companies," 525–526; Coolidge, *Chinese Immigration,* 209–233.

36. Coolidge, *Chinese Immigration,* 409–411; Nee and Nee, *Longtime Californ,'* 228–249; James T. Lee, "The Story of the New York Chinese Consolidated Benevolent Association," *Bridge Magazine,* I (May–June 1972), 15–18; James T. Lee, "The Chinese Benevolent Association: An Assessment," *ibid.,* (July–Aug. 1972), 15–16, 41, 43, 46–47.

37. See Loomis, "The Six Chinese Companies," 222–223; Gibson, *The Chinese in America,* 341–343.

38. For a complete discussion, see Lyman, "The Structure of Chinese Society," 288–328.

39. Gibson, *The Chinese in America,* 339–341; "Report of the Joint Special Committee to Investigate Chinese Immigration," 24; Hoy, *The Chinese Six Companies,* 23; Ivan Light, *Ethnic Enterprise in America: Business and Welfare among Chinese, Japanese, and Blacks* (Berkeley, 1972), 81–100.

40. "Chinese Immigration: Its Social, Moral and Political Effects," *Report to the California State Senate of Its Special Committee on Chinese Immigration* (Sacramento, 1878), 70; *Proceedings of the Numismatic and Antiquarian Society of Philadelphia,* Nov. 7, 1895 (Philadelphia, 1899), 99–100; Fong, "The Chinese Six Companies," 523–524; H. C. Bennett, "The Chinese in California, Their Numbers and Influence," *Sacramento Daily Union* (Nov. 17, 1869), 8; Chinese Chamber of Commerce, *San Francisco's Chinatown,* 5; Loomis, "The Six Chinese Companies," 226; Coolidge, *Chinese Immigration,* 406–407; Rose Hum Lee, *The Chinese in the United States of America* (Hong Kong, 1960), 146, 385–386.

41. Seward, *Chinese Immigration,* 136–158; Coolidge, *Chinese Immigration,* 48–51. Cf., for example, the "Agreement Between the English Merchant and Chinaman" (1849), a contract for transporting Chinese to California. Subsequent translations have pointed out that the "English" merchant was in fact an American. The contract will be found in the Wells Fargo Bank Historical Collection, San Francisco; see also "Letter of the Chinamen," 32–33; Persia Crawford Campbell, *Chinese Coolie*

Emigration to Countries within the British Empire (London, 1923), 27–36, 150–151; Rhoda Hoff, *America's Immigrants: Adventures in Eyewitness History* (New York, 1967), 74–75; "Chinese Immigration: Its Social, Moral, and Political Effects," 70; Fong, "The Chinese Six Companies," 523–524; "Japanese and Other Immigrant Races in the Pacific Coast and Rocky Mountain States," 61 Cong., 2 sess., *S. Doc. 633* (1911), 391–399; Thomas W. Chinn, ed., *A History of the Chinese in America: A Syllabus* (San Francisco, 1969), 11–21; Albert Rhodes, "The Chinese at Beaver Falls," *Lippincott's Magazine,* XIX (June, 1877), 708–714.

42. Chinese Chamber of Commerce, *San Francisco's Chinatown,* 5; Thomas W. Chinn, *A History of the Chinese in America,* 47–54.

43. Rose Hum Lee, *The Chinese in the United States,* 385–386; Leong Gor Yun, *Chinatown Inside Out,* 36–39.

44. Loomis, "The Six Chinese Companies," 223; Fong, "The Chinese Six Companies," 524–525; Culin, "Customs of the Chinese in America," 193; Speer, "Democracy of the Chinese," 836–848.

45. In 1854 the statute prohibiting Negroes and Indians from testifying for or against Caucasians was extended by the California Supreme Court to ban Chinese testimony as well. *People v. Hall,* 4 Cal. 399 (1854). See also *Speer v. See Yup,* 13 Cal. 73 (1855); *People v. Elyea,* 14 Cal. 144 (1859). The statute was revised to admit the testimony of Negroes in 1863, but Mongolians, Chinese, and Indians remained under the ban until January 1, 1873, when the revised California statutes admitted witnesses to the courts regardless of color or nationality. See Chinn, *A History of Chinese in California,* 24; Heizer and Almquist, *The Other Californians,* 47, 129–130, 229–234; Coolidge, *Chinese Immigration,* 75–76. However, during this period Chinese mounted numerous civil rights cases in the courts where testimony against whites was not a factor. The traditional Chinese opposition to employing public courts predates the coming of Chinese to America. See Sybille van der Sprenkel, *Legal Institutions in Manchu China* (London, 1962), 80–111.

46. "Report of Special Committee to the Honorable, the Board of Supervisors of the City and County of San Francisco," in Willard B. Farwell, *The Chinese at Home and Abroad* (San Francisco, 1885), 51–58.

47. For nineteenth-century reports on the Triad Society, see Jean Chesneaux, *Secret Societies in China in the Nineteenth and Twentieth Centuries,* trans. by Gillian Nettle (Ann Arbor, 1971), 1–135; Chesneaux, ed., *Popular Movements and Secret Societies in China, 1840–1950* (Stanford, 1972), 1–144; Gustave Schlegel, *Thian Ti Hwui: The Hung-League or Heaven-Earth-League—A Secret Society with the Chinese in China and India* (Batavia, 1866); William Stanton, *The Triad Society or Heaven and Earth Association* (Shanghai, 1900); J. S. M. Ward and W. G. Stirling, *The Hung Society or the Society of Heaven and Earth* (3 vols., London, 1925); Mervyn Llewelyn Wynne, *Triad and Tabut: A Survey of the Origin and Diffusion of Chinese and Mohammedan Secret Societies in the Malay Peninsula, A.D. 1800–1935* (Singapore, 1941), 1–151, 202–352; Leon Comber, *An*

Introduction to Chinese Secret Societies in Malaya (Singapore, 1957); Comber, *Chinese Secret Societies in Malaya: A Survey of the Triad Society from 1800 to 1900* (Locust Valley, 1959); Wilfred Blythe, *The Impact of Chinese Secret Societies in Malaya: A Historical Study* (London, 1969); W. P. Morgan, *Triad Societies in Hong Kong* (Hong Kong, 1960).

48. Stewart Culin, "Chinese Secret Societies in the United States," *Journal of American Folk-Lore,* III (Jan.-Mar. 1890), 39–43; Culin, "The I Hing or 'Patriotic Rising,' a Secret Society among the Chinese in America," *Proceedings of the Numismatic and Antiquarian Society of Philadelphia for the Years 1887–1889,* III (Nov. 1887), 51–57.

49. Stanford M. Lyman, William Willmott, and Berching Ho, "Rules of a Chinese Secret Society in British Columbia," *Bulletin of the School of Oriental and African Studies,* XXVII (1964), 530–539.

50. *San Francisco Call,* Jan. 9, 1898.

51. See Stanford M. Lyman, "Chinese Secret Societies in the Occident: Notes and Suggestions for Research on the Sociology of Secrecy," *Canadian Review of Sociology and Anthropology,* I (May, 1964), 79–102.

52. Sun Yat Sen, *Memoirs of a Chinese Revolutionary* (London, n.d.), 190–193.

53. A romanticized account of the recruitment and training of Chinese youths for service in the revolution will be found in Carl Glick, *Double Ten: Captain O'Banion's Story of the Chinese Revolution* (New York, 1945). See also Ta-Ling Lee, *Foundations of the Chinese Revolution, 1905–1912* (New York, 1970), 104–109; Carl Glick and Hong Sheng-Hwa, *Swords of Silence: Chinese Secret Societies—Past and Present* (New York, 1947), 94–235; Harold Z. Schiffrin, *Sun Yat-Sen and the Origins of the Chinese Revolution* (Berkeley, 1968), 243–244, 334–338; Philip P. Choy, "Gold Mountain of Lead: The Chinese Experience in California," *California Historical Quarterly,* I (1971), 271.

54. Ta-Ling Lee, *Foundations of the Chinese Revolution,* 106.

55. James Cantlie and Sheridan Jones, *Sun Yat-Sen and the Awakening of China* (New York, 1912), 132–134.

56. Schiffrin, *Sun Yat-Sen and the Origins of the Chinese Revolution,* 331–334.

57. For a discussion and a photograph of the money printed in San Francisco, see Alexander McLeod, *Pigtails and Gold Dust* (Caldwell, 1947), 148–150. On the proposed move of Sun's headquarters from Tokyo to San Francisco, see K. S. Liew, *Struggle for Democracy: Sung Chiao-jen and the 1911 Chinese Revolution* (Berkeley, 1968), 79–80.

58. Veta Griggs, *Chinaman's Chance: The Life Story of Elmer Wok Wai* (New York, 1969).

59. St. Clair McKelway, *True Tales from the Annals of Crime and Rascality* (New York, 1951), 153–169; Eng Ying Gong and Bruce Grant, *Tong War!* (New York, 1930), 27–30.

60. Gong and Grant, *Tong War,* 30–31.

61. *Ibid.,* 31–33, 112–130.

62. *Ibid.,* 39–54.

63. *Ibid.,* 122–130, 161–162.

64. Lyman, "The Structure of Chinese Society," 246–251.

65. According to Wolfram Eberhard, the founders of the Han Dynasty (206 B.C.–220 A.D.), the Later Liang Dynasty (907–922 A.D.), and the Ming Dynasty (1368–1644) were secret society bandit leaders. Eberhard, *Conquerors and Rulers: Social Forces in Medieval China* (Leiden, 1956), 89–106.

66. "Chinese and Japanese Labor in the Mountain and Pacific States," *Reports of the United States Industrial Commission on Immigration,* XV, Part 4 (Washington, D.C., 1901), 773–792; Stewart Culin, "The Gambling Games of the Chinese in America," *Publications of the University of Pennsylvania Series in Philology, Literature, and Archaeology,* I (1891), 1–17.

67. Speer, *The Oldest and Newest Empire,* 603–604.

68. Hoy, *The Chinese Six Companies,* 11, 22–23; Lee, *The Chinese in the United States of America,* 156–160; Gong and Grant, *Tong War,* 211; C. N. Reynolds, "The Chinese Tongs," *American Journal of Sociology,* XL (1935), 623; Dillon, *The Hatchet Men,* 361.

69. "Chinese and Japanese Labor in the Mountain and Pacific States," 777; Reynolds, "The Chinese Tongs," 622.

70. Gong and Grant, *Tong War,* 59–65.

71. Richard H. Dillon, "Little Pete, King of Chinatown," *California Monthly,* LXXIX (Dec. 1968), 42–58.

72. A set of instructions to a "salaried soldier" of a secret society, captured in Victoria, B.C., Canada in 1899, indicates that perjured testimony would be made available for any secret society thug who was charged with a crime committed as part of his societal duties. "Chinese and Japanese Labor in the Mountain and Pacific States," 771; a case of such perjury is reported in Oscar T. Shuck, "Seniors of the Collected Bar—Frank M. Stone," *History of the Bench and Bar of California* (Los Angeles, 1901), 938–942.

73. "Chinese and Japanese Labor in the Mountain and Pacific States," 771; see also Dillon, *The Hatchet Men,* 167–205.

74. See Lyman, *The Asian in the West,* 34–38.

75. "Fine New Home for Chinese Free Masons," *San Francisco Examiner,* Oct. 6, 1907.

76. Lyman, Willmott, and Ho, "Rules of a Chinese Secret Society in British Columbia," 535.

77. "Chinese and Japanese Labor in the Mountain and Pacific States," 771.

78. Lyman, Willmott, and Ho, "Rules of a Chinese Secret Society in British Columbia," 536.

79. Dillon, "Little Pete, King of Chinatown," 52–55.

80. Jake Jackson, "A Chinese War in America," and H. H. Noonan, "Another Version of the Weaverville War," in *Trinity 1957: Yearbook of the Trinity County Historical Society* (Weaverville, 1957), 5–12.

81. Gong and Grant, *Tong War,* 194–202.

82. Lyman, *The Asian in the West,* 29–31.

83. Gong and Grant, *Tong War,* 50; Drayton, "The Chinese Six Companies," 427–477; Dillon, *The Hatchet Men,* 241–340.

84. Gong and Grant, *Tong War,* 50–54.

85. *San Francisco Chronicle,* Nov. 11, 1909, Feb. 7, 1910.

86. Drayton, "The Chinese Six Companies," 475–476.

87. Hoy, *The Chinese Six Companies,* 23–26.

88. Wynne, *Triad and Tabut,* 7–15, 49–113, 202–351.

89. E. J. Eitel, "Outline History of the Hakkas," *The China Review,* II (1873–1874), 160–164; Wynne, *Triad and Tabut,* 59–61, 260–280.

90. In addition to the sources cited in footnote 80, *supra,* see McLeod, *Pigtails and Gold Dust,* 53–56; Joseph Henry Jackson, *Anybody's Gold: The Story of California's Mining Towns* (San Francisco, 1970), 210–223.

91. Stewart Culin, "The I Hing or 'Patriotic Rising,' " 51–57; Liew, *Struggle for Democracy,* 68–103, 172–190; Glick and Hong, *Swords of Silence,* 160–190, 255–262.

92. Gong and Grant, *Tong War,* 194–202; *San Francisco Chronicle,* Nov. 11, 1909, Feb. 7, 1910.

93. Lyman, *The Asian in the West,* 27–31; John E. Bennett, "The Chinese Tong Wars in San Francisco," *Harper's Weekly,* XLIV (Aug. 11, 1900), 746–747.

94. H. H. Bancroft, "Mongolianism in America," *Essays and Miscellany* (San Francisco, 1890), 356; Gibson, *The Chinese in America,* 139–140; Farwell, *The Chinese at Home and Abroad,* 8–14.

95. *San Francisco Chronicle,* Nov. 11, 1909, Feb. 7, 1910; Dillon, *The Hatchet Men,* 227.

96. For the formal theory upon which this section of the paper is based, see the two essays by Georg Simmel, *Conflict and the Web of Group Affiliation,* translated by Kurt H. Wolff and Reinhard Bendix (Glencoe, 1955), 11–195.

97. Lyman, "Structures of Chinese Society," 364–377.

98. Examples of these declarations of war will be found in McLeod, *Pigtails and Gold Dust,* 53–54.

99. Drayton, "The Chinese Six Companies," 475.

100. Dillon, *The Hatchet Men,* 167–206; McLeod, *Pigtails and Gold Dust,* 238–252.

101. "Chinese and Japanese Labor in the Mountain and Pacific States," 771.

102. Lyman, "The Structure of Chinese Society," 352–354.

103. The last major tong war appears to have been fought in 1933. Glick, *Shake Hands with the Dragon,* 265. Twenty-five years later a dispute between the Hop Sing Tong and the Bing Kung Tong threatened to erupt in violence, but after months of negotiations the matter was settled peacefully. *San Francisco Examiner,* Jan. 3, 1958, May 3, 5, 7, and 9, 1958; *San Francisco Chronicle,* Jan. 3 and 4, 1958.

104. The number of secret societies in San Francisco rose and fell as wars continued in the period between 1880 and 1910. See Dillon, *The Hatchet Men,* 243–367. The *hui kuan* experienced a great number of factional disputes resulting in group defections, establishment of new *Landsmannschaften,* and finally a grudging recognition of the rights of secret societies. Nee and Nee, *Longtime Californ',* 13–124, 228–252.

105. Lyman, "The Structure of Chinese Society," 204–221.

106. Simmel, *Conflict and the Web of Group Affiliation,* 11–195; Lewis Coser, *The Functions of Social Conflict* (Glencoe, 1956); Edward A. Ross, *Principles of Sociology* (New York, 1920), 162.

107. Coser, *The Functions of Social Conflict,* 35; Ross, *Principles of Sociology,* 162.

108. One of the finest examples of this solidarity was shown when hundreds of Chinese, under the direction of the Consolidated Benevolent Association, went to jail to protest San Francisco's lodging house ordinance. See *Ho Ah Kow v. Matthew Nunan,* 5 Sawyer 552 (1879); McLeod, *Pigtails and Gold Dust,* 199–212.

109. See William Purviance Fenn, *Ah Sin and his Brethren in American Literature* (Peking, 1933), 1–131; Dorothy B. Jones, *The Image of China and India on the American Screen, 1896–1955* (Cambridge, 1955), 13–42; Colin Watson, *Snobbery with Violence: Crime Stories and Their Audience* (New York, 1971) 109–129.

110. Simmel, *Conflict and the Web of Group Affiliation,* 17–28.

111. Cf. *ibid.,* 25–26.

Contrasts in the Community Organization of Chinese and Japanese in North America

RACE RELATIONS THEORY and policy in North America have for the most part been built upon examination of the experiences and difficulties of European immigrants and Negroes. As a result contrasting ideas and programmes, emphasizing integration for the latter and cultural pluralism for the former, have been generated primarily in consideration of each group's most manifest problems.[1] However, relatively little work has been done to ascertain the conditions under which an ethnic group is likely to follow an integration-oriented or a pluralist-oriented path.[2] Two racial groups found in North America—the Chinese and the Japanese—are likely candidates for the focus of such research, since they have superficially similar outward appearances, a long history as victims of oppression, discrimination, and prejudice, but quite different developments in community orgnization and cohesion.[3] In this paper an attempt is made to ascertain the distinctive features of the culture and social organization of the two immigrant groups that played significant roles in directing the mode of community organization in North America.

There is sound theoretical ground for reconsidering the role of old world culture and social organization in immigrant communities in North America. Even in what might seem the paradigm case of cultural destruction in the New World—that of the Negro—there is evidence to suggest at least vestiges of cultural survival.[4] In those ethnic communities unmarred by so culturally demoralizing a condition as slavery, there survives what Nathan Glazer calls elements of a "ghost nation," so that despite its fires social life goes on at least in part "beyond the melting pot."[5] American ideology has stressed assimilation, but its society is marked by European, Asian, and some African survivals; Canadian ideology has stressed the "mosaic" of cultures, but at least some of its peoples show definite signs of being Canadianized. The immigrants' cultural baggage needs sociological inspection to ascertain its effects on community organization and acculturation. Fortunately, the Chinese and Japanese communities provide opportunities for this research because of new knowledge about the Old Asian World[6] and extensive material on their lives in North America.

The Chinese

In contrast to the Japanese and several European groups, the Chinese in Canada and the United States present an instance of unusually persistent social isolation and preservation of Old World values and institutions.[7] To the present day a great many Chinese work, play, eat, and sleep in the Chinese ghettos known throughout North America as "Chinatowns." The business ethics of Chinatown's restaurants and bazaars are institutionalized in guild and trade associations more reflective of nineteenth-century Cathay than twentieth-century North America. Newly arrived Chinese lads work a twelve- to sixteen-hour day as waiters and busboys totally unprotected by labor unions. Immigrant Chinese mothers sit in rows in tiny "sweatshops" sewing dresses for downtown shops while infants crawl at their feet. In basements below the street level or in rooms high above the colorfully-lit avenue, old men gather round small tables to gamble at *f'an t'an, p'ai kop piu,* or other games of chance. Above the hubbub of activity in the basements, streets, stores, and sweatshops are the offices of clan associations, speech and territorial clubs, and secret societies. And behind the invisible wall that separates Chinatown from the metropolis the élites of these organizations conduct an unofficial government, legislating, executing, and adjudicating matters for their constituents.

Not every Chinese in Canada or the United States today recognizes the sovereignty of Chinatown's power élite or receives its benefits and protections.[8] At one time San Francisco's "Chinese Six Companies" and Vancouver's Chinese Benevolent Association could quite properly claim to speak for all the Chinese in the two countries. But that time is now past. Students from Hong Kong and Taiwan and Chinese intellectuals, separated in social origins, status, and aspirations from other Chinese, have cut themselves off from their Chinatown compatriots. Another segment of the Chinese population, the Canadian-born and American-born, who have acquired citizenship in the country of their birth, not only exhibits outward signs of accultura-

tion in dress, language, and behaviour, but also grants little if any obeisance to Chinatown's élites. Some of this generation now find it possible to penetrate the racial barrier, and pass into the workaday world of the outer society with impunity. Others still work or reside in Chinatown but are too acculturated to be subject to its private law. Still a few others are active in the traditional associations seeking power and status within the framework of the old order.

That North America's Chinatowns are not merely creatures of the American environment is indicated by the relatively similar institutionalization of Chinese communities in other parts of the world.[9] The diaspora of Chinese in the last two centuries has populated Southeast Asia, the Americas, Europe, and Africa with Oriental colonies. Should the tourists who today pass along Grant Avenue in San Francisco, Pender Street in Vancouver, and Pell and Mott Streets in New York City, peering at exotic food and art, and experiencing the sights, sounds, and smells of these cities' Chinatowns, be whisked away to Manila, Bangkok, Singapore, or Semarang, or suddenly find themselves in Calcutta, Liverpool or the capital of the Malagasy Republic, they would discover, amidst the unfamiliarity of the several national cultures, still other "Chinatowns" not unlike their North American counterparts. Recognition of the recalcitrance of overseas Chinese to their surroundings takes different forms in different places. In the United States sociologists marvel at their resistance to the fires of the melting pot; in Indonesia the government questions the loyalty of this alien people; in Malaysia native farmers and laborers resent the vivid contrast between their own poverty and Chinese commercial affluence; in Jamaica Chinese are urged to quit their exclusiveness and become part of the larger community. But everywhere the issue is acculturation. Despite more than a century of migration, the Chinese have not fully adopted the culture, language, behaviour—the ways of life—of the countries in which they have settled. Their cultural exclusiveness—especially as it finds its expression in geographically compact and socially distant communities within the host societies' cities—is a world-historical event deserving far more discussion and research than it has yet been given.

The Japanese

The rapid acculturation of the Japanese in North America has been a source of frequent discussion. The fact that "Japan-town" is not as familiar a term to North Americans as "Chinatown" is an unobtrusive measure of this difference between the two peoples. Such local names as "Li'l Tokyo" or "Li'l Yokohama" have been short-lived references for Japanese communities isolated through discrimination, but these have rarely been characterized by such peculiar institutions and private government as are found in the Chinese quarter. Japanese-owned businesses are not organized on the basis of guilds or *zaibatsu;* perfectural associations exist primarily for nostalgic and ceremonial purposes, playing no effective part in political organization in the community; and secret societies like those so prominent among the Chinese are not found in North American Japanese communities. Neither sweatshops nor gambling houses are established institutions of Japanese-American or Japanese-Canadian communities. Indeed, in the geographic sense, the North American Japanese communities show increasing signs of disintegration.

Although overseas Chinese communities exhibit the characteristics of colonization with a superordinate organization to represent them to the larger society, the Japanese are organized on patterns closer to that of a reluctant minority group.[10] The earliest associations among immigrant Japanese emphasized defense against prejudice and support for the larger society's laws and customs, and these organizations have been supplanted by even more acculturation-oriented organizations in the second generation. Japanese are the only ethnic group to emphasize geo-generational distinctions by a separate nomenclature and a belief in the unique character structure of each generational group. Today the third and fourth generations in North America *(Sansei* and *Yonsei,* respectively) exhibit definite signs of the "Hansen effect"—that is, interest in recovering Old World culture—and also show concern over the appropriate allocation of their energies and activities to things American or Canadian and things Japanese. Ties to a Japanese community are tenuous and find their realization primarily in courtship and marriage and in recreational pursuits.

Although the situation is by no means so clear, overseas Japanese communities outside North America exhibit some patterns similar to and some quite different from those of the continental United States and Canada. In the most extensive study of acculturation among Japanese in pre-war Kona, Hawaii, the community appeared organized less along Japanese than Hawaiian-American lines. Other studies of Japanese in Hawaii have emphasized the innovative food habits, decline of the patriarch, and changing moral bases of family life. On the other hand, Japanese in Peru, where Japan's official policy of emigration played a significant role in establishing the colony and supervising its affairs, had maintained a generally separate though financially successful and occupationally diversified community until 1942; postwar developments indicate that the Peruvian-born Japanese will seek and obtain increasing entrance into Peruvian society and further estrangement from all-Japanese associations. In Brazil, a situation similar to that of Peru developed: sponsored migration reached great heights during the period of Japan's imperialist development, and, although Brazil welcomed Japanese until 1934, a policy of coerced assimilation motivated by suspicion of Japanese intent led to a closing of many all-Japanese institutions before the outbreak of World War II. In the postwar period, Brazilian-born Japanese indicated a greater interest than their parents had in integration into Brazilian society. In Paraguay, where the first Japanese colony began in La Colmena as recently as 1936, signs of acculturation and community break-down have been reported by cultural geographers surveying the area.[11] Generally, this cursory survey of overseas Japanese communities suggests that when such communities are not governed by agencies of the homeland and where, as the researchers of Caudill and de Vos indicate,[12] Japanese values find opportunity for interpenetration and complementarity with those of the host society (as in the United States and Canada), the speed with which community isolation declines is accelerated.

Contrasts between the Chinese and Japanese have been noticed frequently but rarely researched.[13] As early as 1909 Chester Rowell, a Fresno, California journalist, pointed to the Japanese refusal to be losers in unprofitable contracts, to their unwillingness to be tied to a "Jap-town," and to their geniality and politeness; in contrast he praised the Chinese subordination to contracts and headmen, their accommodation to a ghetto existence, and their cold but efficient and loyal service as domestics. Similar observations were made by Winifred Raushenbush, Robert Park's assistant in his famous race relations survey of the Pacific coast. More recently the late Rose Hum Lee has vividly remarked upon the contrast between the two Oriental groups. Professor Lee asserts that the *Nisei* "exhibit within sixty years, greater degrees of integration into American society, than has been the case with the Chinese, whose settlement is twice as long." Other sociologists have frequently commented on the speed with which Japanese adopted at least the outward signs of Occidental culture and attained success in North America. Broom and Kitsuse summed up the impressive record of the Japanese by declaring it "an achievement perhaps rarely equaled in the history of human migration." More recently, Petersen has pointed to the same record of achievement and challenged sociologists to develop a theory which could adequately explain it as well as the less spectacular records of other ethnic groups.

Although the differences between the Chinese and Japanese in North America have excited more comparative comment than concrete investigation, an early statement by Walter G. Beach deserves more attention than it has received. In a much neglected article[14] Beach observed the contrast between the speed of acculturation of Chinese and Japanese and attributed it to those conditions within and extrinsic to the ethnic groups which fostered either segregation and retention of old world culture traits or rapid breakdown of the ethnic community. Noting that ethnic cultures were an important aspect of the kind of community an immigrant group would form he pointed out that the Chinese came to America "before Chinese culture had been greatly influenced by Western Civilization." More specifically, he suggested that "they came from an old, conservative and stationary social organization and system of custom-control of life; and that the great majority came from the lower and least independent social stratum of that life." By contrast, he observed that the Japanese "came at a time when their national political system had felt the influence of Western thought and ambitions." He went on to say: "Japan was recognized among the world's powers, and its people were self-conscious in respect to this fact; their pride was not in a past culture, unintelligible to Americans (as the Chinese), but in a growing position of recognition and authority among the world's powers." It was because of these differences in culture and outlook, Beach argued, that Japanese tended to resist discrimination more vigorously and to adopt Occidental ways more readily, while Chinese produced a "Chopsuey culture" in segregated communities. Stripped of its ethnocentrism, Beach's analysis suggests that acculturation is affected not only by the action of the larger society upon immigrants, but also, and more fundamentally, by the nature and quality of the immigrant culture and institutions.

The present study specifies and clarifies the features of Japanese and Chinese culture which Beach only hinted at, and details the interplay between old-world cultures and North American society. Certain key conditions of life in China and Japan at the times of emigration produced two quite different kinds of immigrant social organization. The responses of the American economy and society to Chinese and Japanese certainly had their effects. But these alone did not shape Chinese and Japanese life. Rather they acted as "accelerators" to the direction of and catalysts or inhibitors of the development of the immigrants' own culture and institutions.[15] Prejudice and discrimination added considerable hardship to the necessarily onerous lives of the immigrating Orientals, but did not wrench away their culture, nor deprive them completely of those familial, political, and social institutions which they had transported across the Pacific.[16] The Chinese and Japanese were never reduced to the wretchedness of the first Africans in America, who experienced a forcible stripping away of their original culture, and then a coercive assimilation into selected and subordinated elements of white America. Thus, although both Chinese and Japanese share a nearly identical distinction from the dominant American racial stock, and although both have been oppressed by prejudice, discrimination, segregation and exclusion, a fundamental source of their markedly different rates of acculturation is to be found in the particular developmental patterns taken by their respective cultures[17] in America.

Emigration

The conditions of emigration for Chinese and Japanese reflected respectively their different cultures. The Chinese migrated from a state that was not a nation, and they conceived of themselves primarily as members of local extended kin units, bound together by ties of blood and language and only secondarily, if at all, as "citizens" of the Chinese empire.[18] Chinese emigration was an organized affair in which kinsmen or fellow villagers who had achieved some wealth or status acted as agents and sponsors for their compatriots. Benevolently despotic, this emigration acted to transfer the loyalties and institutions of the village to the overseas community. In the village, composed for the most part of his kinsmen, the individual looked to elders as leaders; in emigrating the individual reposed his loyalty and submitted his fate to the overseas representative of his clan or village. Loans, protection, and jobs were provided within a framework of kin and language solidarity that stretched from the village in Kwangtung to the clan building in "Chinatown." Emigrants regarded their journey as temporary and their return as certain. Abroad the Chinese, as homeless men, never fully accepted any permanence to their sojourn. They identified themselves with their old-world clan, village, dialect grouping, or secret society whose overseas leaders were recognized as legitimate substitutes for homeland groups. These institutional leaders further insinuated themselves into the overseas immigrant's life by acting as his representative to white society, by pioneering new settlements, and by providing badly-needed goods and services, protection against depredations, and punishment for wrong-doing.

The Japanese emigrant departed from an entirely different kind of society.[19] Japan was a nation as well as a state, and its villages reflected this fact. Village life had long ceased to be circumscribed by kinship, and the individual family rather than the extended kinship group was the focus of loyalty and solidarity. When children departed their homes they left unencumbered by a network of obligations. Unless he had been born first or last, a Japanese son was not obligated as was a Chinese to remain in the home of his parents. After 1868 emigration was sometimes sponsored by the government and certainly encouraged. When Japanese departed the homeland they, like the Chinese, expected only to sojourn, but they were not called back to the home village by the knowledge that a long-patient wife awaited them or that kinsmen fully depended on their return. Moreover, the men who inspired Japanese emigration were not pioneer leaders but exemplary individuals whose singular fame and fortune seemed to promise everyone great opportunity abroad. They did not serve as overseas community leaders or even very often as agents of migration, but only as shining examples of how others might succeed.

Marital Status

The respective marital situation of these two Asian peoples reflected fundamental differences in Chinese and Japanese kinship and profoundly influenced community life overseas. Custom required that a Chinese man sojourn abroad without his wife. A man's return to hearth and village was thus secured, and he laboured overseas in order that he might some day again enjoy the warmth of domesticity and the blessings of children. Abroad he lived a lonely life of labour, dependent on kinsmen and compatriots for fellowship and on prostitutes and vice for outlet and recreation. When in 1882 restrictive American legislation unwittingly converted Chinese custom into legal prohibition by prohibiting the coming of wives of Chinese labourers it exaggerated and lengthened the separation of husbands from wives and, more significantly, delayed for nearly two generations the birth in America of a substantial "second generation" among the immigrant Chinese. Canadian immigration restrictions had a similar consequence.[20] Barred from intermarriage by custom and law and unable to bring wives to Canada or the United States, Chinese men sired children on their infrequent return visits to China, and these China-born sons later partially replenished the Chinese population in North America as they joined their fathers in the overseas venture. Like their fathers the sons also depended on Chinatown institutions. Their lack of independence from the same community controls which had earlier circumscribed the lives of their fathers stood in sharp contrast to the manner of life of the Canadian and American born.

Neither custom nor law barred the Japanese from bringing wives to Canada or America.[21] Within four decades of their arrival the Japanese had brought over enough women to guarantee that, although husbands might be quite a bit older than their wives, a domestic life would be established in America. Japanese thus had little need for the brothels and gambling halls which characterized Chinese communities in the late nineteenth century and which, not incidentally, provided a continuous source of wealth and power to those who owned or controlled them. Japanese quickly produced a second generation in both Canada and the United States, and by 1930 this *Nisei* generation began to claim a place for itself in North America and in Japanese-American and Japanese-Canadian life. The independence and acculturation of the *Nisei* was indicated in their social and political style of life. They did not accept the organizations of their parents' community and established *ad hoc* associations dedicated to civil rights and penetration be-

yond Canada's and America's racial barrier. Some Japanese immigrants educated one of their children in Japan. These few Japan-educated offspring (*Kibei*) did not enjoy the same status in North America as *Nisei,* and in their marginality and problems of adjustment they resembled the China-born offspring of Chinese immigrants. Educated in Canadian or American schools and possessed of Canadian or American culture and values, the *Nisei* found that prejudice and discrimination acted as the most significant obstacle to their success.

Occupations and Locations

Jobs and settlement patterns tended to reinforce and accelerate the different developmental patterns of Chinese and Japanese communities in America.[22] Except for a small but powerful merchant élite the Chinese began and remained as wage labourers. First employed in the arduous and menial tasks of mining and railroad-building, the Chinese later gravitated into unskilled, clerical and service work inside the Chinese community. Such work necessitated living in cities or returning to cities when unemployment drove the contract labourers to seek new jobs. The city always meant the Chinese quarter, a ghetto set aside for Chinese in which their special needs could be met and by which the white population could segregate itself from them. Inside the ghetto old-world societies ministered to their members' wants, exploited their needs, and represented their interests. When primary industry could no longer use Chinese and white hostility drove them out of the labour market and into Chinatown, the power of these associations and their merchant leaders was reconfirmed and enhanced. The single most important feature of the occupations of Chinese immigrants was their tendency to keep the Chinese in a state of dependency on bosses, contractors, merchants—ultimately on the merchant élite of Chinatown.

The Japanese, after a brief stint as labourers in several primary industries then on the wane in western America, pioneered the cultivation of truck crops.[23] Small-scale agriculturalists, separated from one another as well as from the urban anti-Orientalism of the labor unions, Japanese farmers did not retain the kind of ethnic solidarity characteristic of the urban Chinese. Whatever traditional élites had existed among the early Japanese immigrants fell from power or were supplanted. In their place *ad hoc* associations arose to meet particular needs. When Japanese did become labourers and city dwellers they too became segregated in "li'l Tokyos" presided over by old-world associations for a time. But the early concentration in agriculture and the later demands of the *Nisei* tended to weaken the power even of the city-bred immigrant associations.

Community Power and Conflict

Finally, the different bases for solidarity in the two Oriental communities tended to confirm their respective modes of social organization. The Japanese community has remained isolated primarily because of discriminatory barriers to integration and secondarily because of the sense of congregation among fellow Japanese. The isolated Chinese community is, to be sure, a product of white aversion and is also characterized by congregative sentiments, but, much more than that of the Japanese, it rests on communal foundations. Political life in Chinatown has rarely been tranquil.[24] The traditional clans and *Landsmannschaften* controlled immigration, settled disputes, levied taxes and fines, regulated commerce, and meted out punishments. Opposition to their rule took the form it had taken in China. Secret societies, chapters of or modeled after the well-known Triad Society, took over the functions of law, protection, and revenge for their members. In addition the secret societies owned or controlled the gambling houses and brothels which emerged to satisfy the recreational and sex needs of homeless Chinese men and displayed occasional interest in the restive politics of China. Struggles for power, blood feuds, and "wars" of vengeance were not infrequent in the early days of Chinatown. These conflicts entrenched the loyalties of men to their respective associations. More important with respect to non-acculturation, these intramural fights

isolated the Chinese from the uncomprehending larger society and bound them together in antagonistic cooperation. Since the turn of the century, the grounds of such battles have shifted on to a commercial and political plane, but violence is not unknown. Chinatown's organizational solidarity and its intra-community conflicts have thus acted as agents of nonacculturation.

Position and Prospects of the Oriental in North America

The conditions for the political and economic integration of the Chinese appear to be at hand now.[25] This is largely because the forces which spawned and maintained Chinatown are now weakened. The near balancing of the sex ratio has made possible the birth and maturation in America of second and third generation Chinese. Their presence, in greater and greater numbers, poses a serious threat to old-world power élites. The breakdown of discriminatory barriers to occupations and residency brought about by a new assertion of civil rights heralds an end to Chinatown economic and domestic monopoly. The relative openness of Canadian and American society to American-born and Canadian-born Chinese reduces their dependency on traditional goods and services and their recruitment into communal associations. Concomitantly, the *casus belli* of the earlier era disappears and conflict's group-binding and isolating effect loses force. What remains of Chinatown eventually is its new immigrants, its culturally acceptable economic base—restaurants and shops—and its congregative value for ethnic Chinese. Recent events in San Francisco suggest that the young and newly-arrived immigrants from Hong Kong and Taiwan and the American-born Chinese school drop-outs are estranged from both the Chinatown élites and white America. Many of their activities resemble those of protesting and militant Negro groups.

The Japanese are entering a new phase of relations with the larger society in North America. There is a significant amount of anxiety in Japanese circles about the decline of Japanese values and the appearance of the more undesirable features of Canadian and American life—primarily juvenile delinquency but also a certain lack of old-world propriety which had survived through the *Nisei* generation—among the *Sansei* and *Yonsei*.[26] Moreover, like those Negroes who share E. Franklin Frazier's disillusion with the rise of a black bourgeoisie, some Japanese-Americans are questioning the social and personal price paid for entrance into American society. Scholars such as Daisuke Kitagawa have wondered just how *Nisei* and *Sansei* might preserve elements of Japanese culture in America. At the same time one European Japanophile has bitterly assailed the Americanization of the *Nisei*.[27] Nothing similar to a black power movement has developed among the Japanese, and, indeed, such a movement is extremely unlikely given Japanese-American and Canadian material success and the decrease in social distance between Japanese and white Americans. At most there is a quiet concern. But even such mild phenomena are deserving of sociological attention.

Theoretical Considerations

This survey of Oriental community organization suggests the need to take seriously Robert Park's reconsideration of his own race relations cycle. Park at first had supposed that assimilation was a natural and inevitable outcome of race contact marked off by stages of competition, conflict, and accommodation before there occurred the eventual absorption of one people by another.[28] In addition to its faults as a natural history, a criticism so often discussed by other sociologists,[29] Park's original statement of the

cycle took no account of what, in a related context, Wagley and Harris refer to as the "adaptive capacity" of the immigrant group.[30] However, Park himself reconsidered the cycle and in 1937 wrote that it might terminate in one of three outcomes: a caste system as was the case in India; complete assimilation, as he imagined had occurred in China; or a permanent institutionalization of minority status within a larger society, as was the case of Jews in Europe. Park concluded that race relations occur as phases of a cycle "which, once initiated, inevitably continues until it terminates in some predestined racial configuration, and one consistent with the established social order of which it is a part."[31] Park's later emphasis on alternative outcomes and his consideration of the peculiar social context in which any ethnic group's history occurs implicitly recall attention to the interplay between native and host society cultures. As Herskovitz's researches on West African and American Negro cultures indicate, the immigrant group, even if oppressed *in transitu*, does not arrive with a cultural *tabula rasa* waiting to be filled in by the host culture. Rather it possesses a culture and social organization which in contact with and in the several contexts of the host culture will be supplanted, inhibited, subordinated, modified or enhanced. Kinship, occupations, patterns of settlement and community organization are each factors in such developments. Assimilation, or for that matter pluralism, is not simply an inevitable state of human affairs, as those who cling to "natural history" models assert, but rather is an existential possibility. Social factors contribute to the state of being of a people and to changes in that state. The Chinese and Japanese communities in America illustrate two modes of development and suggest the need to refine even further our knowledge of the factors which affect whatever mode of development an immigrant group chooses.

Notes

1. Cf. Horace M. Kallen, *Culture and Democracy in the United States* (New York, 1924) with Gunnar Myrdal, *An American Dilemma* (New York, 1944).

2. See Clyde V. Kiser, "Cultural Pluralism," *The Annals of the American Academy of Political and Social Science,* 262 (March, 1949), 118–129. An approach to such a theory is found in William

Petersen, *Population* (New York. 1961), 114–149.

3. For an extended analysis see Stanford M. Lyman, "The Structure of Chinese Society in Nineteenth-Century America," (unpublished Ph.D. dissertation, University of California, Berkeley, 1961).

4. Melville Herskovitz, *The Myth of the Negro Past* (Boston, 1958). See also Charles Keil, *Urban Blues* (Chicago, 1966), 1–69.

5. Nathan Glazer, "Ethnic Groups in America: From National Culture to Ideology," in Morroe Berger, Theodore Abel, and Charles H. Page, Editors, *Freedom and Control in Modern Society* (New York, 1954), 158–176, Nathan Glazer and Daniel Patrick Moynihan, *Beyond the Melting Pot: The Negroes, Puerto Ricans, Jews, Italians and Irish of New York City* (Cambridge, 1963).

6. The "knowledge explosion" on China has been prodigious since 1949 despite the difficulties in obtaining first-hand field materials. Much research was inspired by interest in the Chinese in Southeast Asia. See Maurice Freedman, "A Chinese Phase in Social Anthropology," *British Journal of Sociology,* XIV, 1 (March, 1963), 1–18.

7. Sources for the material reported are Lyman, "The Structure of Chinese Society in Nineteenth-Century America, *passim;* Leong Gor Yun, *Chinatown Inside Out* (New York, 1936), 26–106, 182–235; Calvin Lee, *Chinatown, U.S.A.: A History and Guide* (Garden City, 1965); Stuart H. Cattell, *Health, Welfare and Social Organization in Chinatown, New York City* (New York, August, 1962), 1–4, 20–68, 81–85. For the origins of organized labour's hostility to the Chinese see Herbert Hill, "The Racial Practices of Organized Labor—The Age of Gompers and After," in Arthur Ross and Herbert Hill, Editors, *Employment, Race and Poverty: A Critical Study of the Disadvantaged Status of Negro Workers from 1865 to 1965* (New York, 1967), 365–402. For a detailed description of Chinese games of chance see the several articles by Stewart Culin, "Chinese Games with Dice" (Philadelphia, 1889), 5–21; "The Gambling Games of the Chinese in America," *Publications of the University of Pennsylvania, Series in Philology, Literature, and Archaeology,* I, 4, 1891; "Chinese Games With Dice and Dominoes," *Report of the United States National Museum, Smithsonian Institution,* 1893, 489–537. The sweatshops of San Francisco's Chinatown are described in James Benet, *A Guide to San Francisco and the Bay Region* (New York, 1963), 73–74.

8. See Rose Hum Lee, *The Chinese in the United States of America* (Hong Kong, 1960), 86–131, 231–251, 373–404. See also *Chinese Students in the United States, 1948–1955: A Study in Government Policy* (New York, March, 1956). For a Canadian-Chinese view of his own generation's adjustment to Chinese and Canadian ways of life see William Wong, "The Younger Generation," *Chinatown News,* XI, 13 (March 18, 1964), 6–7.

9. Material for the following is drawn from Maurice Freedman and William Willmott, "Southeast Asia, with Special Reference to the Chinese," *International Social Science Journal,* XIII, 2 (1961), 245–270; Victor Purcell, *The Chinese in Southeast Asia* (London, 1965), Second edition; Jacques Amyot, S.J., *The Chinese Commu-*

nity of Manila: A Study of Adaptation of Chinese Familism to the Philippine Environment (Chicago, 1960); Richard J. Coughlin, "The Chinese in Bangkok: A Commercial-Oriented Minority," *American Sociological Review,* XX (June, 1955), 311–316; Maurice Freedman, *Chinese Family and Marriage in Singapore* (London, 1957); Donald Willmott, *The Chinese of Semarang: A Changing Minority Community in Indonesia* (Ithaca, 1960); Shelland Bradley, "Calcutta's Chinatown," *Cornhill Magazine,* LVII (September, 1924), 277–285; Christopher Driver, "The Tiger Balm Community," *The Guardian* (January 2, 1962); Tsien Tche-Hao, "La vie sociale des Chinois a Madagascar," *Comparative Studies in Society and History,* III, 2 (January, 1961), 170–181; Justus M. van der Kroef, "Chinese Assimilation in Indonesia," *Social Research,* XX (January, 1954), 445–472; Leonard Broom, "The Social Differentiation of Jamaica," *American Sociological Review,* XIX (April, 1954), 115–124.

10. Material for the following is based on Michinari Fujita, "Japanese Associations in America," *Sociology and Social Research* (January–February, 1929), 211–228; T. Obana, "The American-born Japanese," *Sociology and Social Research* (November–December, 1934), 161–165; Joseph Roucek, "Japanese Americans," in Francis J. Brown and Joseph S. Roucek, Editors, *One America: The History, Contributions, and Present Problems of Our Racial and National Minorities* (New York, 1952), 319–384; Forrest E. La Violette, "Canada and Its Japanese," in Edgar T. Thompson and Everett C. Hughes, Editors, *Race: Individual and Collective Behavior* (Glencoe, 1958), 149–155; Charles Young, Helen R. Y. Reid, and W. A. Carrothers, *The Japanese Canadians* (Toronto, 1938), edited by H. A. Innis; Ken Adachi, *A History of the Japanese Canadians in British Columbia,* (Vancouver (?) 1958); T. Scott Miyakawa, "The Los Angeles Sansei," *Kashu Mainichi* (December 20, 1962), Part 2, 1; Harry Kitano, "Is There Sansei Delinquency?" *Kashu Mainichi* (December 20, 1962), Part 2, 1.

11. For the Japanese in Hawaii, see John Embree, "New and Local Kin Groups Among the Japanese Farmers of Kona, Hawaii," *American Anthropologist,* XLI (July, 1939), 400–407; John Embree "Acculturation Among the Japanese of Kona, Hawaii," *Memoirs of the American Anthropological Association,* No. 59; Supplement to *American Anthropologist,* XLIII, 4:2 (1941); Jitsuichi Masuoka, "The Life Cycle of an Immigrant Institution in Hawaii: The Family," *Social Forces,* 23 (October, 1944) 60–64; Masuoka, "The Japanese Patriarch in Hawaii," *Social Forces,* XVII (December, 1938), 240–248; Masuoka, "Changing Food Habits of the Japanese in Hawaii," *American Sociological Review,* X (December, 1954), 759–765; Masuoka, "Changing Moral Bases of the Japanese Family in Hawaii," *Sociology and Social Research,* XXI (November, 1936), 158–169; Andrew M. Lind, *Hawaii's Japanese: An Experiment in Democracy* (Princeton, 1946). For the Japanese in Peru see Toraji Irie, "History of Japanese Migration to Peru," *Hispanic-American Historical Review,* 32 (August–October. 1951) 437–452, 648–664; (February, 1952), 73–82; Mischa Titiev, "The Japanese Colony in Peru," *Far Eastern Quarterly,* X (May, 1951), 227–247. For Japanese in Brazil see J. F. Normano "Japanese Emigration to Brazil," *Pacific Affairs,* VII (March, 1934), 42–61; Emilio Willems and Herbert Baldus, "Cultural

Change Among Japanese Immigrants in Brazil in the Ribeira Valley of Sao Paulo," *Sociology and Social Research,* XXVI (July, 1943), 525–537; Emilio Willems, "The Japanese in Brazil," *Far Eastern Quarterly,* XVIII (January 12, 1949), 6–8; John P. Augelli, "Cultural and Economic Changes of Bastos, a Japanese colony on Brazil's Paulista Frontier," *Annals of the Association of American Geographers,* XLVIII, 1 (March, 1958), 3–19. For Paraguay see Norman R. Stewart, *Japanese Colonization in Eastern Paraguay,* (Washington, D.C., 1967).

12. William Caudill, "Japanese American Personality and Acculturation," *Genetic Psychology Monographs,* XLV (1952) 3–102; George de Vos, "A Comparison of the Personality Differences in Two Generations of Japanese Americans by Means of the Rorschach Test," *Nagoya Journal of Medicine,* XVII, 3 (August, 1954), 153–265; William Caudill and George de Vos, "Achievement, Culture and Personality: The Case of the Japanese Americans," *American Anthropologist,* LVIII (December, 1956) 1102–1126.

13. Materials in this section are based on Chester Rowell, "Chinese and Japanese Immigrants—a Comparison," *Annals of the American Academy of Political and Social Science,* XXIV, 2 (September, 1909), 223–230; Winifred Raushenbush, "Their Place in the Sun," and "The Great Wall of Chinatown," *The Survey Graphic,* LVI, 3 (May 1, 1926), 141–145, 154–158; Rose Hum Lee, *The Chinese in the United States of America,* 425; Leonard Broom and John I. Kitsuse, "The Validation of Acculturation: A Condition of Ethnic Assimilation," *American Anthropologist,* LVII (1955), 44–48; William Petersen, "Family Structure and Social Mobility Among Japanese Americans," Paper presented at the annual meetings of the American Sociological Association, San Francisco, August, 1967.

14. Walter G. Beach, "Some Considerations in Regard to Race Segregation in California," *Sociology and Social Research,* XVIII (March, 1934), 340–350.

15. See the discussion in Lyman, "The Structure of Chinese Society in Nineteenth-Century America," 370–377.

16. One difference with respect to hostility toward the Chinese and Japanese had to do with whether either was perceived as an "enemy" people. Although the Chinese were occasionally accused of harboring subversive intentions toward America—[See, e.g., P. W. Dooner, *Last Days of the Republic,* (San Francisco, 1880)]—it was the Japanese who suffered a half-century of such suspicions. See Jacobus tenBroek, Edward N. Barnhart, and Floyd Matson, *Prejudice, War and The Constitution* (Berkeley, 1954), 11–99; Forrest E. La Violette, *The Canadian Japanese and World War II* (Toronto, 1948). Undoubtedly these deep-seated suspicions led Japanese to try very hard to prove their loyalty and assimilability. In this respect see Mike Masaoka, "The Japanese American Creed," *Common Ground,* II, 3 (1942), 11; and "A Tribute to Japanese American Military Service in World War II," Speech of Hon. Hiram Fong in the Senate of the United States, *Congressional Record,* 88th Congress, First Session, May 21, 1963, 1–13; "Tributes to Japanese American Military Service in World War II,"

Speeches of Twenty-four Congressmen, *Congressional Record,* 88th Congress, First Session, June 11, 1963, 1–16; Senator Daniel Ken Inouye (with Lawrence Elliott), *Journey to Washington,* (Englewood Cliffs, 1967), 87–200.

17. In the tradition of Max Weber, religion might properly be supposed to have played a significant role in the orientations of overseas Chinese and Japanese. However, certain problems make any adoption of the Weberian thesis difficult. First, although Confucianism was the state religion of China, local villages practiced syncretic forms combining ancestor worship, Buddhism, Christianity, and homage to local deities. Maurice Freedman, *Lineage Organization in Southeastern China* (London, 1958), 116. Abroad Chinese temples were definitely syncretic and functioned to support a non-rationalist idea of luck and the maintenance of merchant power. See A. J. A. Elliott, *Chinese Spirit Medium Cults in Singapore* (London, 1955), 24–45; Stewart Culin, *The Religious Ceremonies of the Chinese in the Eastern Cities of the United States* (Philadelphia, 1887); Wolfram Eberhard, "Economic Activities of a Chinese Temple in California," *Journal of the American Oriental Society,* LXXXII, 3 (July–September, 1962), 362–371. In the case of Japanese, the Tokugawa religion certainly facilitated a limited achievement orientation. Robert Bellah, *Tokugawa Religion: The Values of Pre-industrial Japan* (Glencoe, 1957), 107–132. But both in Japan and the United States Japanese exhibit a remarkable indifference to religious affiliation, even countenancing denominational and church differences within the same nuclear family and relatively little anxiety about religious intermarriage. See Kiyomi Morioka, "Christianity in the Japanese Rural Community: Acceptance and Rejection," *Japanese Sociological Studies. The Sociological Review,* Monograph X (Sept., 1966), 183–198; Leonard D. Cain, Jr., "Japanese American Protestants: Acculturation and Assimilation," *Review of Religious Research* III, 3 (Winter, 1962), 113–121; Cain, "The Integration Dilemma of Japanese-American Protestants," Paper presented at the annual meeting of the Pacific Sociological Association, April 5, 1962.

18. For information on nineteenth-century Chinese social organization in the provinces from which North America's immigrants came see Maurice Freedman, *Chinese Lineage and Society: Fukien and Kwangtung* (New York, 1966); Kung-Chuan Hsiao, *Rural China: Imperial Control in the Nineteenth Century* (Seattle, 1960). On the Chinese as sojourners see Paul C. P. Siu, "The Sojourner," *American Journal of Sociology,* VIII (July, 1952), 32–44 and Siu, "The Isolation of the Chinese Laundryman," in Ernest W. Burgess and Donald Bogue, Editors, *Contributions to Urban Sociology* (Chicago, 1964), 429–442. On the role of immigrant associations see William Hoy, *The Chinese Six Companies* (San Francisco, 1942); Tin-Yuke Char, "Immigrant Chinese Societies in Hawaii," *Sixty-First Annual Report of the Hawaiian Historical Society* (1953), 29–32; William Willmott, "Chinese Clan Associations in Vancouver," *Man,* LXIV, 49 (March–April, 1964), 33–37.

19. Material for the following is based on George B. Sansom, *Japan: A Short Cultural History* (New York, 1943); Takashi Koyama, "The Significance of Relatives at the Turning Point of the Family

System in Japan," *Japanese Sociological Studies. Sociological Review*, X (September, 1966), 95–114; Lafcadio Hearn, *Japan: An Interpretation* (Tokyo, 1955), 81–106; Ronald P. Dore, *City Life in Japan: A Study of A Tokyo Ward* (Berkeley, 1958), 91–190; Irene Taeuber, "Family, Migration, and Industrialization in Japan," *American Sociological Review* (April, 1951), 149–157; Ezra F. Vogel, "Kinship Structure, Migration to the City, and Modernization," in R. P. Dore, *Aspects of Social Change in Modern Japan* (Princeton, 1967), 91–112.

20. For discussions of United States restrictive legislation see Mary Coolidge, *Chinese Immigration* (New York, 1909), 145–336; S. W. Kung, *Chinese in American Life: Some Aspects of Their History, Status, Problems and Contributions* (Seattle, 1962), 64–165. A discussion of both American and Canadian restrictive legislation will be found in Huang Tsen-ming, *The Legal Status of the Chinese Abroad* (Taipei, 1954). See also Tin-Yuke Char, "Legal Restrictions on Chinese in English Speaking Countries, I," *Chinese Social and Political Science Review* (January 4, 1933), 479–494. Careful analyses of Canadian legislation are found in Duncan McArthur, "What is the Immigration Problem?" *Queen's Quarterly* (Autumn, 1928), 603–614; two articles by H. F. Angus, "Canadian Immigration: The Law and its Administration," *American Journal of International Law*, XXVIII, 1 (January, 1934), 74–89; "The Future of Immigration into Canada," *Canadian Journal of Economics and Political Science*, XII (August, 1946), 379–386; Jean Mercier, "Immigration and Provincial Rights," *Canadian Bar Review*, XXII (1944), 856–869; Hugh L. Keenleyside, "Canadian Immigration Policy and Its Administration," *External Affairs* (May 1949), 3–11; Bora Laskin, "Naturalization and Aliens: Immigration, Exclusion, and Deportation," *Canadian Constitutional Law* (Toronto, 1960), 958–977. In general see David C. Corbett, *Canada's Immigration Policy: A Critique* (Toronto, 1957).

21. For Japanese immigration see Yamato Ichihashi, *Japanese in the United States* (Stanford, 1932), 401–409; Dorothy Swaine Thomas, Charles Kikuchi, and J. Sakoda, *The Salvage* (Berkeley, 1952), 3–18, 571–626; H. A. Millis, *The Japanese Problem in the United States* (New York, 1915); K. K. Kawakami, *The Real Japanese Question* (New York, 1921); T. Iyenaga and Kenosuke Sato, *Japan and the California Problem* (New York, 1921); Ichiro Tokutomi, *Japanese-American Relations* (New York, 1922), 65–88 (Translated by Sukeshige Yanagiwara); R. D. McKenzie, *Oriental Exclusion* (Chicago, 1928). For Japanese immigration to Canada see Young, Reid, and Carrothers, *The Japanese Canadians;* A. R. M. Lower, *Canada and the Far East—1940* (New York, 1941), 61–89; H. F. Angus, *Canada and the Far East, 1940–1953* (Toronto, 1953), 99–100. For a statement by a pessimistic *Nisei* see Kazuo Kawai, "Three Roads, and None Easy," *Survey Graphic*, LVI, 3 (May 1, 1926), 164–166. For further discussions see Tsutoma Obana, "Problems of the American-Born Japanese," *Sociology and Social Research*, XIX (November, 1934), 161–165; Emory S. Bogardus, "Current Problems of Japanese Americans," *Sociology and Social Research*, XXV (July, 1941), 562–571; For the development of new associations among *Nisei* see Adachi, *A History of the Japanese in British Columbia, 1877–1958*, 11–14; *Better Americans in a Greater*

America, booklet published by the Japanese American Citizens' League, undated (1967), 24 pp. For an ecological analysis of the distribution and diffusion of achievement orientations among Japanese in America see Paul T. Takagi, "The Japanese Family in the United States: A Hypothesis on the Social Mobility of The Nisei," revision of an earlier paper presented at the annual meeting of the Kroeber Anthropological Society, Berkeley, California (April 30, 1966).

22. For information on occupations and settlement patterns see Lyman, "The Structure of Chinese Society in Nineteenth-Century America," 111–127; Milton L. Barnett, "Kinship as a Factor Affecting Cantonese Economic Adaptation in the United States," *Human Organization*, XIX (Spring, 1960), 40–46; Ping Chiu, *Chinese Labor in California: An Economic Study* (Madison, 1963).

23. For the Japanese as agriculturalists see Masakazu Iwata, "The Japanese Immigrants in California Agriculture," *Agricultural History*, XXXVI (January, 1962), 25–37; Thomas et al., *The Salvage*, 23–25; Adon Poli, *Japanese Farm Holdings on the Pacific Coast* (Berkeley, 1944). For farming and fishing communities in Canada see Tadashi Fukutake, *Man and Society in Japan* (Tokyo, 1962), 146–179. For the rise and decline of urban ghettos among Japanese in the United States see Shotaro Frank Miyamoto, *Social Solidarity Among the Japanese in Seattle*, University of Washington Publications in the Social Sciences XI, 2 (December, 1939), 57–129; Toshio Mori, "Li'l' Yokohama," *Common Ground*, I, 2 (1941), 54–56; Larry Tajiri, "Farewell to Little Tokyo," *Common Ground*, IV, 2 (1944), 90–95; Robert W. O'Brien, "Selective Dispersion as a Factor in the Solution of the Nisei Problem," *Social Forces*, XXIII (Dec., 1944), 140–147.

24. On power and conflict in Chinatown see Lyman, "The Structure of Chinese Society in Nineteenth Century America," 272–369. For secret societies see Stanford M. Lyman, "Chinese Secret Societies in the Occident: Notes and Suggestions for Research in the Sociology of Secrecy," *Canadian Review of Sociology and Anthropology*, I, 2 (1964), 79–102; Stanford M. Lyman, W. E. Willmott, Berching Ho, "Rules of a Chinese Secret Society in British Columbia," *Bulletin of The School of Oriental and African Studies*, XXVII, 3 (1964), 530–539. See also D. Y. Yuan, "Voluntary Segregation: A Study of New Chinatown," *Phylon Quarterly* (Fall, 1963), 255–265.

25. For an extended discussion of the progress in eliminating discrimination in Canada and the United States see Stanford M. Lyman, *The Oriental in North America* (Vancouver, 1962), Lecture No. 11: "Position and Prospects of the Oriental since World War II." On immigration matters to 1962 see S. W. Kung, "Chinese Immigration into North America," *Queen's Quarterly*, LXVIII, 4 (Winter, 1962), 610–620. Information about Chinese in Canada and the United States is regularly reported in the *Chinatown News*, A Vancouver, B.C., publication and in *East-West*, a San Francisco Journal. For problems of recent Chinese immigrants see *San Francisco Chronicle*, (March 18, 1968) 2; for those of American born, *ibid.* (March 19, 1968), 42.

26. On April 15, 1965 in response to a rash of teenage burglaries among Japanese in Sacramento, parents and other interested adults met and discussed how the community might act to prevent delinquency.

27. Daisuke Kitagawa, "Assimilation or Pluralism?" in Arnold M. Rose and Caroline B. Rose, *Minority Problems* (New York, 1965), 285–287. Fosco Maraini has written "The *ni-sei* has generally been taught to despise his Asian roots; on the other hand, all he has taken from the west is a two-dimensional duralumin Christianity, ultra-modernism, the cultivation of jazz as a sacred rite, a California veneer." *Meeting with Japan,* New York, 1960 (Translated by Eric Mosbacher), 169.

28. Robert E. Park, "Our Racial Frontier on the Pacific," *Survey Graphic,* LVI, 3 (May 1, 1926), 196.

29. Seymour Martin Lipset, "Changing Social Status and Prejudice: The Race Theories of a Pioneering American Sociologist," *Commentary,* IX (May, 1950), 475–479; Amitai Etzioni, "The Ghetto—A Re-evaluation," *Social Forces,* XXXVII (March, 1959), 255–262.

30. Charles Wagley and Marvin Harris, *Minorities in the New World* (New York, 1958).

31. Robert E. Park, "The Race Relations Cycle in Hawaii," *Race and Culture* (Glencoe, 1950), 194–195. For an extended discussion of the race cycle see Stanford M. Lyman, "The Race Relations Cycle of Robert E. Park," *Pacific Sociological Review* XI, 1 (Spring, 1968), 16–22.

Social Demography of the Chinese and Japanese in the United States

THIS PAPER FOCUSES on differences in the first phases of Chinese and Japanese contact with the United States. Specifically, it discusses the factors affecting the location and settlement patterns of these two immigrant racial groups. These patterns were affected by 1) the occupational opportunities available for the groups at the time of their arrival in America; 2) the scope and effectiveness of general community controls and the social and economic effects of indebtedness; 3) the social and economic effects of the sex ratio and the availability of husbands and wives. Changes in the patterns first established have occurred because of changes in occupational opportunities, changes necessitated by child-rearing and other familial issues, and sudden politically-inspired enforced movements made involuntarily.

The Chinese and Japanese in the United States

A. Number

Although only a few Chinese had ever come to the United States between 1790 and 1850, a great number began to arrive after news of California's gold strike had reached China. By 1860 the census recorded more than 34,000 Chinese in the United States and in that same year San Francisco's custom house counted over 46,000 passing through its gates.[1] The number continued to grow until 1882, when the United States Congress, influenced by the general anti-Chinese sentiment in California[2] and pressured by the notoriously racist labor unions in the eastern and midwestern cities,[3] passed restrictive legislation prohibiting the coming of Chinese laborers for ten years. This prohibition was renewed every ten years thereafter until total exclusion was achieved in the unlimited extension of the prohibition by the Act of 1904. Thirty-nine years later absolute prohibition was lifted and a very limited quota system was established. After 1943 Chinese entrance to the United States was facilitated by several kinds of special legislation and by private bills.[4] During the Johnson Administration quotas by national origin were lifted and many more Chinese have been eligible to enter the United States.

TABLE I

CHINESE AND JAPANESE IN UNITED STATES, 1790–1950

| | Chinese | | Japanese | Increase | | |
	Census	Other[1]	Census	Chinese		Japanese	
1790	—	—	—	—	—	—	—
1800	—	—	—	—	—	—	—
1810	—	—	—	—	—	—	—
1820	—	—	—	—	—	—	—
1830	—	3[2]	—	—	—	—	—
1840	—	8[2]	—	—	—	—	—
1850	—	450[2]	—	—	—	—	—
1860	34,933	46,897	—	—	—	—	—
1870	63,199	71,083	55	+ 28,266	80.9	—	—
1880	105,465	104,881	148	+ 42,266	66.9	+ 93	—
1890	107,488[33]	—	2,039	+ 2,010 [33]	1.9	+ 1,891	1,277.7
1900	89,863	—	24,326	−17,625	−16.4	+ 22,287	1,093.0
1910	71,531	—	72,157	−18,332	−20.4	+ 47,831	196.6
1920	61,639	—	111,010	−9,892	−13.8	+ 38,853	53.8
1930	74,954	—	138,834	+ 13,316	21.6	+ 27,824	25.1
1940	77,504	—	126,947	+ 2,550	3.4	−11,887	−8.6
1950	117,629	—	141,768	+ 40,125	51.8	+ 14,821	11.7

Source: U.S. Census Data.
[1]Figures in Mary Coolidge, *Chinese Immigration* (New York: Henry Holt, 1909), appendix, p. 489.
[2]Chinese arrivals at San Francisco Custom House, *loc. cit.*
[3]Exclusive of population enumerated in 1890 on Indian reservations: Chinese, 13.

As Table I shows, the absolute number of Chinese declined in the three decades after 1890. Unable to enter the United States after 1882, and also unable, under a special provision of the law, to bring over their wives to join them,[5] the Chinese steadily aged and died off or returned to China with no new Chinese to take their place. "The Chinese population is slowly declining in the United States," wrote Robert E. Park in 1926, "but San Francisco, at any rate, will miss its Chinese quarter when it goes."[6] Park's prophecy proved wrong, however. Chinatown did not disappear. Between 1920 and 1930 the decline in numbers of Chinese was arrested. Some entered the country as members of the categories exempted from prohibition by the law;[7] others were smuggled across the Canadian and Mexican borders,[8] or procured false papers linking them with Chinese families in America;[9] some have been born in the United States from among the few whole families established here. The heavier growth which shows up after 1940 is explained by the lifting of exclusion, the hundreds who entered under the annual quota and special legislation, the "new immigration" which occurred with the end of quotas by national origin after 1966, and by a natural increase following the establishment of more Chinese families on the American mainland.

The Japanese did not start coming to the United States in any great numbers until after 1880. The Exclusion Act of 1882 did not apply to Japanese and they remained unrestricted in their immigration until 1907, when the Immigration Act of that year authorized the President to refuse admission to certain persons if he became satisfied that their coming would be detrimental to labor interests. Although the Japanese Government had begun to discourage immigration to the continental United States, Japanese had obtained visas to Hawaii, Canada, and Mexico, whence they entered the United States. On 14 March, 1907, the President issued a proclamation excluding from the continental United States all "Japanese and Korean la-borers, skilled or unskilled, who had received passports to go to Mexico, Canada, or Hawaii and come therefrom."[10] This executive order was implemented the following year by the so-called Gentle-man's Agreement concluded between the United States and Japan, whereby Japan agreed to issue passports for travel to the United States only to those of its laborers who were former residents thereof, to parents, wives, or children of residents of the United States, and to agriculturists.[11] The Act of 1917 further restricted Oriental immigration by establishing a "barred zone," including parts of China, all of India, Burma, Siam, the Malay States, Asiatic Russia, the Polynesian and East Indian Islands, and parts of Arabia and Afghanistan, from which no natives were admissible.[12] In the Omnibus

TABLE IIA
CHINESE IN THE UNITED STATES BY REGIONS, 1880–1950

	1880	1890	1900	1910	1920	1930	1940	1950
United States Total	105,465	107,488	89,863	71,531	61,639	74,954	77,504	117,629
New England	401	1,488	4,203	3,499	3,602	3,794	3,238	4,684
Middle Atlantic	1,227	4,689	10,490	8,189	8,812	14,005	16,408	24,247
East North Central	390	1,254	2,533	3,415	5,043	6,340	4,799	8,454
West North Central	423	1,097	1,135	1,195	1,678	1,738	1,293	2,192
South Atlantic	74	669	1,791	1,582	1,824	1,869	2,047	4,755
East South Central	90	274	427	414	542	743	944	1,763
West South Central	758	1,173	1,555	1,303	1,534	1,582	1,935	3,950
Mountain	14,274	11,572	7,950	5,614	4,339	3,252	2,853	3,750
Pacific	87,828	85,272	59,779	46,320	34,265	41,631	43,987	63,834

Source: U.S. Census Data.

TABLE IIB
JAPANESE IN THE UNITED STATES BY REGIONS, 1880–1950

	1880	1890	1900	1910	1920	1930	1940	1950
United States Total	148	2,038	24,326	72,157	111,010	138,534	126,947	141,768
New England	14	45	89	272	347	352	340	732
Middle Atlantic	27	202	446	1,643	3,266	3,662	3,060	6,706
East North Central	7	101	126	482	927	1,022	816	15,996
West North Central	1	16	223	1,000	1,215	1,003	755	2,738
South Atlantic	5	55	29	156	360	393	442	1,393
East South Central	—	19	7	26	35	46	43	328
West South Central	—	42	30	428	578	687	564	1,334
Mountain	5	27	5,107	10,447	10,792	11,418	8,574	14,231
Pacific	89	1,532	18,269	57,703	93,490	120,251	112,353	98,310

Source: U.S. Census Data.

Act of 1924 Japanese were excluded from further immigration to the United States by the provision which refused admission to aliens ineligible for citizenship. That category included all those who were not "free white persons," as well as "aliens of African nativity" and "persons of African descent" according to the Naturalization Act of 1906.[13] In 1940 Chinese and a few others were dropped from ineligibility to naturalization, and in 1952 the ineligibility based on race and national origins was dropped altogether. The Act of 1952 established an annual quota for Japan of 185,[14] which lasted until, fourteen years later, a "needed skills" requirement was substituted for the quota system.

B. Distribution and Concentration

Tables II A and B show the Chinese and Japanese population by regions. Although the total number of Chinese in the United States dropped continuously from 1890 through 1920, the seven regions east of the Mountain Region show increases in Chinese population for all but a few decades. On the other hand, the Mountain Region shows a regular decline after 1880 until 1950, when a sharp increase still left the Chinese population below the level of 1920. The Pacific Region shows a decline in Chinese population from 1880 to 1920, when a recovery began. Except for 1950 the Chinese population on the Pacific Coast has, since 1910, been less than 50,000.

Until 1940 only three regions east of the Rocky Mountain area had over 1,000 Japanese—Middle Atlantic, West North Central and East North Central. Of these, only the Middle Atlantic Region sustained a Japanese population of over 1,000 steadily through 1950. By 1950, the relocation necessitated by the wartime exclusion from the Pacific Coast resulted in a Japanese population of over 1,000 in five regions east of the Mountain Region. The Mountain Region, which witnessed a depopulation of Chinese steadily after 1880, showed an irregular increase in Japanese for every decade except 1930–1940. The Pacific Region, similarly, showed a rapid and large increase irregularly after 1880, except for the 1930's and the war years after

1940. Since 1910, when Japanese first outnumbered Chinese in the United States, their population on the Pacific Coast has always exceeded 50,000.

Tables III A and B show the comparative concentration of Chinese and Japanese in the Pacific, Mountain, and Pacific and Mountain Regions, and the rest of the United States. Over 75% of the Japanese in the United States have lived on the Pacific Coast since 1890: 80% or more since 1910. Only in 1950 did the proportion of Japanese on the Pacific Coast drop to 69.5% of the total Japanese population. Since 1900 the Japanese population in the combined Pacific-Mountain Regions has hovered around 95%, except for the drop to 79.5% in 1950.

On the other hand, there has been a greater eastward dispersion of Chinese. From a point of 83.4% in 1880, the proportion of the Chinese population on the Pacific Coast has fallen to slightly more than one-half since 1920. In the Mountain Region, it decreased from 13.5% in 1880 to 3.26% in 1950. During the same period, the proportion of Chinese in the regions east of the Rockies grew from 3.1% in 1880 to 42.5% in 1950. The Chinese have shown, then, a greater emigration from the Pacific and Mountain regions than the Japanese.

Table IV lists cities, with a population of 100,000 or over in 1930, which have ever had a population of 100 or more Chinese or Japanese from 1880 to 1940. Forty-three such cities have had, at some time, over 100 Chinese. But only 14 cities have had over 100 Japanese. Thirty-four of the cities with over 100 Chinese are east of the Mountain Region; five with over 100 Japanese are east of the Mountain Region. Five of the 14 cities with over 100 Japanese are in California; three in Washington; one in Oregon.

C. Rural-Urban Concentration

Table V shows the distribution of Chinese and Japanese in urban and rural areas (with rural-farm and rural non-farm for 1930, 1950) from 1910 to 1950. The Chinese show a great preponderance in urban areas. The proportion of Chinese in urban areas grew steadily from 75.9% urban in 1910 to

TABLE IIIA

CHINESE IN THE UNITED STATES SHOWING NUMBER AND PERCENT OF TOTAL IN THE UNITED STATES, PACIFIC REGION, MOUNTAIN REGION, PACIFIC AND MOUNTAIN REGION, AND REST OF UNITED STATES, 1880–1950

Year	United States Total	%	Pacific Region Total	%	Mountain Region Total	%	Pacific-Mountain Region Total	%	U.S. less Pacific and Mountain Total	%
1880	105,645	100.0	87,828	83.4	14,274	13.5	102,102	96.9	3,543	3.1
1890	107,488	100.0	85,272	79.3	11,572	10.8	96,844	90.1	10,644	9.9
1900	89,863	100.0	59,779	66.5	7,950	8.8	67,729	75.3	22,134	24.7
1910	71,531	100.0	46,320	64.7	5,614	7.8	51,934	72.5	19,597	27.5
1920	61,639	100.0	34,265	55.6	4,339	7.0	38,604	62.6	23,035	37.4
1930	74,954	100.0	41,631	55.4	3,252	4.26	44,883	59.6	30,071	40.4
1940	77,504	100.0	43,987	56.6	2,853	3.69	46,840	60.3	30,664	39.7
1950	117,629	100.0	63,834	54.2	3,750	3.26	67,584	57.5	50,045	42.5

Source: U.S. Census Data.

TABLE IIIB

JAPANESE IN THE UNITED STATES SHOWING NUMBER, AND PERCENT OF TOTAL IN THE UNITED STATES, PACIFIC REGION, MOUNTAIN REGION, PACIFIC AND MOUNTAIN REGION, AND REST OF UNITED STATES, 1880–1950

Year	United States Total	%	Pacific Region Total	%	Mountain Region Total	%	Pacific-Mountain Region Total	%	U.S. less Pacific and Mountain Total	%
1880	148	100.0	89	60.0	5	3.4	94	63.4	54	36.6
1890	2,039	100.0	1,532	75.0	27	1.3	1,559	76.3	480	23.7
1900	24,326	100.0	18,269	75.0	5,107	20.9	23,376	95.9	950	4.1
1910	72,157	100.0	57,703	80.0	10,447	14.4	68,150	94.4	4,007	5.6
1920	111,010	100.0	93,490	85.0	10,792	9.25	104,282	94.25	6,728	5.75
1930	138,834	100.0	120,251	86.5	11,418	8.3	131,669	94.8	7,165	5.2
1940	126,947	100.0	112,353	88.1	8,574	6.7	120,927	94.8	6,020	5.2
1950	141,768	100.0	98,310	69.5	14,231	10.0	112,541	79.5	29,227	20.5

Source: U.S. Census Data.

93.0% urban in 1950. In 1910 barely a quarter of the Chinese population in the United States was rural; in 1950 only 7% remained rural. In 1930 approximately two-thirds of the rural Chinese were non-farm; in 1950 over 70% were rural non-farm.

The number of Japanese in urban and rural areas rose steadily from 1910 to 1930 with the proportion urban rising from just below to just above 50%. In 1940, when the decrease in Japanese population was 11,887, the urban population declined 5,002 and the rural 5,885, revealing the rough static relationship between urban and rural. The sudden increase in urban Japanese in 1950 reflects the effects of the exclusion and relocation when many Japanese lost their land holdings.

Table VI shows the number and percentage of Chinese and Japanese in urban and rural areas by regions from 1910 to 1930. The Chinese show a high degree of urbanization in all regions except two, the East South Central and Mountain. In the latter the degree of urbanization rose from 54.1% in 1910 to 67.3% in 1930. The absolute number of Chinese in this region declined in both rural and urban areas, but more rapidly in rural areas. The East South

TABLE IVA

CITIES WITH OVER 100 CHINESE, OF CITIES WHICH IN 1930
HAD 100,000 POPULATION: 1890–1940

	1890	1900	1910	1920	1930	1940
Boston, Mass.	444	1,186	1,192	1,075	1,595	1,386
Cambridge, Mass.	35	112	83	81	133	133
Fall River, Mass.	24	81	76	45	108	104
Lynn, Mass.	14	62	113	124	69	—
Springfield, Mass.	16	49	55	148	75	41
Worcester, Mass.	27	109	65	80	79	50
Providence, R. I.	43	245	192	135	132	167
Hartford, Conn.	45	122	82	135	75	32
New Haven, Conn.	50	90	86	103	69	71
New York, N.Y.	2,498	6,321	4,614	5,042	8,414	12,753
Jersey City, N.J.	132	218	149	85	152	112
Newark, N.J.	127	261	231	281	667	259
Paterson, N.J.	62	130	86	64	68	60
Philadelphia, Pa.	738	1,165	997	869	1,672	922
Pittsburgh, Pa.	115	182	236	306	296	141
Akron, Ohio	1	2	6	119	107	34
Cincinnati, Ohio	24	14	17	41	135	108
Cleveland, Ohio	36	103	228	275	570	308
Columbus, Ohio	6	8	45	92	126	95
Chicago, Ill.	567	1,209	1,778	2,353	2,757	2,013
Detroit, Mich.	10	2	28	438	710	583
Milwaukee, Wis.	14	21	51	65	176	153
Minneapolis, Minn.	17	24	101	196	221	304
St. Paul, Minn.	36	28	45	95	122	76
Kansas City, Mo.	186	89	62	45	108	56
St. Louis, Mo.	170	312	423	328	484	236
Omaha, Nebr.	89	96	53	126	147	69
Baltimore, Md.	178	477	314	328	438	379
Washington, D. C.	91	415	369	461	398	656
Norfolk, Va.	8	76	59	117	151	80
New Orleans, La.	142	437	344	246	267	230
Oklahoma City, Okla.	8	9	101	124	112	34
El Paso, Texas	210	299	228	117	175	—
San Antonio, Texas	46	54	62	193	316	471
Denver, Colorado	971	306	227	212	154	110
Salt Lake City, Utah	222	214	193	188	155	102
Seattle, Wash.	359	438	924	1,351	1,347	1,781
Spokane, Wash.	341	318	239	139	74	99
Tacoma, Wash.	9	252	23	59	89	48
Portland, Ore.	4,539	7,841	5,699	1,846	1,416	1,569
Los Angeles, Calif.	1,871	2,111	1,954	2,062	3,009	4,736
Oakland, Calif.	1,128	950	3,609	3,821	3,048	3,201
San Diego, Calif.	676	292	348	254	509	451
San Francisco, Calif.	25,833	13,954	10,582	7,744	16,303	17,782

Source: U.S. Census Data

TABLE IVB

CITIES WITH POPULATION OF 100,000 OR MORE IN 1930 WITH
100 OR MORE IN JAPANESE: 1890–1940

	1890	1900	1910	1920	1930	1940
New York	123	286	1,037	2,312	2,356	2,087
Chicago	—	68	233	417	486	390
Philadelphia	7	12	93	130	138	89
Detroit	2	2	30	100	103	63
Washington, D. C.	9	7	47	103	78	68
Seattle	125	2,990	6,127	7,874	8,448	6,975
Spokane	23	51	352	168	393	276
Tacoma	56	606	1,018	1,306	1,193	877
Portland	20	1,189	1,461	1,715	1,864	1,680
Long Beach	—	—	—	375	596	696
Los Angeles	26	150	4,238	11,618	21,081	23,321
Oakland	85	194	1,520	2,709	2,137	1,790
San Diego	9	14	159	772	911	828
San Francisco	590	1,781	4,518	5,358	6,250	5,280

Source: U.S. Census Data.

Central Region shows a regular rise in rural Chinese and an irregular increase in urban Chinese. In general urbanization of Chinese is higher in the Middle Atlantic, East North Central, West North Central and South Atlantic regions than in other regions.

The Japanese show a lower degree of urbanization than the Chinese. It should be noted that in those regions where the urban percentage is high, few Japanese are located. Of the 1,444 urban Japanese in the Middle Atlantic Region in 1910, 1,037 were in New York City; of the 2,979 there in 1920, 2,312 were in New York City; of the 3,233 in 1930, 2,356 were in New York City. There is only a small increase in urbanization on a national scale in the three-decade period. The Pacific Region, in which most Japanese are concentrated, reflects the national proportions; the Mountain Region shows a degree of rural settlement higher than the national average.

D. Summary of Data

The Chinese are a highly urbanized population: over 70% of the total Chinese population is found in cities. Until the forced removal of the Japanese from the Pacific Coast in 1942, subsequent to which 112,000 Japanese were incarcerated in prison camps in the American interior until 1945,[15] the Japanese population had been divided approximately equally between rural and urban aggregates. The degree of urbanization, which until 1940 showed a slight increase, was accelerated by the exclusion from the Pacific coast. The return to the coast which has characterized Japanese internal migration since 1950 has not been accompanied by a resumption of farm activities.

In general the Chinese may be characterized as a small, highly urbanized population, which, although heavily concentrated on the Pacific coast, shows a steady dispersion to areas of concentration in urban eastern and midwestern metropolitan centers. The Japanese are a slightly larger population, which until recently has been far more rural than the Chinese, and which continues to be concentrated in the Pacific Coast and Mountain Regions, although some eastern dispersion is evident since 1945. The significant differences between the Chinese and Japanese are the higher degrees of ruralization and concentration in the west of the latter; the much greater and longer urbanization of the former and their increasing dispersal.

TABLE V

CHINESE AND JAPANESE, RURAL, URBAN WITH RURAL-FARM, RURAL–NON-FARM FOR 1930 AND 1950: 1910–1950

	CHINESE						JAPANESE					
	Urban		Rural					Urban		Rural			
	No.	% Total	No.	% Total	R-F	R N-F	Total R.U.	No.	% Total	No.	% Total	R-F	R N-F	Total R.U.
1910	54,331	75.9	17,200	24.1			71,531	35,181	48.8	36,976	51.2			72,157
1920	50,008	81.1	11,631	18.9			61,639	53,830	48.5	57,180	51.5			111,010
1930	65,778	87.6	9,176	12.4	3,211	5,965	74,954	74,675	53.8	64,159	46.2	46,186	17,973	138,834
1940	70,226	90.6	7,278	9.4	—	—	77,504	69,673	54.8	57,274	45.2	—	—	126,947
1950	109,434	93.0	8,195	7.0	2,351	5,844	117,629	100,735	71.1	41,033	28.9	26,773	14,260	141,768

Source: U.S. Census Data.

TABLE VIA

CHINESE, RURAL AND URBAN, BY REGIONS, AND FOR CALIFORNIA, 1910–1930

	1910				1920				1930			
	Urban		Rural		Urban		Rural		Urban		Rural	
	No.	%	No.	%	No.	%	No.	%	No.	%	No.	%
Total United States	54,331	76.5	17,200	23.5	50,008	81.1	11,631	18.9	65,778	87.3	9,176	12.7
New England	3,441	97.4	58	2.6	3,527	97.9	75	2.1	3,707	97.7	87	2.3
Middle Atlantic	7,917	96.6	272	3.4	8,590	97.5	222	2.5	13,738	98.1	267	1.9
East North Central	3,306	96.8	109	3.2	4,952	98.2	91	1.8	6,252	98.6	88	1.4
West North Central	1,040	87.0	155	13.0	1,521	90.6	157	9.4	1,643	94.5	95	5.5
South Atlantic	1,412	89.3	170	10.7	1,675	91.8	149	8.2	1,755	93.9	114	6.1
East South Central	236	57.0	178	43.0	244	45.0	298	55.0	327	44.0	416	56.0
West South Central	1,111	84.5	192	15.5	1,198	78.1	336	21.9	1,304	82.4	278	17.6
Mountain	3,039	54.1	2,575	45.9	2,603	60.0	1,736	40.0	2,180	67.3	1,072	32.7
Pacific	32,829	70.9	13,491	29.1	25,698	75.0	8,567	25.0	34,872	83.8	6,759	16.2
California	24,262	66.9	11,986	33.1	21,094	72.5	7,718	27.5	31,218	80.9	6,143	19.1

Source: U.S. Census Data.

TABLE VIB

JAPANESE, RURAL AND URBAN, BY REGIONS, AND FOR CALIFORNIA, 1910–1930

	1910 Urban		1910 Rural		1920 Urban		1920 Rural		1930 Urban		1930 Rural	
	No.	%	No.	%	No.	%	No.	%	No.	%	No.	%
Total United States	35,181	46.7	36,976	51.3	53,830	48.5	57,180	51.5	74,675	53.8	64,159	46.2
New England	246	90.4	26	9.6	299	86.2	48	13.8	261	74.1	91	25.9
Middle Atlantic	1,444	87.9	199	12.1	2,979	91.2	287	9.8	3,233	88.3	429	11.7
East North Central	445	92.3	37	7.7	854	92.1	73	7.9	916	89.6	108	10.4
West North Central	622	62.2	378	37.8	701	57.7	514	42.3	467	46.6	536	53.4
South Atlantic	88	56.4	68	43.6	236	65.6	124	34.4	286	72.8	107	27.2
East South Central	17	—	9	—	16	—	19	—	25	—	21	—
West South Central	135	31.5	293	68.5	266	46.0	312	54.0	346	50.4	341	49.6
Mountain	3,438	32.9	7,009	67.1	2,941	27.3	7,851	72.7	2,692	23.5	8,726	76.5
Pacific	28,746	49.8	28,957	50.2	45,538	48.7	47,952	51.3	66,449	55.5	53,802	44.5
California	18,612	45.0	22,744	55.0	33,209	45.6	38,743	54.4	53,397	54.6	44,059	45.4

Source: U.S. Census Data.

TABLE VII

CHINESE POPULATION FOR UNITED STATES FOR CITIES OF 100,000 POPULATION AND OVER AND FOR CITIES 25,000–100,000: 1880–1940

	1880	1890	1900	1910	1920	1930	1940
Total United States	105,465	107,488	88,869	71,531	61,639	74,954	77,504
Total in cities with 100,000 population or over	22,925	32,664	29,630	29,002	34,670	48,608	55,030
Percent in cities with 100,000 population or over	21.6	30.3	33.0	40.5	56.2	64.1	71.0
Total in cities with 25,000–100,000 population	490	13,685	18,062	12,220	7,115	26,886	22,474
Percent in cities with 25,000–100,000 population	.4	12.7	20.1	17.1	11.3	35.8	28.8
Total in cities under 25,000 and rural areas	82,050	61,639	41,971	30,309	19,854	—	—
Percent in cities under 25,000 and rural areas	77.8	56.8	46.8	42.3	32.2	—	—
Total percent	99.8	99.8	99.9	99.8	99.7	99.8	99.9

Source: Rose Hum Lee, "The Decline of Chinatowns in the United States," *American Journal of Sociology*, March, 1949, p. 427.

Social and Economic Elements

The California of 1848–1882 was a different California from that of 1882–1924. Thus, the periods of Chinese and Japanese immigration must be viewed almost as if the two groups were coming to different countries. During the "Chinese period" (1848–1882), California was the scene of two major kinds of economic activity: gold mining and railroad building. The former occupation required long, difficult hand labour and many miners. Labour-saving machinery for mining was almost unknown. When gold mining ceased to be a profitable enterprise and attention was turned to California's other mineral wealth, chiefly quartz, machinery had been invented which replaced much of the labour needed in the early period. This technological revolution coincided, approximately, with the exclusion of the Chinese and the respite before the influx of Japanese. Similarly railroad construction reached its peak in the years prior to the completion of the Transcontinental Railway (1869). When railway construction ended many Chinese were thrown out of work and into the cities on the Pacific Coast, along the lines of the railway, and—because of the desire for cheap labour—into the cities of the East. When the Japanese began arriving in the United States, after 1890, the two occupations which had served as incentives for Chinese immigration were closed to them. Like the Chinese before them, they had to adjust their lives to the available economic opportunities.

A. Factors Affecting the Location Pattern of the Chinese

Chinese immigration was stimulated not only by the apparent opportunities on the American frontier, but also by the Tai Ping Rebellion, which dislocated the economy in South China, causing large numbers of Chinese agricultural labourers in Fukien and Kwangtung Provinces to gather in Canton, Hong Kong and Macao. Unemployment was high, and many Chinese shipped from the latter two ports to the Isthmus of Panama, Cuba and South America as contract labor. Others sailed, especially from the port of Hong Kong, to Britain and America as "free" emigrants. Those who emigrated as contract labor were largely single men, contracted by "Hongs", or corporations, which employed them for long periods of time. Of those who sailed for California, at least 50% were married, leaving their wives behind in accord with the prohibitory Chinese laws and customs concerning women.[16] Payment of passage for free migrants was often obtained by a loan from a Chinese brokerage firm, which accepted the emigrant's wife and family as security.[17]

The Chinese who came to California were largely former agricultural and urban labourers. Agriculture in Kwangtung was carried on from village centres, and village organization and large kinship units have been the standard vehicles of social control. In California the village and province structure was not left behind. Instead district associations, corresponding to the districts from which the immigrants had come, were organized. At first these were separate associations, but in the mid-1850's, as a result of growing anti-Chinese sentiment in California, the lack of an effective organization to represent Chinese interests, and the absence of any regularized diplomatic representation from the Manchu Government, the Chinese Consolidated Benevolent Association, better known as the "Chinese Six Companies" was established.[18] The organization claimed to speak for the entire Chinese population in America and served as a representative, and creditor agency for every Chinese under its jurisdiction. In the words of the Association's authorized historian,

> When, therefore, the seven district groups—which sociologically speaking, constitute the basic social control groups among California Chinese—unite together to form a coordinating organization such as the Chinese Six Companies, the social power that such an agency would wield is practically without limit. By united agreement the Six Companies was empowered to speak and act for all the California Chinese in problems and affairs which affect the majority of the population.[19]

One function of the Association is particularly important since it served, inadvertently, to insure the continuation of an urban Chinese labor force. The Companies assured themselves of membership by meeting each arriving ship and collecting the name and district of departure of each Chinese. These lists were utilized not only for the Companies' census of Chinese, but also to insure payment of debts. No Chinese could return to China without appearing at the offices of the Six Companies, paying all his debts and presenting a "departure fee" to the companies—a reimbursement for the Companies' services and a donation toward the welfare of those Chinese who remained in California.[20]

The Companies were able to exercise effective control over remigration to China through their arrangements with the steamship companies. Until 1880, i.e., until two years prior to the exclusion of Chinese immigrants, the steamship companies agreed not to allow a Chinese to purchase a ticket for China unless he had a certificate from the Six Companies showing he had paid his debts.[21] Thus, although the Chinese labourer may have left wife and family behind, he was compelled to meet his financial obligations before he could rejoin his family. Wage labour, rather than long-term, unpredictable investment in agriculture, was the more sure way of obtaining the financial means to return home.

The Chinese communities outside the Pacific Coast area may well have originated with the reciprocal demand of incipient industrialism for cheap labour and the need by Chinese for money in order to return home. Although the evidence is scanty it is not improbable that the forces which created the early migration of Chinese outside the Pacific region were generated by the decline of mining and railroading after 1880. In 1870 Chinese labourers were shipped from California to North Adams, Massachusetts, to break a strike among shoemakers.[22] Anti-Coolie meetings were held in Boston to protest against reducing American labour

TABLE VIII

MEMBERSHIP IN THE CHINESE SIX COMPANIES

In Six Companies		In United States (various estimates)	
1876[1]		Census: 1870 63,199	
Total	151,300	Coolidge:[3] 1870..................71,083	
Ning Yueng	75,000	Coolidge: 1876 111,971	
Hop Wo	34,000	S.F. Bulletin	
Kong Chow	15,000	April 20, 1876 60,000	
Yeong Wo	12,000		
Sam Yup	11,000	Census: 1880 105,465	
Yan Wo	4,300	Coolidge:[3] 1880.................104,991	
1942[2]		Census: 1940 77,504	
Total	27,500	California............................58,324	
Ning Yueng	13,500	San Francisco......................5,280	
Show Hing	4,000		
Hop Wo	3,000		
Kong Chow	2,500		
Yeong Wo	2,500		
Sam Yup	1,500		
Yan Wo	500		

[1]Cited in Otis Gibson, *The Chinese in America* (1887), and in William Hoy, *The Chinese Six Companies* (San Francisco: Chinese Consolidated Benevolent Association, 1942), p. 16. Hoy believes the figures for 1876 were "jacked up" by the Six Companies.
[2]From Hoy, *op. cit.,* p. 17.
[3]Mary Coolidge, *Chinese Immigration* (New York: Henry Holt, 1909), p. 498 ff.

to the standards of "rice and rats."[23] In 1877 Chinese were sent to break a strike in a cutlery plant in Beaver Falls, Pennsylvania. The Cincinnati *Enquirer* protested against the use of Chinese labour in the cigar-making industry. Many Chinese were imported into the South to develop rice culture and to replace Negroes on railway projects.[24]

Chinese who were brought to the East often discovered economic opportunities for themselves and informed their brethren in the West. The Chinese hand laundry with its methodical care for high quality linen found a place in the metropolis where higher status Caucasians appreciated this service. Perhaps the first Chinese in any great numbers in the East were brought out by a certain Mr. Thomas to work in a laundry in Belleville, New Jersey.

> They quickly discovered, upon their arrival, the field presented by the neighbouring cities for their work, and the news spread rapidly to California and even to China itself. Thousands of Chinese came to the East, until at present there is scarcely a town throughout the whole extent of country where one or more may not be found, while in the large cities colonies have been formed, in which much of their primitive life has been re-established . . .[25]

The fact that the Chinese who first came to America were either single or had left their wives behind served as an added factor in determining their urban location. The laundry business, which has come down as a stereotype of the Chinese, originated because of the absence of women on the frontier. Caucasian males soon discovered through observation of the Chinese that the latter did not possess the scruples about doing "women's work" which inhibited white males from this occupation. Chinese laundries became profitable institutions until Caucasian entrepreneurs sought, with the aid of steam machinery, to invade this ethnically-monopolized occupation.

Moreover the social structure of the Chinatown has been its own undoing. Organized on the basis of four-clan associations or family associations, the organization restricts the choice of mate for marriage. Members of the same clan are considered related by common descent and are prohibited from marriage to one another. Since exogamy must pre-

vail, the Chinese youth in a small Chinatown, inhabited by only one or two clans, must either remain single in his city of birth, or let his parents arrange a marriage through friends in another city, or migrate to another Chinatown to find a mate. As the second and third generation Chinese-Americans reached marriageable age, the first two choices seemed less attractive than the third. Choice of mate and occupational opportunity are greatest in larger urban centres; thus the migration to these centres occurred.[29]

B. Factors Affecting the Location Pattern of the Japanese

The heavy migration of Japanese to the United States beginning in the 1890's was a partial result of the demographic change in Japan caused by industrialization. Overpopulation on the land caused a migration to urban centers and heavy emigration. The United States was but one outlet for this population movement. From 1899 until 1924 emigration companies arranged for the transportation of contract labourers to Peru,[30] Brazil, Mexico, and Hawaii. Although the migrants to other nations and Hawaii where chiefly contract labourers, United States law forbade such importation, so that the Japanese who came to the United States were not formally under contract.

Miyamoto[31] has divided the adjustment of Japanese in America into three intervals. 1) During the Frontier Period, before the Gentleman's Agreement of 1907, the Japanese immigrant *(Issei)* regarded himself as a "sojourner," planning to return to Japan. 2) The Settling Period, from 1907 to the Exclusion Act of 1924, saw semi-permanent and permanent American residence undertaken on farms and in Japanese ghettos. Economic improvement was begun and families were founded. 3) The Second Generation Period began in 1924 and continues with the increase of *Nisei,* the children of immigrants, and *Sansei,* the grandchildren of immigrants.

Secondly, it may be inferred that insofar as a Chinese had left his wife behind he had no desire for any lengthy tenure in the United States. Moreover, many Chinese, even though single, had been sent to America to make their fortune and return to China to support their parents and other relatives. Given this kind of economic incentive, the need was for regularized income without much heavy investment in unmovable capital within the United States. Farms, then, even if available, did not provide the form of occupation suitable for Chinese immigrants. Laundries required little investment and used little or no machinery. The other occupations which early immigrants entered, besides mining and railroad construction, consisted of intra-ethnic services, e.g., sale of Chinese foods—which have also enticed American diners since 1850—and other products, and migratory agricultural labour. With respect to the latter occupation, a well-known economist has argued that Chinese exclusion was in part inspired by the desire of some Californians for small independent farms, rather than large, quasi-feudal estates.[26] If this is true, then the Japanese, with their ability to cultivate a small acreage singly and intensively, provided an ideal agriculture force for California.

C. Factors Affecting the Location of Chinese in the Post-Immigration Period

Professor Rose Hum Lee outlined three phases of Chinese location in the United States:[27] 1) Concentration in the Pacific States and Rocky Mountain areas, 1850–1880; 2) Dispersion to midwestern and eastern parts of the United States, 1880–1910; 3) Reconcentration in larger urban centers in the East and West, 1910–1940. The concentration of the first period and the dispersion following it, as has been stated, were caused by the economic opportunities and their disappearance. The reconcentration, which manifests itself most completely in the decline of Chinatowns in the Rocky Mountain area, is due to the undermining of the economic base upon which such centers exist, and the effect of beliefs about marriage upon a relatively small Chinese population. Actually the period characterized by Professor Lee as dispersion reflects a phase of a

steady movement of concentration of Chinese in larger urban centers.

The size of a city and its ability to maintain a Chinese community within it are reciprocally related. If there are diversified industries, offering varied occupations for both Chinese and Caucasians, and a large enough Caucasian population to support a Chinese community's special services, e.g., hand laundries and exotic restaurants, the Chinese community will thrive. If there are but a few basic industries or sources for occupation, the existence of the Chinese community will reflect the success and size of that industry. The Rocky Mountain Chinatowns have declined as their single industrial base has declined, depopulating the area in general and thus subverting the economic base for a Chinatown.[28]

These periods correspond to periods of occupational change and, consequently, of locational change or concentration. Three periods may be designated correspondingly. 1) During the Sojourner Period, ending roughly at the time of the Gentlemen's Agreement, Japanese were employed as replacements for Chinese in railroading, mining, and as agricultural labourers on a migratory basis. 'n urban enterprise Japanese worked as houseboys and in other domestic service as gardeners, laundrymen, cooks, etc. In this period the decline in railroading and mining effectively decreased job opportunities, while migrant farm labourers competed with Mexicans and immigrants from South Eastern Europe.[32] 2) In the Settlement Period (1907–1930) *Issei* and some *Nisei* began to purchase, lease, or manage farm property and take up residence in the United States. Families were founded as Japanese males arranged for brides from Japan through the "picture system" *(Shashin kekkon).* 3) The Urbanization Period is noticeable with the increase of *Nisei* and *Sansei* of mature years after 1930. Marginal to their Japanese and American cultures, they move out from the essentially *Issei*-dominated agricultural occupations and attempt to move into the areas in which competition with Caucasians occurs. Although the success here is quite small, certain ethnic enclaves develop in urban centres for Japanese. In Los Angeles—a city of heavy

Japanese concentration—these enclaves include the fields of ethnic restaurants and shops (cafes, laundries, and barber shops); fishing and fish canning; wholesale and retail produce business; contract gardening; domestic service.[33] The depression of the thirties resulted in many *Nisei* returning to family enterprises, on farms or in retail fruit businesses.[34]

The factors which affected Chinese occupation and location had a different effect upon the Japanese. Again if one examines the economic conditions in the country at the time of arrival, and the existing institutions within the immigrant community for social control, the reasons for the largely rural and agricultural status of the Japanese becomes clear.

For the first Japanese immigrants to California, only a short period of railroad building remained. Mining had become a diminishing source of employment, as quartz mining replaced gold-mining and machinery displaced men. Urban areas, already "abused" by the influx of Chinese labour did not provide a safe haven for any very remunerative employment. However, California was undergoing an agricultural change toward intensive land usage, a form of farming to which the Japanese peasant was accustomed. During the "sojourner period" the Japanese, like their Chinese predecessors, were nevertheless unwilling to invest in land. There grew up then in the early period, and lasting through the present day, the system of migratory Japanese agricultural labour gangs, under a Japanese boss. These gangs later formed into clubs with secretaries and relatively formalized procedures. They underbid their ethnic competitors and were fairly successful during the period around the turn of the century.[35]

These gangs were replaced by an increase in tenants and sharecroppers after 1900. In 1900, less than 4,000 acres in California were leased to Japanese tenants; by 1905, this had increased to 60,000; by 1910, to 177,000.[36] Tenancy was increased, moreover, as Japanese bosses showed preferential treatment to landowners who permitted Japanese to lease land from them.

The Japanese occupied small holdings and generally cultivated, on an intensive level, berries, vegetables, fruits and other truck crops, and even developed some new crops. Tenancy continued until 1913 when the first of California's Alien Land laws was passed. It was followed by more restrictive measures in 1920 and 1923, including a law which presumed fraud when an ineligible alien bought or leased land in the name of his citizen offspring. If these laws had been strictly enforced Japanese would have been forced out of agriculture and into urban areas or remigration, but evasion was not difficult and only rarely were the laws actively enforced or legitimized in the public eyes.[37] It was not, then, until the wholesale removal of Japanese from the Pacific Coast in 1942 by government order, that the gradual rural to urban migration was upset.

The concentration of Japanese in and around Los Angeles is due to the general shift in intensive agriculture to the southern vegetable growing areas in which the Japanese participated. With this movement south the Japanese, utilizing their special agricultural techniques, obtained a virtual monopoly on vegetable growing in the region.[38]

D. The Japanese Associations

The Japanese family, more than the Association, has acted as an institution of social control for the Japanese. Whereas the Chinese early came under the social influence and economic domination of the Chinese Six Companies, the Japanese Association of America exercised little if any economic domination and had small membership.[39] The Japanese Association of California arose out of discussions on how to combat anti-Japanese activities in California which intensified because of labour agitation and an outbreak of bubonic plague in 1900. Another was organized in New York in 1914 in response to more anti-Japanese agitation. Eventually there were seven such associations in the United States and Hawaii with various numbers of locals.

Sociologically speaking, the chief function of these associations can best be described as accommodation. They engaged in various forms of Americanization programs, taught English and attempted to create an understanding among the Japanese of American society and culture. They gave legal aid to the Japanese, and served as a microcosmic imitation of the United States Department of Agriculture Field Service, providing lectures and reports on improved methods of agriculture. They conducted censuses of the Japanese population in the United States by occupation and business conditions and made these reports available to the Japanese consulates. They aided Japanese who had left the country to obtain re-entry permits, and they acted as agencies, in the absence of Japanese consular officials, for the endorsement of certain certificates. (In this capacity they charged a fee of one to four dollars.) They attempted to educate American-born Japanese about Japan, and to educate non-Japanese about the culture of Japan and Japanese-Americans.

TABLE IX

MEMBERSHIP IN JAPANESE ASSOCIATIONS OF AMERICA[1]

1924

	Members in Association	Number In Area	%
Total (U.S. and Hawaii)	36,792	260,592	12
Japanese Association of America at San Francisco (includes 38 locals)	16,000	63,893	
Central Japanese Association of Southern California (20 locals) in Los Angeles	8,000	38,110	
Northwest American-Japanese Association (Washington and Montana: 14 locals)	6,860	15,768	
Japanese Association of Oregon (Portland; Idaho)	1,250	7,728	
New York	1,200	—	
Denver, Colo., Arizona, Utah, Texas, Illinois (9 locals)	2,127	—	

[1]From Michinari Fujita, "Japanese Associations in America," *Sociology and Social Research,* January–February 1929, pp. 211–228. The figures are derived from a census taken by the Japanese Consulate in Los Angeles.

They did not function, however, as creditor agencies, nor did their membership permit them to exercise dominance in the way that the Chinese Six Companies did. In effect, then the Japanese community was not burdened by a requirement to pay debts on a regularized basis, and thus was not in such great need for regularized wage labour.

It may be inferred then, that in the absence of culturally influential and economically dominant associations and with the family able and expected to provide a haven for those unemployed, the ability to engage in rural activities was enhanced. At the same time the urban Japanese remained relatively concentrated in areas of the west, close to family farms where they could return if necessary, or if needed. Similarly Japanese agriculture was concentrated in areas of accessible markets, and where communication between urban and rural Japanese was facilitated.

The absence of a definite need for regular wages is made more significant by the functions which the Japanese family served. Not only in Japan but in the United States the Japanese family has provided welfare and employment for those members in need.[40] The number of Japanese classified as "unpaid family farm labourer," or "unpaid family workers" reveals the extent of this institutional practice.[41] Urban unemployment could be countered then by a position in the family enterprise or a migration to the farm. The practice of sending children to work as fruit pickers in the summer months is not uncommon among urban Japanese families, and is looked upon, in many instances, as a customary vacation for the children.

E. Marital Status of the Japanese

While there is evidence that at least half of the Chinese who came to America were married, Japanese immigrants appear to have been single. In 1910, 65.1% of the male Japanese 25 to 44 years old reported themselves single, or 15,500 out of an age group of 23,820. Of 3,095 female Japanese in California, aged 25–44, only 275 or 8.9% reported themselves single. Chinese show a higher percentage married and lower percentage single for the same year.

After 1910 the Japanese began the importation of brides from Japan, cutting the sex ratio and providing the possibility of offspring. Before this, the single status of immigrant Japanese was significant. Whereas the Chinese may have been inhibited from land investment because of the desire to return to wife and family in China, the Japanese were not so inhibited. While both Chinese and Japanese paid lip service to their status as "sojourners" in America, the willingness to invest in what might involve long-term settlement—a farm—was greater for the Japanese. Moreover, the importation of Japanese brides from 1910 to 1923 reveals—when coupled with the increase of farm tenancy and management in spite of legal obstacles—the intention to abandon "sojourner" status and take up semi-permanent or permanent residence in the United States. The move into agriculture was made easier by the absence of wives at home, and the ability to stay in agriculture enhanced by the importation of wives.

Conclusion

The Chinese and Japanese occupy different locations and present different degrees of urban and rural concentration because of conditions at the time of the immigration period.

1) The Chinese came to an area of mining, railroading and incipient urbanization. Their occupations were determined by available economic opportunities. The Japanese arrived when mining and railroading began their decline and intensive agriculture—at which the Japanese were adept—began.

2) Chinese institutions of social control made it necessary to pay debts regularly and to pay all debts and fees before leaving for China. Occupying a "sojourner" status the Chinese were in need of ready

TABLE X

MARITAL STATUS CHINESE AND JAPANESE IN CALIFORNIA, 1910. PERSONS 15 YEARS OR OLDER

	Males 15 years of age and older							Females 15 years of age and older						
		Single		Married					Single		Married			
	Total	No.	%	No.	%	Wid.	Div.	Total	No.	%	No.	%	Wid.	Div.
Chinese[1]	31,337	14,751	47.1	13,997	44.7	628	8	2,110	450	21.3	1,455	69.0	188	3
15–24	4,309	3,855	89.5	421	9.8	—	—	602	318	52.8	276	45.8	6	—
25–44	9,670	4,004	41.4	5,262	54.4	99	3	1,061	106	10.0	881	83.0	67	2
45–	16,087	6,826	42.4	8,295	51.6	529	5	438	21	4.8	298	68.0	114	1
Rural	11,231	6,561	58.4	4,242	37.8	265	2	301	52	17.3	216	71.8	28	1
Urban	20,106	8,190	40.7	9,755	48.8	363	6	1,809	398	22.0	1,239	68.5	160	2
Japanese[1]	33,312	23,154	69.5	9,320	28.0	324	45	4,510	522	11.6	3,916	86.8	63	6
15–24	7,094	6,794	95.8	251	3.5	3	1	1,280	235	18.4	1,040	81.3	3	2
25–44	23,820	15,500	65.1	7,900	33.2	232	35	3,095	275	8.9	2,778	89.8	37	4
45–	1,922	667	34.7	1,143	59.5	88	9	117	7	6.0	87	74.4	23	—
Rural	18,993	13,208	69.5	5,404	28.5	226	15	1,968	123	6.3	1,824	92.7	19	1
Urban	14,319	9,946	69.5	3,916	27.3	98	30	2,542	399	15.7	2,092	82.3	44	5

[1]Totals include persons of unknown age.   Source: U.S. Census Data.

TABLE XI

CHINESE AND JAPANESE MALES AND FEMALES, NATIVE AND FOREIGN BORN: 1850–1950

Chinese

Year	Males			Females			Total M-F	M per 100 F
	Native	Foreign	Total	Native	Foreign	Total		
1850	—	—	—	—	—	—	—	—
1860	—	—	33,149	—	—	1,784	34,933	1,858.1
1870	—	—	58,633	—	—	4,566	63,199	1,284.1
1880	—	—	100,686	—	—	4,779	105,465	2,106.8
1890	—	—	103,620	—	—	3,868	107,488	2,678.9
1900	6,657	78,684	85,341	2,353	2,169	4,522	89,863	1,887.2
1910	11,921	54,935	66,856	3,014	1,661	4,675	71,531	1,430.1
1920	13,318	40,573	53,891	5,214	2,534	7,748	61,639	695.5
1930	20,693	39,109	59,802	10,175	4,977	15,152	74,954	394.7
1940	25,702	31,687	57,389	14,560	5,555	20,116	77,504	285.3
1950	—	—	77,008	—	—	40,621	117,629	189.6

Japanese

Year	Males			Females			Total M-F	M per 100 F
	Native	Foreign	Total	Native	Foreign	Total		
1850	—	—	—					
1860	—	—	—	—	—	—	—	—
1870	—	—	47	—	—	8	55	—
1880	—	—	134	—	—	14	148	—
1890	—	—	1,780	—	—	259	2,039	687.3
1900	156	23,185	23,341	113	872	985	24,326	2,369.6
1910	2,340	60,730	63,070	2,162	6,925	9,087	72,157	694.1
1920	15,494	57,213	72,707	14,178	24,125	38,303	111,010	189.8
1930	35,874	45,897	81,771	32,483	24,580	57,063	138,834	143.3
1940	42,316	29,651	71,967	37,326	17,654	54,980	126,947	130.9
1950	—	76,649	—	—	—	65,119	141,768	117.7

Source: U.S. Census Data.

capital which could be obtained by wage labour rather than agriculture. The Japanese Associations did not function so as to require debt payment, and did not command the authority which Chinese Associations did. Hence, in the absence of opportunities for wage labour, and in the presence of opportunities in agriculture, the Japanese were able to enter agriculture more readily than the Chinese.

3) The Chinese and Japanese both regarded themselves first as "sojourners" in America. But this status for Chinese was more real since they had left wives and family behind, sometimes as security for payment of passage to America. The desire to return to wives and family in China inhibited Chinese from investments in land which involved long-term settlement with unpredictable income, and en-hanced their desire to obtain ready capital. The Japanese sojourner status was more readily lost in the presence of agricultural opportunity and the absence of wives awaiting at home.

4) The Chinese need for capital, coupled with the incipient industrialism in the United States, made them more readily exploitable by entrepreneurs. Not tied to the land like the Japanese, they were available and willing to migrate to areas of industrial employment. Their early scattering in the United States, and the continued concentration of Japanese on the Pacific Coast, was due to their availability for spatial mobility. The Japanese, on the other hand, without need of capital, were able to concentrate and intensively build up their agricultural investments.

Notes

1. See Mary Coolidge, *Chinese Immigration* (New York, 1909), pp. 498–499.

2. See Elmer C. Sandmeyer, *The Anti-Chinese Movement in California* (Urbana, Ill., 1939), pp. 25–95.

3. See Herbert Hill, "The Racial Practices of Organized Labor—The Age of Gompers and After," in Arthur M. Ross and Herbert Hill (Eds.), *Employment, Race, and Poverty: A Critical Study of the Disadvantaged Status of Negro Workers from 1865 to 1965* (New York, 1967), pp. 365–402.

4. See S.W. Kung, *Chinese in American Life: Some Aspects of Their History, Status, Problems, and Contributions* (Seattle, 1962), pp. 132–147.

5. "The wife of a Chinese labourer or a Chinese woman not previously a labourer, who married a Chinese labourer, was held to have or acquire the status of the husband, and was not permitted to enter the United States." Huang Tsen-Ming, *The Legal Status of the Chinese Abroad* (Taipei, 1954), p. 84. See *The Case of the Chinese Wife*, 21 Fed. 785 (1884).

6. Robert E. Park, "Our Racial Frontier on the Pacific," *Race and Culture* (Glencoe, Ill., 1950), p. 151.

7. "The 1882 Act which also barred Chinese from naturalization did not prohibit, however, the entry of Chinese teachers, students, merchants, or those 'proceeding to the United States . . . from curiosity'," Frank L. Auerbach, *Immigration Laws of the United States* (Indianapolis, 1961), p. 7.

8. See James G. McCurdy, *By Juan de Fuca's Strait: Pioneering Along the Northwestern Edge of the Continent* (Portland, 1937), pp. 209, 282. For an interesting aspect of the Mexican border problem, see F.B. Worley, "Five Hundred Chinese Refugees," *Overland Monthly*, April 1918, pp. 290–294.

9. Timothy J. Molloy, "A Century of Chinese Immigration: A Brief Review," *Immigration and Naturalization Service Monthly Review*, December 1947, pp. 69–75. For a critique of America's Chinese immigration policy, see Burton H. Wolfe, "The Chinese Immigration Puzzle," *Chicago Jewish Forum*, Fall, 1959, pp. 33–39.

10. Executive Order No. 589, 14 March 1907.

11. See Thomas A. Bailey, *Theodore Roosevelt and the Japanese-American Crises* (Gloucester, Mass., 1964), pp. 150–165, 233–234, 270–280, 305–321.

12. Auerbach, *op. cit.*, pp. 8, 93n.

13. Huang Tsen-Ming, *op. cit.*, pp. 173–175.

14. Auerbach, *op. cit.*, pp. 94–97.

15. See Jacobus tenBroek, Edward N. Barnhart, and Floyd Matson, *Prejudice, War, and the Constitution* (Berkeley, 1954).

16. The Chinese kinship system was patrilineal, patronymic, and patripotestal. A wife was required to live in the home of her husband's parents and to remain there even if the husband should go abroad temporarily. See Wen Yen Tsao, "The Chinese Family from Customary Law to Positive Law," *Hastings Law Journal*, May 1966, pp. 727–765. See also Maurice Freedman, "The Family in China, Past and Present," *Pacific Affairs*, Winter, 1961–1962, pp. 323–336. For the marital status of the early overseas Chinese, see Coolidge, *op. cit.*, pp. 17–20.

17. Russell H. Conwell, *Why and How* (Boston, 1871), pp. 176–196.

18. See William Hoy, *The Chinese Six Companies* (San Francisco, Chinese Consolidated Benevolent Ass'n. 1942); Coolidge, *op. cit.*, pp. 400–410; Everett Wong, "The Exclusion Movement and the Chinese Community in San Francisco" (unpublished Master's Thesis, University of California, 1954), pp. 69 ff.; Anne D. Coulter, "The Economic Aspect of the Chinese Labor Problem" (unpublished Master's Thesis, University of California, 1902), p. 15.

19. Hoy, *op. cit.*, pp. 18–19. See also Nora Sterry, "Social Attitudes of Chinese Immigrants," *Journal of Applied Sociology*, July–August 1923, pp. 328–329.

20. *Ibid.*, pp. 23–25; Coolidge, *op. cit.*, pp. 409–410.

21. Coolidge, *op. cit.*, p. 410.

22. Boston *Transcript*, 13 June 1870, quoted in Carl Wittke, *We Who Built America* (Cleveland, 1939), p. 460.

23. Boston *Transcript*, 30 June 1870, quoted in *ibid.*, p. 460.

24. Cincinnati *Enquirer*, 11 April, 8 January, 24 June 1870); Cleveland *Leader*, 6 June 1870, 19 January, 17, 20, 24 June, 27 July 1867; *Ohio State Journal*, 3 November 1873, quoted in *ibid.*, p. 461.

25. Stewart Culin, "China in America: A Study in the Social Life of the Chinese in the Eastern Cities of the United States," Paper read before the American Association for the Advancement of Science, at the Thirty-Sixth Meeting, New York 1887 (Philadelphia, 1887), pp. 8–9.

26. Paul S. Taylor, "Foundations of California Rural-Society," *California Historical Society Quarterly*, September 1945, pp. 193–228.

27. On this point see Rose Hum Lee, "The Decline of China-towns in the United States," *American Journal of Sociology*, March 1949, pp. 422–432.

28. Lee, *op. cit.*, pp. 422–427.

29. Lee, *op. cit.*, pp. 429–430.

30. Toraji Irie, "History of the Japanese Migration to Peru," *Hispanic American Historical Review*, August–October 1951, pp. 436–452, 648–664 (translated by William Himel).

31. S.F. Miyamoto, "Social Solidarity Among the Japanese in Seattle." *University of Washington Publications in the Social Sciences*, 11

(December 1939), p. 84. Cited in Leonard Bloom and John Kitsuse, *The Managed Casualty* (Berkeley and Los Angeles, 1956), p. 1.

32. D. Thomas, *The Salvage* (Berkeley and Los Angeles, 1952), p. 20.

33. Leonard Bloom and Ruth Riemer, *Removal and Return* (Berkeley and Los Angeles, 1949), pp. 7–31. W.T. Kataoka, "Occupations of Japanese in Los Angeles," *Sociology and Social Research,* May–June 1937, pp. 464–466.

34. Kataoka, *op. cit.,* p. 465.

35. Thomas, *op. cit.,* pp. 23–25.

36. *Ibid.,* p. 22.

37. Thomas, *op. cit.,* pp. 23–24; Bloom and Riemer, *op. cit.,* pp. 69–71.

38. Thomas, *op. cit.,* p. 25. Bloom and Riemer suggest that livestock and dairy farming did not arise among Japanese since they depend on fish for protein, and since Buddhism discourages animal killing, *op. cit.,* p. 73.

39. The following analysis is from Michinari Fujita, "Japanese Associations in America," *Sociology and Social Research,* January–February 1929, pp. 211–228.

40. On Japan, see Irene Taeuber, "Family, Migration and Industrialization in Japan," *American Sociological Review,* April 1951, pp. 149–157.

41. Bloom and Riemer, *op. cit.,* p. 13, 19, note that 1,746 Japanese (of a total of 17,005 employed) were unpaid family farm laborers; of these 605 were native born males, 432 native born females. In a 20% sample of employed Japanese in Los Angeles (1941) 576 unpaid family workers were listed: 161 in clerical and sales, 36 operatives and kindred, 79 service workers, 297 farm and nursery labourers, 3 labourers, except farm. The sample was 3,500; the percent unpaid family workers 16.5.

Generation and Character: The Case of the Japanese Americans

WHEN THE FIRST Japanese Embassy arrived in the United States in 1860, the *Daily Alta Californian,* a San Francisco newspaper, reported with mingled approval and astonishment:

> "Every beholder was struck with the self-possessed demeanor of the Japanese. Though the scenes which now met their gaze must have been of the most intense interest for novelty, they seemed to consider this display as due the august position they held under their Emperor, and not one of them, by sign or word, evinced either surprise or admiration."[1]

Thus, with their first major debarkation in the New World,[2] the Japanese appeared to Americans to lack emotional expression. Indeed, San Francisco's perceptive journalist went on to observe: "This stoicism, however, is a distinguishing feature with the Japanese. It is part of their creed never to appear astonished at anything, and it must be a rare sight indeed which betrays in them any expression of wonder."[3]

In the eighty-five years which passed between Japan's first embassy and the end of the second World War, this "distinguishing feature" of the Japanese became the cardinal element of the anti-

Japanese stereotype. Characterized by journalists, politicians, novelists and film-makers as a dangerous, enemy people, the Japanese were also pictured as mysterious and inscrutable.[4] Supposedly loyal to Japan, cunning and conspiratorial, most of the Japanese Americans were evacuated and incarcerated throughout the second World War. This unusual violation of their fundamental civil rights was justified in the minds of a great many ordinary Americans by the perfidious character they imputed to Japanese.[5]

The anti-Japanese stereotype was so widespread that it affected the judgments of sociologists about the possibilities of Japanese assimilation. Thus, in 1913 Robert E. Park had been sufficiently depressed by the orgy of anti-Japanese legislation and popular prejudice to predict their permanent consignment to minority status: "The Japanese . . . is condemned to remain among us an abstraction, a symbol, and a symbol not merely of his own race, but of the Orient and of that vague ill-defined menace we sometimes refer to as the 'yellow peril'."[6] Although Park later reversed his doleful prediction, his observations on Japanese emphasized their uncommunicative features, stolid faces and apparently blank characters. The Japanese face was a racial mask behind which the individual personality was always hidden. "Orientals live more completely behind the mask than the rest of us," he wrote. "Naturally enough we misinterpret them and attribute to disingenuousness and craft what is actually conformity to an ingrained convention. The American who is flattered at first by the politeness of his Japanese servant will later on, perhaps, cite as a reproach against the race the fact that 'we can never tell what a Japanese is thinking about.' 'We never know what is going on in their heads'."[7]

Since the end of World War II recognition of the evils of racism has reduced the negative and pejorative effects of racial stereotypes, but it has not brought about an end to their popular usage or academic study. Recent scholarship, while eschewing antipathetic and hostile stereotypes, has begun to lay great emphasis on the role of character and character formation for achievement and assimilation. Thus, in one study, the success of Jews in America is attributed in part to their belief "that the world is orderly and amenable to rational mastery;" to their willingness "to leave home to make their way in life;" and to their "preference for individualistic rather than collective credit for work done."[8] Another study points out that the child rearing practices of Jews, Greeks and white Protestants lay the emphasis on independence and achievement, while those of Italians, French-Canadians and Negroes emphasize cooperation and fatalistic resignation.[9]

The remarkable record of achievement by Japanese Americans has been noted frequently in reports of both journalists and sociologists. As early as 1909, Chester Rowell pointed to their refusal to accept unprofitable contracts, their commercial advancement beyond the confines of the ghetto and to their geniality and politeness.[10] Seventeen years later Winifred Raushenbush, Park's assistant in his race relations survey of the Pacific Coast, admonished the Japanese of Florin, California, for their impatience with racial restrictions and praised the Japanese community of Livingston, California, for its propriety.[11] More recently, Rose Hum Lee viv-

idly contrasted the Chinese Americans with their Japanese counterparts, noting that the *Nisei* "exhibit greater degrees of integration into American society, than has been the case with the Chinese, whose settlement is twice as long."[12] Broom and Kitsuse have summed up the impressive record of the Japanese in America by declaring it to be "an achievement perhaps rarely equalled in the history of human migration."[13] The careful statistical measures of Schmid and Nobbe indicate that present-day Japanese in America have outstripped all other "colored" groups in America in occupational achievement and education.[14]

Analyses of Japanese American achievement have laid stress on the same character traits which once made up the notorious stereotype. Thus, Caudill and deVos have pointed out that the *Nisei* appear to be more acculturated than they are in fact because of "a significant compatibility (but by no means identity) between the value systems found in the culture of Japan and the value systems found in American middle class culture."[15] "What appears to have occurred in the case of Japanese-Americans is that the *Nisei* while utilizing to a considerable extent a Japanese set of values and adaptive mechanisms, were able in their prewar life on the Pacific Coast to act in ways that drew favorable comment and recognition from their white middle class peers and made them admirable pupils in the eyes of their middle class teachers."[16]

The experiences of prewar California were repeated in Chicago during the second World War. Personnel managers and fellow workers admired the *Nisei*. "What has happened here," wrote Caudill and deVos, "is that the peers, teachers, employers and fellow workers of the *Nisei* have projected their own values onto the neat, well-dressed and efficient *Nisei* in whom they saw mirrored many of their own ideals."[17] What were these ideals? They included patience, cleanliness, courtesy and "minding their own business,"[18] the same ideals capable of distortion into negative characteristics. Thus, Japanese patience has been taken to be silent contempt; cleanliness and courtesy, as matters for comic ridicule or dark suspicion; minding their own business as unwarranted aloofness and "clannishness."[19] What was once caricature is now recognized as character.

The fact that the same, or very nearly identical, traits can be used to denigrate the Japanese, as well as account for their unprecedented success, suggests the possibility that behind these traits there exists a unique character structure. Indeed, the Japanese Americans themselves believe this and, as we shall presently show, they regard each generation of Japanese Americans as possessed of a unique character. That there should exist a correspondence between a racist stereotype and culturally-created character should not cause too great a concern. The haters of a people have often correctly picked out elements of their enemies' character and spun webs of viciousness out of them. Indeed, one reason for the survival of a stereotype through time and other changes is its origin in a kernel of fundamental truth which it distorts for evil purposes.

Recently a great advance in the understanding of the nature of slavery and Negro personality was made by a recognition of the truth value of personality elements in the "Sambo" stereotype and an attempt to discover just how such a personality could arise.[20] Progress in the social analysis of culture and personality might be enhanced by sociologists and social psychologists undertaking the unpalatable task of assuming for the sake of research that the worst statements made about a people have their origins in some fundamental truth which needs first to be abstracted from its pejorative context and then subjected to behavorial and cultural analysis.

This paper presents an analysis of Japanese American character. Fortunately, no anti-Japanese mood is currently widespread in America, and the analysis may proceed without fear of being distorted for pernicious purposes. A conceptual framework first developed by Alfred Schutz[21] and effectively employed by Clifford Geertz to study the Balinese[22] is here used to analyze Japanese American character. A somewhat similar formulation of concepts by Clyde Kluckhohn has been applied to Japanese character by Caudill and Scarr.[23] Although this paper relies heavily on Schutz, the conceptual schema of Kluckhohn and the findings of Caudill and Scarr will be noted when appropriate. In addition, the findings of numerous researchers on Japan and the Japanese Americans have been employed and interpreted throughout.

Time Person Perspectives

In every culture and in many subcultures there is a predominant time-person perspective. This perspective organizes the relevant temporal and personal categories in order to structure priorities with respect to past, present and future, and to structure orientations with respect to intimacy or impersonality. Any culture may be viewed then with respect to its priorities of predecessors, contemporaries, consociates and successors.[24] *Predecessors* are all those who have lived in some past time, in history, and with whom no contemporary can have direct subjective knowledge. *Successors* are all those who shall live in some future time and with whom no contemporary can share a mutual inter-subjective identity because they have not yet lived. *Contemporaries* are all those fellow men who share the same spatio-temporal environment. Among contemporaries are those about whom one has only categorical but not intersubjective knowledge, and those whom one knows intimately and in regular association. The latter are *consociates*. Now, for any culture or subculture, we may ask how these distinctions appear—not merely as analytic features, but rather as members' understandings of their own world. Note that it is possible for any one of these time-person perspectives to be experienced subjectively by members as prior to, having precedence over, or exclusive from any one or group of the others. The relative subjective weight placed on any one or more of these perspectives over and against the others has profound consequences for the organization of behavior and is, in turn, reciprocally related to other elements of culture and the institutional order.

In the case of the Japanese in America, time and

person are perceived in terms of geographic and generational distance from Japan. The Japanese are the only immigrant group in America who specify by a linguistic term and characterize with a unique personality each generation of descendants from the original immigrant group.[25] In contrast, for example, to the United States Census[26] and the Chinese,[27] the Japanese do not merely distinguish native-born from foreign-born but rather count geogenerationally forward or backward with each new generational grouping. Moreover, from the standpoint of any single living generational group, the others are imputed to have peculiar and distinctive personalities and attendant behavior patterns which are evaluated in positive and negative terms. Each generation removed from Japan is assumed to have its own characterological qualities, qualities which are derived at the outset from its spatio-temporal position, and are thus not subject to voluntaristic adoption or obviation. Thus, each generation is living out a unique, temporally governed lifetime which shall not be seen again after it is gone.

Immigrants from Japan are called *Issei*, literally "first generation," a term referring to all those who were born and nurtured in Japan and who later migrated to the United States. The children of at least one *Issei* parent are called *Nisei*, literally "second generation," and this term encompasses all those born in the United States of immigrant parentage. The grandchildren of *Issei* are called *Sansei*, literally "third generation," and include all those born of *Nisei* or *Kibei* parentage. The great-grandchildren of *Issei* are called *Yonsei*, literally "fourth generation" and include all those born of *Sansei* parentage. The great-great grandchildren of *Issei* are called *Gosei* and include all those born of *Yonsei* parentage. In addition, there is both terminological and characterological distinction imputed to all those persons who were born in the United States of *Issei* parentage, educated in Japan and then returned to the United States. These are called *Kibei*,[28] literally "returned to America," and their children, as mentioned, are considered *Sansei*.

Age and situation may modify the strictness of membership in these generational groups, but while

persons might be informally reassigned to a group to which they do not belong by virtue of geographical or generational criteria, the *idea* of the groups remains intact as a working conception of social reality. Thus, a young Japanese American friend of the author's who enjoys the social status of a *Nisei* jokingly refers to himself as an *Issei* since he was born of *Nisei* parents during their temporary residence in Japan. Older *Nisei* whose social and personal characterisitcs are similar to those of *Issei* are sometimes treated as if they were the latter.[29] *Sansei* age peers of *Nisei* are treated as the latter if they behave accordingly. But *Nisei* who appear to their fellow *Nisei* age peers as "too Japanesy" are sometimes associated in the minds of their more Americanized friends with *Kibei*, while those who are "too American" are associated with *Sansei*. Finally, the offspring of geogenerationally mixed parentage—e.g., *Issei-Nisei, Nisei-Sansei, Nisei-Yonsei*, etc.—and of racially mixed parentage are not easily classifiable. In practice they tend to demonstrate the sociological rule that status is as status does; that is, they enjoy the classification which social relations and personal behavior assign to them and which they assign to themselves.[30]

In terms of the temporal categories with which we began this discussion, the Japanese in America lay great emphasis on contemporaries. This does not mean that they have no sense whatsoever of predecessors, successors and consociates. Rather, their ideas about these categories—in practical terms about the past and history and the future of other generations, as well as about intimates—are vague and diffuse, or in the case of consociates, deemphasized and deprecated. From the point of view of the *Nisei—and especially those Nisei who grew up on the West Coast and received cultural and group reinforcement from the Japanese American communities—Issei*, other *Nisei* and *Sansei*, white Americans, Negroes, Chinese Americans and other persons whom they encounter are contemporaries in the formal sense since they are capable of being known to one another and of sharing similar, but not especially identical, situations. Moreover, while individuals live through an age-demarcated life cycle with *rites de passage* to mark off birth, marriage, death and certain ceremonies, for the *Nisei* it is the common lifetime of the whole generational group that circumscribes social and personal orientations. The generational group has a life cycle of its own internally indicated by its appropriate behavior patterns and externally bounded by the temporal duration of the whole group.

To the *Nisei*—and for the balance of this paper it is this group's perspective we shall be examining—the world of their predecessors is known through whatever their parents have told them about old Japan and what they have learned in afternoon "language" schools, college history courses and Japanese movies. *Nisei* parents are concerned about their own children in particular and the *Sansei* and *Yonsei* successor generations in general, partly in terms of achievement and advancement—which *Nisei* efforts have facilitated—but more significantly they are worried about the future generations' character. *Sansei* and *Yonsei* do not exhibit *Nisei* character, and *Nisei* regard this fact as both inevitable and unfortunate.

It is as and with contemporaries that *Nisei* feel both pride and apprehension. The basic conception of the *Nisei* phenomenon ultimately depends on the objective existence of their own generational group. The *Nisei* geogenerational group inhabits time and space between that of the *Issei* and the *Sansei*. The Japanese community in general and the *Nisei* group in particular provides a *Nisei* with emotional security and a haven from the turbulence and unpredictable elements of the outer world.[31] But the *Nisei* group is threatened by both centripetal and centrifugal forces, by individual withdrawal and acculturative transcendence.[32] Should collective identity be dissolved by the overarching precedence of atomized individuals, dyadic relationships or small cliques, then *Nisei* would lose both its objective existence and its subjective meaning. Should individuals transcend the generational group by moving out into the world of their non-Japanese contemporaries, by "validating their acculturation,"[33] then too would both the objective and subjective senses of *Nisei* identity lose their compelling force. Thus, *Nisei* must worry on two fronts about the risks of intimate association. On the one

hand, the very close contacts inherent in the segregated yet secure Japanese community allow for intimate association "below" the level of the generational group; on the other hand, the breakdown of prejudice and discrimination threatens to seduce the *Nisei* individual away from the confines of his racial group.[34] Hence, it follows that for *Nisei* social and interpersonal relations are governed by a permanent interest in maintaining an appropriate social distance, so that individuals do not "escape" into integration or withdraw themselves from group solidarity. Either of these would jeopardize if not destroy the *Nisei* as a group and an idea.

Nisei do not speak of their social and personal life in this fashion; rather, they exhibit in numerous ways a quiet but deep and pervasive pride in their *Nisei* identity. This pride is not rooted in their material success, as it might be among other ethnic groups in America, but instead in their character. *Nisei* believe that they combine in themselves a perfect balance of Japanese and American traits. They are not "too Japanesy" as are the *Issei* by definition and the *Kibei* by virtue of imposed culture and education; they are not "too American" as are their white American contemporaries and the *Sansei*. *Nisei* character at its best is exhibited in cathectic management and by control over and suppression of spontaneity, emotionalism and inappropriate expressiveness. It is this character itself, in which the *Nisei* take so much pride, that reacts back on the *Nisei* group to maintain its objective existence. It is this character which operates to orient behavior in such a manner that contemporaries are not converted to consociates, that fellow men are not brought *too close* into the intimate circle.

Manners, Mores and Meanings

For the *Nisei* to preserve the objective identity of its own generational group, to deemphasize the biological aging of its members in favor of preserving the single moment-to-moment simultaneity of the generational group, it is necessary to remove interpersonal relations from the intimate or consociate level and push them back toward the formal or contemporary plane. In behalf of this objective, the *Nisei* have a built-in aid, Japanese culture, especially as it had developed by the late Meiji-early Taisho eras, the periods in which the bulk of *Issei* came to America. Although this culture had its origins in an environment far different from that which the *Nisei* experienced, it served the goal of anonymization of persons and immobilization of individual time through its emphasis on etiquette, ceremony and rigid status deference.

The emphasis on etiquette in Japanese culture has been such a frequently mentioned feature that it hardly needs demonstration here.[35] The Japanese language itself is one of social forms, indicative politenesses and status identifiers.[36] Moreover, Japanese language is one of indirection, removing the subject (speaker) in a sentence from direct relation to the predicate, and utilizing stylistic circumlocutions so that the intended object of the particular speech is reached by a circular rather than linear route.[37] The net result of these forms is that individuals are held at arm's length, so to speak, so that potential consociates remain contemporaries—quasi-strangers, quasi-friends.

The *Issei* were able to transmit the basic ideas of this culture to their offspring, but its manifestation took place in an American idiom interpenetrating the only society with which *Nisei* were familiar. Thus, Japanese etiquette appeared in the form of a sometimes seemingly Victorian politeness. Although the bow, whose rigid rules the Japanese imposed upon themselves while exempting all foreigners,[38] did not survive the generational passage, except in a limited vestigial form,[39] other forms especially verbal ones, could be translated into English. Thus, Japanese Americans are likely to pay careful attention to titles, to employ the terms of genteel propriety, to avoid obscenity and to use the passive voice.[40] In all this the *Nisei* succeed simultaneously in keeping associations under management and emotions under control.

The primary concern of a *Nisei* male is the management and control of his emotional economy. He truly cannot countenance an emotional economy governed, or should we say ungoverned, according to principles of behavioristic laissez-faire; he desires ultimately a "socializing" of that economy, and in the absence of complete "socialization," he introduces a constant "Keynesian" watchfulness over it. The human state that is idealized is that of inward quiescence—that is lauded, is an outward appearance of emotional equanimity. An outward appearance that is boisterous, excessively emotional, visibly passionate, obviously fearful, unabashedly vain or blushingly embarrassed, is distasteful and itself shameful, fit perhaps only for children and foreigners.

"Etiquette," as Clifford Geertz has pointed out in his study of Java, provides its user "with a set of rigidly formal ways of doing things which conceals his real feelings from others. In addition, it so regularizes behavior, his own and that of others, as to make it unlikely to provide unpleasant surprises."[41] The manner in which *Nisei* attempt to employ tonal control, euphemisms and circumlocutive forms in speaking English illustrates the role of etiquette in language. Although English-speaking Europeans and most native-born Americans employ tonal change for emphasis and object indication, the *Nisei* strive after a flatness of tone and an equality of metre in their speech. For those who are unfamiliar with this style—as are a great many white Americans—it becomes difficult to distinguish the important from the insignificant items in any speech encounter. For the *Nisei,* it provides a continuous demonstration of the proper state of emotional equanimity; for the uninitiated "foreigner," it presents the *Nisei* as a blank *slate.* Since no one believes that a fellow human is in fact a blank slate, it causes wonder about what "really" is being said and in some instances arouses suspicion of ulterior motives.[42]

Nisei employ euphemisms whenever the simpler and more direct form might indicate a state of emotional involvement or evoke an undesirable emotional response from others. Euphemisms and round-about expressions are especially employed when the direct and precise term would or could be insulting or otherwise emotionally provocative. Where no English euphemism is available, or where one is so awkward as to introduce an embarrassment by its very usage, a Japanese term may be employed. This is especially the case in using nouns to designate racial or ethnic groups. *Nisei* rarely say "white man," "Negro," "Chinese" or "Jew" in their everyday speech. *Nisei* understand that race is a touchy subject in America with ambiguous meanings and ambivalent feelings deeply embedded in the subterranean value structure.

To avoid possible emotional entanglements, they employ substitute and usually neutral terms derived from Japanese. This is the case despite the fact that *Nisei* tend not to speak Japanese to their peers. For "white man," the term "Caucasian" is sometimes used, but one is more likely to hear *Hakujin*, literally "white man," and occasionally one might overhear the pejorative *Keto*, literally a "hairy person," but freely translated as "barbarian." For "Negro," the *Nisei* who combine a culturally derived, mild antipathy to blackness[43] with an unevenly experienced and ambivalent form of the American Negrophobic virus, almost never employ such vulgar terms as "nigger," "coon," "jigaboo" or "black boy." Rather, they use the denotatively pejorative *Kuron-bo*, literally "black boy," usually in a neutral and unpejorative sense, at least on the conscious level. For "Chinese," another people toward whom *Nisei* are ambivalent, the mildly pejorative Hawaiian term, *Pakē*, is quite commonly employed.

For "Jew" the terminology is especially interesting and provides an unusual example of trans-Pacific linguistic transmogrification. Anti-Semitism was almost unknown in Japan at the time the *Issei* came to America, and neither they nor their offspring readily adapted to this essentially European prejudice.[44] While growing up, however, *Nisei* learned of the special attitude held by Americans toward Jews, and in their own inimitable way invented a term whereby they could express one central *idea* of the anti-Jewish stereotype without using the emotion-laden English term, "kike." *Nisei* employ the "Japanese" neologism *ku-ichi* to express this idea. Now, *ku-ichi* in its everyday use among *Nisei* does not refer so much to the Jews as such but rather to the idea of stinginess and miserliness and the representation of "cheapskate." The etymology of *ku-ichi* is the combination of the Japanese numbers "ku," meaning "nine" and "ichi" meaning one. Nine plus one is ten, and the Japanese term for ten is "Ju," the homonym for the English word "Jew." This *Nisei* linguistic innovation is not used or even widely known in Japan. The denotative word for Jew in Japan is *yudaya-jin*.[45] *Nisei* do not apply *ku-ichi* exclusively to Jews, but rather to fellow *Nisei* or to anyone who openly displays an attitude of cheapness or stinginess.

Circumlocutions and indirect speech are regular features of *Nisei* conversations serving to mute one's own feelings and prevent the eruption of another's. In the Chicago researches employing the Rorschach test, *Nisei* males resorted to a significant amount of "confabulatory" responses when faced with a perplexing or emotionally troubling perception.[46] Indirect speech is a regular feature of conversations in Japan and is matched there by the circular placing of household furniture and the use of open space in streets and homes.[47] It also affects the quality of translations from Japanese to another language.[48] Among the *Nisei* English usage is preferred, except when propriety dictates otherwise,[49] and circumlocutions and indirections are not too difficult to develop. Abstract nouns, noncommittal statements and inferential hints at the essential meaning are regular features.

Indirection is also effected by the use of go-betweens to mediate in delicate situations. Anthropologists have emphasized the role of the marriage-arranger (*nakyo-do* or *baishakunin*) in traditional Japan, and some *Nisei* are prevailed upon to employ a *baishakunin* to ceremonialize an engagement *after* it has been effected in the American pattern.[50] On a more personal level, intermediaries may be employed to inform one friend that another wishes to borrow money from him and to sound out the former on his willingness to loan it. In this manner the would-be borrower is prevented from having to go through a direct face-losing refusal should the hoped-for creditor decide not to loan the money, and the borrowee is saved from the mutually embarrassing situation that would arise if he had to refuse his friend the money. An intermediary is also employed, occasionally, to warn someone that he will receive an invitation to a social affair or to inform someone quietly that a "surprise party" is going to be given for him. In the former case, the affective linkage hinted at by the extension of an invitation is blunted, the embarrassment of a refusal to attend is reduced, and the invitee is given the opportunity to mobilize himself for the receipt of the formal invitation. In the latter case, the "surprise" is rendered unprovocative of an undesirable, excessive, emotional display.

Bluntness of speech is not a virtue among *Nisei*. Here again the trait is also found in Japan where it is accompanied by a high tolerance for lengthy monologues and a polite indifference to complete comprehension.[51] Among the *Nisei* as among their forebears in Japan, the main point of a conversational episode is not approached immediately. Moreover, as mentioned earlier, the monotonal flatness of affect prevents it from being readily identifiable to those who, like Europeans and white Americans, are accustomed to a tonal cue which indicates that what is being said now is more important than what has preceded or will follow it. Indeed, conversation among *Nisei* almost always partake of the elements of an information game between persons maintaining decorum by seemingly mystifying one another.[52] It is the duty of the listener to ascertain the context of the speech he hears and to glean from his knowledge of the speaker and the context just what is the important point.

Violations of this tacit ritual speech relationship occur fairly often, sometimes among *Nisei* themselves, but more often in encounters between *Nisei* and *Hakujin*, *Nisei* and *Sansei*, and *Nisei* and other *Gaijin*. Exasperation with the apparent pointlessness of talk, frustration with vain attempts to gauge the meaning of sequential utterances, and the desire to reach a conclusion often lead these non-*Nisei* to ask a pointed question directed at the heart of the matter. *Nisei* are troubled by this; they may refuse to answer, change the subject or, more subtly, redirect the conversation back to its concentric form. The idealized aim in a conversation is to maintain the appropriate ritual and calm state of speaker and audience. To do this, important items (i.e., those charged with potential affect and those likely to disturb speaker-audience homeostasis) are buried

beneath a verbal avalanche of trivia and, in the most perfected of conversations, are never brought to the surface at all—they are silently *apprehended* by the listener.

This emphasis on calmness and composure lends itself to unstated but widely held norms of conversational propriety appropriate to different social occasions. Since it is at informal social occasions—parties, dinners, tête-à-têtes—that one's speech partners and oneself are vulnerable to conversion from contemporaries to consociates, it is precisely such occasions, seemingly just the ones for intimacy and spontaneity, that require careful monitoring for excessive effect.[53] *Nisei* "rules" for social gatherings, therefore, include (1) an emphasis on "democratic participation" in speech; i.e., no one should speak too long or too much and everyone should have an opportunity to speak; (2) circulation; i.e., small clusters of conversationalists are permissible but these should be governed by fusion and fission, regularly decomposing and reforming with new elements; lengthy dyadic conversations at a gathering of ten or twenty people are discouraged; (3) unimportance; i.e., the content of conversations should be restricted to trivial matters, things that can always be kept "external," items that do not reflect directly on either the speaker's or listener's inner life. The most fruitful items for conversation are sports, stocks and bonds and technical subjects, for all of these can be kept "outside" the inner domain of individual personhood and every speaker can be fairly confident that he is not likely to be importuned or embarrassed.[54]

Further exemplification of *Nisei* emotional management is seen in their handling of the erotic and their emphasis on form over function. The erotic is everywhere emotionally exciting and thus is a source of potential emotional discomfiture to *Nisei*. Two examples—that of wedding receptions and pornographic movies—illustrate modes of mitigation and neutralization of the erotic. One "survival" of the rural customs of Japan among current *Nisei* is the employment of a "master of ceremonies" at wedding receptions. Originally, this role was usually enacted by the *baishakunin*,[55] but among *Nisei* a good friend of the groom is often requested to assume this post. At the banquet or reception following the wedding, the master of ceremonies formally introduces the bride and groom and their families to the assembled company, presents one or several toasts to the newlywed couple, calls people out of the audience to perform as comedians, storytellers, or singers, and tells jokes, droll anecdotes and humorous incidents about the groom. Now, in the rural prefectures of traditional Japan, this part of the reception was often accompanied by ribald jokes and risqué stories.[56] When *Issei* participate in such a reception, they sometimes introduce humorous obscenities into them. However, *Nisei* usually instruct their appointed masters of ceremonies to "keep it clean" and to refrain from any drolleries which would "embarrass" bride, groom or company.

Watching pornographic films constitutes one instance of "watching the unwatchable" since they depict activities usually carried out in private with no audience except the participants. Viewing them is not governed by well-known ubiquitous norms.[57] Pornographic films are typical fare at an American stag party for a groom-to-be and his male friends. When *Nisei* are watching such films two kinds of response are prevalent. On the one hand, jibes and catcalls will tease one or another of the assembled company about his excessive interest in the films, alleged similarities or dissimilarities in his behavior and that depicted on the screen, or his remarkable quietness in the presence of an obviously stimulating event. On the other hand, it sometimes happens that a *Nisei* will verbally transform the meaning of the activities on the screen, emphasizing their form irrespective of content. Thus, the nude bodies copulating on the movie screen can be treated in terms of their physical anatomy, aesthetic quality or gymnastic innovation.

Emphasis on form over and against content is not only a protective device against possible emotional disturbance in the presence of the erotic, but also a generally utilized mechanism in the presence of anticipated or actual performance failure. Thus, *Nisei* golfers and bowlers who are performing poorly, or who believe they will do so, may justify their bad scores by pointing out that they are working on their

stance, body form, follow-through, etc. Since it is widely accepted that form and content are analytically separable but related aspects of a variety of activities, the claim to be emphasizing the former irrespective of the latter is an acceptable account.[58] Moreover, it prevents any effective referral of the poor scores to the inner or actual state of the performer. Thus, inner equanimity may be maintained and outer calmness may be exhibited even in the presence of apparently contradictory evidence.

Social and Personal Controls

The ideal *Nisei* is one who has mastered the art of personal control. This requires management of body, mind and feelings.[59] If these are properly under control the outward appearance is that of a calm, collected, blasé sophisticate.[60] This state is rarely reached in fact, but *Nisei* have mechanisms of impression management and mutual monitoring that keep any appearance approximating the ideal from being damaged too much by emotional breakdowns. Among these mechanisms are face controls, dissimulation and avoidance.

The face, as Simmel observed long ago,[61] is the most significant communicator of the inner man. This is especially true of the eyes, nostrils and mouth and of the color exhibited by the face.[62] For *Nisei* the face is a most vulnerable object in any interpersonal encounter, for its uncontrolled expression, if met by the searching gaze of another, may lock them into a consociative relationship from which extrication would be both difficult and embarrassing. *Nisei* faces tend to be "set" at the expressionless level or at least to strive after that effect. This is achieved more easily in America perhaps because of the stereotypical interpretation of Japanese faces by Caucasians and Negroes, and because the epicanthic eye fold and smooth skin make face "readings" difficult. However, some *Nisei* are disturbed over their vulnerability to facial disclosure; they avoid facing others for any length of time or erect barriers and involvement shields against another's gaze.[63] Newspapers and magazines provide objects for scanning during a conversation, and, although too close attention to these might be considered rude, a deft employment of them will serve to reduce eye contact. Finally, the fact that *Nisei* share a common concern over face management facilitates a mutual avoidance of staring or fixed gaze, and a tendency to avert one's eyes.

Dissimulation is a regular feature of everyday life among *Nisei*. Its most elementary form is the self-imposed limitation on disclosure. *Nisei* tend not to volunteer any more information about themselves than they have to. Thus, to a listener, a *Nisei*'s autobiographical statements appear as a series of incompletely presented episodes, separated by voids which are not filled in with events or information unless it is unavoidable.

Beyond silence about much of personal life is the half-truth or "little white lie" which bridges the gap between information requested and personhood protected. Thus, *Nisei* will sometimes not tell about an important event, or will casually dismiss it with a denial or only a partial admission, suggesting by style and tone that it was not important at all. Direct questions are usually answered with vague or mildly meretricious replies.[64] Still another element of dissimulation is concealment of feelings, opinions or activities, especially in the presence of employers, colleagues and guests. As *Nisei* have been promoted into middle-management and other decision-making posts, their colleagues and superiors have sometimes been astonished at their silence during conferences or executive meetings. And, as with the Javanese practice of *etok-etok* (pretense),[65] the *Nisei* do not feel the need to justify these omissions, "white lies" or evasions; rather, the burden would appear to be on the listener to demonstrate why such tact and tactics should not be employed.[66]

Nisei attempt to avoid those persons and situations that are likely to evoke embarrassment, personal disorganization and loss of self-control. When a new line of endeavor is undertaken, especially if it requires learning a new skill or taking a risk, it is usually entered into in secret or with those persons whom the *Nisei* does not know well or wish to know. After it has been mastered, or after the risk has been

evaluated as worthwhile, or sometimes after the endeavor has already begun, the *Nisei* will inform his close associates in a casual manner that he thinks he *might be about to* undertake the line of action in question. To fellow *Nisei* this will be understood not as a probablistic statement, but as an absolute one, and they will further understand that all preparations, rehearsals and calculations have already been made. Later, if his associates see a performance of the new skill, they remain silently aware that it is in fact an exhibition of an already perfected ability.

Persons who are importunate, who demand too much display of interpersonal commitment, or who violate norms of emotional propriety are an ever-present threat to the cathectic equanimity of a *Nisei*. A concept usually employed with respect to Japanese child-rearing practices is relevant here.[67] Japanese speak of *amaeru*, an intransitive verb by which they mean "to depend and presume upon another's benevolence." Not only children but adults suffer from too much *amae*, and their behavior toward those whom they wish to express affection toward them is regarded as overly demanding and excessive. A person suffering from too much *amae* feels himself to be *kodawaru*; i.e., he feels inwardly disturbed over his personal relationships. A recognition of one's own feeling of *kodawari* leads to *sumunai*, guilt over one's failure to do as one should. Behind many Japanese people's feeling of *sumunai*, as Professor Doi has pointed out, lies "much hidden aggression engendered by frustration of their wish to *amaeru*."[68] *Nisei* do not employ this terminology generally, but several studies have pointed to a complex of dependency needs and consequent personal difficulties in *Nisei* individuals, needs which have their roots in the wish to be loved, and the guilt over this wish or the shame over its expression.[69]

For *Nisei*, the entire complex of *amae-kodawari-sumunai* is rarely admitted to be a personal problem; rather it is most frequently perceived to be a problem in another's interpersonal relations. When a *Nisei* recognizes a close associate's excessive *amae* toward him, he may become upset by this fact, retreat even further behind a formal facade of etiquette and attempt to establish greater social distance. Or he might hope, or even clandestinely request, that a third party, recognizing the difficulty between the two friends, tactfully explain the problem to the defalcating party and urge upon him an approach to his friend which is less demanding and less obviously a display of excessive *amaeru*. Still another alternative is to gently but firmly tease the offending party until he realizes that he has overstepped the bounds of propriety. Finally, another tactic is to make sure that all contacts with the offending party will take place with other friends present, so that his excessive affection will be "diffused" among the whole body of friends rather than centered on just one person.[70]

Building Nisei Character

There can be little doubt that the fundamental source of *Nisei* character is to be found in the samurai ethic which developed from the Tokugawa through the Meiji Eras (c. 1601–1912). *Nisei* find representative expression of this ethic in the brilliant epic films made in Japan to celebrate the feats and character of warriors of that period.[71] At one time shown in basements and church social halls in *Nihonmachi* (the Japanese quarter of the city), these movies are now known to many non-Japanese Americans because of their general popularity when exhibited at public theaters. *Chambara* (samurai) stories always emphasize the stoic character of the solitary and often tragic warrior who, though beaten about on every side by personal or clan enemies, political misfortunes and natural disasters, nevertheless retains an outward appearance suggesting inner psychic strength and emotional equanimity.[72] Such characters—poignantly portrayed on the screen in recent years by such actors as Toshiro Mifune and Tatsuya Nakadai—serve as ideal character models and reminders of the appropriate presentation of self.

The patterns of hierarchical society, rigid formalism, etiquette and shame were routinized features of the early life of the *Issei*, who grew up in a

time of great technological and political—but little ethical or interpersonal—change in Japan.[73] The modernization of Japan, actually begun in the Tokugawa Period, was achieved not by over-turning the old cultural order but rather by adapting western industrial, educational and military forms to the framework of that order. "Within this general context," writes Reinhard Bendix, "the samurai were transformed from an estate of independent landed, and self-equipped warriors into one of urbanized, aristocratic retainers, whose privileged social and economic position was universally acknowledged. They remained attached to their tradition of ceremonious conduct, intense pride of rank and the cultivation of physical prowess."[74] The educational system fostered not only study of classics and, later, the more technical subjects, but also, and more importantly, directed its major attention to the development of virtue, humble modesty before superiors, self-control and etiquette.[75] Thus, the *Issei* bore the cultural marks which had been part of the Japanese tradition for at least two centuries.

Few of the *Issei* were of samurai rank,[76] but in the two hundred years before emigration began, a complex melding process had helped to "nationalize" the samurai ethic and remove it from encapsulation within a single status group. First, after 1601 many samurai became displaced *ronin* (masterless warriors) obliged to sell their services to other lords, to cities as policemen or magistrates, even to commoners on occasion or, as a last resort short of suicide, they felt compelled to give up official samurai status entirely and become merchants.[77] All of these acts caused a certain filtering of the samurai ethic through the social order. Second, the educational system founded in the Tokugawa period, and universalized in 1873, though undecided about whether heredity or merit was more conducive to learning, admitted increasing numbers of commoners to the schools, thus affording them direct access to samurai indoctrination.[78] Third, samurai status itself was muddied by the practice, begun after 1700, of selling the right to wear a sword and bear a surname (i.e., the status symbols of samurai) to commoners.[79] Finally, it would appear that a significant portion of America's *Issei* came from prefectures in southeastern, central and western Japan, prefectures in which the "democratization" of "ethical" education had been well advanced at the time of emigration.[80]

In addition to the samurai ethic, elements of the rural farmer's outlook also helped forge the orientation with which the *Issei* reared their children. The *ie* system, by which Japanese farmers represented both the contemporary physical house and the permanent family household, operated through this notion of preservation and continuity to forestall the development of individualism.[81] In Japan's rural villages the *honke-bunke* (stem-branch family system) allowed nuclear families to split off from one another in a partial sense, so that nothing like the extended Chinese clan system developed,[82] but atomization below the *ie,* or household, level was strongly discouraged. Village people spoke of the *iegara,* or *kakaku;* i.e., the "reputation" or "standing" of a family, rather than the *hitogara* or *jinkaku,* the "personality" or social "standing" of individuals. The *ie* "was also far more important than the individuals who at any one time composed it, and hence if 'for the sake of the *ie*' the personal wishes and desires of those individuals had to be ignored or sacrificed, this was looked on as only natural."[83] The *ie* "required its members each to keep their proper place under the authoritarian direction of the householder, resigning themselves to the suppression of personal desires unbecoming to their position. Thus, was order within the *ie* preserved and its harmony guaranteed—a harmony not of liberated cheerfulness, but of smouldering reserve and the frustration of still incompletely repressed desires."[84]

In America the *Issei* men, often married by proxy to women whom they had only seen in pictures *(shashin kekkon)* and who were sometimes quite a bit younger than they,[85] applied the principles of late Tokugawa-early Meiji child rearing to their *Nisei* offspring. In certain respects—notably for the *Issei,* in the lack of Japan's bathhouses and geisha for outlet; for the *Nisei,* in the inhibitions on physical expression and open sensuality, and because of the absence of an indulgent grandmother to assuage the harshness of parental authority—child rearing was more harsh than in Japan. [86] Physical punishments were rarely used, although the *moxa* treatment was sometimes practiced by *Issei* parents not only for punishment and moral training, but also as a curative.[87] In one instance known to the author, an Okinawan *Nisei* reported that his father purposely cut his ears when giving him a haircut. When the boy screamed in pain, his father would slap him across the face with the stern admonition: "You don't scream. Japanese boys do not scream." However, resort to physical punishment is rare among *Issei-Nisei* families. Much more likely is the use of ridicule and teasing.

Several reports on Japanese child rearing have emphasized the role of ridicule.[88] Among these is the common theme of teasing a recalcitrant, noisy, emotionally upset or otherwise obstreporous boy about behaving like a little girl. That a young man should be ashamed of his emotional expressions because they remind him of behavior associated with women is a frequent theme in Japanese biographies.[89] *Nisei* boys were also reprimanded by their parents for acting like little girls.[90] In addition, they were reminded that they were *Japanese* and therefore obligated to avoid *arai* (crudeness); to speak "good" Japanese and not *zuzu* (the dialect characteristic of northern Japan);[91] and to avoid any association with or even mention of *Eta* (Japan's pariah caste, some of whose members had unobtrusively settled in Florin, California, and a few other places).[92]

Moreover, emphasis was placed on individual superiority, achievement and education as criteria for both individual and group maturity.[93] Thus, *Nisei* children were not invited to discuss family matters at the dinner table, but rather were instructed to withdraw from participation until age and achievement had demonstrated their worth. *Nisei* children and adolescents were admonished with the statement, *Nisei wa mada tsumaranai;* that is, they were told that the *Nisei* generation was still worthless. Until manhood had been achieved, a manhood indicated not merely by coming of age but, far more importantly, demonstrated by independent status achieved through steadfastness, determination and single-minded purposefulness, the *Nisei* were treated as immature but developing children.

Central to the demonstration of maturity among growing *Nisei* was self-control. Although independence and real achievement could not be actually demonstrated until adulthood, emotional management was always worthy of exhibition and often tested for its own sake. *Issei* tended to be oriented toward their children in terms of the latter's position in the birth order and their sex.[94] A line of direct authority extended down from the father through the mother to the first-born, second-born, third-born and so on. A line of obligation extended upward from the youngest to the eldest. The authority system was not infrequently tested by an elder brother harshly rebuking his younger brother, sometimes for no apparent reason. Younger brothers learned that if they could "take" these rebukes with an outwardly calm detachment, they would ultimately be rewarded with a recognition of their "maturity." First-born sons received similar treatment from their fathers, and daughters sometimes found that they had to live up to both the precepts of manhood maturity and womanliness.[95] Brothers who threw tantrums or gave way to violent emotional expression were regarded as "immature" and were teased or otherwise maneuvered into conformative cathectic quiescence.

In the case of the *Nisei*, teasing and ridicule are characteristic not only of parent-child discipline but also of intra-group relations. They function to monitor behavior. Among *Nisei,* peer groups begin to share authority over the individual with parents with the onset of adolescense, and they begin to supersede parental authority, though not parental respect, in late adolescence and early manhood. No one who has not been intimately associated with adolescent second generation Japanese groups can testify adequately to the remarkable, pervasive atmosphere and social effect of ridicule among *Nisei* teenagers. A veritable barrage of "cuts," "digs," "put-downs" and embarrassing stories are the stuff of verbal life. Moreover, as if a survival of the cultural collective unconscious,[96] *Nisei* youth, like their Japanese forebears across the sea, have a facility and interest in the organization of clubs, cliques and gangs.[97] These associations are the units through which *Nisei* character is manifested, sustained and reinforced.

Nisei teasing is not randomly directed. Targets for the verbal "cuts" are those fellow *Nisei* and other close friends who exhibit outward signs of tension, embarrassment, excessive emotional display or boisterousness. Persons who blush, tremble, give way to tears or raise their voices too often in anger or too much for emphasis are the "victims" and recipients of jibes and cajolery designed to bring them back into line. Many *Nisei* are self-consciously aware of the didactic purpose of this teasing, and regular "victims" have on occasion reported to me their heartfelt gratefulness for it.

In addition to its teaching and control functions, two other "rules" appear to govern *Nisei* teasing. First, the status position of any particular *Nisei vis-à-vis* his fellow *Nisei* may render him ineligible or preferable for teasing. For instance, in the joking relationship there is a tendency for *Nisei* whose parents hail from peasant and poor prefectures not to tease those whose parents are from urban and socio-economically better-off areas; for *Nisei* from rural parts of California to be somewhat awed by those from San Francisco or Los Angeles; and for clique leaders to be less eligible for "cuts" than ordinary members. The "inferior" statuses are themselves the butt of jokes which earmark offensive behavior and gauche ways as stemming from poor, peasant and rural origins. Thus, *Nisei* whose parents came from Shiga, Kagoshima and a few other prefectures, and those whose parents are from Okinawa and Hokkaido, are often teased mercilessly about their culturally acquired agrestic characters, or are perceived as persons incapable of realizing the *Nisei* characterological ideal. More mild in form, but no less felt, are the ridicule and humor directed at *Nisei* from rural America by their urban compatriots. An informal avoidance and segregation sometimes set boundaries between *Nisei* of different status groups and prevents confrontations that would be mutually embarrassing.[98]

The second so-called "rule" governing teasing centers on that *Nisei* ridicule and joking which must steer a careful course between the Scylla of ineffectiveness and the Charybdis of associative break-up. If jokes and "cuts" are too mild, too obscure, usually misunderstood or always mitigated by apologies and explanations, then the intended objective is frustrated and the defalcating party is not brought to heel. If, on the other hand, the jokes are too damning, too pointed, if they cut to the very heart of a person and leave him no room to maneuver or retreat, then the defalcating party may withdraw from the group in unredeeming shame or anger and be lost, perhaps forever, to its benefits and protections. To indicate that a person has gone too far in his teasing, a *Nisei* "target" may warn him of his offense by directing a telling remark at a third party in earshot of the two. Thus, watching two youthful *Nisei* friends of mine escalate their reciprocal "cuts," I became the third party in such a situation. The offended party turned to me and said, "Man, he's a chilly dude, isn't he?" The warned person recognized the rebuke for what it was and proceeded to deescalate his humorous assaults on the other. And so the appropriate relationship—not too close, not too distant—was maintained.

The characterological ideal of any *Nisei* is best realized when others do not know his emotional state. To achieve this, he must, as one *Nisei* put it to me, build a wall around his emotions so that others cannot see what they are. Their "authoritarian" upbringing on the one hand, and the "samurai" code of stoicism and endurance on the other, helped them to construct this social and psychic edifice. The functions of this wall have been described by Geertz in his study of Java where he found an identical ideal: "If one can calm one's inward feelings . . . one can build a wall around them; one will be able both to conceal them from others and to protect them from outside disturbance. The refinement of inner feeling has thus two aspects: the direct internal attempt to control one's emotions . . . ; and secondly, an external attempt to build a [wall] around them that will protect them. On the one hand, one engages in inward discipline, and on the other in an outward defense."[99] However, while this impregnable "wall" is the ultimately desired objective, most *Nisei* point out that few can fully attain it.

The character displayed or aimed at by *Nisei* in everyday life is not unfamiliar to other Americans. Indeed, while at one time it was thought to be the unique trait of aristocrats, Orientals and urbanites, mature industrial societies seem to require it of everyone today.[100] Ordinary men describe it by such adjectives as "blase," "sophisticated" and in more recent time, "cool." Other related terms describing aspects of this character are "self-possessed," "detached," "aloof," "sang-froid" and "savoir-faire." What is referred to is the "capacity to execute physical acts, including conversation, in a concerted, smooth, self-controlled fashion in risky situations, or [the capacity] to maintain affective detachment during the course of encounters involving considerable emotion."[101] Ideally for the *Nisei,* this means combining courage, a willingness to proceed on a course of action anticipated to be dangerous without any manifestation of fear; gameness, sticking to a line of action despite set-backs, injury, fatigue and even impending failure *(Yamato damashii);*[102] and integrity, the resistance of temptations which would reduce the actor's moral stance. Finally, *Nisei* character places its greatest emphasis on composure, including all its ramifications of physical and mental poise during any act, calmness in the face of disruptions and embarrassing situations, presence of mind and the avoidance of "blocking" under pressure, emotional control during sudden changes of situation, and stage confidence during performances before audiences.[103]

As has been intimated, *Nisei* find it difficult to live up to this ideal. However, there are strategies and tactics whereby its appearance can be generated and its failures avoided or hidden. Thus, courage is balanced by a realistic appraisal of risks and opportunities. Studies of *Nisei* estimates of first salaries, for example, show that they almost always guessed the salary to the nearest dollar,[104] suggesting perhaps a procedure whereby face could be protected from the loss it would suffer by a rejection of an incorrect estimate of self-worth. Gameness is partially mitigated by choosing lines of action—such as jobs, sports, games, etc.—in which one has secretly tested oneself for potentiality and ability. Violations of absolute integrity are neutralized by the practice of situation ethics and the invocation of a layman's version of the international legal principle *rebus sic stantibus*. Composure, as has been mentioned, is guarded by self-discipline, protected by barriers and involvement shields, and tested and supported by teasing and ridicule. Finally, disasters and misfortunes, either personal or collective, may be accepted with equanimity by assigning them to fate (or as the Japanese would say, *shikata-ganai*[105]).

Consequences of Nisei Character

The everyday practice of the *Nisei* way of life has certain consequences which both reflect its essential nature and react back upon *Nisei* as sources of pride or problems. These consequences may be discussed under the headings of perception and projection, communication confusion, stage fright and real and imagined illnesses.

In everyday discussions with *Nisei* any non-*Nisei* listener would be impressed by their pointed perceptions and shrewd observations of others. These perceptions and observations are made about absent third parties and are never uttered in the presence of the party under discussion. Many people would be surprised at how keenly quite ordinary *Nisei* have paid attention to the minute details of interpersonal situations, placed brackets around particular sets of events, and interpreted words and gestures in light of the general "theory" of *Nisei* character. Most *Nisei* analyses of fellow *Nisei* concentrate on the degree to which the latter fail to carry off the appropriate presentation of self and attribute any failings to some inner-lying maladaptation or maladjustment. Parlor "Freudianism" is quite common in these analyses, and one *Nisei* may speak of another in terms of the latter's essential inability to mask his "inferiority complex," "fear of failure" or "feelings of inadequacy."

It is my impression that these "perceptions" are in fact "projections." *Nisei* tend to function as one another's mirror images, showing up the defects in each other's character. This is possible because the "wall" which *Nisei* have built to prevent others from seeing their own emotions is actually only a set of personal blinders keeping the individual from introspection. To put it another way, the *Nisei* have attempted to separate personal feeling from particular action and in doing so have "alienated" their emotional from their behaving selves.[106] This "alienation" gives *Nisei* the peculiar advantage of self-detachment and an angular vision of their fellow men not shared by those not so detached from self. But the angle of perceptive advantage, reinforced by the similarity of life styles among *Nisei* results, as I see it, in the imputation to others of the perceiver's own partly recognized failings. Thus, their common life and general self-alienation permit projections and perceptions to coincide without the latter necessarily being seen as having derived from the former.

Nisei character is an ideal which few *Nisei* in fact ever feel they have achieved. In trying to live up to the ideal, many *Nisei* find they are confused or are confusing to others. These confusions occur over mutual misreadings of intentions or meanings, misunderstandings of jokes and ridicule and problems arising out of the episodic nature of *Nisei* life. Because tonal cues are not used as indicators of significance, *Nisei* sometimes fail to grasp the relevant item in a conversation; more often their non-*Nisei* colleagues or friends miss the important point and fail to act appropriately. Since *Nisei* often take it for granted that those with whom they converse will automatically understand them and will be able to separate the chaff from the wheat of their speech, they are frustrated and exasperated when this fails to happen.[107]

Mention has already been made of the role of jokes and ridicule in *Nisei* social control. Despite their importance, or perhaps because of it, these "cuts" and "digs" create problems. Discussing the problem of what a humorous jibe at another *Nisei* really means, a *Nisei* friend and I distinguished analytically three kinds of barbs: (1) those that are given just in fun; i.e., "pure" humor having neither intent nor consequences beyond the ensuing laughter; (2) those that are didactic; i.e., having as their objective the redirection of another's behavior so that it is no longer embarrassing or inept; and (3) those that are intentionally destructive, having as their object another's degradation.

Nisei tend to disbelieve that many jokes can have no object at all, preferring instead to believe that some intent must lie behind the ostensibly humorous utterance. However, they experience difficulty in ascertaining whether a joke is didactic or destructive, because, in fact, the line between them is difficult to draw. Witty repartee is a well-developed and highly prized art among *Nisei,* but precisely because skill at it is differentially distributed, no *Nisei* can feel entirely comfortable in an encounter.

Beyond adolescence, *Nisei* occasionally confess discomfiture about being permanently locked into a system of competitive relations with fellow *Nisei.* Social visits are occasions for the reciprocal giving and receiving of humorous remarks calling attention to invidious distinctions. Birth, sex and growth of children, richness and style of furniture, occupational advancement, skill at leisure-time activities and many other everyday things may become grist for the wit's mill. Indeed, a young *Nisei* told the author that one reason *Nisei* oppose the continuation of the Japanese residential ghetto is that they "just know" that they would be constantly "looking in each other's windows."

Nisei encounters with friends and colleagues tend to be episodic rather than developmental. Non-*Nisei,* however, usually assume a developmental sequence to be the operative norm in continued interactions. Thus, among non-*Nisei* Americans a sequence of social encounters usually proceeds upon the assumption that each new encounter will begin at the emotional level or feeling-state reached at the end of the last meeting. Among *Nisei,* however, there is a limit to expressed feeling-states that is quickly reached and may not be deepened without loss of inner equanimity or outer poise. Hence, *Nisei* tend to treat each encounter almost as if the participants were meeting for the first time. This permits the limited range of feeling-states to be reached again each time but not transcended. For those content with a permanently established line beyond which interpersonal relations may not go, this pattern may

go unnoticed. However, those who expect that each new encounter will bring increased "depth," or those who expect to open any "second" encounter with a *Nisei* with a reciprocated expression of the warmth typical of Occidental friendships, may be startled or exasperated by an apparent coldness of response. Episodic encounters function to keep potentially consociative relationships at the contemporaneous level, and thus, to protect the integrity of the *Nisei* group.

Unlike many middle-class Occidentals in America, *Nisei* are more conscious of being on display, so to speak, before a hyper-critical audience. "A simile is useful in pointing up the similarities and differences between Japanese American and white middle-class achievement orientations: the ultimate destinations or goals of individuals in the two groups tend to be very similar; but Japanese Americans go toward these destinations along straight, narrow streets lined with crowds of people who observe their every step, while middle class persons go toward the same destinations along wider streets having more room for maneuvering, and lined only with small groups of people who, while watching them do not observe their every movement."[108] People who believe that their every move is under scrutiny are liable to suffer from "stage fright."[109] In the case of *Nisei* this would appear to be an inevitable consequence of their need to exhibit an appearance of poise and equanimity in the face of a constantly intrusive and challenging world. Moreover, the exhibition of "stage fright" is itself a flaw in *Nisei* character management and must be avoided if the illusion of composure is to be maintained. Among *Nisei* one finds a fear—usually mild, occasionally quite intense—that an encounter will be spoiled by a collapse of formality and a revelation of the actual personality hidden behind the facade of etiquette. Nevertheless, *Nisei* lend support to the belief system that generates this fear by observing in quite ordinary conversations, and insisting in their reprimands given to fellow *Nisei,* that the entire community is watching them, and that they must, therefore, behave with circumspection.[110]

It sometimes occurs that ceremony and etiquette collapse and *Nisei* find themselves locked in the mutually embarrassing relationship of consociates. More often this happens to one party who during an encounter is, for some reason, unable to sustain appropriate emotional equipoise. When this does occur, the other parties present will try to repair the psychic bridge which has kept them at the proper social distance from one another by studied non-observation of the other's embarrassment, by aversion of the eyes from the other's discomfiture in order to allow the latter time to repair his social front, or by a warm but unmistakably triumphant grin which simultaneously signals a "victory" in the ever-played "game" of social testing and also the social reinstatement of the "losing" player. Social life for *Nisei* is a contest something like tennis: a single faux pas is a "game" victory; an evening full of them may be a "set," but it takes an entire lifetime to play out the "match."

Many observers have pointed to the noticeable hypochondria in the Japanese character,[111] and at least one has stated that it indicates a remarkably compulsive personality.[112] It is questionable whether, or to what extent, hypochondria is a feature of *Nisei* life; for a sociologist the very question raises problems for which an unambiguous answer is difficult if not impossible.[113] Disease, or the outward signs of disease, threatens the equanimity so cherished by *Nisei*. On the other hand, admission that one has a disease is also potentially damaging. In traditional Japan a history of disease in a family was sufficient reason to cancel a marriage, and it was the task of the *nakyo-do* to discover if such a history existed.[114] Shame over illness is found to some degree among *Nisei* and extends also, with numerous individual variations, of course, to cover any involuntary loss of control over body stasis such as occurs when vomiting or in a state of intoxication. A *Nisei* is vulnerable to "attacks" from his body, which enjoys for him something of the sociological status of the stranger as conceived by Simmel:[115] It is ever with him but is mysterious and not quite subject to perfect control.

It is my impression that the *Nisei* suffer from an unusual amount of that kind of psychosomatic disease—ulcers, colitis, psoriasis, falling hair, etc.—which results from permanent unresolved tensions.[116] That the tensions are real should be clear not only from what I have written thus far, but also from the findings of clinical studies.[117] Proof of the actual existence of these diseases is more difficult to obtain, not only because of the desire on the part of *Nisei* to conceal and deemphasize sickness in themselves, but also because of the structural arrangements in current America which aid them in their efforts. Many of my *Nisei* friends have informed me of the abdominal pains from which they silently suffer. Others are startled by and ashamed of their seemingly incurable mottled fingernails or falling hair. Few *Nisei*, however, visit doctors to have their symptoms analyzed. Instead, they rely on *Nisei* pharmacist friends and colleagues, of whom in California there are a great many, to diagnose their symptoms and prescribe a remedy or a relief. Seeing a *Nisei* pharmacist friend is not too threatening apparently since it keeps the information localized and requires far less elaborate explanation by either "patient" or pharmacist than would or might be required by a physician. The suffering *Nisei* need only hint at his ailment, and the pharmacist, who may suffer from the same problem, will know what not to say and what medicine to prescribe. By eliminating the "middle man"—in this case, the physician—the *Nisei* sufferer preserves his poise while at the same time protecting his health. Moreover, he avoids that source of potentially embarrassing or frustrating information, the doctor or psychiatrist, who might show him that his pain and discomfort arise directly out of the unresolved problems created by his subcultural outlook. That ultimate revelation might be too much to bear; one logical conclusion to be drawn from it is that abandonment of the *Nisei* way of life is the price for permanent relief from pain.

The Crisis of the Future

The geogenerational conception of time and person which predominates in *Nisei* life evokes the recognition that any generation with its attendant character structure will eventually decline and pass away. Although the *Issei* generation has by no means passed out of existence, its influence began to decline after 1942 when the enforced incarceration of all persons of Japanese ancestry propelled the *Nisei* into positions of prison camp and community leadership.[118] At the present time, as the *Sansei* generation comes to maturity and establishes its independent existence and special group identity in America, the *Nisei* group is beginning to sense its own decline and eventual disappearance.

The *Nisei* can clearly see the end of their generational existence in the not too distant future. The census of 1960 reported that 82% of all Japanese in thirteen western states were born in the United States, its territories or possessions; in other words, a little more than eight-tenths of the persons of Japanese descent in that area are *Nisei, Kibei, Sansei, Yonsei* and *Gosei*. The manner of taking the census prohibits any further breakdown of these figures into respective geogenerational groupings. However, by looking at age distribution, we can arrive at a crude approximation. In California, where 159,545 persons of Japanese descent live, the 1960 census recorded 68,015 of these between the ages of zero and twenty-four. Most of these are the children, grandchildren or occasionally great-grandchildren of *Nisei*, and thus will soon equal and then outstrip the latter in number.

The inevitable end of the *Nisei* group has provoked a mild crisis in the *Lebenswelt* ("lifeworld") of the *Nisei*.[119] *Nisei* are coming to realize with a mixture of anxiety, discomfort and disillusion—but primarily with a sense of fatalistic resignation—that the way of life to which they are used, the presentation of self which they have always taken for granted, the arts of self-preservation and impression management which they have so assiduously cultivated and so highly prized, will soon no longer be regular features of everyday existence among the Japanese in America. Thus, *Nisei* perceive that what has been a valid way of living for so many years will not continue to be so, and that what they have accomplished by living this way will no longer be accomplished this way or perhaps at all. The *Sansei*

and, for that matter, the other successor generations will be different from the *Nisei* in certain fundamental respects. Moreover, some of these respects are viewed with considerable misgivings by contemporary *Nisei*.

Nisei have always seemed to recognize the sociocultural and psychic differences between themselves and the *Sansei*. Some of these differences are based on clearly distinguishable generational experiences. Few of the *Sansei* are old enough to remember or have experienced the terrible effects of imprisonment during World War II; most *Sansei* have not grown up in homes marked by a noticeable cultural division between America and Japan; most *Sansei* have benefitted from the relative material success of their parents and have received parental support for their educational pursuits without difficulty; finally, few *Sansei* have borne the oppressive burden of racial discrimination or felt the demoralizing agony of anti-Japanese prejudice. In all these respects *Nisei* recognize that the *Sansei* are the beneficiaries of *Issei* and *Nisei* struggles and perseverance, and they acknowledge that if, because of these things, the *Sansei* do behave differently than an immigrant or oppressed people, then it is only right and proper for them to do so.

There is one aspect of *Sansei* behavior, however, that worries and disappoints *Nisei:* It is their lack of appropriate (that is, *Nisei*) character. Some *Nisei* see this characterological loss as a product of increased urbanization and Americanization; others emphasize the loss of Japanese "culture" among the third generation. Whatever the explanation, many *Nisei* perceive a definite and irremediable loss of character in their successor generation. To illustrate this point, note that *Nisei* often use the term *Sansei* to indicate at one and the same time the existence and cause of social impropriety. Thus, in the face of an individual's continued social errors in my presence, a *Nisei* explained to me, "What can you expect? He's a *Sansei.*"

Ironically, *Nisei* child-rearing and parental practices contribute to the creation of the very *Sansei* character that disappoints them, just as their own

Issei parents helped to lay the groundwork for *Nisei* character.[120] Despite the great general respect and personal deference which the *Nisei* pay to their parents, they tend to see them as negative role models when it comes to rearing their own children. The isolation, loneliness, harshness and language and communication difficulties of their own childhoods are vividly recalled, and a great many *Nisei* have vowed that their children will not experience any of that. As a result, the ethics of samurai stoicism and endurance and the discipline associated with them are rarely emphasized by *Nisei* parents. Rather, they choose to order their childrearing by following the white middle-class ethos of love, equality and companionship. The principles of *Bushido* give way to those of Dr. Spock; the idea of age-graded obligation is supplanted by the agecohort theory of Gesell; the social distance that separated parent and child is replaced by the idea that parents and children should "grow up together."

The resultant product of this upbringing is, of course, quite different from that of its parents. Worse, from the point of view of most *Nisei,* it is a disappointing one. *Nisei* complain that *Sansei* seem to lack the drive and initiative which was once a hallmark of the Japanese; that they have no interest in Japanese culture, especialy its characterological elements; that they are prone to more delinquency and less respect for authority than were the *Nisei;* and that they are "provincial" and bound to the "provincialisms" of Los Angeles, perhaps the city that encloses the single largest aggregate of *Sansei.*[121] *Nisei* often complain of the lack of psychological self-sufficiency and independent capacity for decision-making among *Sansei.* Thus, a *Nisei* scoutmaster pointed out to me how his scout troop, mostly *Sansei,* became emotionally upset and homesick when away for but a week's camping trip, and how their projected wiener roast would have been ruined if he had not stepped in and directed the planning for food purchases. He attributes these "failings" to their *Sansei* background, and he admitted that his own intervention in assisting the scouts in their

plans was a distinct departure from what his own parents would have done in a similar situation during his childhood. *Issei* parents, say many *Nisei,* would probably have "let" their children "fail" in such an endeavor in order to help them cultivate responsibility and initiative. But such a seemingly cold and unfeeling response to their own children is anathema.

Sansei indicate an ambivalence and a mild anxiety over their own situation. They do exhibit a certain "Hansen effect"—that is, a desire to recover selected and specific elements of the culture of old Japan[122]—but in this endeavor itself they discover that their own Americanization has limited the possibility of very effective recovery. If juvenile delinquency among them is on the rise—and the evidence is as yet inconclusive[123]—they attribute it in small part to parental misunderstandings and in greater part to the effects of the great social changes taking place in America. Their parents often appear "old-fashioned" to them, unprepared to understand their "hang-ups" and unwilling to offer sufficient love and understanding to them.[124] Finally, they seem at times to be about to claim the right to dissolve their own geogenerational identity and that of their successor generations in favor of both deeper intimate associations below the level of the generational group and interracial intimacies transcending them.[125] Yet, they also wonder how and in what manner they can or should retain their "Japanese" identity.[126]

Unlike many groups, the *Nisei* do not stand at a crossroads. Their fate is sure and their doom is sealed by the moving hands of the generational clock. They have not merely survived the hatred and oppression of America's racism, they have triumphed over it. In nearly every "objective" measure they outstrip their minority "competitors," and in education they have surpassed the white majority.[127] They have turned almost every adversity into a challenge and met each with courage and cool judgment. In all this their own subcultural character has been an invaluable aid as well as an everpresent source of pride. Now they see the coming of the end of their own generation and of this character, and they can only wonder what psychic supports will provide mental sustenance for future generations. In one sense the *Nisei* are the last of the *Japanese* Americans; the *Sansei* are *American* Japanese. As Jitsuichi Masuoka observed over two decades ago, "It is the members of the *Sansei* who,

having been fully acculturated but having been excluded by the dominant group because of their racial difference, really succeed in presenting a united front against exclusion by the dominant group. A genuine race problem arises at this point in the history of race relations."[128]

Notes

1. Quoted in Lewis Bush, *77 Samurai: Japan's First Embassy to America,* Tokyo and Palo Alto, California: Kodansha International, 1968, p. 132. (Based on the original manuscript in Japanese by Itsuro Hattori.) Bush does not give the date of this newspaper article. It would appear to be April 2, 1860 or thereabouts.

2. The Embassy was not the first visit of Japanese to America. It is probable that a Japanese ship was wrecked off the coast of South America in 3,000 B.C. Betty J. Meggers, Clifford Evans and Emilio Estrada, *Early Formative Period of Coastal Ecuador: The Valdivia and Machalilla Phases,* Washington, D. C.: Smithsonian Institution, 1965, pp. 167–178. The Hashikura Embassy arrived in New Spain in 1614 and some of its members remained until 1615, not returning to Japan until 1620. William Lytle Schurtz, *The Manila Galleon,* New York: E.P. Dutton, 1959, pp. 99–128. Moreover, twenty-four Japanese ships were wrecked off western North America in the period between 1613 and 1850 and some of the survivors resided temporarily among Occidentals. Charles Wolcott Brook, *Japanese Wrecks Stranded and Picked up Adrift in the North Pacific Ocean,* Fairfield, Washington. Ye Galleon Press, 1964 (originally published in 1876); Shunzo Sakamaki, "Japan and the United States, 1790–1853," *The Transactions of the Asiatic Society of Japan,* XVIII (1939), Second Series, pp. 3–204. See also J. Feenstra Kuiper, Ph,D., "Some notes on the Foreign Relations of Japan in the Early Napoleonic Period (1798–1805)," *Ibid.,* I (1923–1924) Second Series, pp. 55–82.

3. Bush, *op. cit.,* p. 132.

4. See Jacobus ten Broek, Edward N. Barnhart and Floyd Matson, *Prejudice, War, and the Constitution,* (Japanese American Evacuation and Resettlement, Vol. III), Berkeley: University of California Press, 1954, pp. 11–98.

5. See Anne Reeploeg Fisher, *Exile of a Race,* Sidney, British Columbia: Peninsula Printing Co., 1965; Morton Grodzins, *Americans Betrayed: Politics and the Japanese Evacuation,* Chicago: University of Chicago Press, 1949, pp. 1–230, 400–422. For a typical example of the rhetoric of that period see Alan Hynd, *Betrayal From the East: The Inside Story of Japanese Spies in America,* New York: Robert M. McBride & Co., 1943.

6. Robert E. Park, "Racial Assimilation in Secondary Groups with Special Reference to the Negro," in *Race and Culture,* Glencoe: The Free Press, 1950, p. 209. (The Collected Papers of Robert E. Park, Vol. I, edited by Everett C. Hughes, *et al.*)

7. Robert E. Park, "Behind Our Masks," *Survey Graphic* LVI (May 1, 1926), p. 137. This essay emphasized its point with photographs of *Noh* masks on each page.

8. Fred L. Strodtbeck, "Family Interaction, Values, and Achievement," in Marshall Sklare, (Editor), *The Jews: Social Patterns of an Ethnic Group,* New York: The Free Press, 1958, pp. 162–163.

9. Bernard C. Rosen, "Race, Ethnicity, and the Achievement Syndrome," *American Sociological Review,* 24 (February, 1959), pp. 47–60.

10. Chester Rowell, "Chinese and Japanese Immigrants—A Comparison," *Annals of the American Academy of Political and Social Science,* XXIV (September, 1909), pp. 223–230.

11. Winifred Raushenbush, "Their Place in the Sun," *Survey Graphic,* LVI (May 1, 1926), pp. 141–145.

12. Rose Hum Lee, *The Chinese in the United States of America,* Hong Kong: Hong Kong University Press, 1960, p. 425.

13. Leonard Broom and John I. Kitsuse, "The Validation of Acculturation: A Condition of Ethnic Assimilation," *American Anthropologist* LVII (February, 1955), p. 45.

14. Calvin F. Schmid and Charles E. Nobbe, "Socioeconomic Differentials Among Nonwhite Races," *American Sociological Review,* 30 (December, 1965), pp. 909–922.

15. William Caudill and George de Vos, "Achievement, Culture, and Personality: The Case of the Japanese Americans," *American Anthropologist,* 58 (December, 1956), p. 1107.

16. *Ibid.,* p. 1116.

17. *Loc. cit.*

18. Alan Jacobson and Lee Rainwater, "A Study of Management Representative Evaluations of Nisei Workers," *Social Forces,* 32 (March, 1953), pp. 35–41.

19. See, e.g., Wallace Irwin, *Letters of a Japanese School Boy,* New York: Doubleday, Page, 1909, pp. 172–173 *et passim.*

So powerful was Irwin's caricature of the Japanese that the distinguished Negro novelist and statesman, James Weldon Johnson, felt he could not be sure whether a letter he received from a Japanese student offering to assist in the Negroes' struggle for equality was genuine or a product of Wallace Irwin's mischievous hand. After a conference attended by Chinese and Japanese diplomats, Johnson noted: "I myself reacted differently to these two peoples; the Japanese left me rather cold. Not during the time I was at the Conference did I form cordial relations with warm friendships." James Weldon Johnson, *Along This Way* New York: Viking, 1968, pp. 399–401.

20. Stanley M. Elkins, *Slavery: A Problem in American Institutional and Intellectual Life,* Chicago: University of Chicago Press, 1959, pp. 81–139.

21. Alfred Schutz, *The Phenomenology of the Social World,* Evanston: Northwestern University Press, 1967, pp. 139–214 (translated by George Walsh and Frederick Lehnert).

22. Clifford Geertz, *Person, Time, and Conduct in Bali: An Essay in Cultural Analysis,* New Haven: Yale University Southeast Asia Studies, Cultural Report Series No. 14, 1966.

23. William Caudill and Henry A. Scarr, "Japanese Value Orientations and Culture Change," *Ethnology,* I (January, 1962), pp. 53–91.

24. Schutz, *op.cit.,* pp. 142–143, 194–214.

25. Cf. Edward Norbeck, *Pineapple Town, Hawaii,* Berkeley: University of California Press, 1959, pp. 5, 86–104.

26. See the interesting discussion in Clyde V. Kiser, "Cultural Pluralism," *The Annals of the American Academy of Political and Social Science,* 262 (March, 1949), pp. 118–129.

27. Chinese prefer to distinguish by a common "middle name" all persons born in the same generational cohort of a single lineage, but they do not continue a genealogical measurement of geo-generational distance from China. See Maurice Freedman, *Chinese Lineage and Society: Fukien and Kwangtung,* New York: Humanities Press, 1966, pp. 44–45, 179–180.

28. The *Kibei* have been the most frequently discussed group among the Japanese Americans because of their socio-cultural marginality and because of their alleged disloyalty to the United States during the Pacific War. See E. K. Strong, Jr., *The Second-Generation Japanese Problem,* Stanford: Stanford University Press, 1934; Andrew W. Lind, *Hawaii's Japanese: An Experiment in Democracy,* Princeton: Princeton University Press, 1946, pp. 33–34, 183–188, 212–213, 245; Carey McWilliams, *Prejudice: Japanese Americans: Symbol of Racial Intolerance,* Boston: Little, Brown, 1944, pp. 321–322; An Intelligence Officer, "The Japanese in America: The Problem and the Solution," *Harper's Magazine,* 185 (October, 1942), pp. 489–497; "Issei, Nisei, Kibei," *Fortune,* XXIX (April, 1944), pp. 8, 21, 32, 74, 78–79, 94, 106, 118; Bradford Smith, *Americans From Japan,* Philadelphia: J. P. Lippincott, 1948, pp.

253–255, 275, 315–321; Dorothy Swaine Thomas and Richard Nishimoto, *The Spoilage,* (Japanese American Evacuation and Resettlement, Vol. I), Berkeley: University of California Press, 1946, pp. 3, 69, 78–81; Dorothy Swaine Thomas, with the assistance of Charles Kikuchi and James Sakoda, *The Salvage,* (Japanese American Evacuation and Resettlement, Vol. II), Berkeley: University of California Press, 1952, *passim;* ten Broek, Barnhart, and Matson, *op. cit.,* pp. 142, 177, 275–285; Alan Bosworth, *America's Concentration Camps,* New York: W. W. Norton, 1967, *passim.*

29. Norbeck, *op. cit.,* p. 94.

30. For a poignant account of the social and personal adjustment of the daughter of an Irish-American mother and an *Issei* father, see Kathleen Tamagawa, *Holy Prayers in a Horse's Ear,* New York: Ray Long and Richard R. Smith, 1932.

31. See Daisuke Kitagawa, *Issei and Nisei: The Internment Years,* New York: Seabury Press, pp. 26–31.

32. The phenomena discussed here are analogous to the issues involved in romantic love and incest on the one hand and group dissolution through loss of function on the other. For perceptive theoretical insights, see Philip Slater, "Social Limitations on Libidinal Withdrawal," *American Journal of Sociology* LXVII (November, 1961), pp. 296–311; and Talcott Parsons, "The Incest Taboo in Relation to Social Structure," *British Journal of Sociology,* V (June, 1954), pp. 101–117; Parsons, "The Superego and the Theory of Social Systems," *Psychiatry,* 15 (February, 1952), pp. 15–25.

33. Broom and Kitsuse, *op. cit.*

34. Discussions of this group breakdown through withdrawal or transcendence usually focus on juvenile delinquency, although the issues clearly go beyond this element of behavior. See, e.g., Harry H. L. Kitano, "Japanese-American Crime and Delinquency." *Journal of Psychology* 66 (1967), pp. 253–263.

35. See, e.g., Ruth Benedict, *The Chrysanthemum and the Sword: Patterns of Japanese Culture,* Boston: Houghton Mifflin, 1946; Nyozekan Hasegawa, *The Japanese Character: A Cultural Profile,* Tokyo: Kodansha International, 1966; Fosco Maraini, *Meeting with Japan,* New York: Viking Press, 1960, pp. 22–23, 217–218 (translated by Eric Mosbacher).

36. Joseph K. Yamagiwa, "Language as an Expression of Japanese Culture," in John W. Hall and Richard K. Beardsley, (Editors), *Twelve Doors to Japan,* New York: McGraw-Hill, 1965, pp. 186–223.

37. Hajime Nakamura, *Ways of Thinking of Eastern Peoples: India-China-Tibet-Japan,* Honolulu: East-West Center Press, 1964, pp. 409–410 (Edited by Philip P. Wiener).

38. See Benedict, *op. cit.,* pp. 48–49. Professor Shuichi Kato informs me that *gaijin* (i.e., foreigners) will be automatically exempted from the rigid requirements of the Japanese bow. *Nisei* in Japan, however, may suffer loss of face for their lack of

knowledge in this area of etiquette, especially if they are not recognized as American-born.

39. Among *Nisei* I have observed a quick jerk of the head in genuflection before elders, *Issei* and visitors from Japan, but this vestigial bow is far from the careful employment of body idiom required of traditional Japanese.

40. Among my *Nisei* associates it is widely professed that the Japanese language contains no obscenities, and many *Nisei* utter English scatological phrases softly and under their breath. In contrast, Chinese Americans of the same generation, especially those who speak *Sz Yup* dialect, employ a rich variety of epithets, curses and obscenities.

41. Clifford Geertz, *The Religion of Java,* London: Collier-Macmillan, The Free Press of Glencoe, 1960, pp. 241–242.

42. As a general phenomenon of human behavior, this suspiciousness has been described by Erving Goffman. See *The Presentation of Self in Everyday Life,* Edinburgh: University of Edinburgh Social Science Research Centre, Monograph No. 2, 1958, pp. 1–46.

43. See Hiroshi Wagatsuma, "The Social Perception of Skin Color in Japan," *Daedalus* 96 (Spring, 1967), pp. 407–443.

44. Jews had reached China as early as the twelfth century, and the synagogue at K'ai-feng was still standing in 1851. See William Charles White, *Chinese Jews: A Compilation of Matters Relating to the Jews of K'ai-feng Fu,* New York: Paragon Book Reprint Corp., 1966 (Second Edition), pp. 9–204. A few Jews came to Japan in the ninth century, and another group in the sixteenth, but it was not until the nineteenth century that the Jewish religion has even a small establishment there. In the early twentieth century Kobe became a center for European Jewish merchants, and this colony was enlarged by refugees from Nazi Germany. See Abraham Kotsuji, *From Tokyo to Jerusalem: The Autobiography of a Japanese Convert to Judaism,* New York: Bernard Geis, Random House, 1964, pp. 58–59, 159–161. The Nazis had a difficult time converting their Japanese allies to anti-Semitism. Kotsuji, (*op. cit.,* pp. 131–200) provides a personal report of his own activities in behalf of Jews in Manchuria and Japan. See also Norman Cohn, *Warrant for Genocide: The Myth of the Jewish World Conspiracy and the Protocols of the Elders of Zion,* New York: Harper and Row, 1966, pp. 242–243.

45. I am indebted to the Rev. Taro Goto and Mr. Nobusuke Fukuda for explaining this term and its origins to me.

46. George de Vos, "A Quantitative Rorschach Assessment of Maladjustment and Rigidity in Acculturating Japanese American," *Genetic Psychology Monographs,* 52 (1955) p. 66.

47. Edward T. Hall, *The Hidden Dimension,* Garden City, Doubleday, 1966, pp. 139–144.

48. Bernard Rudofsky, *The Kimono Mind,* Garden City: Doubleday, 1965, pp. 159–161.

49. Japanese, like English, is a language that betrays the speaker's social and regional origins. Japanese Americans, highly conscious of the poor quality of their spoken Japanese and wary lest it betray peasant origins, tend to rely on English whenever possible.

50. See Ezra Vogel, "The Go-Between in a Developing Society, the Case of the Japanese Marriage Arranger," *Human Organization,* 20 (Fall, 1961), pp. 112–120. For the go-between among Japanese in America, see Shotaro Frank Miyamoto, *Social Solidarity Among the Japanese in Seattle,* Seattle: University of Washington Publications in the Social Sciences, Vol. II (December, 1939), pp. 87–88; Robert H. Ross and Emory S. Bogardus, "Four Types of *Nisei* Marriage Patterns," *Sociology and Social Research,* 25 (September, 1940), pp. 63–66; John F. Embree, "Acculturation Among the Japanese of Kona, Hawaii," Memoirs of the American Anthropological Association. Supplement to *American Anthropologist* 43 (1941), pp. 74–77; Toshio Yatsushiro, "The Japanese Americans," in Milton Barron (Editor), *American Minorities,* New York: Alfred A. Knopf, 1962, p. 324.

51. Rudofsky, *op. cit.,* pp. 161–163.

52. For a discussion of information games, see Stanford M. Lyman and Marvin B. Scott, "Game Frameworks," in *A Sociology of the Absurd,* New York: Appleton-Century-Crofts, 1970.

53. For the most perceptive theoretical analysis of social occasions, and one that is applicable to the Japanese American scene, see Georg Simmel, "The Sociology of Sociability," *American Journal of Sociology,* LV (November, 1949), pp. 254–261 (translated by Everett C. Hughes).

54. Cf. David Riesman, et al., "The Vanishing Host," *Human Organization,* XIX (Spring, 1960), pp. 17–27.

55. John Embree, *The Japanese,* Smithsonian Institution War Background Studies Number Seven. Washington, D.C.: Smithsonian Institution, 1943, p. 25.

56. John Embree, *A Japanese Village: Suye Mura,* London: Kegan Paul, Trench, Trubner, 1946, pp. 155–156.

57. See Lyman and Scott, "Stage Fright and the Problem of Identity," in *A Sociology of the Absurd, op. cit.*

58. See Marvin B. Scott and Stanford M. Lyman, "Accounts," *American Sociological Review,* 33 (February, 1968), pp. 46–62.

59. Cf. Edward Gross and Gregory P. Stone, "Embarrassment and the Analysis of Role Requirements," *American Journal of Sociology,* LXX (July, 1964), pp. 6–10; Erving Goffman, "Embarrassment and Social Organization," *American Journal of Sociology* LXII (November, 1956), pp. 264–271; Stanford M. Lyman and Marvin B. Scott, "Coolness in Everyday Life," in Marcello Truzzi (Editor), *Sociology and Everyday Life,* Englewood Cliffs; Prentice-Hall, 1968, pp. 92–101.

60. Cf. Georg Simmel, "The Metropolis and Mental Life," in *The Sociology of Georg Simmel,* Glencoe: The Free Press, 1950, pp. 409–426 (Edited and translated by Kurt Wolff).

61. Georg Simmel, "The Aesthetic Significance of the Face," in *Georg Simmel, 1858–1918,* Columbus: Ohio State University Press, 1959, pp. 276–281 (Edited by Kurt H. Wolff).

62. Georg Simmel, "Sociology of the Senses: Visual Interaction," in Robert E. Park and Ernest W. Burgess, *Introduction to the Science of Sociology,* Chicago: University of Chicago Press, 1921, pp. 356–361.

63. Cf. Erving Goffman, *Behavior in Public Places: Notes on the Social Organization of Gatherings,* London: Collier-Macmillan, the Free Press of Glencoe, 1963, pp. 38, 42.

64. Cf. Maraini, *op. cit.,* p. 23.

65. See Jerry Enomoto, "Perspectives: Enryo-Syndrome?" *Pacific Citizen,* 64 (June 16, 1967), p. 1; "Perspectives: Enryo," *Ibid.,* 65 (July 7, 1967), p. 1.
In 1953 John H. Burma wrote:

> There is evidence that Nisei leaders are not so aggressive and consistent in their leadership roles as are Caucasion leaders. In their thinking Nisei leaders seem very often to be liberal, progressive, or radical, but these attitudes are often not carried over into aggressive action because such behavior will call down censure from the by-no-means impotent Issei, and because of the tradition that no Japanese leader should assert himself too strongly or too often or place himself in the limelight too frequently. Nevertheless, the leader is expected to be able to speak on his own initiative in keeping things running smoothly, and to speak out when Nisei rights are being infringed upon. The problem involved here is that Nisei are likely to be much concerned with "doing the proper thing," meeting requirements placed upon them, and being careful not to do anything which would too much disturb the Japanese community or disrupt the *status quo.* This tends to penalize initiative and aggressiveness and to slow down the dynamics of leadership as the Caucasian knows it.

"Current Leadership Problems Among Japanese Americans," *Sociology and Social Research,* 37 (January, 1953), p. 162.

66. Geertz, *Religion of Java, op. cit.,* pp. 245–247.

67. See three essays by L. Takeo Doi, "Japanese Language as an Expression of Japanese Psychology," *Western Speech,* 20 (Spring, 1956), pp. 90–96; " 'Amae': A Key Concept for Understanding Japanese Personality Structure," in Robert J. Smith and Richard K. Beardsley (Editors), *Japanese Culture: Its Development and Characteristics,* Chicago: Aldine, 1962, pp. 132–139; "Giri-Ninjo: An Interpretation," in R. P. Dore (Editor), *Aspects of Social Change in Modern Japan,* Princeton: Princeton University Press, 1967, pp. 327–336.

68. Doi, " 'Amae' . . ." *op. cit.,* p. 133.

69. See Charlotte E. Babcock and William Caudill, "Personal and Cultural Factors in Treating a Nisei Man," in Georgene Seward (Editor), *Clinical Studies in Culture Conflict,* New York: Ronald Press, 1958, pp. 409–448; Charlotte E. Babcock, "Reflections on Dependency Phenomena as Seen in Nisei in the United States," in Smith and Beardsley, *op. cit.,* pp. 172–188. See also Katharine Newkirk Handley, "Social Casework and Intercultural

Problems," *Journal of Social Casework,* 28 (February, 1947), pp. 43–50; Mamoru Iga, "The Japanese Social Structure and the Source of Mental Strains of Immigrants in the United States," *Social Forces,* 35 (March, 1957), pp. 271–278.

70. For this last point I am indebted to Hideo Bernard Hata.

71. See Joseph L. Anderson and Donald Richie, *The Japanese Film,* New York: Grove Press, 1960, pp. 63–71, 223–228, 315–331.

72. Cf. Robert Frager, "The Psychology of the Samurai," *Psychology Today,* 2 (January, 1969), pp. 48–53.

73. Douglas G. Haring, "Japanese National Character: Cultural Anthropology, Psychoanalysis, and History," in *Personal Character and Cultural Milieu,* Syracuse: Syracuse University Press, 1956 (Third Edition, compiled and edited by Douglas G. Haring), pp. 424–437; George A. De Vos, "Achievement Orientation, Social Self-Identity, and Japanese Economic Growth," *Asian Survey,* 5 (December, 1965), pp. 575–589.

74. Reinhard Bendix, "A Case Study in Cultural and Educational Mobility: Japan and the Protestant Ethic," in Neil J. Smelser and Seymour Martin Lipset (Editors), *Social Structure and Mobility in Economic Development,* Chicago: Aldine, 1966, pp. 266–267.

75. Herbert Passin, *Society and Education in Japan,* New York: Bureau of Publications, Teachers College, East Asian Institute, Columbia University, 1965, pp. 149–160; R. P. Dore, *Education in Tokugawa Japan,* London: Routledge and Kegan Paul, 1965, pp. 124–251.

76. The early student migration to America was of samurai rank, a fact attested to by their each having two swords. See Charles Lanman, *The Japanese in America,* London: Longmans, Green, Readers, and Dyer, 1872, pp. 67–79. See also Charles F. Thwing, "Japanese and Chinese Students in America," *Scribner's Monthly,* XX (July, 1880), pp. 450–453; John W. Bennet, Herbert Passin, and Robert K. McKnight, *In Search of Identity: The Japanese Overseas Scholar in America and Japan,* Minneapolis: University of Minnesota Press, 1958, pp. 18–46. Although students, some of whom were of samurai rank, continued to migrate to the United States thereafter, the settler and sojourner immigrants who came after 1880 were largely of peasant, handicraft, and merchant origin. Some of these undoubtedly descended from noble lineage or *ronin* (masterless warrior) backgrounds. See Hirokichi Mutsu, "A Japanese View of Certain Japanese-American Relations," *Overland Monthly,* 32 (November, 1898), pp. 406–414; Yosaburo Yoshida, "Sources and Causes of Japanese Emigration," *Annals of the American Academy of Political and Social Science,* XXIV (September, 1909), pp. 157–167. The Japanese American History Project now carrying on research at UCLA may produce more data on the social origins of *Issei.*

77. George Sansom, *A History of Japan, 1334–1615,* Stanford: Stanford University Press, 1961, pp. 333, 398; *A History of Japan, 1615–1867,* Stanford: Stanford University Press, 1963, pp. 32–34, 54–58, 79, 92–93, 133–138; *Japan: A Short Cultural History,* New

York: Appleton-Century-Crofts, 1943 (Revised Edition), pp. 356, 496–498.

78. Passin, *op. cit.,* pp. 117–121, 177–179, 190, 191, 226–228; Dore, *op. cit.,* pp. 214–251.

79. George B. Sansom, *Japan: A Short Cultural History, op. cit.,* pp. 520–521.

80. Paul T. Takagi, "The Japanese Family in the United States: A Hypothesis on the Social Mobility of the Nisei," Revised version of a paper presented at the annual meeting of the Kroeber Anthropological Society, Berkeley, April 30, 1966.

81. Tadashi Fukutake, *Japanese Rural Society,* Tokyo: Oxford University Press, 1967, pp. 39–59, 212–217 (Translated by R.P. Dore).

82. Chie Nakanee, *Kinship and Economic Organization in Rural Japan,* New York: Humanities Press, 1967, shows a distinct difference between Japanese rural social structure and that of China described in Maurice Freedman, *Lineage Organization in Southeastern China,* London: Athlone Press, 1958, and *Chinese Lineage and Society: Fukien and Kwangtung, op. cit.* See also Stanford M. Lyman, "Contrasts in the Community Organization of Chinese and Japanese in North America," *Canadian Review of Sociology and Anthropology,* 5 (May, 1968), pp. 51–67.

83. Fukutake, *op. cit.,* p. 40.

84. *Ibid.,* p. 212. See also Robert J. Smith, "The Japanese Rural Community: Norms, Sanctions, and Ostracism," *American Anthropologist* 63 (June, 1961). Reprinted in Jack M. Potter, et al. (Editors), *Peasant Society: A Reader,* Boston: Little, Brown, 1967, pp. 246–255.

85. Sidney L. Gulick, *The American Japanese Problem,* New York: Charles Scribner's Sons, 1914, pp. 90–96; T. Iyenaga and Kenoske Sato, *Japan and the California Problem,* New York: G. P. Putnam's Sons, 1921, pp. 109–119; Thomas, et al., *The Salvage, op. cit.,* pp. 7–8, 10–12. For a poignant account of the meetings between young brides and their older husbands, see Sessue Hayakawa, *Zen Showed Me the Way.* Indianapolis: Bobbs-Merrill, 1960, pp. 84–88. Accounts of the adjustments to proxy marriages may be found in *Our Christian Testimony,* Loomis, California: First Methodist Church, 1967 (Compiled and translated by Rev. Taro Goto).

86. See William Caudill, "Japanese American Personality and Acculturation," *Genetic Psychology Monographs,* 45 (1952), p. 32. In rural areas and in some of the ghetto residences of urban *Nihonmachi,* the hot bath was transplanted from Japan. I have taken a "Japanese bath" in a traditionally operated boarding house in the Japanese community of Walnut Grove, California. Saké, Japanese rice wine, was also manufactured or purchased by the *Issei.* Drunkenness was a common complaint among the wives of *Issei* settlers. *Our Christian Testimony, op. cit.*

87. Benedict, *op. cit.,* pp. 266–267. Personal interviews with *Nisei* indicate that *moxa* was used or threatened against naughty,

overly-excited, tantrum-throwing children. See also Monica Sone, *Nisei Daughter,* Boston: Little Brown, 1953, p. 28.

88. Douglas G. Haring, "Aspects of Personal Character in Japan," *Personal Character and Cultural Milieu, op. cit.,* pp. 417–419; Betty B. Lanham, "Aspects of Child Care in Japan: Preliminary Report," *Ibid.,* pp. 565–583; Edward and Margaret Norbeck, "Child Training in a Japanese Fishing Community," *Ibid.,* pp. 651–673; Benedict, *op. cit.,* pp. 261–264.

89. See, e.g., *The Autobiography of Yukichi Fukuzawa,* New York: Columbia University Press, 1966, pp. 113–114, (Revised Translation by Eiichi Kiyooka).

90. Caudill, *op. cit.,* p. 30.

91. Takagi, *op. cit.*

92. For the *Eta* in Florin see Winifred Raushenbush, "Their Place in the Sun," *Survey Graphic,* LVI (May 1, 1926), pp. 154–159; Hiroshi Ito (Pseudonym), "Japan's Outcastes in the United States," in George de Vos and Hiroshi Wagatsuma (Editors), *Japan's Invisible Race: Caste in Culture and Personality,* Berkeley: University of California Press, 1966, pp. 200–221.

93. Takagi, *op. cit.*

94. Cf. Edward Norbeck, "Age-Grading in Japan," *American Anthropologist,* 55 (June, 1953), pp. 373–384.

95. Caudill, *op. cit.,* p. 30. On the other hand, in Meiji Japan girls were expected to observe certain proprieties—including a proper body position when sleeping—from which boys were exempted. See Etsu Inagaki Sugimoto, *A Daughter of the Samurai,* Rutland, Vt.: Charles E. Tuttle, 1966, p. 24; Baroness Shidzue Ishimoto, *Facing Two Ways: The Story of My Life,* New York: Farrar and Rinehart, 1935, pp. 13–76.

96. See Edward Sapir, "The Unconscious Patterning of Behavior in Society," in David G. Mandelbaum (editor), *Selected Writings of Edward Sapir in Language, Culture, and Personality* (Berkeley: University of California Press, 1963), pp. 544–559.

97. George A. De Vos and Keiichi Mizushima, "Organization and Social Function of Japanese Gangs: Historical Development and Modern Parallels," in R. P. Dore, (Editor), *Aspects of Social Change in Modern Japan, op. cit.,* pp. 289–326.

98. Takagi, *op. cit.;* Stanford M. Lyman, "The Nisei Personality," *Pacific Citizen,* 62 (January 7, 1966), p. 3.

99. Geertz, *The Religion of Java, op. cit.,* p. 241.

100. Lyman and Scott, "Coolness in Everyday Life," *op. cit.*

101. *Ibid.,* p. 93.

102. Caudill, *op. cit.,* pp. 66–68.

103. For an excellent discussion of these phenomena in general, see Erving Goffman, *Interaction Ritual: Essays on Face-To-Face Behavior,* Chicago: Aldine, 1967, pp. 218–226.

104. William Petersen, "Success Story, Japanese-American

Style," *The New York Times Magazine,* January 9, 1966, p. 40.

105. Professor Harry H. L. Kitano has suggested that most Japanese Americans did not resist incarceration in detention camps during World War II because of their engrained sense of fateful resignation. Joe Grant Masaoka, "Japanese tailor-made for Army order, says Kitano," *Pacific Citizen,* 64 (June 9, 1967), pp. 1–2.

106. There is cultural support for this phenomenon, summed up in the Buddhist ideal of *muga,* carrying on activities effortlessly; that is, having eliminated the observing self in one's acts. The observing self is seen as a hindrance to smooth performance. See Benedict, *op. cit.,* pp. 247–251.

107. Cf. the remark by Sapir: "We do not really know what a man's speech is until we have evaluated his social background. If a Japanese talks in a monotonous voice, we have not the right to assume that he is illustrating the same type of personality that one of us would be if we talked with his sentence melody." "Speech as a Personality Trait," *Selected Writings . . . op. cit.,* p. 539.

108. Caudill and de Vos, *op. cit.,* p. 1117.

109. Geertz, *Person, Time, and Conduct in Bali . . . , op. cit.,* pp. 53–61; Goffman, *Interaction Ritual . . . , op. cit.,* pp. 226–233; Lyman and Scott, "Stage Fright and Social Identity," *A Sociology of the Absurd, op. cit.*

110. The Japanese term *jicho* sums up this sense. Literally "a self that is weighty," it refers to circumspection in social relations. A person loses *jicho* when he commits an impropriety. See Benedict, *op. cit.,* pp. 219–222.
  A nice example is found in the autobiography of a daring, youthful Japanese sailor. Writing of an older sailor whom he admired very much, he tells of his surprise when his "idol" actually spoke to him:

> Takeuchi was a man with a superb record as a yachtsman at Kansai University. He was always one of my idols . . . He seemed like a big shot to me, so much so that I never even used to say "hello" to him because he might not recognize me or return my greeting. But on this day there was something different about him, because he spoke to me first. I was sure that I hadn't done anything wrong, but I still wondered why Takeuchi would want to talk to me.

Kenichi Horie, *Kodoku: Sailing Alone Across the Pacific,* Rutland, Vermont: Charles E. Tuttle, 1964, pp. 26–27. (Translated by Takuichi Ito and Kaoru Ogimi.)

111. George de Vos and Hiroshi Wagatsuma, "Psycho-Cultural Significance of Concern over Death and Illness Among Rural Japanese," *International Journal of Social Psychiatry,* V (Summer, 1959), pp. 5–19; George de Vos, "Social Values and Personal Attitudes in Primary Human Relations in Niike," *Occasional Papers,* Center for Japanese Studies, University of Michigan, 1965; Babcock and Caudill, *op. cit.,* pp. 436–437; Marvin K. Opler, "Cultural Dilemma of a Kibei Youth," *Culture and Social Psychiatry,* New York: Atherton Press, 1967, pp. 360–380.

112. Weston LaBarre, "Some Observations on Character Structure in the Orient: The Japanese," in Bernard S. Silberman (Editor), *Japanese Character and Culture,* Tucson: The University of Arizona Press, 1962, pp. 325–359, esp. pp. 349–351.

113. See Thomas S. Szasz, *The Myth of Mental Illness: Foundations of a Theory of Personal Conduct,* New York: Dell-Delta, 1967, pp. 100, 110, 129–130, 139–143, 248–258.

114. Ezra Vogel, "The Go-Between . . . ," *op. cit.*

115. Georg Simmel, "The Stranger," in *The Sociology of Georg Simmel, op. cit.,* pp. 402–408.

116. See Franz Alexander, "The Psychosomatic Approach in Medical Therapy," *The Scope of Psychoanalysis: Selected Papers of Franz Alexander, 1921–1961,* New York: Basic Books, 1961, pp. 345–358.

117. George de Vos, "A Comparison of the Personality Differences in Two Generations of Japanese Americans By Means of the Rorschach Test," *The Nagoya Journal of Medical Science,* 17 (August, 1954), pp. 153–261. Recent medical evidence lends support to my observations. British psychiatrist Dr. H. H. Wolff reports that psychosomatic illness may be a substitute for "healthy" discharge of aggressive impulses, impulses that arise from fear of loving or being rejected. *San Francisco Chronicle,* November 25, 1968, p. 7.

118. See five articles by Emory S. Bogardus: "Current Problems of Japanese Americans," *Sociology and Social Research,* 25 (July, 1941), pp. 562–571; "Culture Conflicts in Relocation Centers," *Ibid.,* 27 (May, 1943), pp. 381–390; "Relocation Centers as Planned Communities," *Ibid.,* 28 (January, 1944), pp. 218–234; "Resettlement Problems of Japanese Americans," *Ibid.,* 29 (June, 1945), pp. 218–226; "The Japanese Return to the West Coast," *Ibid.,* 31 (January, 1947), pp. 226–233. See also Leonard Bloom, "Familial Adjustments of Japanese-Americans to Relocation: First Phase," *American Sociological Review* 8 (October, 1943), pp. 551–560; Bloom, "Transitional Adjustments of Japanese-American Families to Relocation," *American Sociological Review,* 12 (April, 1947), pp. 201–209; Robert W. O'Brien, "Selective Dispersion as a Factor in the Solution of the Nisei Problem," *Social Forces,* 23 (December, 1944), pp. 140–147; Richard A. Niver, "Americanizing the Issei," *Free World,* 11 (March, 1946), pp. 31–34; John H. Provinse and Solon T. Kimball, "Building New Communities During War Time," *American Sociological Review,* 11 (August, 1946), pp. 396–410; Bernard L. Hormann, "Postwar Problems of Issei in Hawaii," *Far Eastern Survey,* 15 (September 11, 1946), pp. 277–280; John H. Burma, *op. cit.,* pp. 157–163.

119. For this concept, see Alfred Schutz, "Some Structures of the Life-World," *Collected Papers III: Studies in Phenomenological Philosophy,* The Hague: Martinus Nijhoff, 1966, pp. 116–132 (Edited by I. Schutz).

120. Studies of *Issei* with teen-age children in the 1950s suggest that these *Issei* were relaxing their standards and grudgingly accepting the fact of their children's "Americanization." See

Dennie L. Brigges, "Social Adaptations Among Japanese American Youth: A Comparative Study," *Sociology and Social Research,* 38 (May–June, 1954), pp. 293–300; Melvin S. Brooks and Ken Kunihiro, "Education in Assimilation of Japanese: A Study in the Houston Area of Texas," *Sociology and Social Research,* 37 (September, 1952), pp. 16–22; Mamoru Iga, "The Japanese Social Structure . . . ," *op. cit.,* p. 278.

121. See T. Scott Miyakawa, "The Los Angeles Sansei," *Kashu Mainichi,* Holiday Supplement, Christmas Edition, December 20, 1962, Part 2, pp. 1, 4.

122. For the "Hansen Effect," see Marcus Lee Hansen, "The Third Generation in America," *Commentary,* 14 (November, 1952), pp. 492–500; Eugene I. Bender and George Kagiwada, "Hansen's Law of 'Third-Generation Return' and the Study of American Religio-Ethnic Groups," Paper presented at the annual meeting of the Pacific Sociological Association, Vancouver, B.C., Canada, April, 1966. For its application to Japanese Americans, see George Kagiwada, "The Third Generation Hypothesis: Structural Assimilation Among Japanese-Americans," Paper presented at the annual meeting of the Pacific Sociological Association, San Francisco, March, 1968.

123. See Harry H. L. Kitano, "Is There Sansei Delinquency?" *Kashu Mainichi, op. cit.,* p. 1.

124. See "A Sansei's Opinion," *Kashu Mainichi, op. cit.,* p. 2; Ken Yoshida, "Contra Costa Youth Trade Views with Nisei Parents," *Pacific Citizen,* 64 (March 3, 1967), p. 4; Donald Kazama, "On Focus: The Sansei and Nisei," *Pacific Citizen,* 64 (May 26, 1967), p. 4.

125. Recently World War II *Nisei* air ace Ben Kuroki observed that "We're losing our Japanese heritage through intermarriage." His public "blast" at intermarriage [*Pacific Citizen,* 64 (February 17, 1967), p. 1] was criticized in letters to the editor [*Ibid.,* 64 (April 14, 1967), p. 6] and by a young columnist: Ken Kuroiwa, "Mampitsu: Interracial Dating," [*Ibid.,* 64 (March 24, 1967), p. 5.

126. "Sansei in California divided on Integration, FEPC Told," *Pacific Citizen,* 64 (May 19, 1967), p. 1; Jeffrey Matsui, "Sounding Board: Anonymously Integrated," *Ibid.,* p. 4; Bill Strobel, "Japanese Heritage in the United States," *Oakland Tribune,* March, 1966. Reprinted in *Pacific Citizen,* 62 (April 1, 1966), pp. 1, 3, 4. See also Daisuke Kitagawa, "Assimilation or Pluralism?" in Arnold M. Rose and Caroline B. Rose (Editors), *Minority Problems,* New York: 1965, pp. 285–287.

127. Isao Horinouchi, *Educational Values and Preadaptation in the Acculturation of Japanese American,* Sacramento Anthropological Society Paper Number 7, Fall, 1967.

128. Jitsuichi Masuoka, "Race Relations and Nisei Problems," *Sociology and Social Research, 30* (July, 1946), p. 459.

Red Guard on Grant Avenue: The Rise of Youthful Rebellion in Chinatown

ON MAY 7, 1969 visitors to San Francisco's historic Portsmouth Square were startled to see the flag of the Peoples' Republic of China flying over the plaza. The occasion was supposed to be a rally to commemorate the fiftieth anniversary of the May 4th Movement in Peking, an event during which Chinese students demonstrated and protested against ignominious foreign treaties and criticized China's traditional institutions and moribund philosophy. In San Francisco a half century later, however, a group of disaffected Chinatown youth took over the rally from its original sponsors to protest against the community's poverty and neglect and to criticize its anachronistic and conservative power elite. Calling themselves the "Red Guards," these youths listed eleven demands, asserted their right to armed self-defense against the city police and called for the release of all Asians in city, state and federal prisons on the ground that they had had unfair trials. On a more immediate and practical level, the Red Guards announced plans for a remarkably unradical petition campaign to prevent the Chinese Playground from being converted into a garage and for a breakfast program to aid needy children in the Chinatown ghetto. A spokesman for the Red Guards stated, "The Black Panthers is the most revolutionary group in the country and we are patterned after them."

To most San Franciscans the rise of youthful rebellion in the Chinese quarter of the city must have come as a surprise. For the past three decades Chinese-Americans have been stereotypically portrayed in the mass media as quiet, docile and filial, a people who are as unlikely to partake of radicalism as they are to permit delinquency among their juveniles. In the last few years, however, there has been mounting evidence to suggest a discrepancy between that favorable, if somewhat saccharine imagery, and reality. Not only is there an unmistakable increase in delinquent activity among Chinese young people, there is also a growing restlessness among them. Chinatown's young people are experiencing a gnawing sense of frustration over the recalcitrance of local institutions, the powerlessness of youth and their own bleak outlook for the future. The politics as well as the "crimes" of Chinatown are coming to resemble those of the larger society with alienation, race consciousness and restive rebelliousness animating a new generation's social and organizational energies.

The Demographic Equation

A basic cause for the emergence of youthful rebellion among the Chinese is the increase in the youth population itself. In an absolute sense there are simply more Chinese young people in the ghetto now than there ever have been before. Two sources for the increase are discernible: an increasing birth rate among the indigenous population and a sudden rise in immigration from Hong Kong and other Asian centers of Chinese population.

Except for a few sailors, merchants, actors and itinerants, Chinese immigration to the United States did not get underway until 1850. Then, occasioned by the twin developments of disaster in China and opportunity in California, a steady movement of Chinese across the Pacific populated first San Francisco, then California and later the urban areas to the east with Chinese laborers and merchants. The great majority of these were young men eager to try their luck in the "Gold Mountain" and then return, wealthy and esteemed, to wives, sweethearts and kinsmen in their home villages. During the entire period of unrestricted immigration (1850–1882) a total of only 8,848 Chinese women journeyed across the Pacific to San Francisco. Many of the women could not withstand the rigors of life in America and died or returned to China. By 1890 only 3,868 Chinese women were reported to be in the country. During the same period the number of Chinese men emigrating from China to America was much larger. The census reported 33,149 male Chinese in 1860; 58,633 in 1870; 100,686 in 1880; 102,620 in 1890; 85,341 in 1900. The sex ratio; that is, the number of males for every 100 females, reached alarming proportions among the Chinese in America in this period. In 1860 it was 1,858; 1870, 1,284; 1880, 2,106; and in 1890 it reached its highest point, 2,678. In other words, before the turn of the century there were about twenty-seven men for every woman among the Chinese in America.

The settlement abroad by Chinese men unaccompanied by wives was not confined to the United States. Chinese communities in the Straits Settlements, New Zealand, Thailand, Hawaii, Peru and Trinidad were also conspicuous for their superfluity of males. A basic reason for this was the Chinese custom and family law which required that a wife remain in the home of her husband's parents even if her husband sought work elsewhere. Should his parents die during his absence, the wife was expected to perform the appropriate burial and mourning rites in place of her husband.

Villages in Southeastern China were for the most part communities of lineage groups tracing their origins from a common male ancestor. Loyalty to the lineage was expected and encouraged. Often enough village headmen secured an additional insurance of that loyalty by requiring all departing males to marry before they left. Then, it was assumed, these emigrating husbands would be sure to return to their wives in the village and, furthermore, would send remittances to their patiently waiting families throughout the duration of their sojourn abroad. Absences often proved to be far longer than the spouses had anticipated. Not infrequently several decades passed before a husband returned to his wife. Some men became birds-of-passage, returning just so long as it took to sire a child, hopefully a son, and then going back to the immigrant communities abroad. Later the son sometimes followed in his father's footsteps and joined the lonely and homeless men that constituted the Chinese diaspora.

The Chinese custom of leaving the wife behind had begun to erode by the late nineteenth century. However, a new American immigration law brought about a similar result and left Chinese men to work and wait for the great promise of wealth in America—alone. In 1882, under pressure of an anti-Chinese movement that had reached national proportions, Congress passed a law prohibiting Chinese laborers from coming to America for ten years. That prohibition, together with numerous and even more restrictive amendments, was renewed decennially until it became a permanent feature of the law in 1904. It was re-enacted in the Immigration Act of 1924. In effect, Chinese immigrants, except for the few who fell under the exempt classes of merchants, students, itinerants and religious leaders, could not enter the United States legally until the exclusion law was repealed in 1943 and a quota system was substituted in its stead.

In 1884 a United States Federal Court ruled that the Immigration Act of 1882 properly excluded not only a Chinese laborer but his wife as well, so that under the law no Chinese women, except the wives of those in the exempt classes and later the Chinese wives of certain American citizens, could enter the country. Since, according to subsequent judicial rulings and revisions in the Naturalization Act, Chinese immigrants were declared to be aliens ineligible to citizenship in the United States, a status they held until 1943, the lonely Chinese male was rendered helpless in effecting the entry of his wife by legal means.

Chinese men who remained abroad were left to form a homeless men's community within the confines of the Chinatown ghetto. Condemned to a life without intimate family relationships, they joined together in clan associations, *Landsmannschaften,* and secret societies that provided them with a sense of familiarity and solidarity. They participated in Chinese versions of the kinds of recreation that typically arise among men without immediate ties of home and family—gambling, opium smoking and prostitution. And, just as typically, in a society known for its hostile racial stereotypy, the Chinese came to be identified with these vices and in the minds of many white Americans were regarded as lowly, immoral and dangerous.

One important effect of the low number of females in the Chinese communities in the United States was the near inability to produce a second generation of American-born Chinese. In 1890, forty years after Chinese had begun to migrate, the American-born constituted only 2.7 percent of the Chinese population in America. In 1920 this had risen to only 30 percent, and it was not until 1950 that American-born Chinese numbered more than one-half of the total Chinese population in the United States. In 1960, 93,288 Chinese, or more than 35 percent of the total Chinese population in the United States was still foreign-born.

American naturalization laws allowed only those Chinese born on American soil to become citizens of the United States. Thus, inability to procreate in the United States acted as a powerful deterrent to the creation of any sizeable body of Chinese-American citizenry who, had they existed, might have been able to stem the tide of anti-Chinese legislation and discrimination, remove the burdens of non-acculturation which afflicted the immigrants and partake more fully and completely of those benefits that are automatically bestowed on citizens of the United States.

The current increase in the number of Chinese youth in San Francisco's Chinatown is in part a product of the balancing of the sex ratio and the formation of families among America's Chinese in the last three decades. Table 1 below shows the sex ratios for those 10-year periods.

TABLE I

RATIO OF CHINESE MEN TO WOMEN, 1930–1960

Years	Chinese Females in U.S.	Chinese Males in U.S.	Sex Ratio Males per 100 Females
1930	15,512	59,802	394.7
1940	20,115	57,389	285.3
1950	40,621	77,008	189.6
1960	101,743	135,549	133.1

The increase in the number of females by 1950 was made possible by relaxation of restrictive immigration measures against the Chinese. The figures again jumped by 1960, bringing the ratio of males to females to only 133.1. In the San Francisco-Oakland metropolitan area the sex ratio was slightly lower at 128.0. A sufficient balance had been achieved by 1960, however, so that one could predict with fairly good reliability that most Chinese men and women would indeed be able to marry, settle down and rear families in the United States.

The increase in the young among America's Chinese was noticeable even before 1960. Between 1920 and 1940, in part as a result of the illegal immigration of Chinese females to the United States, a small American-born population had been produced. The quota system that was substituted for absolute exclusion in 1943 and a few additional laws in the next fifteen years resulted in the admission of many more Chinese women. In the six years after 1956 the number of births among America's Chinese was significantly higher than during the half-dozen previous years. From 1950 until 1955 there was a total of 28,058 births of which 14,542 were boys and 13,516 girls. But from 1956 to 1961 there was a total of 31,106 births, including 15,694 boys and 15,212 girls. And during the next three years, 19,964 Chinese were born in the United States, comprising 10,686 boys and 8,018 girls. In San Francisco the total number of Chinese births between 1941 and 1947 was 2,383. However, in the next decade the number of Chinese births in San Francisco rose to a total of 9,673.

Enrollments of Chinese in San Francisco's elementary schools numbered 4,995 in 1958; seven years later they had risen to 5,789 of whom 3,174 or nearly 55 percent were attending six schools in or near Chinatown. In 1968 San Francisco's Chinese student population numbered 3,351 in high schools; 2,905 in junior high; and 2,645 in elementary schools. Another 1,120 were distributed in various special, vocational, private, continuation and nursery schools, while 6,863 attended public and private colleges. Of San Francisco's total Chinese population in 1968, believed to be 47,700, no less than 23,984, or about fifty percent, were estimated to be under twenty-one years of age.

A second source for the increase in youthful Chinese is the relaxation of immigration restrictions. After World War II a number of special laws effected the entry of brides, refugees, displaced persons and scientific or technically trained personnel of Chinese ancestry. Between 1956 and 1961 the number of Chinese children entering the United States increased slightly. If we look at the age group of males 5 to 14 in that period; i.e., those who would be 18 to 27 in 1969, the following figures are revealing: 1956, 380; 1957, 362; 1958, 164; 1959, 589; 1960, 289; 1961, 332 for a total during those six years of 2,126. The number of females in that age group admitted for that period totalled 1,772. In 1965 President Johnson signed into law a new immigration act, to become fully effective in July, 1968, which repealed the entire system of quotas based on national origins and substituted in its

place an entry procedure based on skills, and a means for the reuniting of families.

Fears that San Francisco would be "swamped" with Chinese proved unfounded, but the increase since July, 1968, suggested to District Immigration Director C.W. Fullilove that the number entering San Francisco with the intention of remaining there would be approximately 1,200 per year. Although official statistics show that 4,496 Chinese between the ages of ten and nineteen entered the United States in 1967–1968, Fullilove has pointed out that the "problem ages" for Chinese youth are between 16 and 19 and that this comprises about 40% of the total group. Moreover, since about half of those officially listed as arriving immigrants were already residents of the United States who earned the statistical status of "arriving" because of an "adjustment" of their status, Fullilove concludes that the "problem youth;" i.e., newly arrived immigrant youth, number less than 20% of that age group, or about 900 adolescents. Although not all of these remain in San Francisco, a significant portion do become a part of the burgeoning Chinatown population.

Sheer numbers alone do not, of course, account for the rise of rebelliousness among young Chinese in San Francisco. A more significant factor is that conditions of life in Chinatown are by no means pleasant, productive or promising. We must distinguish, however, from among the Chinese those who have escaped the ghetto, those who are American-born but still inhabit Chinatown, and the foreign-born youth who reluctantly find themselves imprisoned within a ghetto not of their own making. Of the first group there are the scholars, scientists, intellectuals and professionals—many of whom hail from regions other than Southeastern China, the original home of the bulk of America's Chinese immigrants—who have found work and residence within the larger society, in university, corporation, professional or government communities. These Chinese do not for the most part feel themselves to be a part of Chinatown and journey there only occasionally for a banquet or for a brief sense of their ethnic origins.

A second and much larger group, although actually quite small in relation to the total number, consists of those American-born Chinese who have successfully completed high school and college and gone on to enter the professions, most frequently pharmacy and engineering. They have joined the American middle class and, when they can evade or circumvent the still prevalent discrimination in housing, the finer neighborhoods or the suburbs. This "gold bourgeoisie"—to paraphrase E. Franklin Frazier whose concept of and eloquence on the black bourgeoisie has so richly informed sociology about middle class life amongst Negroes in America—is also estranged from Chinatown. Proud of his own achievements, wary of any attempt to thrust him back into a confining ghetto existence, and alternately angered, embarrassed or shamed by the presence of alienated, hostile and rebellious youth in Chinatown, the middle class American Chinese holds tenaciously to his newly achieved material and social success.

Middle class native-born Chinese are discovering, however, that the American dream is not an unmixed blessing. On the one hand, the "golden mountain" of American bourgeois promise seems somehow less glittering now that its actual pinnacle has been reached. Chinese, like other descendants of immigrants in America, are discovering that the gold is alloyed more heavily than they had supposed with brass, but, like their second and third generation colleagues among the Jews and Japanese, they are not quite sure what to do about it. The price of success has been great, not the least payments being the abandonment of language, culture and much of their ethnic identity.

For some in this class there is a new search for cultural roots in Chinese history, a strong desire to recover the ancient arts and a renewed interest in speaking Chinese—at least at home. Others emphasize, perhaps with too much protestation, their happiness within the American middle class—they engage in a conspicuous consumption of leisure to prove it. Finally, a few recognize their Chinatown roots and return there with a desire to somehow aid in the advancement of the Chinese ghetto-dwellers. Sometimes their proferred assistance is rejected with epithets and insults, and they begin to wonder about their own motives and also to re-evaluate their abilities to help.

It is this presence of a growing number of restive Chinatowners that constitutes another challenge to the comfort of bouregois existence among the Chinese. In its most primordial sense, the visible contrast between the style of life of the impoverished ghetto dweller and that of the middle class professional promotes a gnawing sense of guilt and shame in the latter. Somehow it seems wrong that one's ethnic compatriots should suffer while one enjoys the benefits of success. Yet, in estimating the sources of their own success, middle class Chinese are quite ready to attribute it to their own diligence, their proverbial habits of thrift and hard work and to their conscious avoidance of delinquent or other kinds of unruly behavior. In the face of this analysis some middle class Chinese charge the angry Chinatown youth with indolence, impropriety and impiety. They sometimes urge the youths to cultivate the old virtues as a sure cure for their personal and social ailments. Yet, some perceive that there is more to these problems than can be solved by the careful nurturance of Confucian or Protestant ethics. The issues of poverty, cultural deprivation and discrimination are seen as more obdurate barriers to the advancement of these ghetto dwellers of today than they were to the more Americanized and less alienated Chinese of the fifties. Moreover, there is an ever deeper and more profound problem. In line with the orientations of other alienated youthful minorities, the youth of Chinatown appear to have adopted a perspective which rejects just that dream which inspired and activated the now bourgeois Chinese. For the middle class Chinese, then, the peak of the "gold mountain" seems to have been just reached when those still below shouted up that the arduous climb wasn't worth the effort.

Among Chinatown's rebellious groups there are two distinguishable types; those who are American-born but have dropped out of school and form part of the under- or unemployed proletariat of the Chinese community; and those recently arrived immigrant youths who, speaking little or no English and having little to offer in the way of salable skills, find themselves unable to enter the city's occupational and social mainstream. Both native- and foreign-born Chinese are included among the ranks of the quasi-criminal and quasi-political gangs that are accused of contributing to the mounting incidence of delinquency in the Chinese quarter. Culture, language and background have divided the native- from the foreign-born Chinese in the past, and it is only recently that there is any sign of a common recognition between the two. (In the 1950s native- and foreign-born Chinese on the University of California campus at Berkeley formed two clubs, the Chinese Students' Club for the American-born and the Chinese Students' Association for the foreign-born. In addition, there was a Chinese-American social fraternity, Pi Alpha Phi, which drew its membership primarily from American-born Chinese.)

It is traditional to focus on Chinatown gangs as an unfortunate form of juvenile delinquency among a people otherwise noted for their social quiescence and honesty. A more fruitful approach, however, would adopt the perspective taken by E.J. Hobsbawm in his discussion of social bandits and primitive rebels. According to Hobsbawm, who has studied these phenomena in Europe, social banditry is a form of pre-ideological rebellion which arises among essentially agrestic, unskilled and unlettered peoples who are at great cultural distance from the official and oppressive power structure. It is led by those who enjoy a certain amount of local notoriety or awe.

Often enough social banditry remains at a stage of petty criminality evoking only the attention of police to what appears to be local acts of homicide, assault, larceny and property damage. A more refined stage includes the formation of predatory gangs that confine their criminal activities to attacks on strangers and officials, and the sharing of any loot obtained thereby with local community members who, though not a party to the depredations, identify with and protect the robbers. Further, bandit gangs may adopt a populist or conservative style: the former represented by a "Robin Hood" ideology of robbing the rich to feed the poor and an attack on civic or state officialdom who are regarded as intruders in the community's traditional way of life; the latter indicated by the cooptation of bandit gangs as the toughs and thugs defending local satrapies and powerful petty interests.

Social banditry may exist side by side with ideological rebellious or revolutionary elements, but it is usually untouched by them except for particular reasons of strategy or tactics. Essentially, social banditry is separated from ideological politics by its deep involvement with local ethnic, rather than cosmopolitan, class interests. It is not, however, impossible for class and ethnic interests to merge, and for the liberation of local groups to become enmeshed within the revolutionary aims of a radically politicized sector of a modern party state.

Looked at under the perspective of "primitive rebellion," Chinatown's gangs take on a greater significance for the understanding of loosely structured pluralistic societies like the United States. Gangs in Chinatown are by no means a new phenomenon but their activities in the past describe mainly the early stages of social banditry. For the most part Chinatown's traditional social banditry has been of a particularly conservative type, identified with the recruitment of young toughs, thugs and bullies into the small criminal arm of Chinatown's secret societies. In this capacity these young men formed the "flying squads" of paid and contracted mercenaries who "protected" brothels, guarded gambling establishments and enforced secret society monopolies over other vice institutions of Chinatown. From their number came assassins and strong-arm men who fought in the so-called "tong wars" that characterized Chinatown's internecine struggles of a half-century ago and which still occasionally threaten to erupt today. Social banditry was an exclusive and private affair of Chinatown. Insofar as Chinatown's violent altercations were circumscribed not only by the invisible wall which separated the ghetto from the metropolis but also by the limited interests of the contending parties for women, wealth and power, the community was isolated by its internal conflicts and, whether manifested in fearful acquiescence or active participation, bound together in a deadly kind of "antagonistic cooperation."

Since 1943 a progressive cycle of rebellion among

Chinatown's youth has metamorphosed from crime to politics, from individual acts of aggression to collective acts of rebellion, and from non-ideological modes of hostility to the beginnings of a movement of ideological proportions. From 1943 until 1949 juvenile crime in Chinatown was largely the activity of a small number of native-born boys about fifteen years of age who experienced some sense of deprivation through unemployment, difficulties in home life or inadequate income. The crimes were typical of the most individualized and inarticulate forms of primitive rebellion. Burglary, auto theft, robberies, larcenies, hold-ups and assault and battery constituted 103 of the 184 offenses for which Chinese male juveniles were referred to San Francisco's juvenile court in those years. There were also gangs of native-born youth, apparently sponsored by or under the protection of secret societies who occasionally assaulted and robbed strangers in Chinatown, not a few of whom, incidently, were Japanese-Americans recently returned from war-time internment camps and also organized into clubs, cliques and gangs.

Petty criminal gangs emerged more frequently among both the native- and foreign-born youth in Chinatown from 1958 to 1964. In some cases these gangs were composed of young men sponsored in their criminal activities by secret societies. Such an instance was found in the "cat" burglary ring broken up by police in 1958 and discovered to be a branch of the Hop Sing Tong. Three years later two gangs—the "Lums" and the "Rabble Rousers," the first composed of boys aged 14 through 17, the second of those aged 17 to 22—were reported to be engaged in auto thefts, extortion, street fights and petty larcenies. In January, 1964, members of a San Francisco Chinatown gang were charged with the $10,000 burglary of a fish market in suburban Mountain View. A year later, the police broke up the "Bugs," a youthful criminal gang dressing entirely in black, with bouffant hair style and raised-heel boots, who over a period of six months committed 48 burglaries and made off with $7,500 in cash and $3,000 in merchandise. The "Bugs" who capitalized on an otherwise stigmatizing aspect of their existence—their short stature—re-emerged a year

later despite an attempt by Chinatown's leaders to quell juvenile gangs by bringing in streetworkers from San Francisco's Youth for Service, a program begun a half-dozen years earlier to channel delinquents toward constructive activities. By the mid-1960s Chinatown's burglary gangs had begun to branch out and were "working" areas of the city outside the Chinese quarter.

The present stage of a more politicized rebellion may be dated from the emergence in May, 1967, of Leway, Incorporated. In its history to date (August, 1969) the Leways experienced almost precisely the pattern of problems and responses that typically gives rise first to non-ideological rebellion and, under certain conditions, to the development of revolutionary ideology. Leway, standing for "legitimate ways" began as a public-spirited self-help group among American-born Chinese teenagers. Aged 17 to 22, these young men organized to unite Chinatown's youth, to combat juvenile delinquency and to improve conditions in the poverty-stricken Chinese ghetto through helping youths to help themselves. In its first months it gained the support of Chinatown luminaries such as Lim P. Lee, now San Francisco's postmaster and a former probation officer, and other prominent citizens. Through raffles, loans and gifts, these youths, many of whom constituted the delinquent members of Chinatown's youngsters, raised $2,000 to rent, temporarily, a pool hall near the Chinatown-Filipino border area and, with the help of the Chinese YMCA and Youth for Service, to outfit it with five pool tables, seven pinball machines, some chairs and a television set. "This is a hangout for hoods," said its president, Denny Lai, to reporter Ken Wong. "Most of us cats are misfits, outcasts with a rap sheet. What we're trying to do is to keep the hoods off the streets, give them something to do instead of raising hell."

Leway was a local autochthonous group seeking to employ its own methods and style to solve its own members' problems; it was precisely this that caused its downfall. Police refused to believe in the efficaciousness of methods that eschewed official surveillance, sporadic shakedowns and the not always occasional beating of a youth "resisting arrest." Leway tried a dialogue with the police, but it broke down over the rights of the latter to enter, search and seize members at Leway's headquarters, a tiny piece of "territory" which the young Chinese had hoped to preserve from alien and hostile intrusion. Leway claimed it wanted to be left alone by this official arm of a society which they saw as already hostile and generally ill-disposed toward them. "We are not trying to bother them (the police) . . . and we won't go out of our way to work with them either."

In addition to continuing problems of police harassment, Leway failed to establish itself as a legitimate association in Chinatown. The Chinese Chamber of Commerce refused it official recognition and, as a result, Leway could not gain access to the local Economic Opportunity Council to obtain much-needed jobs for Chinatown youth. The Tsung Tsin Association which owned the building in which Leway had established its headquarters threatened to raise the rent or lease the premises to another renter. Finally, whether rightly or not, the members of Leway, together with other Chinatown youth groups, were blamed for the increasing violence in Chinatown. Throughout 1968–69 reports of violent assaults on tourists and rival gangs during festivals emanated from Chinatown. Police increased their intrusive surveillance and other heavy-handed tactics. Chinese youth charged them with brutality, but the police replied that they were only carrying out proper procedures in the line of a now more hazardous duty.

In late summer, 1969, the combination of police harassment, rent hikes, its failure to secure jobs for its chronically unemployed members and its general inability to establish itself as a legitimate way of getting Chinatown youth "straightened out" took its final toll. Leway House closed its doors. Smashed were its dreams of establishing on-the-job training for the unskilled, new business ventures for the unemployed, a pleasant soda fountain for Leway adolescents and an education and recreation program for Chinatown teenagers. The bitterness of its defeat stung deep in the hearts of Chinatown young people. "Leway stood for legitimate ways," a fifteen year old youth told reporter Bill Moore. "Helluva lot of good it did them." The closing of Leway did

away with many Chinatown young people's faith in the official culture and its public representatives.

The stage was set for the next phase in the development of rebellion. Out of the shambles of Leway came the Red Guards. It is composed of the so-called "radical" elements of the former Leway. But now Leway's erstwhile search for legitimacy is turned on its head. The Red Guards flout the little red book *Quotations from Chairman Mao Tse-Tung* as their credo, make non-negotiable demands on the power structure of Chinatown and the metropolis and openly espouse a program of disruption, rebellion and occasionally, it seems, revolution.

Leway had been modelled after other San Francisco youthful gang reform groups, but the Red Guards have adopted the organizational form, linguistic style and political mood of the Black Panthers. Cooperation between Chinese and black youth has not been frequent in the past. In the 1960's there were frequent bloody clashes between youthful gangs of Chinese and Negroes; interracial incidents at Samuel Gompers School—a kind of incarceration unit for black and Oriental incorrigibles—had not encouraged friendly relations among the two groups. Nevertheless, it was just these contacts, combined with a growing awareness of Panther tactics and successes and some not-too-secret proselytization by Panther leaders among the disaffected Leway members, that effected an adoption of the black militant style. Whatever prejudices Chinese might harbor against Negroes, Black Panther rhetoric seemed to describe perfectly not only the black but also their own situation. After all, Leway had tried to be good, to play the game according to the white man's rules, and all it had gotten for its pains was a heap of abuse and a few cracked skulls. Now it was time to be realistic, "to stop jiving" and "to tell it like it is." The Panthers provided a language that not only depicted but also evaluated the situation properly. Police were "pigs," white men were "honkies," officially developed reform programs were attempts to "shine on" credulous Chinese youth, and the goal to be attained was not integration or material success, but power. "We're an organization made up mainly of street people and we're tired of asking the government for reforms," said Alex Hing, a 23-year-old Chinese who is the Minister of Information of the Red Guards. "We're going to attain power, so we don't have to beg any more."

The Red Guards are a populist group among Chinatown's "primitive" rebels. They stand against two power structures in their opposition to oppression and poverty, that of old Chinatown and that of the larger metropolis. Ideologically they are located somewhere between the inarticulate rumblings of rustic rebels and the full-scale ideology of unregenerate revolutionaries. They cry out for vengeance against the vague but powerful complex of Chinese and white elites that oppress them. They dream of a world in which they will have sufficient power to curb their exploiters' excesses; meanwhile, they operate as best they can to right local wrongs and to ingratiate themselves with the mass of their Chinatown compatriots. The free breakfast program for indigent youngsters, a copy of a similar program utilized by the Black Panthers, provides a ready means of obtaining popular support among Chinatown's poor at the same time that it shames Chinatown's elites for allowing the community's children to go hungry.

The demand for the release of all imprisoned Asians seems to place the Red Guards squarely on the side of all those "little people" of Chinatown who feel themselves victimized by an alien and oppressive police system. However, their ethnic consciousness usually supersedes and sometimes clashes with their alleged attachment to a class oriented ideology, as it did when the Red Guards accepted the invitation to guard a meeting of the Chinese Garment Contractors' Association against a threatened assault by Teamsters' Union men who sought to organize Chinatown's heavily exploited dressmakers. But it is precisely their parochial dedication to a sense of Chinese ethnicity—which eludes exact definition but encloses individual identity in psychic security against the *angst* of alienation—that limits their political effectiveness at the same time that it endears them to the less hardy of young Chinatowners who secretly share their dilemmas and dreams.

Below this level of semi-articulated ideology are the still existent gangs and social cliques that, although angry and alienated, have not yet thrown in their lot with the Red Guards. Three gangs, the Baby Hwa Ching, the Raiders and the Junior Raiders, attempt to maintain some sense of autonomy despite the fact that they did congregate at Leway's pool hall and youth center. Two other gangs, the Brothers Ten and the Country Club Boys, represent particular school or residential areas, respectively. The Project 895s and the 880s congregate at the addresses represented by their number names. The Drifters, a group of about 20 young men, seem to find their own special outlet in motorcycles. In all these cases there are represented the elementary stages of rebellion, stages that may never progress beyond the limited activities described by social cliquishness, youthful exhuberance and petty criminality. But, it could also happen that some or all of these groups will be absorbed into the new ethnic, radical and populist forms of rebellion that today characterize the Red Guards.

Populist rebellion is not the only form of social politics in Chinatown. In the evolution of the Hwa Ching and the Junior Hwa Ching is illustrated a conservative type of rebelliousness. Hwa Ching emerged in 1967 as a loose association made up mostly of Hong Kong-born youth in Chinatown. Estimates of its size vary from 25 to 300; this fact alone testifies to its low degree of cohesiveness and the sense of drift that characterizes its members. Until very recently Hwa Ching was represented in most public discussions by a "spokesman" (its looseness of organization prevented any greater clarification of title), George Woo, a former photographer who took on the task of bridging the communication gap between the largely Chinese-speaking youths and the officials of the metropolis. What the aims of the association were are difficult to ascertain exactly, partly because common agreement among its members was not great and because spokesman Woo usually tended to a polemical and scare-producing speaking style in order to call attention to Chinatown's immigrant problems. Like many multi-problem groups, Hwa Ching had less of a perfected program than a set of practical problems, less of a coherent perspective than a prevalent condition. Hong Kong youth were insufficiently educated and skilled to obtain jobs outside of Chinatown's dreary positions of waiter, bus boy and sweated laborer, unequipped linguistically to enter the metropolis and, in the beginning, unwilling to accept confinement in a congested, poverty-stricken and despotically ruled ghetto.

Hwa Ching seemed to form itself around El Piccolo, an expresso coffee house opened in Chinatown in 1967 and operated by Dick and Alice Barkley. Alice Barkley, herself a Hong Kong-born Chinese, turned the coffee house into a haven for foreign-born Chinese youth. There they could meet in peace and with the freedom to discuss, argue, complain and occasionally plan some joint activity. Reaction to the clubby fraternization that existed at El Piccolo was mixed. Traditional Chinatowners accused the Barkleys of offering asylum to raffish criminal elements; a newly aroused college and university group of Chinese-Americans praised the establishment of such a place for impoverished immigrants to congregate; most San Franciscans didn't even know the Hwa Ching existed.

Early in 1968 Hwa Ching approached the Human Relations Commission, the Economic Development Council and the Chinese Six Companies to ask for their aid in establishing an educational program for alleviating the misery of Chinatown's immigrant youth. Their approach was frank and practical; it indicated both the growing frustrations and the general problems of these youth, frustrations and problems arising out of a vicious circle of poverty, illiteracy in English, and crime—from all of which they wished somehow to extricate themselves. At the January, 1968, meeting of the Human Relations Commission a spokesman presented their case in Cantonese:

> "The crime rate in Chinatown is increasing. We are partly responsible. We seek a chance to change and be a productive member of the community.
> Frustration is our lot. Housing, job opportunities, recreation facilities in Chinatown are poor. We live in an age of technical advance that requires skill and training to survive.
> We are under the same pressure as other youths. In addition we are subjected to some that are unique because we are foreign born.

> We are frustrated in our pursuit of an education because they do not know how to reach us. As long as we are under-educated and under-trained we will remain under-employed.
> The burgeoning crime rate is largely the result of these problems.

In order to remedy the situation, Hwa Ching proposed the establishment of a comprehensive two year educational program to provide Chinatown's young immigrants with a high school diploma and vocational training in auto repair, business machine operation, construction, sheet metal, electrical installation and plumbing. They closed with a statement that was unfortunately taken as a warning and a threat. "We've been hearing too many promises. The rise and fall of our hopes is tragic and ominous."

The Hwa Ching, unsuccessful in their first bid, spoke to the Chinatown Advisory Board of the Human Relations Commission in late February. Represented this time by the fiery George Woo, the Hwa Ching was more modest in its request for a comprehensive program but more militant in its presentation. Hwa Ching wanted $4,322 to build a club house. Although Woo reiterated the same arguments as other Hwa Chings had presented in January, the tone was different. Speaking of the youths whom he represented, Woo said, "There is a hard core of delinquents in Chinatown who came from China. Their problems are the problems of all poor with the addition that they don't speak English." Then he added, "They're talking about getting guns and rioting. . . . I'm not threatening riots. The situation already exists, but if people in Chinatown don't feel threatened they won't do anything about it."

The mention of guns and the warning of possible riots was too much for John Yehall Chin, former president of the Chinese Six Companies, principal of St. Mary's Chinese Language School and member of the Rights Commission's Chinatown Advisory Board. With respect to the Hwa Ching's request, he gave this advice to the Commission and, indirectly, to the youth. "They have not shown that they are sorry or that they will change their ways. They have threatened the community. If you give in to this group, you are only going to have another hundred immigrants come in and have a whole new series of threats and demands." Although the Commission expressed its interest, Hwa Ching's demand was rejected.

In March the Hwa Ching's President, Stan Wong, presented the immigrant youth's case before the Chinese Six Companies, the oligarchy that controls Chinatown. Speaking in Cantonese, Wong repudiated the threat of riots made at the February meeting. "We made no threats," he said. "They were made by non-members. We need to help ourselves. We look to the future and are mindful of the immigrant youths who will be coming here later. We hope they do not have to go through what we've been through." Later he answered a question about possible communist affiliation: "Hwa Ching is not involved with any political ideology." Although Commissioner Chin pointed out that the Hwa Ching had mended its ways, the Six Companies refused them help, while the Human Rights Commission, under the direction of Chin, organized an establishment-controlled Citizens for Youth in Chinatown. The Hwa Ching felt utterly rejected.

In their bitterness and anger, however, the Hwa Ching did not turn to populist revolt, as had the angry former Leways. Instead they fragmented even more. Their loose coalition at El Piccolo ended when that establishment closed its doors in August, 1968. The Hwa Ching had never in fact professed an ideology. What seemed like such was more a product of the fervid imaginations of alarmed whites and of the fiery invective of George Woo than it was any coherent line of political or revolutionary thought. The Hwa Ching had had a few minor successes outside of Chinatown. They received advice and help from the Mission Rebels, a youth group in San Francisco's Latin-Negro-Oriental area, and almost got their clubhouse built. Woo spoke wherever anyone would listen (he harangued my race and ethnic relations course at Sonoma State College, fifty miles north of San Francisco, and so impressed the mostly white students in the classroom that they spontaneously took up a collection during his talk and at the end of the hour presented him with an envelope filled with small change and a few bills.) A meat packer offered them an abandoned building, but

more than $5,000 in repairs would have been required to put it in habitable condition.

By the end of the year, Hwa Ching was suffering even more than it had in the beginning. All of its demands for help had been rejected or given only token support. The Chinese-American Democratic Club had helped a little, and Hwa Ching had developed some limited cooperation with Leway. But, like the latter group, it had neither established its legitimacy in Chinatown nor was it able to provide its own members with satisfaction. Its spokesman, George Woo, ineffective in his attempts to win substantial support for those for whom he orated so eloquently, if polemically, enrolled at San Francisco State College and became an active member of Inter-collegiate Chinese for Social Action (ICSA), a college-based education and community action group. In January, 1969, he addressed the "Yellow Identity" Conference at the University of California at Berkeley with a rousing call for the students to come away from their books and help in the rehabilitation and liberation of Chinatown.

Hwa Ching's interests could not be channeled into an ideological movement nor could its restive members be organized into a disciplined cadre of revolutionaries. Their practical needs were too immediate, their literacy in English too low, and their limited but practical political experience in Hong Kong and Chinatown was too great for them to accept an organization that used Mao's red book and which, hence, ran the risks of attracting political persecution and possible deportation. As Tom Tom, a 23 year old immigrant who had been one of the earliest members of Hwa Ching explained to a reporter, the immigrant youth were independent of the Leway and all other Chinatown groups, effected none of the hippie-Che-Raoul-Panther styles, and wanted little more than jobs, girls and to be left alone. The Hwa Ching found themselves oppressed by their supposed allies nearly as much as by their condition. Leway boys and other American-born Chinese called them "Chinabugs" and attacked them in gang rumbles; Negroes picked on the diminutive Chinese until they learned to retaliate in numbers and with stealth, strategy and tactics; college students sought to tutor and evangelize them with secular and sometimes political ideas, but succeeded mostly in making them feel inferior and ashamed and in frightening them with a kind of politics which they abhorred.

By the middle of 1969 the Hwa Ching had split into three factions. One portion of the short-lived coalition returned to the streets, to fight, burglarize and assault all those available symbols and representatives of the seemingly monolithic power structure that had scorned them; two other factions apparently accepted co-optation into Chinatown's two most powerful though age-ridden secret societies, the Suey Sing and Hop Sing Tongs. There their anger could find outlet at the same time that their strength could be utilized for traditional aims. The secret societies could pay for the immigrant youths' basic needs and with the same expenditure buy the muscle to keep control of their own interests and institutions. And since the Tongs were part of the complex congeries of associations that make up Chinatown's power elite, it is not surprising that leaders of this same elite gave tacit approval to the Tongs' recruitment of what had appeared in early 1968 to be a serious threat to the old order. Unlike the Leway, who could not join the old order and may have been too Americanized to accept secret society patronage, the immigrant youth find in it a perhaps temporary expedient in their dilemma. They are not a politicized body of young people. Thus, they can more readily join in the protection of old Chinatown. They have assumed a posture typical of Chinatown a half century ago. They form the conservative wing of Chinatown's complex structure of conflict and rebellion.

In other areas of primitive rebellion, conservative and populist factions often fought each other as much as their respectively professed enemies. In traditional nineteenth-century China, for example, the several secret societies that had existed for centuries in Kwangtung and Fukien Provinces fell out with one another over their respective support for wealthy landlords or rebellious peasants during the course of several popular uprisings and the catastrophic Tai Ping Revolution (1850–1864). Similarly in Chinatown, the young toughs who have

become paid guards of the secret society's meetings, are not infrequently arrayed against the Leway-Red Guard gangs and on occasion against the ICSA youth as well. In this sense young Chinatown recapitulates a structure of conflict that characterized that of its earlier generations. Conservative-populist conflicts isolate the contending parties from outside groups and larger issues. The violent fights and smouldering feuds appear to non-comprehending outsiders to be exclusively Chinese in their nature and content. And this intramural conflict in turn circumscribes Chinatown and once again cuts it off from the metropolis.

Connections to the larger society of San Francisco in particular and the United States in general do, however, exist. For the youth the most important one is the Intercollegiate Chinese for Social Action. This group was formed at San Francisco State College from among the more socially concerned and politically aware Chinese American students. For a while it managed the special program by which Chinese students from the ghetto were recruited to the college. This activity, however, had an unintended effect on the originally education-interested ICSA leaders. It forced them into reconsidering the whole relationship of college to community and eventually to reevaluating their priorities of education and service.

Several facets of this relationship came to a head during the long student strike at San Francisco State College in 1968–1969. A loose coalition of non-Anglo and non-white student groups formed under the banner of the Third World Liberation Front. Among the Oriental students two groups stood out. One was the Asian-American Political Alliance (AAPA) which, on other campuses around California, had a more radical rhetoric and more Chinese-American representatives than at State. Although it had its leftward leaning and radical members, AAPA at San Francisco State College came to be more a Japanese-American group and less an outlet for radical expression. Eventually, a few of its leaders put together the Japanese portion of the College's incipient Ethnic Studies Program. ICSA contributed a program for Chinese ethnic studies and, like many of the other programs offered in the Third World proposals, sought to link the educational experience to community development.

The strike, with its violence, terror and excitement, propelled ICSA members into even greater contact with the Chinatown community. They became socially conscious and actively oriented toward conditions about which previously they had been only vaguely aware. For one thing, San Francisco State's language program taught only Mandarin, while the bulk of San Francisco's Chinese spoke one or another of the several dialects of Cantonese. In addition, ICSA asserted with loud emphasis what had been but an open secret for decades: Chinatown was a racial ghetto, poverty-stricken, disease-ridden, overcrowded, under-developed and with a population growing in Malthusian proportions. Finally, they pointed out that no courses, major or program existed to deal specifically with the history, culture, problems and identity of the Chinese in America. They dedicated themselves to the remedy of all these defects and established offices not only in the college but in Chinatown itself.

ICSA functions today as a dualistic communication and cultural bridge. On the one hand it has recreated contacts between the originally bourgeois-oriented Chinese-American college students and the Chinatown dropouts. "The generation before us moved out to the Richmond District and the suburbs," says Jeffrey Chan, a young English instructor at State who supports ICSA. "Now we're moving back into the ghetto." ICSA provides tutoring services to Chinatown's less educated youth and urges that San Francisco State College establish even more programs for community rebahilitation. The community-oriented Chinese college youth will not openly attack Leway or the Red Guards and remain in communication with them as well as with the erstwhile Hwa Ching. But, observes George Woo, now an ICSA member, "We can also see the pitfalls in using too much of the blarney, as the Red Guards did. As a result, they alienated immigrant youths and the whole community in three months' time." ICSA, by keeping open contacts among the native-

and foreign-born, among Hwa Ching and Leway-Red Guards, among status conscious diploma bearers and socially stigmatized delinquents and among the legitimated and the lowly, may yet be able to blunt the deadly edge of conflict and build a durable community for Chinatown.

Such a community, if it is built, will be ethnic without being necessarily Confucian, adaptive without being conformist, race-conscious without being bigoted and economically efficacious without being uncritically bourgeois. What this means specifically is by no means clear even to the ICSA members themselves. Chinese-Americans in particular and youthful ethnic minority members in general are going through an identity crisis of fundamental cultural and psychological proportions. At this moment it is easier for them to state what they are not and what they will refuse to become than it is to indicate precisely the content of an appropriate identity. Echoing the inner nagging question of most of his compatriots, a twenty-one year old college student complained, "I'm still trying to figure out what I am supposed to be as a Chinese-American." And George Woo replied, "I know how you feel. I don't identify with China either and I certainly don't identify with the petty American middle-class values of my aunts and uncles."

In some ways ICSA's approach is reminiscent of an idea for the emancipation of Negroes, formulated over a half-century ago by W.E.B. du Bois, that the minority community must be lifted up and guided by its "talented tenth"; i.e., its educated and professional leaders. "The college students are the only hope," argues Mason Wong, 29 year old ex-Marine and ICSA leader, "because we live in a society where you have to have credentials to do anything." In contrast to the elitist implications that plagued the old program of du Bois, however, ICSA seems to emphasize a two-way learning process between the lettered and the drop-outs and to call for the formulation of a new ethic to replace the Confucian-Protestant ethos of Chinese America. As Mason Wong has said, "Our generation here will no longer accept the old and still prevalent Confucian doctrine of success coming only from hard work and humility." What that ethic will be is not yet known. In the meantime, the Chinese must still contend with the traditional social order that is Chinatown's establishment.

The Old Order . . .

Any person at all conversant about San Francisco's Chinatown will have heard of the Chinese Six Companies. In a vague sense he might know about some of its activities, be able to point out its headquarters, and note that it is a benevolent, protective, and representational body of Chinese who enjoy unofficial but influential standing at City Hall. Beyond this he may know very little, but offer the familiar litany: the Chinese take care of themselves, they contribute little if at all to the welfare rolls or to the city's alarming rate of juvenile delinquency; while the Chinese were perhaps at one time a troublesome minority, they are now safely ensconced in their own quarter of the city where they enjoy a modicum of freedom to practice the peculiar cultural expressions derived from a China that is no more. To him the Six Companies is one aspect of that cultural freedom.

Like many stereotypic images that arise in racist societies, this perspective on the Chinese Six Companies and on Chinatown contains some kernels of truth. The Chinese in San Francisco, like the Chinese in Calcutta, Singapore, Bangkok, Saigon, Manila and, indeed, in almost every large city to which Chinese have migrated, enjoy a measure of home rule that far exceeds that of any other minority group in a metropolis. during the Colonial period in Southeast Asia, the British and Dutch formalized their practices of indirect rule into a specified system of titles. "Kapitan China" was the Dutch designation for the uniformed and be-medalled Chinese who represented his people in the Colonial councils at Batavia, and the "Captain China" system prevailed in British Malaya and other colonies as well.

Indirect rule was for the colonial powers an expedient way of maintaining sufficient control over restless and hostile native peoples in a precariously pluralistic society and a means by which to extract their labor and the colony's natural resources without having to contend with their local, tribal and customary ways and woes. For the subject peoples it meant that they could organize their lives with impunity in accordance with a modicum of traditional practices and customary modes, so long as none of these interfered with the rather limited interests of the imperial powers. Outside of the Colonial area, Chinese immigrant elites also managed to establish a kind of cultural extra-territoriality. They legitimated their traditional control over their fellow-migrants by winning unofficial recognition from white civic elites. In Vancouver, British Columbia, and in New York City, the Chinese Benevolent Association has obtained such prerogatives; in San Francisco it is the Chinese Six Companies. In some cities the leader of this body of Chinatown elites is unofficially referred to as "The Mayor of Chinatown," a perhaps suitable surrogate sobriquet for the more formal and more formidable title of "Kapitan China" that prevailed more than a half-century ago in Southeast Asia.

To more fully understand Chinatown's power structure, it is necessary to analyze the several kinds of traditional associations from which it is composed.

There are three basic types of traditional association established in Chinatown; in addition, there are subsidiary and ancillary groupings, including occupational guilds. At the apex of this complex associational pyramid is a confederation of associations which tends to govern the community.

First, there are clan associations, or "family associations" as Occidental journalists and sociologists usually term them. Clan associations ideally unite all persons descended from a common male ancestor and derive from the lineage communities so prevalent in Kwangtung. Overseas, however, the more manageable lineage unit was replaced by a kinship network with wider influence than that which originally enclosed but a compact village. The clan association includes all who bear the same surname. Its function, with respect to kinship, is to provide the boundaries of the incest taboo by prohibiting marriage within the same surname group. (When I was in high school a Chinese-American friend confided to me that he was dating a girl of the same surname as his own, a fact, he said, which would anger and shame his parents.)

In the early days of Chinese immigration, clan leaders established headquarters and hostelries, and the more formalized association of kinsmen became a particularized kind of immigrant aid society providing the newcomer with food, shelter, employment, protection and advice. Clan leaders reminded the immigrant of his obligations to parents and family in the home village, and in the absence of the village elders, assumed a role *in loco parentis,* settling disputes, arbitrating disagreements and in general containing intra-clan differences within the kinship fold. Some clan associations exercised a monopoly over a trade or profession in Chinatown, effectively resisting encroachments by ambitious Chinese upstarts from other clans. Until the recent arrival of large numbers of immigrants from Hong Kong, the clan associations had been declining in power and authority as a result of the aging of their members and the acculturation of American-born Chinese. However, even their new life-blood of immigrants is less acquiescent than the former sojourner members. Chinatown clan associations are now challenged to provide something more than a paltry benevolence in exchange for their petty despotism.

In addition to clans, however, there developed among overseas Chinese a functionally similar but structurally different type of association. The *hui kuan* united all those who spoke a common dialect, hailed from the same district of origin in China, or belonged to the same tribal or ethnic group. (It is a mistake to suppose, as many Occidentals do, that the peoples of China are culturally homogeneous. In the tiny area around Canton from which most of America's immigrants have come, there are numerous dialects which, while they have a common script, are nearly mutually unintelligible when spoken.) Like the clan association, the *hui kuan* originated in China where, by the middle of the nineteenth century, associations of that type had sprung up in urban areas throughout the empire to minister to the needs of students, merchants and

other migrants from China's many rural villages. Overseas the *hui kuan* was but one more extension of this provincial form of solidarity. In many ways these Chinese associations were similar to those immigrant aid and benevolent societies established by Germans, Irish, Jews and other Europeans in America, and the German name which has been applied to the latter, *Landsmannschaften,* is applicable to them as well.

In San Francisco and other cities in which Chinese dwelt, the *hui kuan,* like the clan association, maintained a headquarters and served as caravansary, hostelry, credit association and employment agency. In all these matters it exercised authoritarian control, and since most of the Chinese in America were debtors, directly or indirectly, to their *hui kuan,* its officers were not infrequently suspected of garnishing an excessive interest or corrupt profit from their charges. The *hui kuan,* again similar to the clan, conducted arbitration and mediation hearings between disputing members, adjudicated conflicts among its factions, managed and collected the debts of its members, and, in addition, charged them various fees for its services. The seniority of its membership and the flight of the American-born to the middle-class districts of the city and to the suburbs tended to undermine *hui kuan* authority, but the old businesses in Chinatown still affiliate with them and accept their mediation and arbitration services. They are especially important in the ownership and control of Chinatown property which they administer in a traditional way quite contrastive to real estate management in the Occidental parts of the city.

The third major type of association in Chinatown is the secret society. Like the clan and the *hui kuan,* the secret society originated in China where for centuries it served as a principal agency for popular protest, violent rebellion and social banditry. The overseas migrants from Kwangtung included not a few members of the Triad Society, the most famous of China's clandestine associations. In nearly every overseas community of significant Chinese population they established chapters of or models based on that order.

In the United States secret societies among the

Chinese were established by the early immigrants in the cities and also in those outlying areas where clans and *hui kuan* could not form a solid base. Inside Chinatown the secret societies soon took over control of gambling and prostitution, institutions which flourished in the absence of wives and domestic habitation and in the presence of the "frontier spirit" that characterized the early West in general. It is with these pursuits, rather than with their political or eleemosynary activities, that they are most often associated in the minds of non-Chinese in America. Clans, *hui kuan,* and the several chapters of secret societies often fell out with one another over their competition for women, wealth, and power inside Chinatown, and these so-called "tong wars" raged intermittently until a Chinatown Peace Association established a still perilous peace between the warring factions in the 1920s. The charitable works of secret societies were confined for the most part to the giving of mutual aid to their own members, the establishment of headquarters and hostelries, and in recent years the building of club houses where their aged bachelor members might find fraternity.

The political activities of the secret societies have consisted in their intermittent interest in the fortunes of China's several regimes, but they have not shown any particular interest in upsetting the national politics of the United States. A vague commitment to restoring the Ming Dynasty in China (deposed in 1644 by the Manchu conquerors), coupled with a pronounced hostility to the Manchu rulers, made it possible for Sun Yat Sen to tap them for financial contributions to his republican revolution in 1911. A few hundred young men (at the most) were even inspired to form eventually abortive drill teams in rural California in anticipation of the fateful day when the revolution would call upon their help. Factionalized again after Sun's Republic proved unable to establish a consensus in China, the overseas secret societies remained only occasionally interested and never effective in solving China's problems. The Triad Society reorganized as a political party in 1947 and, led by aging delegates from the United States and Canada, made a totally unsuccessful attempt to mediate between Chiang Kai-Shek and Mao Tse-Tung. Since then its political interests have subsided considerably. Meanwhile, the secret societies' most successful source of revenue in Chinatown—the control over gambling and prostitution—diminished as the Chinese bachelors aged and died and interest in these vices declined amongst the American-born. The recruitment of the newly arrived and disaffected immigrant youth from Chinatown has undoubtedly done much to rejuvenate these societies, but it remains to be seen whether this will lengthen their institutional life in America or change their function in accordance with new interests and current developments.

At the top of the community power structure of Chinatown is the Chinese Benevolent Association, commonly known as the Chinese Six Companies. It was formed in the late 1850s as a confederation of *hui kuan.* Later it incorporated clans, guilds and, reluctantly, secret societies in order to provide communitywide governance, to promote intra-community harmony and to present at least the appearance of a common Chinese front before the white society. Until the 1870s it functioned as an agency of international diplomacy and as a consulate as well since the Chinese Empire did not provide a specific overseas office for those duties. The Six Companies has been the principal spokesman for the Chinese to white America. It has protested against anti-Chinese legislation, helped fight discriminatory laws in the courts, petitioned federal, state, and local governments in behalf of the Chinese, and generally afforded Chinatown a modest respectability in the face of Sinophobic stereotypy. One of its more recent efforts in defense of Chinese in America was a protest against Secretary of Transportation Volpe's omission of the role that Chinese played in the building of the Transcontinental Railroad when he spoke at the centenary celebration of the railroad's completion.

Gradually the Six Companies established its legitimacy as rightful representatives of the Chinese in San Francisco. Composed of merchants and traders, the confederation's leaders seemed to inspire assurance among civic leaders that the Chinese were not a threat to the city's economic base. The anti-Chinese movement in America was largely made up of small farmers and laborers who acted against what they described as the "unfair competition" of Chinese laborers. Once labor agitation had succeeded in driving Chinese workers out of the city's industries and into the confines of Chinatown, a movement that had largely completed its work by 1910, civic functionaries were quite prepared to negotiate with the Six Companies whatever agreements might have to be reached between the ghetto and the metropolis. For their part, the Six Companies, although they protested the excesses of the movement, must have realized the gain to be made in their own power by having the great majority of Chinese housed and employed in Chinatown. The final establishment of Chinatown as an unofficial but nonetheless fixed quarter of the city consolidated and enhanced the power of the Six Companies over its denizens.

In effect, the Six Companies' authority over Chinese in San Francisco was, until the advent of the American-born and the rise of intra-community rebellion, an institutionalized version of the kind of control Booker T. Washington and his "Tuskegee Machine" exercised over Negroes in America from 1890 until 1915. The slow growth of a second generation prevented an effective counteraction to its powers by an acculturated group demanding a new politics. To be sure, Chinatown's Six Companies had its "DuBoises," men who opposed the despotic benevolence which it excercised, the containment of Chinese in the ghetto which it tacitly espoused and the corruption in its offices which they exposed from time to time. But they were too few in number to be effective, too readily coopted into the controlled violence of Chinatown's secret societies, or too easily frightened into silence by threats of financial loss, deportation or, perhaps, conviction of trumped-up crimes in the white man's courts where Chinese interpreters could be bought and witnesses willing to perjure themselves were easily obtainable. When the American-born generation did reach maturity, many of its members went to college, entered the professions and departed from Chinatown. This caused the Six Companies some loss in

the totality of its constituency, but, since the bourgeoisified Chinese Americans did not challenge the authority of the Six Companies, it did not undermine their control over Chinatown.

Today, in addition to the "illegitimate" rebellion of youth in Chinatown, there is a "legitimate" counteraction of adults against the community-wide authority of the Six Companies. This loyal opposition includes several intra-Chinatown associations composed of "respectable" members of the American-born, and occasionally a foreign born Chinese leader, who opposes the associational oligarchy. Until 1956 the only significant organization among the American-born Chinese was the Chinese-American Citizens' Alliance, (CACA), a group so small that in its early days, more than a half century ago, it was little more than a name promising assimilation. Unlike its Japanese counterpart, the Japanese American Citizens' League, which supplanted the old immigrant organizational federation, the Japanese Association of America, in the 1930s, the CACA has never been able to overturn or replace the Six Companies. Since the mid-1950s, however, a new association has arisen, the Chinese American Democratic Club (CADC). This organization of politically-minded and socially conscious Chinese Americans heralds a shift from communal-oriented traditionalism to civic-minded cosmopolitanism in Chinatown. Through its affiliation with the Democratic Party, CADC has helped to place prominent Chinese Americans in municipal judgeships and other politically-appointed posts in the city and has sponsored some of the candidates for city supervisor that for the first time are coming from Chinatown. Still another organization outside of the domination of the Six Companies is the Concerned Chinese for Action and Change (CCAC), a loose and informal association of middle-class Chinese Americans who live out of the ghetto and who can be counted on to mass for support of more liberal social action in Chinatown. It sponsored a reformist demonstration in Chinatown in August, 1968, fielded one of the two unsuccessful Chinese American candidates in the 1969 election for municipal supervisor, and may become an even greater force in Chinatown if it can continue to muster support. Third, the Chinatown-North Beach Area Youth Council, a product of the Economic Development Agency in Chinatown, seeks to link up the respectable middle-class Chinatowners with the less respectable youth groups. With a coalition of fifteen different youth groups in the area, including ICSA, Leway and some of the street gangs, the Council hopes both to legit..nate youth power and to effect communication between generations in Chinatown, between native- and foreign-born in the city and between the ghetto and the metropolis in general.

Finally, there is one aging Chinese, J.K. Choy, who almost alone has opposed the old order in Chinatown without effective reprisal. A Columbia-educated banker and a professed disciple of Fabianism, Choy has exposed the poverty and neglect hidden beneath the tinseled glitter of Chinatown's neon-lit ghetto. He organized a reading room and English classes for immigrants in the offices next to the branch bank which he oversees as general manager. When in October, 1966, he advised the women employed in Chinatown's sweatshops to organize for better wages, shorter hours and improved conditions, and offered a devastating criticism of the ghetto's poverty program, rumors were started in the community resulting in a three-day run on the bank. Unlike the old Chinese boycotts, which were used so effectively in the early days of the economically isolated Chinatown, this attempt to destroy a Chinatown reformer failed because the bank was protected by its connections to the larger banking system of the state. The failure to silence Choy by traditional methods is an unobtrusive measure of the ghetto's growing interdependence with the nation, and a testimony to the decreasing power of traditional sanctions available to intra-community elites.

The battle arena between the new opposition and the old order in Chinatown has been the poverty board organized under the community action program of the Economic Opportunity Act of 1964. As in other poverty-stricken areas, major competition arose for seats on the board representing the poor in Chinatown. The poor never were effectively represented. The interim board composed of Chinatown elites and charged with the task of providing "maximum feasible participation of the poor," emerged eventually as the permanent board. Including two EOC members and representatives from the Chinese Six Companies, the Chinese American Citizens Alliance, the Chinatown-North Beach District Council, the Greater Chinese Community Service Organization, the Chinese Chamber of Commerce, the Chinese Christian Union and the North Beach Place Improvement Association, the board actually was dominated by the traditional power holders who continued their conservative stewardship over the Chinatown poor.

The Chinatown Board offered no significant opposition to Mayor Shelley during San Francisco's "revolt of the poor" in 1965, and instead favored the immediate establishment of a rather limited area improvement program and an equally limited drive for teaching English to immigrants. To the charge that it failed to involve the poor in solutions to their own problems, a mandate of the original program, the Board replied that an admission of poverty was too shameful for a Chinese to bear, that the Chinese poor worked long hours and could not afford the additional time to attend board meetings and, finally, that many of the Chinatown poor were non-English-speaking immigrants who could not participate effectively in the planning of community programs.

When, after much liberal pressure, the Board expanded to include representatives of the Italian and Filipino communities, a few Chinese-speaking immigrant poor, the ILGWU and, remarkably enough, representatives from two veterans organizations, policies changed but little. Of the four representatives elected to the Board from the Ping Yuen Improvement Association, in April, 1966, the first grass-roots group formed in response to the original EOC mandate, only one, an eighteen year old college freshman, could speak English. In the next three years, and especially following the emergence of the Intercollegiate Chinese for Social Action, the public meetings have been tinged with great drama but few developments. The English-speaking Board controls the outcome of business by its clear mastery of parliamentary procedure; the Chinese-speaking members rarely contribute to the discussions but regularly vote in silent but ineffective opposition to most proposals; the audience, which includes a vociferous element of angry youths and ICSA members, hurls epithets and obscenities at the Board; and the more traditional-minded Chinese are either scared off by these improprieties or shamefully silenced by their humble position before Chinatown's elites.

In April, 1969, after three years of internecine infighting, the liberal opposition, composed largely of the members of the CADC, were finally able to depose the Six Companies Board Member, and to replace him with a chairman more to their liking. The Six Companies charged that the EDA Board was dominated by "left-wing militants," but were unable to secure their complete control over Chinatown's poverty program. However, the Chinatown program, a part of the national policy that Daniel Patrick Moynihan has labeled a "maximum feasible misunderstanding," is budgeted so far only to the beginning of 1970. If the program is scrapped, the arena of conflict and opposition in Chinatown may shift to some other plane.

Another challenge to the old order has been hurled recently by ICSA. In August, 1969, a news reporter interviewed Foo Hum, tea merchant and mogul in the Chinese Six Companies, and representative on the Chinatown EDA, concerning Chinatown's social problems. In addition to denying that the community's problems were either exclusive or very grave, Hum refuted the assertion that they were attributable to newly-arrived immigrants. He then launched into an attack on the native-born youth, especially the Red Guards and the ICSA, and was quoted in the press as saying, "The Red Guards and the Intercollegiate Chinese for Social Action—theirs are Communist activities. They should not be blamed on the new immigrants." ICSA promptly filed a slander suit against Hum for $100,000 general damages and $10,000 punitive damages. Hum, backed by a Six Companies legal defense fund of $10,000, refused to settle out of court to an offer made by Mason Wong, ICSA President, that the suit be dropped in return for Hum writing a letter of apology and publishing it in all local papers, paying all legal fees that have arisen thus far, and donating a "Lai-sze", a token gift of money, to ICSA. The suit is still pending at this writing.

The crust of Chinatown's cake of customary control may be beginning to crumble. The old order must contend not only with the mounting opposition of the community's respectable, professional and American-born younger and middle-aged adults, but also with the militant organization of Chinatown's disaffected youth. In addition, it is by no means clear that the new immigrants will acquiesce to Chinatown's traditional power elite in the future as they have in the past. Whatever the outcome among the parties in the continuing competition for community power, there still remains the burgeoning social problems of the ghetto.

. . . And the New Problems

Chinatown is not only a brightly lit avenue of restaurants and shops, not only a cultural preserve of some institutions of old Cathay, not only a tourist attraction of major civic and economic proportions—it is also a poverty-ridden, over-crowded slum. Similar to Michael Harrington's descriptions of the poor, Chinatown's indigents are not quite visible. They are hidden behind the grandeur of Chinese objets d'art, the glitter of Grant Avenue's neon lights and the gastronomic delights of the ghetto's modestly priced restaurants. Nevertheless, in the recesses of Chinatown's alleys and side streets, in the buildings that rise above the tourist-crowded avenue, and in the basements buried below street level, exist all the elements of poverty and neglect that usually evoke concern, compassion and condemnation when discovered elsewhere. Chinatown suffers from conditions of exploited labor and unemployment, ill-health, bad housing and educational impoverishment. Chinatown is a pocket of poverty secreted within a gilded ghetto.

Chinatown's problems are cultural, social and economic, and they are all rendered more difficult of solution because of the traditional politics that prevail in the ghetto. Linguistically Chinatown is composed of sub-ethnic groups speaking several dialects of Cantonese. Even before the arrival of the new immigrants, the language barrier interfered with educational advancement and occupational opportunities. In 1960 the median education of persons over twenty-five years of age was 1.7 years, which compared unfavorably with a city-wide average of 12 years. New immigrants find themselves trapped in the ghetto because they do not speak English, and the current attempts to teach English have not yet proven effective. Meanwhile the American-born, imbued with a new sense of ethnic consciousness, have discovered that their own speech defects in English are matched as well with their difficulties in communicating in Chinese, and, no longer regarding their native language as inferior, are demanding that Cantonese be taught in public schools and colleges.

Beyond the language barrier is that created by a slum hemmed in by century-old real estate discrimination. Population density in Chinatown is greater than in any other part of the city and is second only to that in Manhattan. City-wide the density is 24.6 persons per gross acre; for Chinatown it ranges from 120 to 179.9 persons per gross acre. Seventy-seven percent of Chinatown's buildings are substandard; most are nearly a half-century old; 60% of the housing lacks bathrooms, many are without heat, closed off from natural light and without facilities for cooking. Electricity is antiquated and any space inside the tiny apartments or single rooms for indoor working or studying is poorly lit and cramped.

The poor housing is inhabited by Chinatown's disproportionately large number of aged bachelors and new immigrants, two groups which either because of age and indigence or newness and non-literacy in English, or both, are unable to make effective claims for better habitation. Medical facilities in Chinatown are inadequate and in some cases substandard, and attempts by committees of compassionate Chinese-American physicians to remedy the defects have only just begun. The Chinese Hospital has only sixty beds; it was not founded until 1924, and did not receive accreditation until 1967. Filth and refuse are still exposed on the streets of Chinatown, and rats are not infrequently seen in the alleys and cellars. Chinatown has the highest suicide and tuberculosis rates in the nation. Finally, the occupations which Chinese have held since their forcible explusion from the jobs protected by labor unions are for the most part menial, non-competitive with those held by whites and highly subject to exploitation. All these conditions are enclosed in the brightly lit ghetto and were until recently, insulated against exposure by an anachronistic system of community politics that does not prevail in any other ethnic community in the United States.

No institution better reveals the scope of Chinatown's seemingly insurmountable problems and its encapsulation within an almost closed community than its garment-making sweat shops. At one time Chinese were employed in many phases of city-wide industry in San Francisco. Cigar-wrapping, gunpowder manufacture, slipper-making, woolen milling and embroidery were the most significant modes of Chinese employment in the city's industries. Then, in the face of labor's open policy of Sinophobia, Chinese were driven out of these industries in a wave a race-baiting strikes and exclusionary contracts that swept over the city from 1875 until 1910. Chinese workers, most of them sojourners beginning to age, fled into Chinatown where, without much choice, they became the exploitable victims of Chinese contractors. One industry which began in this way is garment-making. Today that industry continues in much the same form that it began, in tiny shop-factories, employing immigrant women at rates that are estimated to range from 35 to 75 cents per hour (although official reports present a higher wage), and under conditions of piece-work and "sweated" labor that would make all but an early nineteenth century liberal recoil in horror. In 1921, San Francisco's supervisors established the Chinatown area by ordinance as a place where these shops might continue to operate with impunity, absolutely unprotected by unionization, largely unsupervised by civic inspectors, but occasionally improved because of the benevolence or compassion of the garment contractors. In 1958 an amendment to the city's zoning ordinance legalized those shops that operated outside the specified area of the 1921 zone. The number of factories is hard to ascertain precisely because some are too well hidden from view and a few are actually mobile, but it is estimated today to be between 120 and 180 in the Chinese quarter. The Chinatown garment industry is estimated to be worth $1,500,000.

In the past three years both major newspapers of San Francisco have exposed the conditions that prevail in these workshops, and there have been several claims that the evils would be remedied by quick and coercive trade union action. A few Chinese have been signed up by the ILGWU, there was one short-lived and abortive strike by a few workers, and fresh claims of unionization drives have recently been made by joint teams of ILGWU and Teamster leaders. However, the situation looks less than promising. First, Chinese have good reason to distrust and disbelieve the blandishments of trade union organizers. The labor movement in the West was built upon the exploited and overworked bodies of the Chinese who were excluded from almost every trade union organized, vilified mercilessly as the major source for white workers' woes and employed as scabs by a skillful management that took good advantage over a racially divided labor force. Labor's long hostility to the Chinese is not likely to be forgotten by Chinatowners who know their own history and are properly suspicious of the working-class solidarity propaganda put forth by newly aroused union organizers from the white metropolis.

Second, precisely because of their location inside Chinatown and their employment of immigrant women, the shops are less susceptible to unionization or even union control after successful membership drives. These shops have taken on something of a cultural orientation and social character reflecting their Chinese environment. The language in them is Cantonese, the women often work with their preschool children playing at their feet, and the managers extend a paternalistic benevolence over their despotic exploitation that is hard for the more traditional Chinese to oppose. Attempts by civic officials or union investigators to discover the real wages, actual hours, and existent worker benefits are by no means easy. The non-English speaking women are defeated by the language barrier, disci-plined by Confucian tradition and demeaned in the face of their interrogators. Most often they remain silent, providing mute confirmation to the sometimes false reports turned in by the garment shop contractors.

Finally, Chinatown's more liberal-minded leaders may be self-defeated by their ambiguous support of both progressive policies and a new racial consciousness. The former may call for a need to push for the introduction of unionization and other characteristic features of white America into Chinatown's anachronistic institutions. But the new ethnic consciousness, a consciousness that in its extreme forms opposes both the old order of transplanted Cathay and the middle-class ways of white America, may forbid cooperation with those institutions, progressive or not, that are dominated by Caucasians.

It is in this possible paralysis that Chinatowns' old order coalesces with its new rebels. Both seem to oppose the imposition of the metropolis upon the ghetto, but for quite different reasons. For the old elites any more intrusion might undermine their exclusive and "extra-territorial" power; for the new rebels any intrusion might wrest away their newly-discovered desire for ethnic self-determination. It would not be impossible that Chinatown's garment workers, as well as the community's other unprotected and impoverished denizens, would be caught helplessly in the vice of this excruciatingly cultural conflict.

Discrimination and National Oppression

Beyond the problems of the ghetto itself loom the attitudes and actions of the larger society. Chinatown's myth of social propriety, communal self-help, familial solidarity and a low crime rate was carefully nurtured and designed to counteract the vicious stereotypy of coolie laborers, immoral practices, murderous tong wars and inscrutable cunning that characterized the American white man's perspective. As a pervasive mystique coloring most reports of Chinatown for the past three decades, it has succeeded to a point in its original purpose: to substitute a favorable stereotype for an unfavorable one. It had other latent functions as well, not the least of which was to protect the community's social and political structure from excessive scrutiny and destruction. So long as Chinatown could "contain" its problems, circumscribe its para-govermental institutions with bourgeois or innocuously exotic descriptions and control its members, the community was safe and the city adopted a relaxed attitude toward its own cosmopolitan character.

But Chinatown's safety rests also on America's foreign relations with China. The repeal of the exclusion laws in 1943 was a gesture of reconciliation toward the country's ally during the war against Japan, just as the incarceration of Japanese-Americans during the same war was a hostile move against those Americans who had the misfortune to be physically identifiable with America's enemy. Aware of the vicissitudinal character of America's friendliness toward her racially visible peoples, Chinatown has presented a picture of cultural identity with nineteenth century Cathay and of moral sympathy for the Nationalist Regime in Taiwan. This is not a false picture, for the political identity of the aged aliens is of very low intensity. But if it must be linked to old China, it is most probably attuned to the Republic founded by Sun Yat Sen and continued under Chiang Kai-Shek. American-born Chinese are not "zionists" to any degree and, therefore, feel themselves to be Americans politically and socially. They do not identify with either China. Even the Red Guard's rhetorical usage of Mao's book is more a symbol of an American rebellion than the substance of communist affiliation. And the new immigrants have shown a profound disinterest in associating even with the symbols of Maoism.

Nevertheless, the fires of fear and prejudice are still kindled in America. Not only are acts of prejudice and discrimination still visited upon Chinese-Americans in everyday life, in jobs, housing, schools and inter-personal relations, at least one agency of the government itself is still not wholly satisfied with the loyalty of Chinese in America. On April 17, 1969, J. Edgar Hoover testified before a Subcommittee of the House Committee on Appropriations that "the blatant, belligerent and illogical statements made by Red China's spokesmen during the past year leave no doubt that the United States is Communist China's No. 1 enemy." Hoover went on to warn the Subcommittee that Chinese Communist intelligence functions in ways "overt and covert, to obtain needed material, particularly in the scientific field." After hinting darkly that a Chinese-American who served a 60-day prison sentence for making a false customs declaration about electronic parts being sent to Hong Kong might have been an agent of a communist country, Hoover asserted, "We are being confronted with a growing amount of work in being alert for Chinese Americans and others in this country who would assist Red China in supplying needed material or promoting Red Chinese propaganda." "For one thing," he continued, "Red China has been flooding the country with its propaganda and there are over 300,000 Chinese in the United States, some of whom could be susceptible to recruitment either through ethnic ties or hostage situations because of relatives in Communist China." "In addition," he added, "up to 20,000 Chinese immigrants can come into the United States each year and this provides a means to send illegal agents into our Nation." Hoover concluded his testimony on this point by asserting, "There are active Chinese Communist sympathizers in the Western Hemisphere in a position to aid in operations against the United States."

Thus, the Chinese in America were reminded that perhaps all their efforts at convincing white America that they were a peaceable, law-abiding, family-minded and docile people who contributed much and asked little in return had gone for nought. In time of crisis they too might suffer the same fate that overtook the highly acculturated Japanese Americans a quarter century before—wholesale incarceration. When Hoover's remarks are coupled with the widespread report in 1966 that China's atomic bomb was "fathered" by Dr. Tsien Hwue-shen, an American-educated Chinese who was persecuted here for five years during the McCarthy era, and then allowed to return to the country of his birth and citizenship, and with the fact that under Title II of the Emergency Detention Act of 1950 any person or group who is deemed to be a "threat to the internal security of the United

States", may be incarcerated in the same detention camps in which the American Japanese were imprisoned, the safety of the Chinese in America from official persecution is by no means assured. The Chinese, of course, protested Hoover's comments and one San Francisco paper labeled his testimony an irresponsible slur on "a large and substantial segment of American citizens." Meanwhile, Japanese American, Chinese American and several other kinds of organizations have joined together to attempt to get Congress to repeal the infamous Title II.

Race prejudice, as Herbert Blumer has reminded us, is a sense of group position. It arises out of the belief, supported and legitimated by various elites, that a racial group is both inferior and threatening. Such a belief may lie dormant beneath the facade of a long-term racial accommodation, made benign by a minority group's tacit agreement to live behind the invisible wall of an urban ghetto. Then, when circumstances seem to call for new meanings and different explanations, the allegedly evil picture and supposedly threatening posture may be resuscitated to account for political difficulties or social problems that seem to defy explanation.

History, however, does not simply repeat itself. There is a new Chinatown and new sorts of Chinese in America. The old order holds its power precariously in the ghetto; the new liberals and the now vocal radicals bid fair to supplant them and try new solutions to the old problems. Finally, the experience of 1942 may not be repeated either because the United States has learned that lesson too well, or because too many Americans would not let it happen again.

Ethnicity: Strategies of Collective and Individual Impression Management

(with WILLIAM A. DOUGLASS)

ANTHROPOLOGISTS AND SOCIOLOGISTS have long considered race and ethnicity in terms of social process. However, while such a perspective has avoided the static and overly structural bias that characterized earlier biological theories, it nevertheless failed to grasp the full implications of a truly dynamic conception of these phenomena. By emphasizing acculturation and assimilation, by conceiving these processes to be evolutionary and, with rare exception, unidirectional, the sciences of man have eschewed the strategic and tactical employment of racial and ethnic identities by which groups and individuals work through situations and careers.[1] Understanding of race and ethnicity has certainly been advanced by a thoroughgoing processual approach; however, further advances can be made if we widen the understanding of social process itself to include those individual and group modes which invoke, modify, qualify, or revoke racial and ethnic identities.

Ethnicity, Impression Management, and the Group

At the group level of social organization ethnic relations usually translate themselves into sets and series of strategic and tactical situations played out over time as contending ethnic groups seek to alter their respective statuses vis-à-vis one another. In a plural society at least six general aims of such strategies may be noted. A minority might attempt to: (1) become fully incorporated into the larger society; (2) participate actively in the public life of the larger society while retaining significant aspects of its own cultural identity; (3) emphasize ethnic identity in the creation of new social positions and patterned activities not formerly found within the society; (4) retain confederational ties with the larger society at the same time that it secures territorial and communal control for itself; (5) secede from the larger society and form a new state or enter into the plural structure of another state; (6) establish its own hegemony over the society in which it lives. [2] The actual conduct of any or all of these strategies by any one or several of the ethnic groups in a plural society is likely to be a source of societal disruption and, as such, to be a source of political, social, and personal problems as well.

If a Hobbesian state of nature is to be avoided, there must be a degree of accommodation and association, at least at a minimal level of adherence to a set of rules governing interaction and relationships between the members of the several groups composing the plural social order. These rules constitute a deeply ingrained understanding transcending the cultural differences which divide groups while at the same time binding them at the level of a basic social contract. Typically these rules are embedded in a common language, in a set of basic shared understandings, and in the codes of conduct that operate at the subliminal levels of consciousness. Social order in a pluralistic society is woven in a fine net of minute threads of understanding. Although the mesh is thick, the threads are fragile, so that fractured sociation is an ever-present threat.

If, on the one hand, a kind of fundamental "social contract" binds disparate groups together in a plural society, a kind of uncommunicable essence of ethnic solidarity prevents full acculturation. Beyond the biological, cultural, and social traits that characterize the exterior quality of ethnic differences, there is also a certain sense of ineffableness with which members define the boundaries of their own ethnic group. This silent but shared understanding constitutes the symbolic estate "inherited" by the in-group. It can neither be communicated to nor adopted by the outsider. A recent but by no means unique example is the current emphasis on "soul" among blacks in America. "Soul" can be experienced by blacks, but not explained to whites. At best, a fellow traveler of the black community can, after long and intimate association, develop an empathic understanding, while never sharing fully in the communion which "soul" provides for those who "have" it. "Soul" constitutes an invisible social cement binding blacks together and separating them and their unique experience from other groups. [3]

Sharing in such an ethnic estate is taken as a sign of his ethnicity by a member. Moreover, the outsider signals his nonmembership by his ignorance of precisely those ethnic things that cannot be explained but only silently apprehended. Every ethnic recognizes this quality of "insider" understanding in himself; at the same time, he is often perplexed and chagrined when he observes it in members of other ethnic groups. This tacit symbolic estate of ethnicity is the taproot of ethnocentrism.

In a plural society characterized by an official culture and many racial groups in varying states of cultural and social distance from it, the interplay between the forces favoring the social contract and those favoring cultural and social apartheid often produces societal instability and anguished personal ambivalence. Social order rests upon shared understandings and common conventions. The necessity for a commonly agreed upon set of conventions governing interethnic relations usually results in racial and ethnic stereotypes—generalizations about the various ethnic groups that both define and indicate appropriate attitudes toward them. Although an egalitarian and melioristic social science has tended to reject stereotypes as allegedly biased distortions of social and personal reality, they may not be dismissed out of hand since they are also the folk categories which underlie and condition interethnic relations.

The content of stereotypes constitutes the definition of peoples and situations, while the attitudes contained in them make up orientations which actors feel they are ordinarily obliged to take. Even if stereotypes are frequently distorted for pernicious purposes, they are based upon the perceptions or misperceptions, understandings or misunderstandings, of certain behavioral realities. An ethnic's own generalizations about the group to which he belongs are also stereotypes in that they too emphasize certain features and relegate others to unimportance. The anxieties and stress that occur in multiethnic societies arise not so much out of a one-sided use of stereotypes by a dominant group, but rather out of the nonreciprocal structures of emphasis and priorities about similar stereotypes employed by members of all the ethnic groups. In a plural society that has had sufficient continuity over generations, there is often a high degree of consensus about the general character of stereotypes, but widespread disagreement about the relevance and rank order of values and sentiments within each stereotype. Taken as a body, the several sources of stereotypes constitute the field of saliencies for an ethnic identity.

What is important, then, is that in a pluralistic society the membership of any ethnic group is aware that outsiders hold stereotypes of them and have knowledge of their content. Moreover, the members see themselves as inheritors of a symbolic ethnic estate whose saliencies and rank order of priorities are sharply and sometimes inversely differentiated from the perspective of the larger group. In orienting themselves to the social world of stereotypy in which they live, members of an ethnic group usually attempt some form of collective impression management as they seek to defuse potentially dangerous aspects of the stereotypic saliencies, arouse sympathy for their position as a minority, and influence outsiders toward a more appreciative and tolerant attitude. The strategies and tactics of such a scheme of impression management are many and varied. In general, however, they include, on the one hand, attempts to restrict public displays of ethnicity among their own members to those aspects which are acceptable to the larger society and, on the other hand, to cast the dominant group into a role which is advantageous to itself. An example of the former is frequently noticed in the United States, where the dominant society is relatively closed with respect to adaptation of foreign culture items unless they are in the realms of dance, dress, or diet. The "cafeteria culture" which constitutes the American gastronomic way allows the possibility for a "foreign" group to ingratiate itself further with the host society by contributing a new dish.[4] Indeed the "success" of immigrant groups in America would appear to rest upon their ability to make "contributions" to America, that is, to bring into the society just those elements which it is prepared to accept

while withholding from presentation any element which challenges or subverts cherished values or sacred institutions.[5]

If, however, contributions are in short supply, or if the group seeking a better image has used up its contributional assets without yet attaining sufficient satisfaction, it may attempt to recast the image the larger society has of it, hoping to foist upon the latter a self-image that has distinctive payoffs. Recently, blacks in America have emphasized the centuries of white oppression which have characterized their group life in America, and in so doing they have laid claim to various kinds of compensation owed to them for their suffering. Thus stereotypes and group identities become the "focal" elements through which claims and adjustments may be mobilized, adjudicated, and compromised.

Ethnicity, Impression Management, and the Individual

The very same conditions that give rise to a plurality of ethnic groups in varying kinds and degrees of relationship with one another also evoke a plurality of identities and saliencies for individuals. There is one sense in which membership in an ethnic group, and hence access to an ethnic identity, is ascriptive, with the result that ethnic groupings have a tendency to be closed social groupings. This is true insofar as accident of birth introduces an actor to a lengthy process of socialization into the ethnic heritage. However, despite its anchorage in ascription, there is also a very important sense in which ethnic identity, and the several saliencies of any ethnic identity, are qualities of individual personification which may be inferred, assumed, manipulated, or in some cases avoided altogether. Just as an ethnic group must affirm and reaffirm its boundaries (or be reminded by others of what they are) in order for such boundaries to retain social relevance,[6] so also individual ethnics must affirm and reaffirm an ethnic identity (or have it reaffirmed by outsiders) in order for it to be a feature of any social situation in which they are participants. From the ethnic actor's perspective, ethnicity is both a mental state and a potential ploy in any encounter, but it will be neither if it cannot be invoked or activated. Ethnic boundaries are not impregnable barriers to trespass or escape. If persons can neither be admitted nor excluded on the grounds of obvious and unambiguous physical differences (where such differences are vested by the members with ethnic importance), "passing" behavior is possible for those who possess ambiguous physical characteristics and who acquire sufficient behavioral versatility to function at some level in more than one ethnic milieu. Parenthetically, it should also be noted that ethnic boundaries are partially penetrable by those whom Goffman calls "the wise," i.e., persons who, though clearly not hereditary bearers of the ethnic group's culture or symbolic estate, nevertheless come to share sufficient experiences with members and to indicate such complete empathy with them that they are awarded honorary membership in the group.[7]

Treating ethnic identity strictly as a group phenomenon in which recruitment of membership is ascriptive forecloses study of the process whereby individuals make use of ethnicity as a maneuver or strategem in working out their own life chances in an ethnically pluralistic social setting. When ethnicity is regarded as purely ascriptive, those actors who escape from or deny their "birthright" tend to be defined as "passers"—or even "traitors" or "cowards"—while those who acquire one or several ethnic identities are regarded as "impostors." In both cases an air of fraudulence and "bad faith"[8] pervades the analysis. While ethnic "fraudulence" may pose a problem for persons in a plural society, it is precisely that phenomenon which should be seen as a datum for analysis by the researcher. Ethnicity is an *acquired* and *used* feature of human identity, available for employment by either participant in an encounter and subject to presentation, inhibition, manipulation, and exploitation. However, the individual's manipulation of ethnic identity and ethnic saliencies is not totally unrestricted. Barth recognizes

both the potential for identity ploys and their limitations when he states:

> Different circumstances obviously favour different performances. Since ethnic identity is associated with a culturally specific set of value standards, it follows that there are circumstances where such an identity can be moderately successfully realized, and limits beyond which such success is precluded. I will agree that ethnic identities will not be retained beyond these limits, because allegiance to basic value standards will not be sustained where one's own comparative performance is utterly inadequate. The two components in this relative measure of success are, first, the performance of others and, secondly, the alternatives open to oneself . . . What matters is how well the others, with whom one interacts and to whom one is compared, manage to perform, and what alternative identities and sets of standards are available to the individual.[9]

Constraints in Ethnic Impression Management

There are several sources of constraint upon the actor's freedom to manipulate the negotiation of acceptable and at least somewhat mutually complementary ethnic identities or saliencies appropriate to a particular context of social interaction.

First, in a society where visual cues are imbued with ethnic significance there are limits beyond which individual actors cannot hope to affirm or deny a particular identity (at least at the broadest level such as black, white, Oriental) without going to extreme measures to modify such cues—e.g., a white's use of skin-darkening agents to pass as a black.[10]

Second, ethnic identity is rarely if ever the sole aspect of self that is relevant and requisite to initiating any social relationship. Other dimensions, such as socioeconomic status, will likely introduce a sense of superordinacy—subordinacy into the evaluations of the parties concerned, thereby affecting their own background expectancies concerning the behaviors that each deems appropriate to their relationship. Similar to socioeconomic status, ethnic identities—and saliencies within them—are likely to be positively or negatively weighted and ranked within the ideology of the wider society. The awareness of weights and ranks on the part of the parties to the relationship becomes itself a factor in their identity negotiations.

Third, it has been noted by sociologists that the kinds of role differentiation and specificity characteristic of modern society are likely to produce inconsistent individual behavior in the area of race relations.[11] Thus in the context of American race relations, a particular white might reside in a neighborhood opposed to equal housing for blacks, attend a church in which black participation is welcomed, belong to a labor union with covert discriminatory practices, and yet work for an equal opportunity employer. In each of these contexts the use of ethnic identity and identity saliencies will likely be conditioned by the structural considerations of specific role requirements. However, such structural requirements are best viewed as parameters upon rather than determinants of manipulativeness on the actor's part. Furthermore, such parameters are not to be regarded as inviolable. In fact, it is in their violation, with the attendant breakdown in background expectancies, that we encounter much of the tragedy, tension, and the potentially explosive element in race relations.

Fourth, individuals in a plural society are likely to be in possession of less than complete information about the fundamental nature of the several ethnic groups and saliencies in their society. Such information becomes a body of personal knowledge derived from socialization for any particular group, while learning it in later life constitutes acculturation for anyone brought up in a different milieu. In most societies the dominant culture pattern is one which most closely approximates that of the most powerful ethnic group. Hence it is probably that members of ethnic groups other than the dominant group are at a disadvantage in interaction with the latter, since they are likely to be imperfectly acquainted with the rules, roles, and relationships that pertain to interethnic interaction. Moreover, they may lack confidence in their ability to manipulate identities to

their own advantage and hold something less than exclusive commitment to the rules of propriety appropriate to their own predesignated status in the society. Indeed, one of the great personal frustrations for the individual ethnic actor arises out of his difficulty in conveying the richness of his own ethnic self, as well as the humanity that encompasses his total identity, to those who insist on imputing stereotypic characteristics to him and all members of his group. But in addition to majority-minority encounters, interethnic relations go on between members of the several minorities as well. Hence it is very likely that in a plural society two actors of different ethnic groups, neither of which is dominant in the society, will possess very incomplete information concerning the nature of the other's ethnic heritage and the cultural nuances characteristic of the other's behavior. In lieu of these, such actors may consequently resort to their own understanding of the larger society's stereotypes of each other's ethnic group. Plural societies are likely to be characterized by pluralistic ignorance, reinforcing stereotypy and restricting the respective repertoires of all of their actors.

Finally, the actor's ability to enter into any particular ethnic identity or to manipulate its saliencies may be restricted by his skills in role playing and limited because of his failure of nerve. Skill in ethnic role repertory may be acquired by experience and experiment, but those bereft of both may have little capacity to carry off a performance in a new or strange setting. Once confident of these skills, however, an individual may regard ethnic role and saliency manipulation as something that not only *can* be done, but that in certain circumstances *ought to be*. When conscious dissembling is part of one's mode of impression management, any single instance of it constitutes the declaration of a moral holiday; such holidays are likely when the definitions of status and role among the several ethnic groups do not enjoy mutual agreement and alternate definitions abound.

Even when skills are well developed, however, the individual may lack the mental state requisite for undertaking such hazardous activity as ethnic role manipulation. The new experience to be had through a different presentation of self might be euphoric, but undertaking the activity is by no means simple. However, some minority group members are so dominated by the rules and prejudices of their society that they feel themselves to be members of the wretched of the earth.[12] A mood of fatalism sets in, and when oppression becomes so total in scope that desperation describes the individual's mental state, only the resort to acts of mastery will restore the preferred mood of humanism. At such moments the will to enter into identity manipulations and saliency experimentation may be activated. Thus, many who experience the indignities and outrages of racial ignominy suffer in silence: The potential pain and anxious doubt which surround racial and ethnic identities in plural societies may produce a paralysis of the will to change. Perhaps only those who are both skilled and desperate will hazard the new fortunes of a change in identity.

Incomplete control over the projection of ethnic cues, the presence of ethnic stereotypes as a part of the wider social ideology, the structural requirements and limits of role specificities, and the potential differential access to information due to varying degrees in the acculturative experiences of actors, are all possible limitations upon the individual's ability to manipulate his own ethnic identity. This is particularly the case when he is placed in the role of subordinate. No amount of individual manipulation of identity saliencies would, at present, secure for a Bantu a home in a white district of South Africa. Thus, while we contend that individual ethnics are capable of dragging the anchor of ethnic identity, there *is* an anchor which is being dragged.

Opportunities in Ethnic Impression Management

While it must be acknowledged that there are many structural and personal limitations upon the individual's potential manipulations of ethnic iden-

tity saliencies, there is certainly a greater range and occurrence of such behavior than social scientists have heretofore suggested. Depending upon the particular situation, an individual is likely to assume none, one, or several ethnic identities or saliencies available to him. The Basque people (whose Old World homeland encompasses a portion of both Spain and France) in America provide several examples of this phenomenon. When interacting with fellow ethnics from Spain, a Spanish-born Basque is likely to invoke his *regional* subethnic identity—e.g., to remind his audience that he is a *Vizcayan;* with fellow ethnics from France his *national* ethnic identity—e.g., a *Spanish* Basque; with non-Basques, his general ethnic identity—e.g., *a Basque;* with Old World Basques on a return trip to the Pyrenees region, his adopted civic and social identity—e.g., and *Amerikanue.* Then there is the case of the Puerto Rican-born European-educated person of Vizcayan Basque descent who in addition to the above is a *continental* gentleman when functioning in American high society, a fellow *Latin American* when dealing with an intellectual from any Latin American country, and a *Puerto Rican* when dealing with U.S. consular officials (Puerto Ricans are, if they accuse officials of discrimination, more likely to receive preferential treatment in U.S. embassies than other bearers of U.S. passports).

There are many other examples in which situations seem to dictate an appropriate ethnic choice so that an individual responds by casting himself in the apparently appropriate role. Thus, the American-born son of immigrant parents from Canton might find it advantageous to invoke his membership in the *Sam Yup* speech group when interacting with a speaker of *Sz Yup* dialect; in the Cantonese regional group, when encountering a fellow from Shanghai; in the Chinese "race," when confronting whites; in the Asian peoples, when forming an ethnic studies program; and as an Oriental, when discussing the influence of cultures on behavior. Moreover, he may find it to be fun or profitable to be "Japanese" when seeking a date with a nisei girl; to be "Hawaiian" when confronting people interested in peoples from exotic and tropical environments; and to be "just plain American" when seeking a job.

It is important to note that while the gross racial or national terms often suffice to differentiate and identify persons in *inter*ethnic relations, the subethnic identities are crucial in *intra*ethnic situations. Thus, in his relations with whites the American-born son of immigrants from Japan might be "Oriental," "Asian," "Japanese," or "Japanese-American," but in his relations with fellow ethnics he might wish to invoke his generational identity as a nisei, since that has consequences in character imputation; his geoethnic background as a son of immigrants from Hiroshima, since that has status payoffs; or his "American" qualities, which might ratify his desire for an acculturated identity.[13]

The ethnographic literature provides examples of individual manipulation of ethnic identity. The new nations of Southeast Asia and Africa in many instances provide particularly rich examples of ethnic pluralism.[14] In his study of social relations in two ethnically pluralistic Malay communities, Provencher finds that Malays emphasize "behavior as a validation of ethnicity" and that what he calls "subethnicity" is "situationally variable."[15] According to Provencher, "Whether it was better to be a Malacca Malay, a Sumatran, or a Javanese became less a matter of static community opinion, and more a matter of personal taste and specific social context as affected by possible ways of interpreting consanguineal and affinal relationships."[16] Thus, "A single individual may claim several sub-ethnic identities, each in its appropriate situation, through ability to perform the characteristic behavior and through claim of affinal or distant consanguineal relationship."[17]

The social significance of such identity-switching in Malay society appears to be relatively low key for the simple reason that these particular subethnic distinctions are not themselves vested with great social import in the Malay worldview.[18] However, there are other ethnographic examples which suggest that ethnic identity switching need not be a socially marginal activity. D'Azevedo reports on a region of Liberia where the mingling of Gola, De, Vai, and Mandingo peoples has produced an ethnically pluralistic society characterized historically by a significant amount of intermarriage. Political

integration of the region turns less upon the supremacy of any one ethnic group than upon the ability of political leaders to avoid total entrapment in any ethnic category. D'Azevedo states: "Leading families seem to be preserving the ethnic 'neutrality' of their lineages as a strategy of expedience. Golaness, Deness, or Vainess is asserted when some advantage can be gained in doing so."[19] In the words of one political leader:

> "It was my desire in life to become a Paramount Chief over many people and gain their respect among other people and in the eye of the Liberian Government. I am fortunate in this because my family's house has many rooms where you can find people from all the main tribes in this section. My father was a real Gola man, but he had many wives and other relatives from different people. No one can say I am not real Gola, but also no one can say that I am not Madingo, De, or even Vai. In Gbo where I was Clan Chief you could not rule unless all the people of your big family were satisfied with you. I learned to be a leader of many kinds of people, and I was able to show them that I could turn my face to each of them and be one of them. This is how I kept peace in my family and how I managed to become Paramount Chief of all this country. My Mandingo people wanted me to join them and make Gbo part of their country. My De people wanted me to go with them. My Gola people told me I must show that I was real Gola from my father's line. I waited to see which was the best way for all my people before I decided which way to go."[20]

Beyond the assumption of a particular ethnic identity by an individual, there are the related phenomena of identity switching and alter-casting. Identity switching is a common tactic when the particular identity of the actor becomes distinctly disadvantageous and another seems to promise better payoffs in the encounter. In many societies, all ethnic identities are regarded as particularities within a universal identity embracing the entire human species. Thus in America a person who has been cast or has cast himself into the "Negro" role may find that it is more profitable to deny that identity in favor of the more universal one of "human being." The shift from any particular ethnic identity to a universal one is tactically wise when the former identity burdens the bearer with a stigma. On the other hand, it often happens that there are alternative particularist identities each having distinctive nuances of meaning. Shifting from one to another may signal a change in status, in attitude, or in orientation toward others. Ethnic stereotypy is a multisided game in which an actor seeks to restrict himself only to those aspects which are advantageous to his aims in the particular situation. Thus in his relations with a welfare worker a man may lay claim to "poor Negro" status while clearly not encumbering himself with potentially associated saliencies such as "black militant," "lazy Negro," "lusty savage," or "superstitious Sambo." But in his conversations with a white liberal, the same man might seek to validate his claim to "black militant" or "soul brother" while staving off or openly attacking all other saliencies. The world of ethnicity holds out opportunities for dramatic shifts in an individual's own chosen role. He may assume one ethnic identity, switch to a universal identity in mid-conversation, and then change, again, taking over a different saliency of the earlier identity.

Individuals not only cast their own parts in life's daily dramas but also seek to cast others in roles suitable to the scenario to be enacted. *Alter-casting* is the formal term used to describe this process.[21] In terms of race and ethnicity, an individual may seek not only to impose his own definition of himself on a situation but, perhaps even more importantly, to establish agreement on the other's exact identity as well. For purposes of exploitation it is useful to restrict the range of identities available to another since, by doing so, one also restricts the chances for noncompliance.[22] On the other hand, those who wish to preserve freedom of action in a potentially exploitative situation may seek to maintain a repertoire of roles ready for assumption as wisdom or discretion indicates. The man who can successfully impose a single identity on another can usually extract considerable compliance from him as well; the man who maintains a multiplicity of roles can usually escape the onerous burden of any one of them by adopting another.[23]

Gross ethnic identity alone is often insufficient for manipulation and goal achievement. Alter must be cast into the correct saliency or saliencies as well. Here the question is not what race I am dealing with, but rather what mode of racial identity is facing me? To achieve his aims, an adept actor may need to cast the entire company in the life drama of which he is a part. His ability to exact saliency compliance and allegiance from his role partners may determine his success or failure. Hence power, with all its subtleties, is a feature of all such negotiations, and the maximization of power includes the possibility that not only one's own but also others' identities can be shaped and controlled. Absolute power to cast self and others is a rare feature of everyday life, even in rigid status and caste societies, but relative power, bargains, and compromise may well characterize most encounters.

Alter-casting of saliencies on a group level may be an instrument of policy with political and economic as well as social and personal consequences. The case of the Indians in North America provides a telling example. So long as they were interested in trading with them and converting them to Christianity, English explorers emphasized those aspects of the already developed complex Indian stereotype appropriate to these activities. Indians were seen then as Richard Hakluyt described them in 1585: "Simple and rude in manners, and destitute of the knowledge of God or any good lawes, yet of nature gentle and tractable, and most apt to receive the Christian Religion, and to subject themselves to some good government."[24] When permanent settlement became the object of British endeavors, however, the Indian was recast as naked, lascivious, brutish, knavish, meretricious, and uncooperative.[25] And this aspect of his imputed identity justified conquest and the consequent system of reservations to pen in the Indians' "dangerous" character.

Discussion

Since every social relationship ultimately turns on the identities of the actors involved, every relationship includes this implicit or explicit negotiation of identities. Each actor has a stake in assuming the identity most advantageous to him and in casting the other into a reciprocally related identity as well.

Identity switching and alter-casting thus become essential tactics in establishing consensus, securing compliance, and avoiding conflict. They are also elements in the creation of dissensus, the avoidance of cooperation, and the development of conflict. Ethnic identities in a plural society are thus part of a repertory in the drama of everyday encounters and crucial situations. Any ethnic identity available to an actor may be invoked or hidden, projected or rejected, affirmed or denied. The scenario of life is not written in advance. Only the parts are available, and among human actors there is a differentially distributed skill in assuming them and in casting others into their roles.

The process of identity assumption and alter-casting entails a mutual exchange of what might be called ethnic cues and clues, [26] a kind of information game.[27] Ethnic cues are those aspects of appearance and behavior (e.g., physiognomic features, color of skin, texture of hair, accent in speech, style of expression, etc.) which can be assumed to be vested with ethnic significance but over the projection of which each actor has little or no control. While ordinary men might assume generally that ethnic cues are both definite and precise, there is often insufficient information transmitted in any *particular* cue transfer situation to make ethnic identification unambiguous. A man encountered on a busy New York City street with dark skin, frizzly hair, and wearing a *daishiki* might be a Harlem Negro, but he might also be a Falasha Jew from Ethiopia.[28] Hitler required Jews to wear the Star of David not only as a badge of ignominy but also because other Germans could not identify them without it.[29]

If ethnic cues belong to that category of information that Goffman refers to as "given off,"[30] ethnic clues are those bits and pieces of information that an actor consciously provides for another in order to project a particular image, present a specific ethnic self. Since cues are often insufficient or ambiguous, a person may seek to aid his own purpose by providing further clues to his ethnic identity. Moreover, since fellow interactants usually feel the need to ascertain another's ethnicity in order to know how to proceed in any situation, they may seek to elicit more information by a selective reference to an inter-

pretation of available cues. A conversation between John Howard Griffin, a white American Catholic who used skin-darkening agents to make it possible for him to "pass" as a Negro, and Christophe, a light-skinned Negro whom he met on a bus outside of Louisiana, reveals some of the dynamics of this process:

> "Let's see," Christophe said, eyeing me speculatively. "What blood have you got? Give me a minute. Christophe never makes a mistake. I can always tell what kind of blood a man's got in him." He took my face between his hands and examined me closely. I waited, certain this strange man would expose me. Finally, he nodded gravely to indicate he had deciphered my blood background. "I have it now." His eyes glowed and he hesitated before making his dramatic announcement to the world. I cringed, preparing explanations, and then decided to try to stop him from exposing me.
> "Wait—let me—"
> "Florida Navaho," he interrupted triumphantly. "Your mother was part Florida Navaho, wasn't she?"
> I felt like laughing, first with relief and then at the thought of my Dutch-Irish mother being anything as exotic as Florida-Navaho. At the same time, I felt vaguely disappointed to find Christophe no brighter than the rest of us.
> He waited for my answer.
> "You're pretty sharp," I said.
> "Ha! I never miss."[31]

Ethnic clues are the "feelers" which any actor may put forth in order to project a particular identity. However, since ethnicity itself is a tender subject in many societies, an actor may introduce tentative clues toward a particular ethnic identity while seeking to discover whether the identity which he is seeking to invoke is acceptable. Should it turn out that the identity has disadvantageous consequences, the actor must be capable of withdrawing or redesignating the indicators already given so as to create a more favorable impression. Ideally the situation amounts to reciprocally escalating presentation of relevant information by which one actor enhances the risk of ethnically labeling himself in order to ascertain the acceptability of the label to another. The negotiation of identities is concluded when the actor has satisfied himself as to the acceptability of the ethnic identity put forward and drops all inhibitions about it, or when the initiator of the clues decides that the tentatively proffered identity is disadvantageous and determines upon a strategy to salvage the remnants of his own honor and perhaps to offer a new ethnic identity.

However, ethnic relations in a plural society must proceed even at times when individuals fail to strike a mutually satisfactory agreement on ethnicity. Individuals may have to deal with one another under conditions of duress, subordination, or grudging accommodation. A Chinese-American, for example, may find that he cannot cast off the multidimensional label of "Oriental," a term which he knows is used to refer not only to members of his own ethnic group, but also to Japanese, Koreans, Burmese, and peoples of the Middle East. In such cases, the undesired ethnic identity may have to be exploited rather than expelled. The identity may then be carefully looked over for its possibilities and opportunities. Even subordinate statuses and ignominious identities have their favorable aspects, and these may be seized upon when no other identity is available. Thus the "Sambo" character attributed to nineteenth-century Negro slaves was of course degrading and debasing, but it lent itself to covert sabotage of the system of slavery as well.[32]

For members of ethnic groups with long histories of oppression, the art of identity assumption, switching, and alter-casting may be highly developed. Indeed it may be an individual's only weapon in the arsenal of racial defense in a rigid caste society.[33] On the other hand, members of majority groups, though adept at adopting, switching, and enjoining *nonethnic* aspects of identity, might be relatively unskilled in the art of *ethnic* dissembling. In this respect, ethnically conditioned social interaction may be characterized by a differentiation in actor skills, as members of a minority group exploit the possibilities in "putting on ol' Massa,"[34] while majority group actors rely more heavily on open, direct, and forceful coercion.

Finally it is important to note that ethnic cue and clue transfers rarely occur in isolation from other nonethnic aspects of identity negotiations. In multiethnic societies one of the problematics of social relationships arises precisely out of the condition that interactants cannot ascertain the relevance of racial and ethnic identity with any degree of certitude. Rather, they must try to gauge its importance for any encounter, and sort out its relative weight in relation to other aspects of identity. The chances for error in assigning weight to ethnicity are very high, and the possibilities of nonmutual evaluations in the same encounter are extremely likely. Conflict and communicative misunderstandings are an ever-present feature of plural societies, then, because men do not have a clearly marked scale with which to measure the value of the multiplicity of identities and saliencies available to them. The subtleties of ethnicity and their rhetorical and strategic employment may constitute one of the basic understandings of a whole culture. To be a socialized member in such a culture is to be competent and matter-of-fact in the situation appropriate to racial and ethnic usages. Competency is not perfection, however, and identity assumption, alter-casting, correct invocations and inhibitions are sources of strain and difficulty even for those who are full-fledged members. This is especially the case if, as in American society, there is a cultural contradiction between ideals of equality on the one hand and prejudices about race and ethnicity on the other.

Ethnicity, viewed either as a phenomenon of individual or group life, is not a static factor in human affairs. The importance of ethnic boundaries resides more in their viscosity and mutability than in their persistence. Whether operating at the level of identity assumption or alter-casting, ethnic identity can be used either by groups or individuals as one aspect of the tactical arrangements whereby they work through life strategies. It is not the nature of ethnicity that it provides agony for some while it promotes opportunity for others. Rather, ethnicity is likely to provide both agony and opportunity for all with the specifics varying according to the unraveling of individual life histories. To view race and ethnicity as an unchangeable aspect of man's ascriptive estate is to ignore the important consideration that in living out their lives human actors do not merely accept a given world but rather engage regularly in the construction, manipulation, and modification of social reality.[35]

Notes

1. Stanford M. Lyman, *The Black American in Sociological Thought* (New York: G. P. Putnam's Sons, 1972).

2. Louis Wirth, "The Problems of Minority Groups," in Ralph Linton, ed., *The Science of Man in the World Crisis* (New York: Columbia University Press, 1945), pp. 347–372; Fredrik Barth, *Ethnic Groups and Boundaries: The Social Organization of Culture Difference* (Boston: Little, Brown, 1969), p. 33.

3. Ulf Hannerz, "The Significance of Soul," in Lee Rainwater, ed., *Soul* (Chicago: Aldine, 1970), pp. 15–30.

4. A good example of such marketing of an ethnic cuisine and "folk" form of entertainment is reported from Detroit, where the favorite plates of Hungarian immigrant construction workers and the talent of Hungarian gypsies (who originally entered the United States to provide music for the weddings and festivals of the Hungarian colony), in combination, provided the basis for luxury restaurants aimed at a non-Hungarian, nongypsy trade. See Erdmann D. Beynon, "The Gypsy in a Non-Gypsy Economy," *American Journal of Sociology*, XLII (November 1936), 358–370.

5. Francis J. Brown and Joseph S. Roucek, eds., *Our America: The History, Contributions, and Present Problems of Our Racial and National Minorities* (New York: Prentice-Hall, 1952).

6. Barth, *Ethnic Groups and Boundaries*, pp. 9–10.

7. Erving Goffman, *Stigma: Notes on the Management of Spoiled Identity* (Englewood Cliffs, N.J.: Prentice-Hall, 1963), pp. 19–31.

8. Jean-Paul Sartre, *Being and Nothingness: An Essay on Phenomenological Consciousness*, translated by Hazel E. Barnes (New York: Philosophical Library, 1956), pp. 47–72.

9. Barth, *Ethnic Groups and Boundaries*, p. 25.

10. John Howard Griffin, *Black Like Me* (New York: Signet, 1962), pp. 7–17.

11. Nahum Z. Medalia, "Myrdal's Assumptions on Race Relations: A Conceptual Commentary," *Social Forces*, XL (March 1962), 226.

12. Frantz Fanon, *The Wretched of the Earth* (New York: Grove Press, 1963).

13. Stanford M. Lyman, *The Asian in the West*, Social Science and Humanities Publication No. 4, Western Studies Center, Desert Research Insititute (Reno: University of Nevada System, 1970), pp. 81–98.

14. F.K. Lehman, "Ethnic Categories in Burma and the Theory of Social Systems," in Pater Kunstadter, ed., *Southeast Asian Tribes, Minorities, and Nations* (Princeton: Princeton University Press, 1967), I, 93–124; Abner Cohen, *Custom and Politics in Urban Affairs: A Study of Hausa Migrants in Yoruba Towns* (Berkeley: University of California Press, 1969); Joan Vincent, *African Elite: The Big Men of a Small Town* (New York and London: Columbia University Press, 1971).

15. Ronald Provencher, "Two Malay Communities in Selangor: An Urban-Rural Comparison of Social Habitats and Interaction," unpublished Ph.D. dissertation, University of California at Berkeley, 1968, pp. 170, 177.

16. *Ibid.*, p. 176.

17. *Ibid.*, p. 183.

18. *Ibid.*, pp. 169–192.

19. Warren D'Azevedo, "A Tribal Reaction to Nationalism (Part 4)," *Liberian Studies Journal*, Vol. III, No. I (1970–71), p. 10.

20. *Ibid.*, p. 11.

21. Eugene A. Weinstein and Paul Deutschberger, "Tasks, Bargains, and Identities in Social Interaction," *Social Forces*, XLII (May 1964), 451–456.

22. Cf. Talcott Parsons, "On the Concept of Influence," in *Sociological Theory and Modern Society* (New York: Free Press, 1967), pp. 355–382.

23. Stanford M. Lyman and Marvin B. Scott, *A Sociology of the Absurd* (New York: Appleton-Century-Crofts, 1970), pp. 135–141.

24. Richard Hakluyt, *Divers Voyages Touching the Discovery of America and the Islands Adjacent . . . ,* Hakluyt Society Publications, First Series, VII (London, 1850), p. 23.

25. Gary Nash, "Red, White, and Black: The Origins of Racism in Colonial America," in Gary B. Nash and Richard Weiss, eds., *The Great Fear: Race in the Mind of America* (New York: Holt, Rinehart and Winston, 1970), pp. 2–5.

26. Erving Goffman, *The Presentation of Self in Everyday Life* (Edinburgh: University of Edinburgh Social Science Research Centre, Monograph No. 2, 1958).

27. Lyman and Scott, *A Sociology of the Absurd*, pp. 58–66.

28. Wolf Leslau, tr., *Falasha Anthology: The Black Jews of Ethiopia* (New York: Schocken Books, 1969), pp. ix–xliii.

29. Philip Mason, *Race Relations* (London: Oxford University Press, 1970), p. 3.

30. Goffman, *The Presentation of Self in Everyday Life*, pp. 1–46.

31. Griffin, *Black Like Me*, p. 58.

32. Stanley Elkins, *Slavery: A Problem in American Institutional and Intellectual Life* (Chicago: University of Chicago Press, 1959), pp. 81–139.

33. John Dollard, *Caste and Class in Southern Society*, 3d ed. (Garden City, N.Y.: Doubleday, 1957).

34. Gilbert Osofsky, ed., *Putting On Ol' Massa: The Slave Narratives of Henry Bibb, William Wells Brown, and Solomon Northrup* (New York: Harper and Row, 1969).

35. Field research relevant to this article was conducted by William Douglass with National Institute of Mental Health grant 5 K02 MH24303-01 and the field materials were analyzed with 1 R01 MH18913-01.

Essays and Reviews

Overseas Chinese in America and Indonesia

THE STUDY OF overseas Chinese has come into its own in the last decade. The flow of publications since the appearance of Purcell's monumental work in 1951 is impressive. Since that date monographs have appeared on the Chinese in Malaya, Singapore, Thailand, Indonesia, Sarawak, New Zealand, and the Philippines. In 1958 the Institute of Pacific Relations published the proceedings of a *Colloquium on Overseas Chinese*. Two valuable specialized studies have recently been issued, one on Chinese spirit-medium cults in Singapore, the other on Chinese secret societies in Malaya. The two books[1] under review here add to this store of knowledge and hasten the day when comparative analysis may be undertaken. Professor Lee attempts to analyze the present position and problems of Chinese throughout the United States. More modest in scope, more scholarly in approach, Dr. Willmott's study examines a single Chinese community in a large Indonesian city.

The contrast between the styles of these two books is striking. Dr. Willmott has approached Semarang's Chinese community with a detachment not usually exhibited even by social scientists in the study of ethnic relations. Professor Lee, on the other hand, writes with missionary fervor about the possibility and desirability of unreserved assimilation for America's Chinese. Not committed to championing the further integration of Indonesia's Chinese, Dr. Willmott dispassionately describes the present social, economic, political, religious, and familial life of his subjects in standard ethnological and sociological form. Motivated by the conviction that her fellow Chinese ought to unshackle the institutional chains of their Asian past, Professor Lee vigorously attacks those persons and associations which retard the "acculturation, assimilation, and integration" of the Chinese into American society. Dr. Willmott is least effective when he tries to fit his rather limited case study on to the Procrustean bed of a general theory of "sociocultural change." Professor Lee is never able to balance the sociological superstructure of her book against the "message" which she seeks to convey and the policies she advocates.

Semarang's Chinese have resided there for at least three centuries and perhaps more. The earlier Chinese came unaccompanied by wives and not infrequently took wives from among the native Indonesian women. As a result several generations of *Peranakan* Chinese have grown up with a mixed heritage. Newer immigrants and those who remain culturally Chinese are known as *Totoks*. But both *Peranakans* and *Totoks* are regarded as Chinese and in that sense distinguishable from the Indonesian and Dutch residents. More and more women have found it possible to emigrate from China in the last half century, and, as a result, endogamy has been more firmly reestablished among Semarang's Chinese.

Indonesia is a tri-cultural nation. Dutch, native, and Chinese influences have inter-penetrated one another so that no single ethnic group has been untouched by the culture of its neighbours. The Chinese have changed in response to their economic position vis-à-vis the local population and in accordance with the subtle but effective consequences of intermarriage with Indonesian women. The practices, prejudices, and political power of the Dutch rulers affected the Chinese greatly: they admired the advanced ways of the Dutch and resented the measures directed at restricting their opportunities to acquire the benefits of Western life. In addition, Indonesia's Chinese have been persistently responsive to China's changing political fortunes. The anti-Manchu revolt had its counterpart (with local issues in the foreground, to be sure) in Indonesia. Chinese schools, chambers of commerce, Nationalist organizations, consular officials, and visitors from China, all played important roles in the development of Semarang's Chinese community. More recently, Communist China has also made itself felt. Publications, travel and exchanges, and schools express interest in the Peking regime. The emotional loyalties of Indonesia's Chinese are divided: many admire the new strength of the erstwhile "paper tiger" though they are not ideologically committed to it.

As they have done elsewhere in Southeast Asia, Semarang's Chinese have made their greatest economic gains in commercial activities. In 1955 "the Semarang Chinese owned and managed from three-quarters to four-fifths of Semarang's retail, transport, manufacturing, service, and wholesale enterprises. They were less important in banking and finance, and their position in the import-export field, always secondary to the European firms, was being challenged by Indonesian or part-Indonesian companies." Familistic enterprise is the characteristic Chinese business form, though exceptions to this are to be found in Semarang. Chinese businesses tend to be small enough for a single family to handle, but expand horizontally into newer lines of operation. Though reputed to be successful, the Chinese suffer severe setbacks and business instability is endemic. Businesses are owned and staffed by family members and organized informally. Informal organization also is found in loan and credit facilities where mutual trust prevails over contractural relations. Similarly (though this point is not emphasized by Willmott) Chinese settle business disputes by arbitration proceedings before the *Chung Hua Tsung Hui* (Federation of the Chinese Associations) or the *Sianghwee* (Chinese Chamber of Commerce) but rarely by official court proceedings.

It is fruitful to compare the manner in which Dr. Willmott and Professor Lee treat Chinese political structure. As a student of Southeast Asian colonial and post-colonial society, Dr. Willmott is neither surprised nor angered by the "extraterritorial" rights which Indonesian Chinese possess. The system of indirect rule by which European powers dominated their multi-ethnic colonies had as a natural consequence the establishment of a semblance of internal self-government by each minority group. Professor Lee, however, is dismayed by her discovery of an internal, and largely undemocratic, "government" among Chinese *within* the non-colonial United States. It reveals incomplete acculturation on the one hand and suggests self-serving corruption on the other.

In Semarang's Chinese community power is today more diffusely spread than was once the case. At one time the day-to-day administration of the Chinese community, representation to the Chinese, Dutch, and Indonesian governments, business leadership, and community-wide organizational leadership were all in the hands of the several *kapitans* and *majors China*. From 1900–1931 commercial and business leadership passed into the hands of the *Sianghwee*. Administrative leadership of the Chinese community has passed from the Chinese *wijkmeesters* (neighborhood heads) into the hands of the Indonesian *lurah* and other direct Indonesian administrations. The representation of the Chinese community is now a task of the *Chung Hua Tsung Hui,* though other political groups dispute this organization's claim to represent the Chinese community. Clans, *landsmannschaften,* and secret societies appear to have declined in importance in Indonesia, though a fuller examination of the structure of the *Chung Hua Tsung Hui* might have clarified their status. Secret societies have assumed a ritual place in Semarang's Chinese society—but not in America's—and apparently no longer play the revolutionary and criminal role they once did.[2]

The Chinese in the United States present an unusual instance of low acculturation. To the present day a great many Chinese are crowded into ghettos in America's largest cities where they live out their lives isolated and insulated from dominant American values and practices. Behind the invisible wall which separates Chinatown from the metropolis, an unofficial government legislates, executes, and adjudicates matters for its denizens. An interlocking directorate of secret-society moguls, clan leaders, and merchants possessing "face and favor," the power élite of Chinatown is the descendant (with many important changes, to be sure) of the once-powerful *landsmannschaften* élite which ruled in China's pre-modern cities. The steadily increasing centralization of government has eroded the power of local élites in China's cities, but among the overseas Chinese this traditional form of government has survived—a reminder of dynastic China's past transplanted overseas.

Not every Chinese immigrant in America recognizes the sovereignty of Chinatown's ruling group or receives its protection. Students and intellectuals, separated in social origins, status, and aspirations from the mass of Chinese immigrants, have segregated themselves from their fellow Chinese. Living in close contact with academics, professionals, and Caucasians generally unlikely to be possessed of prejudices, this group of Chinese has had to face problems quite different from those of the peasants and artisans who journeyed to America to make a

fortune. Since 1949 many Chinese students have been stranded in the United States. Unwilling to return to mainland China, or to take up residence in Formosa, they have been forced to make an unforeseen adjustment to American life. Not infrequently this has meant a reduction in social status, a deferment of aspirations, and the acceptance of menial occupations. In addition, many of the stranded were cut off from contact with wives and family in China. Unable to effect the entry of wives into the United States, some of the stranded students have entered into bigamous marriages in the United States; others have suffered divorce from their wives. Nevertheless, Professor Lee concludes that most of the stranded "have made the best adjustment of which they are capable under trying circumstances."

A second and by far larger group who have emancipated themselves in part from Chinatown are the American-Chinese, those Chinese who by birth are citizens of the United States. Penetration of the dominant American occupational structure has been followed by upward mobility and residential relocation outside and away from Chinatown. Not all American-Chinese have moved out of the ghetto, and many of those who have, maintain social, economic, or political contacts with Chinatown. For even the most assimilated Chinese, Cantonese cuisine holds an attraction that apparently has not been stifled by acceptance of American patterns of dress, language and outward social behaviour.

The trait-by-trait acculturation that has characterized the adjustment of the American-Chinese has some interesting features worthy of further sociological investigation. The religious divisions which characterize American society, and which have been recently documented and discussed by Will Herberg, have not been taken over by the Chinese. Within the same conjugal unit may be found Catholics and Protestants, and several different denominations of Protestantism. On the other hand, some of the alleged "cultural conflicts" of the American-Chinese appear to have their counterpart within the dominant society. The extent to which chastity and virginity are to be preserved prior to marriage, the invidious comparisons which children make between their own parents and those of their peers, and the dilemmas which young adults face in choosing to satisfy their material, emotional, and intellectual needs, are all characteristic strains of American as well as Chinese-American society.

Given their isolation and insulation from American values, the Chinatowners deserve attention as deviants from that pattern usually followed by immigrants in America. The cycle of conflict, accommodation, assimilation, and (less frequently) amalgamation has been experienced by most of America's immigrants. Why have the Chinese failed to follow suit? This question haunts Professor Lee's book, but it is never fully answered. Professor Lee is not a disinterested observer of the Chinatown scene. She has a deep and abiding desire to see the full integration of her people into American society. The entire book is pervaded by a sense of mission and exhortation. On the second page the clarion call is sounded: ". . . the conditions favouring total integration are at hand." But the "Chinese need to comprehend the nature, composition and problems of their group. . . . (However,) the most unfortunate aspect is that the persons who have the most pressing need to 'see themselves as others see them' cannot read English. . . . The other persons who should benefit from this book are the China-oriented leaders and followers, most of whom have spent their lives in the U.S., or were born there, but whose prestige, power and influence are involved in promoting separatism." The book ends as it began. Despite her observation that the audience to whom the book is directed may never read nor understand it, Professor Lee is unflagging in her zeal. "Now is the most auspicious time to strive for total and unreserved integration into the American society. . . . Although the road ahead may be rough, the attempt must be made, with the Chinese themselves taking the initiative, because the members of the larger society have demonstrated their good will by removing the barriers, one by one. . . . The American-born, especially, must resist the pressure of the older Chinese who try to impose Chinese norms, values, and attitudes on them or who woo their loyalty by exhortation to 'save the face of the Chinese'. . . . Finally, . . . Americans must help,

too, by thinking of them (i.e., the Chinese) as fellow citizens and be less concerned with their ancestry." The author is not one to tolerate cultural relativism or a pluralistic society: "There should be but one set of norms which apply to human beings anywhere, encompassing sincerity, honesty, integrity, humanity, dignity, humbleness and concern for the general welfare." Apparently, Professor Lee believes this set of norms is more closely approximated in American society than in Chinese.

Given this moralistic approach and a firm discipleship in the Chicago school of sociology, Professor Lee is led ultimately to attribute the failure of acculturation on the part of the contemporary Chinese primarily to a lack of will, and secondarily to the corruption and evil practices of Chinatown's leaders. At one point she offers the extraordinary suggestion that the leaders are acting contrary to their own private inclinations. "Their vested interests have superseded their personal motivation and wholehearted attempts at effective integration."

Though Professor Lee has not presented a careful *sociological* examination of the causes for the low rate of acculturation among the Chinese, her book is replete with data and implicit suggestions which might be used for such a study. Important for future studies is the distinction made early in the book between intramural and external barriers to acculturation. Segregation and isolation may have important positive functions for a minority group. The preservation of old world values and unusual practices is certainly enhanced when contact with foreigners is kept to a minimum. The same can be said for traditional ruling élites who are insulated against loss of power by becoming the recognized spokesmen of an alien group to the larger society. (In this connection, I should add that a comparison of the informal legitimacy granted to Chinatown élites by American police and municipal leaders with the practices followed in the British and Dutch *Kapitan China* system would reveal some striking similarities.) Unfortunately, Professor Lee is too interested in presenting the negative consequences of isolation. The latent functions of Chinatown's private government in many ways resemble those of the political machine in a metropolitan ward. As R. K.

Merton has observed, on the basis of his own investigation of the political machine, one must examine the reasons for its persistence *in the face of* its acknowledged evils.

Professor Lee has called attention to the fact that the Japanese have responded quite differently from the Chinese to the challenge of life in America. Second generation Japanese "exhibit, within sixty years, greater degrees of integration into the American society, than has been the case with the Chinese, whose settlement is twice as long." A full-scale study of the Japanese and Chinese in the United States would reveal certain important differences, differences which I believe could be used in part to explain the different extent of acculturation for these two groups. Chinese and Japanese share in common their visible physical distinction from the dominant American racial stocks, and have both been victims of racial discrimination. They differ in kinship systems, occupational status, concentration of settlement and intra-community structure. In a review article I can only suggest the relation of these differences to acculturation.[3]

The kinship system of nineteenth century southeastern China was patrilineal, patripotestal and patrilocal. A single large-scale lineage not infrequently inhabited an entire village. Local village loyalties were buttressed by their kinship ties. The decentralization which characterized the dynasty's political control over the rural villages enhanced village loyalties over against loyalty to the state. Though the lot of women was better than certain writers have described, wives were in effect the property of the lineage more than they were the helpmates of the husbands. Women did not travel abroad with their husbands. Emigrants regarded their journey as temporary and their return as certain. Abroad the Chinese lived as homeless men, never fully accepting the permanence of their sojourn. They identified themselves with their clan, village, and dialect grouping. The overseas clan, village, or prefectural leaders were accepted as legitimate substitutes for the village council. The immigrant's country of residence was not regarded as home, but as a "job" eventually to be terminated.

The Japanese kinship system, on the other hand, was neo-local for all but the first-born or last-born son. Village loyalties were disconnected from ties of kinship, and had been severely weakened with the political centralization carried on by the Tokugawa and Meiji regimes. Japanese emigrants did not live long as homeless men. As soon as they had a sufficient competency, they sent for wives from Japan and established domestic life in the new country. They soon disobliged themselves from old world societies *(kenjinkai),* except for social and recreational purposes, and accepted the legitimacy of American institutions. Gradually the immigrant country came to be accepted as a permanent home, especially after the birth and rearing of children. To the extent that Chinese have been able to marry women in the country of adoption and settle down and raise a family in relative isolation from Chinese immigrant institutions, they too have responded like the Japanese. Comparative study of marriage among Chinese in Southeast Asia and the United States would throw further light on this point.

The Chinese came and remained wage workers or merchants in America. This necessitated living in the city and inevitably in the ghetto set aside for Chinese. There their personal economic and social needs could be met. There individual recognition and response, denied to them by the categorical treatment of white men, were possible. There Chinese religious, social, and political practices could be carried on without the intruding stare of the foreigner. There protection from and representation to the white society could be obtained from benevolently despotic elites.

The Japanese, after a brief stint as laborers in several primary industries then on the wane in western America, pioneered the cultivation of truck crops. Small-scale agriculturalists, separated from one another as well as from the urban anti-Orientalism of the labour unions, Japanese farmers did not retain the kind of ethnic solidarity characteristic of the Chinese. Whatever traditional power elites had existed among the early Japanese immigrants quickly fell into desuetude. In their place *ad hoc* associations arose to meet particular needs. The most important of these were the Japanese Associations of America, the Japanese-American Citizens'

League, and the Japanese-Canadian Citizens' Association. These organizations aimed at the integration of Japanese into North American society.

Japanese immigrants quickly produced a generation of American-born children. By the 1920's the *Nisei* generation began to claim a place for itself in American and Japanese-American society. The severely unbalanced sex-ratio of the Chinese, and the infrequency of inter-racial unions, sufficed to deter the growth of an effective second generation until quite recently. The Chinese population in America was replenished by immigration rather than natural increase for most of the century after 1850. Immigrants sired children on their infrequent visits to China, and these China-born children later emigrated to America. Their dependence on Chinatown institutions stood in sharp contrast to the independence of the "emancipated" *Nisei*.

Political life in Chinatown was not tranquil. The traditional clans and *landsmannschaften* controlled immigration, settled disputes, levied fines and "taxes," regulated commerce, and meted out punishment. Opposition to their rule took the form it had taken in China. Secret societies were established, modeled along the lines of the well-known Triad Society, and these took over the functions of law, protection, and revenge for their members. In addition the secret societies owned or controlled the gambling houses and brothels which emerged to satisfy the recreational and sex needs of homeless Chinese men. Struggles for power, blood feuds, and "wars" of vengeance were not infrequent in the early days of Chinatown. These conflicts entrenched the loyalties of men to their respective associations. More important in accounting for non-acculturation, these intramural fights isolated the Chinese from the uncomprehending larger society and bound them together in antagonistic cooperation. This was as true for the passive non-participant who silently acquiesced (because he had no place to which to retreat) as it was for the combatant. Since the turn of the century, as Professor Lee's data indicate, the grounds of battle have shifted on to a political and commercial plane, but violence is not unknown. (In this connection one is led to question whether Semarang's secret societies, once so politi-

cally and criminally active, are as innocuous today as Dr. Willmott indicates.) An uneasy truce has existed in America's Chinatowns since 1913, when secret society and *landsmannschaften* leaders joined forces to control Chinatown. Periodically this truce has been broken by the outbreak of "tong wars" in which not a few Chinese have been murdered or injured. Allegedly, bitter rivalry has recently arisen over control of illegal immigration and over adherence to various factions in the Taiwan-Mainland China struggle.

In distinct contrast to Chinatowns, "Little Tokyos" have not experienced inner-directed, internecine power struggles. Rather the Japanese have organized and insisted on equal rights with Caucasian Americans. No tradition of old-world rule has survived the immigrant generation, and even that generation threw off the fetters of old world institutions as soon as conditions permitted.

The conditions for the integration of Chinese into American society may indeed be at hand. But it is not by wishes and hopes, exhortations or denunciations that such integration will be achieved. The rise of second- and third-generation American-born Chinese who have the opportunity to penetrate the white man's world occupationally and residentially heralds a change. The closing of China to return-migration has hastened the severing of old-world ties. (Paradoxically, the integration of overseas Chinese might be slowed by the return of a Nationalist Chinese government to mainland China.) However, it should not be overlooked that, for all its inequities, Chinatown ministered to a sex-starved, footloose population whose needs could not be met by the institutions of the larger society.

Finally, this writer must query the alleged advantages arising from "total and unreserved integration into the American society." Professor Lee paints the status-seeking, other-directed way of life as an unmixed blessing. Among the successful Chinese personalities who are held up as models for other Chinese to emulate are an anthropologist "whose studies . . . are widely used," two Nobel-Prize physicists who "have a huge following," the "most renowned" author Lin Yutang, a cameraman "whose sensitive photography places him in great demand by Hollywood's leading movie stars," the "Chinese movie queen" Anna May Wong, the artist and teacher whose "classes at Columbia are well attended." Chinese women may also succeed: "Dolly Gee [is] the manager of the Bank of America's Chinatown branch in San Francisco," and the "present writer is the only American of Chinese ancestry to head a university department of Sociology, and her text-book is widely used." In fields where Chinese are often found one-upmanship is encouraged: "Dr. Louise Chin teaches mathematics at the University of Arizona. Glenn Ginn has taught law at the latter institution and at Shiel's institute in Chicago as well as English at Park College in Missouri; he has a degree in English as well as one in jurisprudence." Serving on the civic committees and organizations of the dominant society is praiseworthy, but is to be more highly prized in a

larger city. "In small cities and sparsely settled states the competition is not so keen and the Chinese have opportunities to be better integrated, if they so desire." But in "super-cities like Chicago and New York, the first person of Chinese ancestry to be invited to serve on civic committees must have unusual experience, education, and personal qualifications." In a remarkable passage early in the book, Professor Lee apparently accepts birth control as desirable in order to forestall the "dominant fears held by the larger society in respect of 'The Yellow Peril.'" Another scholar in the field of American racial relations, E. Franklin Frazier, has already documented the barrenness of the over-assimilated life for the Negro. Must the Chinese in the United States look forward to the emergence of a Yellow bourgeoisie to stand beside that of the Black man?

Notes

1. Donald Earl Willmott, *The Chinese of Semarang: A Changing Minority Community in Indonesia,* Ithaca: Cornell University Press. Published under the auspices of the Modern Indonesia Project, Southeast Asia Program, Cornell University. 1960. 374 pp. $6.00.

Rose Hum Lee, *The Chinese in the United States of America.* Hong Kong: Hong Kong University Press. New York: Oxford University Press. 1960. 465 pp. $7.25.

2. Dr. Willmott's study is marred by an unnecessary and misleading amount of terminological confusion with respect to organizational designation. The fault is compounded because the reader is nowhere presented with a Chinese glossary to help him unscramble or check the English transliterations. For example, the Chinese term for organization or association is variously rendered in different spellings *(hui, hwe, hwee)* and sometimes as a separate term *(Hwa Joe Hwee Kwan),* other times as a suffix *(Sianghwee).* The Chinese term for "Chinese" is transliterated

Tiong Hoa, Tiong Hwa, and *Chung Hua.* Other Chinese terms are also transliterated in different ways in different parts of the book. Dr. Willmott explains in the preface that Chinese terms are rendered as is the current practice in Semarang. This seems, however, to obscure rather than clarify Chinese organizational structure. This point is more than semantical. Since Occidentals first began to study Chinese society they have been plagued by an inability to comprehend Chinese social organization. Part of this difficulty is due to the incorrect labeling of organizations and the identification of two or more different organizations as the same or vice versa. A standardized spelling and a sociological investigation of the etymology of Chinese association names would go far to enhance future Sinology.

3. For a more complete discussion, see Stanford M. Lyman, *The Structure of Chinese Society in Nineteenth Century America* (unpublished Ph.D. Dissertation), University of California, Berkeley, 1961.

Up from the "Hatchet Man"

ALTHOUGH THEY HAVE been inhabitants of the United States for more than one hundred years, the Chinese there have not been the objects of extensive sociological or anthropological research. Much is known about the history and social organization of the Chinese in Southeast Asia from the recent writings of American and British anthropologists but these same scholars have generally eschewed analysis of the Chinese communities close to home. The 1909 edition of Mary Coolidge's *Chinese Immigration* is still considered a classic in America despite the fact that it contains but the briefest mention of Chinese clans, *landsmannschaften,* and secret societies, and even that is distorted by the author's benevolent attempt to counterbalance the outrageous sinophobia of the day. Thirty years after Professor Coolidge's work was published, Elmer Sandmeyer produced his well-documented *Anti-Chinese Movement in California* but, like his predecessor, Sandmeyer concentrated on the political and legislative reactions to the presence of Chinese immigrants. Since 1944, with the exception of an occasional article on inter-marriage, dating or courtship, America's Chinese have been largely the academic preserve of Professor Rose Hum Lee. However, her indefatigable efforts to appraise their position and prospects suffer from limitations imposed by her discipleship in the "Chicago school" of sociology and by her unqualified insistance on their immediate "acculturation, assimilation and integration."[1]

The two books[2] under review here are not the products of sinological scholarship. Dr. Kung is associated with the Central Trust of China in New York City and is better known for his efforts in international trade than for the sociological analysis which he has here attempted. Mr. Dillon is head of the Sutro Library in San Francisco and is highly regarded as a writer and lecturer on the social history of San Francisco. "In preparing this book," Dr. Kung tells us, "the author had no intention of dwelling at length upon the history of the Chinese immigration into this country. Rather, the aim has been to bring up to date the material for the study of comtemporary Chinese immigrants and of Chinese-Americans in the United States." Mr. Dillon, on the other hand, concentrates on the origins, rise and decline of secret society warfare in San Francisco's

Chinatown between the years 1848 and 1906. Both works gain and suffer from the limits of their authors' intentions. Dr. Kung's critical and precise handling of statistical materials on Chinese immigration contrasts so sharply with his lack of sophistication in discussing sociological matters that one wishes that he had dwelt at even greater length upon the history of Chinese immigration. Mr. Dillon's excellently researched history of the sanguinary encounters of Chinese secret societies rarely emerges from the simplified mold in which it is cast: "The book attempts to tell the story of the high cost of bigotry and intolerance. It is no condemnation of San Francisco's Chinatown nor of its citizens, past or present; it is a condemnation of the criminal classes which flourished there." The "decent" citizens, posed against the "criminal classes," constitute the whole of its frame of reference. The book fills a wide gap in the history of America's Chinese. Most writers on the subject have avoided or deemphasized the role of secret societies in Chinatown. Yet they played such a vital part in the social life of the early Chinese that no student of the subject can afford to overlook the role of these important associations.

Secret societies, chapters of or modelled after China's famous Triad Society, appeared in San Francisco during the first decade of Chinese immigration. For a few years these societies went unnoticed because of the refusal on the part of Californians to differentiate in any way among Chinese and because of the clandestine nature of the societies' activities. However, certain of their more unsavory practices were called to the attention of law enforcement officials as early as 1854. In the summer of 1862 a notice published in a Sacramento newspaper gave the first public indications of how disputing Chinese associations (not all of which were secret societies) sought to coopt California courts as unwitting allies in their intra-community struggles. When a secret society leader who had aroused the enmity of the "See Yup" people was murdered, his associates sought the public prosecution of one Chu Pak, who, they alleged, had given the orders to kill their leader. The "President Directors of the Five Chinese Companies of California"

published a denial, asserting that the murdered man's followers were trying to use the courts to continue their oppression and begging the court "to pass a righteous judgment" in the matter.

In 1861 the first opium was imported into San Francisco and a flourishing demand for the narcotic sprang up not only among some of the residents of Chinatown but also among certain white groups of other parts of the city. Although the evidence is by no means conclusive, it appears that the narcotics traffic was managed by several of the secret societies. Attempts to restrict the trade in opium by duties and inspections drove operations underground, and it may be presumed that the secret societies continued to obtain considerable profit through the sale of narcotics. Secret societies also appear to have owned or controlled, through tributary payments, the gambling houses and brothels that honeycombed early Chinatown. Living in enforced bachelor status and denied access to the amenities and recreations available to white settlers in California, the Chinese laborers were hardly immune to the promise and pleasure available in the *pai kop piu* parlors and bagnios. Provision of these heavily demanded illicit goods and services undoubtedly was a lucrative occupation, well worth the entailed risks of fine and imprisonment.

As the secret societies increased in number and operations, their competition for control of gambling and prostitution in Chinatown expanded into a struggle for power in the socially isolated ghetto. "Salaried soldiers" were employed by the "tongs" (as the societies were designated) to carry out vendettas against rivals and to fight the now more frequent "wars" between opposed societies. Called "highbinders" or "hatchet men" by outraged white citizens, these mercenaries seem to have been drawn from the ranks of alienated and disaffected Chinese.[3] Although they were regarded by white society as dangerous criminals, some of these hired gunmen aroused the sympathy and admiration of contemporary and later Chinese who attempted to communicate this feeling to non-Chinese through apocryphal tales about San Francisco's tong wars.[4] The secret societies protected their mercenaries well, providing them with insurance and welfare benefits in case of wounding or death, and with perjured testimony when apprehended by the police.

According to Dillon the height of internecine strife was reached in the last two decades of the nineteenth century. When the "Chinese Six Companies"—the confederation of "speech" associations whose leaders were recognized as the spokesmen for the Chinese in America—failed in its attempt to have the infamous Geary Act declared unconstitutional (1893), all of Chinatown was caught up in the tong struggle to wrest community power from the "Companies." Intervention by the Chinese consul on behalf of the merchant élite, and violent but clumsy repression by San Francisco's police, did little to halt the violence. It was in this period that Chinatown's most colorful criminal, Fong Ching (alias Little Pete), by manipulating the belligerent parties and by using to his own advantage elements of a bribed or deceived police department, rose to power only to be shot to death by his bitter opponents.

Dillon believes that the back of tong rule was broken in 1906 by San Francisco's fire and earthquake which destroyed Chinatown's rickety structures, brothels and gambling dens. Actually, as he shows in his final chapter, tong strife continued well into the twenties. By 1913 the heads of the tongs had formed a Peace Association to end inter-tong strife. As early as 1909 the Six Companies began sponsoring tourism in the newly rebuilt Chinatown, advertising its safety to the white visitor. Tong suppression was supposedly completed by the inspector of police, John J. Manion, whom Dillon credits with driving out the gunmen and closing down prostitution and gambling operations. "For all its dark alleys," concludes Dillon, "there is nothing sinister about modern 1962 Chinatown."

Sanguine though his conclusion may be, Mr. Dillon's final remarks are a more accurate description of the contemporary image than of the actual institutions of Chinatown. Though fewer in number, Chinese secret societies have by no means disappeared and at least six tongs continue operations in San Francisco. The *Chih Kung T'ang,* descen-

dant of the once-powerful Triad Society, is today recognized as the "Chinese Freemasons." And, as any close observer of Chinatown can testify, tiny gambling houses are still to be found in the recesses of restaurants and hotels. Violence has certainly declined but, though not reported in Dillon's book, contemporary inter-tong disputes have, on occasion, led to the threat of forceful measures.[5] As recently as 1958 the Bing Kung and Hop Sing Tongs in San Francisco fell out with one another over the brutal beating of two members of the former society. Older unsettled issues between the societies were revived and the police feared an open tong war. The Bing Kung leaders demanded that a public apology from the Hop Sing members be published in the Chinatown newspapers and that a cash indemnity be paid for the injuries suffered. Eventually, after negotiations had dragged on for months and pressure had been brought to bear by Chinese merchants, police and the Peace Association, the Hop Sing leaders agreed to comply with all of the demands of the Bing Kung.

Sociologists and sinologists will find in Mr. Dillon's book rich materials for the analysis of overseas Chinese social structure. It is doubtful, however, if his frame of reference can be of much value in the understanding of the relations between community associations. In the first place, to say that the "story of the Six Companies' success is the story of Chinatown's growth; the story of the Six Companies' failure is the key to Chinatown's shame—the tong wars"—is to beg the whole question of power and conflict and their intricately woven web in Chinatown. Moreover, the "Six Companies" should hardly be allowed to enter the analysis with such clean hands and the tongs with such dirty ones as Mr. Dillon (and as we shall see below, Dr. Kung) allows. For the purposes of sociological analysis, adding a value element of oversimplified goodness or badness, seems to obscure rather than enlighten. It remains to be demonstrated, however, whether present-day uncritical interest in racial tolerance in America will allow an unbiased analysis of Chinatown.

In a sense Dr. Kung's book begins where Mr.

Dillon's leaves off. It is largely an account of the Chinese today and their "contributions" to America. Tongs and tong wars are things of the past, mentioned but parenthetically. The first notes of Dr. Kung's theme are sounded in the opening chapter: "Since Chinese civilization goes back more than four thousand years, the Chinese have had ample opportunity to utilize many forms of communication with the world." But "the Chinese abroad have been unable to offer much in comparison to the contributions of exceptional European immigrants. No Chinese scientist received the Nobel prize until late in 1957."

Atrocities and discrimination were among the factors hindering the Chinese from "contributing" to the nations in which they settled. Dr. Kung offers an unusual and provocative explanation for the harsh treatment accorded to overseas Chinese: it was the indifference of the imperial Chinese government toward its nationals abroad which subjected them to so much misery. "The Manchu rulers did not regard the emigrants as true sons of China, but instead chose to assume that they were defying the imperial prohibition [against emigration]." In another passage he speaks of "the Manchu throne's complete ignorance of, and utter stupidity toward, the Chinese living abroad. . . ." Still later, "had the Ming and Manchu dynasties paid due attention to Chinese nationals abroad, and had they given them continuous diplomatic protection instead of adopting a foolish policy of recriminatory prohibition while taking an attitude of indifference toward Chinese overseas, the history of Chinese immigration might have been altogether different." The "pusillanimous attitude" of the Ming Emperor who refused to attack the Philippines after Chinese oarsmen had murdered the Spanish governor "tempted" the Spaniards to massacre 23,000 Chinese in 1603. Though "the Manchus were just then at the very height of their military power," the Manchu government "declined to interfere after the massacre at Batavia" in 1740. Despite the cruelties of the coolie trade, the "Celestial Empire had, as usual, been turning a deaf ear to what was going on in Macao and neighboring cities." When in a later chapter he comments on outrages against Chinese

in the United States, Dr. Kung states, "The imperial government, to be sure, did protest regularly all acts of injustice and violence committed, but seldom if ever took a strong stand." Dr. Kung admires the policy adopted by Japan to protect its nationals in America. "Compared with Japanese tactics of prolonged negotiations with American authorities on all matters pertaining to Japanese in the United States, Chinese diplomacy was certainly a fiasco."

However, Dr. Kung does not demand that the Chinese governments of today do what their predecessors failed to do. Although "overcoming the difficulties will require cooperation on both sides," contemporary Chinese are warned about the unfortunate effects of their own "ultranationalism." As a solution Dr. Kung proposes an even greater separation of Chinese immigrants from their homeland: "Those who wish to settle permanently should realize that it is to their advantage to be naturalized and participate in politics." Apparently Dr. Kung believes that citizenship and community activity will accomplish today what he asserts force and threats of force might have accomplished yesterday. Whatever the merits of the argument, its motives are not hard to discern. The only strong Chinese government today is that in Peking. Chinese in the United States would suffer greatly and gain nothing by identification with the communist regime. On the other hand, Chinese citizens of the United States who show concern for the fate of the government in Taiwan would probably be admired for the fact that their national loyalty is compatible with American foreign policy.[6]

Despite his disclaimer about writing a history of Chinese immigration to the United States, Dr. Kung devotes one hundred pages—more than one-third of the text—to the subject. Though in part summarized from extant sources and brief in its treatment of Chinese social organization, this section is superior in style and content to the rest of the book. During the period of "free immigration" (1820–1882) several hundred thousand Chinese arrived in the United States. Most re-migrated to China but a substantial minority remained in America, many as long-term sojourners awaiting the day when they might be wealthy enough to return home. After an initial but short-lived period of welcome, the Chinese became the objects of an intense hatred compounded of racial antipathy and economic competition. They became the victims of individual and collective abuse. Their mines were attacked and they were forced to flee; their lives were seldom protected by the law; newspapers heaped abuse upon them; mobs descended upon the Chinese quarters of west coast cities to rob, pillage, burn, and murder. Concomitant with this unchecked violence, municipalities and states enacted numerous forms of anti-Chinese legislation. Most of these laws were designed to prohibit entirely or restrict the numbers of Chinese in certain occupations; some, however, like the "cubic air" ordinance and the "anti-queue" provision appear to have been motivated largely by the vindictive attitudes of outraged whites. Ultimately, the forces of sinophobia were able to secure the revision of the Burlingame Treaty and the passage of the Chinese Restriction Act of 1882.

In 1904 the United States government converted the Chinese Restriction Act to an order of permanent exclusion. The Immigration Act of 1924 confirmed this order, added further rules and regulations and extended the exclusion to all Asians. Nevertheless, the statistics, revised and corrected by Dr. Kung, indicate that 24,580 Chinese entered the United States between 1904 and 1943. In a trenchant analysis, Dr. Kung shows that these numbers are composed of the so-called "exempt classes"— those Chinese not excluded by the several American laws: Chinese wives and children of U.S. citizens, treaty traders, members of merchant families, and a very few professors, ministers and their families. The much larger official figure is fallacious in several respects: different methods of calculating arrivals have been used at different times—prior to 1906 data on arrivals referred to the country of national origin and not the last country of permanent residence; prior to 1908 emigration figures were not included. In addition, returning resident aliens have been counted as if they were new arrivals, students have been included as non-quota immigrants, and non-Chinese, born in China, have been counted in the "Chinese" figures. Throughout this period, ineligi-

ble Chinese attempted to enter the United States through subterfuge, illegal entry, or other circumvention of the law. Undoubtedly, many Chinese successfully masqueraded as treaty-traders before the definition of that status was clarified in 1924; others were smuggled across the Canadian or Mexican borders; still others falsely declared themselves to be the wives or children of United States citizens. Several thousand Chinese were debarred or deported before repeal of the exclusion law.

In 1943 the United States government established an annual quota of 105 for persons of Chinese ancestry regardless of birthplace. In addition Chinese have benefited from certain features of the McCarran-Walter Act, the admission of non-quota immigrants, the War Brides and Fiancees Act, the Displaced Persons Act, the Refugee Relief Act of 1953, and three other minor modifications of the immigration regulations. The complicated and confusing features of each of these acts are examined and partially clarified by Dr. Kung in an objective and uncritical manner. One point is made abundantly clear, however. The seemingly great discrepancy between the official quota and the number of Chinese listed as admitted arises not because so many more Chinese actually have been allowed to enter the country but because so many old residents have "adjusted" their status under special provisions. These long-time residents are categorized in a manner which gives them the statistical status of new arrivals.

It is unfortunate that Dr. Kung does not make explicit what his history of immigration reveals—the slow metamorphosis of a right into a prerogative. In the Burlingame Treaty of 1868 the United States and China agreed to "cordially recognize the inherent and inalienable right of man to change his home and allegiance, and also the mutual advantage of the free immigration and emigration of their citizens and subjects, respectively, from one country to the other, for purposes of curiosity, of trade, or as permanent residents." Twelve years later the United States Congress demonstrated that, whatever were the inherent and inalienable rights of man, there was no natural right of Chinese laborers to immigrate to, or become permanent residents of, the

United States. Free immigration to the United States has never been restored to the high place it held at the time the Treaty of 1868 was ratified. Instead more and more restrictions—on numbers, races, nationalities, and more recently on political groups—have been added, until today admission is accorded primarily to those possessed of designated inborn traits or acquired skills. Between 1944 and 1956 the United States Congress rejected 1,016 private bills designed to effect the entrance of 1,423 Chinese persons to the United States, while it granted entrance to 182 others who would otherwise have been ineligible to enter the country. Even more indicative of the fall of the once-inherent and inalienable right of man to cross national borders without hindrance is Dr. Kung's disclosure—unaccompanied by comment or criticism—of the lengths to which the U.S. federal authorities have gone in order to discover unqualified applicants among those Chinese seeking admission to the country. The Attorney-General's attempt to confiscate the records, membership rolls, personal files and photographs of San Francisco's Chinese family associations was halted only when the federal court ruled that the subpoenas had the effect of being a mass inquisition and constituted an unreasonable search and seizure. To distinguish "paper" from genuine offspring of Chinese fathers who are United States citizens, the Immigration Service imposed a blood test, first on all Chinese applicants, and later, when claims of unconstitutional racial discrimination were lodged in the courts, on white persons as well. In addition, x-ray and dental examinations have been undertaken to test the claims of Chinese aspiring to enter the United States. What was once a right derived from one's membership in the human race may now be a crime because of one's membership in one of its divisions.

Except for the chapters on immigration Dr. Kung's book is largely a plea, illustrated by statistics and homely commentary, for Chinese to be recognized by and accepted into American society. The grounds for recognition are the many "contributions" to America made by Chinese; for acceptance, the many virtues and few vices of the Chinese. So

interested is Dr. Kung in pursuing this issue that he eschews all scholarly analysis of his subject.

There is serious inaccuracy and embarrassing gaucherie displayed in the pleasing qualities gratuitously assigned to America's Chinese, past and present. In discussing crime among the Chinese, Dr. Kung assures us that the arrests of Chinese are for petty offenses *if tong wars are not counted.* Indeed, his entire discussion of crime is pervaded by his attempt to "prove" that Chinese are, at best, the smallest group contributing to crime in the United States and, at worst, petty offenders. In order to prove this statement, he employs whatever number, index or ratio is most useful, without regard to meaning or consistency. Thus, for the twenties Dr. Kung proudly cites Walter G. Beach's ratio of total Oriental serious offenses to total Oriental offenses. Later for "serious crimes" he uses absolute numbers of arrests, and still later for larcenies the arrest rate of Chinese compared to that of whites and to that of the nation as a whole. The large number of foreign-born and aged Chinese arrested for drunkenness is explained thus: "To the older people who are isolated in Chinatown, drinking is a form of discharging a complex sickness that may have been caused by medical, domestic, moral, or spiritual factors." Noting that the greatest number of arrests of Chinese between 1934 and 1960 were for violation of narcotics laws, Dr. Kung redefines that behavior as "an offense against public health, which may breed other crimes." "Excepting professional gambling and violations of narcotic drug laws," the other offenses noticeable among Chinese—vagrancy, gambling, and drunkenness—"represent nuisances rather than crimes."

It is difficult to validate Dr. Kung's claim, reiterated several times in the book, that the Chinese adolescent is rarely a delinquent. ("There is," writes Mr. Dillon, "ironically, a tendency toward juvenile delinquency as today's Chinatown children become so completely Americanized.") In support of his assertion Dr. Kung cites the praise heaped upon New York's Chinese children by a congressman and the single statistic that in 1954, out of a total of 7,700 delinquents brought into New York's Children's Court, only nine were Chinese. Yet according to figures presented earlier in the same chapter, there were but 4,375 Chinese children in the United States under five years of age in 1940. This cohort would form the bulk of Chinese teenagers in the country in 1954. To obtain a reasonably accurate measure, it would be necessary to know the ratio of arrested Chinese teenagers to total Chinese adolescents as well as the comparative non-Chinese ratio. Curiously, Dr. Kung later cites Professor Rose Hum Lee's account of 225 cases of Chinese juvenile delinquency in San Francisco between 1943 and 1949 as evidence that delinquency arises from cultural and parent-youth conflicts. But one paragraph earlier he asserts that "The Chinese family system helps make the low delinquency rate possible." In place of the critical eye with which he surveyed immigration statistics and related arguments, Dr. Kung substitutes a laconic homily: "The prime cure for juvenile delinquency is found in the home." Even here statistics raise grave doubts about the virtuous effects of the Chinese family system which Dr. Kung would have us acknowledge. In 1940 barely more than one-half of all Chinese males in the United States, fifteen years of age and over, were married, and this was the highest percentage to that date. Perhaps here is one reason for the few arrests of Chinese children in the recent past.

Dr. Kung's insistence on demonstrating the favorable attributes of Chinese leads him into further difficulties when he discusses mental illness. Assuming that the low absolute number of Chinese admitted to state mental hospitals or deported for physical and mental defects is a measure of the incidence of mental disease, Dr. Kung, apparently having forgotten what he just wrote about the causes of alcoholism among Chinese, explains "the Chinese as a group are less tense in facing problems; accepting life as it is, they are less vulnerable to mental suffering." But, confronted one paragraph later with the fact that the suicide rate among Chinese in the years 1950–1958 was almost two and one half times that of the nation, he is forced to conclude that whatever are the immunities of the Chinese as a group, some Chinese are quite vulnera-

ble to the ultimate effect of mental anguish. "One explanation [for the high suicide rate] is that with the mainland lost to the Communists, old people planning to return to China are unable to do so. Life is hard for others because of family separation." Cautiously he ventures, "It is possible that some suicides were mentally ill."

Platitudes continue in a chapter entitled "problems of second generation Chinese,"—a chapter remarkable for its refusal to take up any problem specifically that of second-generation Chinese. Here Dr. Kung discusses the "problem of race prejudice," "the pattern of discrimination in the United States" and "the question of assimilation." The first two issues are disposed of by an inconclusive review of misleading and sometimes contradictory comments and quotations from authorities ranging in interest and expertise from novelists (Pearl Buck) to sociologists (E. Franklin Frazier). Assimilation remains mystifyingly undefined throughout Dr. Kung's cursory survey of that process in emergent Africa, traditional China and Hawaii. With the tenor of his argument thus far, it is not surprising to find Dr. Kung concluding his six sentence account of six hundred years of Chinese social history with this succinct statement: "We may say that the fundamental solution [to the problem of assimilating China's heterogeneous population] lay in the family system."

Sections on the occupational status of Chinese appear three times in the book. The first two sections are previews anticipating Dr. Kung's *coup de grace*—a twenty-four page description of Chinese "contributions and achievements." In the earlier sections statistics demonstrate the change from the days when Chinese were employed as laborers, cooks, laundrymen—and, incidentally, as "hatchet men"—to the present when some Chinese occupy professional and managerial positions. (It ought to be noted, though, that laundries will constitute the largest single unit of employment for Chinese in America.) In his final chapter on this subject, Dr. Kung celebrates the "achievements" of some ninety-five Chinese in the United States. To each of these is given a paragraph honoring his "contribution" to

America. Although with the exception, perhaps, of a Nobel Prize-winning discovery, the bulk of these achievements and contributions constitute little more than the successful completion of routine occupational tasks, a few of the activities which Dr. Kung would have us acclaim are remarkable. For instance, Dr. Anthony Koo of Michigan State University has been elected as the "most distinguished teacher of the year" by his students who presented a gold watch to him. Although "Chinese movie actors and actresses for the most part play merely supporting roles," Anna May Wong "has appeared on television." Dr. Loh-Seng Tsai is credited with the solemn pronouncement, "The world can lead to survival through cooperation," after he completed experiments which "proved that a habitually rat-killing cat could be made to live, eat, and play with a hooded rat." Dr. Kung gratefully adds that Professor Tsai's experiment "may have laid a biological foundation for a theoretical possibility of world peace."

Throughout the book Dr. Kung has been wrestling with a dilemma created by his own theme. He desires that America welcome its Chinese residents into its warm embrace but feels that the Chinese must prove themselves worthy of this affection. In Chinese activities before World War II, Dr. Kung finds little to praise and much to forget. To resolve the dilemma he concentrates his attention on recent and praiseworthy events and people. His allusions to China's "ancient traditions" and the "Chinese family system" are designed to show that Chinese institutions can be used to achieve American aims. Thus, China's tradition of scholarship can be used to mold the children of laundrymen into American physicists and engineers; the Chinese family, which, it turns out, embodies in exaggerated form all the values cherished by American middle-class mothers, can be used to combat juvenile delinquency; Chinese clan, speech, and secret societies, appropriately disguised to look like associations familiar to businessmen and welfare agents, can be used to promote trade and at the same time provide relief for the aged and indigent.

Dr. Kung's prescription for the Chinese is tragically reminiscent of that program advocated for European Jews in the eighteenth and nineteenth century.[7] Assimilation, re-defined to mean acceptance by American society, is to be granted insofar as the Chinese individual is a distinguished exception from the Chinese masses. Chinese are asked to demonstrate that they are exceptional, that is, that they are Chinese but not *like* Chinese. In effect the aspiring Chinese is requested to become as "educated" as the American and, although he need not behave *like* an ordinary Chinese, he should *be* and *produce* something extraordinary (a "contribution") since after all he *is* Chinese. But, both for the Jew and the Chinese, this promising new status depends precisely upon the existence of a lowly, poverty-stricken, pariah ghetto group with whom the enterprising parvenu can be contrasted. His "exotic" characteristics are of course the source of his appeal. When, after the advent of Napoleon, the emancipation of all Jews became a real possibility, the "assimilated" Jews, realizing that emancipation would wipe out the distinction upon which their social status was based, escaped their fate by conversion to Christianity. In America the political and legal emancipation of the Chinese is already at hand. It only awaits ratification by the acculturation or death of the ghetto Chinese. But Chinese, whose separate social life depends in large part on physical as well as social characteristics, cannot "convert" to escape. What will the "assimilated" Chinese do in the age of equality?

Notes

1. See Stanford Lyman, "Overseas Chinese in America and Indonesia: A Review Article," *Pacific Affairs,* Winter 1961–1962, pp. 380–389.

2. S. W. Kung, *Chinese in American Life: Some Aspects of Their History, Status, Problems, and Contributions.* Seattle: University of Washington Press. 1961. 352 pp. $7.50.
Richard H. Dillon, *The Hatchet Men: The Story of the Tong Wars in San Francisco's Chinatown.* New York: Coward-McCann, Inc. 1962. 375 pp. $5.95.

3. Dillon treats this point inadequately; for some discussion of it see Stanford Lyman, *The Structure of Chinese Society in Nineteenth Century America* (unpublished Ph.D. dissertation), University of California, Berkeley, 1961, pp. 246–251.

4. See, e.g., Eng Ying Gong and Bruce Grant, *Tong War!,* New York: Nicholas I. Brown, 1930.

5. Lyman, op. cit., p. 266n.

6. Recently the Chinese Ambassador to the United States, Dr. T. F. Tsiang, was reported to have said that the acquisition of local citizenship and its attendant rights does not prevent Overseas Chinese from holding sympathy for the mother country. *Asian Student,* January 12, 1963, p. 1.

7. For a brilliant analysis on which I have here liberally drawn, see Hannah Arendt, *The Origins of Totalitarianism* (New York: Meridian Books, 1958), pp. 56–68.

Review of *The Indispensable Enemy*

THE INDISPENSABLE ENEMY: LABOR AND THE ANTI-CHINESE MOVEMENT IN CALIFORNIA. By Alexander Saxton. (Berkeley, Ca., University of California Press, 1971). Bibliography. Index. Notes. 401 pages.

Until recently the events surrounding the anti-Chinese movement in America have been regarded as regional history peculiar to the West and having little national significance except for their effect on immigration legislation. Certainly such early works as Mary Coolidge's *Chinese Immigration* (1909) and Elmer C. Sandmeyer's *The Anti-Chinese Movement in America* (1939) presented the regional themes. Gunther Barth's *Bitter Strength* (1964) did little to dispel the local importance of the Chinese story. But a fundamental departure from this perspective appears to be emerging in the writings of recent investigators of the subject. Thus, Stuart Creighton Miller's *The Unwelcome Immigrant* (1969) documented the Sinophobic character of national American thought from 1785 to 1882. Stanford M. Lyman's *The Asian in the West* (1970) suggested the significance of Chinese immigration for changing the bases of institutional racism in America. With Alexander Saxton's work brilliantly re-analyzing the role of labor in the anti-Chinese movement, it is

fair to say that a full scale revision is in progress. The history of the West is to be integrated in national history, and Chinese immigration is a fundamental part of that integration.

The cultural baggage which the Californians carried with them from the East, Midwest, and South was an uncomfortable amalgam of Jeffersonian yeomanry, Jacksonian populism, and anti-monopolistic individualism. Central to this potpourri of ideas was a general xenophobia and a particular anxiety over non-white peoples. Many of the pioneers of California were fleeing both slavery and abolitionism, cities and banks, foreigners and old Americans. In the shortlived bonanza mines of California they celebrated their independence, not only by popular elections and tribunals, but also by restricting the activities of Chinese laborers to menial tasks. They did not absolutely remove the Chinese, for so long as the latter were willing to wash clothes, cook meals, and do the daily drudgery, and, more importantly, so long as they could be confined to tasks that were too dangerous for whites to tackle or which would create a wage floor from which whites could rise, their presence would be tolerated.

The ideologies of the major parties led ultimately to racial hostility toward the Chinese and a resurgence of that Negrophobia that had been dampened by the Civil War. The Democrats had pioneered in the development of the "producer ethic," which, extended to include not only yeomen farmers but also artisans, workingmen, businessmen, promoters, and independent manufacturers, locked these "carriers of value" in relentless warfare against the monopolists and bankers. However, the producer ethic, although egalitarian on its face, proved to be racist in practice. The Negro was declared to be unequal and, hence, unable to compete with the supposedly superior white men in the pursuit of happiness. Some Democrats became active defenders of slavery; others, though they did not support the American system of bondage, feared the exploitative use of Negroes by "monopolists" and an inevitable subversion of the producer class. Northern workingmen were most subject to anti-Negro sentiment since they encountered free Negroes as competitors and worried that emancipation would swamp the labor market. Immigrants and their children, who comprised the bulk of the California labor force, were even more prone to a racist stance. Fearful of being reduced to the lowest point on the social and economic ladder, they opposed abolitionism and flocked to the Democrats who assured them that it was permissible to hate Negroes. In California, Chinese replaced Negroes as the objects of this hatred, and indeed, Sinophobia helped to resuscitate the Democracy in the post-bellum period when the spirit of Reconstruction forbade open denunciation of blacks.

The Republican Party inherited the egalitarian philosophy of Locke and Jefferson but linked it to order and the preservation of property. The egalitarian ethics was further sullied by Nativism, which attracted workingmen to Republican ranks, and by the free soil and unionist aspects of its anti-slavery position. Free-soilers were also Negrophobes, linking the settlement of the territories to the liberation of white men. Unionists opposed separation of the Republic but were silent on the issue of Negro rights. The principled civil rights orientation of the Republicans rapidly disappeared in the post-bellum period. The death knell was sounded early. On July 4, 1870 Charles Sumner appealed to his colleagues to eliminate the word "white" in the naturalization clause of the Immigration Act so that Chinese in the West might become citizens; his amendment was defeated 30 to 14.

Ideology within the labor force favored republicanism, socialism and the producer ethic. Although these three tendencies did not always coalesce, they seemed to suggest an egalitarian outlook. However, again the race question eroded the purity of the ethic. Trade unionism faltered on the Negro question, and in 1868 the National Labor Union voted to exclude blacks. However, it was the Chinese question which animated labor's racist spirit. Labor's emancipation of the workingman would be confined to the white worker. The solidarity of the working class would be bifurcated by the color of the working men.

Saxton's contribution is in telling the story of labor's devolution from a principled position of class unity to a practical one of racial division. By identifying Chinese laborers as the agents and tools of the monopolists, by accepting the racist imagery of the Chinese, and by refusing to adopt a class position undifferentiated by race, the house of labor missed the opportunity to solidify its forces and strike a blow against the racism rampant in America. Radicalism, trade unionism, and racism coalesced on the Chinese issue and the Chinese—already the objects of merciless exploitation by capital, demeaning patronage by missionaries, and destructive discrimination in the courts and legislatures—were left to fend for themselves as best they could. Their own cultural orientation and old-world organizational forms—especially the vertical guilds which permitted and even encouraged exploitation of laborers and artisans—were strengthened. The Chinese ghetto was reinforced by pressures from within and without.

As for labor, its promise of universalism and equality were permanently compromised. The practices worked out to exclude the Chinese—the boycott, union label, and even the most potent weapon, the strike—were put into service not only to shorten hours and increase wages, but also to drive out Asians. Later this same arsenal would be used to exclude Negroes, ignore Mexicans and Indians, and in general restrict labor's interests to those of the white workingman. California was the setting for the beginnings of this tragic story; the nation is the inheritor of the California legacy. Alexander Saxton is to be congratulated for uncovering this awful truth and making it available in careful detail and objective analysis for all of us to ponder.

Review of *Chinese Labor in California, 1850–1880*

CHINESE LABOR IN CALIFORNIA, 1850–1880. Ping Chu. Madison: The State Historical Society of Wisconsin (for the Department of History, University of Wisconsin). 1963. 180 pps.

This is an important book for students of Chinese life in America. The author has assembled a remarkable amount of data on the employment of Chinese in California during the first three decades of their immigration. Included are chapters on Chinese laborers in the gold mines, as railway builders, in agriculture, and in the woolen, textile, shoe, cigar, and other smaller industries. All the data are subjected to a classical economic analysis in order to demonstrate that the economic arguments in support of California's anti-Chinese movement were not valid. The attempt to exonerate the Chinese from blame for California's economic difficulties is not new—Mary Coolidge attempted the same thing in her book, *Chinese Immigration,* in 1909—but the sophistication of the economic techniques is unusual and, given the admitted lacunae in and unreliability of the data, its theoretical reach is probably beyond its empirical grasp.

The principal argument of the book is that Chinese labor was not a liability to California's economy but an asset. The accusations by labor unions and small manufacturers and farmers that Chinese depressed wages or were unfair competition are not sustained by economic analysis of the industries involved or of the external factors that in fact determined the vicissitudes of California's alternate cycles of prosperity and depression. Thus, the popular assertion that 10,000 Chinese were discharged at the completion of the Central Pacific Railway in 1869 glutting the urban labor market is untrue. The teeming Chinese population of San Francisco was composed of new immigrants drawn there by alleged opportunities while most of the railroad laborers continued to work on trunk lines in California and Nevada. Further, the author argues, the Sinophobia of the workers made it impossible for them to form what he asserts would have been an effective anti-monopoly alliance with the farmers. Finally, the urban clothing, shoe, and cigar industries in which Chinese first labored and against which they later formed competing manufactories were "sick" industries beyond the cure which anti-Chinese demagogues promised.

The author's economic analysis brings his conclusions strikingly into line with those employers, entrepreneurs, and large-scale agriculturists who were in need of a cheap, efficient, and docile labor force. Although he does opt for the cooperation of farmers and laborers as a more effective alternative to Sinophobia, he does not suggest that laborers, white and Chinese, might have combined to demand better wages, working conditions, etc. Apparently a racially divided labor force—which Marx predicted would negate the possibility of socialism in America—did not impress itself as significant on the author. Yet the alleged docility of the Chinese laborer is revealed as by no means certain. Chinese railroad workers once sat down all along the line, and urban factory-owners were not immune to occasional strikes from the Chinese employees. The book contains but the briefest reference to Chinese contractors and no mention whatsoever of the role of Chinese community institutions—clans, *landsmannschaften,* and secret societies—on the organization of Chinese labor. But the intra-ethnic exploitation of fellow Chinese by these agencies and the limitations they presented to a united labor front were surely important aspects of the Chinese labor question.

Finally the author's insistence on strict adherence to "pure" economic analysis indicates the limits of that procedure. Sociological and psychological factors are formally excluded in the introduction but then re-admitted by the back door of ad hoc suggestions to account for the economically unsound behavior of Californians.

Review of *Bitter Strength*

BITTER STRENGTH: A HISTORY OF THE CHINESE IN THE UNITED STATES, 1850–1870. By Gunther Barth. (Cambridge: Harvard University Press. 1964. 305 pps.)

Professor Barth's book is a welcome addition to the recent but growing literature on Chinese in America. For many years those interested in the subject almost had to rely on either Mary Coolidge's spirited and Sinophilic *Chinese Immigration* (1909), or Elmer Sandmeyer's more detached account, *The Anti-Chinese Movement in California* (1939). In general, works on the Chinese have suffered from one of two basic distortions. They were either overzealous in portraying Chinese simply as the undeserving victims of racist demagogues and unscrupulous white capitalists, or they accepted the one-sided arguments of the Sinophobes and regarded the Chinese as inimical to labor and morals. The general climate of racial tolerance since the end of World War II has stilled the xenophobic voices almost completely but unintentionally give unwarranted credence to a so-called 'liberal' interpretation. Thus, Mrs. Coolidge's refusal to regard Chinese merchants as any different from American petit-bourgeois entrepreneurs has gone virtually unchallenged except by racists, and recent works, such as Richard Dillon's colorful *Hatchet Men,* reinforce that myth. Similarly, excessive filiopietism mars Ping Chiu's *Chinese Labor in California* and S. W. Kung's *Chinese in American Life.* On the other hand, Rose Hum Lee's *Chinese in the United States of America* suffers from a roseate view of assimilation that fails to comprehend the issues before the nonassimilated Chinese minority. Harold Isaacs' *Scratches on our Minds,* Kwang Chiu's *Americans and Chinese,* and Professor Barth's study are each in their own way scholarly works that rise above the view that American history is a kind of vicissitudinal morality play depicting the opposed forces of Absolute Good and Absolute Evil, total assimilation and total prejudice.

Professor Barth's thesis is that rather than a direct confrontation, the early contact of Chinese and Californians emerged as an abrasive encounter between two peoples with quite divergent aims. The forty-niners who came to California were intent on realizing an idealized America free of the twin evils of fettered labor and unscrupulous exploitation. The Chinese who crossed the perilous Pacific wished to sojourn only long enough at the "Golden Mountain" to acquire a competence sufficient to retire without worry in their native village. To the Americans fleeing from both slavery and abolitionism, the Chinese, even more than Indians, Mexicans, Negroes, and "foreigners," reminded them of those features of the United States they wished to avoid. To the Chinese the temporary, onerous burden of indentured servitude on the American frontier was a price worth paying in return for the envisioned comforts of an honorable and secure old age, surrounded by admiring kinsmen and respectful offspring. Independent miners and—later—Irish, Scandinavian, and other Anglo-Saxon trade unionists regarded the seemingly docile Chinese as anathema. On the other hand, certain capitalists and agriculturalists viewed the Chinese as a race eligible for the very treatment that believers in the California dream did not wish to inflict on white laborers, American or foreign. A few Catholic and several Protestant missionaries regarded the Chinese as worthy of special efforts in proselytism. Not all the Chinese were debt-ridden laboring sojourners. A merchant elite among them held their indenture and controlled their labor, domestic life, and departure. The work camps and Chinatowns, emblematic respectively of the servile control and social distance of the Chinese from other settlers in "El Dorado," excited the attention and aggression of the latter and reinforced the already closed society of Chinese California.

Chinese California, as Barth designates the network of control over Chinese in the state, consisted primarily of the associations established by the merchant elite that encompassed Chinese life. Clans and *hui kuans,* representing, respectively, the lineage and the territory, tribe, or language of the immigrants, enrolled nearly all the Chinese who came to the state. Secret societies, chapters of or modeled after the mainland Triad Society, formed the basis for opposition to the clan-*hui-kuan* oligarchy and also controlled gambling and prostitution, vital aspects of the homeless Chinese man's lonely sojourn. The relations between these associations were fraught with conflict, and they were not above co-opting elements of the uncomprehending larger society as unwitting accomplices to their feuds. Professor Barth describes all of this with painstaking attention to detail and documentation, and yet he never loses sight of his point: Chinese California shut itself out from the mainstream of American life at the same time that its denizens contributed to the development of the American West. His is the first published study of the Chinese in the United States to comprehend the complex origins, as well as the poignancy, of Chinatown's isolation.

Barth's duodecennial history concludes with his argument that the forces which spawned Chinese California began to erode after 1870. "Acculturation," in the form of conversion to Christianity, did not occur in numbers enough to encourage the missionary's zeal or to dampen the nativism of white Californians, but the learning of English and tool adaptation indicated the selective interest of the Chinese. The movement of Chinese beyond California—the importation of Chinese into the southern states is but one of the revelations from Professor Barth's indefatigable research—escalated the "Chinese problem" to a national issue but also weakened traditional controls over them and encouraged individuals to convert from sojourners to immigrants. Unfortunately, this *dénouement* is the weakest part of the argument and the least validated by the evidence. In fact, the net effect of nationalizing the Chinese issue was to exclude the Chinese from immigrating to the United States, from naturalization, and from realizing the benefits of trade unionism. Excluded from citizenship, prevented from procreating offspring in America, and barred from corporations, public works, free professions, and union membership, the steadily aging and diminishing population of Chinese was forced more and more behind the invisible walls of Chinatown and its benevolently despotic elites. Not until after 1930 was the sex ratio sufficiently balanced to permit normal domestic life and the birth of a substantial second generation. Chinatown survived Sinophobia; it is threatened today by equal opportunity and assimilation.

The anachronistic conclusion to Barth's work

should not detract from its otherwise excellent presentation. His detailed description of social life and labor among the early Chinese is unsurpassed in other available accounts. Although Barth's distinctions between the Chinese terms, *hui, hui kuan,* and *kongsi,* might not satisfy the Sinologist seeking etymological exactitude, they are enough to make his analysis clear and to suggest that Chinese probably used certain roughly equivalent terms interchangeably. Bibliography and footnotes are excellent and, although Barth might have been better served by an editor who obviated certain wordy obfuscations and the redundant "match-cutting" that connects chapters, his is an altogether fine contribution to history, Sinology, and sociology.

Review of *"Chink"*

"CHINK": A DOCUMENTARY HISTORY OF ANTI-CHINESE PREJUDICE IN AMERICA. Edited and with an Introduction by Cheng-Tsu Wu. Ethnic Prejudice in America Series. New York: The World Publishing Company. 1972. IX–XIV + 290 pp.

One of the most positive benefits of the new ethnic consciousness in America is the increasing interest in uncovering the nature and varieties of racism spawned in this country. The Sinopobic crusade was one of the most significant developments of American society; yet, until recently, it has received little attention, all too often being consigned to a footnote in the regional history of the West and treated as a short-lived phenomenon as well.

Professor Wu has brought together an excellent collection of documents, accounts, laws, and articles that, read intensively and with care, should help to dispel two prevailing myths: 1) That the anti-Chinese movement was a peculiar product of the West having little or nothing to do with national and industrial developments in the nation as a whole; and 2) That prejudice and discrimination against the Chinese is now a thing of the past. In providing this service, Professor Wu has presented us with a welcome addition to the growing literature on Asians in America.

"Chink" might properly serve as the documentary companion to the three most recent attempts at reversing the traditional historians' verdict on the importance of Chinese in American history: Miller's *The Unwelcome Immigrant,* Saxton's *The Indispensable Enemy,* and Lyman's *The Asian in the West.* Wu quite rightly begins with the institutionalization of prejudice in the laws, first of California and then of the nation as a whole. Chinese were desired as laborers provided they worked in jobs avoided by whites, lived apart in joyless ghettos unprotected by police and devoid of the amenities necessary to life, and behaved in a docile and tractable manner.

To insure these limitations, Chinese were singled out for taxation as miners, coerced into an unpleasant urban enclosure and then punished for living in overcrowded conditions, forbidden from testifying in court cases involving white men, prevented from uniting their families, proscribed from certain occupations and public works, and eventually, when their labor was no longer in demand they were excluded—except for certain so-called "exempt" classes—from entering the United States.

The official treatment of the Chinese by civic, state and national authorities constitutes the beginnings of *modern* racism in America. Nonwhite peoples could no longer be exploited by being kept in place in total institutions such as the slave plantation and the reservation. Henceforth, as the ignoble experiment with anti-Chinese legislation indicated, the presence of nonwhites would be acceptable in the formally free urban industrial settings, but their lives would be hedged about with severe restrictions and social isolation.

However, legislation was not enough. The Chinese did not supinely accept their designation as mudsills and pariahs; they actively and sometimes successfully opposed their treatment by mounting cases in the Supreme Court. To legislation, therefore, was added a vicious stereotypy and riotous terror. The former was not the product of the ignorant classes, but rather the proclaimed "truths" expressed by governors, congressmen, merchants, medical doctors and scholars.

Inspired by these racist teachings and turned against their fellow workers by demagogic speeches—not the least of which were given by union leaders—mobs attacked the Chinese in Los Angeles in 1871, Rock Springs in 1885, and Seattle and Tacoma in 1885 and 1886. Many Chinese were killed; others were maimed; and in general the Chinese of this period were subjected to crimes comparable to those committed against "free" blacks in America and Jews in Czarist Russia. The term "pogrom" is aptly and correctly applied by Professor Wu to these outrages.

But, it is popularly believed, these things are part of the past. The Chinese, it is often said, are now one of the nation's model minorities, having succeeded in climbing out of the ghetto and up the ladder of success. One of the most valuable sections of his book is Professor Wu's refutation of this excessively happy *denouement* to the Chinese-American story.

With documentary and eyewitness reports, Professor Wu reveals the real condition of Chinese in America. Despite the repeal of the Exclusion Act in 1943, the development of a small but significant Chinese-American middle class, and the claim that racial bias against Chinese in America has subsided, Chinese are still the victims of subtle prejudices, social exclusion, and occupational restrictions.

Not only are Chinese still popularly designated by the hated epithet "Chinaman" in the mass media, they are also humorously or insultingly demeaned in countless caricatures. This imagery has consequences that go far beyond the incalculable personal hurt that they produce. Even more important, Chinese have been denied entrance to certain labor unions, passed over for promotions that their efforts clearly merited, and discriminated against in both private employment and public service. Sanguine beliefs about the end of the anti-Chinese movement must be chastened by recognition of the evidence presented here that institutionalized racism still exists in America's major industries and many of its centers of government.

Professor Wu's compilation is an important corrective to the optimistic bias that prevails in the most popular conceptions of America's minorities. It should be part of every serious reader's library on the subject.

An addendum about the arresting but ambiguous cover photo. Professor Wu has disclaimed personal responsibility for the picture of a tee-shirted, hirsute, Chinese youth with a sullen but enigmatic expression on his face, holding a dead rat in his chopsticks while on the plate before him there lies a coiled dead snake. My own view is that the picture constitutes a dialectical desublimation of culture, (as described by Marcuse in *An Essay on Liberation*, pp. 34–36.) By boldly presenting a symbolic stereotype on the cover of a book whose contents refute it, the photo reverses its own negative imagery. Thus, the picture becomes an act of rebellion against the very system that first evoked its original pejorative meaning. Interpreted in this manner, the cover manifests an open rupture with the continuum of racist repression.

The same holds true for the book title, *"Chink."* Of course, I cannot be sure this was the intention of the jacket designers. I can only hope that readers will see it this way, or failing this, that they will not be so offended as to overlook an important book because of its controversial cover.

Review of *Learning to Be Chinese*

LEARNING TO BE CHINESE: THE POLITICAL SOCIALIZATION OF CHILDREN IN TAIWAN, by Richard W. Wilson, Cambridge, Mass.: The MIT Press, 1970. 203 pps.

Studies of socialization typically pose the question of the relationship between mental states (attitudes) and action without answering it. Does the orientation of childhood implant fixed ways of thinking about and doing things? In particular, political socialization studies usually beg whether the orientation toward authority implants a fixed relationship to the state. The present study is no exception to this generally overlooked issue, but it does provide a view of the role of schools in socializing Chinese on Taiwan.

Children in a country school, an urban public school, and an urban private school were subjected to projective tests, a questionnaire, interviewing, and on occasion observation in their daily curricular and extracurricular activities. Particular emphasis was placed on authority and hostility so that the children were shown pictures of a meeting, an encounter between a policeman and a vendor, a schoolroom scene, and a scene at home. Questions turned always to the authoritative relationship: the rectitude of doubting, disobeying, or refusing commands; and the moral, social, or personal justifications for obedience or dissent. Although the author is familiar with the Chinese (Formosan) scene, his methodology and theoretical insight are derived from the Occident. The familiar Western researchers—Erikson, Bandura, Walters, Child, Coleman, Hyman—provide in a rather random way the hypotheses to be tested or, more startlingly, the explanations for why certain hypotheses proved to be incorrect. There seems to have been no thought given to the possibility that the Chinese scene is *sui generis,* although the study rests its case on the ramifications of a shame ("face") culture for political orientations.

The Chinese are oriented around the maintenance of "face," the loss of which is either to have no *mien-tzu* (prestige or reputation based on achievement) or, far worse, no *lien* (group respect owned to a man with a good moral reputation). Face is essentially a group phenomenon so that a sense of we-they, insider-outsider, prevails over the organization of actions and attitudes whereby face may be lost or maintained. At the apex is the Chinese people among whom face can be lost by incorrect behavior toward foreigners. But below that a congeries of sub-groups—family, clan, friends, schoolmates, colleagues, etc.—provide the associational base for loyalty, obedience, obligation, trust, and shame. In learning to be Chinese, a child is constantly checked in his actions by the potential loss of face that untoward behavior might produce. Not only acts of commission but errors of omission can cost a person his *lien*. Thus, hedged about in his possibilities for political leadership, dissent, criticism, and opposition, the Chinese find outlet in tolerated deviance, situational and sanctioned departures from norms, a hyper-conscious sense of gamesmanship in social and political relationships, cynicism, and, ultimately in rebellion.

Despite the author's objectivity, it is difficult to escape the pervasive presence of the authoritarian state. The author acknowledges his own fear of asking questions about Chiang. The responses of the children show a keen awareness of the dangers of candid utterances, of acknowledging criticism or opposition, or of open criticism of the President. Teachers correct students in such minute details of speech as the correct way to refer to the political party on the mainland—"Communist bandits" not "Communist party." That a special awareness takes hold early is revealed in an interview with a first grader:

> Question: "What happens if a policeman makes a mistake?"
>
> Response: "We ask someone higher up to arrest him and kill him."
>
> Question: "Can we criticize a policeman?"

> Response: (frightened) "No. We must say he is good. If we say he's bad, we'll be arrested" (p. 103).

The strategies available to a people who must protect the face of their sub-group and their nation, who must be outwardly obedient to authority, and who must repress impulses to rebel or criticize are not fully explored in this study. Cynicism, deviance, and situational ethics do not exhaust the possibilities. Students of traditional China will recognize in the child's answer quoted above another, and more prevalent, approach—to utilize the hierarchy itself to get rid of enemies or, to repeat the child's phrase, "We ask someone higher up to arrest him and kill him." Over one hundred years ago, Thomas Taylor Meadows emphasized this and related approaches to show why the Chinese had a great many rebellions but very few revolutions. Rebellions oppose the incumbents but not the system by which they hold office; revolutions attack the system as such and may even forgive the incumbents as dupes or victims. The Chinese have been traditionally the masters of the intrigue against the incumbent and thus preserve obedience to authority at the same time that they resist the oppression of officials.

The conclusion to the monograph mutes the authoritarian culture in which it was carried out even further. Suddenly the author is interested in "social change," "development," and "modernization." Taiwan's economic miracle is seen as perhaps deriving from the authoritarian shame culture which the author has described. No further attention is given to culture, personality, individual, or even political change. Perhaps the author has said enough. The responses of the children will remain with the reader, a haunting reminder of tact and tactics in an oppressive society.

Scholars and Partisans

Chinatown in American History

LONGTIME CALIFORN': A DOCUMENTARY STUDY OF AN AMERICAN CHINATOWN by Victor G. and Brett de Bary Nee. Pantheon Books, New York, 1973. ix–xxvii + 411 pps.

When Nathan Glazer set out to write his "Social Characteristics of American Jews, 1654–1954, he remarked that "For the first half of the three hundred years of Jewish experience in America, there were so few Jews that it has been possible to track down almost every scrap of information that exists about each of them; . . ." Unfortunately, no similar situation exists for the Chinese in the United States. Despite the fact that their settlement in America has been less than half as long as that of the Jews, our knowledge about them is scanty, superficial, and, still, stereotyped. Much of the data from which a comprehensive picture might be drawn is as yet unanalyzed, and some of it undiscovered. Diaries, letters, and documents lie untouched in trunks and chests in basements of San Francisco's Chinatown. The trans-Pacific correspondence of the first Chinese immigrants is probably lost to us forever; although it is not impossible that some of these letters are kept in the family files of a clan-conscious person living in China. It is not yet a decade since the founding of the Chinese Historical Society of America, but thus far, despite efforts to open long-buried basements and preserve artifacts and documents from the early settlements, its outlook has remained largely antiquarian. Still another possibility is oral history. The recently completed Japanese American history project provides a model for such research, and when the University of California Press publishes the long awaited volumes revealing the findings, there should be a stir to replicate the study among the Chinese. Meanwhile, the Nees, a husband-and-wife research team, have more than filled the gap. Theirs is a fine synthesis of history, sociology, and biography—an integrated analysis of Chinatown that is the best book on the subject to date.

Victor and Brett de Bary Nee did not have an easy time of it. At first conceiving of their project as the gathering of a living record of the significant memories and current issues among Chinese in San Francisco's Chinatown, they discovered a much more complicated setting than they had imagined, found themselves beset and frustrated by their own language handicaps (speakers of Mandarin, they could not converse with the Cantonese speaking Chinatowners), and eventually determined that a social and economic history would have to inform their interviews. Undaunted by these difficulties, the Nees succeeded admirably. Not only have they captured the human element of today's Chinatown, but also they have unraveled its complex institutional structures. Their book presents, in addition to a biography of the study, and a "prologue: Portsmouth Square," which describes with clarity and empathy the setting in which Chinese oldsters gather each day, five sections—the bachelor society; the refugees; the family society; the emergence of a new working class; radicals and the new vision—each describing a segment of the community. To each section the authors have written a brief but excellent socio-historical introduction—and then let the people speak for themselves, in the form of autobiographies that were taped and transcribed by the Nees during their months of residence in Chinatown. In the back of the book H. Mark Lai, historian of Chinatown, has provided a set of clear and comprehensive organizational charts depicting the community's power structure. Appendices give profiles of Chinatown's class structure, highlights of recent immigration legislation, and a map of the districts of southeastern China from which the Chinese in America originated. The book is, fortunately, beyond the constrictions of dead history or dry social science; for the poignancy, humor, tragedy, and rage that inform the biographies cannot help but move all but the most insensitive reader. Rarely have natural literary expressions, moral suasion, oral history, and social science been so wonderfully combined.

America's conflict with Chinese immigrants aroused the interest of white and black leaders and thinkers throughout the second half of the nineteenth century. Although consideration of their thought was beyond the scope of the Nees' study, it is relevant to understanding the setting of "The Chinese Question." The Chinese presence challenged prevailing ideas about the chances for racial harmony and class conflict in America. Such luminaries as Josiah Royce, Hinton R. Helper, Mark Twain, and Henry George among the whites, and Frederick Douglass, John Roy Lynch, and James Weldon Johnson among the blacks discussed the social and economic issues that first arose out of California's racial cockpit and later engulfed the nation. Royce and Helper, from quite different perspectives, thought California a dreadful mistake. Although not particularly alarmed by the Chinese immigrants, Royce pointed to the lawlessness bred into white Californians by the doctrine of popular sovereignty and the extensive settlement of some-time slaveholders in the state; Helper, an abolitionist who was nonetheless a racist with pronounced prejudices in favor of Anglo-Saxon superiority, despised California because of its mosaic of peoples and cultures—especially the Chinese ("I cannot perceive what more right or business these semi-barbarians have in California than flocks of blackbirds have in a wheatfield") about whom he concluded, "No inferior race of men can exist in these United States without becoming sub-ordinate [sic] to the will of the Anglo-Saxons, or foregoing many of the necessities and comforts of life." Mark Twain documented the cruelties, petty and grave, against the Chinese in San Francisco and pointed openly to the cause of them—systematic vilification by political leaders, legislative enactments, and a Sinophobic press. Before he fully developed his famous theories of land economics and taxation, Henry George had distinguished himself by a widely publicized letter to the New York *Tribune* on May 1, 1869 entitled "The Chinese on the Pacific Coast." George provided an intellectual patina to American Sinophobia, presenting the most impressive statement to date in behalf of the argument that China's inexhaustible supply of cheap workers would drag down the price of white labor, take over every basic occupation, withdraw needed capital from the United States in the form of remittances to China, populate America with a familyless group of alien, unassimilable, subsistence laborers, and, ultimately, rebalance the distribution of productive return in favor of capitalists and landlords. A die had been cast.

Black intellectuals and leaders were perplexed, chagrined, and divided in their opinions over the

Chinese presence. On the one hand, they discerned that Chinese shared many of the same ignominies and much of the maltreatment previously reserved for Negroes and Indians; on the other hand, they could not but perceive the Chinese laborer as a competitor in the struggle for advancement in America. Thus, the California correspondent for *Frederick Douglass' Paper,* while opposed to the injustices heaped upon them, commented in 1854 that the Chinese "are filthy, immoral and licentious—according to our notions of such things. . . . The Chinaman, under the most favorable aspects, is calculated to excite a smile. His vacant Know Knothing face is expressive of nothing but stupidity." In later issues this correspondent complained about placing Negroes under the same ban as Chinese, especially, he asserted, since the latter, unlike blacks, could never amalgamate with Americans, were willing to remain "coolies," and lived at such a low standard.

Douglass himself adopted a position consistent with his own stand on civil rights. Opposed to the cruelties of the coolie trade, which he compared in its horrors to the trials of the middle passage, he nevertheless sought to refute those who believed that the Chinese worker in America was incapable of rising above the condition of a mudsill. "The Chinese laborer," he wrote in 1871, "who, at home, thinks himself a rich man, with earnings averaging two dollars per month, will not in this country long be satisfied with twenty." From the beginning Douglass joined with those who favored equal rights for all persons regardless of race. With stunning accuracy he stated the fundamental issues in the conflict in a letter to Senator Charles Sumner on July 6, 1870:

> Upon the Chinese question I rejoice to see you in the right place, far in the advance and the country as usual behind you.
>
> A bitter contest, I fear, is before us on this question. Prejudice, pride of race, narrow views of political economy, are on one, humanity, civilization and sound policy are on the other.

And the opposition to Chinese in California, Douglass asserted, was a feature of America's "color line": "Our Californian brothers, of Hibernian descent,

hate the Chinaman, and kill him, and when asked why they do so, their answer is that a Chinaman is so industrious he will do all the work, and can live by wages upon which other people would starve. When the same people and others are asked why they hate the colored people, the answer is that they are indolent and wasteful, and cannot take care of themselves." Douglass hoped for interracial harmony: "We are made up of a variety of nations—Chinese, Jews, Africans, Europeans, and all sorts. These different races give the Government a powerful arm to defend it. They will vie with each other in hardship and peril, and will be united in defending it from all enemies, whether from within or without."

However, blacks, Chinese, and European immigrants found themselves in competition with one another for opportunities in America. To journalists, demagogues and intellectuals their competition was assessed as the struggle for *assimilation,* a term whose capacity to cow and excite proved far greater than its ability to define or clarify. Leading members of the several minorities all too often accepted the terms of this struggle without giving them critical analysis. They then sought to demonstrate their own fitness for assimilation in contrast to other groups who, they argued, were less able to meet the requirements of life in America. Thus, after visiting San Francisco in 1906, John R. Lynch, first Negro to be elected to the United States Congress from Mississippi and a staunch advocate of civil rights was sure "That the colored American is gradually reaching that point where he insists upon the same rate of wages for himself that is paid to a white man for the same kind of service." But, on the other hand he "found . . . that the situation with reference to the Japanese and Chinese is not so much racial as it is industrial. The apprehension is that, as competitors in the field of labor with the American man, they are liable to bring about, if they should be there in large numbers, a reduction in the wages of the American laborer or throw him out of employment and thus degrade the American standard of wages and labor."

For those not involved in the problem of job opportunities the issue of social acceptance loomed large. Even in the generally fair-minded judgments of James Weldon Johnson we may discover doubts about certain peoples from Asia, coupled with praise for others. After attending an international conference in the Far East in 1929 Johnson wrote:

> Intelligent Japanese and Chinese are both stung to the quick by our Exclusion Act, and both resent it, but it appeared to me that, while Japanese smart under it, the Chinese are able to rise above it. One reason for this, I thought, was the fact that the Chinese are more self-contained and not so solicitous of the approbation of the white world as are the Japanese. I myself reacted differently to these two peoples; the Japanese left me rather cold. Not during the time I was at the Conference did I form cordial relations with any Japanese. Among the Chinese at the Conference, I formed some warm friendships.

And when American Indian intellectuals entered the competition, they, too, felt the need to compare and contrast and make invidious distinctions. Arthur C. Parker, Seneca Indian, anthropologist, and president of the Society of American Indians, seeking to exculpate the Indians for their allegedly slow assimilation, contrasted their chances with those of Negroes and *European* immigrants, but scarely paid attention to Chinese. After all, Asiatics had been declared aliens ineligible for citizenship, and thus they had already lost out in one important area of the contest. Perhaps the final irony—and tragedy—of this contest emerged in 1960 when Rose Hum Lee, Chinese American, sociologist, and keen student of Chinese America, summed up her years of researches on the subject with the bitter complaint that despite a century of habitation within the United States the Chinese had not assimilated as rapidly or as completely as the Japanese whose time of settlement had been only half as long. The strife over assimilation not only divided the old American stock from blacks and the newer immigrants from Europe and Asia but also fractured whatever unity the minorities might have forged out of their common plight.

Of all the opposition to the Chinese in America the bitterest cries arose from the incipient labor movement and most of the politically radical sects. Samuel Gompers epitomized the nonradical workingman's hostility to the Chinese. Himself an immi-

grant, Gompers drew a distinction between those elements among the newcomers to America who were assimilable and those who were not. The latter, he felt, should be excluded both from the protections of organized labor and from the United States altogether. For example, Gompers distinguished between Eastern European Jews, whose habits and customs seemed so alien to other Americans and to the earlier Jewish immigrant groups, and the Chinese, also foreign and exotic but, he argued, dangerous and unassimilable as well. About the Russian and Eastern European Jews Gompers was understanding and solicitous:

> They were strangers in a new land. They had to provide subsistence for tomorrow in whatever opportunity it could be found. They crowded into unskilled callings and worked at starvation wages. They undermined standards and labor organizations, but they were under the urge of dire necessity. They were the products of decades of persecution.

When it came to the Chinese laborers in America, however, Gompers could find nothing to say in their favor. Professing to have no anti-Chinese prejudices, Gompers nevertheless aligned himself with the most vitriolic, demagogic, and Sinophobic voices in the labor movement, co-authored with Hermann Gustadt the infamous racist tract *Meat vs Rice: American Manhood Against Asiatic Coolieism—Which Shall Survive?*, and worked incessantly from the 1880s onward for the total exclusion of Chinese and Japanese from the United States. ("I have always opposed Chinese immigration not only because of the effect of Chinese standards of life and work but because of the racial problem created when Chinese and white workers were brought into the close contact of living and working side by side.") Equally significant was Gompers' ironclad opposition to organizing Chinese workers or to enrolling already established locals with Chinese members in the A.F. of L. Gompers stated his position unequivocally in a letter to a local organizer:

> I am inclined to believe that it would be unwise and impractical, to unionize a Chinese restaurant. Of course I realize the desirability of having every establishment possible unionized, and to organize our fellow workers, but you must take under consideration the further fact

that the American labor movement has set its face against the Chinese coming to this country, and upon our demands the law has been passed for the exclusion of the Chinese from the United States or from any of the territories or possessions of the United States. . . . In other words, the American labor movement stands committed against the Chinese coming to our country or any possession of our country.

It would be the height of inconsistency of our movement to unionize the Chinese against whom we have declared.

Prominent leaders in the right wing of the American radical movement also spoke out against the Chinese. Victor Berger, Ernest Untermann, and Max Hayes led the attack on Asian immigrants, despite a plea from Japan's Socialist Party to remain faithful to Marx's dictum, "Workingmen of all countries, unite." Berger warned that if Oriental immigration were allowed to continue, the United States "is absolutely sure to become a black-and-yellow country within five generations." Untermann agreed and stated boldly, "I am determined that my race shall be supreme in this country and in the world." Hayes went further than most, asserting—quite incorrectly as it turns out—that Marx's call for international workingmen's unity was made without knowledge of conditions on the Pacific Coast. Although the right wing did not succeed in dominating the American radical movement, its virulent racism sullied the principle of workingmen's unity.

At times labor's hostility to Chinese immigration combined with an ill-concealed anti-Semitism in a general attack on certain classes of foreign laborers. Thus, in 1886 W. C. Owen justified socialist support for California's anti-Chinese agitation by accusing Jews and Chinese of failing to live up to the requirements of national solidarity:

So it is with the anti-Chinese crusade; a great part of the repugnance to them upon this coast is that they do not act as citizens, that they have no concern in the solidarity of the nation. A precisely similar sentiment has dictated the persecutions of Jews in Germany, Austria, and Russia, persecutions which have been justified precisely on this ground. . . . It is, in short, but the public method of voicing the sentiment, "no rights without duties," or as Comte puts it, "Man has no rights except to fulfill his duties."

And, in the same year, as anti-Semitism merged with Sinophobia into a selective division of the working class, a lone, brave, tragic figure in the labor movement, the Jewish barber and seaman Sigismund Danielewicz, sacrificed his important position and few perquisites to denounce the anti-Chinese stance of the International Workingmen's Association, which he served as secretary. A contemporary newspaper account tells of this dramatic—and lost—moment as Danielewicz, hooted and jeered, gave labor a chance to redeem its principles. He

tried the patience of the convention by reading several pyramids of words about the equality of men. He said that he belonged to a race which had been persecuted for hundreds of years and was still persecuted—the Jews; and he called upon all of his people to consider whether "the persecution of the Chinese" was more justifiable than theirs had been. And he left it upon the Irish to say whether it was more justifiable than their persecutions in New York had been; upon the Germans to make a similar comparison upon their condition somewhere else. . . .

Danielewicz was repaid for his stand on interracial equality by being driven off the speaker's platform. His statement, according to the newsman covering the convention "would have proved a defense of the Chinese if it had been completed." He was last heard of in California in 1910, twenty-four years after his vain attempt to halt the rush to racism by western labor radicals. Out of work and deserted by his erstwhile comrades, he set out on foot for the East.

What in fact happened to the United States because of its short-lived (1850–1882) policy of unrestricted Chinese immigration? Despite the apocalyptic visions of ruin or reinvigoration, nothing quite so dramatic occurred. California, where the Chinese at first were concentrated, suffered neither an economic collapse nor a cultural renaissance. The "mongrelization" of the races, a primordial fear in white America, was prevented by anti-miscegenation statutes, directed in fourteen of the thirty states wherein they were enacted specifically at "Mongolians." Organized labor's fears about the degradation of *white* workingmen were assuaged by four decades of race-baiting strikes and riots which, by 1910, had achieved their aim of evicting Chinese workingmen from just about every nonghetto occupation in which they had obtained a foothold. The passage of the Chinese Exclusion Act in 1882, which with a succession of even more stringent amendments, remained in force until 1943, not only cut off the immigration of laborers from China but also prevented the coming of their wives, denied Chinese the right to naturalization, halted the propagation of a second generation, and insured a dwindling population of aging sojourners in Chinatown for the next fifty years. Spokesmen for the unions took most of the credit for "saving" America from the "Mongolian" evil, as is indicated in this remarkably candid statement by Selig Perlman, the distinguished labor economist, in 1920: "The anti-Chinese agitation in California, culminating as it did in the Exclusion Law, passed by Congress in 1882, was doubtless the most important single factor in the history of American labor, for without it the entire country might have been overrun by Mongolian labor and the labor movement might have become a conflict of races instead of one of classes."

And what of the Chinese in San Francisco? The Nees have documented with life histories the full story to date. Despite predictions of their imminent demise throughout the 1920s, the Chinese in America have endured. Denied the chance to form families in the United States, Chinese men labored in America and paid infrequent visits to their wives in China, sired children, hopefully sons, and when these boys reached young manhood they were encouraged to join their fathers overseas. Other Chinese were smuggled into the United States on false papers or over the borders from Canada and Mexico. During the period when the male population was youthful and women scarce, prostitution flourished in Chinatown. The girls, often illegal entrants, were indentured servants whose contract was owned by the brothel keeper, and they were carefully watched over by the secret societies who guarded the bordellos. Recreation for this homeless men's colony included gambling, whoring, and, for some, an escape into the euphoric fantasies induced by opium. It was a dreary existence.

A smaller group formed families in the third and

fourth decades of the twentieth century. Merchants, who could bring wives from China legally, fathered a small second generation. Born in San Francisco, educated in the public schools and in Chinese language schools in the late afternoon, these first Chinese Americans were encouraged to think of themselves as sojourners like their parents. Learn American techniques, their parents urged, and then go to China and use them to build up the homeland. During the 1920s and 1930s opportunities for Chinese in America were largely confined to menial positions as waiters, busboys, clerks, and garment workers in Chinatown. Educated Chinese could not hope to reach middle class status in the United States. But they could not but help imbibe American values, ideals, practices, and language. And thus they were caught in between the two cultures—products of both, full-fledged members of neither.

In the forties everything suddenly changed. The war with Japan made the United States and China allies. The Chinese Exclusion Act was repealed, naturalization permitted, and a quota of 105 allowed to enter the United States each year. Subsequently a series of bills extended opportunities for Chinese immigration until, in 1965, President Johnson ushered in a new era by signing into law the repeal of all national origins quotas on immigration. A rush of new immigrants from Hong Kong threatened to swamp the aging and seemingly enfeebled complex of institutions that controlled the Chinese community. A balance in the sex ratio promised new generations of Chinese Americans. American Chinese and the new immigrants both proved restive under the anachronistic despotism of the old Chinatown order.

During the 1940s and 1950s job opportunities for Chinese Americans opened up in the war industries and in the defense oriented expansion occasioned by the Cold War. Those who went to college and majored in physics, chemistry, engineering, pharmacy, dentistry, and medicine achieved professional status, moved out of the ghetto, and in some instances became suburbanites. Meanwhile, the establishment of the Peoples' Republic of China closed the mainland to those aged sojourners and few "zionists" who had sought to return to the homeland, created a new class of refugees and overseas students (some of whom were harshly treated during the McCarthy era), and induced a more permanent sense of exile among the overseas Chinese.

But just as the success of the small middle class of Chinese Americans seemed to herald the fulfillment of the immigrants' golden dream, a new set of problems emerged. The exploited classes of the Chinatown labor force—especially the garment workers—became a force in a new eruption of ethnic class consciousness. At the same time youths from Hong Kong and Taiwan, champing under the restraints imposed by a crowded and unpromising ghetto, formed rival gangs, fought each other, roamed the streets, terrorized tourists, and extorted money from Chinese shopkeepers. American born youths also formed associations, but, not subject to deportation, their formations took on a radical, populist, and political character, emulated the Black Panthers for a while, espoused "yellow power," ethnic liberation, and, occasionally, a rhetorical Maoism. The traditional Chinatown power elite, associated since the 1930s with the Kuomin-

tang and supportive of the commercial and industrial status quo in the ghetto, reacted harshly, opposing the youths, the labor unions, the O.E.O., and, seemingly all programs of amelioration except those sponsored by itself. Middle class Chinese, drawn to the old ghetto by a desire to help their less fortunate peers, sometimes found themselves estranged from all camps, unwilling to wholly abandon the Confucian ethic of hard work and filial responsibility which served them so well, yet sensitive to the enormous anguish, alienation, and anger of the radical and rebellious young people.

It has been fashionable to treat the Chinese in America as a "model minority"—quiet, hardworking, unassuming, and infrequent contributors to either the welfare rolls or juvenile delinquency. The Nees have shown that all that is a bourgeois mystique, a comfortable illusion that a closer look at harsh realities must shatter. In disenchanting the conventional wisdom about Chinatown they have called upon all of us to see our history, culture, institutions, and peoples as they really are. Truth is not always beautiful—it is necessary.

In Memoriam: Rose Hum Lee (1904–1964)

American sociology lost one of its outstanding contributors when Rose Hum Lee passed away in Phoenix, Ariz., on March 25, 1964, at the age of 59. She was born on August 20, 1904, in Butte, Montana.

Lee received her bachelor's degree from the Carnegie Institute of Technology in 1942. Her graduate work was completed at the University of Chicago where she earned the master's degree in 1943 and the doctorate in sociology in 1947. Her dissertation, "The Chinese Communities of the Rocky Mountain Region," described the cultural elements peculiar to these communities, and analyzed the social and economic factors affecting their rise and decline. From this early work flowed a series of articles that became minor classics in the field. Her most famous essay, "The Decline of Chinatowns in the United States" (*American Journal of Sociology,* March, 1949), is reprinted in numerous anthologies on racial relations, unban problems, and the sociology of minorities. Less well known but more significant for its ethnographic description was her earlier essay, "Social Institutions of a Rocky Mountain Chinatown" (*Social Forces,* October, 1948).

Before World War II, Lee lived in China, engaged in social work and in the study of missionary social welfare. (Her master's thesis described the work of the 19th-century medical missionary and diplomat in China, Peter Parker.) After obtaining her doctorate she continued her active interest in improving racial and human relations. She served on the Education Committee of the Chicago Commission of Human Relations and with the National Conference of Christians and Jews. She was a board member of the Hyde-Park Kenwood Community Conference, and in 1959 she served as National Secretary of the Society for the Study of Social Problems. In the same year she received the B'nai B'rith Woman of Achievement Award for Greater Chicago.

As a sociologist Lee utilized the theoretical approach and conceptual apparatus developed by Robert E. Park and his colleagues at the University of Chicago. "Chinatowns" were communities that arose from the conflict, competition, and accommodation of the Chinese in white America. In one essay—"Occupational Invasion, Succession, and Accommodation of the Chinese of Butte, Montana"

259

(American Journal of Sociology, July, 1949)—she explored changes in the employment of Chinese in her birthplace from 1890 to 1945 in terms of the perspectives familiar to students of the Chicago school. In another essay, "The Marginal Man" *(Journal of Public Relations,* Spring, 1956), she enhanced the theoretical precision of the concept first developed by Stonequist. In 1949–1950 she received a Social Science Research Council grant to study the new immigrant Chinese families in the San Francisco-Oakland area. Out of this research came four short monographs describing the social characteristics of established, immigrant, stranded, and delinquent Chinese. In 1960 she combined her exhaustive researches in her book, *The Chinese in the United States of America.*

This book is her most important published work. (Her earlier book, *The City: Urbanism and Urbanization in Major World Regions,* 1955, received critical acclaim and was singled out as a contemporary example of the pervasive influences of the Chicago school on urban sociology by Don Martindale in his important critique of that school's approach.) In *The Chinese in the United States of America* Lee asked why the Chinese had not yet entered the final phase of Park's racial cycle—assimilation—and she exhorted the Chinese in America to unshackle themselves from the parochial and limiting associations of Chinatown. Chinatowns were understandable as a reaction to the hostility of white America, but made no sense once that hostility had abated. In the absence of anti-Chinese prejudice the only explanation for the continued viability of closed Chinese communities was a failure of will on the part of the Chinese themselves. Chinatown leaders had a vested interest in segregation, she suggested, but the Chinatown masses were being exploited by these interests and should escape them by unreserved entrance into American society. "Now is the most auspicious time to strive for total and unreserved integration into the American society," she wrote. "Although the road ahead may be rough, the attempt must be made, with the Chinese themselves taking the initiative, because the members of the larger society have demonstrated their good will by removing the barriers, one by one. . . ."

In 1961 Lee took an extended leave from Roosevelt University in Chicago, where she had risen to full Professor and Chairman of the Department of Sociology—the first American of Chinese descent to do so. She returned to the West and took up residence at Phoenix College in Arizona. There she studied local problems of social welfare but devoted herself to writing a book-length monograph about her father, an immigrant from China who had worked as a ranch worker, miner, laundryman, and merchant. Hopefully this manuscript will be published posthumously. At the time of her death she was also working on research concerning the adoption of Indian children by whites.

Rose Hum Lee died leaving a rich legacy of research and many questions requiring further work. For over 20 years she was the only American sociologist studying the Chinese in America. Her work challenges those who follow her to unravel the complex skein of ethnic and immigrant life in this country and to formulate from the biographies and histories of its peoples more adequate sociological basis for understanding American society.

Review of *The Story of the Chinese in America*

THE STORY OF THE CHINESE IN AMERICA. By Betty Lee Sung. (Orig. pub. in 1967 as *Mountain of Gold:* rpt. New York: Collier Books, 1971. viii + 341 pps. Appendix and index.)

Professor Sung's book is a celebration of Chinese success in America. Although it has the superficial trappings of a sociological analysis—statistical tables, demographic data, and discussions of assimilation—these are but scientistic shibboleths that frame and justify a Chinese American's telling of America's perpetual morality tale about its minorities. With but a few changes in detail, the same fable can be—and has been—told about the Japanese, Irish, Jews, Italians, Greeks, Swedes and many more. Its form is always the same: a people beset by hardships and oppression in their own country bravely cross the seas to America, a land which promises freedom and opportunity. Once arrived, however, they encounter prejudice, oppression, and difficult times. However, they never lose faith in the dream that originally compelled them. They work hard, refuse to be discouraged by the abuses that harm their lives and hinder their progress, and eventually—usually in the second, or sometimes the third generation—succeed. The success is recognized in "contributions" made to the host country and ratified by a

general social acceptance of the once-despised people. These tales resonate not only with the children's stories that affect our adult outlook more than we care to imagine, but also with the largely mercantilist (not capitalist) mystique of small town ambition that forms a great part of the American socioeconomic gospel. History is, thus, nicely encapsulated within the American Protestant ethic: all the "bad" things happened in the past; sensible courage and patient fortitude were shown in moments of danger; proper diligence and prodigious effort proved the worthiness of a people who were at first sorely tested; ultimately—that is *now*—the rewards for these virtues are granted.

Professor Sung's version is true to this form. Indeed, were it not that the book is presented as a serious effort, it might be a parody of its theme. According to her presentation, it was mostly the Chinese from Toishan, a district of Kwangtung, who responded to the gold rush in California, while the rest of the Chinese, "resigned to toil and deprivation," and constrained by family ties that were "too

261

strong," stayed home. Once arrived in America, these Chinese were taken benevolently in hand by the Chinese Six Companies, who hired out their labor, loaned money and collected debts, and in general looked after their charges. However, an anti-Chinese movement, supported by politicians, organized labor, businessmen and farmers, ultimately succeeded in restricting Chinese labor by excluding workers and their wives from coming to America and by oppressing those who remained. Chinese responded to this treatment, "taking the consequences," as Ms. Sung puts it, by engaging in "an honorable deception," i.e., illegally smuggling family and friends into the United States, until a "crack in the door" appeared in 1943 with the congressional establishment of an immigrant quota for China and eventually widened into the fissure made possible by the Johnson Immigration Act of 1968. With the Chinese family slowly and painfully transplanted to America, Chinese settled at first into laundries which were a "haven and a prison," restaurants, which we learn were a "natural inclination," and obtained spiritual succor through "a practical view of religion" which indicated that there were "many roads to heaven." As a reward for their ardor and arduousness, the Chinese today "get into the best places," are rapidly "joining the mainstream," and are finding that their compatriots there are a "distinguished company." Moreover, the Chinese are deserving of their current wonderful condition because, among other things, they "view prejudice with a very healthy attitude," they "are not as clannish as they used to be," and they "have transferred their allegiance and loyalty to the United States." Of course there are some problems still to be solved, but these are minor. Professor Sung notes two bad traits among the Chinese: lack of punctuality at ceremonial affairs, and excessive apathy and individualism among the elderly. Presumably these too will pass away with further acculturation among the American-born and the death of the aged sojourners. Thus, all's well that ends well.

Scholars interested in the life of Chinese in America can learn little from this fable. Its evidence is marshalled from lively anecdotes, not careful appraisal. Its purpose is to lay the ghost of the parlor variety of anti-Chinese prejudice. Its method is to substitute a mythical Chinese bourgeoisie for the once hated "coolie," with the curious and unanalyzed assumption that *embourgeoisement* of the Chinese will allay the fears about them.

Everything we should want to know about the Chinese in America is left out or covered with a syrupy gloss. Chinese secret society activity is casually disposed of as a thing of the past—which it is not—and as too overlaid with pejorative stereotyping to analyze. The overseas clans are inadequately described and all too cozily redeemed as "family associations." The *hui kuan* are not treated beyond their own myth-making protective propaganda. The significance of institutional racism is wholly neglected by the remarkable avoidance of any analysis of Chinese life in America between 1910 and 1943, the period in which ghettoization became secure and the controls of the Chinatown power elite were consolidated. The current malaise among Chinese American youth is dismissed in the foreword to the 1971 edition as too recent to cope with, but this excuse won't do: the failure here is one of sociological imagination. The author is too much a part of the generation she seeks to apotheosize. What is required is an optimum distance, a socio-cultural understanding of the American racism, a thorough knowledge of overseas Chinese institutions, and a clear-eyed judgment independent of national and cultural imperatives. Unfortunately, none of these is present in this work.

Hopefully, a new generation will carry out the necessary next step: an historically and culturally informed analysis of Chinese in the United States. This generation should mark the end of fabled innocence.

THE HATCHET MEN: THE STORY OF THE TONG WARS IN SAN FRANCISCO'S CHINATOWN. By Richard H. Dillon. New York: Coward-McCann, 1962. 375 pps.

The author of this work is a locally well-known historian and bibliographer of San Franciscana. He has assembled from the dusty archives of California history a massive and imposing amount of data and written a lively account of the internecine struggles that took place in San Francisco's Chinese quarter in the latter decades of the 19th century. Material on the "tong" wars has hitherto found its way into serious historical or sociological works only rarely. Rather, it was confined to the pious aphorisms of a handful of 19th-century missionaries, usually reaching its widest audience in the Sunday rotogravure, a few movies, and the tales of Sax Rohmer. Now given this imprimatur of seriousness, perhaps sociologists and anthropologists will turn their attention to this data, rich in the stuff from which theory might arise.

To say that the book takes its subject matter seriously is not to say that it is good scholarship. The complexity of Chinese social institutions is filtered through a simplifying sieve. "This book attempts to tell the story of the high cost of bigotry and intolerance. It is no condemnation of San Francisco's Chinatown nor of its citizens, past or present; it is a condemnation of the criminal classes which flourished there." Throughout the book this thin, moralistic theme is reiterated. The "good" Chinese citizens (mostly mechants) are pitted against the Chinese "criminal classes." As with children's fiction and bad movies, "good" triumphs over "evil." The Chinese "tongs" are destroyed by the great earthquake of 1906 and the perseverance of certain able policemen and the honest Chinese merchants.

There are two serious errors here. The first is that of factual coverage. The material on the period covered is good and comprehensive, but an absence of data and a desire to "close the case" should not have led the author into the romantic and hardly credible *denouement* with which he closes his book. Chinese secret societies did not disappear after 1906. Their membership was instrumental in raising the funds for Sun Yat-Sen's revolution of 1911. In 1949, delegates from Canadian and American chapters of the Triad Society vainly attempted to negotiate a compromise between the forces of Chiang Kai-Shek

263

and Mao Tse-tung. Recently a convention of the so-called "Chinese Freemasons"—an Occidental euphemism adopted by the Triad Society—was held in Victoria, B.C. (Even in his assertion of the end of Chinese tong "criminality" he is in error. As recently as 1958 an open inter-tong fight between the Hop Sing and Bing Kung Associations of San Francisco was narrowly averted by months of negotiation and arbitration.)

The second error stems from his frame of reference. Dillon omits any effective analysis of the "tongs" as radical societies. Imprisoned by his facile view of them as criminal associations, he can only treat them as organized criminal gangs. The relation between criminality and rebellious or revolutionary activity has never been fully appreciated in America: Dillon's error is no different from that of many criminologists who perceive Chinese tong depredations as a social problem caused by an unhealthy environment of prejudice and misunderstanding.

Dillon is clearly very concerned lest he revive the once-popular stereotype of the Chinese as cunning, crafty, and dangerous. He wishes simultaneously to write a history of Chinatown's "criminal classes" and to absolve the Chinese of any collective cultural or hereditary guilt. But a less parochial and more detached point of view would have saved him from this dilemma, which after all, is of his own making. Secret associations of outcasts have been a traditional instrument of rebellion and a mechanism for the redress of grievances among the Chinese. As Hobsbawm has shown in his brilliant treatise *Social Bandits and Primitive Rebels,* non-ideological bandit movements are not uncommon among peasant peoples at great social distance from a central government that has only formal legitimacy to them. Such movements, if they survive, may become institu-tionalized, conservative, and even attempt a veneer of respectability. In their struggle for survival and immediate gains, bandit movements co-opt legitimate agencies as temporary allies. Such co-optation has mutual advantages, as Dillon's discussion of the relations between police and tongmen implies and as Hobsbawm has made explicit.

Two factors that contribute to the institutionalization of bandit movements are their own successes and migration. The former needs little comment since it follows a pattern similar to that laid out by Michels in *Political Parties.* Migration to a new society imposes certain survival problems upon a non-ideological radical movement. To survive it must often resort to robbery or control of illicit goods and services demanded by fellow immigrants. Dillon documents the secret societies' oligopoly over the supply of narcotics, women, and games of chance. Feuds between would-be monopolists tended to develop among the societies. Thus originated some of the tong wars of Chinatown and incidentally, under similar conditions, the gang wars between the overseas chapters of the Mafia in America.

"Local history," Louis Wirth once remarked, "has been regarded as the province of the amateur and of historians of lesser breed." Yet local history provides material as rich as that from which historians have written in the grand manner and from which sociologists have constructed macrocosmic theory. British and American social anthropologists and sociologists working in Southeast Asia and China have shown greater theoretical appreciation and comprehensiveness than writers on the same subject in the United States. Hopefully, Dillon's book may stir more sociologists to apply themselves to "domestic" Chinese communities. Dillon certainly has provided the opportunity.

CHINESE-AMERICANS: SCHOOL AND COMMUNITY PROBLEMS. By Integrated Education Associates. Chicago, Ill.: Integrated Education Associates, 1972. 76 pps.

This modest but fine anthology contains a dozen essays and a bibliography on the current social, educational, and economic problems of Chinese in America. The discussions cover conditions in San Francisco, New York City, Boston, and Honolulu and its environs, and thus include the major settlement areas of Chinese in the United States. Essays in this collection vary in depth, scope, and style. Several are in fact printed statements of testimony before various investigating committees: the Senate Committee on Equal Educational Opportunity; the Subcommittee on Employment, Manpower, and Poverty of the U. S. Senate Committee on Labor and Public Welfare; the Subcommittee on Education of the U. S. Senate Committee on Labor and Public Welfare. The others are reprinted from local journals concerned with civil rights, social change, and Asian American problems.

The fact that Chinese American community leaders, spokesmen, and reformers are testifying before committees of the Congress indicates a major development in this ethnic group. Among tradi-tional Chinese the resort to public law for the redress of inequities was discouraged. Public law invited an invasion of privacy, threatened local authority, and upset cherished values. To invoke legal authority was to bring shame on all those involved. The erosion of traditional values through acculturation of the American born, and the inability of the old Chinatown elites to solve burgeoning social problems has let to the current resort to Congress and public opinion. Moreover, among some of the younger Chinese American groups, the clan. *Landsmann-schaften,* and secret society elites are not only incapable of meeting the needs of Chinatown's denizens, but are themselves part of the problem. A wholesale reconstitution of the community—of its values, institutions, practices, relationship to the metropolis, and its self-image—seems to be the preferred order of the day. Yet, there is also a powerful strain toward retaining old world customs, continuing the teaching of Chinese (both Mandarin and the several Cantonese dialects), and preserving some semblance of the ancient virtues. A synthesis of the old traditions and the new progressivism, and, it should be added, a reevaluation of their attitudes toward the social, cultural and economic experiment in the People's Republic of China, are matters of dramatic moment in America's Chinatowns.

The practical and vexing social problems facing those who would seek reconstitution in Chinatown are many and varied. Priorities are difficult to establish, and claims upon the energy, resourcefulness, imagination, and skills of the new Chinese American critics and reformers seem almost beyond the capacity of those who must bear the burden of leadership. Yet there are in these essays a sense of vigor and of mission. America is witness to a new generation of Chinese and a new demand for response to their conditions and problems. These Chinese Americans see themselves not only as a vanguard of rediscovered race consciousness, but also as an element in the general development of ethnic pluralism in America. The problems of the Chinese are in some sense unique, but in a larger perspective they are problems of non-whites and non-WASPs throughout the United States. Blacks, Chicanos, Native Americans, Puerto Ricans, Filipinos, Korean Americans, and Samoans are among the people who—seeking redefinition and response—speak of themselves as members of America's indigenous "Third World" and redesignate their condition as that of "ghetto colonialism."

Specifically the essays in this book reveal that Chinatowns are tinseled pockets of poverty and neglect in the nation's most affluent cities. Within these tiny communities—usually thought of solely in terms of their popularity as tourist attractions and places to visit for an inexpensive meal of exotic cuisine—there dwell aged sojourners who suffer pangs of loneliness, illness, and remorse that lead to a deplorably high suicide rate. Restive youth, newly enlarged by the increased immigration from Hong Kong and Taiwan, roam the streets and terrorize tourists and local businesses with their demands for money and deference, and their criminal and quasi-political gangs are a new cause for fear and personal insecurity. Students from Asia have crippling language handicaps preventing them from participating in the larger society. There are the unemployed and underemployed, including common laborers, craftsmen, skilled mechanics, waiters, busboys, and garment makers, as well as sometime jurists, doctors, and pharmacists whose immigration has resulted in an enormous plunge in social and occupational status; women of all ages who are under- or uneducated, exploited as members of Chinatown's hidden labor force, and abused in loveless marriages, coercive concubinage, or, occasionally, as prostitutes. Responsible education, remunerative employment, and real opportunity are hard to find in Chinatown, although its citizens have proven for over a century their capacity to learn, their willingness to work under the most egregious conditions, and their investment in the hope that once animated America's appeal to the peoples of Europe and Asia.

One cannot read these essays without experiencing a mixture of emotions: anger, concern, sympathy, and finally, admiration for the courage of the writers and the subjects of their writing. These essays strip away the myth and mystique of America's Chinatowns and reveal the essential humanity and erosive squalor that exists behind the glittering lights of this gilded ghetto. They also reveal a new perspective, a developed imagination, and a social activism that does credit to those who still seek freedom and liberation in this once new nation.

Review of *The Politics of Prejudice*

THE POLITICS OF PREJUDICE: THE ANTI-JAPANESE MOVEMENT IN CALIFORNIA AND THE STRUGGLE FOR JAPANESE EXCLUSION. By Roger Daniels. Berkeley and Los Angeles: University of California Press. 1962. 165 pps.

This study covers the development of the anti-Japanese movement in California from its inception in the late nineteenth century until its "victory" in the passage of the immigration act excluding Japanese from entering the United States in 1924. The author, a historian, has chronicled the story of the California exclusionists, groups of men and women active in California politics and society, often divided on many issues and interests but united in their desire to halt forever the coming of Japanese to American shores. The passage of the immigration legislation of 1924 brought to an end the most pressing of their demands and the Japanophobes retired temporarily only to emerge after the outbreak of the Pacific War in 1941 to demand the evacuation and incarceration of America's Japanese.

The forces which pressed for exclusion of the Japanese were not united ideologically, socially, economically, or politically. Radicals and reactionaries, liberals and conservatives, Democrats and Republicans, farmers and workers were caught up in California's peculiar xenophobia. The chorus of demands for Japanese exclusion included such otherwise disharmonious voices as Henry George, Jack London, William Randolph Hearst, Democratic Senator James Phelan, Republican Governor Hiram Johnson, and even carried into the White House in the ambiguous notes of Theodore Roosevelt and the wavering reverberations of Woodrow Wilson. But the main agitation arose and remained in California.

The labor movement, from its inception a political force to be reckoned with in the cities of California, had early concentrated its efforts on the exclusion of Orientals. The Chinese were the first target but, after the abrogation of the Burlingame Treaty in the Exclusion act of 1882, attention turned to the newly-arriving Japanese. In 1888 the *Coast Seaman's Journal* sounded the first labor tocsin against the "recently developed phase of the Mongolian Issue." Two decades later not only the conservative American Federation of Labor but also such important radical leaders and labor sympathizers as Morris Hillquit and Victor Berger were fulminating against the Japanese. Labor's opposition to the Japanese was to continue with spasmodic fervor for the next four decades. The occupational shift of the Japanese after 1910 into farming and small business caused new enemies to raise the exclusionist cry, though the older ones continued to agitate against them.

Political pressure and diplomatic necessities sometimes aided and sometimes hindered the anti-Japanese forces. The attempt to segregate Japanese high school students in San Francisco was halted by President Theodore Roosevelt, who agreed in return for the end of this agitation to negotiate the "Gentlemen's Agreement" with Japan. Intervention by the President and by secretaries of state was able to postpone but ultimately not prevent the passage of some state laws which would have embarrassed American-Japanese diplomatic relations. Woodrow Wilson as a writer of history in 1902 had unflinchingly criticized the Sinophobia of nineteenth century Californians but as a presidential candidate in 1912 he succumbed to the demands of California politics and subscribed to Senator Phelan's latest anti-Japanese diatribe. The Republican Progressives, dedicated to the elimination of certain social and economic evils in American life, unhesitatingly joined the popular anti-Japanese movement. Despite the pleas and protestations of the organizers of the Panama-Pacific International Exposition, who feared for the success of their forthcoming enterprise, Governor Hiram Johnson allowed the Alien Land Law to pass.

Although Professor Daniels has told the political story of the anti-Japanese movement in California with precision as well as brevity (the text of the book is but 107 pages), he has not dealt with the overall meaning of his study. With the historian's eye for biography and interest in the motives of the actors on the historical stage, he confines his analyses to why James Phelan was a Japanophobe, why Hiram Johnson allowed the legislature to override demands from Washington, why Charles Evans Hughes sub-

mitted the Hanihara letter, and so on. (In a lengthy footnote he exposes the legend of "General" Homer Lea by a scathing critical examination of this alleged hero's biographers and worshippers.) Daniels heaps criticism on the progressives, liberals and those (unnamed) "liberal historians" who "too often make the American past a sort of perpetual morality play in which the wicked conservatives continually thwart the democratic aspirations of the people." "Demos has a dark side too," he concludes; "the anti-Japanese movement was one of its aspects."

One need not quarrel with this conservative thesis to note that for all its sound and fury the anti-Japanese movement succeeded in only two pieces of legislation: the Alien Land Law, which, happily, contained so many loopholes that a great many Japanese were able to circumvent its intent; and the exclusion provision of the Immigration Act of 1924, which, although it halted Japanese migration to the United States for twenty-eight years, came sufficiently late so that a great many *Issei* had acquired wives, settled down in America, and begun to raise families. The real effect of the movement, it seems to me, was to provide a legitimation for local prejudices and discriminations, the brunt of which individual *Issei* must have experienced. Unfortunately, Daniels provides us with but the briefest glimpse of this aspect of *Issei* life.

In the preface Daniels asserts his "firm conviction that the largest single causal component" of the elimination of anti-Orientalism from California's statute books "was the undeniable fact that the vast bulk of California *Issei* and their descendents were, despite almost continuous abuse and provocation, superlatively good citizens." The good citizenship of the Japanese is not in question here, nor was it ever; for the Japanese—despite their ineligibility to naturalization—were as good "citizens" in 1913 and 1924 as they are today. It is difficult to see why Dr. Daniels, who distrusts the liberals and white citizens of the first three decades of the twentieth century, should claim that those of the fifth and sixth decades are any better. It is not, as Daniels would have it, that Japanese good citizenship has at last been recognized but rather that race no longer occupies the high position it once did as a device to account for historical, social, political, or personal phenomena. Race prejudice has lost its public legitimacy in the postwar United States, though it continues in the minds of certain individuals and those private sectors of society. The Japanese, as well as the Negro, is reaping the benefit of this recent normative change. One cannot but wonder, however, how permanent this contemporary rejection of race as an explanatory factor will be, and how secure the American minorities will remain in their long overdue emancipation.

Nihonism and Judaism: A Dissent

THE JAPANESE AND THE JEWS, by Isaiah Ben-Dasan. Translated from the Japanese by Richard L. Gage. John Weatherhill, Inc. New York, 1972. 193 pps.

In 1970 a remarkable book was published in Japan, *Nihonjin to Yudayajin;* two years later, the book was translated into English and released in the United States as *The Japanese and the Jews.* Everything about the book is perplexing, puzzling and a cause for concern if not consternation. "Isaiah Ben-Dasan," the author, employs a pseudonym; his real name, nationality and religion are features of a celebrated mystery in Japan. Despite the exotic subject and peculiar thesis of the book, it has been not only a *succès d'estime,* winning the Oya Prize in literature and earning the praise of Rabbi Tokayer of the Jewish community in Japan, but also something of a best-seller as well. As a knowledgeable analysis of the cultures of Jews or Japanese, the book is at best embarrassing; yet it has not aroused much critical condemnation among either Jewish or Japanese scholars.

Much discussion has been generated about the actual identity of the author. No one seems to know him or even to have seen him; when he was awarded Japan's most distinguished prize for literature, he sent a proxy to receive it. According to his own statements in the book he is a Jew, born and reared in Kobe, Japan, but not currently resident there. He also says that he worked for the United States government as a translator of documents during the Pacific War. Other than this we know nothing. Some believe he is a Japanese using a Jewish foil to critically appraise manners, morals, and policies of his native land; others believe he is a gentile who manages to make telling points while misunderstanding both Japanese and Jews; and of course some believe that he is a Jew but wonder what intellectual, cultural, and religious qualifications should be attached to that claim. This reviewer has no special knowledge about the author, and so the mystery will not be solved in this essay. The book could be an elaborate hoax. However, it will be evaluated here with reference to its actual content.

Why should such a book be written at all? The author's justification for doing so is both vague and vacuous:

I know both the Japanese and the Jews well and I am only

too keenly aware of the difficulties involved in comparing them if the aim of the examination is to discern similarities. There are simply too few to bother hunting for them. Moreover, I believe that the only meaningful comparisons are those that attempt to find and analyze differences. By discovering wherein one entity differs from another related one, it is possible not only to learn much about both things, but also to draw certain broad conclusions about the general class to which they belong. In short, by turning the light of inquiry on the distinctive traits of the Japanese and the Jews, I think I can illuminate their national personalities while simultaneously shedding a ray or two on some interesting aspects of humanity.

Well, perhaps the book is intended as a dilettante's approach to the comparative study of national character. If it were only intent on such, we should be content with showing how it fares against the scholarly investigation of, let us say, Douglas Haring or Geoffrey Gorer. But, alas, there is in this book a subtle, serious—and darker—purpose, buried amidst the author's glittering generalization, glib assertions, and garrulous accusations. In fact, the work is a clever piece of propaganda in behalf of modifying Japan's current defense and foreign policies to suit American cold war aims in Asia and the Middle East. "Jewish" ethics, history, culture, and philosophy are pressed into service less—it seems to this reviewer—to explicate or illuminate the differences between Japanese and Jews than to assert the priority of an Occidental (i.e. Judaeo-Christian) "realism" over an Asian ascetic "idealism." Ultimately and repeatedly Ben-Dasan reiterates his cold war thesis and warns the Japanese about the perils in their failure to face up to the dangers of today's international power struggles. He justifies his fears and caveats with an elaborate and foolish argument about the Jews' historical concern for security and Japan's culturally derived insensitivity to the issues involved in establishing or maintaining a decent world order.

However, it is one thing for the author to have written the book, quite another for it to have been so widely accepted. The explanation of the former will not suffice for the latter. Why should Japan have taken up the book with such acclaim? There is no Jewish minority problem there. Japan's relations with Israel are not a cause for major concern. The Japanese are quite able to debate the merits of cold war policy without the additional overlay of a "Jewish" ethic. Why then the fuss?

It is not possible to give an unambiguously clear answer to this question. Perhaps it is best to offer an educated guess. Whatever Ben-Dasan's real intention, his book contributes to what might be called the "optometric" view of their own society that Japanese like so much. It has often been remarked that the Japanese prefer to examine their world from the multiplicity of angles of vision that wisdom, knowledge, and culture can provide. In this tradition Ben-Dasan has contributed a new set of lenses. Japanese character and customs can now be magnified or miniaturized (the happy comparison of *Bonsai* comes to mind) through the perspective provided by a "Jewish" view. The "Jewish" angle of vision enlightens, enlarges, exaggerates—like any other frame of reference, but in its own unique way. There is no assumption of objective truth in the statements derived from any particular perspective, only the sensitivity to interesting nuance, unusual style, and fascinating manner that it innocuously provides. Thus, it is precisely in the novelty of things Jewish that we find an explanation for this book's attraction to the Japanese.

Ben-Dasan's contrastive thesis is new to Japan, but acquaintance with the Jews and theories about them are occasional to Japanese religious writings. Not only have small numbers of Jews lived in Japan for ten centuries, but more recently there has been a flurry of excitement over Japanese conversions to Judaism. (Indeed Ben-Dasan would be far more convincing if he provided illustration of his thesis with examples from among the Japanese Jews). Moreover, comparisons of Japanese and Jewish ethics do not begin with the work of Ben-Dasan. In 1879 one N. McLeod, a sometime businessman and intellectual, published a proof that the Japanese nation descended from the ten lost tribes of Israel. He further advised the Japanese government to liberalize its naturalization laws to permit citizenship to Jews, and then to admit a few Rothschilds so that they might "soon turn the tables of political economy in favor of Japan." A half century later Professor Chikao Fujisawa published "The Spiritual and Cultural Affinity of the Japanese and Jewish People" in which he not only cited other Japanese scholars' beliefs that the first emperor of Japan was a descendant of the House of King David, that the term Mikado can be traced back to the tribe of God, and that Elijah might have been a precursor of the Emperor Tenno Jimmu, but also asserted a common spiritual character to Shintoism and Judaism. In 1939 Bishop Juji Nakada of the Holiness Church wrote:

> Japan alone has never done the Jewish people any harm. Therefore, God intends to use this sun-rising country (Japan) to save the elected (the Jews) and to give great blessings of the Kingdom of God for a reward. To this end all people must convert, become devout believers in God, and cleanse their sins through receiving the brilliant light from Jesus Christ, the sum of righteousness.

In 1959 a sixty-year-old Japanese, descended from a long line of Shinto priests, journeyed to Jerusalem so that Dr. Nahum Cook of Sha'rei Zedek Hospital could perform the ritual of circumcision, signifying his conversion to Judaism. Since that time, visitors to the Wailing Wall have included contingents of Japanese Jews who add their numbers to multiethnic world Jewry.

Stereotypic identifications of Jews with the Orient have been common and are not confined to a few Oriental theorists. When Dietrich Schaefer, a German anti-Semite intellectual of the late nineteenth century, denounced Georg Simmel as a "dyed-in-the-wool Israelite" who attracted to his lectures "an extraordinarily numerous contingent of the oriental world, drawing on those who have already settled here as well as on those who are still flooding in semester after semester from the countries to the East," he was speaking to an audience already prepared to identify Jews with Asia. As European imperialism carried Occidental beliefs to the Far East, ideas of anti-Semitism were spread as well. They took root in curious ways. Thus, in 1914 Vajiravudh, Rama VI, King of Siam, seeking an expression that would denigrate the Chinese merchants in his country, referred to them as "Jews of the Orient." However, the *Protocols of the Elders of Zion*, even when translated into the vernacular,

apparently did not take hold in Asia with the same tenacity as they did in Europe. White Russians in Japan had published an edition of the infamous forgery after the murder of the Czar and his family in 1918, but apparently it aroused little popular interest. In 1938, the Japanese delegate to the *Weltdienst* Congress urged that his country's soldiers in China were dying not for Japan's interests but for the sake of the whole world, which they were valiantly attempting to save from "the Judaeo-Masonic-Bolshevik claws." By 1939, through the apparent conversion of General Shioden to the Nazi cause, the Protocols as well as other anti-Semitic documents had been translated into Japanese in order to "contribute to the enlightenment of the Japanese about the Jewish plan for world domination. . . ." Some attempt to purge Jews in Japan, Shanghai, and Manchuria followed, but a few Japanese—including Abraham Kotsuji, who later was tortured for his efforts—worked from within the government to rescue Jews, halt the worst abuses, and prevent the terror of Asian anti-Semitism from merging wholly with the Holocaust.

That anti-Semitism among Japanese did not predate the Nazi alliance is also revealed by the experiences of Japanese in America. The immigrant generation—*Issei*—arriving in the United States largely during the three decades between 1890 and 1920 harbored no noticeable antipathy toward Jews. No pejorative term for Jews existed then in the Japanese language, and for a period none was needed overseas. However, by the time the children of these immigrants *(Nisei)* had begun to reach adolescence, the essentially European prejudice had been learned about—but not internalized. The *Nisei*, not possessed of any particular hatred toward Jews, felt the need for an expression which indicated the stereotypic characterology attributed by gentiles to Jews in America. However, no word in Japanese expressed that precisely, and a deeply engrained *Nisei* cultural propriety dictated that an English word could not be employed. *Nisei*, therefore, invented a word—*ku-ichi*—to express the newly learned idea. Literally, *"ku-ichi"* means "nine plus one," or "ten." The term in Japanese for the latter number is *"ju,"* the homonym for the English "Jew." However,

Nisei seldom apply *ku-ichi* to Jews; rather they use it to refer to anyone—most often their own ethnic compeers—who possess the traits stereotypically attributed to Jews. Thus even in their complex linguistic transmogrification, the Japanese Americans appear reluctant to adopt a full-scale anti-Semitism as a feature of their acculturation.

Though anti-Semitism does not appear to have flourished in the Far East before 1938, Jewish settlements there go back at least ten centuries. The Middle Eastern communities of Jews there, from which the great Sassoon family sprang, date back at least to the seventeenth and perhaps as far as the twelfth century. By the nineteenth century, Sassoon interests included factories on the southeastern Chinese seacoast and the involvement of the family in the terrible opium trade forced upon China. In Cochin, in southern India, a Jewish colony had apparently existed for eight centuries before it came to the attention of anthropologists who noticed how its Judaism had incorporated certain features of the Hindu caste system. Perhaps most interesting is the Jewish community of Kai-feng-fu in China which dates back to the twelfth century and had retained elements of a basic Judaism at least until 1933. The Chinese Jews have aroused much scholarly interest and considerable philanthropic endeavor. Perhaps the thaw in relations between the United States and the People's Republic of China will permit further investigations of this group's history and remarkable endurance.

None of the foregoing appears in Ben-Dasan's book or appears to be of any interest to him. Rather his work seeks to highlight certain remarkable contrasts between the Japanese and the Jews and to use these as a strategic entry point for a criticism of Japanese social customs and national—especially national security—policies. The contrasts, according to Ben-Dasan number no less than thirteen, to each of which he has devoted a chapter.

1. Every phase of Jewish life is influenced by a desperate search for security, "while relative ignorance of the cost of security has done much to mold the Japanese mind."
2. Jews revere animals and even allow them to be symbols of God, while Japanese, because of their lack of a nomadic tradition, conceive of animals as impure. For the same reason, extended to the human animal, Japanese never kept slaves.
3. Japanese, influenced by the exigencies of rice agriculture, are always in a desperate race with time, fleeing before the threatening fangs of Chronos, while Jews, as a nomadic people, have learned to wait and to ride the back of time rather than run before it.
4. Because they have never really faced a true war, never been exiled or lost their homeland, the Japanese have become both "spoiled" about the actual nature of international relations and over-reliant on other people.
5. "The entire Japanese nation is a body of faithful followers of Nihonism, which is based on human experience instead of on a covenant or body of dogma. . . . The Jews, the Crusaders, the Company of the Saints, the Americans, the Soviet Russians, and Milovan Djilas consider the goal of politics to be the realization of an absolute or divine justice. But the Japanese concern themselves entirely with concrete goals."
6. While Jews are a people who adhere to a fixed code of ethics and an absolute acceptance of divine law, Japanese are constrained by an existential orientation lending itself to a situational ethics.
7. Although Jews, forced by the Diaspora into an exclusive and unique sense of identity and a careful relationship with gentiles, are largely correct in their wary attitude, Japanese, never having undergone such a dispersal, are unjustified in holding to their own attitudes of exclusive clannishness. Moreover, they are ignorant of their ethnocentric usages and fail to see that these constitute a "religion"—Nihonism.
8. Both the Judaeo-Christian and Nihonist traditions have produced martyrs, but the former arise from a belief in a finite universe and eternal life while the latter derive from principles that are just the reverse.
9. Although the Jewish relationship with God is contractual, the Japanese sense of a relationship with a deity is as to a parent.
10. As a desert people, Jews believe all men are equal before God and that conditions of birth—including virgin birth—do not convey a special distinction. Japanese also reject the idea of virgin births but only because it contravenes the principle of the lineage, central to Nihonist thought.
11. Whereas persecutions of all Jews, overseas Chinese, and Arabs in Black Africa arise chiefly out of a "scapegoat" syndrome, Japanese persecution of minorities—Koreans, for the most part—are "animalistic," i.e., underived from realistic economic appraisals and rooted instead in primordial antipathies. However, since Japanese have recently elected to become the middlemen protectors of non-white peoples, they too are potential victims of a scapegoat persecution.

12. Common Japanese misconceptions of Jews include a) ignorance of the origins and tradition of the Wailing Wall; b) belief that the quarrel between Arabs and Israelis is solely one of rival land claims; c) an erroneous reading of the biblical *lex talionis* as an incitation to vengeance rather than a demand for equal justice for all.
13. Japanese language is courteous and full of circumlocutions and careful programmatic etiquette. This betrays an optimism about human relations and a belief in harmony arising from close contact. Jewish history has revealed this sanguinary feeling to be both doubtful and dangerous.

What shall we make of all this? At first blush, one is tempted to dismiss it all as a melange of half-truth, much ignorance, glaring stereotype, and thinly disguised prejudice; and it is all of these. Moreover, the arguments and examples offered in behalf of the thirteen theses just cited are directed in behalf of servicing not only an Occidental ethnocentric orientation, but also—and more specifically—the last two decades of American cold war policy in Asia. The basic proposals presented by Ben-Dasan are that Japan should accept the American exhortation to build up its "self-defense forces" (even modifying its Constitution to do so), but refuse to become an Asian power in its own right representing the anticolonial interests of the restive peoples still in some state of thralldom. Finally, out of recognition of its own cultural blinders—which Ben-Dasan has happily lifted—Japan should wholeheartedly support the state of Israel in its opposition to its Arab opponents. While support for such policy positions is not beyond the bounds of reason or *raison d'état,* here they are subordinated to a pseudo-anthropophilosophical panegyric designed to demonstrate the superiority of Judaism over Nihonism. Jewish ideas, half-digested and exaggerated, become both a panache and a weapon in a seemingly exotic polemic against both Japanese tradition and Japanese left-wing opposition to America's role in Asia.

The reader wishing to know more about Japanese culture and its relation to Judean ethics will find little to aid and much to confuse him in *The Japanese and the Jews.* The main argument of Ben-Dasan is a species of cultural neo-Lamarckism: Jews once a

nomadic people, have continued to bear the culture necessitated by that early form of existence, while Japanese, living in an insular paradise, have been blinded by their cultural inheritance to the realities and dangers that exist in an increasingly interdependent world. Why either culture should be regarded as so static is never even explained. The changes in and debates over Jewish perspectives, however, are too well known to need recitation here. Perhaps more should be said about the Japanese. To be brief: Ben-Dasan is dead wrong when he ascribes no sense of insecurity to Japanese. In the past two decades several careful studies and reports have indicated the enormous importance attributed to—and almost unbearable apprehension about—psychosocial security among Japanese. The alleged docility and inscrutability of Japanese are forms of a culturally encouraged mask over the manifestation of cathexes, which, if they were to be openly expressed, would produce the most acute discomfort among Japanese. Holding their feelings in reserve and ever mindful of being on display before others, Japanese try to monitor their presentation of self in order to give off an impression of stoic neutrality and emotional equilibrium.

Ben-Dasan is equally incorrect in his equation of Japanese politeness and circumlocutions with an optimistic and unrealistic harmony. Rather, there is a norm, closely related to the interest in personal security, which indicates a preference for assisting others in emotional controls. A kind of interpersonal altruism operates to prevent excessive eruptions of temper, embarrassment, or humor. The lengths to which this interest in equanimity will lead are indicated by the linguistic innovations in ethnic pejoratives described above and in the extent of psychosomatic illness among Japanese—a price they pay for holding everything in. To suppose—as Ben-Dasan does—that the Japanese are a serene unrealistic people without knowledge or concern for personal and collective security is utter nonsense.

There is a need for a comparative and contrastive analysis of Japanese and Jews. It would highlight and explain the differential variation of cathexis and cognition among these two peoples. Analyses of the senses of time, place, and manner among Japanese and Jews would throw new light on the culture and philosophy as well as the daily praxis among two of the most fascinating peoples of the world. Although Ben-Dasan's work is unacceptable in these respects, perhaps it will spark the interests of other and better scholars to enter the field.

An Interview with Stanford M. Lyman

Staten W. Webster, Ph.D., who conducted the interview, is a Professor of Education at the University of California, Berkeley. Currently, he is actively involved in research, publishing, community and university services, and consulting activities. He is a member of the newly formed State of California Commission on Teacher Preparation and Licensing. From 1967 to 1969 he served as a consultant to the United States Commission on Civil Rights and periodically serves as a consultant to the United States Office of Education and the California State Department of Education. His areas of concern cover urban education, educational programs and curricula for the socially disadvantaged, ethnic minority groups, and human relations.

WEBSTER: How did it happen that you ended up concentrating on Orientals as an area of academic study?

LYMAN: It was an accident of my own youth. I grew up in San Francisco and went to one of the high schools that was partly integrated because of traffic patterns. And there were a lot of Chinese kids in the school . . .

WEBSTER: Which school was that?

LYMAN: That was George Washington High School. The Chinese kids came all the way across town from Chinatown. I became friends with a group of these Chinese students and began to hang around Chinatown. I developed a personal familiarity with Chinatown. I never thought of my interest as

academic; it was just part of my personal life. And my interest has sustained itself all these years.

With the Japanese it was a curious offshoot of that. My father's grocery story was located in the heart of the Fillmore District in San Francisco and we had mostly black customers. We did have a few Japanese customers as well. But that really didn't throw me in with any Japanese group. What happened was that one of my Chinese friends introduced me to a Japanese friend of his, and shortly after that—this was in my freshman year of college—I developed a considerable number of Nisei friends. I began to move in a circle of friends of this Japanese

277

fellow—it was almost a club—and began hanging around *Nihonmachi,* the Japanese quarter of the city, an area that was already very familiar to me. In a period of about ten years, or a little more than that, I became very close to, very intimate with, a great many Chinese and Japanese people. Most of them belonged to the same generation I did—that is, they were also children of immigrants as I was. And that's how it began.

I never thought of these experiences in terms of sociology until my doctoral work when I was examined in racial and ethnic relations. My instructors told me that they felt that this was the area in which I was most competent. I then began to do serious academic research into that with which I already had a personal familiarity. It built from that into my present researches, summed up in my book *The Asian in the West.*

WEBSTER: So, Stan, you have seen Chinatown and the Japanese community, in San Francisco in particular, over the last 15 or 20 years.

LYMAN: Right.

WEBSTER: People seem to always be speculating on whether or not one can tell a Chinese from a Japanese. On the basis of your experiences are there distinct differences between these two ethnic groups?

LYMAN: I would say that there are definite cultural and personality differences that one can distinctly locate. An anthropologist or a person who is a student of culture and personality can perceive certain differences in presentation of self, in the style of character, and so on.

In the Japanese case this is most pronounced because the Japanese are self-conscious about it. That is, each generation of Japanese—and the Japanese are the only ethnic group in America, that I know of, that has a self-concept based on generational differences—has a sense of how it should appear, . . .

WEBSTER: How does this develop, Stan? How do they develop this?

LYMAN: It develops primarily in child rearing and peer group socialization. The immigrant generation of Japanese, the *Issei,* brought with them the ideas of child rearing of Tokugawa, Meiji, and Taisho, Japan. The latter two eras were periods in which there was a high degree of emphasis on democratization of education, but that education and upbringing had to be extremely moral and ethical. The *Issei* brought their children up that way. They brought their children up employing a complex of authoritarian controls and emphasizing that the child would demonstrate maturity by showing that he could "take it." By showing that, in American terms, he didn't throw tantrums, he didn't become red in the face, he didn't burst into tears, he didn't get violently angry, the young man showed that he was assuming the proper role of an adult. Among Japanese Americans, through the second generation, through, that is, the *Nisei* generation, maturity is defined in terms of self-control, in terms of emotional controls.

Issei parents used a considerable amount of ridicule and teasing in bringing up their children. There's very little physical or corporal punishment used by Japanese parents; it is almost never used. Occasional use of a pseudo-medical treatment called moxa—ashes are used to burn the arm—is found, but that's not regularly done with little children. Primarily, *Issei* parents ridiculed and teased their children into conformity, and at the time when peer groups take over social controls from parents, at adolescence, the teasing was continued by friends. Japanese teenagers are great formers of associations, groups, gangs, clubs. I've had some close association with at least one of these clubs. One salient feature about *Nisei* teenagers is that they're constantly teasing one another, that is the members of a club or group teasing one another. But the teasing isn't random, the teasing is always concerned with bringing a person around, into what I would call the *Nisei* characterological line. I was teased, always, by my *Nisei* friends in this club because what they saw—quite correctly by the way—was that I had certain Jewish mannerisms which I was unself-conscious about. To me they were "just natural." And they would tell me, "Oh you're acting very Jewish; we understand that, but it's not very mature." Maturity for the Jewish boy is very different from maturity for the Japanese boy. Maturity for the Jewish boy—especially the son of Eastern European parents, such as mine—was defined in part by demonstrating that one had a moral stake in the world. This could be shown by a character that expressed the verve and feeling that moved one. Just the opposite for the Japanese! To do that was a sign that you were immature. My Japanese friends would always tease me, gently and with good fellowship. They would say, "Stan, you're getting carried away with things." And so on. As a result of his moral and ethical upbringing (and, by the way, this has certain negative consequences that maybe we can come to later) the *Nisei* strives after an ideal character—which he rarely achieves— one of absolute emotional self-control.

There are all kinds of techniques employed, trying always to appear composed. These include relying on mutual reinforcement by fellows, and carefully planning things so they won't go awry in public. It's been shown in one study that Japanese-American college students always guessed their salary for their first job within a dollar or two. Now some people saw this as a sign of a proper adjustment to America. I think it's a quite different thing; I think it's a sign that Japanese Americans carefully calculated what their salary might be so they wouldn't be embarrassed if it turned out to be lower. That is, they didn't set aspirations too high and so avoided suffering embarrassment. It would be a terrible embarrassment to one's parents and friends to come home and admit that one had overestimated his worth. But

perhaps I'm going on too long on the Japanese . . .

WEBSTER: Why is it that at times you see a pile-up in certain professions and occupations of Orientals, particularly Japanese? What accounts for this?

LYMAN: Several things. In both the Chinese and Japanese cases, in the second generation, the pile-up appears to be in engineering, pharmacy, and to some extent dentistry. Pharmacy and engineering are very prominent in the occupations of second generation of Asians in California. I think the reasons for this are as follows: First, although I don't have sufficient evidence to prove this, I believe it to be the case that, in searching about for occupations which were safe from discrimination and persecution, both Japanese and Chinese discovered the security available in pharmacy and engineering.

Engineering for Orientals is for the most part mechanical and civil engineering. Working for the city or working for the state in jobs protected against discrimination by civic and state law, Orientals could truly achieve on the basis of merit. Second, with respect to pharmacy. I believe it was an accidental discovery. The stereotype of the pharmacist and the stereotype of the Oriental coincide.

WEBSTER: How so?

LYMAN: The pharmacist is perceived as clean, correct, and careful. The Oriental is perceived as clean, correct, and careful. Now, you'll find very few black pharmacists in California and I suspect, though I don't know for certain, that one of the reasons for this is that the stereotype of the black and the stereotype of the pharmacist don't go together. To put it another way, let's look at it from the white customer's point of view: When he goes into a pharmacy and he sees an Oriental behind the counter he has no hesitancies or ambivalencies. Immediately there comes into play in his mind the positive image of the Oriental—he's very careful, he's very clean, he's going to get me the right pills. But if he carries with him stereotypes about blacks—as almost everybody does in America, I suppose—if he sees a black man behind the counter, the white coat that he wears is a kind of contradiction to what he "knows" about black people. I want to emphasize that this is only an hypotheses. I need to do much more research on the first Japanese pharmacists and on the relevance of stereotypes to occupational choice.

Now there were famous early Japanese pharmacists who set a kind of tone. The most famous was Takamine, a Japanese immigrant who came at the turn of the Century, and he developed a widely used medicine—Takadiastase. He also is reputed to be the man who developed the formula for Canadian Club whiskey and sold it in Canada for a million dollars. He became a very famous figure in Japanese-American circles in the 1900's and 1920's and that may have provided that kind of exemplary action that led others to go into the field. That often happens in occupations—where there's an exemplary figure, other people follow in his footsteps.

But I do know that there are other aspects related to this occupation among Orientals. We know something about pharmacists; pharmacists, for the most part, are people who did not get accepted into medical school or who decided against medicine after seeing the competition in entrance to medical schools. Now many Chinese and Japanese students that I knew in college in the '50's were majoring in medicine or pre-medicine. The competition was very stiff; they didn't always have the grades to qualify, and for various reasons, they didn't make it into medical school. Some opted, by the junior year, for pharmacy. They began to see that they weren't going to qualify for medical school, and they began to shift their aspirations accordingly. In the medical field you shift "down" from medicine to dentistry or

optometry to pharmacy. Or sometimes you bypass dentistry or optometry because it just doesn't appeal to you, and you shift directly to pharmacy. I think a great deal of that kind of shifting took place among Orientals.

But once the idea of going into pharmacy became popular it developed its own inertia, so to speak. Big brothers passed down advice on it to little brothers, friends to friends, and so on, so that by the late '50's when you met Oriental kids starting at the University of California, Berkeley, and asked them what they were majoring in they often replied Pharmacy. And if I inquired: "Why are you in pharmacy?" they answered, "Well, you know—all my friends are in pharmacy, it's a lucrative field, it's easy to get into," and so on. I think that had a great deal to do with it.

I remember talking to my own dentist who, it happened, sat on the Board of Entrance to UC Pharmacy School and Dentistry School. He was telling me how many Orientals there were, and he was jokingly saying that it used to be all Jews in those professions. Now it's Orientals as well as Jews and Jewish students are having to compete with some very bright Orientals. But all that is changing anew in the third generation. We're seeing another great shift.

WEBSTER: Where are we going?

LYMAN: The shift, and I think it's representative of a more general shift, occurs in the third generation. We're seeing, both with the *Sansei*—the third generation Japanese—and with the third generation Chinese, or those second generation Chinese who happen to be the same age as the third generation Chinese, a much broader and wider interest in things. They are no longer concerned only with the safe, secure occupation. They are no longer motivated by studying something which will guarantee them a profession.

In that sense Jews, Chinese, and Japanese have been somewhat similar in that the parental aspirations for their children were similar. The parents were grocers or farmers or shop-keepers in all three groups, and they urged their children to go to college and to study to be, in the Jewish case, a doctor or lawyer or an engineer, in the Oriental case, to be a professional. The emphasis was on the technical professions; they were safe and open.

But in the third generation this is all changed. First the parents aren't pushing that same kind of aspiration as hard anymore on their children. The second generation parents don't push that hard. Anyway, the third generation are much more independent, so you're now finding what you didn't find in the '50's. Chinese and Japanese students majoring in history and sociology and literature . . .

WEBSTER: . . . in education . . .

LYMAN: . . . in education . . . Ah, you did find Chinese and Japanese *girls* in education in the '50's—you know, like many girls they thought, first go into teaching, then get married, move out of it eventually—but now you are finding men in education, and what's interesting about it, men studying in the social sciences. There was a very small group of Japanese studying in the social sciences in the 1920's and '30's, but they were few in number. There was then only a small Japanese population going to school, and they were doing good work. USC has a number of MA theses in sociology which were done in the 1930's under the great sociologist Emory Bogardus. He was a lightning rod, attracting a considerable number of Japanese students apparently. What happened to this interest on the part of Japanese students we don't know. The second generation of students from this group did not pursue such studies. But in the third generation, we're finding this interest in history, literature, sociology, and political science. It's no longer the concern with the safe technical profession—there's even a certain amount of resentment against that.

WEBSTER: Do you think that can be partly at-

tributed, at least in the case of the Japanese, to the fact that they have achieved a level of social acceptance to the extent that the other orientation is no longer really necessary?

LYMAN: This is certainly true of the Japanese; however, it is less true of the Chinese. It's awfully important to make the distinction between the Japanese and Chinese here. Each group, the Japanese and the Chinese in this new third generation, a generation which is primarily concerned with liberation in all its forms, is facing different and unique problems. The third generation Japanese are for the most part beneficiaries of the acceptance, well-being, and acculturation of their parents, and yet they feel estranged and alienated both from white America and from their parents' version of Japanese America.

Now the Chinese of the third generation have something more concrete with which to deal—the ghetto, poverty, and racism. Japanese kids suffer more in a poignant psychic way because they can't put their finger on what it is exactly that they're upset with.

WEBSTER: Earlier you were saying that the generational thing was a kind of a cement that really gave a cohesiveness to the Japanese. Now in the case of the Chinese are you saying that there's another mechanism which operates in their case? What is it?

LYMAN: If generation means what it does to the Japanese, and I think it does, I would say community and revolt against community means more to the Chinese, a very different thing.

The idea of generation is not a prominent idea among the Chinese. All Chinese born in America, as far as Chinese are concerned, are just Chinese Americans or American Chinese—they have one Chinese word for it and that's it. Whereas the Japanese count each generation removed from Japan—you know, *Issei, Nisei, Sansei*—they can go on counting this way forever.

The Chinese situation resolves around the ambivalence and ambiguity of the Chinese community, Chinatown. And here we find a kind of escape and return. The second generation Chinese grew up with the idea for the most part that they were going to escape Chinatown. They were going to get out of the ghetto, become engineers or pharmacists, get as far away from the ghetto as they could. But they still retained Chinese ties which were natural to them, but which they weren't so conscious about. The Chinese ties to the community were ratified very easily by visits to the folks, by eating in Chinatown, by knowing the people there, and so on. Residential restriction made it more difficult for Chinese to get as far from Chinatown as they thought they could get, even when they had achieved on the professional level.

Chinese-American friends of mine told me about discriminatory housing restrictions they ran into in San Francisco, restrictions which they didn't think they'd run into. One couple told me about the time they went out to a tract area and walked into an open house. All the flags are flying, the salesmen are anxious to sell, and a Chinese couple walks in—a Chinese-American couple—he's a professional man working for the Bell Telephone Co. as an engineer—and they are noticeably ignored by the salesman. They watch for a long time. The salesman *runs* to everyone who comes in, presents them with brochures, talks to them, and so on. They are absolutely and completely ignored—just given non-person treatment. They finally saw the score—they waited around to watch it for a while, to make sure they were right, and then they left.

Another instance really upset me personally when I saw it happen. A Chinese-American friend of mine, a pharmacist, graduate of the University of California, a Doctor of Pharmacy, was buying a home. I happened to be there when he was calling the real estate person and I listened to the conversation. He had found the house he was interested in and he said, *he said* to the realtor, "I

want you to go talk to the neighbors; I want you to tell them that I'm Chinese and I want you to find out if they object. If they object I won't buy it. But please go and find out for me, I don't want the trouble of moving in and having objections come in." To have to go through all of this is very severe on one's sensibilities.

Nevertheless some Chinese Americans, those whom I call in my book the "gold-bourgeoisie," have moved out of the ghetto, have achieved middle-class status, have become pharmacists, or optometrists or dentists, or engineers. Now their children, at least a vocal minority group of their children, are interested in returning to the ghetto—to rebuild it, to reorganize it, to participate in some way in reestablishing both ties of community and ties of ethnicity. I think ties of enthnicity are more important to them. That is, in an age, suddenly thrust on us, where everyone feels he ought to know his ethnic heritage these third generation Chinese find they can't realize their ethnicity in a suburb, like Walnut Creek, for example. As one Chinese, a friend of mine, who lives in Walnut Creek told me. "I worked all my life to get out of Chinatown and I finally got to Walnut Creek. And my children want to go back to Chinatown. I don't understand this."

WEBSTER: How do you explain this? Everywhere we look at ethnic groups, including my own, blacks, there's this tremendous, intensive search to reestablish what seems to be a certain type of identification that has been lost or washed away. The Indians are looking back and saying, "The hell with Anglo-Saxon ways," the Chicanos are saying, "Look, we're beautiful," . . . the Orientals too, as you pointed out. As a sociologist what do you think is causing this?

LYMAN: Well, there was an argument made by an historical sociologist, Marcus Lee Hansen, about 30 years ago, that I think explains this. But we didn't believe it or we didn't pay serious attention to it then, and we're now realizing that what he called Hansen's Law of Third Generation Return is perhaps true.

Marcus Lee Hansen argued that, "What the second generation wishes to forget the third generation wishes to remember." He got the idea from studying Swedes in America. He noticed that in the third generation of Swedish Americans there began to be founded Swedish historical societies. Swedish Americans began to go hunting for artifacts of their old world life and having little shows. It was a very mild and a very innocuous phenomenon, but he took it very seriously and he raised the question, why has this occurred?

The answer he gave was that the third generation is the recipient of full-fledged Americanization and, having gotten that, so to speak, simply by being born in America, it discovers the emptiness of it. Third generation people experience a lack of verve, excitement, interest. They discover in one sense that "the trip" wasn't worth it, only they didn't take the trip, it was their grandparents who took the trip. And this is the cruel irony of the third generation. They are the recipients of a dream of their parents and grandparents which they find is not quite a nightmare but is not exactly a beautiful thing, either.

Now the specifics of this vary, I suppose, but it comes down to saying things like, well, life in middle-class America is dull. There's nothing very exciting. Everyone is just alike. It is the dullness and mediocrity of homogeneity that bothers the third generation, I think.

Now this has been given an added sociopolitical impetus, I think, by the rise of black power or just the whole black movement, by everything that occurred since what I call the end of the civil rights integration movement, which I date as ending around '63, '64.

WEBSTER: That early?

LYMAN: Yes . . . I'm sure people will argue about

when it ended. But there was this big push from '54 to '63 when we were all interested and working on integration; when we assumed it was an unalloyed blessing. Only a few people were beginning to raise very serious questions, questions like what does this integration mean. But anyway, that period seems to be over now, though we don't know exactly what to do next.

In one sense a new twist has been added. Blacks had never been, as far as I could tell, models for other peoples in America. That is, positive models. But they have become that. It is my contention that the black has become the model for all other minorities, although other minorities might deny this in their desire to demonstrate independence. And so blacks, through their movement, with its often very powerful, grandiose, beautiful, and occasionally romantic statements about black ethnicity—a group which was originally supposed to be the least ethnically inclined—suddenly created a model and added a new vitality that, I think, all the other ethnic groups are now imitating.

It's also true of the white new left. Portions of the white new left are secretly desiring to be or to model themselves after black militants or Indians. The black militants are role models for other minorities; there's no question in my mind about that; and this has very probably had an effect on youthful minority students, young people, whether they're Oriental, Mexican, Indian, and so on. That blacks are leading the way as exemplary models of what young people should be is of fundamental importance. So when that occurred, combined with the existence of a third generation which would suffer, if Hansen was correct, and I think he was, a general disillusion with American society, there arose a new ethnic interest.

Of course there are other specific dissatisfactions that they can turn to but I suspect that if the specific dissatisfactions were all wiped away we'd still have this—if there were no Viet Nam war; if conditions of poverty were not as extreme as they are, I still think we would find a vague but powerful disillusion with the idea of a homogeneous America.

We're really entering into a new era in American history. That era was characterized almost in the fashion of Frederick Jackson Turner's frontier thesis by the announcement in the 1970 census that more people now live in the suburbs than live in the cities. Now that is a world historical event for America just as the end of the frontier was in 1890. Now, I saw that as something which signals a whole host of things.

WEBSTER: What will be some implications of this, Stan? I also feel that this is a most important event.

LYMAN: One is the changing function of the city. The city is becoming a place now to realize ethnic identity. It was a place for a while to escape ethnic identity. You escaped outward. The classical view of the Chicago school of sociology was that the city grew out from its center. As people successively removed themselves from their ethnic background and from poverty they moved further and further on a straight line distance from the center of the city.

Well, they were partly right, certainly as far as the suburbs were concerned. So the suburbs are essentially the home of the white middle-class, several generations removed from their European forbears, at least three generations removed. Now some of these white suburbanites are also suffering from a pang of emptiness, but perhaps we ought to stick to Orientals.

The Orientals, in so far as they were able to get to the suburbs—and some of them have, not very many, but there are some. Friends of mine, Asians, in the suburbs feel a certain amount of guiltiness. And their children, especially in the case of Chinese, want to return to Chinatown.

Now, they may have romantic illusions

about Chinatown, and they have romantic illusions about many things, but this is the irony of "third generation return." The irony of the third generation return is that the very group that seeks to recover its lost heritage is least equipped to do so.

WEBSTER: How are they least equipped?

LYMAN: They're least equipped in the sense that the nuances and the essential feelings that make up a true ethnic heritage have really been lost. The last group that had those was the second generation—which didn't have to prove its ethnicity by announcing it. They felt it, they knew they were Chinese. They knew they were Japanese. They were struggling to be somehow other than that. The third generation knows they're American. The second generation was the last generation of Chinese Americans; the third generation is the first generation of American Chinese. And that difference is a very powerful one. They lack the little things; for example, Jews know that if you can say certain things in Yiddish you can express them in a way that is meaningful to the in-group. This is true also for blacks in terms of the concept *soul* which, as I understand it, sums up a very powerful sense of ethnic identity whose essence is that it is uncommunicable to outsiders.

Now the Orientals, Asians, also have this sense but by the third generation it is becoming so diffuse, so unrecognizable, so unfelt, that they're not adequately equipped to return to their native identity.

Now in addition to that psycho-emotional sense, the third generation is the best educated in American schools. And that raises a question: What do they know of their own history? Well, they know U.S. History, world history. Which means they know next to nothing about Asians, nothing about Africans. They know almost nothing about their historical and cultural backgrounds. It is an embarrassment which I often see in young Asians when they ask me to teach them Chinese history. I realize that they sometimes feel chagrined having to ask a Caucasian to do that. I've given lectures to groups of Chinese on Chinese-American history and to *Sansei* on Japanese-American history and I have seen the embarrassment, and sometimes the anger. And occasionally they get very angry: "Well what are *you* doing here," they ask, referring to my non-Asian ancestry.

One can really sense the poignancy of the situation if a whole people has been educated in America but not been similarly educated in their own heritage. The second generation had either a home education or an afternoon school education that provided some semblance, some vestige of ethnic identity. There were Hebrew schools, Chinese schools, and Japanese schools. But, often enough the parents of the third generation have felt "Well, I hated Oriental school; I'm not going to force that on to my kids." (Some of them have begun to change their minds, I've noticed, recently. When they realize that their children can't even read a Chinese menu when they go to Chinatown, they're embarrassed for them; they can't even order food.)

The third generation, despite its eagerness, is the least equipped; they don't have the historical, the cultural, or even the rather poor education of the afternoon schools. The afternoon schools generally gave a bad education—but even that bad education provided the pupils with a kind of internal feeling of ethnicity; now much of that's gone.

WEBSTER: Stan, what's going to be the ultimate outcome of this? What prediction would you make about this third generation and its quest to reestablish its roots?

LYMAN: Well, you see there's been thus far three basic approaches to the reestablishment of ethnicity. I don't think they've ever been analytically separated and appraised although they ought to be. But the protagonists of each of these approaches sometimes

quarrel with each other in the schools. Certainly this is the case in the colleges, and I suspect in the high schools, too.

First let me say, was the demand—originally voiced by blacks and then taken up by other minorities—that it was the duty of the public sector of the society, essentially the school systems, to supply the lost or forgotten heritage of the ethnic past. What is interesting in this demand is that blacks, Asians, Chicanos, and Indians are the first groups to my knowledge to ask the public sector to supply the ethnic heritage. There's a reason for this. The other ethnic groups supplied their heritage through funded private schools which they were fortunate enough to be able to put together. This was also true of Asians, they had Chinese and Japanese schools. This same solution was impossible for blacks, essentially for reasons of poverty. However, it should be pointed out that the black church played a role, as the Jewish Sunday school did, in fostering a sense of ethnicity. But at any rate, afternoon schools are either absent or insufficient for the third generation, and so the third generation, and—we really are in a kind of third generation from slavery which is a way of noting that this is the third generation for blacks too—the third generation is demanding now that the public sector supply what used to be called the private heritage.

The argument, and I think it's correct, is that this is not a private heritage; this is part of the history of America, part of the culture of America. But other groups have not made this demand in the past, or if they've made it, they've couched it in such modest or euphemistic terms that it hasn't gone recognized as such.

WEBSTER: But are those who call for these studies in complete agreement as to what they want?

LYMAN: Some, who might be called the conservatives, and I think I would probably be classed among these, strangely enough, see the appropriate mode as the establishment of a wide-ranging set of what amounts to historical and cultural studies, at every level of education, dealing with the cultures and histories of the various groups. They see it, in other words, in academic terms, as an academic program, as an academic addition to the curriculum, as well as a needed integration of the old standard school program.

But there are two other views. One is essentially a psychological view. According to this position it is the duty of the public sector, the schools, to provide psychic shoring up for those minority peoples who have suffered psychically by being in a deprived and oppressed condition. This can be done, so the argument runs, through curricular and extracurricular activities that ought to be a part of the regular school program. This means courses whose primary function isn't to provide knowledge and skills, but rather to provide psychic uplift. And psychic uplift of an ethnic kind should generate the feeling "Be proud of the Japanese," "It's good to be Chinese," etc. Nobody knows exactly what a program like this would look like. There are all kinds of suggestions. But that is an aim and the aim specifically is psychic and emotional uplift.

Third, there is what might be called the aim of community reorganization. Here, again under the heading of ethnic studies, the desire is not to provide historical knowledge, not to provide psychic uplift, but rather to provide the tools, mechanisms, and the bodies to go out into the ethnic community and reorganize it so that it can become a participating and powerful member of the larger society. This ranges in political persuasion from the moderate middle to the radical left. What community reorganization means varies according to the ideology of the person.

WEBSTER: Now, this line of thinking was very forcefully stated as an argument by black students when they were arguing for Afro-American studies and what have you. But I wonder what has happened to these youngsters who were saying we want to go back into the ghetto and throw our bodies back in there. But I haven't seen many of them emerge out in the community doing things. Am I wrong?

LYMAN: Well, in the Chinese and Japanese cases, though it hasn't been as dramatic and exciting as some of the news from the black ghetto, there have been attempts to reorganize and to solidify the communities. I can speak about the Bay Area where these movements really got started. In fact the origins of the movements were in Berkeley and at San Francisco State College. It's perhaps no accident that Asians got into the act there because there's such large Asian communities there. As one part of the San Francisco State College strike there was an Asian group, combining Japanese and Chinese, the Asian-American Political Alliance . . .

WEBSTER: . . . that's unusual isn't it? . . .

LYMAN: Yes, as a matter of fact it has been unusual and that's something we ought to come back to—the integration or disintegration of Chinese and Japanese cooperation. But there was this AAPA group at SF State and it was different from the chapter at AAPA at Berkeley. AAPA at Berkeley was very "political," AAPA at SF State was less political, or perhaps I should say, less radical. Anyway, what grew out of that situation was Chinese-American, middle-class students going down into Chinatown and rediscovering Chinatown. And they rediscovered Chinatown because they came in contact with Chinese Americans and with Hong Kong born youth in Chinatown, both of whom were drop-outs.

The Chinese-American drop-out, a much neglected figure by the way in discussions of the Chinese, and Hong Kong born youth are separated by culture and intramural hostility from each other. What happened was that these students from SF State "discovered" them and found out about the many kinds of troubles and problems they were having. And in the process they discovered a sense of kinship, of community. Well, the Chinese and Japanese eventually split, not hostilely, but in terms of their respective interests in their own communities.

The Chinese utilized their association called the Intercollegiate Chinese for Social Action to set up headquarters both in Chinatown and at SF State College. And, at the level at which they set them up, there has been an attempt to try and effect some kind of community-wide rapprochement between youth, whether they were Hong Kong born, Chinese-American drop-outs, or college kids. They have tried to link up the diploma bearer with the drop-out, and to do something about the community. The Chinese community, however, is fraught with all kinds of difficulties. We can talk about that if you want to.

WEBSTER: Yes, I'd like to hear your analysis.

LYMAN: We can look at it from the point of view of the youth because they're the ones who have been trying to force certain changes.

It's fair to say that we're seeing the era of maturity of the second generation Chinese only now. The rise of a teenage and 20-year-old third generation is taking place now because, for about 80 years, there was no large number of Chinese families in America. That in turn was caused first because Chinese custom and then American law prevented women of Chinese extraction from coming to America. The restriction act of 1882 forbade not only the coming of laborers from China, but also the laborers' wives. That situation with only a few modifications was in order until 1943. The quota of 105 set in 1943 did not do much to change things.

On the other hand an unknown number of Chinese were smuggled into the United States all during the period of restriction. We can only guess as to how many, and a good many of them were women. But if we use census figures, which are probably incorrect in an absolute sense but not necessarily unreliable in their proportions, we can say that there weren't very many Chinese families in America, in the sense that Americans think of a family—mama, papa, and the kids—until after 1930.

WEBSTER: That's an amazing thing.

LYMAN: Yes, it is amazing. Chinese came to America as early as 1850, but there was not the foundation of large numbers of Chinese families until 1930. The sex ratio was, in 1900, about 27 to 1, I think, and it was still about 3 to 1 as late as 1930. It's still out of balance today, but much less so than it has ever been. So you can see, beginning in 1930 children are being born of Chinese extraction and these children reach their maturity in the '40's and '50's. And they were the ones who went to college when I went to college and studied pharmacy and engineering. Now some of them in turn have children now who are in their 20's and going to college and they are the new third generation of Chinese.

Of that third generation of American Chinese, we can roughly distinguish two categories: Those who made it to college and those who didn't. And those who didn't make it to college find themselves trapped in a Chinatown which they neither like nor understand. Now they're trapped because of lack of skills and poor education. I'm speaking here of the drop-out. They're the students who went to Galileo High School in San Francisco, who had troubles with the school, and who quit or were expelled. There are a lot of troubles in that school, very complex problems involving misunderstanding and, perhaps, downright discrimination, problems involving the staff and the administration. Anyway, these kids drop out or are thrown out of school. They lack a high school diploma, and therefore they lack the kind of skills that can get them out of Chinatown and into the mainstream.

They can't get a good job—they're hanging around Chinatown. Now in hanging around Chinatown they went through a set of stages, which I would call the route from delinquency to politics. First they were just angry and disillusioned kids hanging around, playing pool, occasionally stealing a car or perhaps robbing somebody. There was at that time a rise in juvenile delinquency among Chinese.

WEBSTER: But, Stan, don't most people assume that there is little or no juvenile delinquency among Oriental groups?

LYMAN: Yes. For a long time the rise in delinquency was hidden because of a special relationship between Chinatown and the police department in which Chinese children who were apprehended were not booked. They were brought to a Chinese officer and he reprimanded them and took them home. There was no official record kept. Hence, statistically the Chinese remained low on the juvenile delinquency records when actually the number of offenses rose.

In the middle '60's there began the formation of new Chinatown gangs. Now there were Chinatown gangs before—the few youths there were had organized gangs, and even in the '20's there were Chinatown gangs—but these gangs were co-opted in the '20's and '30's and '40's by secret societies. The bullies and tough guys of Chinatown became the thugs and guards of secret society meetings, gambling dens, and brothels. In the '60's the new gangs at first became more independent. Many of the American-born Chinese were not interested in those things. Some of the youngsters became second-story men, some of them were "rolling" people on the street in Chinatown, especially tourists.

They split up into smaller gangs after the failure to get aid, and some of them were co-opted by the old secret societies, who found in these young China-born youth, who would not become politically radical, just the kind of toughs and thugs that could be used to maintain the old Chinatown status quo.

And so right now you find a split between two groups of young Chinese—the Chinese Americans who are more politicized, more angry and make openly radical statements, and who utilize the language of Mao and Che Guevara and Malcolm X on the one side, and the foreign-born Chinese who don't openly speak that kind of language and who now wish to be left alone. These two groups fight each other. There are "rumbles" in Chinatown between foreign-born and native-born Chinese.

The educational problems are enormous, by the way. It's very interesting to note that foreign-born Chinese and the native-born Chinese have different educational backgrounds but similar problems. The foreign born need to learn English and, although this seems incomprehensible to me, apparently no one has devised an effective way to teach English to Chinese young people. But there should be and there must be a way. I'm convinced of that—I wish I knew more of the pedagogy of language. Now, in addition to their problems in English, their Chinese is often not sophisticated—they can't write it, for example, so they are becoming functionally illiterate in two languages and literate in none. Now this is an irony and a tragedy that I've just discovered is true of other peoples as well. I recently saw a television program on Eskimoes in which it was shown that they do not learn the Eskimo language adequately and they do not learn English very well at all. Now this same problem is very severe in Chinatown, for both the native and foreign born.

The Chinese students from the State College tried to develop a program, tried coming down and teaching English to the Chinatowners. But it was very amateurish. It was also suffused often enough with political and social aims, or with interest in getting a date, or with interest in meeting somebody new, or, occasionally, with a kind of ethnic slumming. It has not been an effective program thus far.

Now the Chinese-American drop-outs do not have adequate command of either Chinese or English; as ethnics they demand that they be taught Chinese in the public schools. As Americans, they suffer because they cannot communicate effectively in the language of the country in which they have been born.

WEBSTER: Well, this thing of education seems to be a major problem with all non-Anglo groups. It's a tough one. Stan, what should a non-Oriental know or understand about these groups if he is to have any chance of effective interaction with them?

There was a movement among the kids to stop this. A group called Le-Way—Legitimate Ways, Inc., they called themselves—was formed ostensibly to stop crime in Chinatown, to set up a club house to try and develop a kind of self-administered socio-educational, cultural, recreational program for the Chinese-American drop-out. It never got very far, the police didn't trust it, the elders of the community didn't trust it, and it was harassed. It was soon politicized from within by persons who were interested in seeing less of a social welfare orientation and more of a political orientation. Eventually Le-Way fell apart, disintegrated. Some of its members, not all, became the leaders and members of a new political group in Chinatown, the Red Guard, which is modeled after the Black Panthers, and uses similar rhetoric. The Red Guard demands general political and communal change.

But there was another group in Chinatown at the same time, the Hong Kong-born youths. When the Johnson Immigration Act—originally the Kennedy Immigration Act which finally was passed under President Johnson—came into force in July 1968, it opened the doors to immigration from Taiwan, and especially from Hong Kong. A large number of Chinese youth, teen-agers, entered the United States.

These youth were often sophisticated but they were uneducated in English and often unskilled in industrial pursuits. So they also found themselves trapped in Chinatown, and they didn't like their situation at all. Chinatown was a reminder to them of a China that they thought had disappeared a hundred years ago. I've interviewed many foreign youths who said it was the strangest thing they had ever seen; they'd read about it in books but didn't think it actually existed. Chinatown *is* a very good replication of the cities of 19th Century China. It's one of our last vestiges of 19th Century China—you can't find it in China anymore.

These youths were unhappy, lonely, and unemployed. Being foreign born, new immigrants, uneducated, and without citizenship papers, they weren't likely to gravitate toward the "Maoist" Red Guard movement, a movement which might get them into trouble with the immigration service. Their gang and group formation took a more conservative orientation, conservative, that is, if you see that the Red Guard is representative of a kind of populist movement.

The foreign-born groups asked the community to help find them jobs, to help them build a club house, and to assist in their education. But they were unsuccessful—the community didn't respond at all. And when they escalated their language it only hurt them more. They called themselves the Hwa-Ching, which is a Chinese term for "Young China." Their first demands—which were very reasonable—were for a program whereby they could obtain a high school diploma. They thought it should be possible for a person from China to get a high school diploma. They especially wanted education with an emphasis on technical training, vocations—they named what they wanted: engineering, drafting, plumbing, carpentry and machine tool work.

LYMAN: One thing that is very important, I think, the non-Oriental has to develop a new way of looking at Chinatown. When he is on tour there, he has to realize that Chinatown is more than what he immediately sees. It is *above* him in the form of old men who live out their days in dark, dank little rooms without relatives to comfort them. It is *below* their feet in the basement sweatshops where countless women work at grinding tasks for incomes far below those required by national standards. They have to realize that in that "good" Chinese restaurant, there perhaps works an immigrant whose chances are extremely limited because of his inadequate language skills, lack of labor union protection, and poor job training. They have to start by giving up a romantic view of Chinatown and the Chinese. They can, as a starter, see Chinatown for what it really is. The same is true in the case of the Japanese community. A Japanese community in San Francisco is now actually being created for "white man's consumption." It is now being rebuilt by commercial interests—actually mostly from Japan—and not by the local Japanese community. It's being rebuilt as a tourist attraction, and it should be seen in terms of who they really are, as persons as well as members of a culture which now flows through three or four generations in America, with appropriate generational differences. You can't sum up either the Japanese or Chinese Americans in the doll-like image of the positive stereotype, that is, as a people who use those cute little sticks and who are very "sweet" and "docile."

Another thing to remember—our history books have been extremely deficient in telling us the story of the Chinese and Japanese in America. For that we need to turn to the special studies that are being republished today and to the new researches, such as my own *The Asian in the West*. It is not true to say that either the Chinese or the Japanese simply accepted the early phases of discrimination and hostility. That is not at all true. And if we want to find the actual facts, the facts that should be in the history books, we have to turn our attention away from the "presidential history" our public school textbooks use—and toward the story of the Supreme Court.

Our textbooks are full of the stories of one more perfect president replacing another—American history is chopped up into four year periods. Supposing we shifted the institutional base of United States history from the Presidency to the Supreme Court. And this might be the thesis: The Supreme Court is the agency designed to bridge the gap between the promise of the Constitution and the performance of American institutions.

WEBSTER: Beautiful, beautiful.

LYMAN: And what we will learn, then, about minority peoples—and the Chinese and Japanese are the ones I know about—is that in case after case after case an individual or a small group of Chinese or Japanese came before the Court and asked that the Constitution be obeyed. And if we knew that, we'd know that these people were not lying down, were not simply accepting prejudice, were not docile, were not, as one recent book on the Japanese-Americans calls them, the "quiet Americans."

WEBSTER: That's a very excellent idea. I never thought of it that way but it's true. That would really let it all hang out and show what the struggles were; the Indians' petitions for recognition of treaties, the blacks petitioning . . .

LYMAN: That wonderful book by a black judge in LA—*The Petitioners*—it's a history of blacks before the Supreme Court. It's beautiful. He did it for blacks, the history runs up through 1920, and when I read that I thought, well, we could recapture history this way for each of the ethnic groups.

WEBSTER: That's a beautiful idea. And it would be *objective* too!

LYMAN: Well, you know, there's one reason we

don't do it this way, and it has to do with our academic knowledge of the law. The lawyers have maintained for years that only lawyers know how to read and find Supreme Court cases—and they are right, because we do not teach teachers how to do reasearch in the archives of the courts. You can only learn that in law school.

Now what we have to do—and it would be a very good thing for teachers and educators, I think, would be to teach them how to read the cases of the Supreme Court. Teach that in school, in education departments, and begin to put together textbooks or supplementary readings using law cases which would tell the story very nicely. It would focus on people rather than leaders. The cases involving Asians are marvelous; sometimes the 14th Amendment to the Constitution gets defined by a "little man."

One Chinese case is instructive—*Yick Wo vs. Hopkins* (118 U.S.356). A Chinese in San Francisco in 1885 had been running a laundry for 20 years. San Francisco passed a laundry licensing act actually designed to get rid of the Chinese laundry. The act stipulates that no person running a laundry in a wooden building may continue to operate it unless he has a license from the Board of Supervisors.

Yick Wo goes down to get his license and the Board says no, you can't have one. So he continues running his laundry without a license until he is arrested. He is convicted and fined $10; he refuses to pay, and carries his appeal all the way to the United States Supreme Court.

That case helped to define the 14th Amendment—every law student has to read *Yick Wo vs Hopkins.* It's a landmark case among other reasons because the Court did a sociological investigation. They took a look at San Francisco's laundries; they counted all the laundries in San Francisco and noted that several hundred of them were run by Chinese and only a few by whites. But every time a Chinese man asked for a license he didn't get it. The Court asked, what is the purpose of San Francisco's laundry licensing ordinance?

The Court said in effect, we believe, despite what the city claims as the purpose of this law, namely, prevention of fires, that this law is administered with an "evil eye." That's the language of the Court, I really love that passage. The intent, the Court went on, is to drive a whole people out of a business—now, the Court rules, that is an impermissible thing in law. And they wipe out the administration of the law. In doing so they cite the 14th Amendment—they talk about the equal protections clause. Yick Wo was an immigrant, he wasn't a citizen, but he's still protected by the 14th Amendment, so that this "little man" with his little laundry helped define the Constitution of the United States as well as represent the Chinese people in what was to be a long series of court fights about equal justice. It's a whole history that nobody knows—because it isn't taught that way. Perhaps, now we can begin . . .

Index

Index

The Asian in the West was composed in 10-point Baskerville text
and Baskerville display
by Computer Typesetting Services, Inc., Glendale, Calif.
The body was printed on a 31-inch web offset press by
R. R. Donnelley and Sons Company,
Crawfordsville, Ind.,
using a 55 # cream white antique stock bulking at 350 pages to the inch.
Binding, also by Donnelley, uses a .080 pasted oak board, over which
printed casesides of Permacote cambric have been applied.
Cover design was prepared by Jack Swartz,
text design by Shelly Lowenkopf;
proofing by Paulette Wamego, Jean Holzinger and Gail Marceaux.
The index was prepared by Marianne Morgan.